Constable
The Great Landscapes

With essays by Sarah Cove,
John Gage, Anne Lyles and
Charles Rhyne and additional
catalogue contributions
by Franklin Kelly
Edited by Anne Lyles

Constable

The Great Landscapes

Tate Publishing

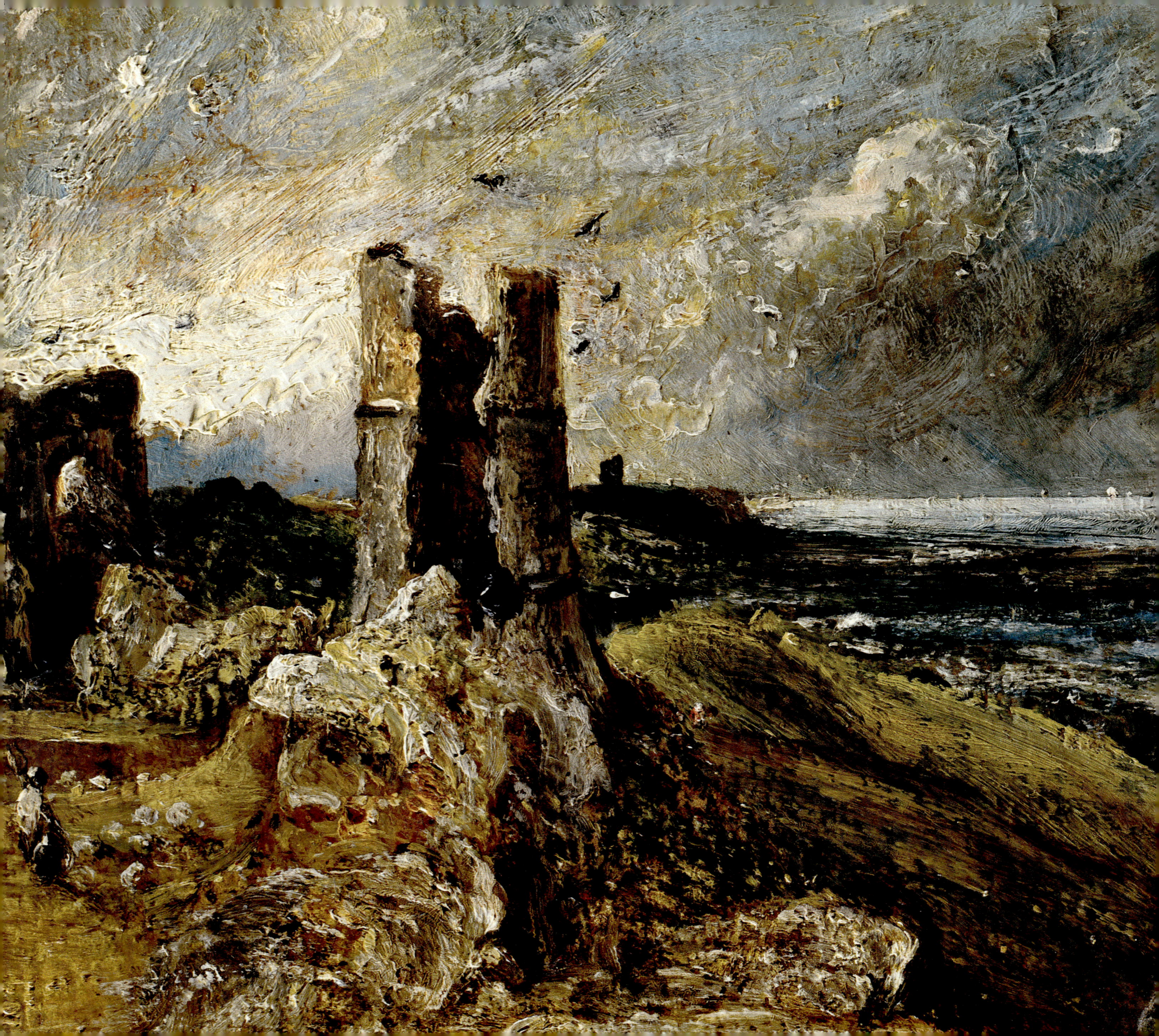

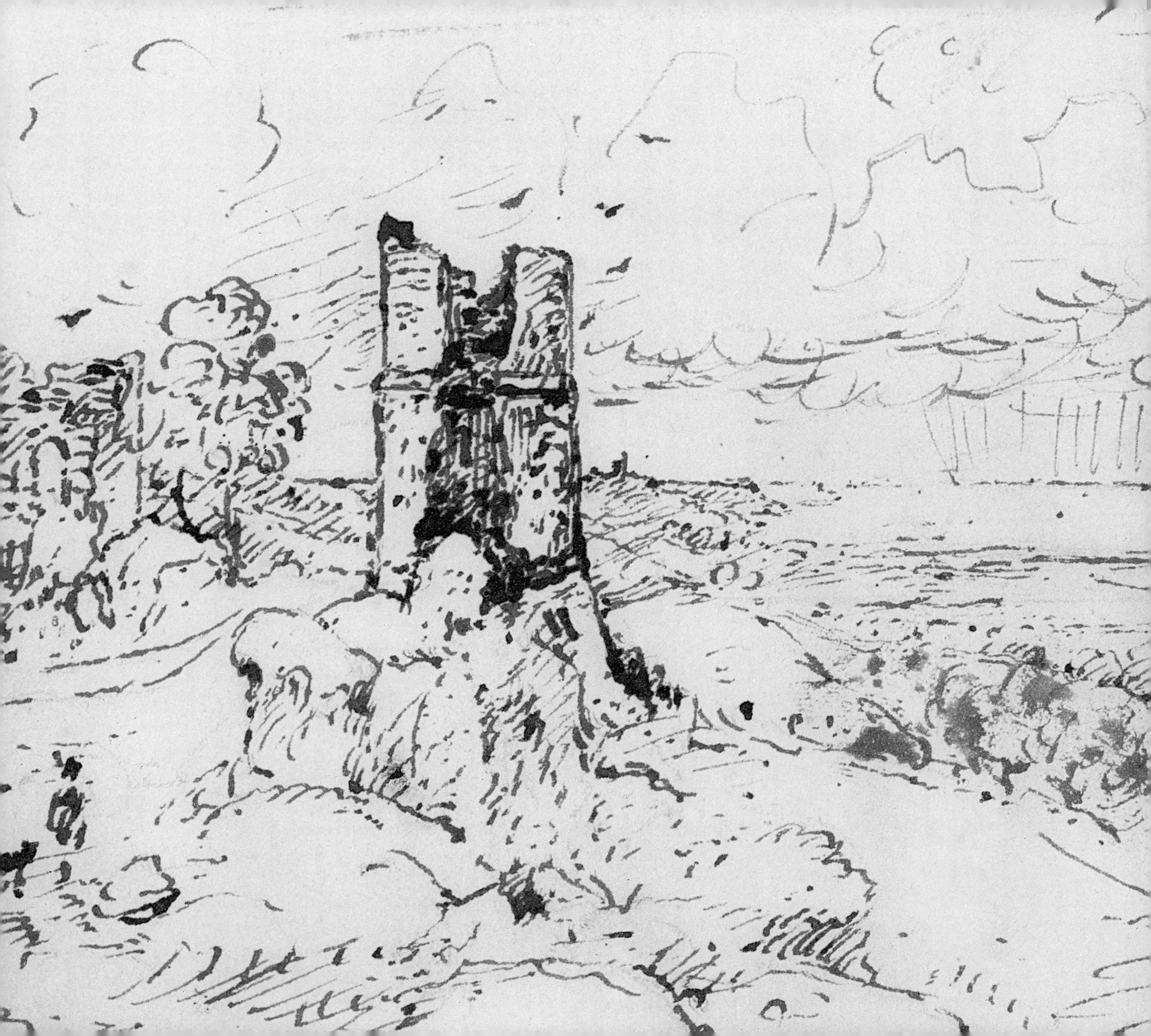

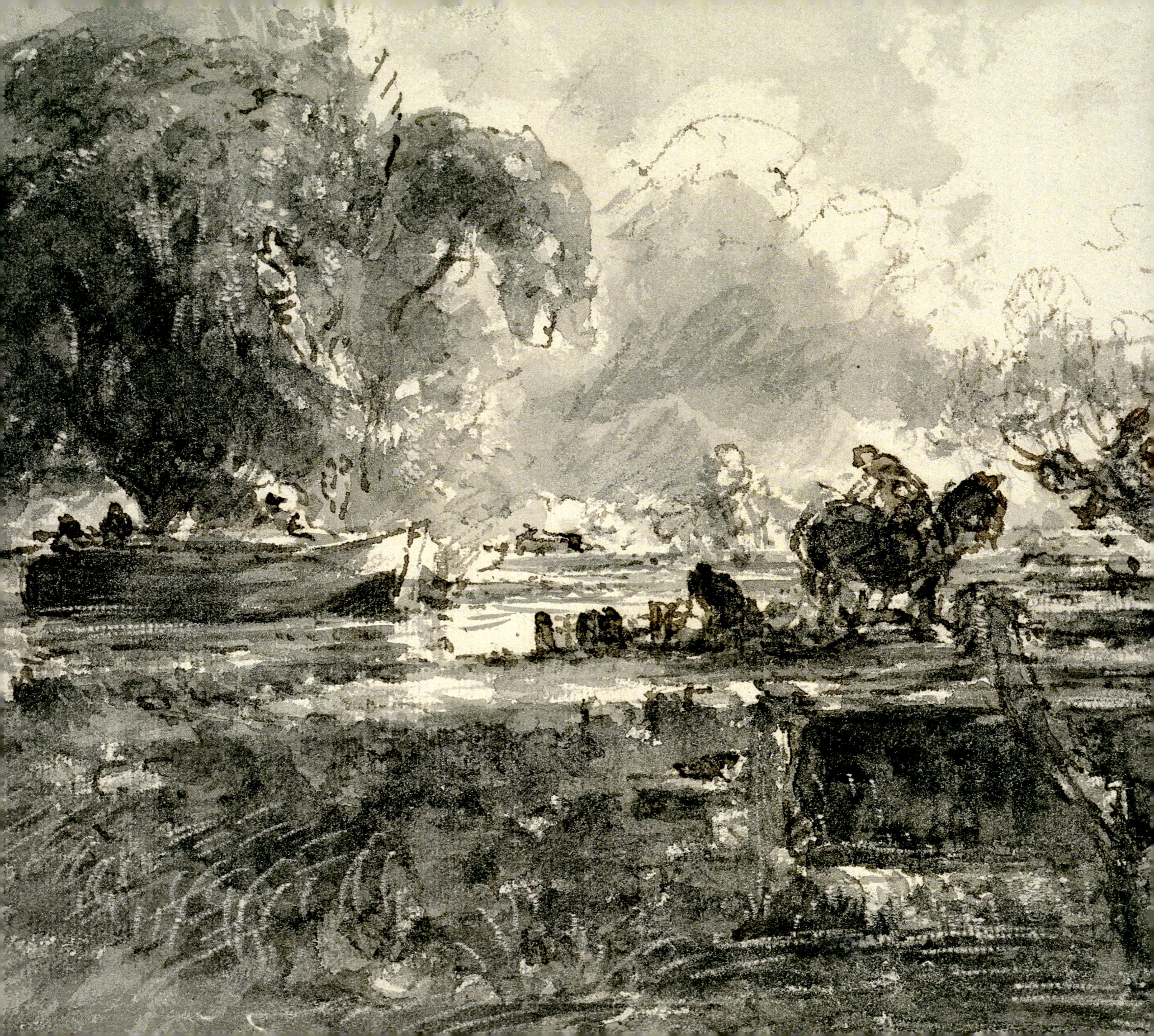

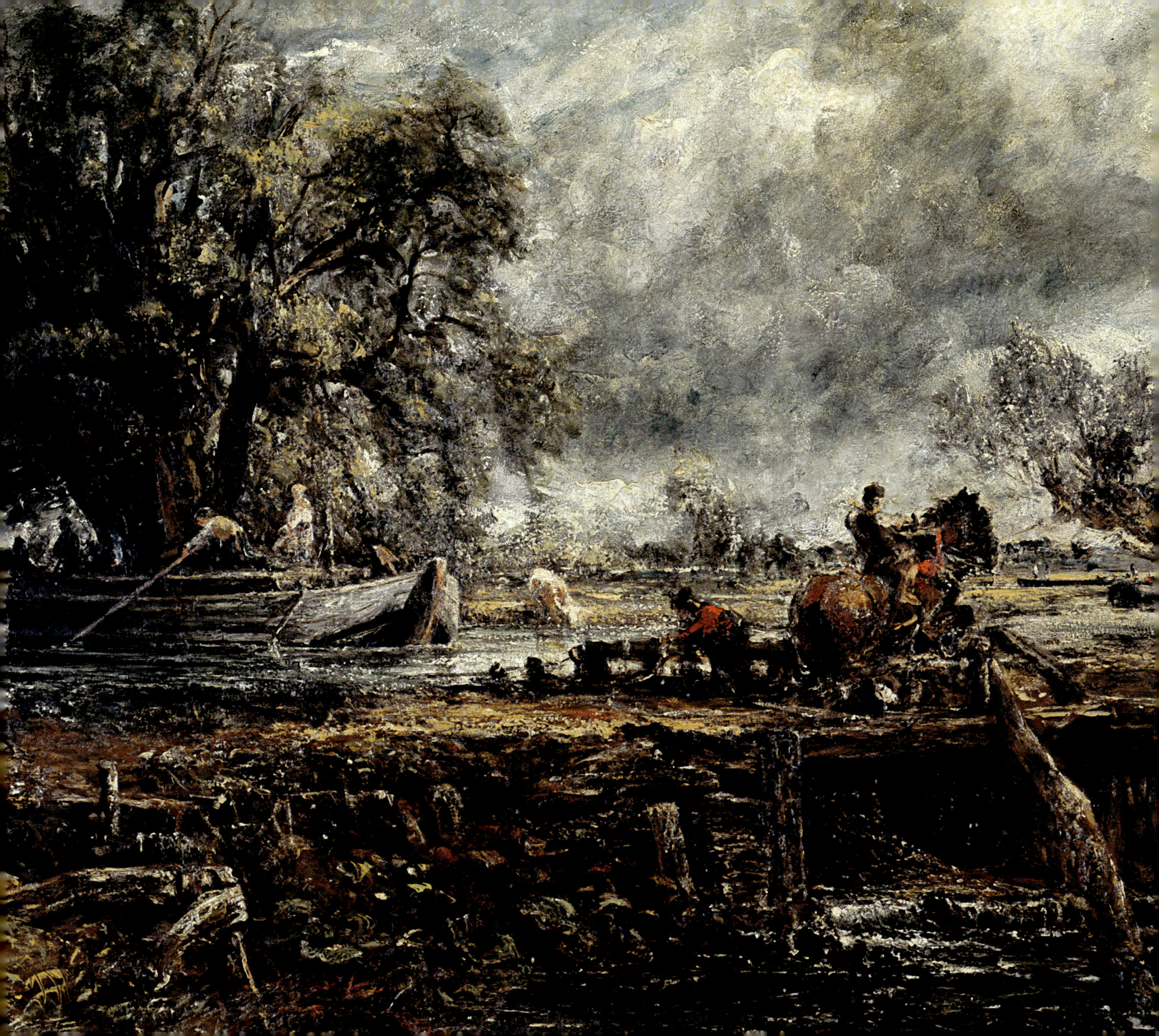

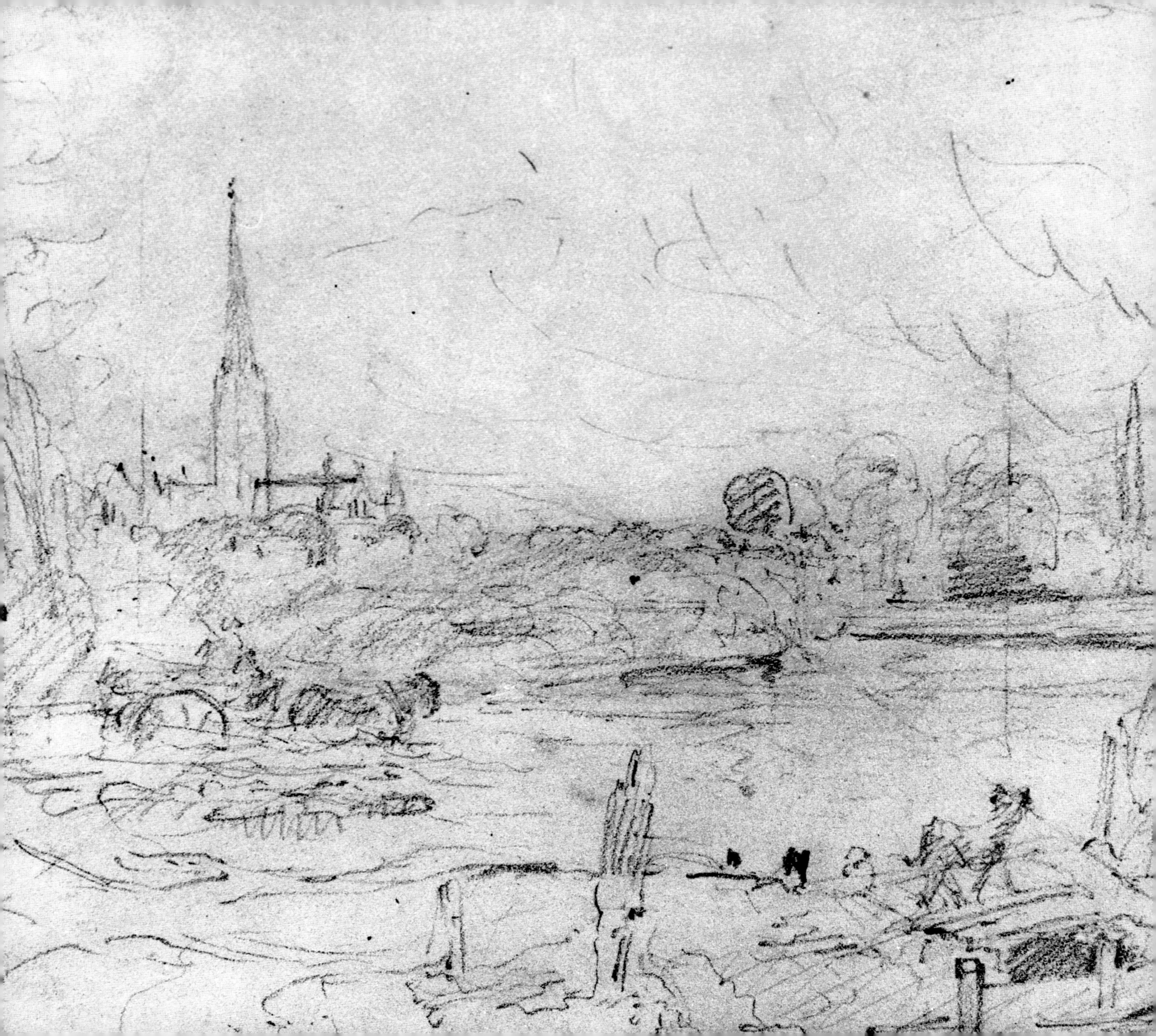

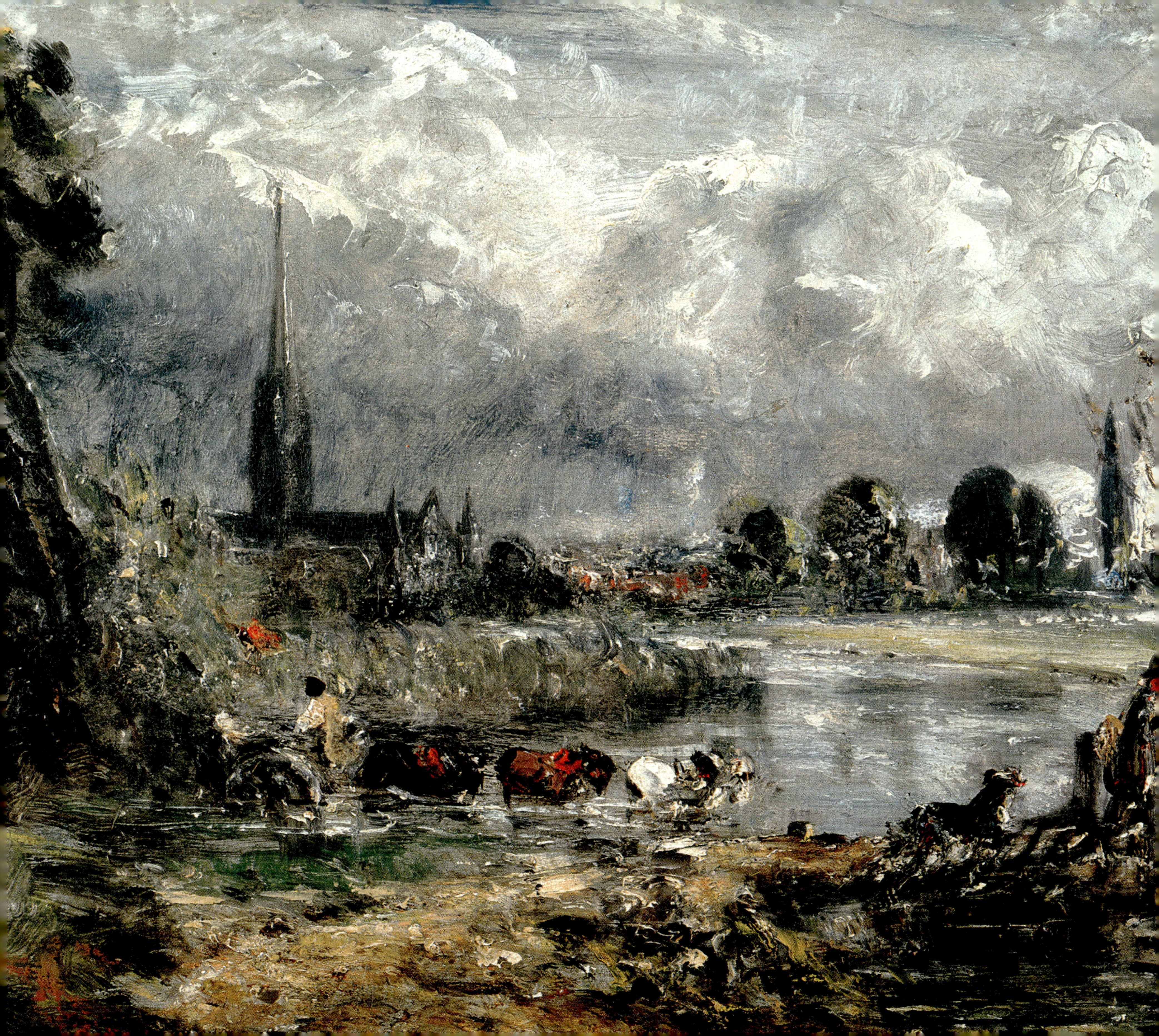

First published 2006 by order of the Tate Trustees
by Tate Publishing, a division of Tate Enterprises Ltd,
Millbank, London SW1P 4RG
www.tate.org.uk/publishing

on the occasion of the exhibition
Constable: The Great Landscapes
Tate Britain, London
1 June – 28 August 2006

Constable's Great Landscapes: The Six-Foot Paintings
National Gallery of Art, Washington
1 October – 31 December 2006

Huntington Art Gallery, San Marino
3 February – 29 April 2007

British Library Cataloguing in Publication Data
A catalogue record for this book is available
from the British Library

ISBN-13 978-185437-635-0 (hbk)
ISBN-13 978-185437-583-4 (pbk)
ISBN-10 1-85437-635-7 (hbk)
ISBN-10 1-85437-583-0 (pbk)

Distributed in the United States and Canada
by Harry N. Abrams, Inc., New York

Library of Congress Cataloging in Publication Data
Library of Congress Control Number: 2006926361

Jon Hill Design & Art Direction with Matt Brown
Printed in Spain by Grafos S.A.

PAPERBACK COVER
The White Horse 1819 (no.29, detail)
HARDBACK JACKET
front: *The White Horse* 1819 (no.29, detail)
back: *The White Horse (full-size sketch)* c.1818 (no.28)

DETAILS
p.4 *Sketch for 'Hadleigh Castle'* c.1828 (no.54)
p.5 *Sketch for 'Hadleigh Castle'* c.1828 (no.55)
p.6 *First Study for 'The Leaping Horse'* 1824 (no.42)
p.7 *The Leaping Horse (full-size sketch)* c.1824 (no.46)
p.8 *Salisbury Cathedral from Long Bridge* 1829 (no.58)
p.9 *Sketch for 'Salisbury Cathedral from the Meadows'*
c.1829 (no.59)
pp. 18–19 *The Hay Wain* 1821 (no.37)
pp.30–1 *Stratford Mill* 1820 (no.31)
pp.40–1 *Hadleigh Castle (full-size sketch)* c.1828–9 (no.56)
pp.50–1 *The Opening of Waterloo Bridge*
('Whitehall Stairs, June 18th, 1817') 1832 (no.67)
pp.68–9 *The Lock* 1824 (no.41)
pp.74–5 *The Mill Stream* c.1810–14 (no.9)
pp.100–1 *Dedham Lock and Mill* c.1816–17 (no.23)
pp.126–7 *The White Horse* 1819 (no.29)
pp.162–3 *Salisbury Cathedral from the*
Meadows 1831 (no.61)
pp.198–9 *Chain Pier, Brighton* 1827 (no.51)

Sponsor's Foreword

AIG is pleased to sponsor *Constable: The Great Landscapes* in memory of the late Sir Edwin Manton, a long-time executive of AIG and benefactor of Tate. I can think of no finer tribute to Sir Edwin than sponsorship of this exceptional exhibition of Constable paintings. Sir Edwin was one of the founding fathers of AIG and one of the most respected figures in the global insurance business. His enthusiasm and insights for the business were never diminished, nor was his enthusiasm for British paintings, particularly the work of John Constable. In appreciation of Sir Edwin's remarkable generosity to Tate Britain, all of us at AIG are delighted to support this exhibition, which we hope you will enjoy.

Martin J. Sullivan
President and Chief Executive Officer
American International Group, Inc.

Director's Note

Sir Edwin Manton (1909–2005), whose many benefactions to Tate were the most generous in the history of the Gallery, was a passionate enthusiast for the work of John Constable. 'Jim' Manton, as he was known to his English friends, was born twenty miles from Constable's own birthplace and, although he moved to America as a young man, he always retained an affection for the wide horizons and open skies of Suffolk and Essex. When success in business allowed him to begin making a collection after the Second World War it was natural that he should begin with Constable. Over the years he assembled one of the best collections of Constable's work in private hands, and it was this enthusiasm that brought him into close contact with our Constable specialist, Leslie Parris. Jim became a friend of Leslie, who sadly died in 2000, but also a friend of Tate. His support for the Appeal to assist Tate in acquiring *The Opening of Waterloo Bridge* 1832 in 1987 was followed by major benefactions that created The American Fund for the Tate Gallery and laid the foundation for the Centenary Development at Tate Britain. Jim also left a bequest to Tate including, appropriately, Constable's *The Glebe Farm* c.1830. Tate and its audiences are enormously in his debt and he would have been thrilled to see this exhibition in the museum, which has been transformed by his generosity.

Nicholas Serota
Director, Tate

Foreword

John Constable (1776–1837) is the most celebrated of all painters of the English landscape; indeed, his vision and representation of his native countryside have become bound up with the identity of the nation itself. Yet his own focus was, at one level, determinedly local: he was born and brought up in Suffolk's Stour Valley, and a relatively narrow stretch of land there between East Bergholt and Dedham Vale was to serve as the primary source of his lifelong artistic inspiration. Though he enrolled at the Royal Academy Schools in London in 1799, he set up his studio back in Suffolk from 1802 and was to spend much of the next twenty years in an intensive engagement with the natural world of his birthplace, sketching in oils, sometimes in *plein air*, translating constant pictorial experimentation into finished works for sale or exhibition. His insistence on drawing inspiration directly from nature was balanced and enriched by his close knowledge of, and admiration for, great European art of the past – Claude Lorraine, Jacob van Ruisdael, Peter Paul Rubens – and he longed to see his work accepted alongside theirs in the highest realms of the history of art. It is in the light of this ambition that his best-known and most important group of works should be seen: the succession of six monumental 'six-footer' canvases depicting Stour Valley canal scenes, which were exhibited at the Royal Academy between 1819 and 1825.

Passionately local in subject, these works were both epic in intent and international in their impact. The exhibition of one of them, *The Hay Wain*, at the Paris Salon of 1824, brought Constable an immediate measure of the acclaim the picture and its companions were later to enjoy more widely at home. Though it may be argued that the 'six-footers' lie at the very heart of Romantic landscape painting in Europe, it is the contention of this exhibition that their significance in Constable's *oeuvre* lies as much in the extraordinary processes of their individual evolution as in their latter-day status as cultural icons. Above all, an analysis of the relationship between the finished works and the remarkable and unprecedented full-scale six-foot sketches that Constable produced for each of them, far from the public eye, has provided a new but central route to understanding the methods, practices and accomplishments of a great artist. The six Stour Valley 'pairs' from 1819–25 are here assembled in one place for the first time ever, supplemented by three further 'pairs' of six-footers – full-scale sketches and finished works – from 1829–32, as well as the *Chain Pier, Brighton* 1827 (which has no full-scale study) and a final large late sketch, *Stoke-by-Nayland* c.1835–7. Accompanied by a further fifty or so works shedding light on Constable's wider practice, these twenty pictures form the central core and narrative of the exhibition. Not viewed by Constable as finished works of art in their own right, the sketches were little known or remarked upon in his lifetime and they became widely dispersed after his death. The exhibited six-footers, meanwhile, were more highly valued but also found homes in many separate collections. Today, these twenty works belong to no fewer than fifteen different collections internationally.

The idea of attempting to bring together this body of work came originally from the National Gallery of Art, Washington, in the late 1990s, inspired by its cleaning of the full-scale sketch for *The White Horse*. Not only did the cleaning serve to restore the original appearance of the very first of Constable's large sketches, which had been overpainted by another hand in the nineteenth century; it also had dramatic results for our understanding of Constable's working procedures at this critical turning point in his career. However, the National Gallery of Art's attempt to persuade all fifteen collections to lend at the same time foundered and was ultimately defeated by a number of conflicting commitments. In 2003, however, in partnership with Tate Britain and the Huntington Library and Art Gallery, renewed approaches were made and extraordinary indulgence begged. The remarkable result of this endeavour, the product of great generosity from public and private collections alike, is today's exhibition – one that is touring to all three venues. We are especially indebted to The National Gallery, London, the Victoria and Albert Museum, London, and the Yale Center for British Art, New Haven, which have each lent two six-footers apiece: to do so for a period of nearly a year represents public-spirited generosity of the highest order. To them and to all our lenders, we record our profound gratitude. We also pay tribute to the curators and writers who conceived, assembled and presented the exhibition. They have been inspirationally led by Anne Lyles, Tate Britain's Constable specialist, who worked tirelessly with Franklin Kelly, Senior Curator of American and British Paintings at the National Gallery of Art, Washington, in developing a remarkable show through all its stages and securing all the loans. We are also grateful to Shelley Bennett, Curator of British and European Art at the Huntington for overseeing the myriad details of presenting the exhibition in San Marino. The curators' acknowledgements to their many collaborators are made elsewhere, but here we wish especially to underscore the contributions made to the project by John Gage, Sarah Cove and Charles Rhyne: their advice and insight, and their written contributions to this catalogue, have been deeply appreciated.

This is the third major Constable exhibition at Tate (after those in 1976 and 1991) but the first for both Washington and the Huntington. We hope that those who love Constable already may learn more, and those who are meeting him in depth for the first time will enjoy his acquaintance through this historic gathering of the six-foot canvases – an unprecedented event that may never be repeated.

The exhibition is staged at Tate Britain thanks to the generous sponsorship of AIG. We are delighted that they have chosen to support the project as a tribute to their former director, Sir Edwin Manton, whose love for Constable and commitment to Tate Britain were so remarkable.

The exhibition in Washington is generously supported by General Dynamics and its subsidiary, General Dynamics United Kingdom, Ltd. The National Gallery of Art is extremely grateful to General Dynamics for its support of this exhibition and for its partnership over the years.

All three organising institutions wish to acknowledge with respect and gratitude the enabling role played by Robert F. Erburu, former Chairman of the Huntington and present Chairman of the National Gallery of Art, in early international discussions about this exhibition.

Stephen Deuchar
Director, Tate Britain
Earl A. Powell III
Director, National Gallery of Art, Washington
John Murdoch
Director, Huntington Art Collections, San Marino

Any exhibition on John Constable owes an immense debt to the research and publications of previous scholars, in particular to the catalogue of the artist's entire output of paintings and drawings compiled by Graham Reynolds and published by Yale University Press in 1984 and 1996. These volumes, together with the indispensable catalogue by Leslie Parris and Ian Fleming-Williams that accompanied the last exhibition of Constable's work at the Tate Gallery in 1991, and the catalogue they co-authored with Conal Shields for the Tate's bicentenary exhibition in 1976, form the essential foundations for any serious presentation of Constable's art. Another vital addition to the literature in 1991 was Judy Ivy's compilation of contemporary critical responses to the artist's exhibited work. This has provided a rich vein of original source material on which to draw, which has been especially valuable for an exhibition that focuses on the presentation of the artist's most important pictures in the public arena. It sits as a valuable resource alongside the magisterial volumes of the artist's correspondence that appeared in the 1960s and 1970s, for the most part edited by Ronald Beckett, under the guiding hand of Norman Scarfe, also published by the Suffolk Records Society. Meanwhile, we look forward to the appearance this year of Anthony Bailey's new biography of the artist, the first full study of its sort since the appearance of C.R.Leslie's famous *Memoirs* in 1843, a later edition of which happily remains in print to this day.

We are also indebted to a wealth of other publications on Constable that are too numerous to list here, though many of those most relevant to the theme of this exhibition appear in the bibliography. We would however like to draw attention to the important monographs on the artist written by Michael Rosenthal and Malcolm Cormack in the 1980s and, more recently, to the revelatory exhibition at the Courtauld Institute of Art in London, *Art on the Line*, masterminded in 2001–2 by David Solkin, with its valuable accompanying book on the subject. Focusing on the public display of pictures, drawings, prints and sculpture submitted for exhibition at the Royal Academy during the years it was located at Somerset House, this exhibition provoked many stimulating ideas about the context in which artists' work was shown and received during the period, a very relevant topic to the theme of our current show .

We should also like to extend our warmest thanks to the contributors to the catalogue. We are most grateful to John Gage, for his wide-ranging and stimulating essay on the important role played by the great landscapes within the context of Constable's own achievements, as well as within the wider tradition of European landscape painting. That John was able to spare the time to contribute to our publication is the more remarkable when one bears in mind that he was also committed to work on another exhibition about Constable in Australia, co-curated with Anne Gray, the catalogue of which unfortunately appeared too late for its findings to be taken into account in this publication (*Constable: Impressions of Land, Sea and Sky*, National Gallery of Australia, Canberra, 3 March – 12 June 2006; Museum of New Zealand Te Papa Tongarewa, Wellington, 5 July – 8 October 2006).

We were also delighted that we were able to persuade the well-known Constable specialist Charles Rhyne to contribute to this catalogue. Charles has written widely about Constable over the years, and in the early 1980s was awarded a Kress fellowship at the Center for Advanced Study in the Visual Arts at the National Gallery of Art, Washington, in connection with his Constable research. It was during this period that he persuaded the Gallery to analyse, and take x-radiographs of, the then disputed sketch for *The White Horse* (no.28). Not only did this investigation serve to confirm an existing suspicion that the sketch had been overpainted in the nineteenth century by another hand (see fig.18, p.45), but it also led to the entirely unsuspected discovery that the (partly obscured) original full-scale sketch had in turn been painted by Constable over an abandoned composition (fig.21, p.45). The latter discovery encouraged Charles to publish a pioneering article in 1990, focusing primarily on the origins of the first of Constable's 'six-foot' landscapes, *The White Horse*, in The Frick Collection (no.29). Shortly afterwards, the National Gallery of Art decided to undertake the cleaning of the large sketch for *The White Horse* in order to return it to its original appearance, a formidable task of interpretation and labour entrusted to Michael Swicklik, Senior Conservator in the National Gallery of Art's Paintings Conservation Department. We should like to extend our thanks to Michael for his careful cleaning of the picture between 1992 and 1997, an achievement that led directly to the original idea for this exhibition, in which the newly cleaned sketch and finished picture of *The White Horse* will be reunited for the first time since Constable's day.

Finally, we would like to express our profound gratitude for the remarkable contribution made by Sarah Cove. Sarah is the internationally recognised authority on Constable's materials and techniques. Given that the artist was committed to the unique practice of making full-scale sketches for the majority of his later large landscapes, much of the emphasis of this exhibition has necessarily been on his working procedures, and it is therefore difficult to imagine how we could have managed to do justice to the subject without Sarah's contribution. She has collaborated with a wide range of conservators and curators in the UK and the US in the collation of information relating to Constable's methods of working (her own tributes to those who have offered advice are given in her notes section). She has also examined many paintings afresh or even for the first time. She has been passionately committed to the project from the start, whether helping to shape the exhibition by advising on key loans, or finding the time to undertake a careful reading of the entire catalogue with an eagle eye for detail. We are most grateful to David Thomson for allowing Sarah to be diverted from her regular studio work to become such an important participant in the exhibition and its accompanying catalogue.

Within Tate, as well as Stephen Deuchar and Judith Nesbitt, Head of Exhibitions and Displays at Tate Britain, we should particularly like to thank Rachel Tant, who has seen the project through from its earliest stages with characteristic imagination, perceptiveness, efficiency and calmness under pressure. She was succeeded in this role in its later stages by Tim Batchelor with great professionalism and attention to detail. Cathy Putz and Gillian Buttimer have attended to the complex matters of contractual arrangements between the venues and transport planning. Jacqueline Ridge was instrumental in making it possible for Tate conservator Natasha Duff to take on the important technical examination of many of Tate's own pictures for the exhibition, in close liaison with Sarah Cove, and we are also grateful to Natasha for arranging for many of the works to have x-radiographs taken, with very exciting results for the project. Gerry Alabone has helped with aspects of framing, greatly benefiting from research into historic framing styles undertaken by the late John Anderson.

In Tate Publishing, meanwhile, the catalogue has been steered from the outset with dedication and patience by Nicola Bion. The production has been managed by Sarah Tucker, Sarah Brown and Tim Holton; Lillian Davies has diligently overseen the picture research for the catalogue; and Mary Scott has been an attentive and sensitive editor. With the assistance of Matt Brown, Jon Hill has produced a design for the catalogue combining elegance with clean modern design, a spirit followed through by John Hewitt with his neat and graceful maps. Jon has also advised on important aspects of the exhibition's installation, which was overseen by Andy Shiel and Liam Tebbs. Research for the exhibition's interpretation and educational brief was undertaken in the early stages by Sarah Hyde, and taken up later with great enthusiasm and commitment by Richard Humphreys with invaluable technical advice from James Davis, and assisted by Christina Bagatavicius. Among other Tate staff who have helped in different ways, we should like to thank Heather Birchall in particular, and also: James Attlee, Rosie Bass, Anne Beckwith-Smith, Helen Beeckmans, David Blayney Brown, Sue Breakell, Krzysztof Cieszkowski, Michael Eldred, Adrian Glew, Melanie Greenwood, Richard Hamilton, Robin Hamlyn, Karen Hearn, Rebecca Hellen, Matthew Imms, Anna-Lena Johnsson, Rica Jones, Siobhan McCracken, Daisy Mallabar, Lynn Murfitt, Martin Postle, Sean Rainbird, Lara Raymond, Nicholas Serota, Joyce Townsend, Piers Townshend, Ian Warrell and Vajira Wignarajah.

At the National Gallery of Art in Washington we should also like to thank: Earl A. Powell III, Director; Alan Shestack, Deputy Director; D. Dodge Thompson, Chief of Exhibitions, Naomi Remes, Exhibition Officer, Laura Cunningham, Exhibition Assistant, Department of Exhibitions; Abbie Sprague, Research Assistant, Charles Brock, Assistant Curator, Kate Kooistra, summer intern, Department of American and British Paintings; Mark Leithauser, Senior Curator and Chief of Design, Gordon Anson, Deputy Chief of Design, Donna Kirk, architect, Elma Hajiric, architect, Bill Bowser, Production Coordinator, Barbara Keyes, Head of Graphics, Department of Design; Christine Myers, Chief Corporate Relations Officer, Susan McCullough, Corporate Relations Associate, Office of Corporate Relations; Sally Freitag, Chief Registrar, Melissa Stegeman, Assistant Registrar for Exhibitions, Office of the Registrar; Michael Pierce, Senior Conservator for Loans and Exhibitions, Michael Swicklik, Senior Conservator, Hugh Phibbs, Coordinator of Matting-Framing Services, Department of Conservation; Elizabeth A. Croog, Secretary and General

Counsel, Lara Levinson, Associate General Counsel, Office of the Secretary and General Counsel; Susan Arensberg, Head of Exhibition Programs, Margaret Doyle, Assistant Curator, Department of Exhibition Programs; Judy Metro, Editor in Chief; Faya Causey, Head of Academic Programs, Ana Maria Zavala, Administrator for Academic Programs, Department of Academic Programs; Deborah Ziska, Chief Press and Public Information Officer, Anabeth Guthrie, Publicist, Press and Public Information Office.

At the Huntington Art Gallery, as well as John Murdoch and Shelley Bennett, we should also like to thank Jacqueline Dugas, who has undertaken much of the responsibility for the administration of the loans to the third venue of the exhibition, and Gregg Bayne, Abigail Haskell, Joyce Liu, Brian Mains, Melinda McCurdy and Genevieve Preston.

Although in their joint foreword the Directors have already expressed their thanks to all the lenders to the exhibition, we should like to single out here for special mention the following museum and gallery colleagues who have helped in many different ways to make the loans possible: Antony Griffiths, Sheila O'Connell and Kim Sloan at the British Museum, London; James Cuno at the Art Institute of Chicago; Julia Blanks at the Courtauld Institute of Art, London; Susan Strickler, Kurt Sundstrom and Andrew Spahr at the Currier Art Gallery, New Hampshire; Colin Bailey and Susan Galassi at The Frick, New York; Vivien Knight and Vicky Leanse at the Guildhall Art Gallery, London; Sally Dummer at Ipswich Museum and Art Gallery, Suffolk; Sandra Penketh at the Lady Lever Art Gallery, Port Sunlight, Liverpool; Charles Saumarez Smith, Susan Foister and Martin Wyld at The National Gallery, London; Alastair Laing, Tina Sitwell and Chezzy Brownen at the National Trust; Joseph Rishel, Jennifer Thompson and Mark S. Tucker at the Philadelphia Museum of Art; Mary-Anne Stevens and Helen Valentine at the Royal Academy of Arts, London; Tòmas Llorens at the Thyssen collection, Madrid; Mark Jones, Mark Evans, Nicola Costaras and Helen Whitcombe at the Victoria and Albert Museum, London, and in earlier stages of the project Susan Lambert and Janet Skidmore; and Amy Meyers, Angus Trumble and Timothy Goodhue at the Yale Center for British Art, New Haven.

For other valuable advice or support, we would also like to thank: Tania Adams, Brian Allen, Charles Armstrong, Anthony Bailey, Anthony Battersby, Marina Bezrukova, Alan Bowness, Martin Butlin, Henry Christiansen III, Judith Colton, Richard Constable, Valerie Constable, Sasha Constable, David Dallas, Andrew Dempsey, William Feaver, Elizabeth Einberg, Patrick Elliott, Rachel Feilden, Melissa Gastgaber, Dan Glaser, the late Richard Godfrey, Alan Hobart, Sarah Hoborough, Robert Hoozee, Sophie Jackson, Bette Jane Jacobus, Karen Jordan, Ed Kanfer, Michael Kauffmann, Peter Kennedy Scott, Catherine Kinley, Julia Krapf, David Landau, Lowell Libson, Michael Liversidge, Kelly Lyles, Denise McColgan, Nicola Maclennan, Richard and Sandra Melville, David Moore-Gwyn, Susan Morris, Diana Morton, Rosemary Muir, Jane Munro, Angus Neill, Sandra Morton Niles, Charles Noble, Felicity Owen, Pippa Parris, Diane Perkins, Steven Rautenberg, Charles Rhodes, Andrea Rose, Ian St John, Larry Salander, David Solkin, Anthony Spink, Lindsay Stainton, Martin Sullivan, David Thomson, Nicholas Walsh, David Wardlaw, Henry Wemyss, Timothy Wilcox and Andrew Wyld.
Anne Lyles and Franklin Kelly

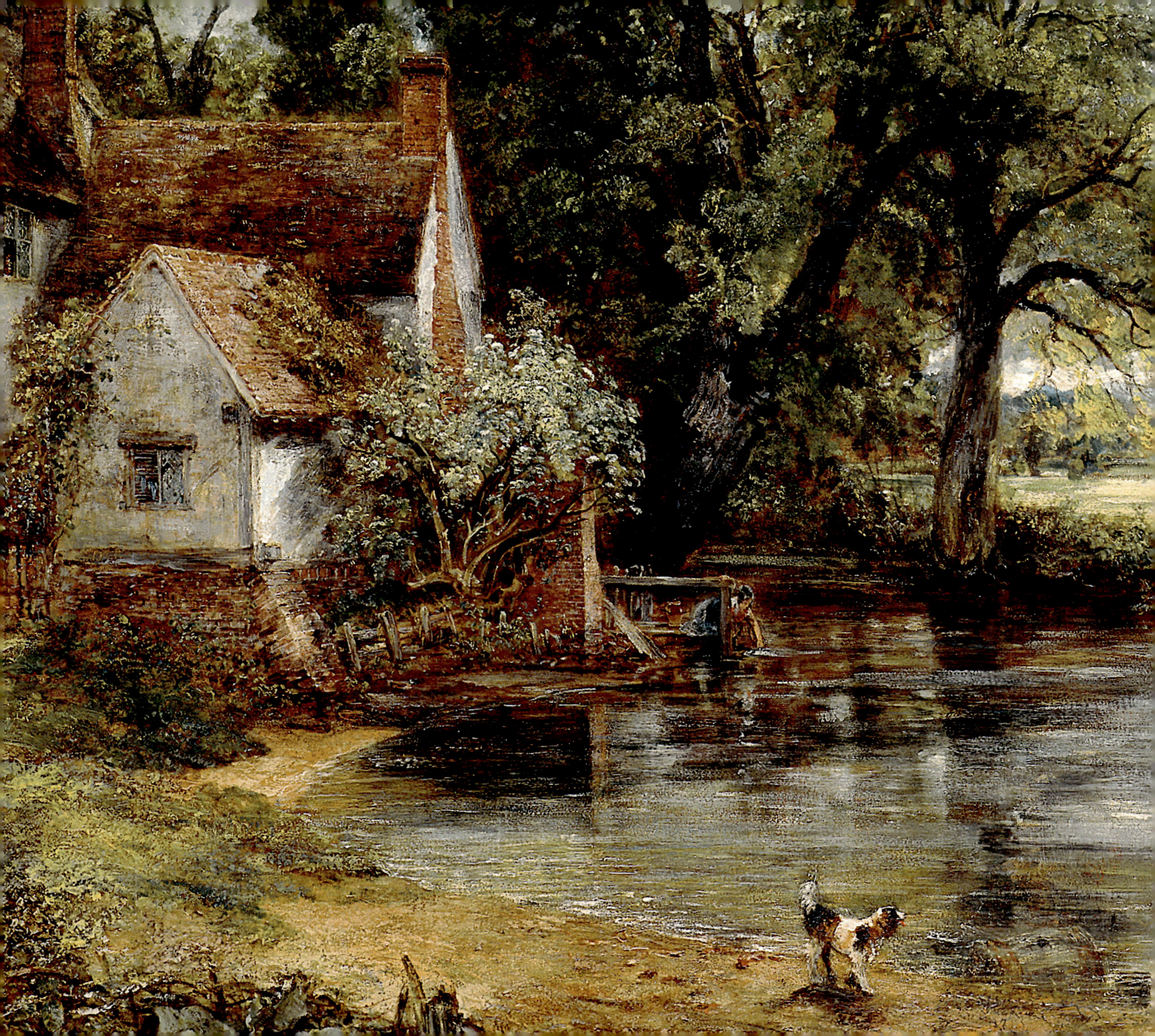

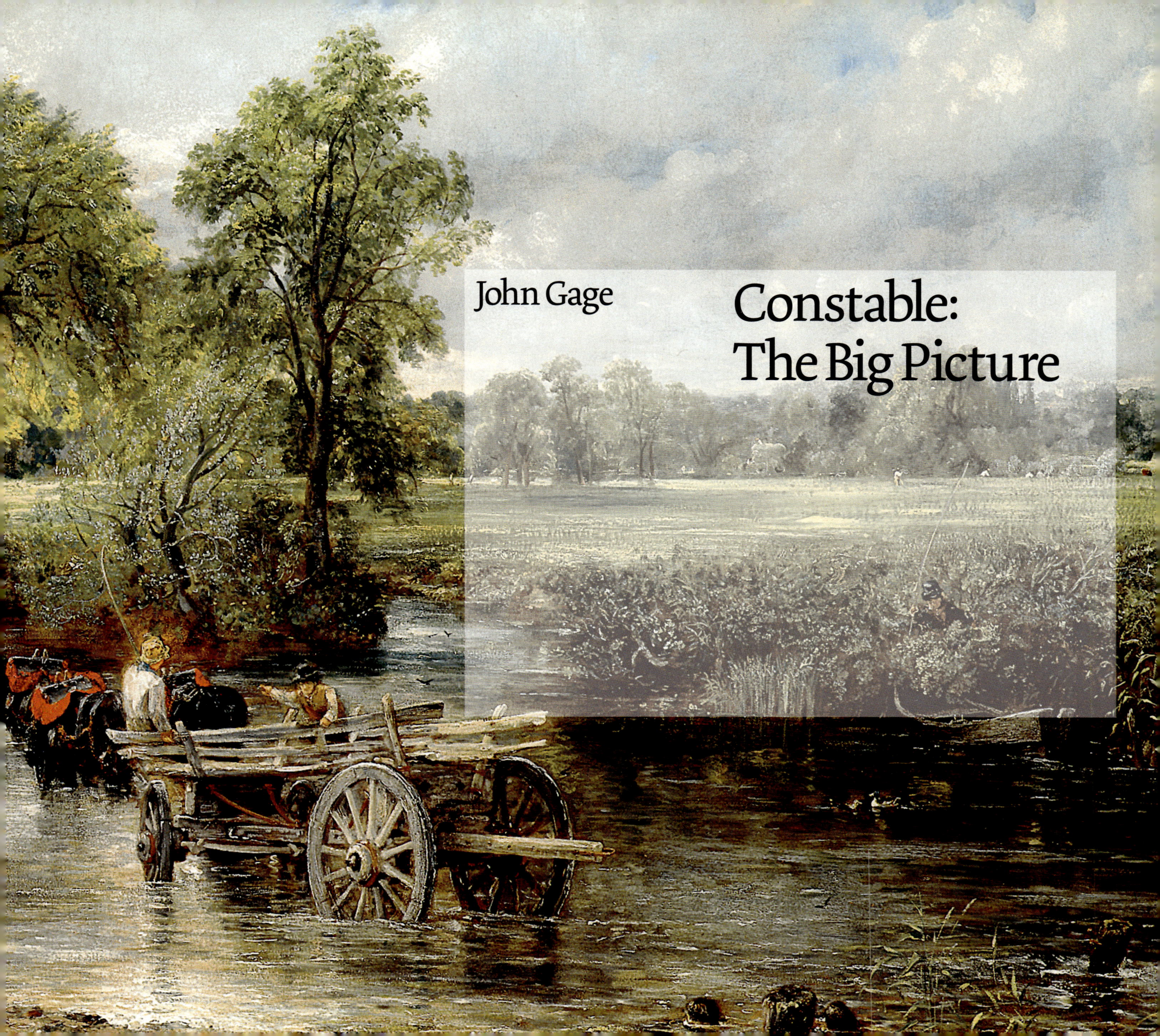
John Gage
Constable:
The Big Picture

Constable:
The Big Picture
John Gage

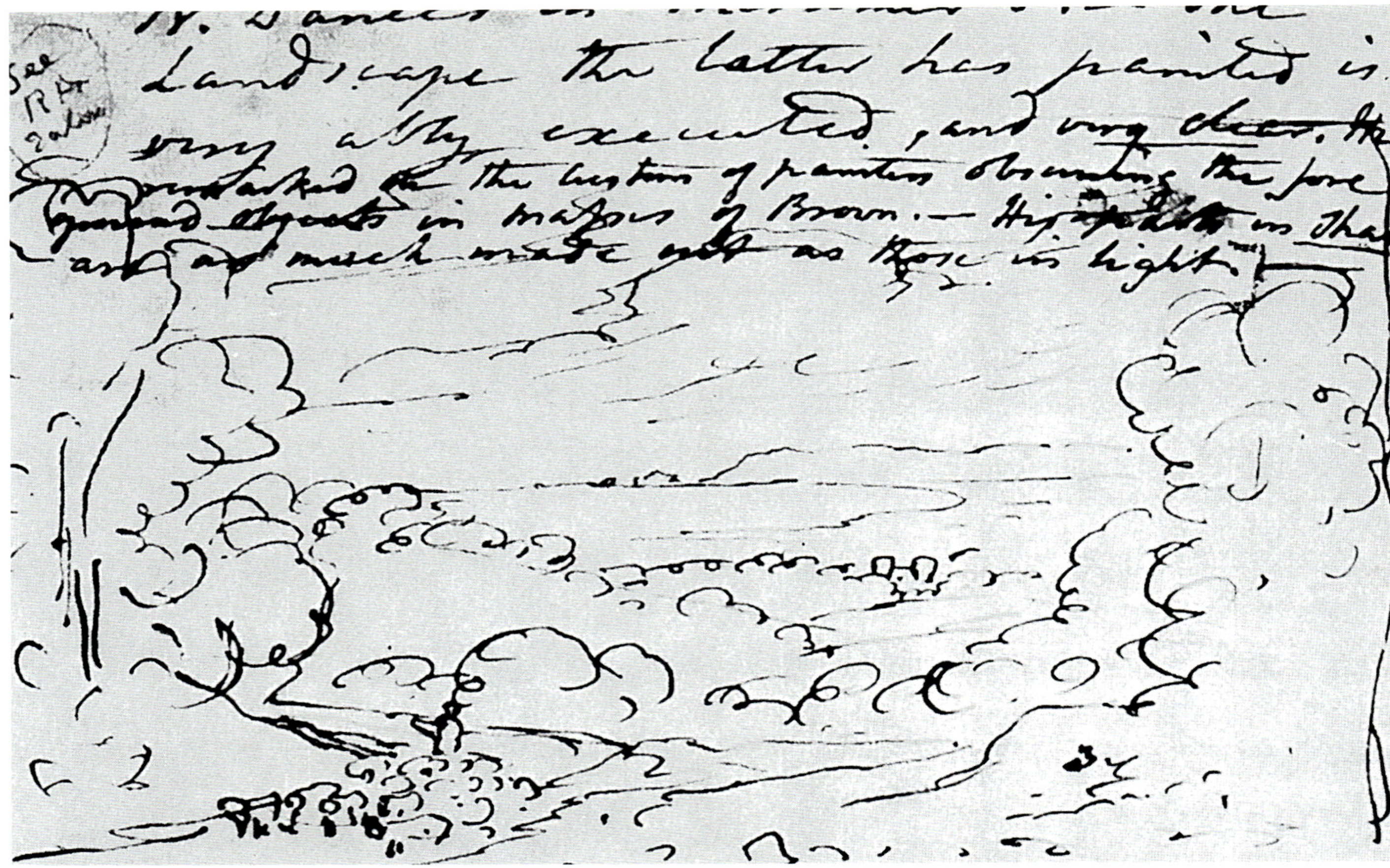

FIGURE 1

Ever since the late nineteenth century, Constable's reputation as an innovator has rested substantially on his unprecedented range of small oil sketches which, from the 1880s, became increasingly known through public collections. As Roger Fry noted in 1934, every one of these sketches 'is a discovery', and in them we 'find the real Constable';[1] a decade later Kenneth Clark pronounced them to be 'a full record of his sensations … which are nowadays the most admired part of his work'.[2] For the painter himself, however, precisely the opposite was the case. He wrote from Hampstead in a celebrated letter of October 1821 to Archdeacon John Fisher: 'I am most anxious to get into my London painting room, for I do not consider myself at work without I am before a six-foot canvas';[3] and in a later letter to another friend, George Constable (no relation), he characterised his large exhibition canvases as 'the dreams of a happy but unpropitious life'.[4] Already determined to bid for associate membership of the Royal Academy, and a decade before he achieved it with *The White Horse* 1819 (no.29), Constable was painting large pictures for exhibition. He had toured the Lake District in 1806 and made many watercolours in the open air, some of which he later squared for enlargement, presumably with exhibition pictures in mind (fig.6, p.27). In April 1809, the diarist and amateur artist Joseph Farington saw in Constable's studio a Lake District scene, five feet (1.52m) wide, which he was planning to send to the Academy. Farington advised him against it, 'as being in appearance only like a preparation for finishing, wanting variety of colour & effect'. This seems to be a remarkable anticipation of the handling of the full-size sketches of the 1820s.[5] The recent discovery of a full-scale unfinished version of *Dedham from Gun Hill* on the canvas later used for the six-foot *White Horse* sketch in Washington (fig.21, p.45; no.28), shows Constable already preparing 'six-footers' as early as the mid-1810s, no doubt also in connection with his bid for Academic recognition.[6]

Constable's experience with *The White Horse* in 1819 did indeed assure him that size could help to make a splash at the Royal Academy exhibition, and that being noticed was one important criterion for election to the Academy. But his six-footers were by no means the first large-scale rural landscapes to be shown in London. One particularly striking example, now unhappily untraced, was the first of a series of landscapes to be exhibited by the portrait painter Nathaniel Dance, in 1792 (fig.1). It was a canvas of about four feet by six feet (1.2 × 1.8m) showing, according to one critic, 'an English scene in oils, all in greens, a summer sun at midday'. Several critics emphasised the painting's unusually cool tonality. As one wrote:

There is certainly too blue a cast through the whole, though we must confess that this imperfection gradually abates and a pleasing idea of truth and simplicity finally steals upon the mind. The foliage of the respective trees is given with character but without undignified minuteness. The scenery is beautifully in keeping and presents an interesting portrait of English landscape.[7]

When Dance took Farington to see this painting in October 1799,

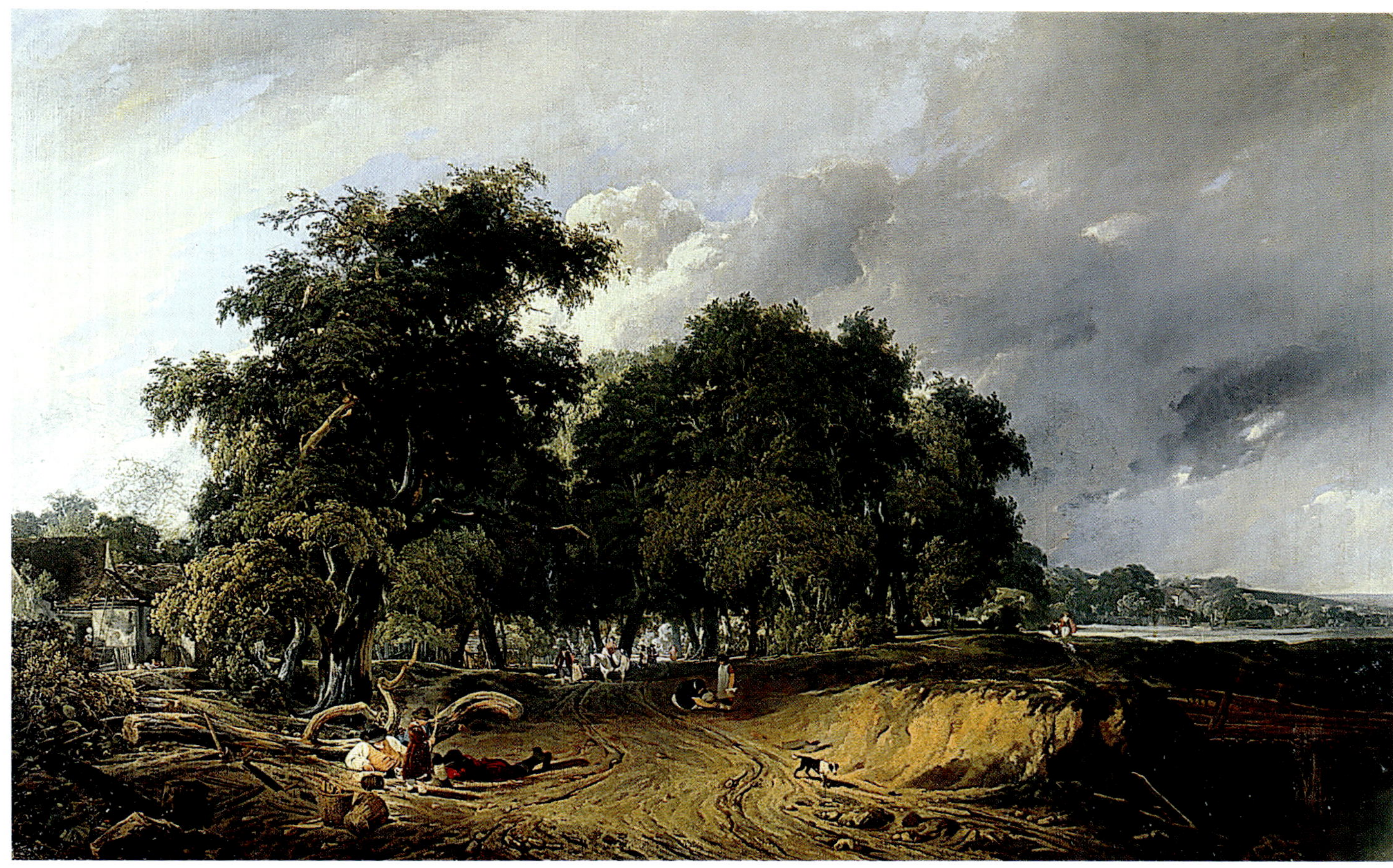

FIGURE 2

he alluded to these early criticisms by saying that it 'did not appear to him cooler than nature', and William Daniell, who was also of the party, conceded that, although the picture had 'a weak, pea-green color', this might be true.[8] Since Constable had come to London with an introduction to Farington at the beginning of that year, and remained in touch with him throughout it, it is highly likely that he knew of, and had even seen, Dance's work, which was so prophetic of his own large noonday subjects of the 1820s.

However this may be, Constable was certainly only too familiar with the very large (1.47 × 2.56m/4ft 10in × 8ft 5in) pastoral but stormy landscape, *Landscape – Market Day* (fig.2), exhibited at the Royal Academy in 1807 by Augustus Wall Callcott, three years younger than Constable but already an associate member of the institution, and to be elected to full membership only three years later. Constable had seen this picture in March 1807 before its exhibition, and was highly critical of it. He reported to Farington that:

it was a fine picture, but treated in a *pedantick manner*, every part seeming to wish to shew itself; that it had not an air of *nature*; that the trees appeared crumbly – as if they might be rubbed in the hand like bread; not loose & waving, but as if the parts if bent would break; the whole not lucid like Wilson's pictures, in which the objects appear floating in sunshine.

A few weeks later he told Farington that he thought Callcott's picture was 'apparently too much of a work of art & labour, not an *effusion*.

His smaller pictures he thought better in that respect'.[9] It was conceivably Callcott's example in *Landscape – Market Day* that stimulated the large Lake District subjects exhibited at the Royal Academy in 1807 and 1808 and, although Constable was soon to find in his own small paintings the means of expressing his feelings through an effusive swiftness of handling, it was to be many years before he was able to convey that effusiveness on a scale as large as that of Callcott.

Large English rural subjects were thus not unfamiliar in London during Constable's formative years; yet it was probably not modern painting that gave him the courage to embark on his campaign of six-footers in the 1810s and 1820s but, rather, the example of the Old Masters, and most of all, Peter Paul Rubens. The two large Rubens landscapes, *The Rainbow Landscape* c.1636–7 (fig.3, p.22) and *A View of Het Steen in the Early Morning* c.1636 (fig.4, p.23) , brought to England from a Genoese collection in 1803, were a major talking-point that year in the art circles of the capital. Constable saw the first in February of the following year in the studio of the President of the Royal Academy, Benjamin West, and judged it to be 'the finest of the Master that He had seen'.[10] Since West was not above giving technical advice to the young painter, it is more than likely that he discussed with him the technique of this painting, as he had done the year before in the company of a group of painters, including Farington, who reported:

West said the process of painting it was to *scumble* & wash it with thin colours, and gradually encrease the effect by repetition of thin colours,

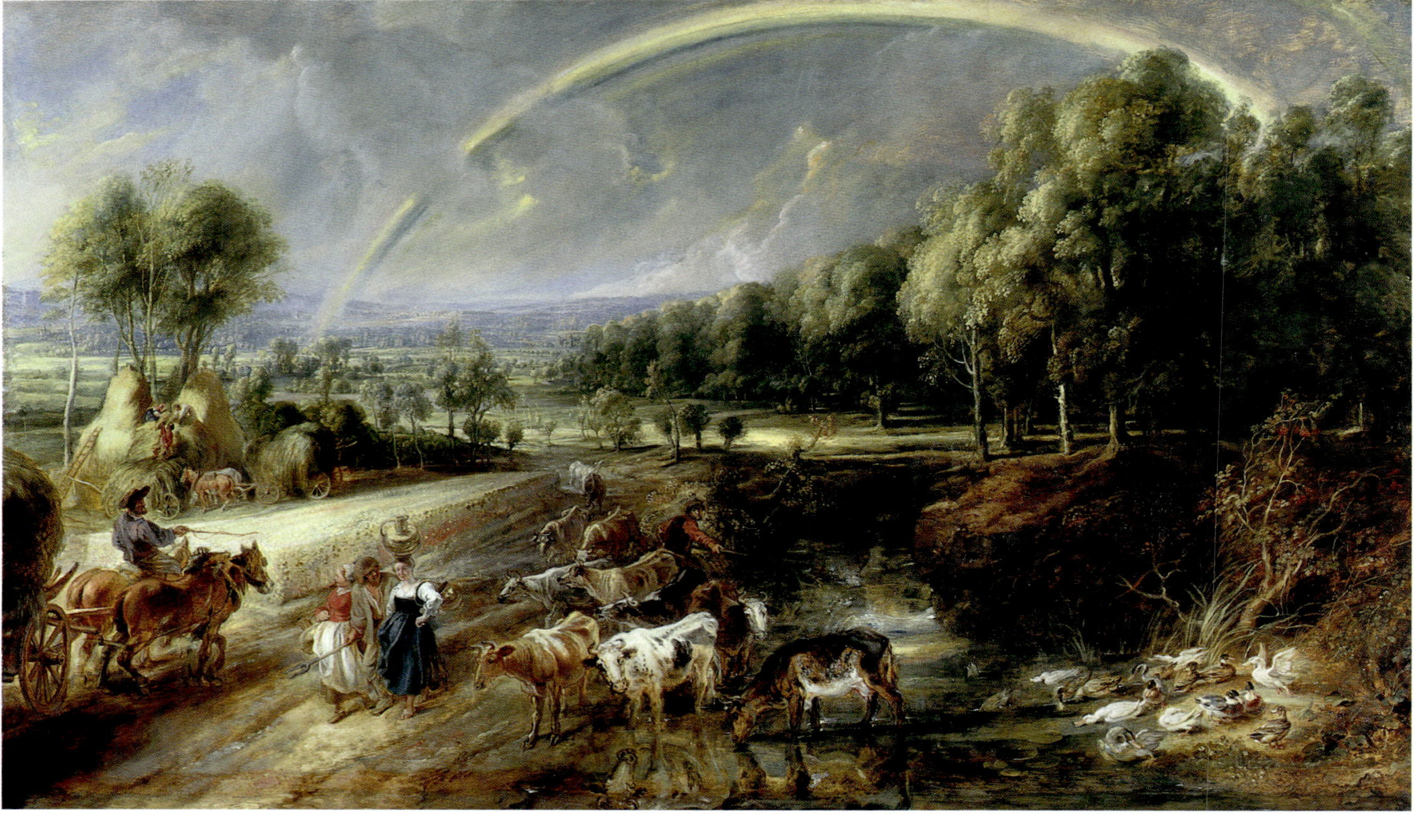

FIGURE 3

preserving the ground on which it was painted as much as possible. At the last urging on thicker colours & dragging and touching in the highest lights to give strength and spirit to the whole. He thought the ground might be made by glazing over a *white ground* a thin coat of Burnt Umber softened by a little blue.[11]

This was a process to whet Constable's appetite. A group of freely and thinly painted sketches of c.1810–12 has long been recognised as showing the effect of his study of Rubens, and two of them, at least, appear to have a blue priming, derived perhaps from the sky in a re-used canvas (fig.7, p.27).[12]

The two Rubens landscapes were probably conceived as a pair,[13] and Constable certainly considered them as such. In his third lecture on landscape at the Royal Institution in 1836, he spoke eloquently of their relationship:

In no other branch of the art is Rubens greater than in landscape; the freshness and dewy light, the joyous and animated character which he has imparted to it, impressing on the level monotonous scenery of Flanders all the richness which belongs to its noblest features. Rubens delighted in phenomena; rainbows upon a stormy sky – bursts of sunshine – moonlight – meteors and impetuous torrents mingling their sound with wind and waves. Among his finest works are a pair of landscapes, which came to England from Genoa, one of which is now in the National Gallery.

By the rainbow of Rubens, I do not allude to a particular picture, for Rubens often introduced it; I mean, indeed, more than the rainbow itself, I mean dewy light and freshness, the departing shower, with the exhilaration of the returning sun, effects which Rubens, more than any other painter, has perfected on canvas. The companion of the landscape in the National Gallery was doubtless painted to give more effect to it by contrast. When pictures painted as companions are separated, the purchaser of one, without being aware of it, is sometimes only buying half a picture. Companion pictures should never be parted, unless they are by different hands, and then, in general, the sooner they are divorced the better.[14]

Constable was here alluding to a common practice in his time, when collectors would commission a modern artist to paint a 'companion' to an Old Master in their collection, as the Duke of Bridgewater, for example, had done with the young J.M.W. Turner in 1801, and by so doing had influenced Turner's whole approach to the art of the past. Constable himself in the 1820s had been quite prepared to alter the shape of his earlier canvas, *A Summerland* (fig.5, p.24; R.24.81), for John Allnutt , in order to make it a fitting companion to a Callcott landscape, *Open Landscape: Sheep Grazing* 1812 (York City Art Gallery).[15]

But the Rubens pair had been separated as soon as they arrived in England, and Constable, who had probably seen *The Rainbow Landscape* on exhibition at the British Institution in 1815 and at a Christie's sale in 1823, had a particular interest in the companionship of his own large compositions, which owed so much to Rubens. In 1822 he told Fisher that the owner of *Stratford Mill* 1820 (no.31), Fisher's solicitor John Pern Tinney, had commissioned a companion to it: 'it will enable me to do another large work as a certainty – thus to keep up & add to my reputation'.[16] In the event this offer came to nothing, but the following

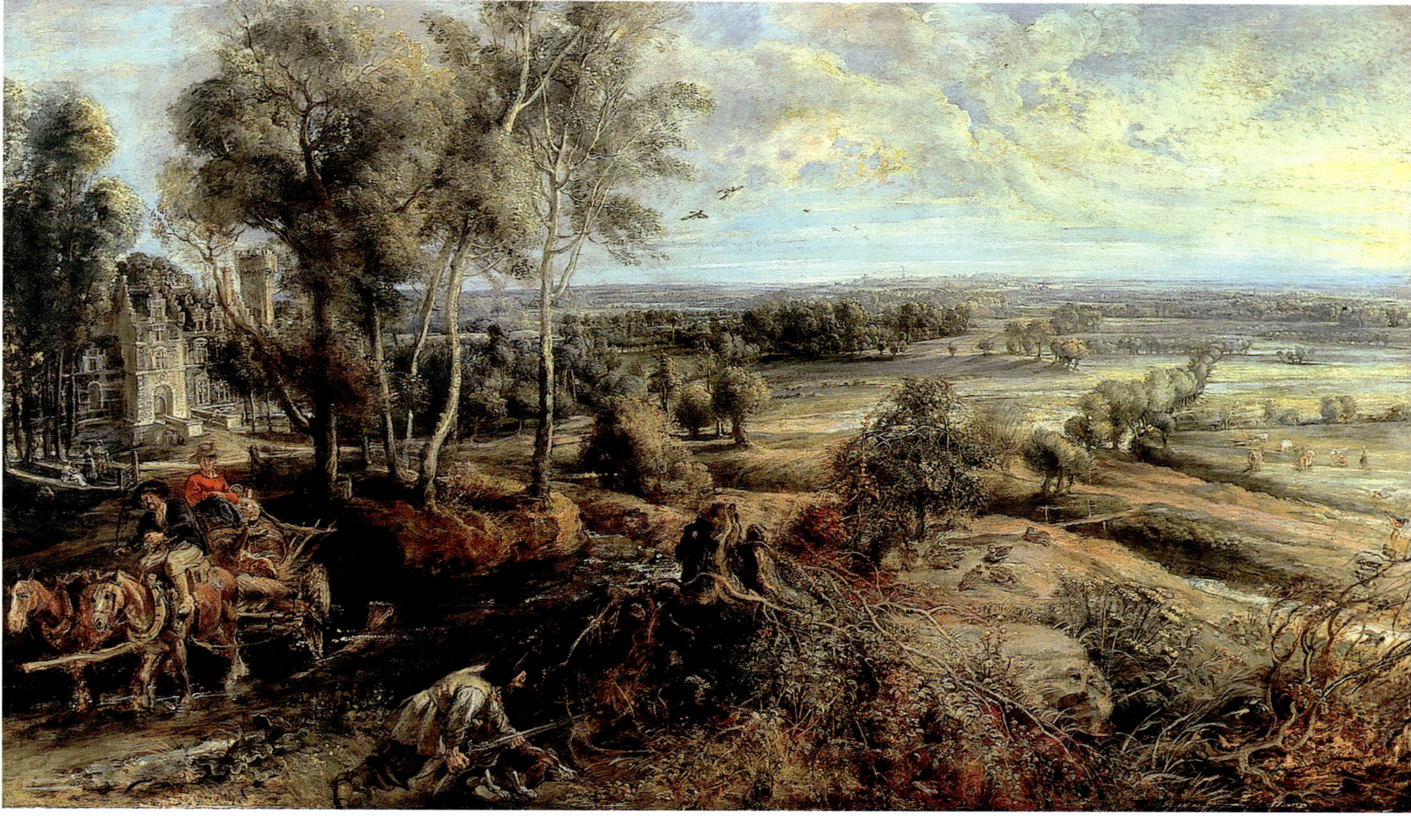

FIGURE 4

year Constable wrote to Fisher that *The Hay Wain* (no.37) 'was born a companion to your picture [*The White Horse*, no.29] in sentiment. It must be yours'.[17] Constable was still thinking of Tinney's proposal, which 'will enable me to paint another large picture for the Exhibition', but, as Fisher had explained, he could not afford *The Hay Wain* at that time, and it soon found its way across the Channel and into a number of French collections.

Yet, as Judy Egerton has shrewdly observed in her exemplary account of *The Hay Wain* that Constable had exhibited in 1821 as *Landscape: Noon*, which has so often been related to Rubens's *Autumn Landscape*, 'there is, surely, more "original observation of nature" in *The Hay Wain* than there is a "re-interpretation" of Rubens'.[18] Rubens was, after all, very much a seventeenth-century landscapist, and his handling of, for example, aerial perspective, was still, unlike Constable's, rather formulaic, in the Venetian and Flemish tradition of blue distances and green middle grounds. Equally within seventeenth-century conventions was Rubens's choice of the extreme times of day, morning and evening, which yielded an obvious 'effect' and often helped to weld the composition together with long shadows. As Constable noted in his lecture, Rubens offered striking phenomena of nature, effects which he himself chose for his most Rubensian sketches; but for his large exhibition pictures, at least until the stormy morning of *Hadleigh Castle* 1829 (no.57), with its animated rooks and gulls, and the symbolic rainbow in *Salisbury Cathedral from the Meadows* 1831 (no.61), Constable more often preferred the undramatic moment of noon. As with *The Hay Wain*, Constable gave the title *Landscape: Noon* to

The Cornfield 1826 (fig.59, p.116; R.26.1) when it was re-exhibited at the British Institution in 1827. As the Redgrave brothers recognised in their early history of British painting (1866):

Landscape painters had hitherto usually painted with the sun at their backs, to the right, or to the left, out of the picture, looking to the landscape, as the sun looks on it … Many had painted the sun *in* the picture, gradually sinking in the low horizon, and casting a dreamy mist and glow over all the earth. Such treatments Claude loved and painted finely; Cuyp also loved them, and gave them with unequalled breadth and beauty. But Constable chose the time when the sun was high in the heavens, far above, out of his canvas, but still in front of him, and painted almost always under the sun; and much that is peculiar in his art arose from this cause.[19]

Before the mid-1820s the energy of the large paintings was established rather by the staffage than by the weather. With *The Leaping Horse* 1825 (no.47) and the second, horizontal version of *The Lock, A Boat Passing a Lock* c.1823–6 (fig.8, p.28), sky, trees and figures together begin to take part in the more general agitation that is so characteristic of Constable's late work.

More striking than the avoidance of extremes of light and weather in the six-footers of the early 1820s is the marked difference between Constable's and Rubens's handling of their medium. As an experienced painter in oils, Rubens cultivated in these autograph landscapes an elegant handling that is often rather akin to drawing; his most notable English follower in this respect was Thomas Gainsborough. Constable, who famously remarked that he saw 'no handling in nature',[20] did not, at least until the works of his last years, settle on any style of painterly handwriting, and thus his works show a greater variety of touch perhaps than those of any other painter. That this was a thoroughly conscious objective is suggested by Constable's delight in 1824 at hearing that the French Salon authorities had lowered his two exhibits – *The Hay Wain* (no.37) and *View on the Stour near Dedham* (no.39) – to eye level, so that the public could now acknowledge 'the richness of the texture – and the attention to the surface of objects in these paintings'.[21] This may seem to be a trivial formal point, but for Constable it was far from trivial, for it allowed him to submit each and every movement of his brush not simply to the demands of representation, but also to the expression of feeling, that key to his aesthetic to which he referred in the celebrated letter to Fisher of October 1821:

I should paint my own places best – Painting is but another word for feeling [C.R. Leslie weakens the effect of this by inserting 'with me' into this sentence; but Constable is quite clear that this is so with *all* painting]. I associate my 'careless boyhood' to all that lies on the banks of the *Stour*. They made me a painter (& I am grateful) that is I had often thought of pictures of them before I had ever touched a pencil [i.e. brush], and your picture [*The White Horse*] is one of the strongest instances I can recollect of it.[22]

It is not surprising that this reminiscence has led commentators, from Leslie onwards, to focus primarily on the significance to the artist of local subject matter. But the tortuous progress of his career shows that Constable was not 'made a painter' simply by thinking about subjects; he had to find ways of rendering his thoughts, and the emotions bound up with them, in terms of drawing and painting.

It was his genius for transforming representation into expression that made him the original painter he became, and this transformation was bound up with the complex relationship of sketching and 'finish'. Since 'finish' was an issue that arose very largely in the context of exhibition pictures, it is a central concern of the present exhibition.

Constable became notorious and then famous for the sketch-like qualities of his surfaces, but he was not himself much interested in the sketch as a category of painting. As he wrote to Fisher apropos a copy of a Claude he was making in 1823, 'in a sketch there is nothing but the one state of mind – that which you were in at the time'; it would 'not serve to drink at again & again'.[23] He did not regard his sketches as saleable works; they were simply aids to picture-making. He would sell the corn, he said, but not the field that grew it.[24] It is an irony that the first Constable to reach France, with all the important implications of that event, was an *esquisse* (sketch), noticed by Eugène Delacroix in the studio of the landscape painter F.-J.Régnier as early as November 1823, but it remains a mystery how it arrived there, and so far it has not been traced.[25] For all their brilliance and variety of touch, Constable's outdoor sketches are the most traditional element in his armory of painting procedures. *Plein-air* painting had been well established in Italy since Rubens's day, and in the eighteenth century it was particularly cultivated by young artists based in Rome.[26] Nor was it a practice unknown in the Royal Academy when Constable was a student there. Amongst his circle of friends was the Scottish painter Andrew Robertson, who – only a few months after Constable had written his well-known letter to John Dunthorne, in which he said he proposed to return to Suffolk and 'make some laborious studies from nature', which would help him 'with respect to colour particularly'[27] –

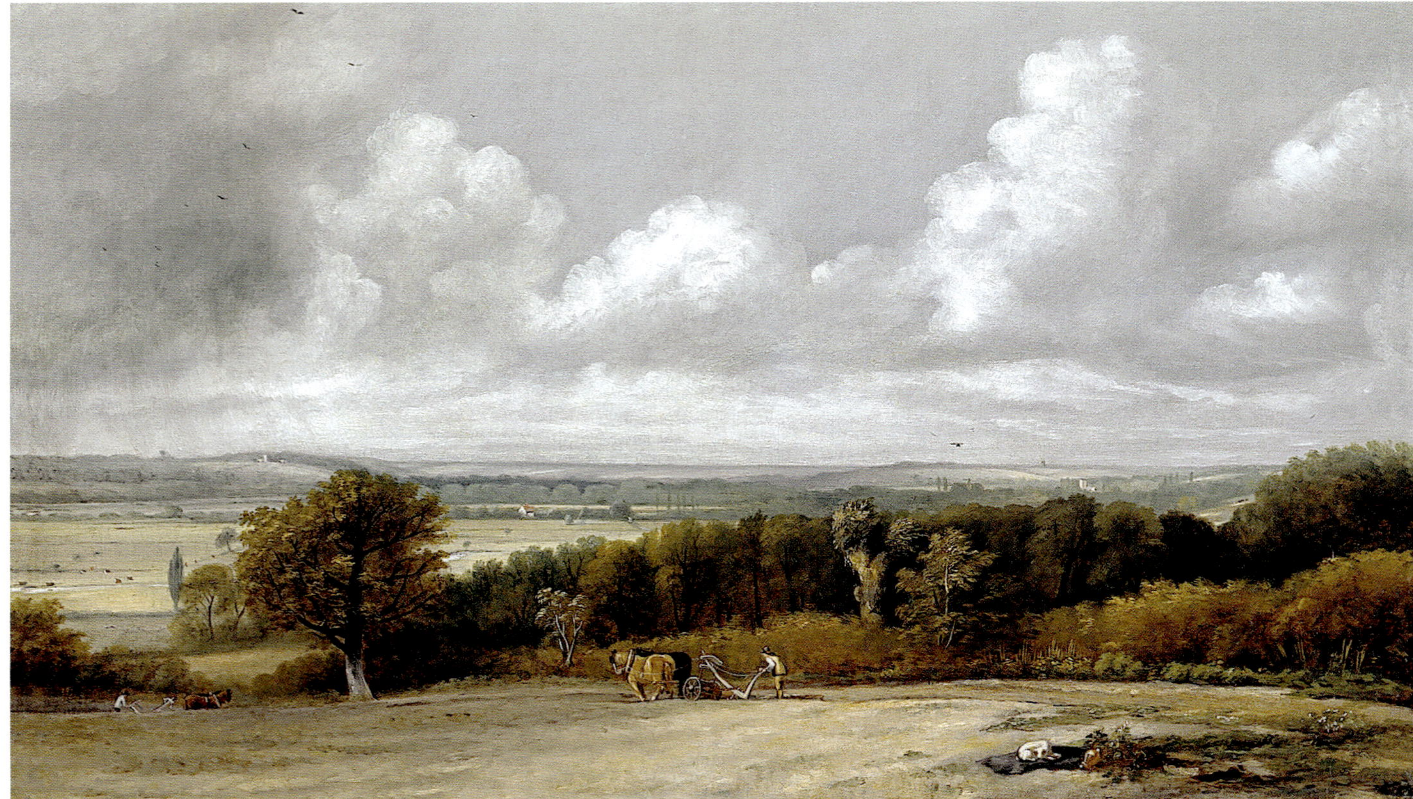

FIGURE 5

was advising his brother that he should:

Draw and copy the colouring of rocks, stumps, foregrounds, plants etc. … Clouds if sketched as they pass, will always carry something to distinguish them from ideal conceptions … It is not sketching but finishing from nature that makes the great artist.

Two years later he wrote, in an even more Constable-like vein: 'All *manner of touch* is bad. Manner makes pictures look like family pictures. Poussin, Claude and Rosa had a manner of *composing* but none of touch.'[28]

So Constable was neither isolated nor innovative in his approach to studying nature; likewise his method of incorporating outdoor sketches and studies into large exhibition paintings, and making small preparatory studies of their compositions, was thoroughly conventional. What was not at all traditional, and what constitutes his most original contribution to landscape art, was precisely the development of the full-size sketch for ten or a dozen of his large exhibition canvases, which Kenneth Clark has called Constable's 'supreme achievement'.[29] That this was no ordinary achievement may be gauged from its high cost. In 1822 Constable was begging from Fisher a loan of £20 or £30, 'as painting these large pictures have [*sic*] much impoverished me at this time'.[30] The large sketches involved at least double the cost of time and materials, and since only one version would be exhibitable and saleable, Constable was effectively painting one picture for the price of two. Sarah Cove has proposed in this catalogue (p.56) that Constable worked on the sketch canvases pinned to the wall, so at least for them he would have been spared the cost of stretchers; but she has also shown that there was no distinction in the types of canvas used for 'sketch' and 'exhibition' work.

Most of the full-size sketches were dispersed at the painter's posthumous sale in 1838, but we hear little or nothing of them for twenty years after that until, with the rise to popularity of French Barbizon landscape, some of them began to appear in public exhibitions in England. Probably the first, and certainly the most interesting instance of this, was the showing of *The Hay Wain* (no.36) and *The Leaping Horse* (no.46) sketches, close to (but not in the same gallery as) their respective pictures (nos.37, 47) at the International Exhibition held in South Kensington in 1862. Here they were noticed by the Redgrave brothers, who were both artists (Richard an RA), and who had worked on the selection of the exhibits. Four years later they gave what must be the first analysis of the role of these sketches in Constable's art:

These are commencements for two of Constable's pictures, which are invaluable, not only for their intrinsic qualities, but as illustrations of his mode of conducting his pictures … The subjects are laid in with the knife, with great breadth and in a grand and large manner. Various glazings have then been passed over the parts, to bring together and enrich them (even the skies are glazed); and then the whole has again had enhancing points of colour added, brightness and daylight being obtained by further draggings and knife touches. With the exception of the glazings, it would seem as if the brush had not been used upon them; hence there is a complete absence of any sort of detail.

When Constable had carried his study thus far, and was pleased with the indications it contained, he would leave it without further completion, perhaps fearing to lose what he was so satisfied with – for it must be confessed, that Constable was a man who had sufficient self-esteem, in the language of the phrenologists, to think well of his own

works – he would leave it without completion, and begin again on a new canvas, endeavouring to retain the fine qualities of the studied sketch, adding to it such an amount of completeness and detail as could be given without loss of the higher qualities of breadth and general truth. How completely this was effected would be at once seen by comparing the incomplete with the completed work … It was a lesson [in 1862] that might be most valuable to young artists if they could read it aright. And to the despisers of the method followed by the older masters of our school [?the Pre-Raphaelite Brotherhood], Constable himself knew the value of such studies, for he rarely parted with them.[31]

This is an interesting analysis, but it gives no sense of the struggle Constable evidently had with the full-size sketches, and then with the exhibition paintings, all of which show many signs of changes of mind. We are able to follow this struggle in some detail, because the painter opened himself readily to Fisher, who purchased the first exhibited six-footer in 1819, but had to wait many months for its delivery, since Constable wanted to work 'a good deal' on it for a proposed second exhibition, apparently 'to subdue a few lights and cool [the] trees'.[32] This was to be a recurrent pattern. As Sarah Cove shows, Constable in the later 1820s was to work on paintings such as *The Leaping Horse* (no.47; see p.64) and *Chain Pier, Brighton* (no.51; see p.56) after their exhibition, in a style far broader than that of the original painting, which suggests that the 'sketch' style was becoming increasingly satisfying to him.

The sketch for *The White Horse* (no.28), when it was exhibited at the Old Masters Exhibition at the Royal Academy ten years after the South Kensington International Exhibition, aroused, it seems, none of the Redgraves' reflections on 'completed' and 'uncompleted' paintings. The painter James Smetham, despite his closeness to Ruskin, Constable's chief detractor in the nineteenth century, wrote rhapsodically of:

that solemn reflective grandeur of rural peace, 'ancient peace', in the two cottages, the river bank, the disappearing barge with the white horse *in it*, not pulling it. Men might paint ten thousand pictures with two cottages by a river, a barge, and a white horse, and they should be feeble and worthless. Nay, more, hundreds of painters since Constable could have united the material of the picture better. That is a blotch, and not much like a dock leaf in the foreground, and the rest of the work is equally obscure as a mere matter of photographic resemblance. Whence, then, that mystic overruling charm? Have we not felt something of the same influence when in some recess of life, far away in the country's heart, on a gray afternoon we have dreamily watched the rain-waggons of the sky, the large clouds of silver gray, slow moving, drawn by their slow 'White Horses'? … We may burn our copy of Shakespeare, but we must not lay hands on Constable's 'White Horse' when the hoary tints of true fame gather (as the lichens and weather stains encrust and gild an abbey) over a picture that has touched the heart of the world.

Although *The White Horse* canvas (no.29) had been re-exhibited at the Manchester Art Treasures Exhibition in 1857, Smetham thought the sketch was in fact the painting bought by Fisher, and sent to France in 1825, where it 'began to form a French school of landscape when as yet in his mother country her rustic [!] son was unregarded and depreciated'.[33] Despite Smetham's talk of 'blotches', it may well be that hands had indeed already been laid on the sketch, to bring it up to a saleable finish, as Charles Rhyne has revealed in this catalogue (p.43).

Throughout the early 1820s the relationship of Constable's full-scale sketches to the exhibited pictures underwent a constant transformation, and they came closer and closer together. When Constable wrote to Fisher about *View on the Stour near Dedham* (no.39) early in April 1822, he referred to the 'composition' his friend had seen two or three months before, which he had now changed substantially. Some of the changes had already been made in the 'sketch' (no.38), for example, the painting out of the large sail towards the left (fig.40, p.61); others, such as the adding of a barge and lighterman, only appear in the final version, to give the picture 'a rich centre', thereby taking away the emphasis on the bridge to the right (Constable first thought of the work as *The Bridge*) and making it 'only an accessory'.[34] What made this exhibited work 'better than any I have yet done' was, it seems, that 'some of the parts were very nicely finished',[35] and this is certainly so. The enforced speed of painting this second canvas helped the finish, as in *The Hay Wain*, for it is hard to see how the finesse and freedom of touch could have been achieved on top of the much revised and heavily impasted sketch.

A far more radical process of revision took place with Constable's next six-foot RA submission, *The Lock* (no.41). Not only are there many pentimenti in the full-scale sketch for the composition in Philadelphia (no.40), but as the x-radiograph of the latter indicates (fig.72, p.153), the format was changed during execution from a horizontal to a vertical composition. Some experiments with format are also a feature of two related drawings of the subject (R.23.8; fig.71, p.153, R.26.17, usually dated 1826, but possibly earlier). The horizontal format re-established itself two years later in the unfinished oil in Melbourne (fig.8, p.28; R.26.16) and in Constable's RA Diploma Painting (fig.70, p.152; R.26.15), which differs from all the previous versions in the position of the lighterman's crowbar. The handling of the two upright versions is closer than before, and Constable drew Fisher's attention to this:

My execution annoys most of [the RAs] and all the scholastic ones – perhaps the sacrifices I make for *lightness* and *brightness* is too much, but these things are the essence of landscape.[36]

Some of the underpainting of the Philadelphia version is more refined than the upper layers, and it has therefore been suggested that Constable had not decided which version was to be 'finished' until a late stage.[37] However, as Franklin Kelly points out (p.152), the bold handling of the large sketch might well indicate that it was always intended only ever to be a study, and it now seems more likely that the more refined areas underneath must belong to what remains of the abandoned (horizontal) earlier version of the composition.

In the case of Constable's last great Stour landscape, *The Leaping Horse*, exhibited at the RA in 1825 (no.47), C.R. Leslie conjectured that the painter did not decide which version to send to the exhibition until the last minute, in other words that both canvases were worked on simultaneously until a late stage in their evolution. It is true that both versions are full of changes, and the 'bustle incident' described to Fisher at the end of January 1825: 'four or five boats passing with dogs, horses, boys & men & women & children, and best of all old timber-props, water-plants, willow stumps, sedges, old nets &c &c &c',[38] has been considerably simplified even in the Victoria and Albert full-size sketch (no.46). Furthermore, Constable found it hard to know when the exhibited version was finished; as he told Fisher, 'I must say that no picture ever departed from my easil with more anxiety on my part with

it … it should have been on my easil a few weeks longer'.[39] However, there are other instances when Constable sent in pictures to the Academy exhibition before he had finished working on them, *The Opening of Waterloo Bridge* 1832 (no.67) being a case in point. Furthermore, it may be significant that Leslie's comment about Constable's uncertainty as to which version of *The Leaping Horse* to exhibit was dropped from all subsequent editions of the *Memoirs*, perhaps because he (Leslie) changed his mind about this point. If, however, at any stage Constable had wondered whether to try to work up the Victoria and Albert version as the exhibition example, it is difficult to imagine how he could have recovered it from its present appearance, caked in impasto, and thus succeed in creating the calm fresh effect he was after.

This last Stour landscape was also the last for a number of years for which Constable prepared a full-size sketch version. For his later large exhibition landscapes – *The Cornfield* 1826 (fig.59, p.116), *Chain Pier, Brighton* 1827 (no.51), *Dedham Vale* 1828 (fig.74, p.164) – he made do with complete compositional sketches or alternative studies on a smaller (usually half-size) scale, partly perhaps because he was now so confident in his management of these large compositions that he could save himself the time and expense of full-scale studies. It may be significant that he returned to the earlier practice with *Hadleigh Castle* (nos.56, 57), an unusually sublime, and hence more obviously academic, subject, which in 1829 marked his final acceptance as a full Academician. The painting's subtitle, *morning, after a stormy night*, has led scholars to link the unusual subject with Constable's depression after the death of his wife the previous November, but the accompanying extract from the 1744 edition of James Thomson's 'Summer' from *The Seasons* (1727), with its opening lines:

The desert joys
Wildly, through all his melancholy bounds
Rude ruins glitter …

gives an upbeat interpretation to the scene, which is a prelude to the rainbow inserted into the exhibited version of *Salisbury Cathedral from the Meadows* two years later (no.61), also accompanied by an optimistic passage from Thomson's 'Summer', concluding:

… as if in sign
Of danger past, a glittering robe of joy,
Set off abundant by the yellow ray,
Invests the fields, and nature smiles reviv'd.

In these two compositions, the 'sketch' versions are far more unrelentingly turbulent than the exhibited paintings.

Kenneth Clark has argued that the whole procedure of making full-size sketches was, for Constable, more psychological than technical:

The boldness and freedom of touch were partly a means of rendering effects of light, partly a means of expressing emotion; and it was only possible to conserve the vividness of the original emotion on this scale if he felt free from all anxieties of finish and logical composition. The full-size studies were not so much dress rehearsals as emotional discharges which allowed him to attack his final canvas without a feeling of frustration.[40]

We have seen that such a tidy explanation does not fit each case, and that it remains the case that the full-scale sketches are puzzling. Charles Rhyne, the leading modern student of the large sketches, has suggested that, at least in the case of the full-size sketch of *The White Horse* (no.28),

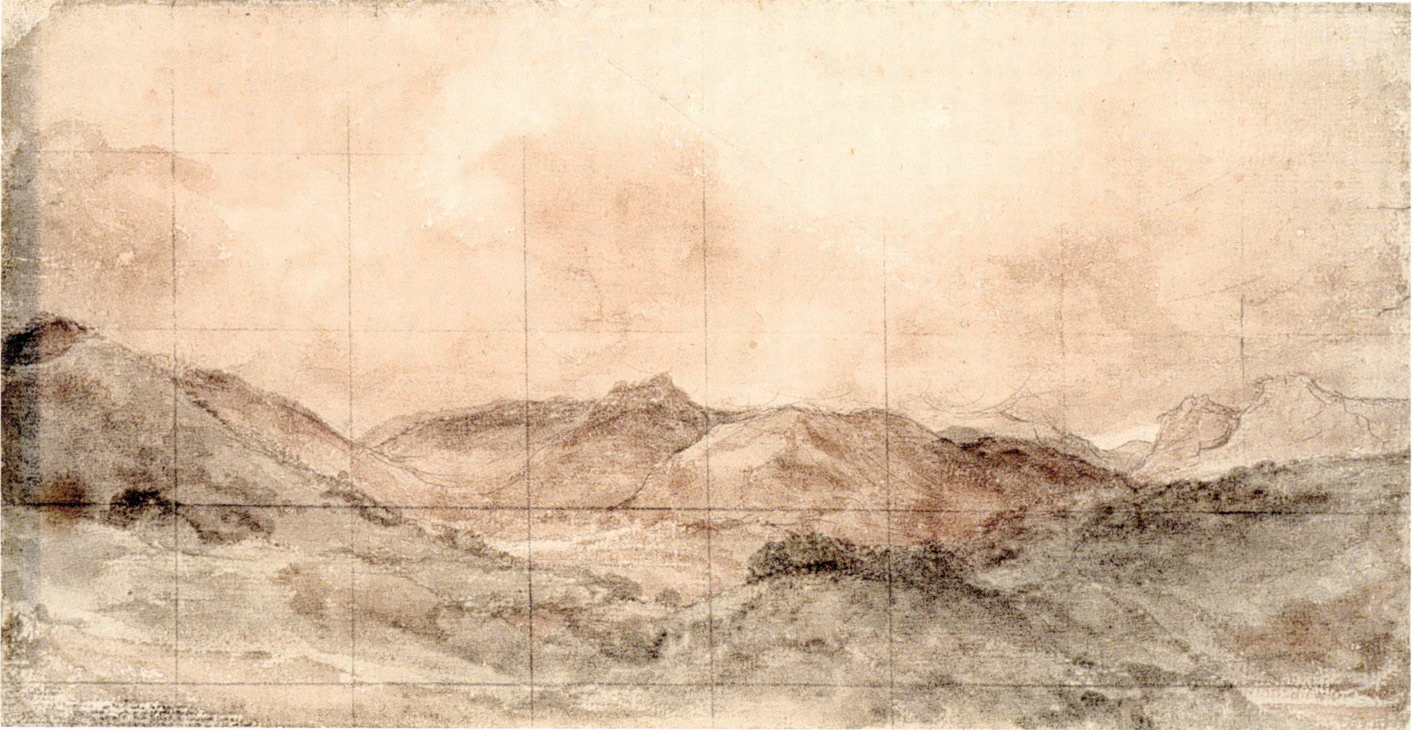

FIGURE 6

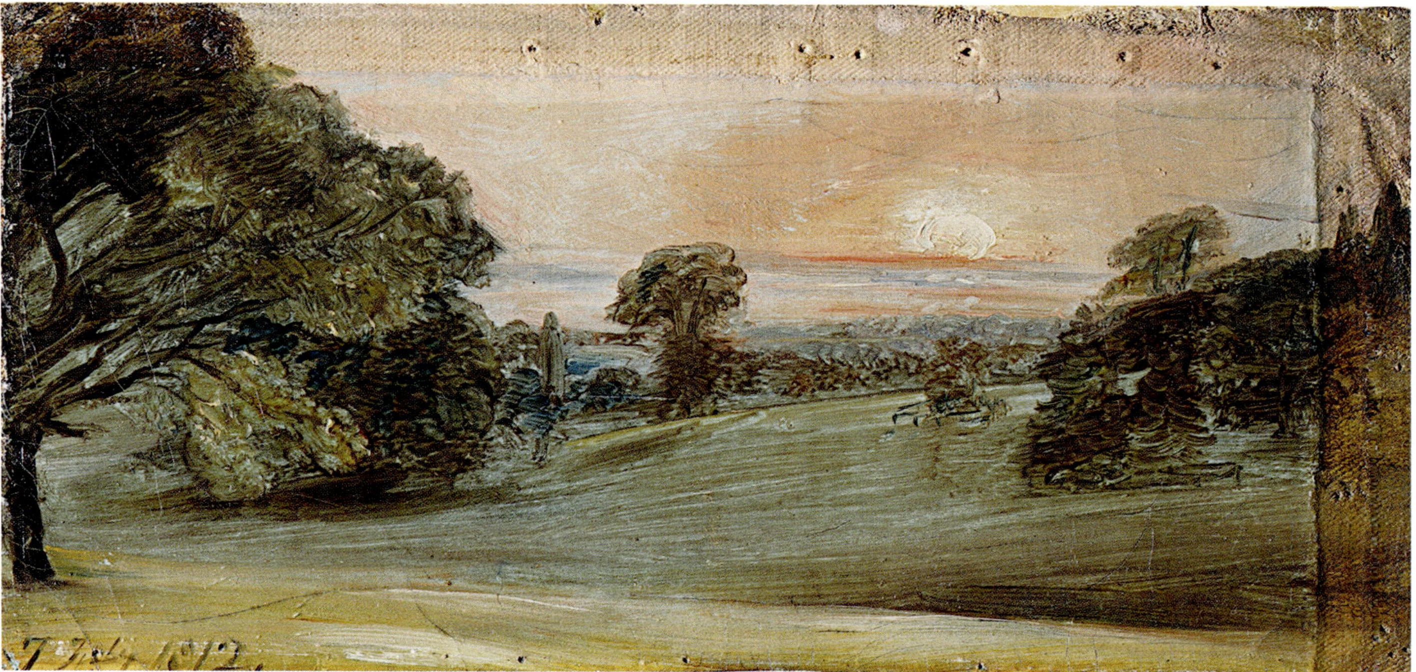

FIGURE 7

Figure 8
A Boat Passing a Lock
c.1823–6
Oil on canvas
103.5 × 129.9 (40¾ × 51⅛)
NATIONAL GALLERY OF VICTORIA,
MELBOURNE. FELTON BEQUEST, 1950

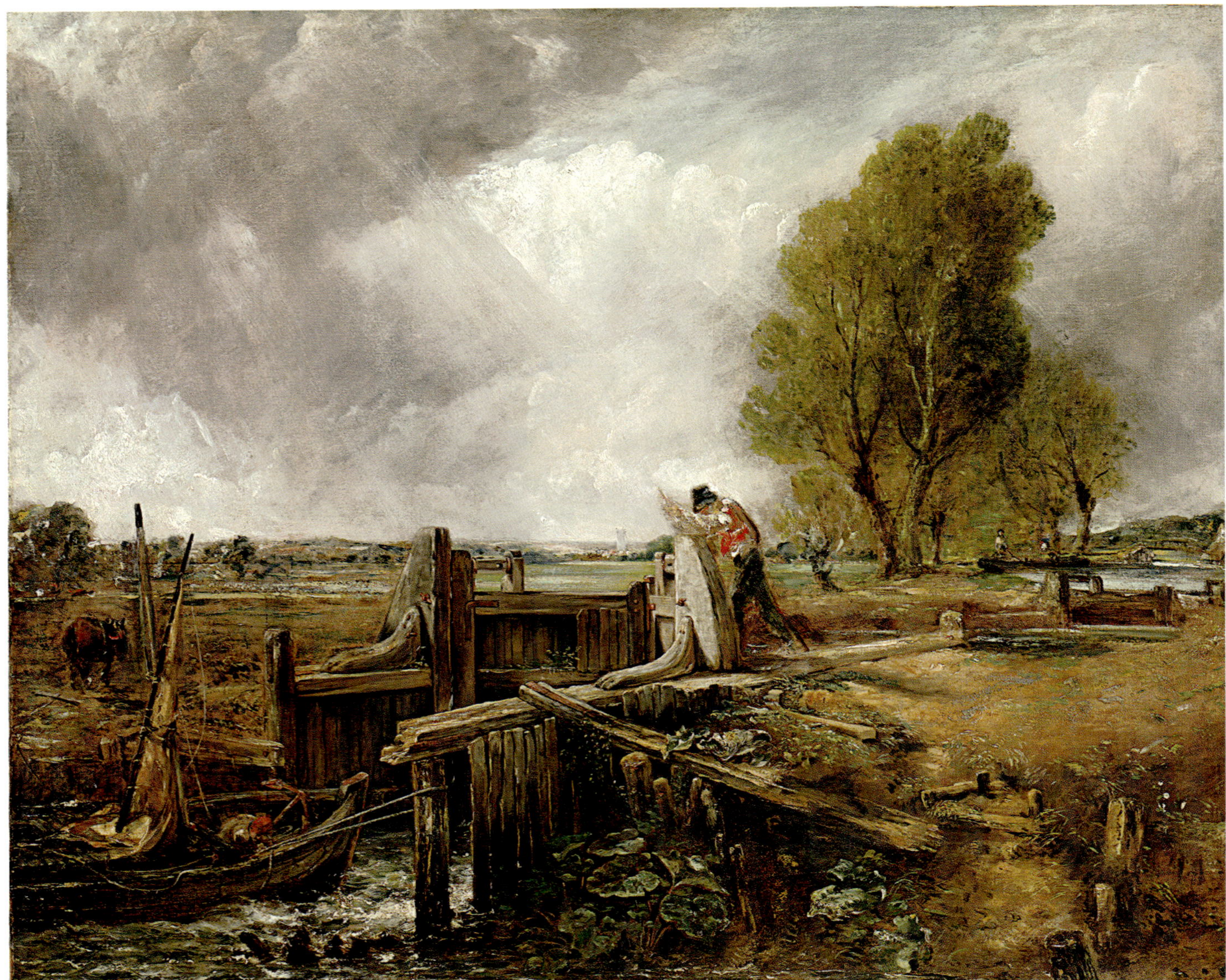

FIGURE 8

his main purpose … was not to preserve the vigor of the small sketches, but to solve the compositional problems posed when he attempted to base his first six-foot exhibition piece on a two-foot oil sketch and other small drawings and sketches done from nature, which did not automatically provide an integrated composition on so large a scale.

The lack of references to Constable's full-size sketches, even in his extensive correspondence with intimate friends, must surely indicate their private nature and therefore their importance in attempting to understand the psychology of Constable's working procedure.[41]

Although it is now clear that Constable did not regard his sketches quite so privately as was previously thought (see p.52), the references to psychology by both Clark and Rhyne are surely crucial. For Constable was not only a highly emotional person, but also an artist capable of weaving his feelings intimately into his work. Not only was his subject matter dependent on an intense love of his family's countryside, and of the places to which he was taken by friendships or the needs of his wife and children, but he was also deeply obsessed with himself and with his reputation, which in his day was to be made largely at the Royal Academy. As Leslie wrote of Constable, more candidly than usual, in his own autobiography:

No man more earnestly desired to stand well with the world; no artist was more solicitous of popularity. He had, as the phrenologists would say, *the love of approbation* very strongly developed.[42]

We have seen how much the six-foot format was a function of Constable's yearning for Academic recognition. Long before the arrival of the six-footers – but after he had acquired facility with pencil and brush – Constable saw the countryside around him in terms of pictures: the 1813 and 1814 sketchbooks are full not only of details, but also of thumbnail sketches of whole compositions, several of which, including *Hadleigh Castle* (no.53), later became large paintings. And long before the development of the six-foot sketch, Constable had found a supremely various and flexible way of working in oil, so that brushmarks became indices of feeling. Constable was a painter – probably the first in landscape – able to transform his love of country and weather directly into technique. The terms he used for the movement of nature: fresh, blowy, sparkle, found their equivalents in the movement of brush or pencil. He wrote to Fisher in 1830:

I have filled my head with certain notions of *freshness – sparkle – brightness* – till it has influenced my practice in no small degree, & is in fact taking the place of truth so invidious in manner, in all things – it is a species of self-worship – which should always be combated – & we have nature (another word for moral feeling) always in our reach to do it with – if we will have the resolution to look at her.[43]

But 'nature', for Constable, now took on a more abstract, more generalising, aspect.[44]

Academic recognition, financial security, the urge to promote landscape more widely through lectures and the publication of *English Landscape*, as well as failing health, all led Constable to restrict his production to less ambitious formats. The last of his six-footers, *The Opening of Waterloo Bridge* (no.67), had caused him trouble for more than a decade, and he was still 'brushing it up' two years after its exhibition in 1832. In the letter to George Constable in which he mentioned this, the painter added: 'The difficulty is to find a subject fit for the largest of my sizes. I will talk to you about one, either a canal or a rural affair, or a wood, or a harvest scene.'[45]

In the end it was to be a quintessentially Constable rural scene, including a wood, which occupied him in his final years, *Stoke-by-Nayland* c.1835–7 (no.68), now recognised as the last of the full-scale sketches. This final, strenuous effort to immortalise the Suffolk landscape, already known as 'Constable Country', came about largely through the stimulus of a late friendship with the amateur landscape painter William Purton, a Hampstead neighbour who became one of Constable's most sensitive supporters. It was in a letter to Purton that he spoke of his 'great Salisbury' (no.61), on which he was still working for another exhibition in 1834; and Purton proposed, after the artist's death, that it should be acquired by subscription for the nation.[46] Constable and Purton clearly discussed the problems of large paintings, for Purton passed on one of the painter's aphorisms: 'A large canvas will show you what you cannot do, a small one will only show you what you can.'[47]

It may well be that it was the *Stoke-by-Nayland* that was in question when Constable wrote to Purton late in 1834 that 'I seem foolishly bent on a large canvas'; certainly he wrote the following year appreciating Purton's encouragement to continue with the project.[48] Just as *English Landscape* included a fair sample of six-footer images (though not all of them were published in Constable's lifetime, see no.2), so the *Stoke*, closely related to plate 7 of that work, is a kind of summing-up of Constable's favourite motifs. Listing them to Purton, he concluded with a characteristically rural metaphor: 'the size of the canvas sufficient to try one's strength, and keep one at full collar.'

After Constable's death in 1837, Purton and Leslie toured Constable Country, very much with the images of the six-footers in mind. They found that some of the motifs, such as the cottage and bridge in *View on the Stour* (no.39), were exactly as he had painted them, while others, such as the river in *The White Horse* (no.29) and *The Hay Wain* (no.37) had been widened by him 'to great advantage'. Purton summed up Constable's achievement by noting all the difficulties he had overcome to reach the 'highest attainments of art', but he recognised that these attainments were due, most of all, to 'the purest and warmest admiration and affection for the scenes and effects which he represented'.[49]

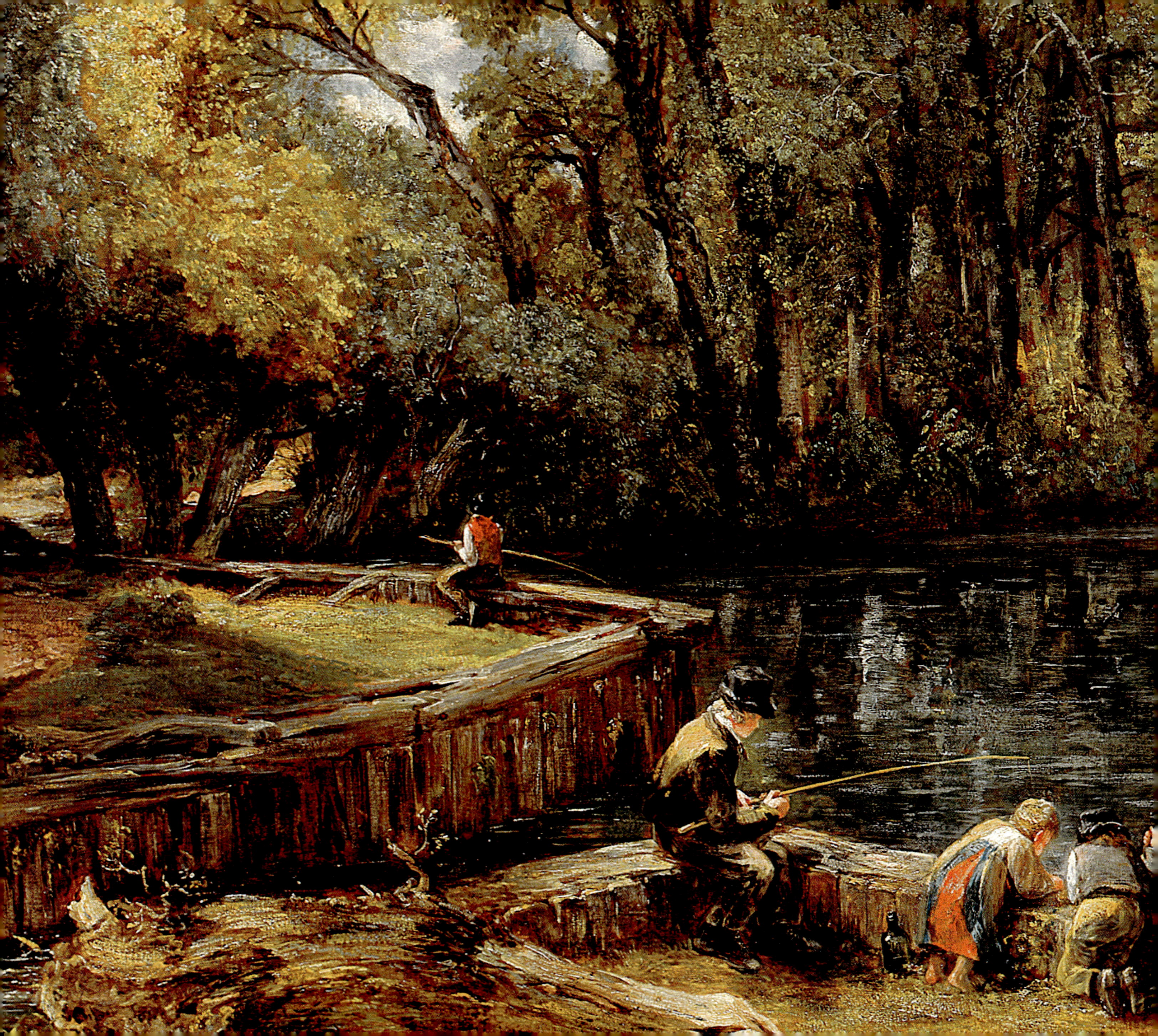

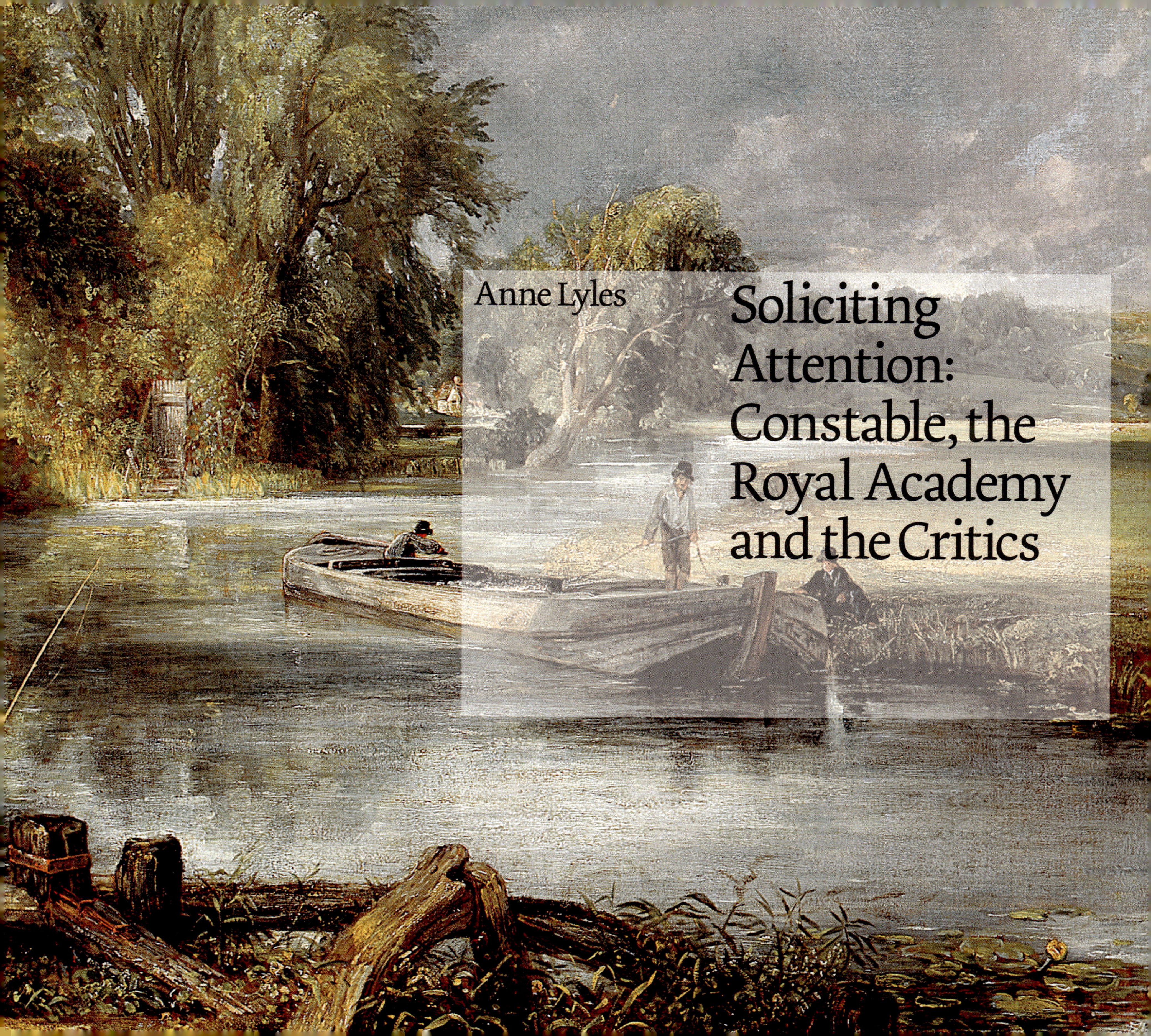
Anne Lyles
Soliciting Attention: Constable, the Royal Academy and the Critics

Soliciting Attention: Constable, the Royal Academy and the Critics
Anne Lyles

It was at about sixteen or seventeen years of age that Constable first apparently developed a fondness for painting.[1] It took him seven years to persuade his father, a prosperous mill owner and coal merchant in Suffolk, to allow him to pursue an artistic career, and he was already in his early twenties when he arrived in London in 1799 to join the Royal Academy Schools. In one of his earliest surviving letters, Constable writes excitedly to his East Bergholt friend the elder John Dunthorne to tell him that he has been accepted as a student in the Schools, and mentions the pictures he has recently seen or intends to copy, as well as the lodgings he has taken close to the Academy in the Strand.[2] One wonders, at this stage, if Constable had any inkling of the long struggle for recognition that lay ahead.

The Royal Academy had been founded in 1768, with backing from George III, by thirty-four leading painters, sculptors and architects under the presidency of the portrait painter Joshua Reynolds. It was a fully constitutional body run by its own members. As well as a President, it had Academicians, Associate Academicians, and Professors who lectured on the fine arts as well as on academic subjects such as ancient history and literature. It ran the first school in Britain for the professional training of painters, sculptors and architects. Above all, from as early as 1769, it organised a self-financing Annual Exhibition of works by living artists, which were selected by a jury made up from the members. On the crowded walls of the Academy's exhibition spaces, an aspiring artist would hope, not only in the first instance for his (or occasionally her) pictures to be noticed, but also to attract favourable commentary in the press as well as feedback from fellow artists, especially the Academicians. During the exhibitions, which usually opened on 1 May and which, by Constable's day, lasted for up to ten weeks, an artist might also hope to meet potential patrons interested either in buying their pictures or perhaps commissioning alternative ones, for art dealers at this date still generally only handled pictures by the Old Masters. In short, until well into the nineteenth century, the Royal Academy was the main exhibition venue for an aspiring artist hoping to build a professional reputation and to make a living.[3]

The first treasurer of the Royal Academy had been the neo-classical architect, William Chambers, who in 1775 won the commission to design London's new Somerset House on the Strand. The north wing of the new building, the Strand façade, was given over to purpose-built accommodation for the recently founded Academy (fig.9). On the ground floor a room was designed as the space where artists would make drawings from the life model (the Academy of the Living Model; see room 1, fig.9). On the first floor there were rooms to house the Library (room 2, fig.9) and the Academy's collection of plaster casts taken from classical and antique statuary (the Antique Academy, room 3). There was also a Council Room (room 4), later used to display the paintings presented as 'Diploma' works by newly elected Academicians. Most significantly, however, on the top floor of the building Chambers designed an elegant and functional top-lit gallery known as the Great Room, for the annual display of paintings by living artists (room 6, fig.9). An engraving of 1787, showing a crowd of fashionable visitors gathered in the Great Room with Reynolds and the Prince of Wales in the foreground, gives a good impression of how pictures were hung there (fig.10). The gallery contained a wooden moulding running around the walls at the height of the doors, situated some eight feet (2.5m) from the ground. This was designed to serve

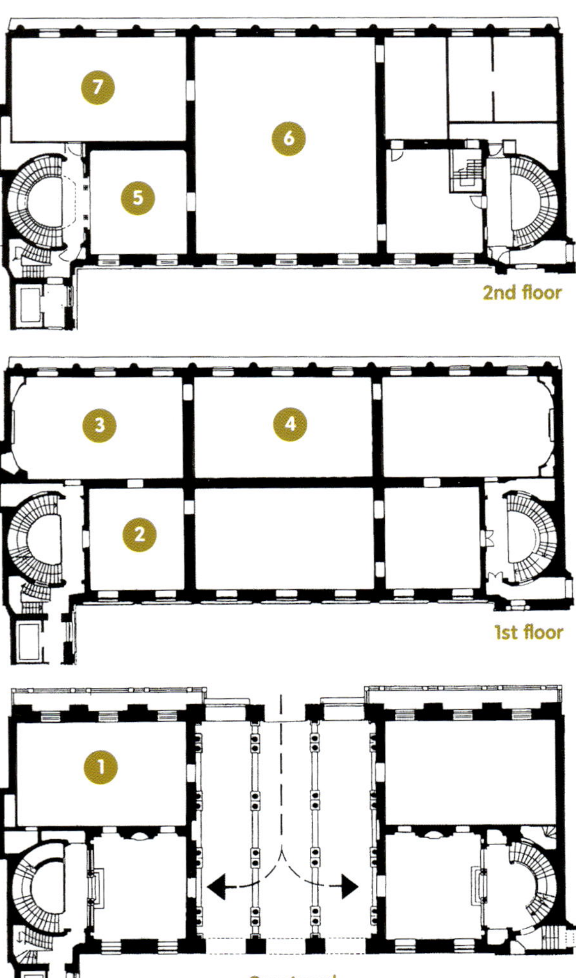

FIGURE 9

as a way of establishing a common base-line height for the largest canvases. However the moulding also had a practical function in helping to support the weight of the pictures. With the help of a wooden armature, the pictures could also be locked into position on to the moulding in such a way that their tops could hang forwards and outwards to avoid reflections caused by daylight flooding into the gallery from the windows and glass skylight above.[4]

A position 'on the line' – that is, a position with the bottom edge of the frame resting on the moulding – thus came to be seen as one of the most prestigious placings, something that can only, in turn, have encouraged artists to paint pictures on a deliberately larger scale in an attempt to secure such a placing. Meanwhile, smaller and more highly worked canvases tended to be hung at eye level in the Great Room, or else somewhat lower beneath it. What artists most dreaded, it seems, was to find that their paintings had been placed at the highest level in the gallery, and were thus barely visible at all. It is nevertheless debatable whether it was a worse fate to have a work 'skied' in the Great Room or else to have it hung, perhaps more advantageously, in an alternative space such as the Ante-room adjacent (room 5, fig.9).

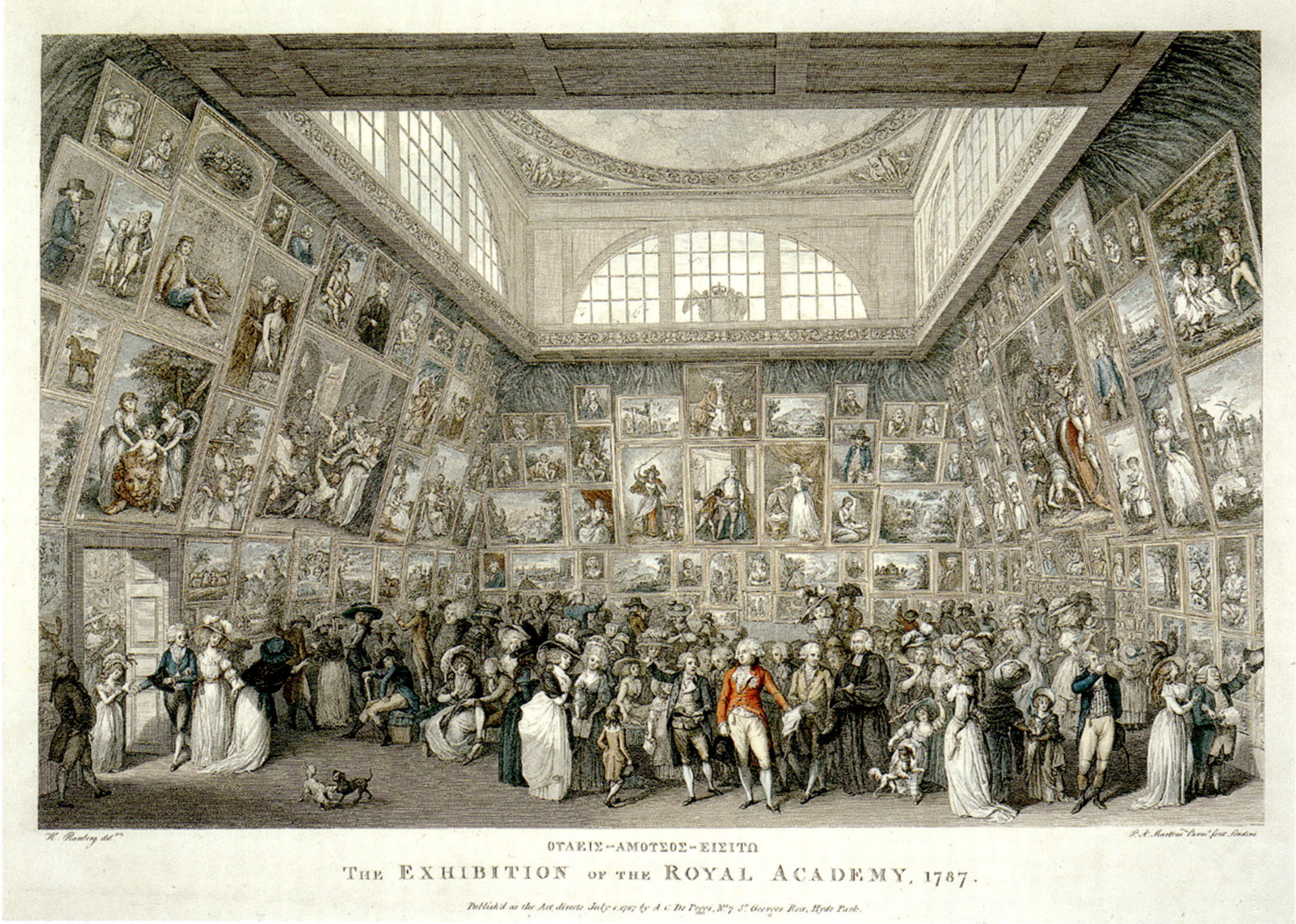

FIGURE 10

Indeed, as the Academy exhibitions grew larger, some paintings, whether large or small, came to be placed in another room on the upper level known as the Inner Room (room 7, fig.9). This was first brought into use as an exhibition space in 1811, though it was referred to in the Academy catalogues from 1818 as the School of Painting (as it was also used from 1816 to teach the practice and technique of oil painting).[5] Smaller pictures, however, might be placed on a different level altogether, usually on the first floor, in the Library or in the Antique Academy. Watercolours and drawings were routinely placed in these latter rooms to the annoyance of the artists concerned, most especially as these spaces were side lit, which tended to cause glare or else bad reflections if a work was glazed.[6] Meanwhile, other works, again usually drawings, were hung in the room on the ground floor used during the rest of the year for drawing from the living model. Constable's exhibition watercolour of *His Majesty's Ship Victory, Capt. E. Harvey, in the Memorable battle of Trafalgar, between two French ships of the Line* (Victoria and Albert Museum; R.06.1) for example, was exhibited in the Academy of the Living Model in 1806 (see no.3).

A good or a bad placing could make the difference between an artist being noticed or entirely overlooked. Thus for any young painter at the start of their career – and this was especially the case for Constable – each spring was accompanied by anxieties as to whether their pictures submitted for the Academy exhibition would be accepted by the jury, whether they would receive favourable placings, and how they might be judged by critics and fellow artists. Early in his career, Constable had the advantage of being given a letter of introduction to the Academician Joseph Farington, a landscape painter of moderate talent better known today for his famous *Diary*, but a key figure in the Academy's politics and thus an invaluable contact. Farington took kindly to the young Constable and offered him regular encouragement and advice. Constable would often call on him – though sometimes it was vice versa – to show him the latest picture he was planning or, perhaps, had already painted in East Bergholt the previous summer, and ask his opinion as to whether it was of sufficient merit to submit to the exhibition. In the spring of 1802, for example, when Constable was planning to exhibit at the Academy for the first time, he asked Farington's advice about the landscape he was planning to submit to the jury. Farington told him he thought the painting had 'a great deal

Figure 11
Dedham Vale: Morning
1811
Oil on canvas
78.8×129.5 (31×51)
PRIVATE COLLECTION

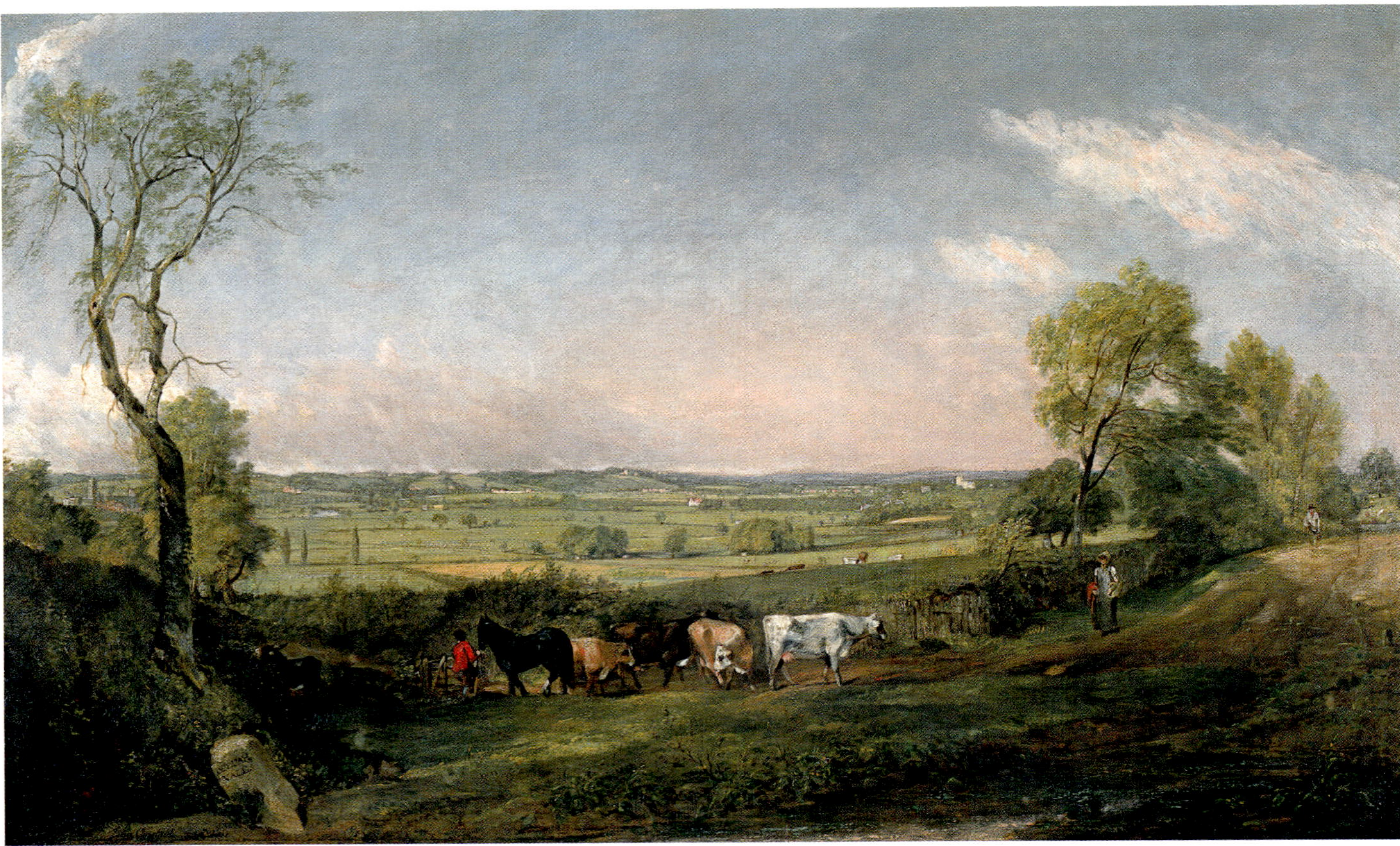

FIGURE 11

of merit but is rather too cold'.[7] However, we know from the Academy catalogue that the picture, *A Landscape*, was not only accepted for exhibition but also allocated a place in the Great Room.[8]

Indeed, with the exception of three works accepted for exhibition at the Academy in 1803, until 1811 all Constable's oil paintings (as opposed to watercolours or drawings) received placings in the Great Room. Even in 1803, when these three works were hung in the Library, the fourth picture accepted for exhibition, *A study from Nature*, conceivably identifiable with the famous early *Dedham Vale* closely modelled on a landscape by the seventeenth-century French painter Claude Lorraine (see figs.50, 51, pp.76–7), was allocated a position in the Great Room. It was not until 1807, however, that Constable's work received any individual notice in the press. As Judy Ivy has pointed out, the fact that his earliest exhibition landscapes appear to have made so little impact on the reviewers may reflect less on the paintings themselves than on the reviewing practices of the time. For the daily newspapers and frequently published periodicals, such as the *Morning Chronicle* or *The Examiner*, tended to concentrate on works by Academicians, Associates or honorary exhibitors, whose status was singled out by abbreviations in the accompanying catalogue, and rarely turned their attention to lesser known or younger artists with no newsworthy commissions or sales.[9] In this context it may be significant that when, for example, Constable achieved what appears to have been his first exhibition sale in 1810, *A landscape*, purchased that year by the Earl of Dysart for 30 guineas, he received no fewer than four different notices

in the press, albeit two of these were in the local *Ipswich Journal*.[10] Indeed, thanks to two of the reviewers' descriptions of the picture, as well as the fact that we also know it was painted on a 'kit-kat' scale (36×28in/91.5×71cm), we can conjecture that it may be identifiable with *The Mill Stream* c.1810–14 now at Ipswich (no.9). Meanwhile, Constable's first securely identified exhibit at the Academy, the more modestly sized *A church-yard* (no.4), also shown in 1810, seems to have escaped any critical notice whatsoever.

Just when it was looking as though Constable was beginning to attract some notice at the Academy, in 1811 he suffered a serious setback. Over the autumn and winter of 1810 to 1811 he had been hard at work on his most ambitious portrayal of a Suffolk subject to date, *Dedham Vale: Morning* (fig.11). It was a picture on which he appears to have ventured a great deal. By 1810 he was already contemplating marriage to Maria Bicknell, and therefore under increasing pressure to establish himself in his profession and thus secure financial stability. Indeed in June that year he followed Farington's advice in entering his name for the first time in the lists for the annual election of new associate members the following November.[11] Perhaps as a result of failing to be elected, Constable then became especially anxious about the reception of *Dedham Vale: Morning*, when he sent it to the Academy the following spring, for – at 31×51 in– this was his largest exhibition picture submitted so far. As it happened, that year Constable was to receive one of the worst placings of his entire career for the painting. On 23 April, Farington noted in his *Diary* that:

It is hard to deduce from this whether, for Constable, the bigger insult was to have had his picture hung so low or for it to have been placed in the Ante-room, having so far enjoyed positions in the Great Room for all his oils since 1805. Perhaps it was the combination of these two facts that led Constable to draw such a demoralising conclusion. Farington did his best to reassure him by telling him that the portrait painter Thomas Lawrence had twice noticed his picture with great approval.[13] However, Constable's worst fears must have been realised when, as a likely consequence of the poor placing, his view of *Dedham Vale: Morning* failed to receive a single notice in the press, and perhaps for the same reason did not find a buyer.[14]

Whether Constable was right in interpreting the poor placement of *Dedham Vale: Morning* as an implied rebuff is difficult to say. Passionate about his profession and ambitious to succeed in it, he was prone to take offence too easily. He also had a tendency to speak his mind, and some of his caustic comments about art and other artists seem to have alienated him from some of his colleagues over the years, one or two of whom would no doubt have served from time to time on the 'Committee of Arrangement' (hanging committee), whose job it was to decide where works should be placed. However, there may be a more straightforward explanation in this case. Constable had given his painting a title in the catalogue that located its subject in a very specific geographical area, Dedham Vale in Essex. By contrast, all his landscape oils that had received placings in the Great Room in previous years had been submitted with more generalised titles such as *A landscape* or *A church-yard*. An exception to this was the group of Lake District oils that Constable exhibited at the Academy in 1807 and 1808, all of which were similarly given positions in the Great Room. However this mountainous region in the northwest of England had for many years been a fashionable destination for tourists and artists in search of picturesque and sublime scenery, and Lakeland subjects would therefore have been held in higher regard than a landscape like *Dedham Vale: Morning*, which showed the flatter and more unassuming landscape of the Suffolk–Essex border.

Thus, although Constable's *Dedham Vale: Morning* owes something to Claude Lorraine in its representation of early morning light and the careful placing of the foreground tree, thanks to its title, those serving on the hanging committee in 1811 may have classified it as a topographical work. Topographical landscape was dedicated to the rather literal task of accurately describing a particular location or, as Henry Fuseli once so famously dubbed it, 'the tame delineation of a given spot'.[15] It stood at the very lowest end of the hierarchy of landscape types, and certainly below ideal or imaginative landscape as practised by the Old Masters such as Claude, Nicolas Poussin, Salvator Rosa or Peter Paul Rubens, on whom most landscape painters in this period attempted to model their work. Meanwhile, as defined by Joshua Reynolds himself in his influential series of *Discourses*, lectures on the theory of art delivered when President of the Royal Academy, landscape as a subject category stood well below history painting, which, of all branches of art, was the one he thought most suited to elevating and enriching the mind. In theory, history painting

was therefore the subject best suited to bring an artist professional success in this period. In practice however it was usually portrait painting that was more likely to enable an artist to earn a respectable living. This explains why Constable was under pressure at the beginning of his career from his family to specialise in portraiture rather than landscape, even though portraiture and landscape probably fell into a similar category in terms of their perceived – that is, relatively low – status.

Constable was a great admirer of Reynolds and knew the *Discourses* well, and he was also a loyal supporter of the Royal Academy.[16] In addition, he greatly valued the example of the Old Masters.[17] However he also knew that he had to make his own way in landscape, and to some extent this meant rejecting the art of the past, particularly any formulaic or slavish imitation of the methods or styles of other artists. In 1802, for example, he wrote to the elder John Dunthorne that there were no landscapes in that year's Academy exhibition even 'worth looking up to', for, he said, 'the great vice of the present day is *bravura*, an attempt at something beyond the truth … *Fashion* always had, & will have its day – but *Truth* (in all things) only will last and can have just claims on posterity'.[18] Constable disliked anything that he felt was derivative in landscape, and was vehemently opposed to 'manner' in painting, that is, the close imitation of another artist's style resulting in a uniform 'touch' or handling. He knew that he himself had to paint more directly from nature than artists had tended to do before him. He also felt an attraction to his native East Anglian landscape, partly of course because he had lived there and knew it so well, hence his admiration for the Dutch seventeenth-century painters such as Jacob van Ruisdael, whom he praised for being what he called 'stay-at-home' people.[19] It is also clear, however, that following his trip to the more dramatic mountainous scenery of the Lake District in 1806, Constable realised that he felt more at home in a landscape that was more modest and unemphatic, and one which, as he told C.R. Leslie, abounded in human associations.[20] To project his ideas – and, more especially, his feelings – about landscape meant dealing with the scenery he knew and loved best, and with a familiar landscape he would surely be in a better position to present what he called 'the truth'. Constable once said that his 'limited art …[was] to be found under every hedge, and in every lane, and therefore nobody thinks it worth picking up'.[21]

In the context of the times, and most especially in the context of the Academy exhibitions, these were radical ideas. The sort of landscape Constable felt compelled to paint was one potentially more challenging to the establishment of the day than that practised, for example, by J.M.W. Turner, who would generally paint landscapes with historical, classical, biblical or mythological themes, which were thus seen to carry a more elevated message. Turner's precocious talent apart, this difference goes a long way to explaining why, for example, he was elected a full Academician in 1802, whilst Constable had to wait until 1829, even though there was only a year's difference between the two artists in age. Bearing all this in mind, it would seem highly likely, then, that when in 1811 Constable received such a disappointing placing for his *Dedham Vale: Morning*, he was probably contending with a prejudice against topographical view-making from members of the hanging committee, who may have incorrectly associated his work with that landscape genre. Indeed only the following year, another of Constable's exhibits whose location was identified by title, *Salisbury: Morning*, was similarly hung in the Ante-room, when three other landscapes by him with more generalised titles received more favourable placings in the Great Room.[22] Whilst in future years Constable did not necessarily shy away from using an identifying place name in the titles of his exhibited works, whether of Suffolk subjects or otherwise, it is nevertheless the case that he exhibited four out of six of his large River Stour paintings between 1819 and 1825 under generalised titles that in no way linked them with the Stour region: for example, *Stratford Mill* (no.31) was exhibited at the Academy under the title *Landscape*; *The Hay Wain* (no.37) as *Landscape: Noon*; *The Lock* (no.41) as *A boat passing a lock*; and *The Leaping Horse* (no.47) as *Landscape*.[23]

There was, however, another problem affecting Constable's work in general around this date, according to his great friend John Fisher, on whom Constable could always rely for helpful but honest advice. In November 1812 Fisher wrote to Constable to acknowledge receipt of a letter and of a painting by Constable which he had once admired in Constable's presence, and which Constable had subsequently sent him as a gift. Fisher told Constable in his letter about some of the comments this painting had elicited from various friends and acquaintances in Salisbury, both positive and negative. He then summed up his own mixed feelings about the picture in the following terms:

It is most pleasing when you are directed to look at it – but you must be *taken* to it. It does not *sollicit attention* – And this I think true of all your pictures & the real cause of your want of popularity.

By contrast, Fisher went on to say, a picture by Rubens 'pleases before you examine it or even know the subject', and also '*illuminates* a room'. How Rubens achieved such an effect, Fisher could not say: '*hic labor, hoc opus est*'; this was the difficulty.[24] The message, however, was clear. Constable needed to make his paintings attract more attention both at first glance and also from a distance. He would surely have realised that if his work was failing to 'sollicit attention' in the enclosed domestic environment of Fisher's house in Salisbury, it would be under even greater pressure to do so in the much larger rooms, and on the more crowded walls, of the Academy exhibition space itself.

As John Gage has pointed out, Constable was a great admirer of Rubens, particularly of his two large landscapes, *An Autumn Landscape with a View of Het Steen in the Early Morning* and *The Rainbow Landscape*, both of which had been brought to England from Italy in 1803 (see figs.3, 4, pp.22–3). In later years, Constable was to single out some of the most impressive characteristics of Rubens's landscapes as 'freshness' and 'dewy light', or the 'bursts of sunshine' and the 'departing shower' that would invariably accompany his representations of the rainbow.[25] These were to become important features of Constable's own art in his later career, as he sought to capture the 'chiaro'scuro' (light and shade) in nature that gave landscape its expressive voice. No doubt they were also the features that gave Rubens's paintings the power, as Fisher said, to 'illuminate' a room, and from the 1820s they would increasingly confer a similar quality on Constable's landscapes as well. In the first instance, however, Constable needed to apply himself to another aspect of Rubens's art, and in this respect these two particular landscapes set an important example. He needed to paint on a larger scale.

Given that Farington had dissuaded Constable in 1809 from exhibiting a Lake District painting measuring five feet wide (1.52m), by 1811 the artist's largest exhibited canvas to date was *Dedham Vale: Morning*. Despite – or, perhaps, partly because of – the setback he

received over the placing of that work at the Academy exhibition in 1811, by the autumn and winter of 1812 to 1813 Constable decided to paint an exhibition canvas on a larger canvas, a 'half-length' (50×40 in/1.27×1.02m) turned to a horizontal format, *Landscape: Boys Fishing* (National Trust, Anglesey Abbey, Cambridgeshire; R.13.1A), submitting it to the Academy in 1813. Although placed in the Inner Room, which had now been brought into use as an exhibition space on the upper floor, Constable was told by Farington that the picture was greatly 'approved', and was later informed by the President of the Royal Academy, Benjamin West, that the entire Council was agreed that he had recently made remarkable strides in his art.[26] Constable even managed to sell the picture the following year when he sent it to the exhibition at the British Institution, another exhibiting venue in London showing the work of living artists (as well as Old Masters), which had been founded in 1805 and was governed by a group of wealthy, mostly aristocratic collectors.[27] However, when Constable tried to repeat his success at the Royal Academy in 1814 with another picture on the same scale, *The Ferry* (no.15), this time the critics rebuked it for 'lack of finish'. On the same basis Farington now warned Constable that his chances of being elected an Associate Academician later in the year were looking compromised, 'as the objection made to His pictures was their being unfinished'.[28]

For the next two or three years, therefore, Constable reverted to painting smaller pictures, this time as much as possible from the motif, to improve his powers of finishing (see especially nos.16, 17, 20, 21). By the summer of 1816, however, he again felt sufficiently confident to embark on a canvas on the same ('half-length') scale, and in 1817 he sent to the Academy a picture of this size, *Flatford Mill* (no.19), under the general title *Scene on a Navigable River*. Although again placed in the Inner Room rather than the Great Room, this time the critics were agreed, especially when the picture was shown again at the British Institution the following year, that Constable's previous coarseness of execution had now given way to a 'very improved style', and one critic actually praised his 'pencilling' (brushwork) for being 'extraordinary' (meaning extraordinary in its detail).[29] When in 1819 Constable sent *The White Horse* (no.29) to the Academy, this time measuring six feet (1.84m) in width, the critics to some extent simply treated the picture as just another example of what they had come to expect from the artist, albeit one with larger dimensions.[30] Significantly, however, for the first time a reviewer referred to the need for more distance between the viewer and the painting. This was the sort of comment that was to occur with more frequency with the critics over the years, as they felt Constable's handling became increasingly indecipherable. It cannot have helped that, like *Flatford Mill* two years earlier, *The White Horse* had also been hung in the smaller Inner Room, now referred to as the 'School of Painting', where there was less space than in the Great Room to stand back from a large picture. Two additional new strands entered their criticism as well. For the first time a reviewer compared Constable's art with Turner's (concluding that whilst Turner had 'the poetry of Nature', Constable had 'more of her portraiture'); and, again for the first time, a critic attempted to liken Constable's painting with the great tradition of rustic landscape associated with Ruisdael and Meindert Hobbema.[31] These remarks imply that, perhaps without fully realising it, the reviewers were now beginning to take Constable's art more seriously. So, apparently, were the Academicians themselves, as later in the year they elected him an Associate Member.

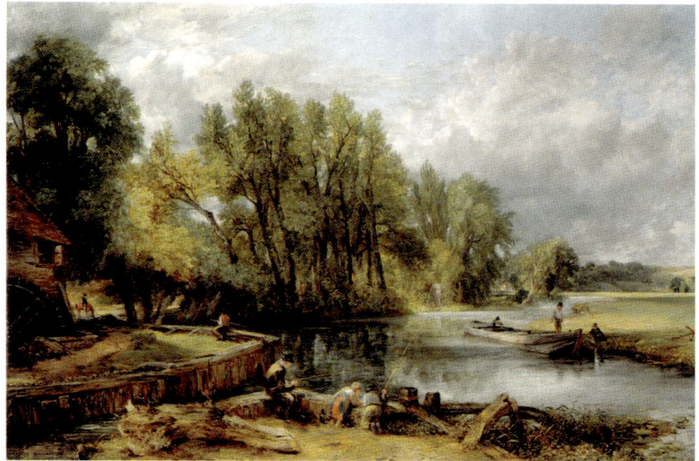

FIGURE 12

These new strands of commentary from the reviewers in connection with *The White Horse* tend to predict the tone of their criticism in future years as well, when they would tend to concentrate on matters of style and manner of execution, or were prone to compare Constable's work with earlier or contemporary landscape painters. They might also talk about the general 'effect' of his pictures, or to what extent they carried the 'air of nature'. What they rarely commented on, however, was the content, least of all the narrative content, of Constable's pictures, even if they might sometimes pause to discuss their rustic charm. In 1822, for example, one reviewer wrote that the *View on the Stour near Dedham* (no.39) helped revive 'the most delightful images and associations that mingle with the recollections of our early years', whilst another felt it evoked 'the consoling recollection of the charms of nature'.[32] In 1820, however, a reviewer for the *British Freeholder* described *Stratford Mill* (fig.12, no.31) at some length, singling out the mill, the boys fishing, the boat with two men pulled in on the opposite bank, the tiny cottage in the distance, 'the brink ... enriched with aquatic plants and herbage', as well as the picture's weather effects, supposing it to be 'a day after recent rain, and the sky is not yet wholly cleared up'.[33] Even then, however, the reviewer missed one of the key details in the painting, which Constable himself once pointed out to David Lucas as being part of the 'natural history' of the picture, and which no doubt explains why he and Fisher were to nickname it 'The Touchwood Tree':

when water reaches the roots of plants or trees the action in the extremities of their roots is such that they no longer vegetate but die which explains the appearance of the dead tree on the edge of the stream.[34]

Furthermore, although the trees that Constable represents in his pictures are, until about 1821, almost always identifiable individually by species, whether black poplars in *Flatford Mill* and *The Hay Wain*, or elms and what is probably a hybrid black poplar, identifiable by its yellowish foliage, in *Stratford Mill*,[35] the critics never attempted to single them out by name. Assuming they had noticed them, or were even capable of identifying them, they may have thought such an exercise unworthy of their column inches, even though Constable's attention to botanical accuracy was highly unusual for this date.

Perhaps because Constable had been elected an Associate at the end of 1819, *Stratford Mill*, his main exhibit in 1820, was given a position in the Great Room. However, his other large landscapes were not automatically hung in the Great Room after his election. Indeed, of the six great River Stour landscapes exhibited between 1819 and 1825, three – *Stratford Mill*, *View on the Stour near Dedham* (no.39) and *The Lock* (no.41) – were placed in the Great Room; whilst the other three – *The White Horse*, *The Hay Wain* (no.37) and *The Leaping Horse* (no.47) – were all hung in the School of Painting. Judging by the installation of paintings shown in the Great Room in 1787 (see fig.10, p.33), a symmetrical arrangement tended to depend on including a substantial number of full-length portraits, which were of course almost invariably in an upright format. Such an arrangement also needed to accommodate large ambitious historical canvases which, as it has been seen, were more highly esteemed than either portraits or landscapes. Large horizontal landscapes like those painted by Constable were therefore probably quite difficult to place in the Great Room, uprights perhaps somewhat easier. In this respect it is interesting to observe that, with the exception of *The Cornfield* 1826 (fig.59, p.116), all Constable's later landscapes painted on an upright format were hung in the Great Room: *The Lock* in 1824 (no.41); probably also *Dedham Vale* in 1828 (fig.74, p.164); *The Valley Farm* in 1835 (Tate; R.35.1); and *The Cenotaph* (fig.13, p.38; R.36.1) in 1836.[36] Assuming a more or less symmetrical hang, these would probably have been placed towards the centre of a wall, which can only have increased their visibility and, potentially, the possibility of a sale. Indeed, uniquely for Constable, *The Lock* sold on the first day of the exhibition in 1824 and, though Fisher was not surprised, believing it to be 'one of [Constable's] best pictures', a favourable placing can only have helped to promote the sale.[37]

The Lock also elicited one of the earliest references to what the critics came to see as Constable's 'spotty manner of laying on his colour', with the effect that it seemed, in this particular critic's view, as though it had been '*dredged* upon the canvas', meaning, presumably, like flour over pastry.[38] What the reviewer seems to have been referring to here were the impasted strokes of paint that Constable applied to the final layer of the canvas as flickering highlights – whether in white, yellow or very pale green, for example – which, as Sarah Cove has pointed out, would have looked quite raw when freshly applied and before they had had a chance to mellow with time or to be toned down during later reworking.[39] In later years, as critics became increasingly bemused by Constable's handling, comments like these would proliferate, although the terms used to describe this aspect of his late style varied from 'spottiness' to 'showers of sleet', 'snow', 'soap-suds', 'whitewash fallen from a ceiling' and even, in the case of *Hadleigh Castle* (no.57), as resembling 'chopped hay'.[40] Incapable of reading Constable's handling in terms of its individual expressive force, they rather dismissed it as a deliberate mannerism, even a form of 'trickery', by which he would wilfully distort the original quality of the painting and in the process sacrifice its 'freshness' and 'truth'.[41] Allied to this was the critics' notion that Constable's pictures needed to be viewed from a 'proper' distance to become fully 'legible'. Perhaps inevitably, comments about an appropriate viewing distance tended to be more numerous in years when Constable's large paintings were hung in the more confined space of the School of Painting, and thus arose in particular with *The Hay Wain* (no.37), *The Leaping Horse* (no.47), *Hadleigh Castle* and *The Opening of Waterloo Bridge* (no.67).[42] As John Gage has pointed out with reference to Constable's representation at the Paris Salon in 1824,

Figure 13
The Cenotaph
1836
Oil on canvas
132 × 108.5 (52 × 42 ¾)
THE NATIONAL GALLERY, LONDON

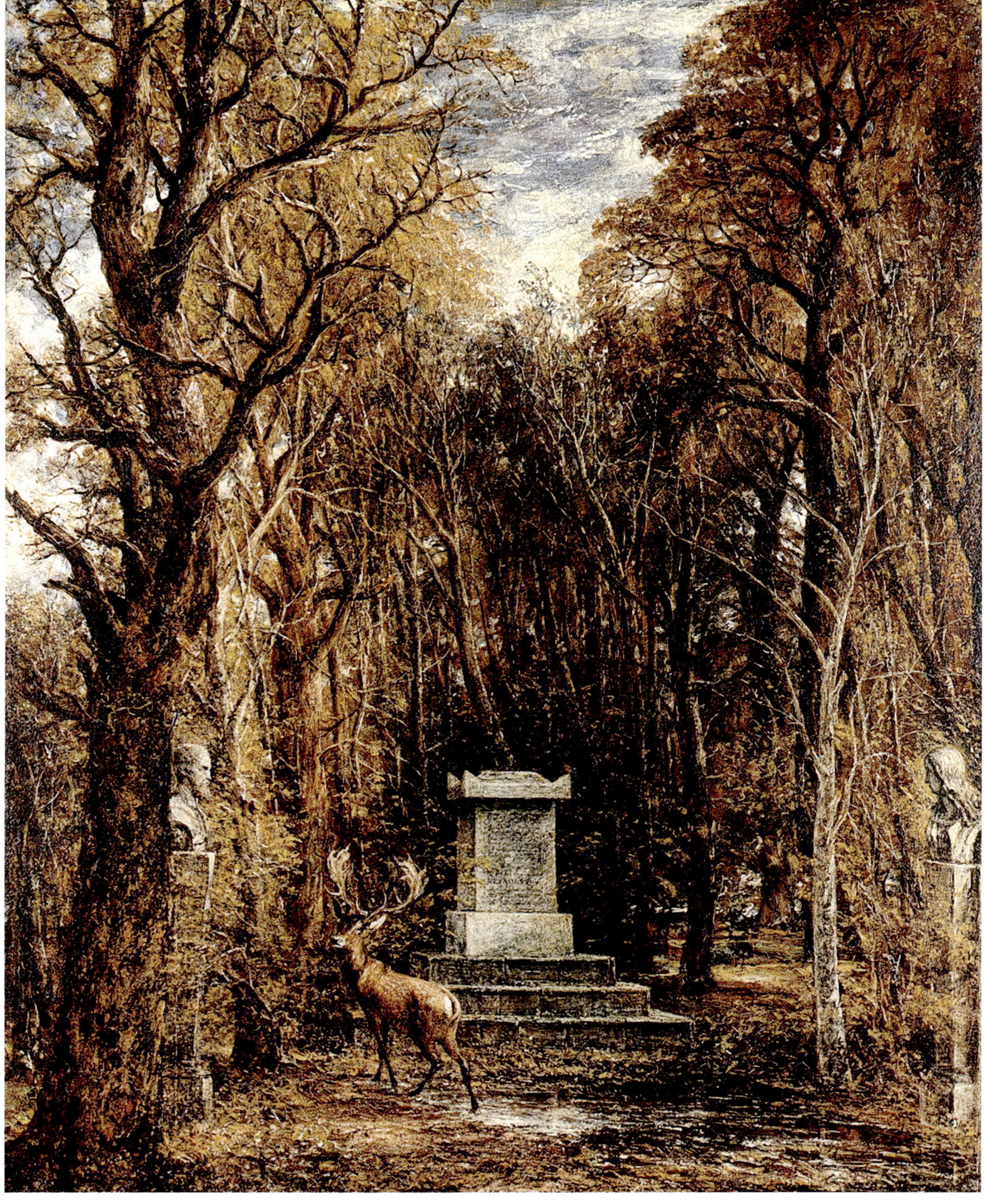

FIGURE 13

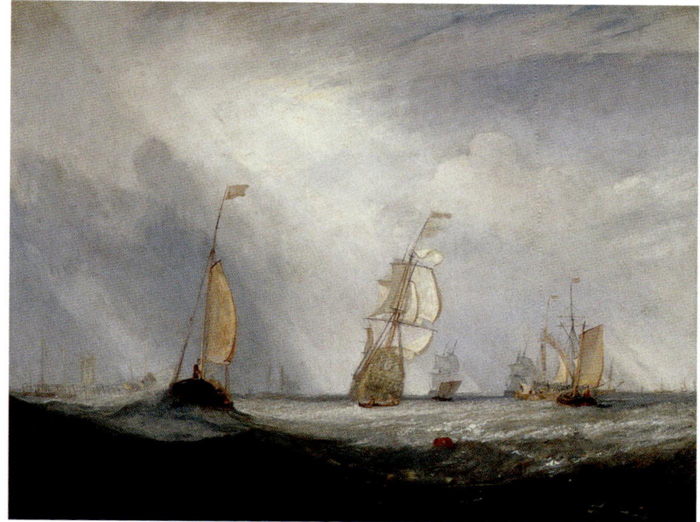

FIGURE 14

this perception about a proper viewing distance was common among French critics as well (see p.24).

Indeed, it was in response to the French authorities having originally hung Constable's *Hay Wain* and *View on the Stour near Dedham* (no.39) too high at the Salon (only subsequently to lower them) that we know Constable actually wanted the public to relish the richness of the texture of his paintings, which they could only do if they were able to come up close to them.[43] Of course, as Judy Ivy has pointed out, Constable would also have wanted the viewer to be able to step back from his paintings – for at a suitable distance all the 'spots' would then blend in the eye – and thus be able to appreciate the look of nature that, as even his most outspoken critics were willing to acknowledge, he was able to create.[44] Given a choice, therefore, Constable would probably have preferred his large pictures to hang in the Great Room, preferably with good situations, at the Academy exhibitions. For here a viewer would have been better able than in the School of Painting both to get up close to a picture and also stand well back, large crowds permitting. It may have been a coincidence, but during the two years that Constable himself served on the hanging committee for the Academy exhibitions, in 1830 and 1831, both of his key exhibits during those years, *Helmingham Dell* (Nelson-Atkins Museum of Art, Kansas City; R.30.1) and *Salisbury Cathedral from the Meadows* (no.61), received placings in the Great Room. Indeed in 1831, in his capacity as a member of the hanging committee, Constable apparently replaced a Turner with his own *Salisbury Cathedral from the Meadows* after the arrangement of the hang had been virtually fixed (though whether this involved displacing the Turner in question to another room is not clear). Nevertheless, it has been suggested that the famous incident in 1832, when Turner found one of his silver-toned marines, *Helvoetsluys;*

– the City of Utrecht, 64, going to Sea 1832 (fig.14), hanging immediately adjacent to Constable's more hotly coloured *Opening of Waterloo Bridge* in the School of Painting, he deliberately painted a red buoy into his own picture on one of the varnishing days, so as to throw the effect of Constable's painting and thus wreak his sweet revenge (see also nos.63–7).[45]

Such a story provides evidence of Turner's competitiveness. However, a bit of artistic jousting like this would probably have been entered into by him in a spirit of friendly rivalry. It was not seriously intended to damage the reception of Constable's *Opening of Waterloo Bridge*. Indeed, in this particular year, 1832, one critic, though disturbed by the picture's white highlights, proceeded to remark that 'we have no hesitation in pronouncing it one of the proudest productions of the English pencil [i.e. brush]'.[46] For, much as the critics may have been puzzled about Constable's late manner of execution – indeed they were often tempted to mock it – they were never for a moment in any doubt about the force and power of his paintings, nor of his originality; the critic for *The Athenaeum* in 1835 declared that 'Constable is an original in everything: he must be compared with nature, and not with art'.[47] Nor, for his part, did the reception of his pictures at the Academy exhibitions ever cause Constable to deviate from his chosen path, or indeed threaten his loyalty to the Academy itself as an institution; on the contrary. In 1836, Constable knew that that year's exhibition was to be the last at Somerset House before the Academy moved to new premises in Trafalgar Square the following year. He therefore decided to send in a picture, *The Cenotaph* (fig.13), showing the avenue at Coleorton House in Leicestershire where his much-respected former patron, Sir George Beaumont, had erected a commemorative mounument to Joshua Reynolds, with busts of Michelangelo and Raphael on either side. Reynolds had of course been the first President of the Royal Academy, and Sir George Beaumont a firm supporter and benefactor of the institution,[48] and there can be no doubt that *The Cenotaph* represents Constable's personal homage to them as well as to the Academy itself. He told a friend that 'I preferred to see Sir Joshua Reynolds's name and Sir George Beaumont's once more in the catalogue, for the last time in the old house'.[49]

Constable died unexpectedly in March 1837 before he was able to finish his next exhibition picture, a view of *Arundel Mill and Castle* (Toledo Museum of Art, Ohio; R.37.1). However, the Royal Academy permitted the inclusion of a deceased member's work in the exhibition immediately following his death. *Arundel Mill* therefore appeared posthumously in the 1837 Academy exhibition at Trafalgar Square. In discussing the painting, a reviewer for the periodical press, by a happy coincidence writing for a publication called *John Bull*, spoke of:

how great a loss the Academy and the public have experienced by [Constable's] decease … as an artist of feeling, and science, and power, he stood very high. His early works are truth and nature themselves; and, unless we much mistake, *all* his works, now that he is gone, will be held in very great estimation.[50]

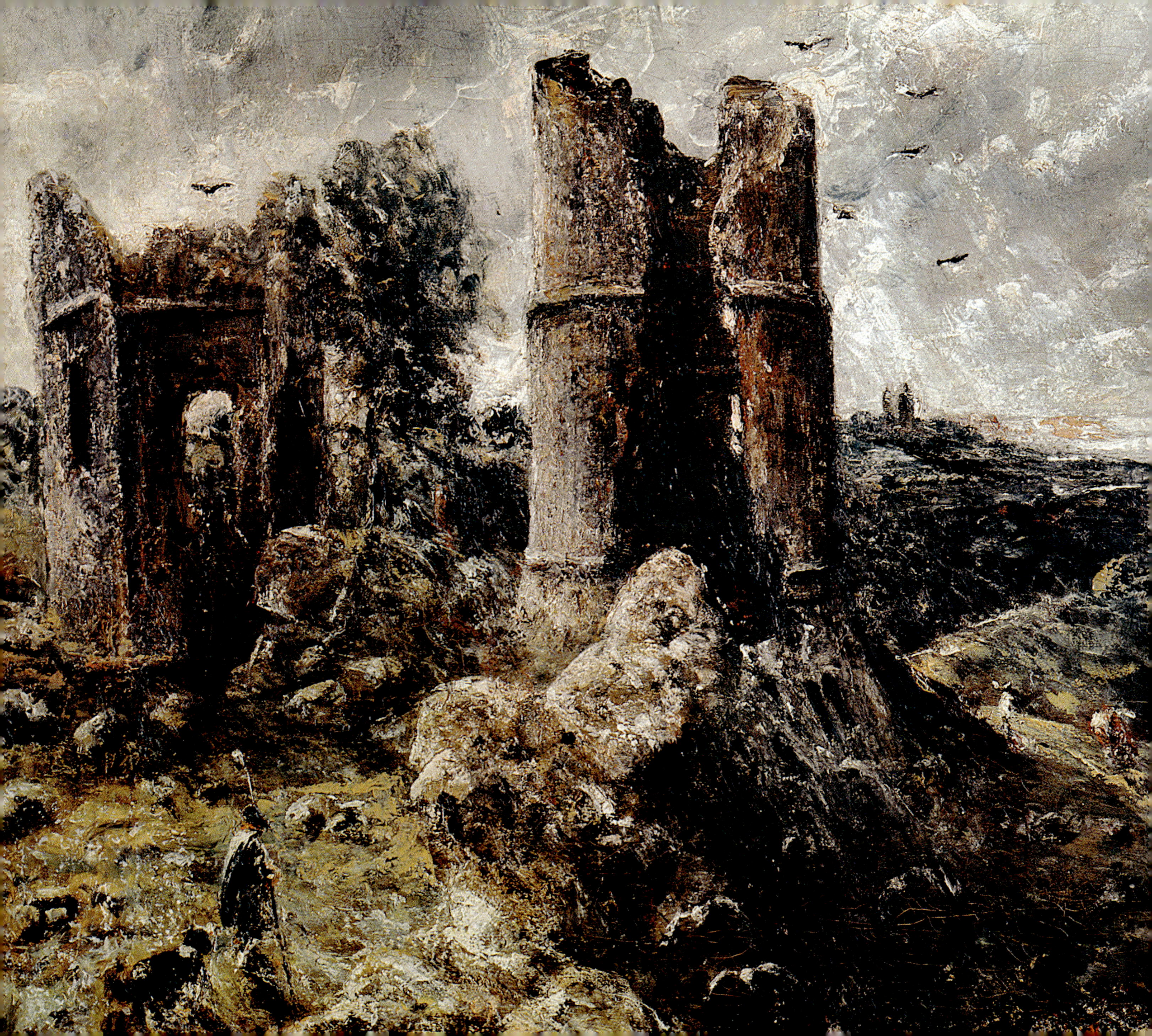

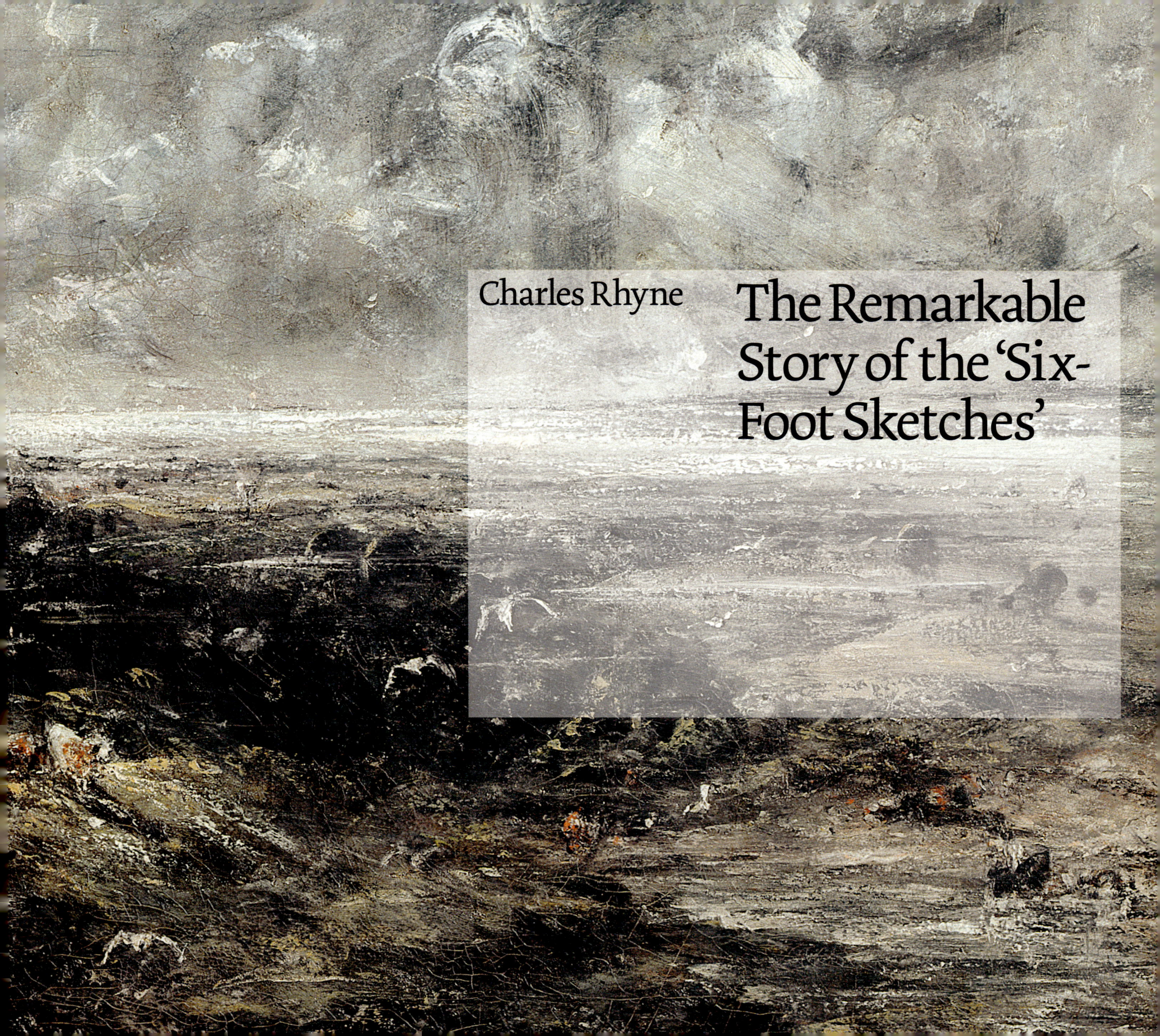

Charles Rhyne
The Remarkable Story of the 'Six-Foot Sketches'

The Remarkable Story of the 'Six-Foot Sketches'
Charles Rhyne

Some of the most challenging questions about Constable's art concern the meaning of his so-called 'six-foot sketches'. What was their purpose? What was their relationship to his matching exhibition pictures? Are they preparatory studies or alternative versions of the exhibited paintings? Do they disclose the 'real Constable'?[1] To what extent do they constitute an unprecedented form of art? Why is there not a single reference to the idea of full-size sketches in Constable's voluminous correspondence, even with his family and intimate friends? Why, at auction, did they sell at almost giveaway prices? Why has a distinguished authority described them as 'Constable's supreme achievement', and even 'the greatest thing in English art'?[2] Why has the authenticity of so many of them been doubted even by leading scholars? Why has it taken so long for them to be considered as a group? To what extent do we understand them even today?

Identifying the Full-Size Sketches

Even identifying which objects should be considered large, full-size sketches is problematic. In spite of C.R. Leslie's defining 1855 statement that 'Constable made a sketch of the full size of every large picture he painted',[3] we are still struggling to identify the sketches to which Leslie referred. Often called Constable's 'six-foot sketches' by later authors, only six of his large, full-size sketches correspond closely with this measurement.[4] Of the others often thought of as part of the series, one is significantly larger,[5] and two are about a half-foot shorter.[6] In addition, three are under five feet, thus clearly not six-footers, though as large, full-size sketches, they are instructive to consider as part of the series.[7] Two of these large, full-size sketches, one exactly six feet, date from the last decade of Constable's life, calling attention to the endurance of this concept in his mind and working procedure.[8]

We recognise quickly that more important than the exact six-foot length was the unprecedented concept of painting a large studio sketch on a separate canvas the same size as a matching finished painting. In other ways, the six-foot sketches vary greatly. Even the full-size sketches for *The Hay Wain* c.1820 (no.36) and *The Leaping Horse* c.1824 (no.46), which for decades served almost exclusively to represent this aspect of Constable's art, are so different in appearance, complexity and purpose, that very few things can be said that apply equally to both.

There are other, even more challenging, reasons that scholars have been slow to identify the full-size sketches to which Leslie referred. As discussed in the sections below, some of these sketches have not been included in past publications because they were unknown to the museum and academic worlds; others because they were judged not to be by Constable; still others because they were considered unfinished paintings rather than full-size sketches.

References during Constable's Life

How were Constable's large, full-size sketches seen and understood during his life? Astonishingly, the concept of a full-size sketch is never mentioned in Constable's extensive correspondence, even with his intimate friend, Archdeacon John Fisher, with whom he regularly discussed his artistic ideas. During Constable's life, there are two nearly certain and two possible references to individual full-size sketches, though these must be surmised from related information.[9] We long to know to what extent Constable considered his large,

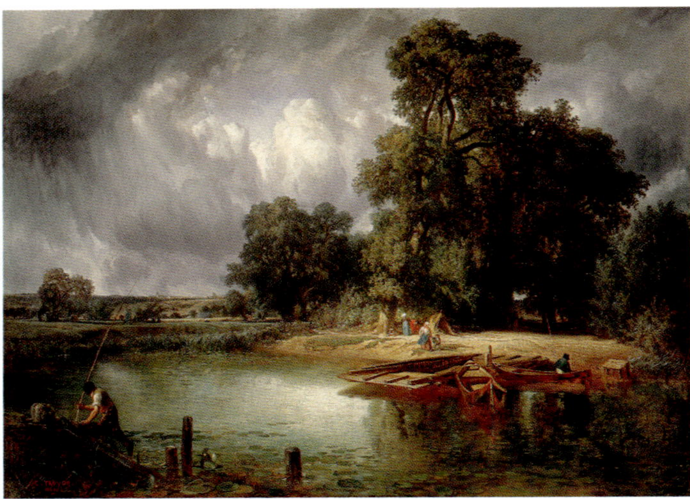

FIGURE 15

full-size sketches private. Did he show them to, or discuss them with, intimate friends or visitors to his studio?

Various friends, collectors, dealers and artists visited Constable at his studio at No. 35 Charlotte Street in London, though there is no evidence of what they saw.[10] Some recent authors have written that the existence of the full-size sketches was 'probably unsuspected even by his friends until some were included in the 1838 sale',[11] but this is surely too categorical. It is nearly certain that the full-size sketch for *View on the Stour near Dedham* c.1821 (no.38) was seen by Fisher. In a note to Fisher on a now lost piece of paper, recorded by Leslie, Constable refers to an earlier version, probably the full-size sketch. This is a rare and instructive description by Constable of the changes from, in all probability, one of his full-size sketches to the matching painting (nos.38, 39):

The composition is almost totally changed from what you saw. I have taken away the sail, and added another barge in the middle of the picture, with a principal figure, altered the group of trees, and made the bridge entire. The picture has now a rich centre, and the right-hand side becomes only an accessory.[12]

Constable's note describes compositional changes, partly details, but more importantly the overall structure and impact of the image.

Nineteenth-Century Evidence

It is nearly certain that several of the large, full-size sketches were listed in the auction catalogue of the Constable family collection at Foster and Sons in London in 1838, one year after Constable's death.[13] This was the first public showing of these sketches, but there is no evidence that they made any impression, and those that sold went for almost giveaway prices. The first secure descriptive reference to any of the large, full-size sketches appeared in the 1843 first edition of C.R. Leslie's *Memoirs of the Life of John Constable*, in which Leslie was describing Constable's *The Leaping Horse* (no.47), exhibited at the Royal Academy in 1825.[14]

Before he sold them in 1853, the dealer D.T. White showed *The Hay Wain* and *The Leaping Horse* sketches to viewers, including the French landscape painter Constant Troyon (fig.15), whom Henry Vaughan noted 'came frequently to see these studies and desired much to become the owner of them had circumstance permitted'.[15] Thirteen years later, in their 1866 *A Century of Painters of the English School*, Richard and Samuel Redgrave provided the first extensive description of any of the full-size sketches (see p.25), and the subject has been a fixture in Constable studies ever since. The Redgraves' two-page account far exceeds all other nineteenth-century descriptions of Constable's full-size sketches in length and perception, helping us to relive their experience of these remarkable paintings.[16]

The most influential event for the full-size sketches was the long-term loan in 1862 (bequeathed 1900) by Henry Vaughan of the full-size sketches for *The Hay Wain* and *The Leaping Horse* to the South Kensington Museum (which became the Victoria and Albert Museum in 1899), where, except for brief periods, they have been on display ever since.[17] Moreover, the two matching finished paintings were given to London's National Gallery in 1886 (*The Hay Wain*) and the Royal Academy in 1889 (*The Leaping Horse*). Possibly because they provided such a convenient set piece, these two sketches and their matching exhibition paintings served for decades as the basis for all discussions of Constable's large, full-size sketches. While the recent ease of air travel has significantly reduced the problem of studying the full-size

sketches, we should note that one of them is in Paris (*Helmingham Dell*, R.30.3); one each are in Washington (no.28), New Haven (no.30), Philadelphia (no.40) and Chicago (no.68); and in Great Britain, one is at Anglesey Abbey near Cambridge (no.65), and one, previously at the Royal Holloway College, University of London, is in a private collection (no.38). A further possible full-size sketch, though more likely an unfinished painting, is in Melbourne (fig.8, p.28).

The lack of evidence relating to the history of these full-size sketches is emphasised by the fact that *The White Horse* sketch c.1818 was not recorded, as far as we know, until 1872, in the catalogue of the Old Master exhibition at the Royal Academy, in which, not surprisingly, it was listed with no mention that it might be a large sketch.[18] An engraving of it, illustrated in the *Magazine of Art* in June 1883, shows that by then it had been extensively overpainted, no doubt to make it more saleable as a finished painting (fig.16).[19] This is key evidence, indicating both that all overpainting of *The White Horse* sketch had taken place by 1872, and also that so few participants in the market understood the range of Constable's art or recognised his hand that uncharacteristic changes could be made without calling their authorship into question. The recent, thoroughly researched and

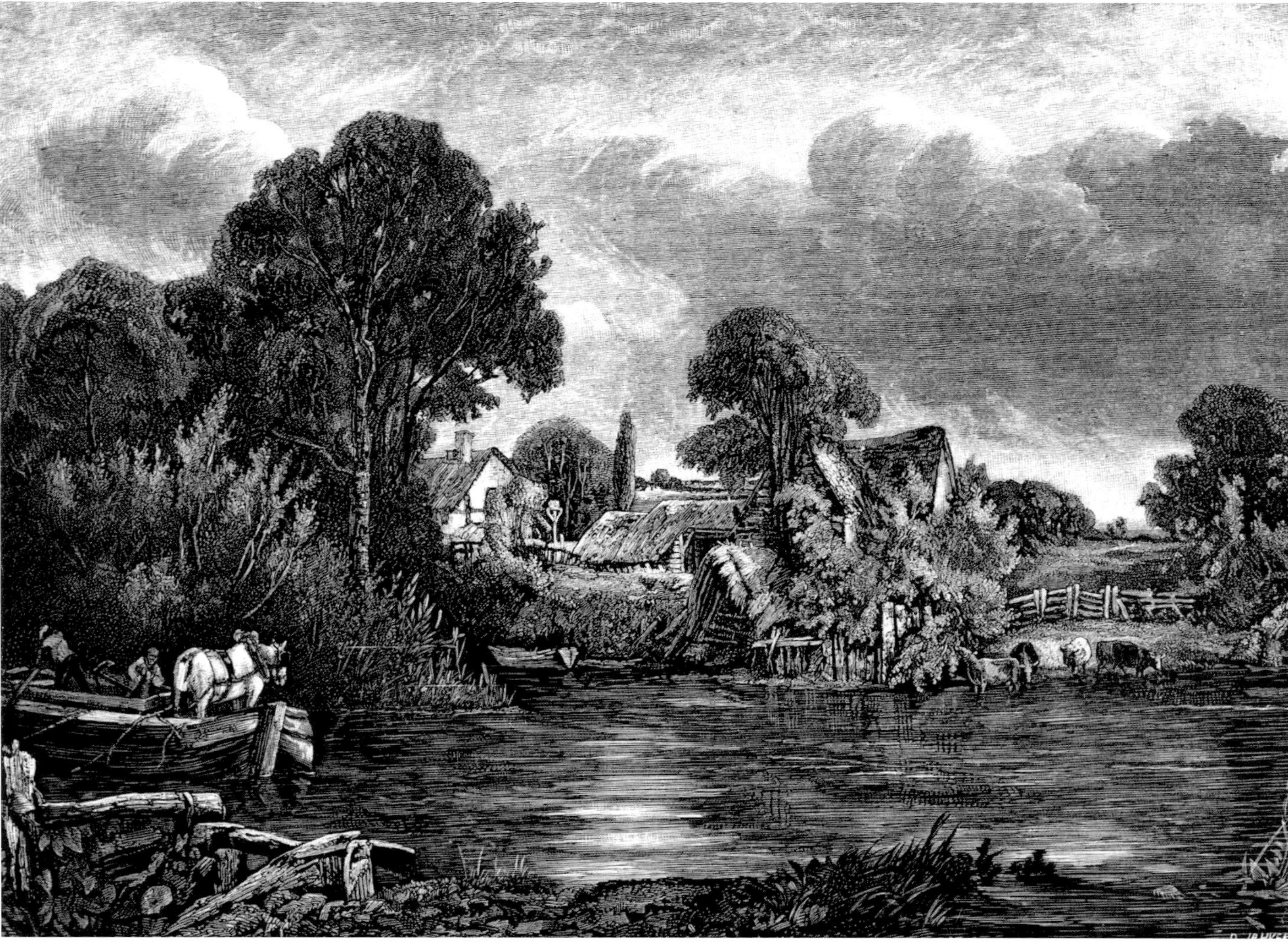

FIGURE 16

Figure 17
Full-size sketch of *Salisbury Cathedral from the Meadows* c.1829–31 (no.60) before cleaning
GUILDHALL ART GALLERY, CITY OF LONDON

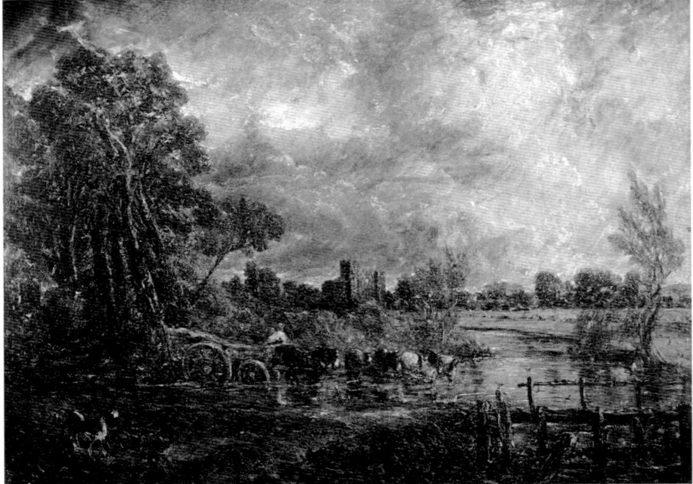

impressively skilled cleaning by Michael Swicklik at the National Gallery of Art, Washington, has provided the first opportunity for over a century to see approximately what the painting looked like during Constable's life, and to reconsider what it tells us about the origin of these famous sketches (figs.18, 19).[20]

A somewhat comparable situation was the overpainting of most of Salisbury Cathedral in the full-size sketch for *Salisbury Cathedral from the Meadows* (fig.17), finally removed in 1951, forty-nine years after its bequest to the Guildhall Art Gallery in London.[21] Such 'finishings' have contributed ever since to the confusion regarding the attribution of Constable's full-size sketches.

At the beginning of the twentieth century, Constable studies were brought suddenly into the modern era with the 1902 publication of Charles Holmes's major monograph, *Constable and His Influence on Landscape Painting*, which included the first chronological catalogue of the artist's work.[22] In this catalogue, Holmes mentions five of the large, full-size sketches. His descriptions constitute the earliest statement that some of the full-size sketches capture 'pictorial breadth and harmony' more successfully than the matching finished paintings, which, he writes, sometimes suffer in the pursuit of detail.[23]

Full-Size Sketches Versus Finished Paintings

During the twentieth century, critics and scholars have disagreed most about two aspects of Constable's large, full-size sketches: the authenticity, or not, of many of these sketches, and their superiority, or not, in relation to their matching finished paintings. During the first half of the twentieth century, critical and scholarly opinion moved swiftly to prefer the full-size sketches and, correspondingly, to denounce the more detailed exhibition pictures. In the 1930s and 1940s, three internationally recognised authorities voiced the most compelling claims for the full-size sketches. In a burst of critical enthusiasm, almost as if in competition, they described highly perceptive and deeply felt responses to the full-size sketches, set against rigid condemnation of the corresponding finished paintings.

In his *Reflections on British Painting* (1934), Roger Fry wrote that:
the influence of his ambience impelled [Constable] to spend most of his time in London elaborating those great machines which were calculated to produce an effect in the Academy exhibitions. The habit of making these was entirely bad. They are almost always compromises with his real idea. He watered that down, filling it out with redundant statements of detail which merely satisfy an idle curiosity and inevitably obscures the essential theme … Fortunately, however, he frequently did full-size studies for these pictures, and it is to those and to the sketches that we must turn to find the real Constable.[24]

Even for those of us who do not agree with his denunciation of the finished paintings, Fry's fifteen short pages of Constable criticism constitute some of the most perceptive writing on his full-size images. Like others, he depended entirely on *The Hay Wain* and *The Leaping Horse* sketches. Two years later, in a brief foreword to an exhibition of English art held in Amsterdam, Kenneth Clark wrote:
His first versions (they cannot be called sketches) of *The Hay Wain* and *The Leaping Horse* are the greatest thing in English art, and it is tragic to think that much of his time was spent in making from them dull replicas, finished for exhibition according to the timid taste of the day.[25]

Eleven years later, in two books published in 1947, Lionello Venturi provided the most extended presentation of this extreme critical view.[26]

Objections to these views appeared soon after. In the preface to his 1951 edition of Leslie's *Life*, Jonathan Mayne provided an early rejoinder:
Some critics now even suggest that the oil-studies, which he made as preliminaries to all his larger paintings, not only are superior to the completed works, but were considered to be so by Constable himself. Such a view is in danger of missing the point. There is no documentary evidence for attributing it to Constable, and those who adopt it themselves tend to lose sight of one of his most remarkable powers – his architectonic ability to carry over into large compositions of an almost classical poise the admired lyricism of the sketches. The small sketches and the full-sized studies show us the substance of his art in its most immediately assimilable form; but they were made with one constantly expressed intention – the construction from them of large finished pictures; and it is in these, 'The Hay Wain', and 'The Leaping Horse', 'the Chain Pier', and the others, that we see the artist's capacities most fully expressed.[27]

A telling refutation of the views of Fry, Clark and Venturi appeared in an excellent, seldom referred-to 1976 book, *Constable and His Country*, in which Alastair Smart wrote:
Certainly it is fantastic to suppose that Constable ever considered the brown and yellow meadows and blue-grey skies of the full-size sketch for *The Hay Wain* as in any sense a realization of his deepest feelings in front of nature.[28]

The Purpose of the Full-Size Sketches

Closely tied to these conflicting values are different readings of the purposes for which the full-size sketches were made. In a famous passage, Basil Taylor wrote that 'the only certain conclusions are that we *cannot* establish the function of these paintings with any certainty'.[29] But let us try. There are several possible explanations for this unique practice, more than one of which is probably operative at any one time. Moreover, Constable's primary reason for continuing this practice, somewhat irregularly, for eighteen years, almost certainly evolved over time.

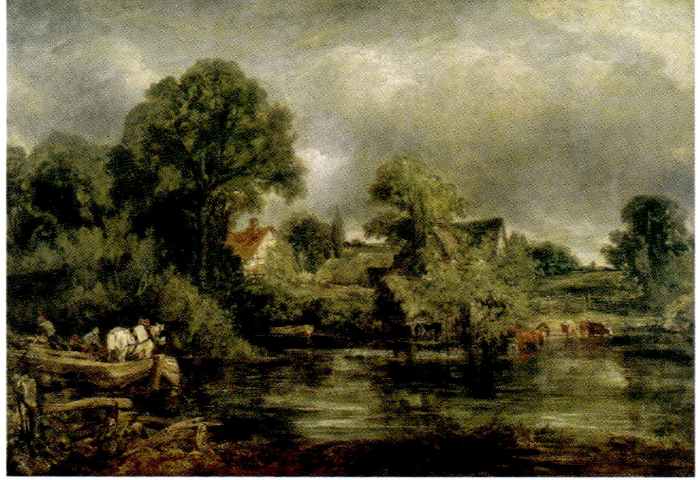

Figure 18
Full-size sketch of *The White Horse*
c.1818 (no.28) before cleaning
NATIONAL GALLERY OF ART,
WASHINGTON

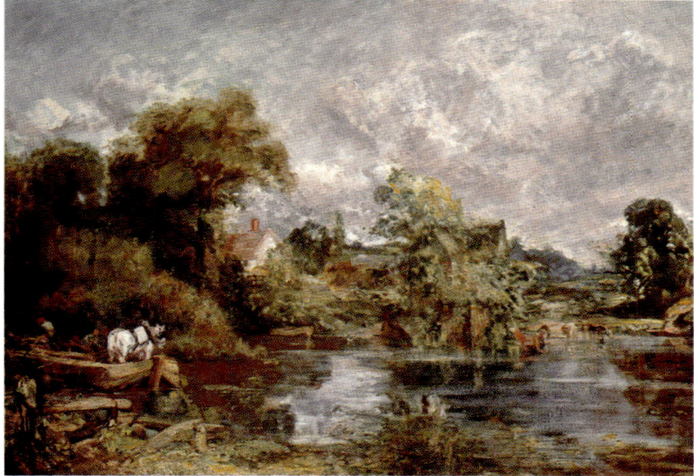

Figure 19
Full-size sketch of *The White Horse*
(no.28) after cleaning
NATIONAL GALLERY OF ART,
WASHINGTON

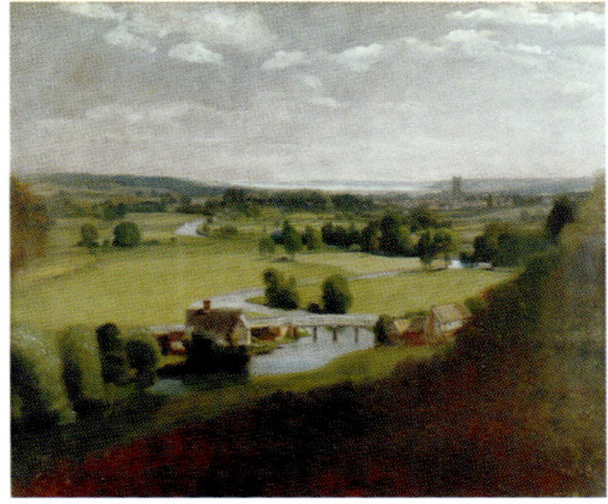

FIGURE 20

Figure 20
The Valley of the Stour
(Dedham from Gun Hill)
c.1805–9
Oil on paper laid on canvas
48.8×59.8 (19⅛×23½)
The river, buildings and bridge in the
centre of this sketch are clearly
visible on the x-ray of *The White Horse*
(fig.21).
VICTORIA AND ALBERT MUSEUM,
LONDON

Figure 21
X-ray of the full-size sketch of
The White Horse (no.28), showing
the image of the abandoned
composition of *Dedham from Gun Hill*
underneath
VICTORIA AND ALBERT MUSEUM,
LONDON

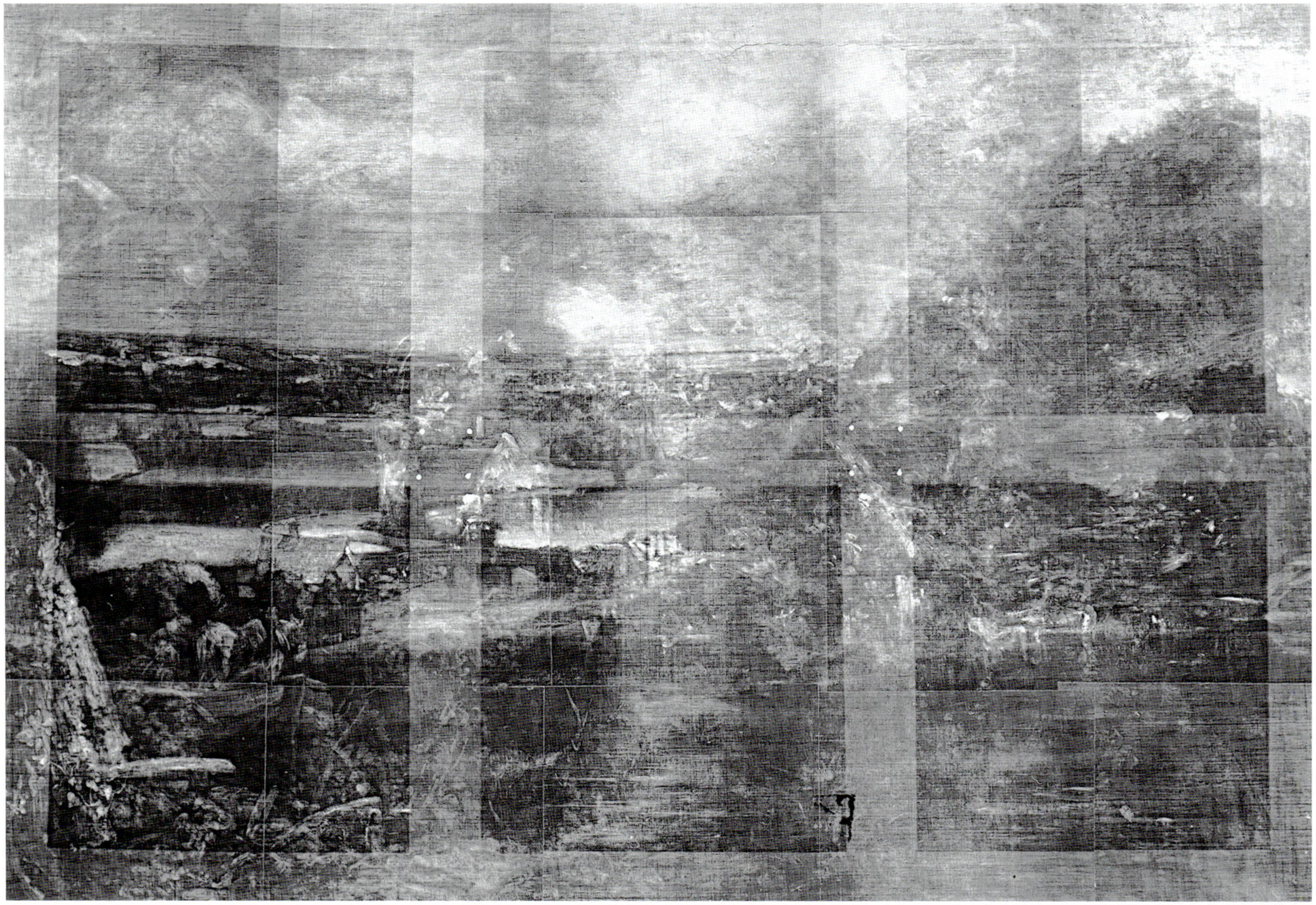

FIGURE 21

45 | The Remarkable Story of the 'Six-Foot Sketches'

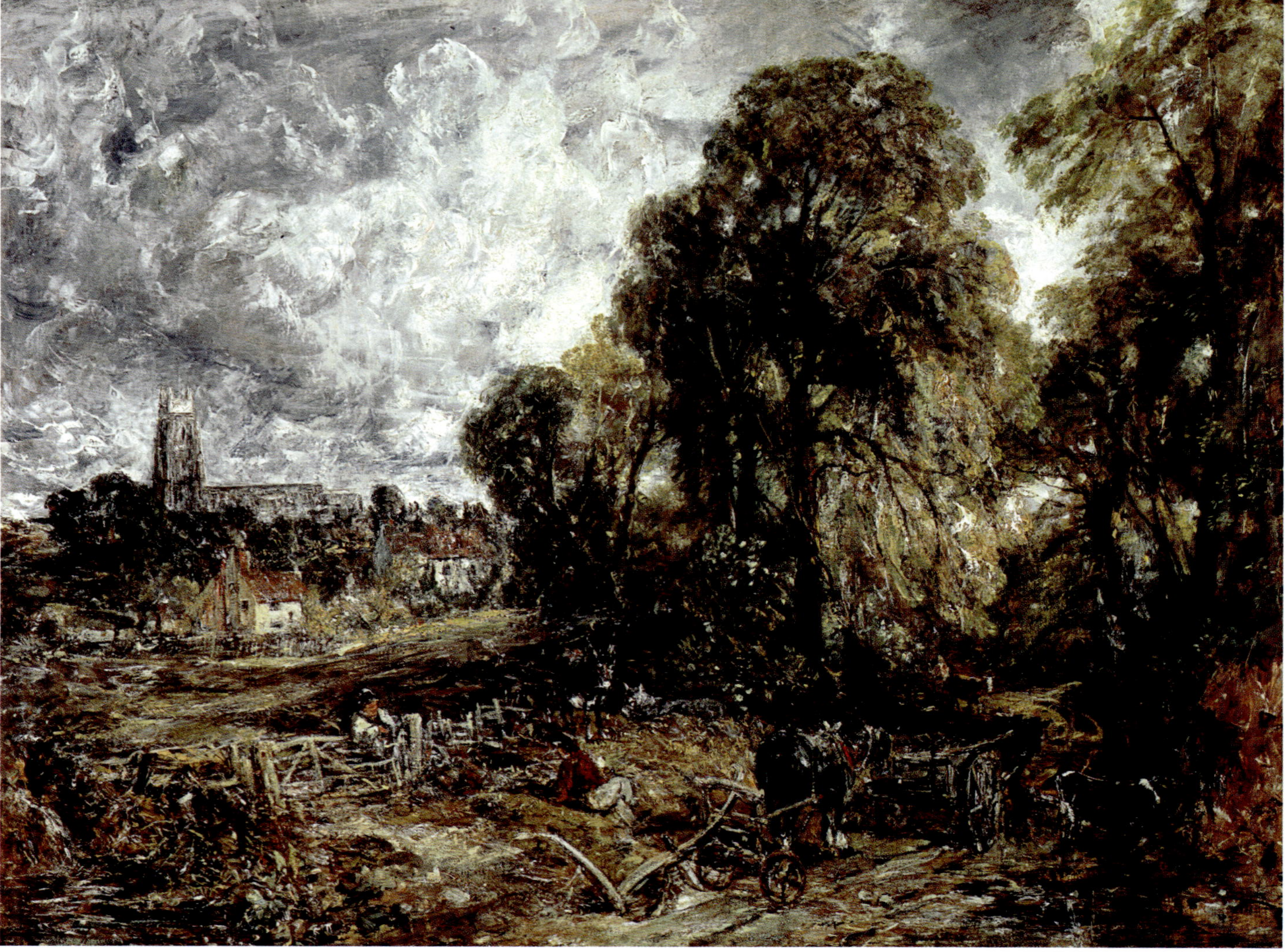

FIGURE 22

In an article on *The White Horse* sketch at the National Gallery of Art, Washington, I attempted to describe why Constable seems to have begun this practice.[30] New x-radiographs had revealed a previously unsuspected image of *Dedham from Gun Hill* beneath *The White Horse* sketch (fig.21, p.45).[31] Judging by the X-rays, it looked as if, in attempting his first landscape at so large a size, Constable had failed to pull the composition together and had clearly stopped work on the canvas. It seems likely that, before beginning another six-foot exhibition piece, he decided to work out the problems first in a large sketch. Perhaps a slightly smaller sketch would have served but, with a full-size, rejected canvas at hand, he re-used it. Judging by the fact that he did not cover much of the *Dedham* image with ground before beginning *The White Horse* image, it is likely that he began *The White Horse* image consciously as a sketch, not intending it as the beginning of an exhibition piece. We cannot be certain of Constable's intentions, but it seems probable that his methodical working process and need for step-by-step progression from open-air drawings, sketches and studies to finished exhibition paintings help us to understand his seminal decision to paint a six-foot sketch and then to paint an exhibition painting of the same subject on a separate canvas of the same size.[32]

Because the finished painting of *The White Horse* was such a success at the 1819 Royal Academy exhibition, and because it led to Constable's election as an Associate of the Royal Academy, it is easy to understand why Constable continued the practice of a full-size sketch for his RA exhibits for at least the next year or two. But what about after Constable began to gain confidence with his six-foot paintings? It appears that the function of the full-size sketch primarily as preparation for a finished painting was evolving. John Sunderland has put extremely well one possible explanation for Constable's later, fuller development of his paintings and full-size sketches:

It … seems possible that as Constable grew older the extensive working and reworking of a canvas and the resultant complex texture of paint layers took on a meaning of its own for him, so that he found it difficult to stop adding to the depth and richness of his work.[33]

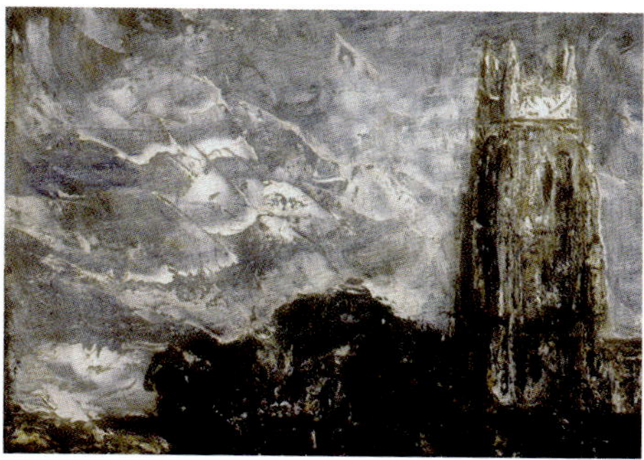

FIGURE 23

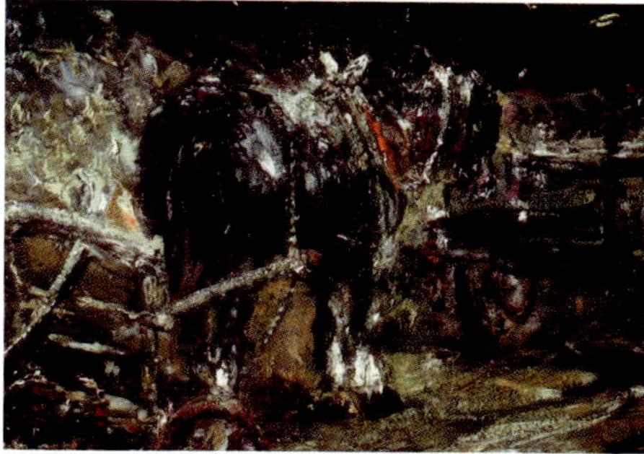

FIGURE 24

Figures 23–5
Details from the full-size
sketch for *Stoke-by-
Nayland* c.1835–7 (no.68)
THE ART INSTITUTE
OF CHICAGO,
MR AND MRS W.W.
KIMBALL COLLECTION

Full-Size Sketches Misinterpreted as Paintings

In his 1855 *Hand-Book for Young Painters*, Leslie wrote that:

Constable made a sketch of the full size of every large picture he painted, and as these sketches are sometimes complete in effect, though not in detail, they are sometimes mistaken for pictures, and a false notion is therefore conveyed of his Art.[34]

The most dramatic and informative example of this mistake concerns the full-size sketch for *Stoke-by-Nayland* (figs.22–5; no.68). The misinterpretation of this full-size sketch as a painting lasted for over sixty years after its entry into a public collection in 1922. Moreover, recognition that it was a full-size sketch rather than a painting did not result from misleading overpainting by other hands or information later discovered through X-ray study.

Until 1986, no scholar had mentioned that the large *Stoke-by-Nayland* might be a full-size sketch. It had even served as the exemplar of Constable's late style in world histories of art. In his landmark *History of Art*, first published in 1962, H.W. Janson included an illustration of *Stoke-by-Nayland*, about which he wrote: 'The full-scale compositions of Constable's final years retain more and more of the quality of his oil sketches.'[35] In the 1993 edition of his *History of Painting, Sculpture and Architecture*, first published in 1976, Frederick Hartt continued to illustrate the picture and wrote: 'One of these late pictures is *Stoke-by-Nayland*, of 1836–37 … The symphonic breadth of the picture … bring[s] to the finished painting the immediacy of the color sketch.'[36]

In 1986, I was invited to the Art Institute of Chicago to confer on the cleaning and technical study of the picture, and to lecture and write an article on it for their *Bulletin*. Although the article was never published, the Art Institute retains a copy in their files and I shared it with other Constable scholars.[37] I could see no reason to think it a finished or nearly finished painting. There was no documentary evidence to support the idea. In fact Leslie's oft-quoted statement that 'The large picture of "Stoke" was never painted' no longer presented a conflict, since Leslie was presumably referring to a painting rather than a full-size sketch.[38] The X-ray and technical study, while of value for comparison with other works by Constable, produced nothing to indicate that it was either a sketch or painting.

Thus, judgment depended on visual comparison with other late sketches and paintings. For comparison, from the 1830s there are no fewer than five finished landscapes over four feet (over 1.2m), two of them certainly finished in 1835 and 1836, in addition to two under four feet finished in 1836 and 1837.[39] None of them look anything like the Chicago sketch, nor do any of them suggest an underpainting with the character of the Chicago canvas. On the other hand, the vigorous handling, brilliant work with the palette knife and thick impasto of *Stoke-by-Nayland* accord closely with full-size sketches such as the Tate's *Hadleigh Castle* c.1829 (no.56), nearly identical in size, and with other sketches from the 1830s. The fence, plough and cart, and the position of the reclining figure, which are sometimes interpreted as later, inept finishings by another hand, do not accord with details in Constable's finished paintings, but are natural as integral parts of a boldly painted sketch and are consistent with his other late full-size sketches. The evidence seemed clear and I described it as such in two 1990 articles.[40] The next year, in their catalogue of the major Constable exhibition at the Tate Gallery, Parris and Fleming-Williams provided an extensive summary of these findings and support for its identification as a full-size sketch entirely in Constable's hand.[41]

It is instructive to ask how it was possible that this misleading concept for so important a painting (illustrated in histories of world art, not just nineteenth-century or British art) survived until 1986. There was no evidence or comparative material to support the misinterpretation. We must recognise first that traditional attributions, dating and other judgments have a certain standing, justified or not, and tend to be continued until evidence appears to the contrary. Partly because it was not in London, the sketch had never been studied in depth by British scholars. Because Constable's full-size sketches are so greatly reduced in illustrations, the distinctive character of his remarkable technique can only be fully experienced in front of the original canvases (figs.23–5). I was privileged to study the *Stoke* picture for three days out of its frame in the Conservation Department at the Art Institute, in consultation with outstanding professional conservators; ideal conditions for studying a painting and not one that can often be provided.[42]

It seems clear that the main reason for the misinterpretation was the oversimplified concept that Constable's handling of paint became bolder and freer late in life. This survey-type generalisation, true of Constable's sketches but not of his detailed and intensely worked finished paintings, needed a major finished painting as an exemplar. The Chicago *Stoke-by-Nayland* made it possible to tell the story.

In a few cases, it has even been claimed that in 'Constable's late style … the difference between a sketch and a finished exhibition piece is almost nonexistent'.[43] Constable's known RA painting exhibits from the last years of his life were *Salisbury Cathedral from the Meadows* 1831 (no.61), *The Opening of Waterloo Bridge* 1832 (no.67), *Englefield House* 1833 (Private Collection; R.33.1), *The Valley Farm* 1835 (Tate, R.35.1), *The Cenotaph* 1836 (fig.13, p.38), and *Arundel Mill and Castle* 1837 (Toledo Museum of Art, Ohio; R.37.1), all extensively developed and finished, unlike any of his sketches.

Authenticity

As discussed above, the question of whether any given work is by Constable or not has troubled the market, museum practice, and

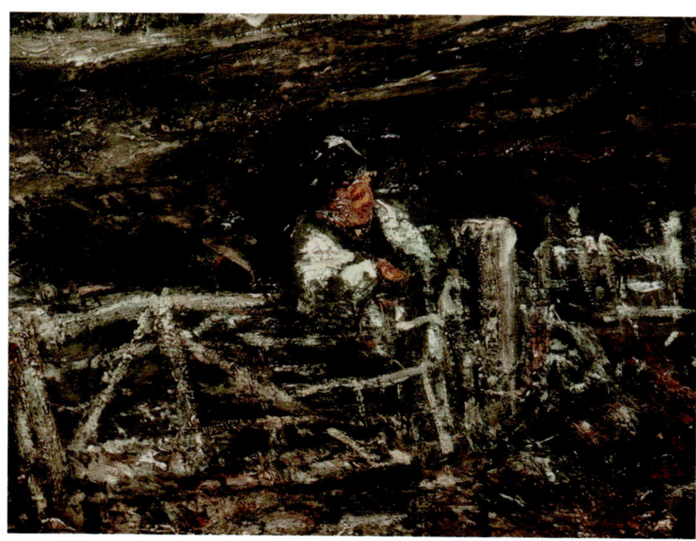

FIGURE 25

Constable scholarship since the artist's death. His large, full-size sketches have been at the centre of this debate.

Evidence from documentation and, increasingly, from technical studies, have played an important role in judgments of authenticity.[44] However, all types of evidence require interpretation and can be misleading if taken on their own. It is too rarely explained that there are many ways to prove that a painting is not by an artist, but only one way to show that it is. All other characteristics of a painting, including technical evidence, can be true also of a contemporary copy. Documents are often unreliable. Only the hand of the artist is unique to the artist's work, and the more distinctive the artist's hand the more reliable the judgment. Constable's hand is very distinctive, but it is also very varied. Judgments depend above all on scholars who have looked long and hard, and critically, over many years, at the full range of original works by a given artist. For one who has lived through forty years of such experience, I am amazed at the extent to which these judgments have been clarified and refined over the years, not only for Constable but across the full range of world art.

Decisions regarding authorship are forced by the appearance of new works on the market. All but one of Constable's full-size sketches had reappeared before the second half of the twentieth century and, although scattered, were on public view. Then, in 1983, the newly discovered full-size sketch for *Stratford Mill* c.1819–20 (no.30) came up for auction.[45] Experts were divided over its attribution to Constable, indicating the extent to which judgments regarding Constable's full-size sketches were unsettled, until the publication the next year of Graham Reynolds's definitive catalogue, *The Later Paintings and Drawings of John Constable*.[46]

Problems of attribution are most comprehensively pressed by research for and publication of scholarly catalogues. During the past half-century, a series of major Constable catalogues have appeared. The great leap forward was provided by the publication in 1960 of Reynolds's catalogue of all paintings and drawings in the Victoria and Albert Museum.[47] Although this catalogue produced no new information directly on any of the full-size sketches, the astonishingly detailed contextual material has been essential for all later Constable studies.

Sixteen years later, the Tate Gallery mounted the first comprehensive exhibition of Constable's work, a highly successful exhibition with a catalogue by Leslie Parris and Ian Fleming-Williams.[48] For the study of the full-size sketches, most important was not only the addition of the full-size sketch of *View on the Stour near Dedham* c.1821 (no.38), at that time still in the collection of Royal Holloway College, London, but, even more so, the inclusion of the finished painting of *Hadleigh Castle* 1829 (no.57), on loan from Mr and Mrs Paul Mellon. This allowed, for the first time, comparison of a major full-size sketch with its matching painting, other than the standard *Hay Wain* and *Leaping Horse* comparisons. The *Hadleigh Castle* pair had recently been illustrated on facing pages in a splendid double-page spread, along with a small drawing and oil sketch on which they were based, in Basil Taylor's innovative *Constable* volume of 1973 (fig.26).[49] Previously, only one publication had illustrated any full-size sketch and matching painting on the same or facing pages.[50]

Remarkably, the next major catalogue was written by a Belgian scholar and published only in Italian. In his 1979 *L'opera completa di Constable*, Robert Hoozee doubted or questioned four of the full-size sketches.[51] These were doubts that had been shared, often verbally, among other scholars, so that Hoozee's bold approach was instrumental in opening up the debate that had been hovering behind the scenes. In addition, his volume was notable for including, for the first time, illustrations (very small) and brief catalogue information for all twelve of the full-size sketches.[52]

In 1981, the Tate Constable Collection catalogue by Leslie Parris was published, providing large colour illustrations and detailed catalogue information for all works in the Tate Constable Collection by and previously attributed to Constable.[53] This included a six-page review of all information related to the full-size sketch for *Hadleigh Castle* (no.56), the type of in-depth study needed for each of the full-size sketches.[54] Amazing as it may seem, this entry included the first publication of an X-ray photograph for any of these full-size sketches, many of which have multiple changes. These x-radiographs, taken in 1975, revealed that strips of canvas, about 4 inches (10cm) wide, had been added to the left side and bottom of the main canvas, which were then painted as part of the overall composition. In his 1981 entry for the full-size sketch, Parris presented reasons for concluding that 'there can be little doubt that someone other than Constable was responsible for the additions'. In his catalogue raisonné of Constable's later paintings and drawings, published three years later, Graham Reynolds disagreed, reaffirming that the two strips were painted by Constable. Strangely, no paint samples had been taken to determine if the paint on the added strips was significantly later than that on the main canvas. In connection with the current exhibition, the picture was thoroughly re-examined by Tate conservator Natasha Duff, paint samples and new x-radiographs taken. Duff has recently published her research on-line as part of a series of Tate papers, presenting convincing evidence that the paint on the strips is significantly later than that on the main canvas, very likely early twentieth-century additions. She proposes that the strips were probably added as part of a project, instigated by the art dealer and connoisseur Percy Moore Turner, to restore the picture before it was sold to the National Gallery, London, in 1935, perhaps because at that time the sketch was thought to be the exhibited version (see nos.53–7).[55]

The defining document for all Constable studies is now Graham Reynolds's four-volume catalogue raisonné, containing abundant colour illustrations and information for every work known and considered by Reynolds to be by Constable.[56] The entries for the twelve large, full-size sketches provide the comprehensive in-depth information necessary for any attempt to answer the questions posed at the beginning of this essay. The full-page, high-quality colour illustrations of every pair of full-size sketch and matching painting, wonderfully reproduced on facing pages, was itself a major contribution.[57] Reynolds reaffirmed the authenticity of all twelve of the large, full-size sketches.

By far the largest and most spectacular exhibition of Constable's art ever held was mounted at the Tate Gallery in 1991. The exhibition was matched by an equally spectacular catalogue by Leslie Parris and Ian Fleming-Williams, impressively bringing together much research from recent years and providing new information of their own.[58] It included eight of the twelve full-size sketches, the largest number ever brought together, possibly since the auction of works

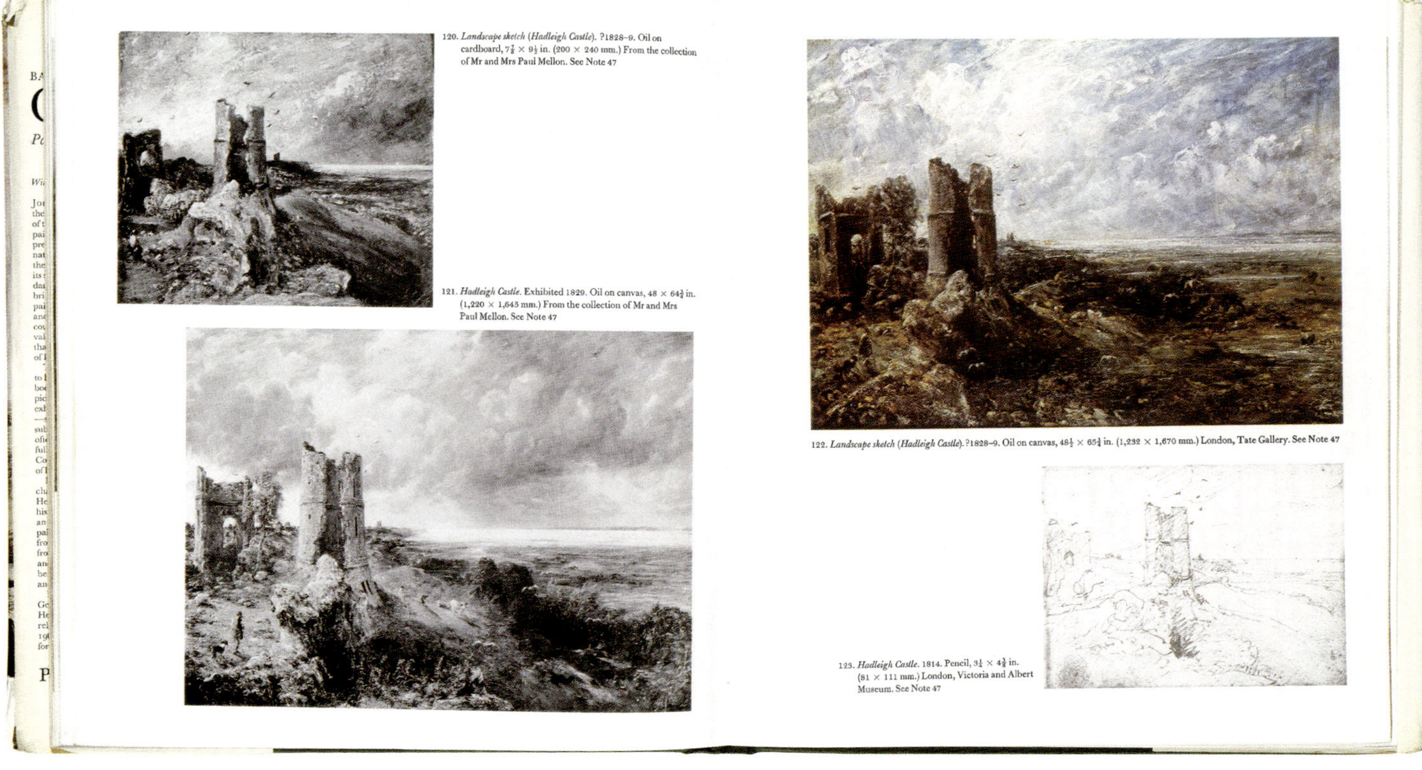

FIGURE 26

from the family collection the year after his death. On display together for the first time were no fewer than four pairs of the full-size sketches with their matching paintings: *Stratford Mill* (nos.30–1), *The Lock* (nos.40–1), *Helmingham Dell* (Louvre, Paris, R.30.3; Nelson-Atkins Museum of Art, Kansas City, R.30.1), and *Salisbury Cathedral from the Meadows* (nos.60–1). Moreover, these were joined by two other pairs that had previously been displayed together: *The Leaping Horse* (nos.46–7) and *A Boat Passing a Lock* (figs.8, 70). Altogether six paired full-size sketches and matching paintings were on display. I had assumed that this was a once-in-a-lifetime experience.

Once again, attribution questions were brought to the fore by the full-size sketches. No fewer than four of Constable's large, full-size sketches, previously doubted in whole or in part by the catalogue's authors, were reaffirmed as genuine Constables. The reasons for the re-evaluation of these sketches were closely related. The authors described the basis for their revised judgment in the entries for the sketches. About the *Stratford Mill* sketch they wrote:

There are also passages that can only be described as crude … Constable is working for his eyes only and does not need to spend time refining the details and solving every problem at this stage. It has taken students of the artist some time to accept this fact.[59]

On the *Salisbury Cathedral from the Meadows* sketch they wrote: doubts, shared by the present authors, still remained as to the authenticity of the work. For some of the more awkward passages … it is still difficult to find a satisfactory explanation. One or two similarly ungainly passages in a work of undoubted authenticity,

the 'Stratford Mill' sketch, have made it easier to accept such lapses in a preparatory sketch, however, and [the *Salisbury Cathedral from the Meadows* sketch] is now accepted as fully authentic.[60]

About the *Stoke-by-Nayland* sketch they wrote:

Certain odd features … were regarded by some writers as a ham-fisted attempt by a later hand … to complete the picture. Rhyne convincingly proposed that [*Stoke-by-Nayland*] is in fact a sketch for a painting that Constable never executed and that it must therefore be accessed by different criteria … Constable seems to have been willing to sacrifice many of his usual skills when trying to pull together the sketch for a large composition.[61]

Acceptance of these four works has made possible, for the first time, scholarly agreement for the full sequence of Constable's known large, full-size sketches.

The full story of Constable's six-foot sketches has only recently begun to emerge. Each time a new work appears in the marketplace, we face new judgments of authenticity and value. Each time a scholar publishes the results of in-depth research, we struggle to incorporate new evidence. Each time X-ray study reveals previously invisible alterations, we expand our view of Constable's creative process. Each time a newly formulated critical statement is presented, we are challenged to think anew. Each time an exhibition brings together works previously separated, new relationships emerge. Each time a restoration cleans away later overpainting or discoloured varnish, we must look again. This essay attempts to explore these evolving perspectives so that our own attempts to see these extraordinary paintings might be more richly informed.

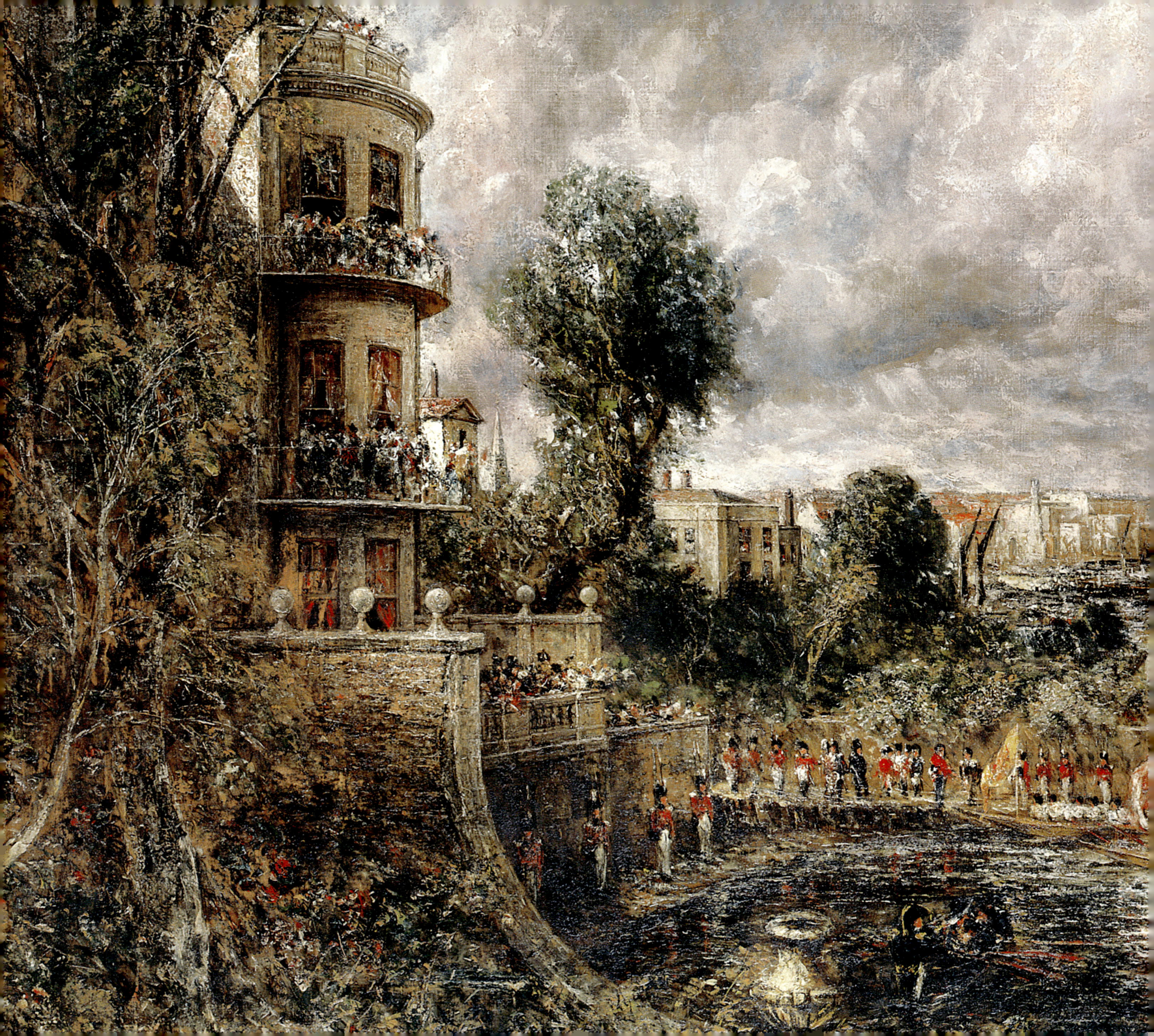

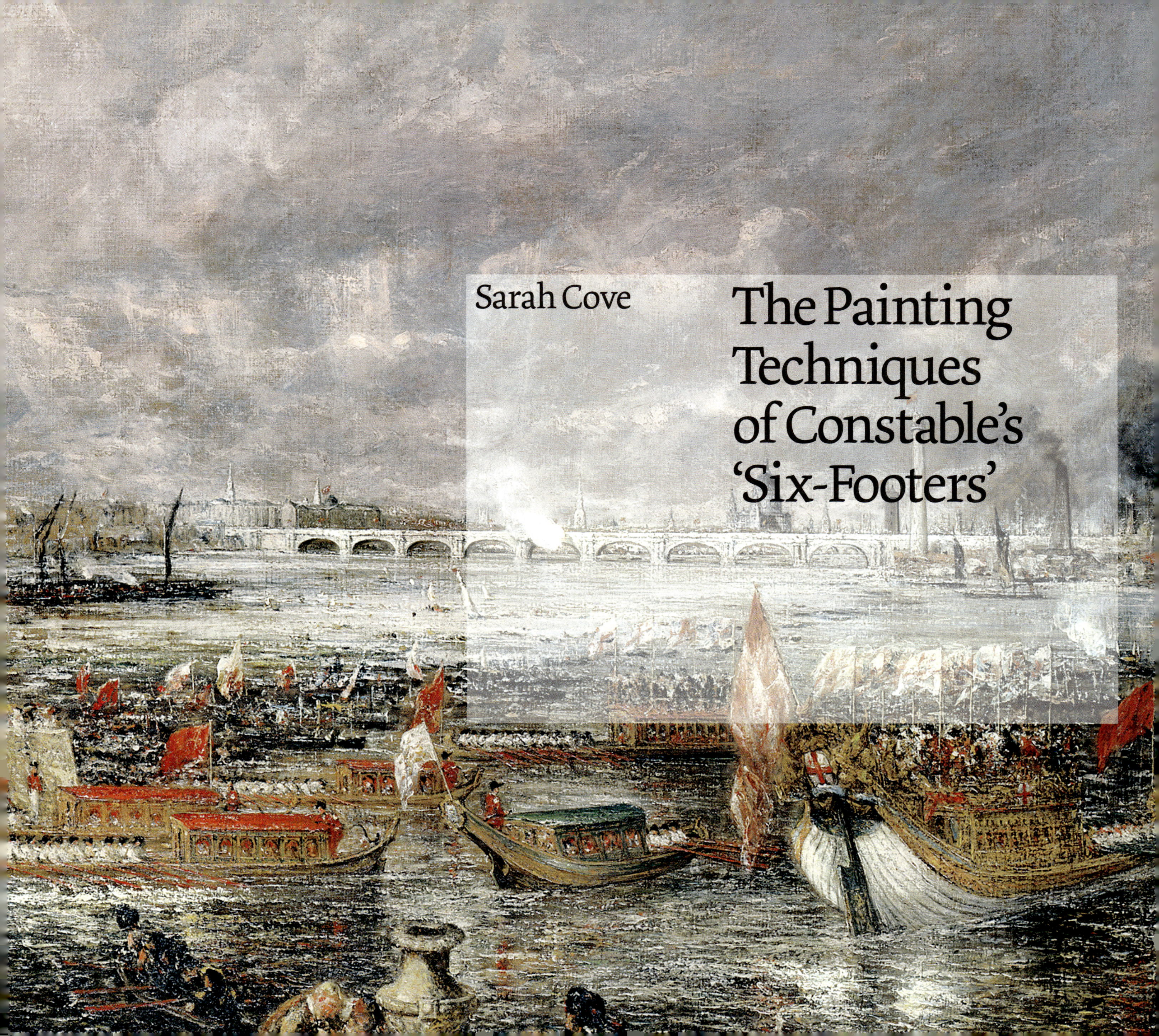

Sarah Cove
The Painting Techniques of Constable's 'Six-Footers'

The Painting Techniques of Constable's 'Six-Footers'

Sarah Cove

In preparation for this exhibition, the majority of Constable's exhibited six-foot paintings and their full-size sketches have undergone technical examination and scientific analysis as part of the Constable Research Project.[1] Together with technical reports supplied by the lending institutions, this has provided a substantial body of new information on Constable's working methods of the 1820s and 1830s.[2] The relationship between the full-size sketches and exhibited works has also been clarified by consideration of this technical data in the light of recent art historical scholarship, as each type of painting has significant characteristics that make it possible to differentiate between them clearly in terms of materials and techniques. In addition, Constable's extensive and detailed correspondence reveals his artistic temperament and the extent to which his physical environment and domestic circumstances affected his work.[3]

In the nineteenth century, a 'finished' landscape was expected to exhibit a 'harmony' not found in nature, to portray fine detail and have a smooth surface, not traits generally associated with Constable's oils of the 1820s and 1830s.[4] At the Royal Academy 'finish' was considered the difference between excellence and mediocrity, so success or failure at this final stage of painting was reflected in critical responses at the annual exhibition. Constable tried hard in his own way to create high 'finish', with flickering highlights and subtle glazing, but he could not be true to himself using a conventional, relatively smooth, manner. In 1819, when the first 'six-footer', *The White Horse* (no.29), was exhibited, a critical debate began regarding the proper viewing distance for his pictures.[5] This was prompted both by the size of the canvas and the unconventional technique. His paintings were apt to receive a censorious response from the critics if they were not advantageously hung, as the numerous small strokes used in the 'finishing' layers only blend in the eye at a certain distance. In 1832 Constable complained that *The Opening of Waterloo Bridge* (no.67) was 'put where it can only be seen to the greatest disadvantage, in the traffic between the doors in the new room [the School of Painting] – the light of the worst kind for my unfortunate "manner"'.[6]

When painting a six-foot sketch Constable was no longer shackled by the rigours of academic 'finish', and could express his personal vision by engaging in a more physical way with the act of painting on a large canvas. He soon needed more room to work, bigger brushes, more paint, more speed, and always more time. It has often been assumed that he kept the six-foot sketches private, even secret, during his lifetime, as there are no specific references in his correspondence to anything other than 'sketches'.[7] It is now clear that this was not the case, as Constable had definitely shown the full-size sketch for *View on the Stour near Dedham* (no.38) to his closest friend, Archdeacon John Fisher, in January 1822, before telling him later of alterations to the composition that have been recently identified by technical examination.[8] We also know that he wrote at length to his close friend in later life, the amateur painter William Purton, in 1835 regarding the six-foot *Stoke-by-Nayland* sketch (no.68).[9] Why, then, was Constable not more explicit about the full-size sketches in his letters? With our modern perspective, where preparatory works are often preferred to 'finished' pictures, it is easy to forget that the full-size sketches did not have the iconic status to Constable and his contemporaries that they have enjoyed since the late nineteenth century.[10] Constable did not single out *six-foot* sketches from others for special mention because to him a sketch was simply a sketch, whatever its size. He had a practical and workmanlike approach to their creation, and no doubt considered them to be just one aspect of his ordinary working method, little of which is described in his letters. He could not have known that they would come to be recognised as unique in the history of British landscape painting, let alone global art history, and would later be seen as completely innovative and revolutionary.

Constable in Context:
Domestic Concerns and Studio Environment

Many people's impression of Constable as the serene painter of 'chocolate-box' landscapes is far from the truth. He was a complex and troubled soul, whose genius was far ahead of his time and went largely unrecognised and unacknowledged by his peers. He was full of contradictions: he could be arrogant and abrasive, yet he was deeply insecure and desperately sought approval and recognition from family, friends and colleagues. He was a loving husband and devoted father, but he was also moody, sulky and had a sharp temper. He was passionate about painting, but trying to express his personal vision drove him to distraction. He strove for artistic and financial success, yet he cultivated an individual style that was unsuited to the tastes of the day. Many of his anxieties were due to his personality and temperament, though his personal circumstances also exerted significant external pressures that strongly affected his moods and, as a result, his paintings.

The environment of a painter's studio can be very significant to the work he produces. In 1817–18, when Constable embarked upon the series of six-footers, he lived with his wife and children in a rented house in Keppel Street, Bloomsbury, just around the corner from the British Museum.[11] The house was small, as he later commented: 'In Keppel Street we wanted room – & were like bottled wasps.'[12] The cramped space certainly affected his temper and no doubt his painting too. Little beyond general information is known of the size and layout of the house, and none regarding the specifics of his studio. There are hints that it was in an upstairs room, which would have given him the best light: 'I am now in the plight of moving. All well, my largest things are gone & safely upstairs.'[13] Another remark, reporting the removal of *The Hay Wain* (no.37) to the Royal Academy in 1821, indicates that the hall and stairwell were too narrow for a six-footer to come down the stairs: 'My picture goes to the Academy on the tenth. At the same time (as the window on the stairs must be taken out) I shall send Mr Tinney's picture [*Stratford Mill* 1820, no.31] to Mr Woodburns – to be packed as the large case is there.'[14] Evidently *Stratford Mill* had to be moved elsewhere to be crated for the journey to its new home in Salisbury. Working from a six-foot sketch side-by-side with a final canvas must have highlighted and exacerbated Constable's problems of space, quite apart from the noise and distractions of young children in the house. In the summer of 1821 the family took temporary lodgings in Hampstead (as they had done the previous two years), then a country village some miles outside London on a hill overlooking the Thames valley. There Constable set up a workshop in a 'small shed in the garden … that is literally a coal hole'. However, this was undoubtedly too small to accommodate the next 'large picture', as he called it, the sketch for *View on the Stour near Dedham* c.1821 (no.38), so he rented 'a room at a glazier's down town [in London] as a workshop'.[15] Despite spending the summer sketching on Hampstead Heath and working in his shed, the arrangement proved unsatisfactory and, by September, he

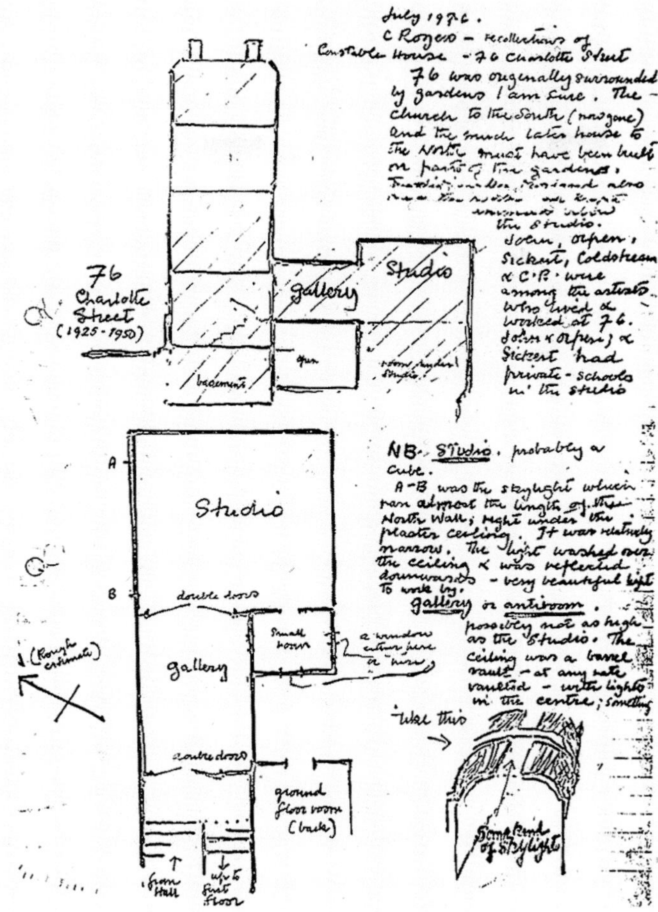

FIGURE 27

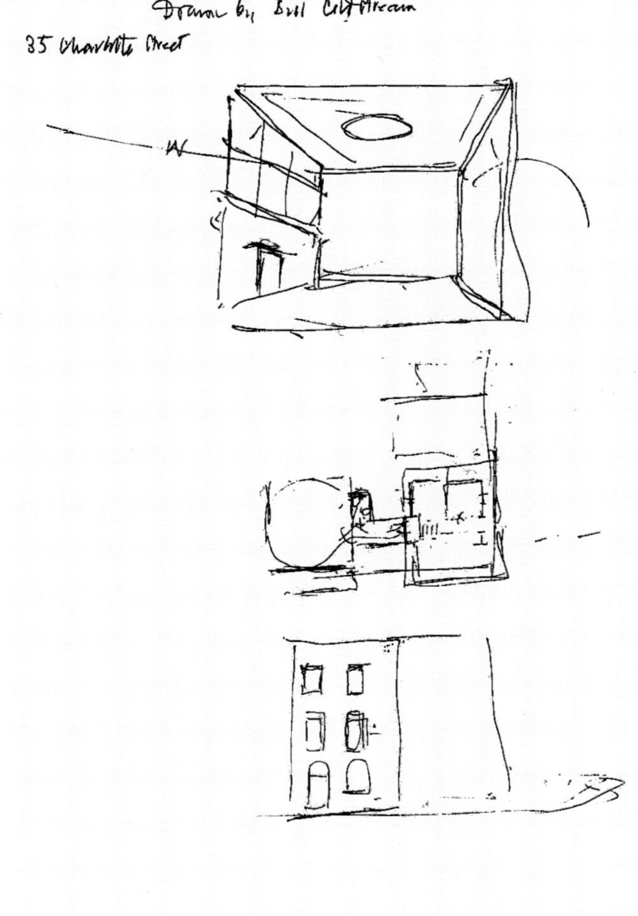

FIGURE 28

complained to Fisher that he was 'so behind with the Bridge [*View on the Stour*] which I have great hindrances in. I cannot do it here – & must leave my family & work in London', and later he wrote that Hampstead was 'a ruinous place to me – I lose time sadly here'.[16] Still torn between work and family in 1825, he told Fisher that Hampstead 'was so near I made my home at neither place – I was between two chairs – & could do nothing'.[17] The separation from his wife and family and anxiety about his work (and thus his finances too) must have caused him tremendous additional stress.

In October 1822, the family moved to the house of Constable's late mentor, the famous diarist and amateur artist Joseph Farington, in Charlotte Street, on the edge of London's burgeoning 'West End', where they lived until 1827.[18] It must have been a godsend, as it had substantial family accommodation and a large, purpose-built studio and gallery in a back extension to the ground floor (fig.27).[19] Constable initially bemoaned the disruption to his work after the move: 'We left Hampstead a fortnight ago last Tuesday – and I have not had my pencil [brush] in my hand one day yet. I have had an immense trouble to get the house habitable.'[20] Once settled he was very happy with the new premises: 'I have got this room (the large painting room) into excellent order. It is light-airy-*sweet* [smelling] and warm.'[21] In 1825 he made alterations to the studio to increase his privacy and improve the heating and lighting. With concerns for propriety and the first impressions of prospective purchasers, he had the door into the studio from the 'gallery', where clients perused saleable paintings, re-hung from the other side of the door-frame, 'by which my easil [*sic*] is not exposed even if the door is three quarters open, and none of the washhand part of my room seen, as it was before, at first sight'.[22] Though he selectively invited friends and fellow artists to visit his studio, the contents were evidently not for public consumption. In the same year he reported the sale of his old stove to his friend George Field, the colourmaker: 'I have now got my [new] painting room stove so compleat that it makes the painting room more warm & comfortable than any room in the house.'[23]

The Charlotte Street studio was particularly well lit by north light from a high window: 'the light washed over the ceiling and was reflected downwards – a very beautiful light to work by' (fig.28)[24] In 1825 Constable found that new 'shutters, add[ed] very much to it in the evening' and that he could 'accommodate my light a great deal better'.[25] Despite the well-positioned windows, the lack of good daylight was a significant constraint, since the six-footers were painted in the studio over the winter and early spring.[26] One December Constable complained that it was 'so dark that we had a candle on the table at 10. in the morning' and that he 'could not paint'.[27] This considerably reduced the time available to work up a large composition and, together with family sickness that usually accompanied the winter months, caused numerous delays and 'hindrances'. This became a matter of increasing concern to Fisher: 'I yearn to see you tranquilly and collectedly at work on your next great picture ... when the glands of the body are unobstructed by the cold ... You choose February and March for composition; when the strongest men get irritable & uncomfortable ... Sep: Oct: & Nov: are our healthiest months in England ...   The season you select for composition is the chief reason of the unfinished, abandoned state of your surface on the first of May. Your pictures look then like fine handsome women given up to recklessness & all abominations.'[28]

Constable not only needed good daylight to paint; he also intended his paintings to be viewed in these same light conditions, as he was aware that they looked better or worse at different times of the day and in certain types of weather.[29] *Stratford Mill* (no.31) was hung to particular advantage in John Tinney's drawing room in Salisbury, according to Fisher: 'The light on your picture is excellent, it receives the South sun, standing on a Western wall ... it puts out all the other pictures and attracts general attention.'[30] Though the light was wonderful the surroundings were 'exactly like the best parlour of an opulent pawnbroker', and the picture looked like 'an emerald in a dish of rubbish'. Fisher felt that 'villanous company' – Tinney's other pictures – detracted from its effect.[31]

Despite the relative seclusion, privacy and comfort of the large Charlotte Street studio, Constable's work was hindered by his own inner demons, together with growing family responsibilities, his wife's worsening illness and her untimely death in 1828. He told Fisher that the younger John Dunthorne, his assistant in the 1820s, was 'grieved at his master having so much of the devil about him'.[32] Only during the tranquil luxury of a month's visit to the country residence of his mentor and amateur painter Sir George Beaumont in 1823 did he fully relax and find some peace. In a touching letter to Maria, in which he accuses himself by implication, he noted that Sir George was never 'angry or pettish or peevish and though he loves painting it does not harass him', and he swore that on his return 'my temper will be so much improved'.[33]

Painting Supports: Canvas
Despite using a range of supports, including canvas, paper, panel and board for his outdoor oil sketches, Constable used plain weave linen canvas for all but one of the full-size sketches and exhibited six-footers.[34] There seems to be no correlation between the weight of the canvas and whether it was intended for a sketch or a 'finished' picture.[35] Most of the canvases are slightly finer than those used earlier in his career and are moderately loosely woven, with thick and thin

threads and numerous slubs that give a rough and uneven texture to the surface.[36] A few of the canvases are more tightly and evenly woven; for example, that of the first six-footer, the full-size sketch for *The White Horse* c.1818 (no.28).[37] This was originally intended for a 'finished' version of *Dedham from Gun Hill*, which is under *The White Horse* sketch (fig.21, p.45).[38] The use of a finer canvas may indicate Constable's initial intention to use better quality materials for his large exhibited works, though he was inconsistent in this, as the finest canvas of all is found in the full-size sketch for *View on the Stour near Dedham* c.1821 (no.38).[39]

The only example of a different type of canvas is the full-size sketch for *Hadleigh Castle* c.1829 (no.56), which is painted on a medium-weight twill, measuring approximately 44×62 inches (1.12×1.57m), somewhat smaller than the other six-footers.[40] It was enlarged after Constable's death with strips of primed, painted plain weave canvas on two sides, to extend it to its present size.[41] The illness and death of Constable's wife in November 1828, followed by his own illness, meant that by late January 1829, less than three months before the Academy exhibition, he was bemoaning not being 'afloat on a canvas of six feet'.[42] He evidently did not have a six-foot canvas prepared, so he started work on this slightly smaller twill canvas that he may have already had in his studio. Although not his most frequent choice of support, there are similar examples of his occasional use of twill weave canvas *in extremis* throughout his career.[43]

It is ironic that the paintings in this exhibition are called 'six-footers', since the majority of them no longer have a single dimension measuring six feet (72in). A six-footer seems anecdotally to have been thought to be four by six feet, or 48×72 inches. Constable only used one canvas of exactly this size, for the full-size sketch of *The Leaping Horse* 1824–5 (no.46), though he later enlarged it. It appears that the majority of the six-foot canvases were slightly larger, measuring 50×72 inches (4ft 2in $\times$ 6ft). Their present dimensions are complicated by Constable having regularly extended canvases, by the loss of original edges during lining and by restretching on non-original stretchers, which have resulted in there being no two six-footers of identical size today.[44]

Constable's preferred canvas, 50×72 inches, was not a standard size for landscape or portraiture, according to contemporary lists published by 'Primed Cloth Manufacturer[s]' Brown of High Holborn and Middleton of St Martin's Lane, London.[45] These also state that 'Landscapes have no settled dimensions, but are often painted on the *given sizes*, placing them on their sides instead of upright'.[46] This was Constable's regular practice before c.1818, when he used standard 'kit-kat' canvases (36×28in/91.4×71.1cm) turned sideways, as in *Dedham Lock and Mill* c.1817–18 (no.24).[47] He deviated from this straightforward method when he commenced the series of six-footers, as he wanted to paint a much larger picture that would make a strong impression at the Royal Academy, where there was a tradition of sizeable landscapes by eminent predecessors such as Thomas Gainsborough, Richard Wilson and Joseph Farington, as well as contemporaries such as Augustus Wall Callcott.[48] However, in 1819 his ambition was likely tempered by the practical constraints of getting a large canvas in and out of the small Keppel Street house. Probably he could not use the largest off-the-shelf portrait canvas, a 'full-length' (94×54in) because it was too big. In 1817 he had used the next size down, a 'half-length' (50×40in), for *Flatford Mill* 1817 (no.19), but by 1819 he presumably no longer felt that this size was sufficiently imposing. Ultimately, he settled for

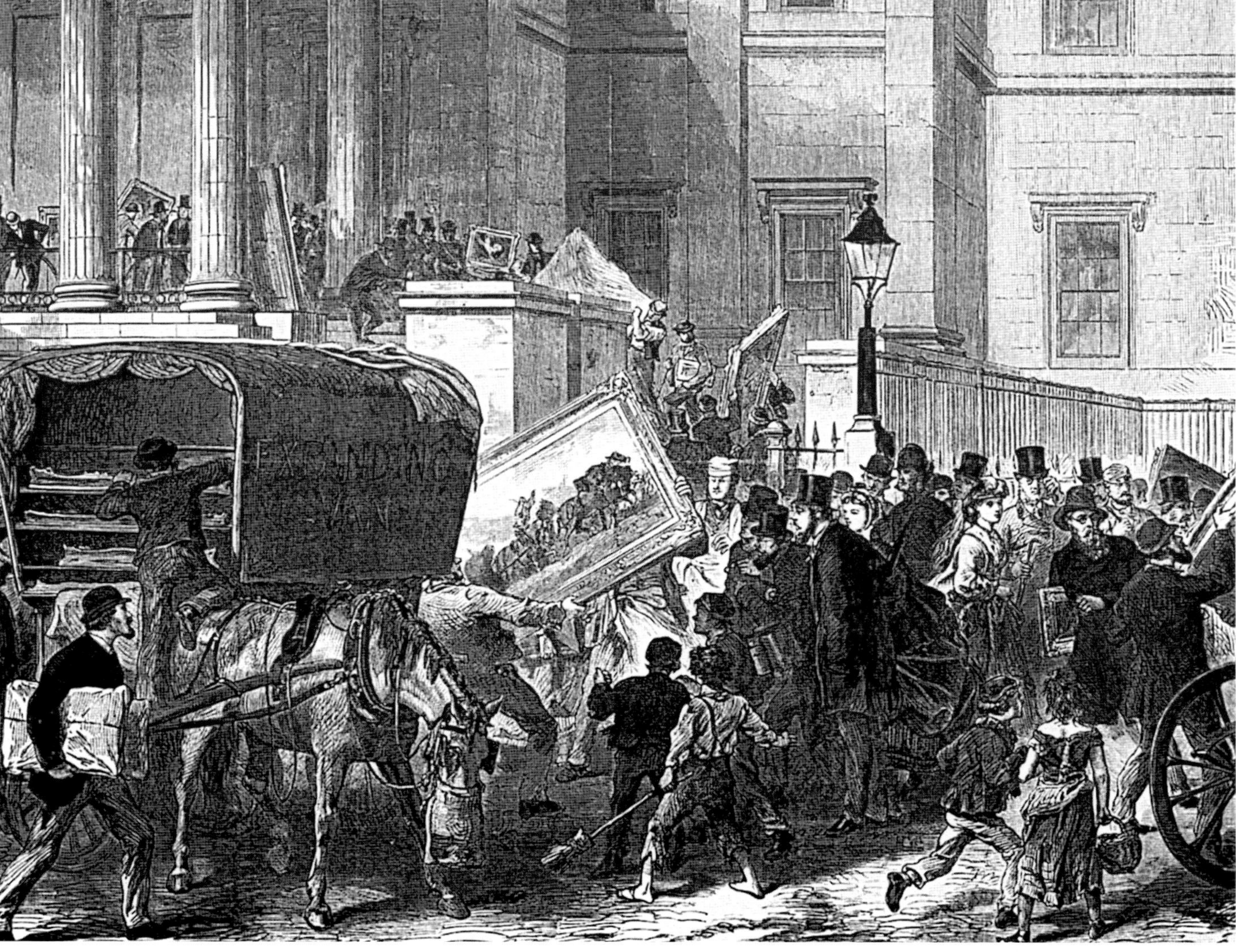

FIGURE 29

something in between. In making the final decision on size he must have considered the time it would take to paint a large canvas, since he also intended to do a full-size sketch. There was also the expense of a suitable frame and the difficulty and cost of transporting a large, heavy work to the Academy. This was by horse-drawn wagon and does not bear thinking about in an age of acclimatised air-ride vehicles (fig.29)![49] He no doubt felt that a framed six-footer was reasonably easy to handle and transport, yet sufficiently large and attractive to gain critical recognition, and hopefully a sale, at the Academy.

A canvas could have been purchased from a colourman as a 'primed piece', or Constable may have bought all or part of a 'six yard' roll, as primed rolls 'six yards long' (216in/5.5m) were sold in various widths throughout the nineteenth century.[50] Selvedges, indicating the original roll width, are rarely seen on the six-footers, as their tacking edges have invariably been removed. However, scalloped threads, known as 'cusping', created by pinning out the long sides of a roll during commercial preparation with size and ground layers, suggest

that the six-foot canvases came from a 'four feet six inch' wide roll (54in), which was a standard width.[51] When stretched on to a 'six-foot' stretcher, with 2-inch tacking margins top and bottom, this gives dimensions of 50 × 72 inches, matching most of the full-size sketches and exhibition works. It is notable that the standard 54-inch 'six-yard roll' (18ft/216in) provides exactly two six-footers and a remnant that stretches up to 50 × 60 inches. When turned upright this is exactly the size of *The Lock* 1824 (see no.41), and it could have provided supports for *The Cornfield* 1826 (fig.59, p.116; R.35.1), *Dedham Vale* 1828 (fig.74, p.164) and *The Valley Farm* 1835 (Tate; R.31.1), which are almost the same size, suggesting that Constable could have used up several six-yard rolls over the years.[52]

In 1820 Constable began work on his largest canvas, Anglesey Abbey's *The Opening of Waterloo Bridge* c.1820–5 (5ft ¹⁄₂in × 8ft ⁵⁄₈in; no.65). No doubt this reflected his increased confidence and ambition following the positive response to the first six-footer, *The White Horse* (no.29), the previous year. Constable failed to complete the painting, and it is possible that it was removed from its stretcher and rolled up for the move to Charlotte Street in 1822. When it was restretched, the previous tacking edges were incorporated into the picture plane before painting recommenced, possibly as late as c.1830.[53] At Charlotte Street canvas size was less of a problem, so Constable could buy large stretched canvases off-the-shelf and 'to order'.[54] Colourmen's stamps show that he bought the canvas for *The Leaping Horse* 1825 (no.47) and the *Chain Pier, Brighton* 1827 (no.51) from Brown of High Holborn.[55] In 1824 he ordered a special new canvas for the exhibited *Opening of Waterloo Bridge* 1832 (no.67), though we do not know who supplied it.[56] Despite no longer facing the practical constraints of his earlier premises, he never chose to paint on the really huge canvases favoured by some of his contemporaries.[57]

During painting Constable routinely made alterations to the size of a canvas, particularly in the process of developing the composition in the full-size sketches. Most frequently this was to increase the overall dimensions by unfolding the tacking edges on one or more sides, flattening them and incorporating them into the picture plane, for example in the full-size sketches for *The Hay Wain* c.1820 (no.36), *View on the Stour near Dedham* c.1821 (no.38) and *Salisbury Cathedral from the Meadows* c.1829–31 (no.60). Crudely executed extensions are understandable in a full-size sketch in which Constable was finalising the composition, but less so in a 'finished' picture, intended for exhibition, when the initial set of tack holes can be seen on unfolded edges. Some of the full-size sketches were removed from their stretchers and worked on whilst pinned out flat on a wooden strainer, board, or to a wall, rather than being permanently stretched. For example, on *The Leaping Horse* sketch c.1824 (no.46), there are round holes visible on the x-radiograph (an image created when X-rays are transmitted through an artwork on to a sensitised film) along the top edge indicating that, as the sky was worked up using thick impasto, tacks were present that Constable painted over. These were subsequently removed leaving holes in the paint layer.[58] Constable kept all the six-foot sketches until the end of his life, and they may never have been permanently stretched since they would have taken up a considerable

amount of valuable studio space.[59] It appears that after his death some of them, including *The Leaping Horse* sketch, were harshly trimmed around the edges, extended with new canvas additions and probably lined at the same time.[60] The additions were then painted in imitation of Constable's 'late' style, in an attempt to make them look more like the exhibited six-footers, and no doubt more saleable.

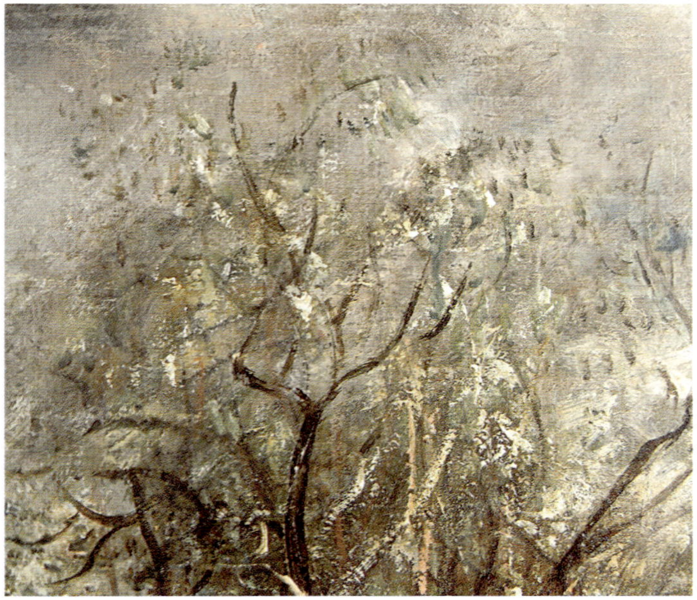

As well as pinning out sketches, 'finished' canvases may not have been permanently stretched during 'squaring-up', drawing or painting. Between October and December 1825, Constable and Dunthorne put the 'intricate outline' on the new canvas for *The Opening of Waterloo Bridge* (no.67).[61] We hear nothing more of it after July 1826 for five-and-a-half years, until late February 1832, when Constable had it 'very beautifully strained on a new frame – keeping every inch of the canvas'.[62] Before this it is not known whether it had ever been properly stretched or only pinned out. If he had been working on it over the winter of 1831 to 1832, as was his usual practice, stretching the canvas covered in thick semi-dry impasto would have been difficult. This either suggests that he had not worked on it for some time to allow it to dry, or that he had not even started the major work at this point. If the latter is the case, and he left himself less than three months to complete this hugely ambitious project, it is not surprising that he was even more anxious than usual when it went to the Academy unfinished: 'This is a sad affair to me – but I am rightly served – I should not have sent my scrambling affair.'[63]

As well as routinely enlarging canvases, Constable occasionally cut them down, as he did with the exhibited *Chain Pier, Brighton* 1827 (no.51) by approximately nine inches on the left and one inch on the right, to make it a six-footer. He did this relatively soon after the picture was exhibited, probably in 1828–9, when the paint was still slightly soft.[64] After it was cut down, the boat on the left and the sky and right edge were reworked with broad impasto applied with a palette knife in Constable's 'late' manner, completely out of keeping with the rest of the painting. By cutting it down to the size of a regular six-footer, Constable may have hoped to find a buyer, though it still failed to sell during his lifetime.[65]

Constable was always desperate to start work as soon as an idea had crystallised in his mind, and this sometimes led him to make unconventional or ill-advised choices of materials if he did not have the correct item to hand.[66] He was less concerned with the condition of a canvas for a sketch than for a 'finished' painting and this, together with his impetuous temperament, led him to re-use discarded or abandoned canvases, such as those for the full-size sketches for *The White Horse* c.1818 (no.28) and *The Lock* c.1823 (no.40). He sometimes turned this to his advantage as, having only oiled-out the surface of an unfinished *Dedham from Gun Hill* to prepare it for *The White Horse* sketch, he cleverly incorporated areas of the earlier composition into the new sky and foliage with hardly any reworking (fig.21, p.45).[67] In the full-size sketch for *The Lock*, he changed the format from 'landscape' to 'portrait' during the evolution of the composition. The support was originally a 'half-length' portrait canvas (50 × 40in). He had already painted an unfinished figure on it when he restretched it back to front and laid-in the composition in landscape format.[68] He subsequently changed his mind, removed the canvas from its stretcher again, flattened the tacking edges and glued an 11¼-inch (28.5cm) canvas addition to the underside of the unprimed top edge of the original canvas. He then cut a strip off the right side and

Figure 30
Detail from *The Leaping Horse* 1825 (no.47), showing the top of the large tree on the left. The neat horizontal join in the canvas is just visible at the top. Comparatively un-'finished' brushwork and strokes of almost pure Prussian blue and muddy greys were used to rework the tree and sky over and around the extension.
ROYAL ACADEMY OF ARTS, LONDON

FIGURE 30

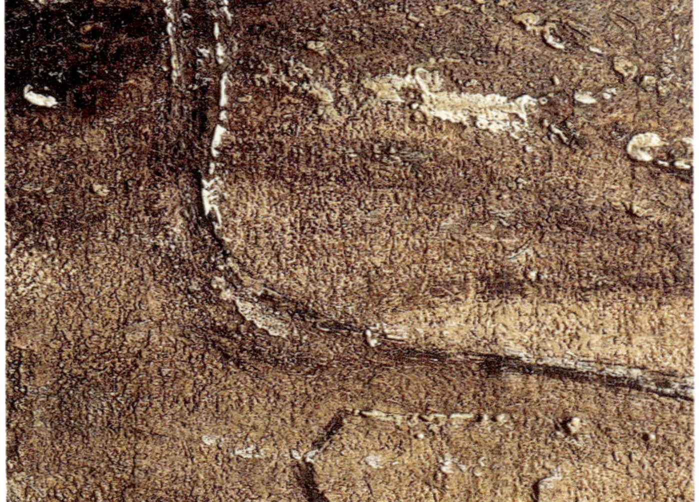

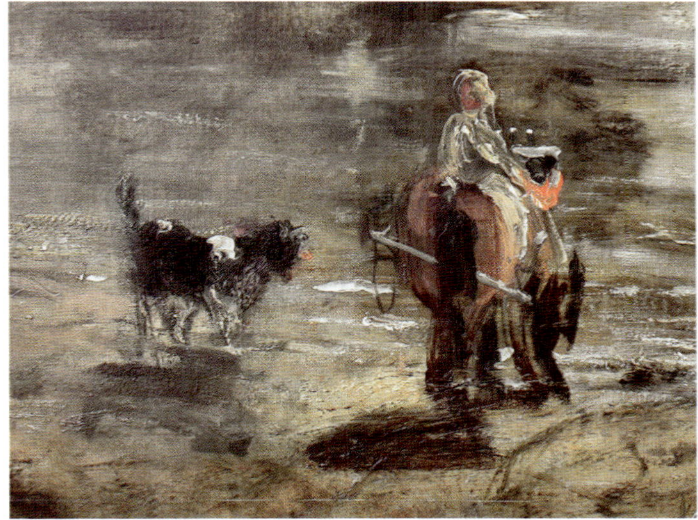

Figure 31
Detail from the foreground beach in the *Chain Pier, Brighton* 1827 (no.51), showing dragged brushwork over the 'stippled' priming.

TATE. PURCHASED 1950

Figure 32
Detail from the full-size sketch of *The Hay Wain* c.1820 (no.36), showing the modelled brown *imprimatura* over a pink ground. The principal elements are drawn in fluid brown paint, highlighted with minimal local colour.

VICTORIA AND ALBERT MUSEUM, LONDON

restretched the canvas in vertical format, turning some of the paint over the stretcher edge on the right. Before recommencing painting he cursorily primed the new top portion and then carried on painting. The thick layer of glue on the underside of the join has caused the paint to repeatedly crack and flake off in a strip across the sky.[69]

This almost total disregard for the niceties of the painter's craft is typical of Constable's approach to his canvases, particularly in the sketches, though this was not always the case. In September 1825, two months after *The Leaping Horse* returned from the Academy, he radically altered the composition.[70] Instead of crudely glueing an additional canvas piece to the top edge, a neater, stronger method was used. The tacking edge was unfolded and flattened, and a similar piece of fine plain weave canvas 2½ inches wide was cut to match, butt-joined (edge-to-edge) and neatly stitched across the width of the canvas (fig.30). Though not visible on the surface, the tiny stitches can clearly be seen on the x-radiograph.[71] This level of care is uncharacteristic, and the method strongly suggests that the extension was carried out professionally by a commercial firm.[72]

Preparation of the Canvas: Grounds and Primings

In the early nineteenth century, 'Prepared' canvases were available from colourmen with 'Oil or Absorbent Grounds', the latter probably chalk and glue. These were often pure white but they could be tinted at extra cost.[73] Over a commercial ground an artist could apply a coloured priming, or a modelled or tonal underpainting, or *imprimatura*, in preparation for the final image. Constable's early method was to use canvas prepared with a double oil-bound ground, usually containing lead white and chalk, which is thin enough to just fill the interstices of the canvas weave. Over this he applied an overall coat of opaque brown or pink priming, as can be seen in *Flatford Mill from the Lock* 1812 (no.14) and *Dedham Lock and Mill* c.1817–18 (no.24).[74] He continued with this method until c.1820, and it can be seen in the first three large pictures he planned, *The White Horse* sketch c.1818 (no.28), *The White Horse* 1819 (no.29) and the *Stratford Mill* sketch c.1819 (no.30).[75] The Anglesey Abbey *Opening of Waterloo Bridge* c.1820–5 (no.65) is prepared with a flat opaque reddish-brown priming, characteristic of works before 1820,

and closely resembling the c.1819 sketch for *Stratford Mill* (no.30). This strongly suggests that it is the 'Thames on a large canvas' that Constable was putting in hand in September 1820, as by 1821 he was employing alternative methods.[76]

From 1820 to 1821 Constable used several different types of light-toned ground without an overall brown priming. This gave more luminosity to the paint, particularly in skies in which he sought a greater range of 'effects'. During the summers of 1821 and 1822 he made numerous sky and cloud sketches, in which he developed techniques for painting on a light ground that fed directly into his large studio works.[77] Until the mid-1820s he used both off-white and pale pink grounds, as can be seen in the full-size sketches for *The Hay Wain* c.1820 (no.36), *View on the Stour near Dedham* c.1821 (no.38) and *The Leaping Horse* c.1824 (no.46), the 'finished' *View on the Stour* 1822 (no.39) and the horizontal *Lock* of 1826 (fig.70, p.152).[78]

However, from 1820 to 1827 Constable predominantly used an idiosyncratic 'stippled' off-white or pale pink priming that has a characteristic texture of tiny peaks and rivulets, similar to the effect created by a modern paint roller.[79] At this date it is likely to have been applied with a particular type of brush that leaves a light stippled texture, similar to those used by decorators today.[80] This priming is present on more than half the six-foot canvases: the earliest in 1820 (*Stratford Mill*, no.31), the latest in 1827 (*Chain Pier, Brighton*, fig.31, no.51). It consists of a semi-translucent mixture of chalk, lightly pigmented with ochres or synthetic iron oxides (Mars colours), bound to a stiff consistency with an emulsion of egg and oil, and possibly a little glue.[81] It appears pink in contrast to the blues of the sky. Where it remains visible its obvious texture enlivens the surface, and it also gives considerable 'tooth' to the brush, creating an intrinsic drag in Constable's layered paint strokes. This method of preparation appears unique, as it has not been identified in works by Constable's contemporaries, and artists' manuals of the time only comment on the smoothness of grounds and methods for obtaining this.[82] The consistent use of identical materials and their application suggests that the 'stippled' priming derives from a single source. It is present on the canvas for *The Leaping Horse* (no.47) and the *Chain Pier, Brighton*

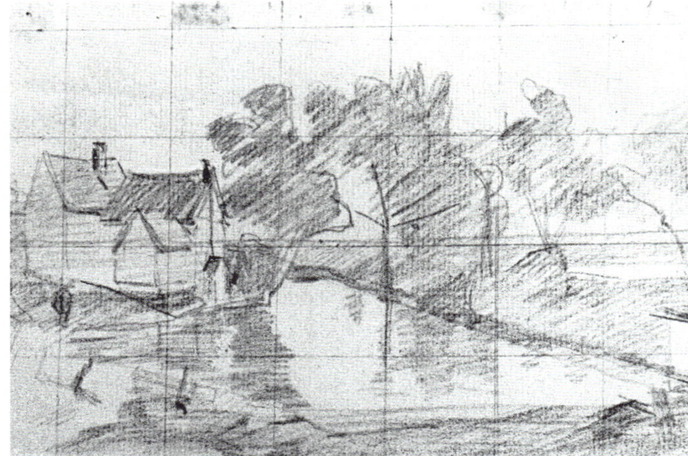

FIGURE 33

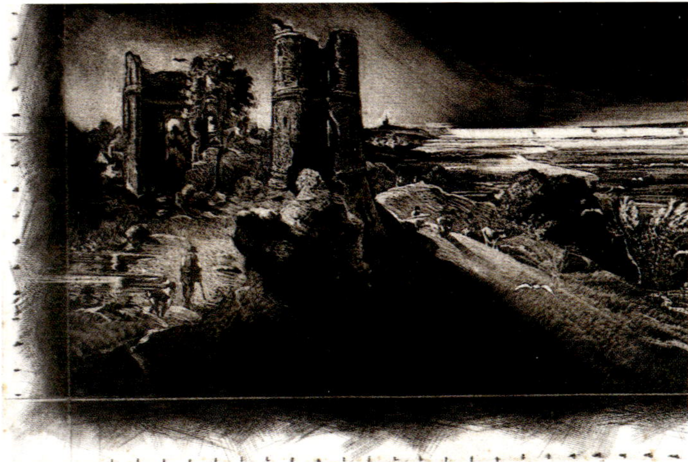

FIGURE 34

(no.51), which were both supplied by Brown of High Holborn, so it is possible that it is a commercial preparation. However, its use also precisely coincides with Dunthorne's main period of employment with Constable (c.1820–7), so it is possible, likely even, that this method is his work.[83] It is tantalising to wonder whether he, the son of a Suffolk house-painter, introduced Constable to an innovative method of priming canvas using some kind of decorators' tool or technique that enabled him to prepare large canvases relatively fast with a quick-drying priming.

From 1827 onwards Dunthorne gradually moved to independent employment, so Constable either had to prime his own canvases, or use commercially prepared ones if he lacked time or the inclination to prime his own. From around this time until the end of his life, he favoured a smooth, absorbent, distemper-type ground that he could easily have applied himself, though it could equally be a quick-drying commercial preparation. These grounds appear to be bound with glue, or a glue-oil mixture, and exhibit a characteristic small-scale rectilinear cracquelure, related to the canvas weave, which is in keeping with the relatively brittle nature of distemper-type paints.[84] This white ground was sometimes modified with a smooth pink priming over the sky.[85] In the half-size study for *The Opening of Waterloo Bridge* c.1829 (no.66), the white ground and pink priming are separated by a thin size layer that may have aided the drying process.[86]

Both the 'stippled' priming and the later white grounds were especially lean and absorbent, and were particularly suited to Constable's painting technique in the 1820s and 1830s. An absorbent ground or priming speeds up the drying time of paint and helps keep it crisp 'by absorbing the oils or vehicles with which the colours are tempered' [mixed].[87] It also reputedly keeps 'the colours more pure'.[88] There was tremendous interest in absorbent grounds in the early nineteenth century, because they were reputedly used by revered Venetians painters such as Titian and Veronese.[89] Constable had been touched by this avid interest as, in 1824, Sir George Beaumont had asked him to try out the 'Venetian Secret of Colouring' discovered by 'Miss Cleaver'.[90] However, there were drawbacks to using an absorbent ground, and these were discussed in contemporary artists' manuals. Evidently the paint would 'sink-in' too much, leaving the surface dead and matt until it was resaturated, and thus enlivened, with 'finishing'

glazes or 'toning', and ultimately, some time later, a varnish.[91] Constable's paintings no doubt suffered these drying defects that compounded his innate compulsion to constantly rework the surfaces after exhibition.

Throughout the 1820s and 1830s Constable applied a translucent brown wash, or *imprimatura*, to seal the ground and priming, and tone areas of landscape, trees and foliage.[92] In some paintings it is a flat, even layer of dark reddish-brown, in others it varies from a thin, pale 'tan', created with the addition of a little lead white or ochre, to a very dark glossy brown, and is tonally modelled to lay in the masses of the composition. This is the 'faint dead colouring, in which the masses only are laid in' mentioned by the artist C.R. Leslie, Constable's friend and biographer, and is most clearly seen in the full-size sketch for *The Hay Wain* c.1820 (fig.32, p.57; no.36).[93] The influence of Rubens's technique, studied by Constable early in his career, can be seen in the use of this method, which is one of the most important factors in the creation of a mellow appearance in his 'late' paintings.[94]

Transferring the Design: 'Squaring-up'

An elaborate six-foot composition required considerable work before painting commenced. Constable's preparatory material ranges from ink and pencil drawings to outdoor oil sketches and studio studies. Usually elements from several of these were brought together in a large oil sketch (quarter-, half- or full-size), in which he mapped out basic ideas and then made alterations and additions to the composition as necessary. Only occasionally did he make a small compositional oil study that was directly copied and 'squared-up'.

'Squaring-up' is a method of copying or enlarging a design that has been used by artists for hundreds of years. It consists of dividing an image with evenly spaced horizontal and vertical lines using a variety of methods. The design is then copied on to a larger support with a grid in the same ratio. The easiest method of squaring-up is to draw lines directly on to the image, but this permanently defaces it. Constable did this to enlarge compositional drawings and oil studies for early exhibited pictures, for example the sketches for *The Mill Stream* c.1809–14 (fig.33) and *Flatford Mill* c.1814–16 (no.18).[95] After his permanent move from Suffolk to London in 1816 he used methods of squaring-up that preserved his early sketches, as they were valuable

Figure 35
Detail from the full-size sketch of *Salisbury Cathedral from the Meadows* c.1829–31 (no.60), showing the sky at the top edge, above the trees, with fine horizontal and vertical pencil 'squaring-up' lines drawn directly over the ground, under the paint. The paint was scraped back in places, exposing the pink priming, ground and canvas weave. Palette-knife strokes are visible, lower left.
GUILDHALL ART GALLERY, LONDON

Figure 36
Half-size sketch of *The Opening of Waterloo Bridge* c.1829 (no.66), which has a horizontal ink 'squaring-up' line running through the window of the bay-fronted house. Ruled ink lines can be seen in the buildings to the right and on the top rail of the balcony. Constable did not slavishly follow the drawn outline, having only indicated the balcony with a few lines incised into the wet paint revealing the white ground. The crowd is depicted with impressionistic strokes of neat colour.
YALE CENTER FOR BRITISH ART

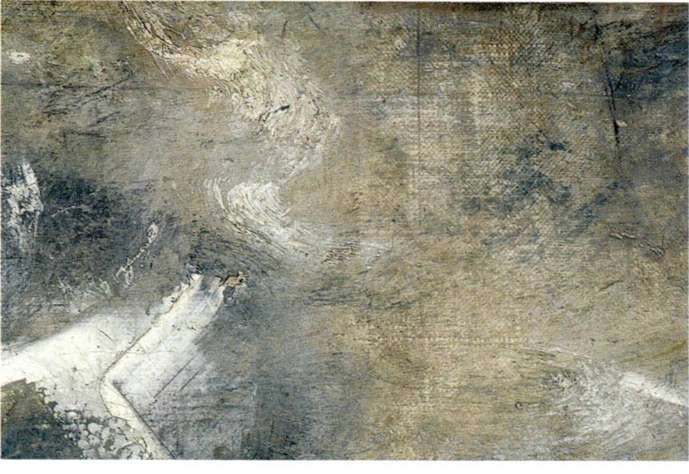

FIGURE 35

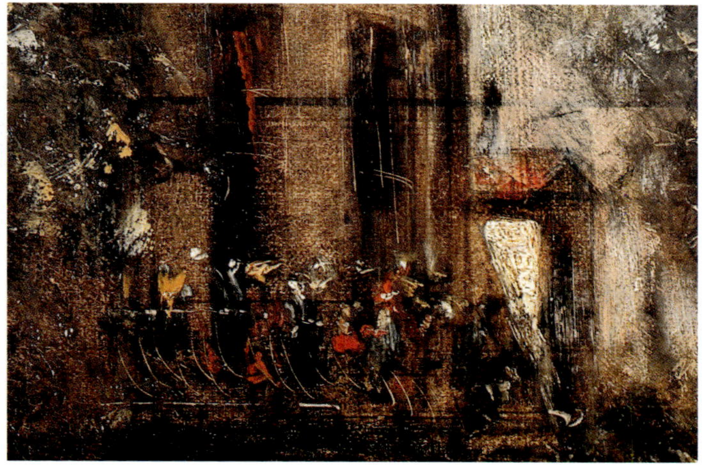

FIGURE 36

source material for his later studio works. One method that he probably used involved a wooden frame with horizontal and vertical threads stretched across it. This was placed over the front of a picture and lined up against ink or pencil marks around the edges.[96] This method is suggested in the copies of *Dedham Lock and Mill* c.1817–18 (no.24).[97]

The method that Constable used most frequently to square-up the six-footers involved stretching threads over the front of the canvas from evenly spaced tacks around the edges. The threads were removed after the design was copied, leaving the image unmarked apart from the tell-tale tack holes. Presumably he disliked the disfiguring effect of drawn grids on earlier works and elected to square-up his large canvases with this relatively non-invasive method. Few of the six-footers retain all of their original tacking edges, so evidence for this method has mostly been lost. However, there are clear indications of its use on some remaining edges, including those on the full-size sketch for *View on the Stour near Dedham* c.1821 (no.38), which has regularly spaced tack holes two inches (5cm) apart. On *The Hay Wain* 1821 (no.37), there is one sequence of holes two inches apart and, on the top edge of *The Lock* 1824 (no.41), there are holes three inches (7.5cm) apart. These indicate that both full-size sketches and final canvases were squared-up in this way. 'Finished' canvases would have been squared-up before painting to copy the design from the full-size sketch, and in some cases after exhibition in the preparation of a mezzotint. Regularly spaced 'marks' are visible around the edges of many of Constable's printed mezzotints. These are squaring-up marks on the plate that originally related to thread-grids on the large canvases (fig.34). In 1836 Constable mentioned taking the 'threads' off the large *Dedham Vale* of 1828 that David Lucas was engraving.[98] Earlier, in 1831, he had given Lucas specific instructions for squaring-up 'a slight outline of the "Nore"' (*Hadleigh Castle*) with a sketch showing how to divide it into sixteen rectangles crossed by diagonals, similar to that used on the pencil and oil studies for *Salisbury Cathedral from the Meadows* 1831 (no.61).[99] On the *Chain Pier, Brighton* canvas 1827 (no.51), there are regular tack holes present that do not extend right across the canvas. This indicates that small areas were squared-up locally for the transfer of individual design elements, presumably taken from preparatory sketches. Evidence for this is seen in the area of the Albion

Hotel on the left of the promenade and the large sailing boat on the right.[100]

Two of the preliminary works for *Salisbury Cathedral from the Meadows* 1831 are examples of fully resolved compositional studies where squaring-up was done directly on the work itself. The pencil drawing, *Salisbury Cathedral from Long Bridge* 1829 (no.58), has horizontal, vertical and diagonal pencil lines drawn over the image. The design was copied on to the larger canvas for the oil study c.1829 (no.59) using ruled and freehand pencil ('black lead' or graphite) drawing, which is visible with the naked eye. The oil study was subsequently squared-up using threads to transfer the composition to the canvas for the six-foot sketch c.1829–31 (no.60), which has a corresponding pencil grid drawn directly on to the white ground (fig.35). There are also pencil and ink grids on most of the preparatory works for *The Opening of Waterloo Bridge* 1832 (no.67). In the early oil study c.1819 (no.63), a pencil grid was drawn on the opaque pink priming, whereas on the half-size sketch c.1829 (no.66) lines were drawn over the pink ground in brown ink (fig.36).

Transferring the Design: Underdrawing
Little underdrawing has been detected on Constable's early paintings, though almost certainly there is more than we can now see.[101] Its apparent absence strongly suggests that it was carried out in chalk, which is clearly visible over a strongly coloured priming, though it is obscured by subsequent oil paint layers.[102] As Constable moved away from brown and pink primings towards lighter preparations in the early 1820s, he used pencil, ink and dilute paint or watercolour for underdrawing, as recommended in contemporary artists' manuals.[103] Some of his earliest detectable underdrawing can be seen on the small compositional oil study for *The Opening of Waterloo Bridge* c.1819 (no.63).[104] In this work, extensive pencil drawing over the pink ground was used to detail the architecture to the left of the bridge, and there are expressive freehand squiggles in the clouds. The large c.1820–5 *Opening of Waterloo Bridge* (no.65) was taken directly from this small oil study yet, despite its size and elaborate detail, there is no visible underdrawing, suggesting the use of chalk over the dark brown priming.

Detailed underdrawing not only helps the transfer or enlargement of a composition, it also assists a less competent painter to achieve

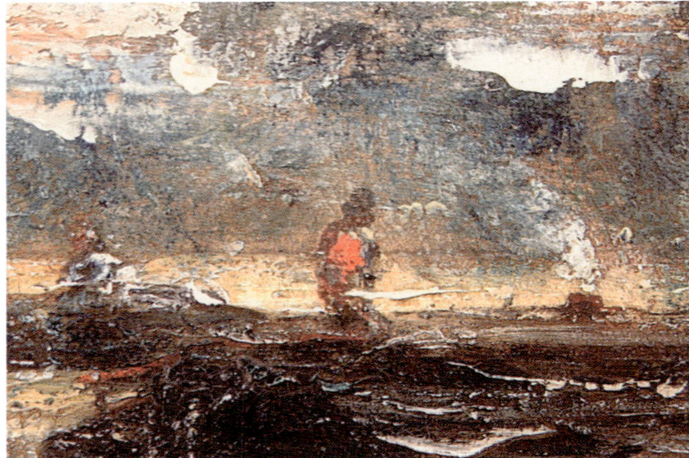

FIGURE 37

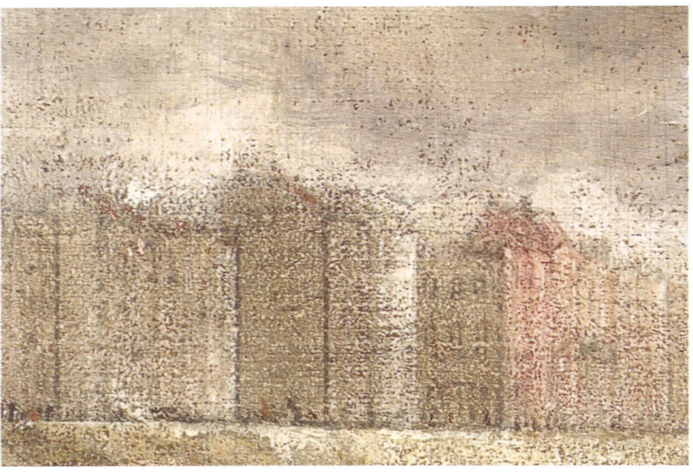

FIGURE 38

a reasonable copy. Dunthorne's employment during the 1820s, together with an increase in demand for copies and commissions, may explain the greater incidence of underdrawing during this period. Dunthorne did much of the 'subordinate' technical work in the studio, such as 'tracing, squaring and copying', and even painted some of the less important areas.[105] Laboured handling, which closely follows the underdrawing, is characteristic of copies from the 1820s, in which Dunthorne probably had a hand.[106] After 1827, when Dunthorne was no longer employed, Constable did not stick to initial drawing lines in many compositions, nor to numerous reinforcing lines he drew into the wet paint. In the exhibited *Hadleigh Castle* 1829 (no.57), drawing can be seen in the shepherd to the right of the tower and along the coastline. Constable did not keep to the drawn outlines of the rocks, and painted them about an inch lower down.

The earliest drawing detected on a six-footer is in the exhibited *View on the Stour near Dedham* (no.39) of 1822. It depicts 'a boat that was initially drawn in a very rough, scratchy style' and the exposed roots of a tree trunk, drawn in a more 'refined' line.[107] This may describe the difference between ink and pencil drawing, with the pencil as the more 'refined' line, since a sharp pencil point is characteristic of Constable's underdrawing. In addition to pencil, Constable used dilute brown paint or ink applied with a quill pen to create thick, dense lines that are now easy to see. Pencil and water-based materials are ideal for underdrawing as they do not dissolve in oil paint or turpentine. In addition, Constable's use of a brown oil-bound *imprimatura* in the foreground and landscape sealed the surface and stopped the drawing from being rubbed out by vigorous brushing.[108] These drawing media are frequently used together in rapid, freehand strokes, except in areas with architectural elements where straight lines are usually ruled (fig.36, p.59; fig.38). Where drawing is identified on the six-footers, there is generally a ruled pencil line along the horizon (fig.37). This is often barely visible with the naked eye; however, the bright sparkle of graphite particles can be detected at high magnification.

Among the six-footers, the most extensive drawing is found where there is a substantial and detailed architectural component, for example in the *Chain Pier, Brighton*; *Salisbury Cathedral from the Meadows* and *The Opening of Waterloo Bridge*. In the *Chain Pier, Brighton* 1827 (no.51), there is detailed pencil underdrawing that can be seen with

the naked eye in the buildings on Marine Parade, the pier and many of the boats (fig.38). The boat on the far right was initially drawn with its sail hoisted.[109] The drawing of the buildings and pier was taken from a meticulous pencil sketch, enlarged almost two-and-a-half times by squaring-up (no.49).[110] In the full-size sketch for *Salisbury Cathedral from the Meadows* c.1829–31 (no.60), the steeple and porch are emphatically redrawn with ruled lines through the wet paint, but Constable did not stick to this outline, as he rubbed back the sky and painted the façade of the church, porch and steeple leaning backwards to one side of the drawn outline (fig.41, p.62). The most extensive underdrawing of all is visible in the 1832 *The Opening of Waterloo Bridge* (no.67).[111] Constable and Dunthorne put the 'intricate outline' on the 'real' canvas in 1825.[112] It was drawn directly on to the off-white ground in pencil followed by either thinned paint, possibly watercolour, or dilute ink, applied with a quill pen and brush, probably in several stages (see nos.63–7). The outline is visible with the naked eye in the buildings on the left, the arches of the bridge, the Shot Tower and church steeples on the right. Architectural details, notably in the bay-fronted house and terrace, were ruled with brown ink and a quill pen (fig.36, p.59).[113] During the painting process, ruled pencil lines were redrawn over and into the wet paint to reinstate the horizontals and verticals of the bridge, towers and buildings.

The Six-Foot Sketches

Constable usually planned a new composition during the late summer to autumn of the year before a 'finished' picture was due to be exhibited, giving himself six or seven months to complete the final canvas. Frequently the best-laid plans went awry, leaving him with significantly less time to paint both the sketch and the exhibited version.

The sketch for *The Hay Wain* c.1820 (no.36) is the third of the full-size sketches. It was not begun until late 1820 due to a last-minute change of mind regarding subject matter.[114] The necessity for economy of both time and technique is reflected in its broad, rapid execution, since the amount of paint on the surface is minimal compared to the other six-foot sketches. Over a smooth pink absorbent priming, the tonal masses were blocked-in with fluid semi-opaque browns and a two-inch (5cm) bristle brush. Much of the pink ground is left

Detail from the full-size sketch of *The Hay Wain* c.1820 (no.36), showing the elder tree to the right of Willy Lott's cottage. Constable's years of constant oil sketching gave him a rich vocabulary of effects to draw on in the full-size sketches. Here, he uses a rapid personal notation, including bristle brushwork, white dabs from the tip of a palette knife and fluid green paint, to depict the flowering elder tree.

THE NATIONAL GALLERY, LONDON

Figure 40
In this detail from the full-size sketch of *View on the Stour near Dedham* c.1821 (no.38), a raised triangular sail on the central barge above the foremost figures is clearly visible with the naked eye. It was altered and then painted out during development of the composition.

PRIVATE COLLECTION

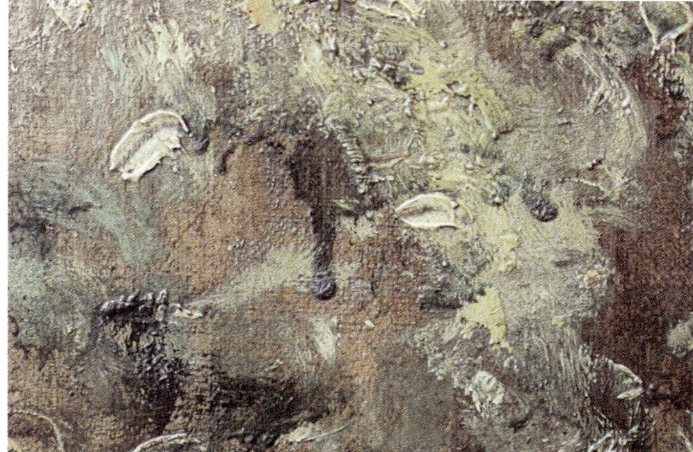

FIGURE 39

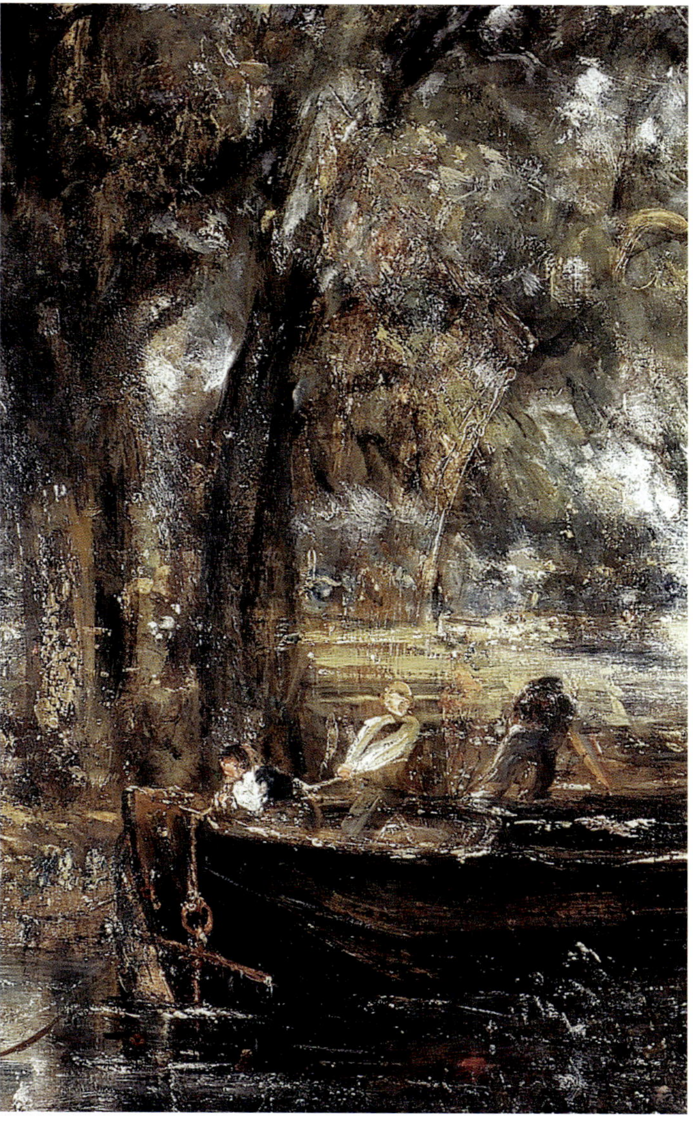

FIGURE 40

unpainted or shows through the thinner washes of this modelled *imprimatura*. The sky is the most thickly painted area. It was worked up using sweeping strokes of creamy white paint applied in a swirling, wiggling motion with a two-inch bristle brush.[115] There is also some very thick, crusty dragged impasto, though some of this has been partially flattened, possibly by lining.[116] The sky is quite strongly cracked in places, indicating that too much thick reworking was carried out without leaving the paint sufficient time to dry. The main elements of the landscape were 'drawn' with smaller bristle brushes using stiff, lean opaque paint and a limited range of colours (fig.32, p.57).[117] Finally, the figures, cart, cottage, dog and highlights in the trees were worked up with thickly impasted blobs of barely mixed paint, applied by brush and with the tip of a palette knife (fig.32, p.57; fig.39).

Having laid-in the composition and sometimes worked it up quite fully, Constable made numerous major and minor changes (pentimenti) in most of the six-foot sketches. Occasionally he took care to reprime an area before repainting, so pentimenti are not visible on the surface, though they are often detected by x-radiography. In the sketch for *View on the Stour near Dedham* c.1821 (no.38), the central barge originally had a raised sail that was altered twice (fig.40). There were originally two seated figures in the centre, a barge-building dock and a small figure on the right, and a boat with raised sail in the bottom left corner (see fig.69, p.149). Constable described some of these alterations in a letter that clearly indicates that Fisher had seen the sketch in its earlier incarnation.[118] More often than not Constable did not prepare the surface carefully before making changes and he painted too much, too thickly, too soon. As a result numerous pentimenti can now be seen with the naked eye due to drying cracks in the upper paint layers. Sometimes changes are also visible as unrelated brushwork under the surface, for example, the fishing rod of the standing boy seen in the full-size sketch for *Stratford Mill* c.1819–20 (no.30) is clearly visible higher up and to the left in the final version (no.31), into which he was originally painted and then painted out by Constable.[119]

Constable's sketches of the 1830s are extraordinarily modern for their time, and have earned him the title 'the Jackson Pollock of the 1830s' for the wild use of thick impasto and flecks of pure colour.[120] His powerful and expressive handling reached its climax in the full-size sketches for *Salisbury Cathedral from the Meadows* c.1829–31 (no.61) and *Stoke-by-Nayland* c.1835–7 (no.68). In the *Salisbury* sketch, Constable drew the outlines with dilute paint, possibly watercolour, and filled them in with dragged strokes, dramatic scratching and scumbling, with local colour applied wet-in-wet and wet-over-semi-dry by brush and palette knife.[121] A knife tip was used to 'draw' in the wet paint, revealing the underlayers, to create light streaks and lines. A flat tapered stick or brush handle covered in paint was pressed into the trees to make black and white 'branches'. Constable moved from one area to another, working up the surface over a long period, with the paint becoming 'touch-dry' between sessions. Consequently it dried well overall and remains in exceptional condition. Recent cleaning has revealed the intentionally stark colouring and the staggering texture which is relatively undamaged (fig.35, p.59; figs.41, 42, p.62).

One notable aspect of the colouring of Constable's late sketches is that much of the 'ochre-coloured' paint is Patent yellow (lead

Figure 41
Detail from the full-size sketch of
Salisbury Cathedral from the Meadows
c.1829–31 (no.60), in which Constable's
powerful rendering of the imposing
cathedral front and dramatic sky is
created with furious bristle brushwork
and exhilarating palette-knife strokes.
Note that the steeple leans very slightly
to the left.
GUILDHALL ART GALLERY, LONDON

Figure 42
Another detail from the full-size sketch
of *Salisbury Cathedral from the Meadows*
(no.60), with the bushes and main tree
on the left showing the 'lattice' of highly
textured strokes, including discoloured
Patent yellow, used to depict dense
foliage.
GUILDHALL ART GALLERY, LONDON

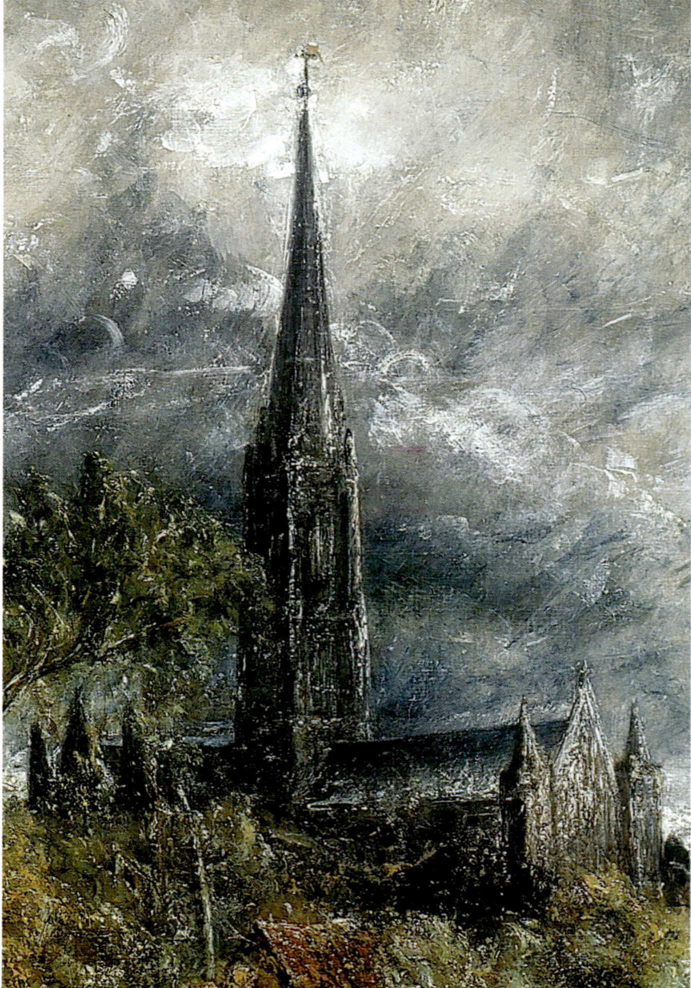

FIGURE 41

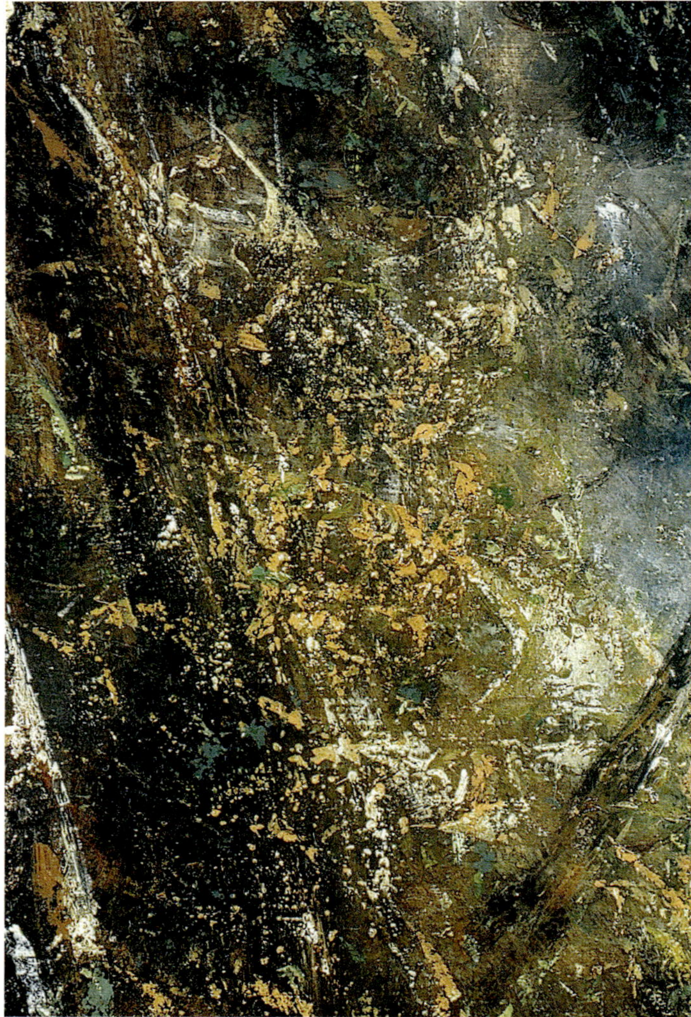

FIGURE 42

oxychloride), originally an 'acid' lemon yellow pigment that discolours
to a dull ochre with time and impure air.[122] This is visible in the
mustard-coloured strokes on the fields on the far side of the river and
in many of the splattered 'leaves' in the trees and the foreground
foliage of the full-size sketch for *Salisbury Cathedral* (fig.42). When it
was applied it would have been significantly more vivid than it appears
today, brightening the overall colour of works that are already striking
in their effect.

In addition to the battery of painting techniques described above,
in the *Stoke-by-Nayland* sketch (no.68), Constable used a method
developed to extend the range of subtle effects he could achieve in
skies. First he applied a wash of purplish brown-black to mask the
luminosity of the white ground in the manner of his earlier dark
primings.[123] Over this, the clouds are described in a flurry of furious
bristle brushstrokes, rubbings out, scrubbing, scratching, and dotting
on to the surface in a patchwork of overlapping strokes, dabs and
swirls. The dark underlayer allowed Constable to exploit the turbid
medium effect to create 'optical' purples that cannot be straight-
forwardly mixed on the palette.[124] In the landscape the forms are

'drawn' with small bristle brushes and worked up using touches
of local colour: vermilion and a red lake, chrome yellow, Prussian and
cobalt blues, together with vivid bright greens, including verdigris.[125]
In addition there are stiff, crusty impastos, heavily loaded on to a
palette knife, then smeared, squeezed, dabbed and cut-through with
the knife edge and tip.

The Six-Footers: 'Finished' Works

Stratford Mill 1820 (no.31) is a particularly good example of Constable's
technique in the 'finished' six-footers before 1829. Encouraged by the
success of *The White Horse* (no.29) the previous year, his new-found
confidence is evident in the clarity and precision of the paint
application. The composition was worked up in a sensible, practical
manner, allowing reasonable drying time. The design was copied from
the six-foot sketch to the final canvas and the masses laid-in with a
tonal *imprimatura*. First, the sky was broadly painted with sweeping
strokes of a large bristle brush to set the overall tone.[126] The small
unfinished *Hove Beach* gives an impression of this stage (fig.43).[127]
The landscape was worked up tonally from dark to light, using thin,

lean, opaque colours, starting with the middle-distance and large forms, with the foreground last. The coloured priming was left visible, particularly in the foreground and middle-distance, and provides a unifying, warm mid-tone. Constable took care in making alterations, allowing each layer the necessary time to dry, thus avoiding the numerous technical defects visible in sketches and paintings that were executed more rapidly. Once the forms were established, and their tonal relationships defined, he refined and subdued the sky with subtle scumbles, including the prized blue pigment natural ultramarine.[128] The landscape was worked up and 'finished' with glazing and touches of local colour, applied with increasingly small and meticulous brushstrokes, to work up the detail. He used light delicate touches and crisp feathery strokes of quarter-inch bristle brushes and small soft-haired brushes to apply lightly impasted highlights and coloured accents (fig.44, p.64). Glazing was carried out, possibly using a resin-containing medium, to tone the shadows and subdue stark

highlights.[129] Minor adjustments and 'toning' that he carried out after exhibition in 1820 and in 1823–4 are in keeping with the original, and as a result the surface looks 'all-of-a-piece'.[130] He was sufficiently pleased with *Stratford Mill* to send it to the Academy without first showing it to his usual mentors.[131] Sadly, his confidence was not reflected in the reviews, which criticised it for its 'want of finish', 'specky' manner, its 'scattered appearance, wanting unity and *point d'appui*' [point of emphasis] and 'busy and flickered' brushwork, which was not to the public taste.[132]

Criticism for 'want of finish' did not just refer to Constable's comparatively rough surfaces and 'specky' manner. The public also expected a high level of detail and realistic depiction of the foreground staffage, the figures and animals that invite close inspection and are key to the narrative of a picture. Popular genre scenes by Constable's contemporaries David Wilkie (fig.46, p.65) and C.R. Leslie showed lifelike, near-photographic detail, while animals by Henry Bernard

Figure 43
Hove Beach
1824
Oil on canvas
40.6 × 51.1 (16 × 20⅛)
The unfinished condition of this painting shows the preliminary stages of Constable's working method for 'finished' paintings, revealing the ground, modelled *imprimatura*, underdrawing and initial lay-in of the sky, which are usually hidden as a composition is worked up.
MUSÉES ROYAUX DES BEAUX ARTS DE BELGIQUE

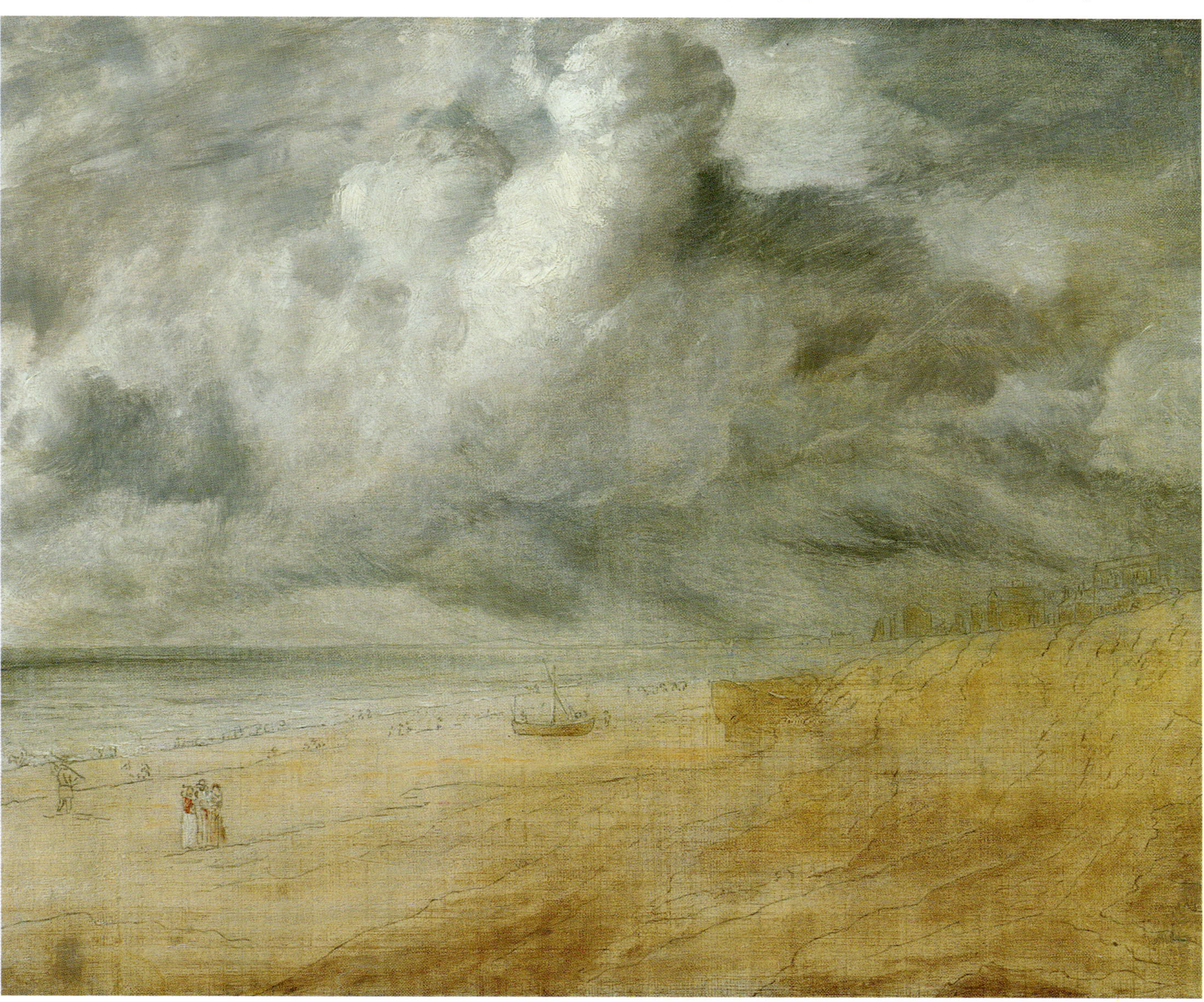

FIGURE 43

Chalon and Edwin Landseer (fig.45, p.65) might almost walk out of the canvas. Constable's foreground figures and animals, though often on the same scale, are crude by comparison. For example, on close inspection, the boy in the cart in *The Hay Wain* (no.37) has indistinct features, while the two huddled women on the beach in the *Chain Pier, Brighton* (no.51) are little more than thickly encrusted relatively abstract paint strokes (fig.47).

Constable usually worked on a 'finished' painting in numerous sittings over several months. There was only so much he could do in a day, even on a large canvas, working around the picture from area to area for, depending on the thickness of the paint, the pigment and the medium, it could take anything from a few hours to several days to dry. This meant that he could not necessarily work on it every day without fear of the surface becoming muddied if fresh paint picked up the semi-dry underlayers. Occasionally there were weeks when he did not paint due to family commitments, visits or sickness, and this enabled the paint to dry thoroughly. As paint dries, the medium (oil, sometimes with resin) is absorbed into the underlying ground and paint layers. This is known as 'sinking-in'. This happens more with some pigments than with others, leaving the surface patchy and unevenly matt after drying. In order to even up a surface before repainting, Constable applied thinned oil, probably linseed, to 'wet-up' the matt areas, a process known as 'oiling-out'.[133]

Despite having supposedly established the composition in a preliminary sketch, Constable usually made major changes while working up the 'finished' six-footers. He often changed the emphasis of a picture by moving, adding or subtracting figures or animals, and amending details that distracted the eye from the main narrative. Depending on whether he reprimed the surface before repainting an area, these pentimenti are more or less visible today. In *Stratford Mill* 1820 (no.31), he took great care to paint out a large standing boy in the foreground, copied directly from the sketch (no.30), so that this figure was only discovered when the painting was x-radiographed in the 1990s (see fig.64, p.137).[134] This change probably took place relatively early in the painting process, when Constable had the time and inclination to do things properly. However, the following year when he was short of time on *The Hay Wain* 1821 (no.37), he made several major changes to the foreground that are visible today because they were only thinly painted over and the paint has cracked and become more transparent with age (fig.48, p.66).[135] Separation cracks caused by reworking over insufficiently dry paint are especially characteristic of Constable's hastily finished Academy exhibits, and can be seen as early as 1812 in *Flatford Mill from the Lock* (no.14).[136] It is not possible to say precisely when he made certain late alterations, as he usually reworked the pictures after exhibition, sometimes on several occasions. Only if there is a detailed description of the subject matter in a letter or an exhibition review, a contemporary engraving (as in the case of the *Chain Pier, Brighton*, see no.52) or a dated account of his having made changes, as with *The Leaping Horse* (no.47), do we know exactly when he did what.

When *The Leaping Horse* went to the Academy in 1825, it looked nothing like it does today (no.47). There was a large willow to the right of the horse, as in the full-size sketch; its finely painted branches are just visible in the finished work under the sky (see fig.73, p.156). There was no central willow, and the tallest tree on the left was much smaller. The canvas was several inches shorter and it was worked up

to the high level of 'finish' typical of the early 1820s, similar to *Stratford Mill*. In September 1825, a couple of months after it returned from exhibition, Constable 'Got up early … Took out the old willow stump by my horse, which has improved the picture much … [and] made one or two other alterations'.[137] The other 'alterations' consisted of extending the height of the canvas by stitching a strip of matching primed canvas across the top (see p.57), extending the large tree and sky on to the addition, and painting in the central willow over the lighterman (the man who worked the barges) in the red jacket. This repainting was carried out using large bristle brushes and a palette knife, the latter not previously used at all, with different pigments from those used in the 'first conception'.[138] For example, the sky had been skilfully 'finished' with translucent scumbles of natural ultramarine in accordance with Constable's usual practice for 'finished' paintings. Later, it was reworked in large, coarse strokes of ill-matched Prussian blue and muddied greys. Brash white impasto, totally unlike anything else on the picture, was applied with a knife over the canvas join in the sky. Once the difference between the original 'neat' brushwork and the later repainting is noted, the reworked areas appear unusually jarring (fig.30, p.56). This aberration was no doubt intended to improve the composition, but the comparatively crude reworking is so out of keeping with contemporary expectations of 'finish' that it must have rendered the painting completely unsaleable thereafter.

From the late 1820s Constable developed a richly physical technique that is particularly expressive and 'impressionistic' for its time. Almost abstract splashes of pure pigment were worked up to create a heavily textured lattice of dragged coloured strokes. The picking-up of semi-dry paint was intrinsic to this method, so Constable used paint bound with slow-drying poppy oil that enabled him to repeatedly rework the surface with little concern for drying time between painting sessions.[139] He also used a wider range of brightly coloured pigments.[140] *Salisbury Cathedral from the Meadows* 1831 (no.61) and *The Opening of Waterloo Bridge* 1832 (pp.50–1, no.67) are fine examples of his 'late' technique. The sky was painted first with large brushes. It was worked up with numerous scumbles of semi-transparent paint and then scraped back in places, exposing the canvas weave. Skies were 'finished' with rich ultramarine and smalt washes, and translucent purple scumbles containing vermilion and a pink madder. Highlights were added in broad strokes of stiff white paint, mainly by brush. The buildings and landscape were broadly laid-in and initially worked up by brush. The modelling is not always explicit: for example the figures on the balconies of the bay-fronted house in the *Waterloo* canvas consist of numerous 'abstract' splashes of colour (fig.49, p.67). Stiff paint, probably bound with poppy oil, egg yolk and beeswax, was used for crisp highlights, created with tiny brushes and a knife tip on foliage, buildings and water (and regalia in the *Waterloo*) and flecks of bright colour in the foreground.[141] Much of the foreground and stark impasto was 'glazed down' and 'harmonised' with glossy translucent browns, greens, reds and yellows.

Contrary to previous assertions, Constable hardly used a palette knife before 1829 in the exhibited six-footers, apart from *The Lock* 1824 (no.41).[142] He used it mainly during reworking in the studio *after* exhibition, as in *The Leaping Horse* 1825 (no.47) and the *Chain Pier, Brighton* 1827 (no.51). However, following the tragic death of his beloved wife in November 1828, and his long-awaited election as a Royal

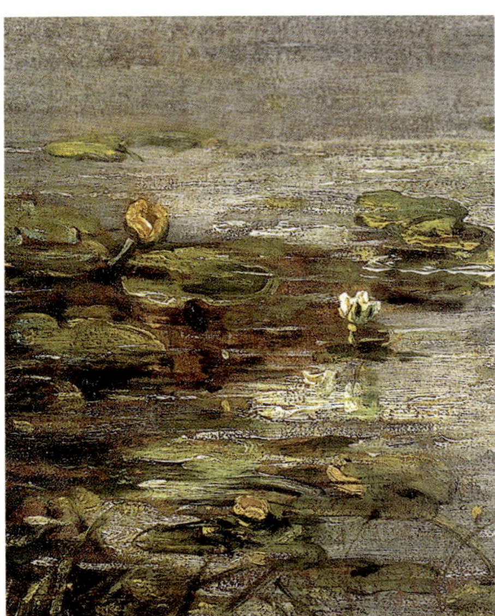

Realistic depictions of sentimental domestic scenes and animals were especially popular in the nineteenth century. *The Highland Family* was exhibited at the Royal Academy in the same year as Constable's *The Lock* (no.41); *Ratcatchers*, reputedly Queen Victoria's favourite picture, in the same year as *The Hay Wain* (no.37). Constable's figures and animals did not compare favourably with these in the eyes of the viewing public.

This detail from the *Chain Pier, Brighton* 1827 (no.51) shows two huddled women on the beach, fighting against the wind, are approximately 4 ½ inches (11.5cm) high (reproduced life-size here). For figures of this size and prominence they are very roughly delineated with broad crusty paint strokes, and were totally out of keeping with contemporary expectations of a 'finished' picture.

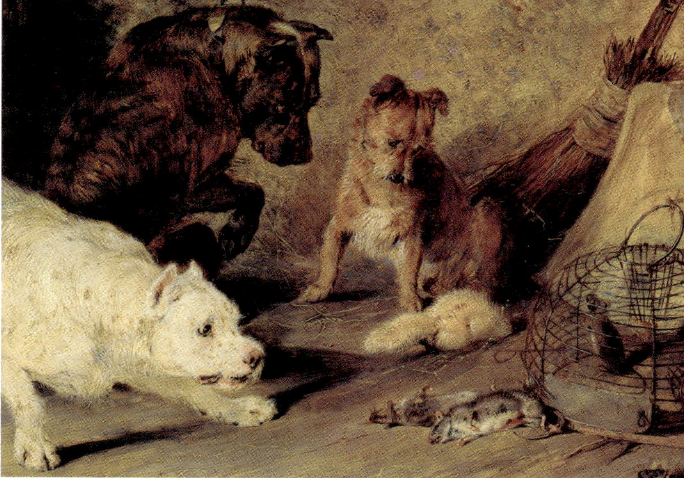

FIGURE 45

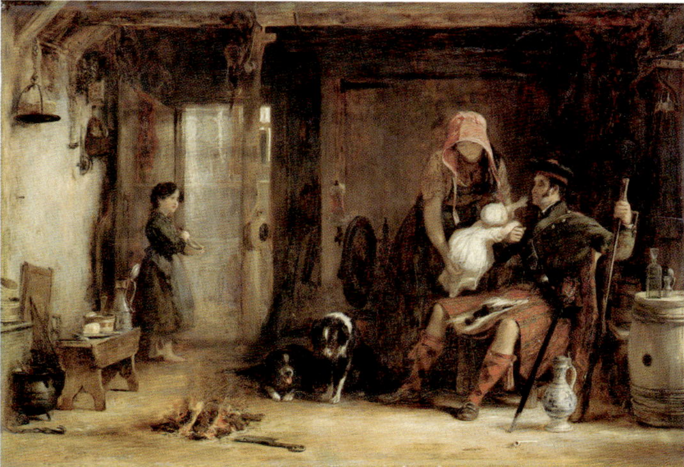

FIGURE 46

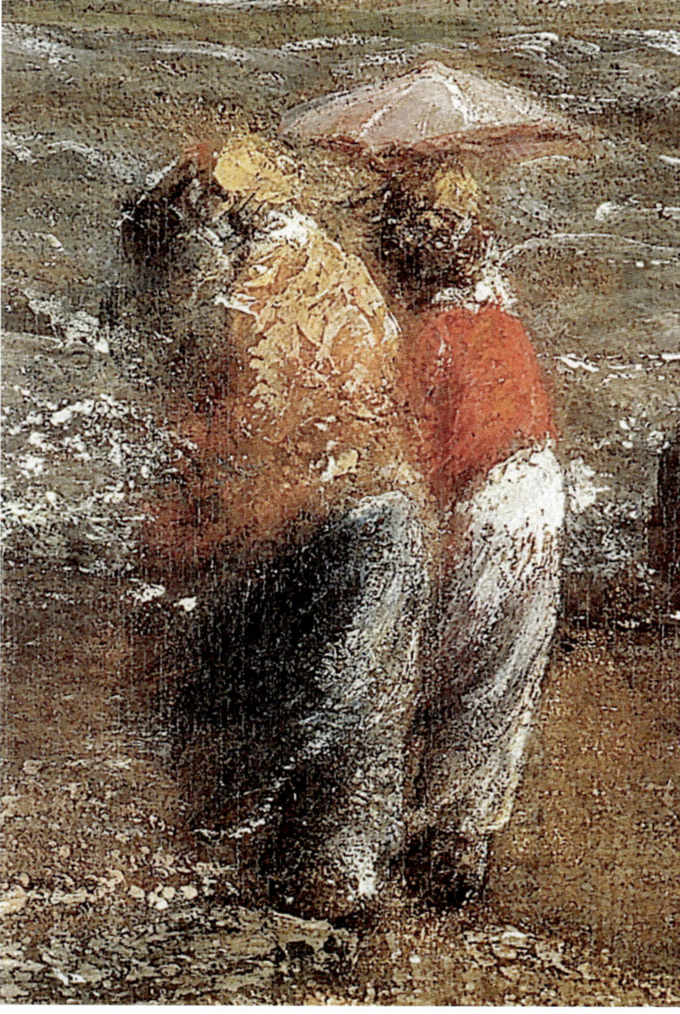

FIGURE 47

Academician in February 1829, he appears to have felt free of earlier constraints regarding 'finish' in his exhibited works. Fuelled by a great well of emotion, from this time onwards he wielded a palette knife with great virtuosity and expressiveness, to add touches of highly textured pure colour to the surfaces of all the large canvases. This technique appears superficially reckless but is, in fact, precisely calculated for maximum effect. Comparison of *Salisbury Cathedral from the Meadows* 1831 (no.61) with its full-size sketch (no.60) shows its relatively controlled 'finish' by comparison with the wild handling in the sketch. The 'power and force' of the exhibited picture was almost grudgingly recognised by the critics in 1831, though they were 'genuinely puzzled by [Constable's] apparent abdication of a fresh and healthy rendering of natural landscape scenery in favour of an exaggerated, indiscreet, coarse (and hence unnatural) style … complaints about his white spots proliferated and for the first time since 1823 their effects were likened to snow.'[143]

Though Constable's apparently un-'finished' technique initially caused popular offence, he was certain that over time the objectionable 'sparkle' would gradually subside due to chemical changes in the paint caused by impure nineteenth-century air.[144] This particularly affected the lead-based white and yellow pigments that he used, no doubt intentionally, for 'finishing'.[145] He knew that his paintings would gradually take on a pleasing and harmonious aspect, for he saw such alterations on several occasions: 'My Lock is now on my Easil … and is wonderfully *got together* after only this one year.'[146] While he anticipated and welcomed such a change in exhibited paintings, he had been alarmed on first moving to Charlotte Street to discover 'a real grievance – a hollow wall – which communicated with the floors of my [painting] room … immediately over the *well* of the *privy*. This would have played the devil with the oxygen of my colours'.[147] It is notable that significant discoloration has occurred in Patent yellow (see p.61), but not in lead white. Inevitably this has upset the careful nuances of colour and tone in Constable's 'finished' paintings.

When paintings returned from exhibition Constable invariably started work on them again. Even on the few occasions when he seemed happy with a picture, he still reworked it afterwards, as with *Stratford Mill* (no.31). He usually planned to do this, and communicated his intentions to Fisher.[148] His reasons were probably both

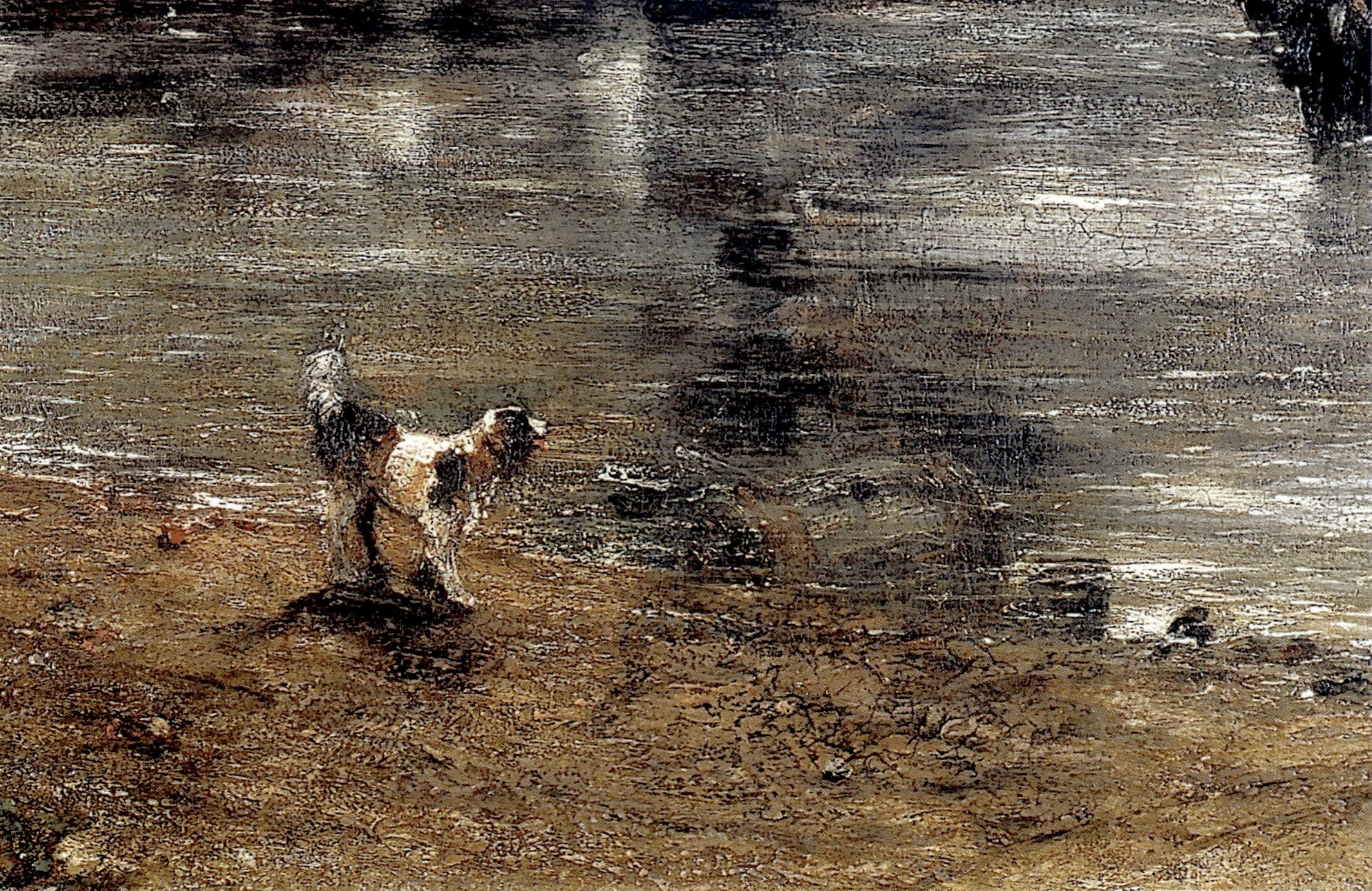

FIGURE 48

psychological and technical. The main reason for reworking was that he hardly ever sent a completed picture to the Academy. Fear of failure may have held him back from starting early enough to 'finish' a painting properly, for then he could excuse himself if an incomplete work went to the Academy and was not well received. In July 1821 Fisher begged him to start earlier so he had proper 'opportunity for correction & polish'.[149] He had an almost pathological inability to allow sufficient time for painting, and family responsibilities always caused delays. At the same time he was terrified that his works would *not* be well received, so he went over and over them, worrying and niggling until the very last minute.

There are also significant technical reasons why he may have needed to rework his pictures after exhibition. Ideally, a painting should be left to dry for several months, then 'toned' (glazed), followed by more drying, then more toning if needed. Finally, after a year or so, a glossy varnish is applied to even the surface and saturate the paint, giving full depth of colour and tone. In most cases Constable painted the *whole* picture in the few months before the Royal Academy exhibition, so it had no time to dry thoroughly. Though he attempted to 'finish' it, the final glazes, which were often hastily applied before the body-colour was fully dry, cracked and sank-in. During exhibition the surface would inevitably develop a matt and patchy appearance as it dried.

In order to produce a properly 'finished' painting, Constable had no choice but to carry out remedial 'toning' of the matt parts to wet-out and even the surface. He was sometimes carried away during reworking and 'toning' and caused areas to lose definition, as in *Salisbury Cathedral from the Meadows* (no.61), where numerous confusing specks of colour and drying cracks break up the image, especially in the cottages on the left edge, which were repainted with thick impasto that has cracked and separated.

It was always Constable's intention that 'finished' paintings should be varnished, and he made numerous references to how much better they looked for it: *The Lock* 'looked beautifully fresh when it was varnished'.[150] Varnishing was recommended at least a year after 'finishing', when the paint was fully dry.[151] The 'Varnishing Days' at the Academy were held five or six days before the exhibition, during which time artists could adjust, or varnish, their pictures in their final hanging position. Constable was always too busy *painting* the picture for it to be conventionally varnished with a resin-spirit varnish. If the paint was sufficiently dry before exhibition he could have applied a water-based varnish, such as that made from egg white and alcohol, which was commonly recommended in contemporary painting manuals.[152] This was thin and watery, and though it would have temporarily 'wet-up' the image, it would not have evened out the

Figure 49
In this detail from *The Opening of Waterloo Bridge* 1832 (no.67), the crowd on the balcony of the bow-fronted house is painted in almost abstract strokes of somewhat muddied impasto. This is superficially similar to the half-size sketch (fig.36, p.59), though in the 'finished' painting the working up is thicker and more elaborate. At a distance the specks blend in the eye to create an impression of movement in the excited spectators.

TATE. PURCHASED WITH ASSISTANCE FROM THE NATIONAL HERITAGE MEMORIAL FUND, THE CLORE FOUNDATION, THE NATIONAL ART COLLECTIONS FUND, THE FRIENDS OF THE TATE GALLERY AND OTHERS 1987

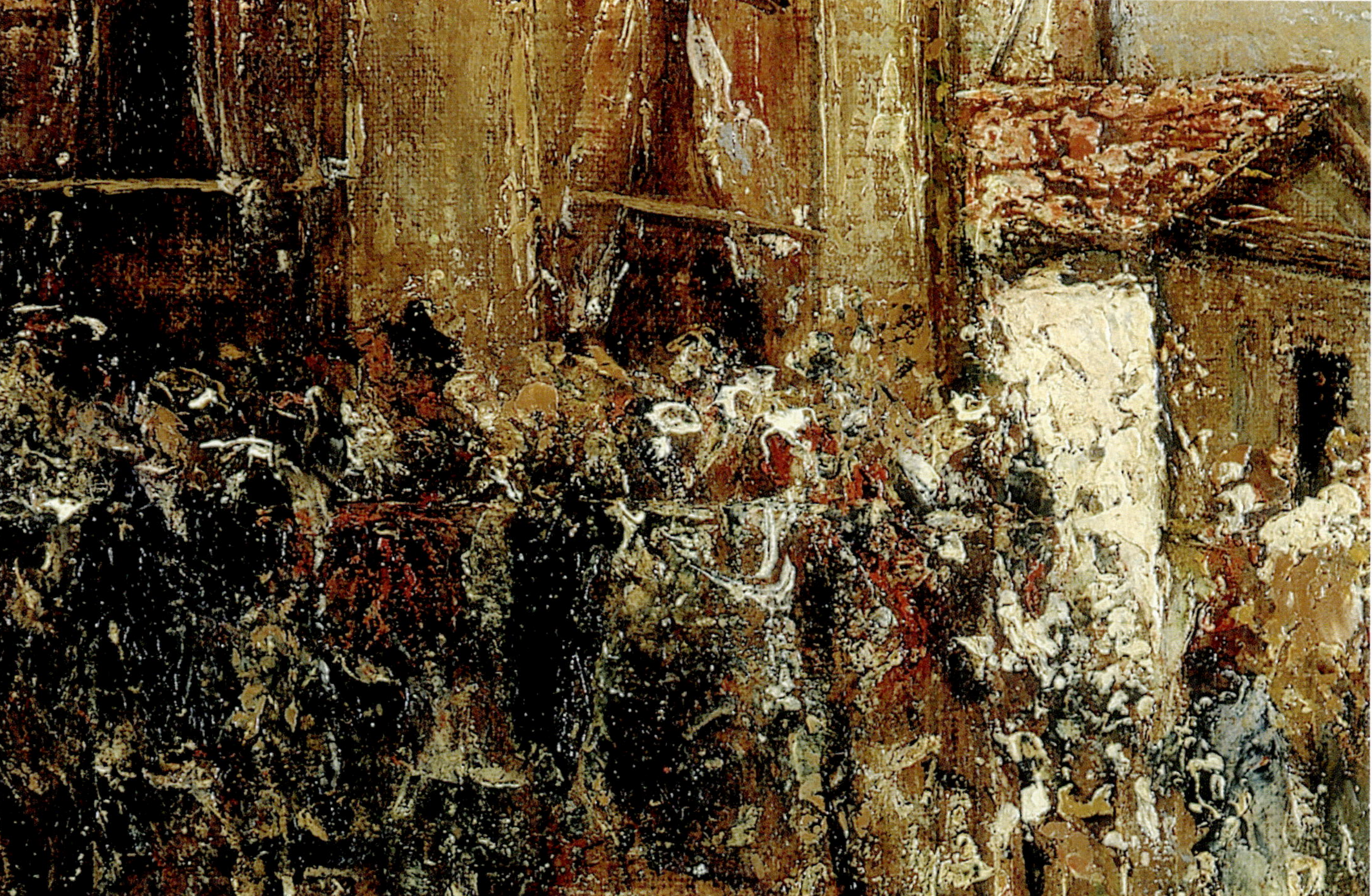

FIGURE 49

surface. Some of the criticism of the 'unfinished' look of his pictures was undoubtedly due to their patchy and unvarnished surface.[153] Nevertheless, the six-footers were all varnished some time later, often by Dunthorne. Constable was meticulous about recalling pictures from their owners specifically for this purpose: in 1825 Fisher noted that *The White Horse* 1819 (no.29) returned to Salisbury 'wonderfully improved by Dunthorne's coat of varnish'.[154] It is certain that, after drying, cracking, reworking and toning, chemical alterations to some of the colours, and finally varnishing, Constable's 'finished' six-footers did not take on their final, intended aspect until several years after their first exhibition.

Constable's Heritage: The Six-Footers Today

As we see them today Constable's six-footers are no longer at the peak of their maturity, as they have continued to alter over time. Natural ageing of the paint, together with the chemical degradation of some pigments, has changed the colour balance and increased the tonal contrasts in both sketches and exhibited pictures. This inevitably undermines the carefully orchestrated 'harmony' of the 'finished' works. The paintings have also suffered from various human interventions: canvas exposed when Constable rubbed back the paint has darkened due to impregnation from lining adhesives, and now appears as disfiguring spots in light areas; much impasto has been 'moated', smeared and abraded by harsh nineteenth-century lining treatments; subtle colouring and glazing is lost beneath old insensitive retouching and patchy discoloured varnish; degraded varnish distorts tonal values, causing dark areas to appear light and desaturated. On canvases with a 'stippled' priming, the varnish 'pools' in the hollows of the textured surface and discolours to form disfiguring spots. Where aged varnish is thick, it surrounds impastos with brown 'haloes', smoothing out the carefully calculated texture. When Constable's paintings have not been cleaned for decades, they are often marred by some or all of these defects. This significantly detracts from their appearance, and it can also skew interpretations of handling and attribution. Among many superb examples of recent conservation in the exhibition are the sketches for *The White Horse* (no.28), *Salisbury Cathedral from the Meadows* (no.60) and *Stoke-by-Nayland* (no.68), and the magnificent exhibited *Opening of Waterloo Bridge* (no.67). These brilliantly coloured masterpieces enable us to appreciate Constable's original vision and virtuoso technique most fully.

In Memoriam Caroline Villers 1948–2004

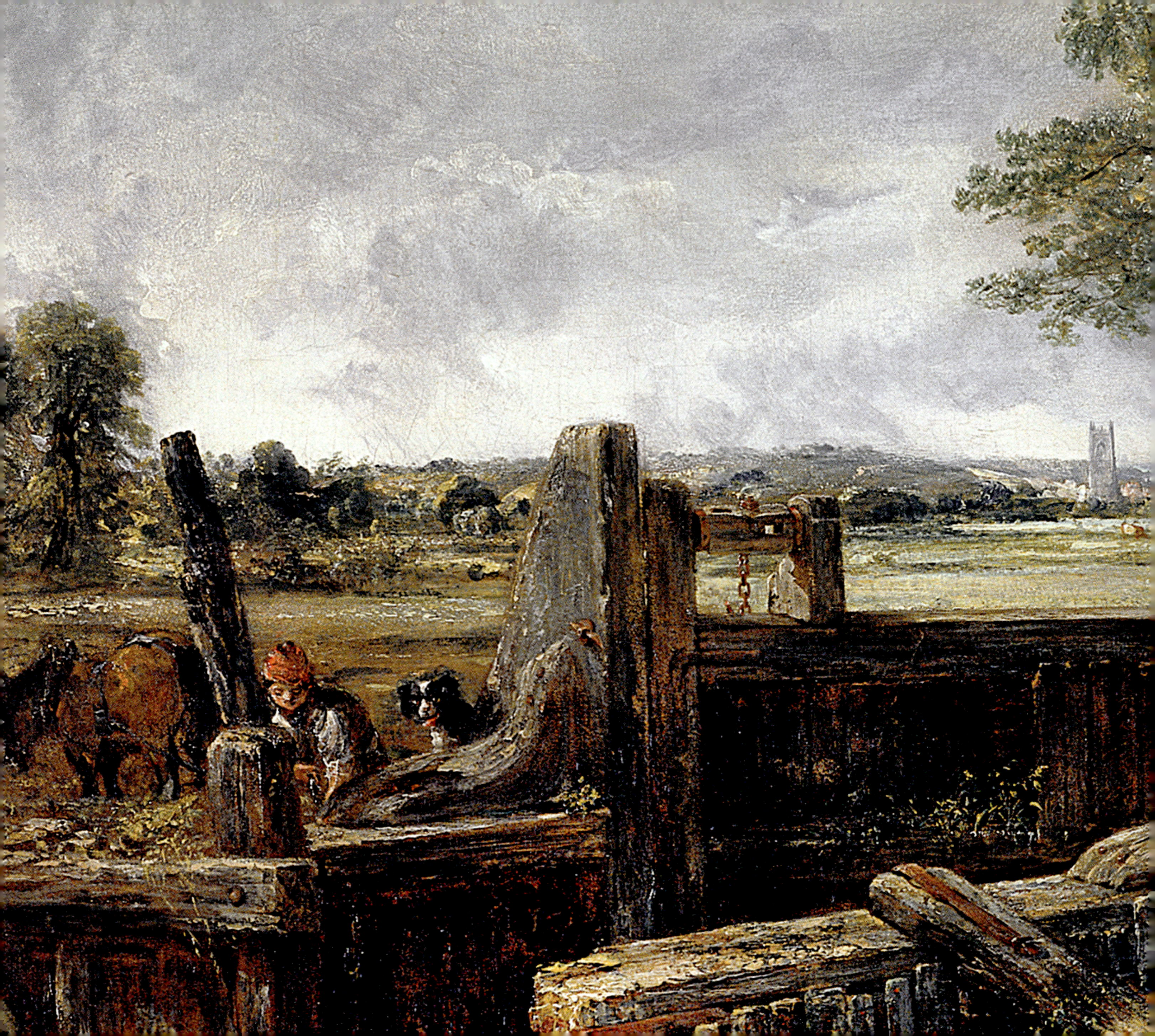

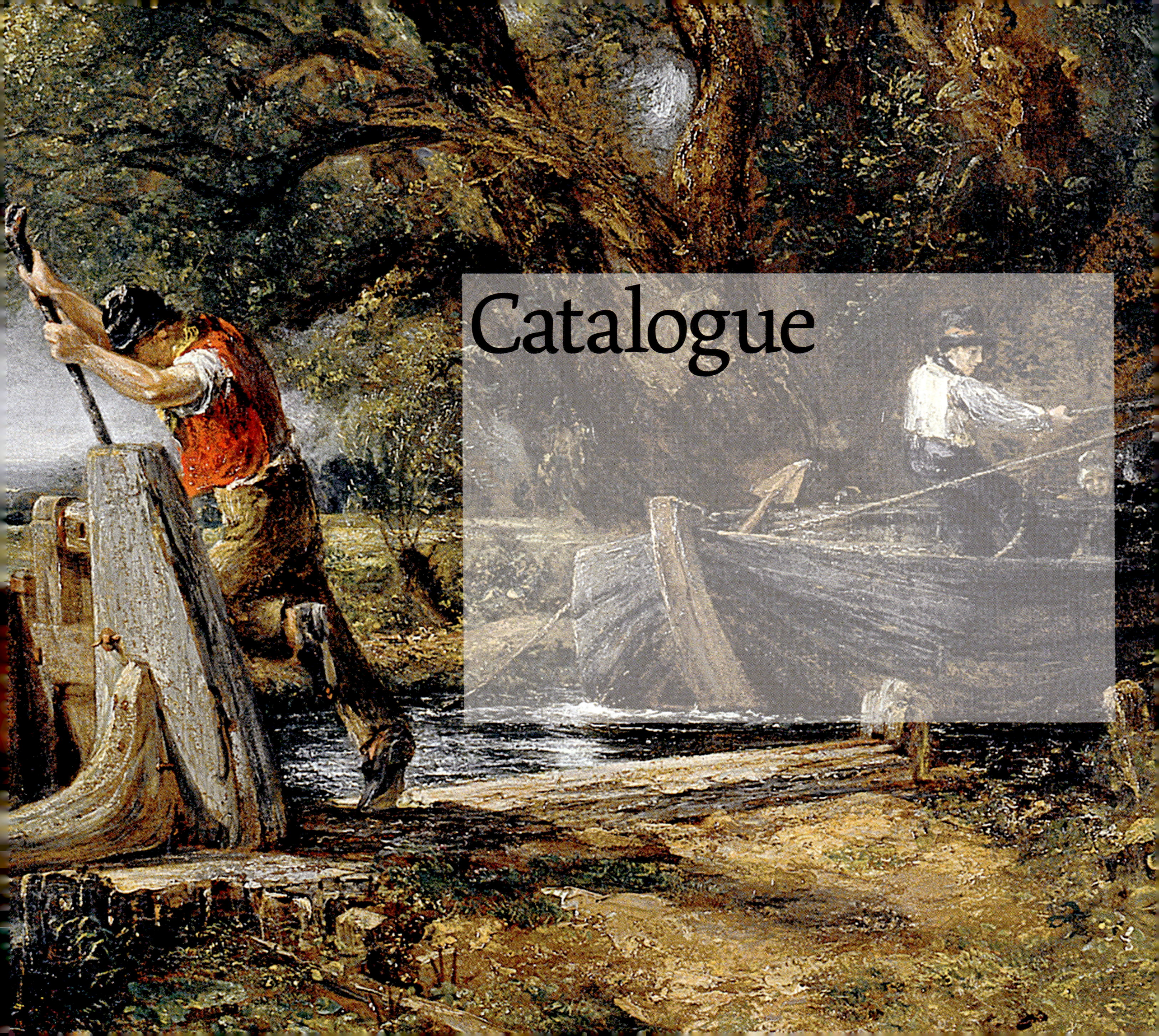

Catalogue

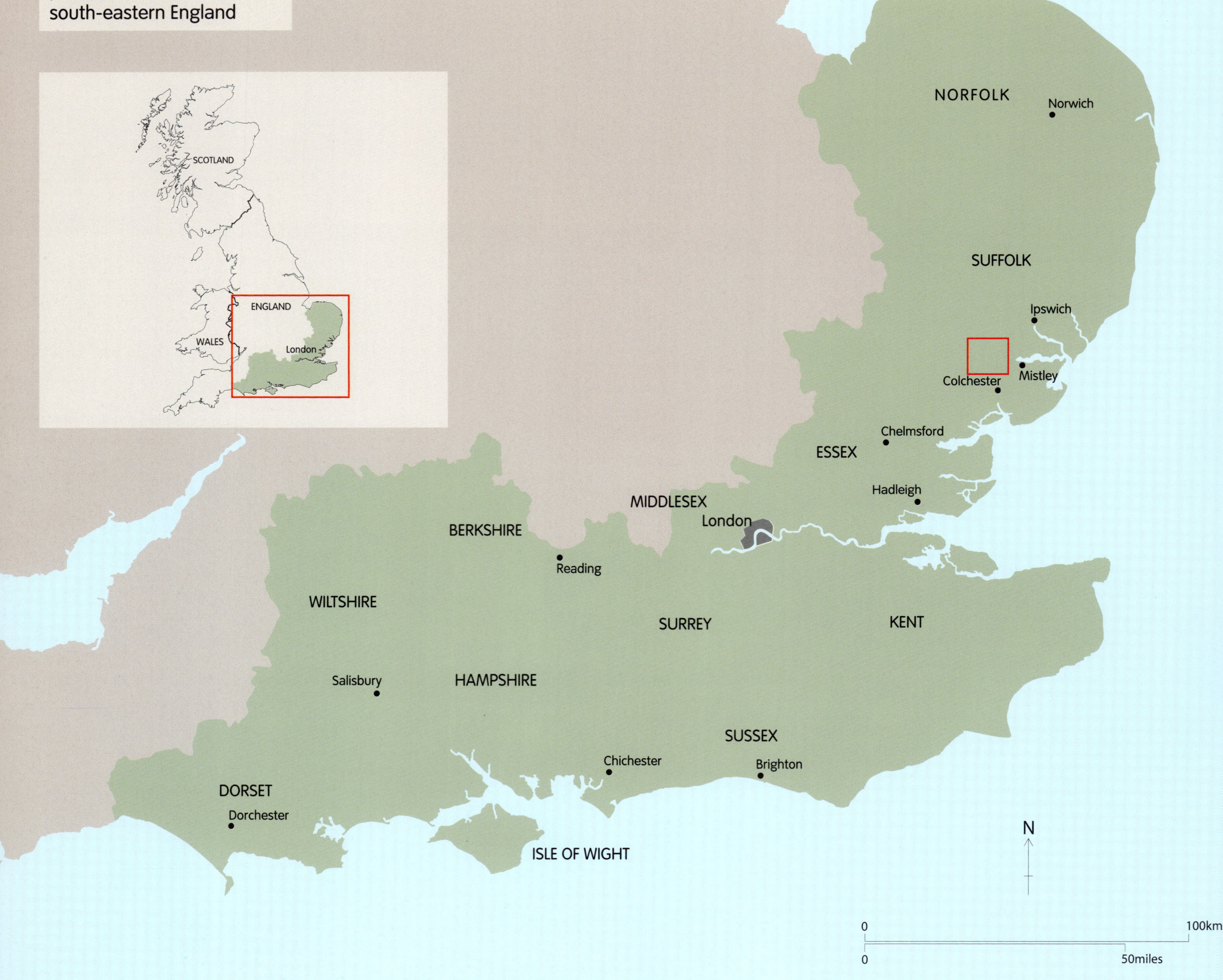

Maps of Britain showing the locations where Constable painted in southern and south-eastern England
SCOTLAND
ENGLAND
WALES
London
NORFOLK
Norwich
SUFFOLK
Ipswich
Colchester
Mistley
Chelmsford
ESSEX
Hadleigh
MIDDLESEX
London
BERKSHIRE
Reading
WILTSHIRE
SURREY
KENT
Salisbury
HAMPSHIRE
SUSSEX
Chichester
Brighton
DORSET
Dorchester
ISLE OF WIGHT
N
0
100km
0
50miles

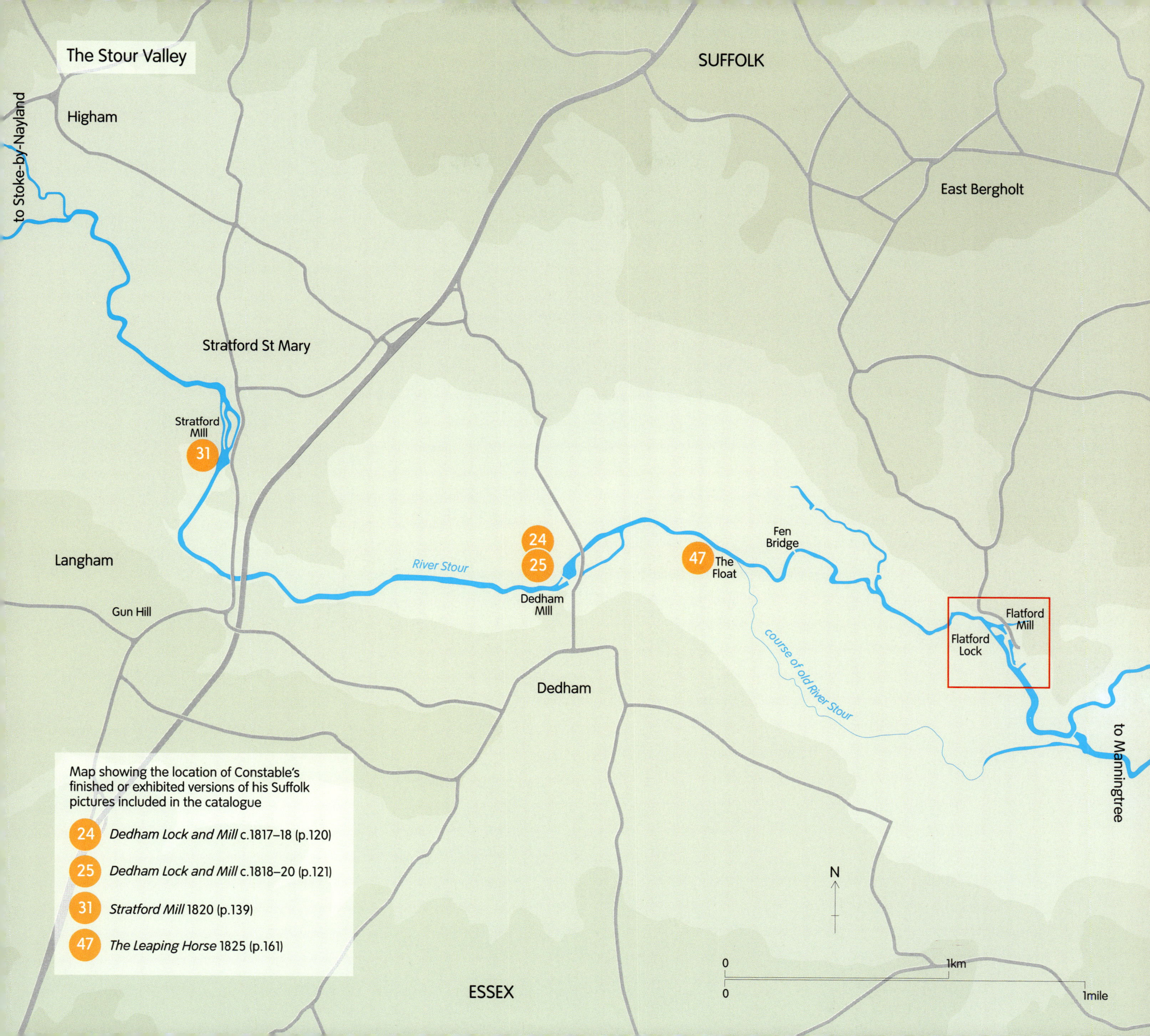

The Stour Valley
SUFFOLK
to Stoke-by-Nayland
Higham
East Bergholt
Stratford St Mary
Stratford Mill
31
Langham
River Stour
24
25
Fen Bridge
47 The Float
Gun Hill
Dedham Mill
Flatford Mill
Flatford Lock
course of old River Stour
Dedham
to Manningtree
Map showing the location of Constable's finished or exhibited versions of his Suffolk pictures included in the catalogue
24 Dedham Lock and Mill c.1817–18 (p.120)
25 Dedham Lock and Mill c.1818–20 (p.121)
31 Stratford Mill 1820 (p.139)
47 The Leaping Horse 1825 (p.161)
N
0   1km
0   1mile
ESSEX

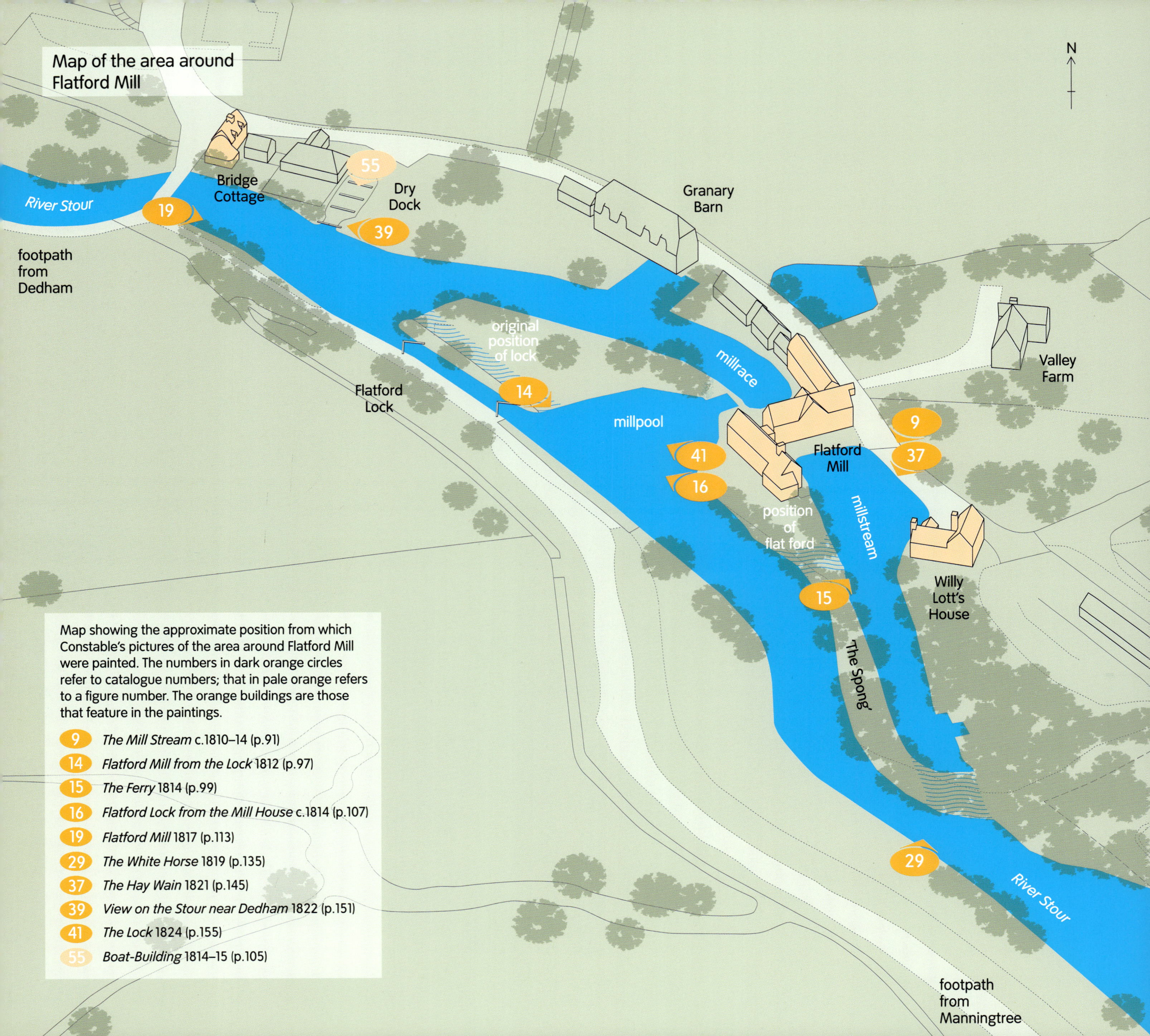

Map of the area around Flatford Mill
N
River Stour
footpath from Dedham
Bridge Cottage
55
19
Dry Dock
39
Granary Barn
original position of lock
Flatford Lock
14
millrace
millpool
Valley Farm
9
41
Flatford Mill
37
16
position of flat ford
millstream
15
Willy Lott's House
"The Spong"
29
River Stour
footpath from Manningtree
Map showing the approximate position from which Constable's pictures of the area around Flatford Mill were painted. The numbers in dark orange circles refer to catalogue numbers; that in pale orange refers to a figure number. The orange buildings are those that feature in the paintings.
9   The Mill Stream c.1810–14 (p.91)
14   Flatford Mill from the Lock 1812 (p.97)
15   The Ferry 1814 (p.99)
16   Flatford Lock from the Mill House c.1814 (p.107)
19   Flatford Mill 1817 (p.113)
29   The White Horse 1819 (p.135)
37   The Hay Wain 1821 (p.145)
39   View on the Stour near Dedham 1822 (p.151)
41   The Lock 1824 (p.155)
55   Boat-Building 1814–15 (p.105)

All works are by John Constable unless otherwise specified.

Pictures shown by Constable at the Royal Academy are dated to the year of their exhibition, even though often started the previous year or, conceivably, earlier.

Dimensions are given in centimetres followed by inches, height before width. Some paintings have been re-measured in connection with this exhibition, and so dimensions given here will sometimes differ from those cited in previous catalogues of the artist's work. Inscriptions are only given if in the artist's hand, or possibly in the artist's hand.

Exhibition history is given only for works exhibited during Constable's lifetime. 'RA' denotes that a work was exhibited at the Royal Academy, 'BI' that it was shown at the British Institution.

An 'R' number indicates the listing of the work in the catalogue raisonné of Constable's work compiled by Graham Reynolds in 1984 and 1996 (see bibliography), where a fuller exhibition history and provenance for individual works can be found.

'Ivy' indicates the listing of a contemporary review for an exhibited work in Judy Ivy, Constable and the Critics 1802–1837, 1991. A listing is only given for a specific mention of the exhibited work in question.

'Shirley' indicates the listing of the work in the catalogue of Constable's mezzotints by Andrew Shirley (see bibliography).

The authors of the entries are denoted by their initials: AL (Anne Lyles), FK (Franklin Kelly) and SC (Sarah Cove).

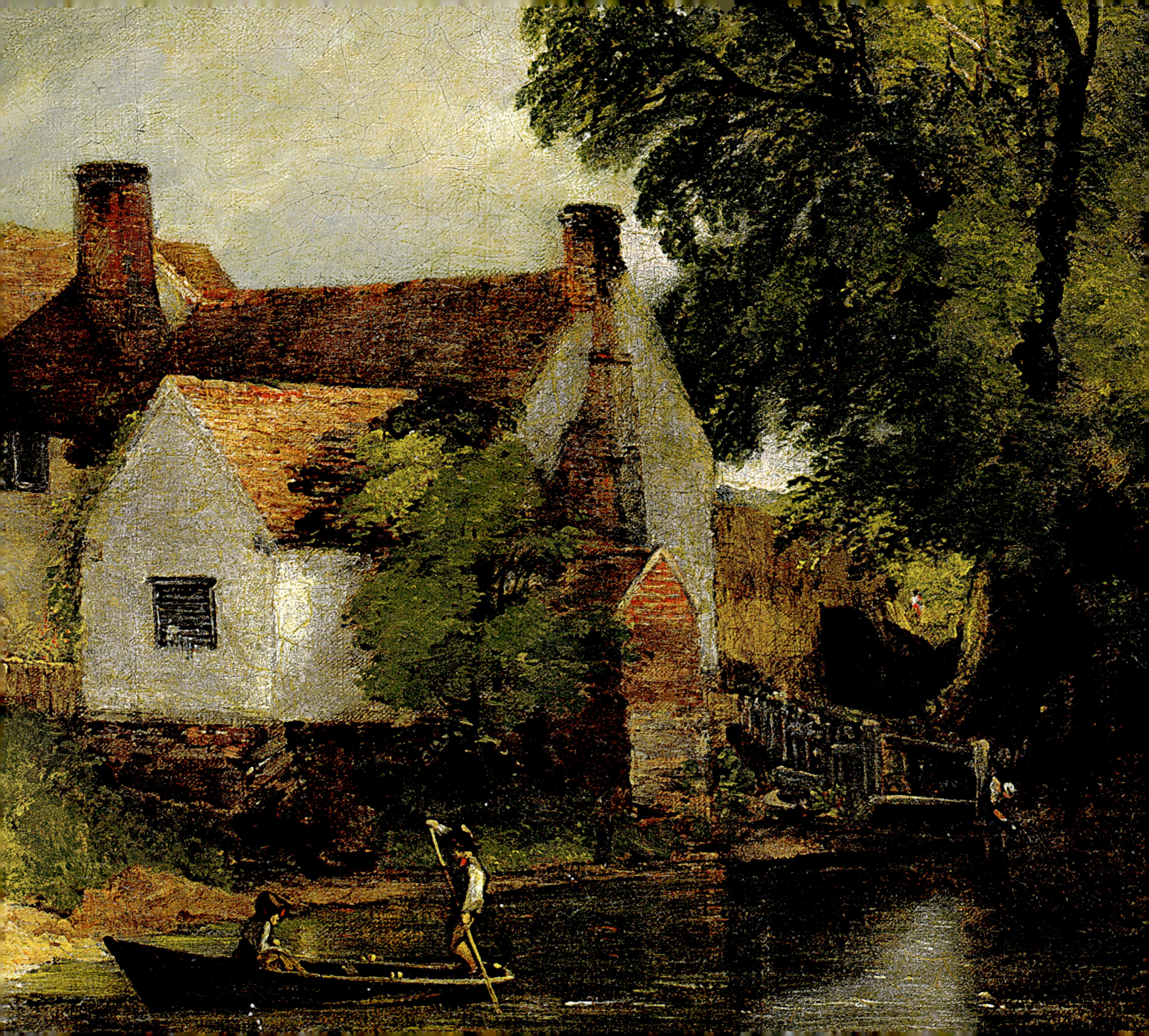

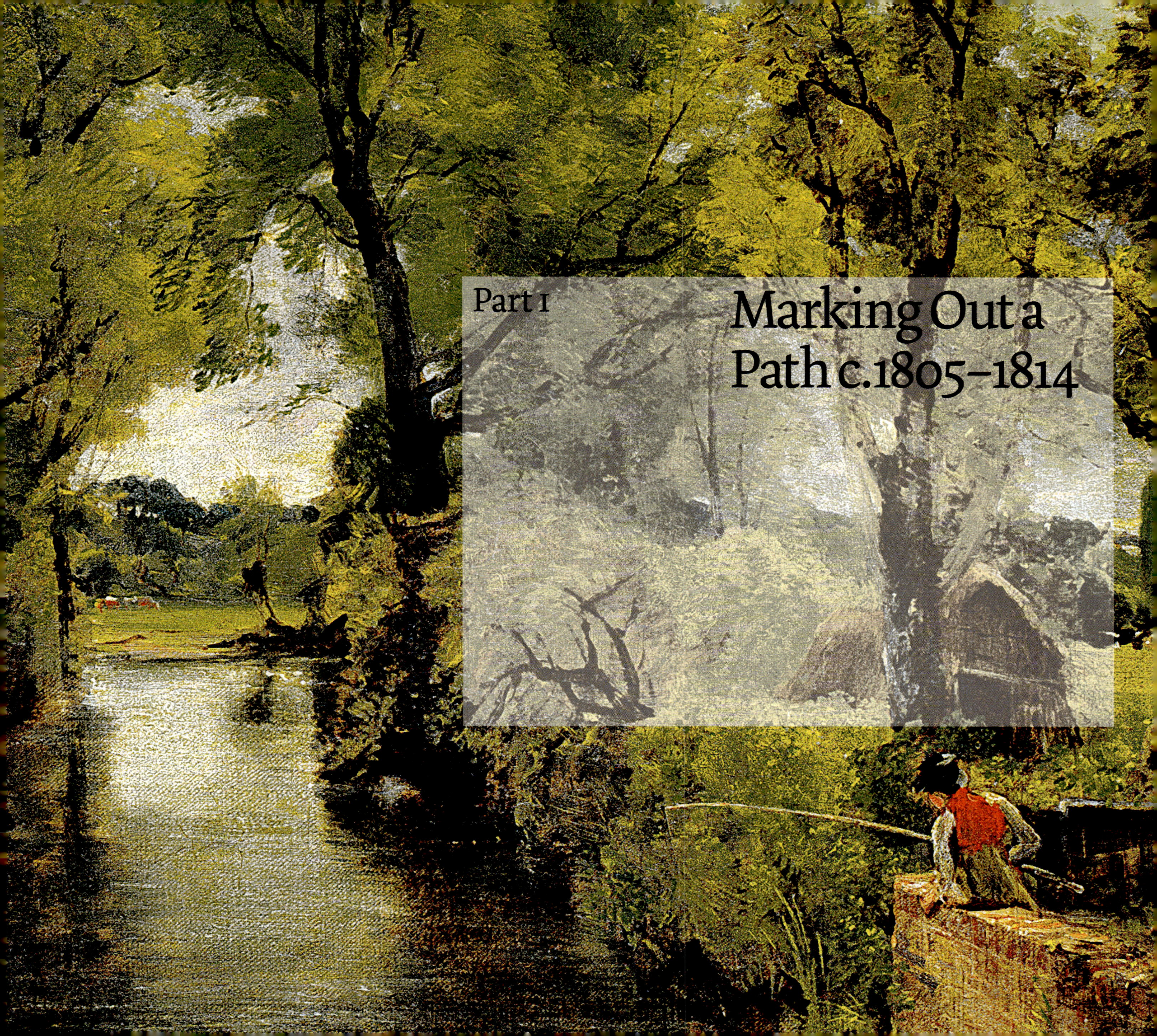

Part 1

Marking Out a
Path c.1805–1814

Towards the end of Constable's life, the stretch of the Stour Valley in Suffolk that formed the subject matter of so many of his paintings was already beginning to be described as 'Constable's country' (JCC IV, p.387). Yet Constable's success in establishing himself as one of the foremost landscape painters of his day had never been a foregone conclusion. As well as having to overcome parental opposition to his chosen profession in his early years, he also had to learn how to paint and to decide in which branch of the art – portraiture, history painting or landscape – to specialise. He was to prove a particularly slow developer.

Constable was born in 1776 in the Suffolk village of East Bergholt, situated, as he himself was to write many years later, in the most cultivated part of the county, and overlooking the fertile valley of the River Stour. It was an agricultural region, prosperous but workmanlike, and without the sort of obvious pictorial potential that attracted artists and

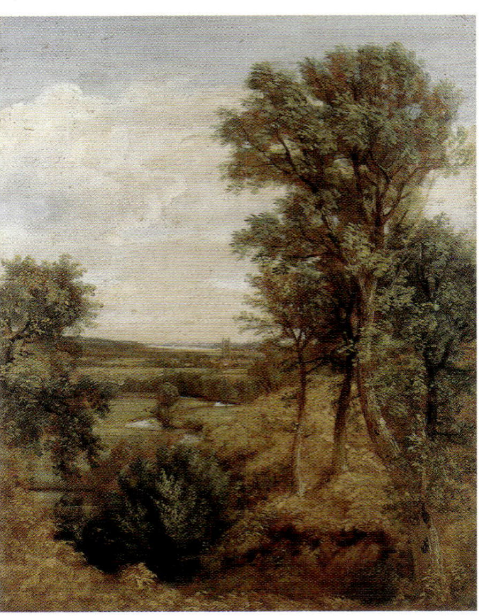

FIGURE 50

Figure 50
Dedham Vale
1802
Oil on canvas
43.5 × 34.4 (17 $\frac{1}{8}$ × 13 $\frac{1}{2}$)
VICTORIA AND ALBERT
MUSEUM, LONDON

visitors in extensive numbers to other regions in England such as the Lake District or North Wales (see Tate 2005, p.158). However, Constable admired this essentially flat and unemphatic landscape, with 'its gentle declivities, its woods and rivers … numerous villages and churches, farms and picturesque cottages' (JCD, pp.12–13). These unassuming landscape features were all, indeed, to provide fruitful subjects for his art.

He was the fourth child of Ann and Golding Constable; his father was a prosperous corn and coal merchant who owned mills at Flatford and Dedham (see nos.14, 19, 23–5). Corn ground at these mills was transported by barge eastwards along a stretch of the River Stour, made navigable in the early eighteenth century by the construction of a series of locks and associated sluices, bridges and dams. The corn was carried as far as Manningtree in Essex and then Mistley, the port on the Stour estuary from which it would be shipped onward to London. Returning barges would bring coal and other imported cargoes upstream. Many years later Constable was to write to his great friend John Fisher that it was the scenes he associated with his childhood years spent on the banks of the canalised Stour – 'the sound of water escaping from Mill dams … Willows, Old rotten Banks, slimy posts, & brickwork' – which had originally inspired him to become a painter (JCC VI, p.77). Indeed, it was scenes like these that were to provide the subjects for his famous series of 'six-foot' canvases showing views on the River Stour (nos.28–47), which helped to secure his professional reputation at the Royal Academy in the 1820s.

Golding Constable was initially reluctant for his son to become a professional painter, and in the early years Constable's artistic interests were nurtured by the local plumber and glazier, John Dunthorne, a keen amateur

artist. In 1799, however, Golding finally relented and Constable – already by now in his early twenties – joined the Royal Academy Schools in London as a probationary student. The Academy at this date devoted no part of its curriculum to the teaching of oil painting (least of all to the study of landscape), its core teaching revolving around drawing from plaster casts or from the living model (the 'Life Academy'). Constable therefore had to pursue his own path in landscape. He took advice from fellow Academicians, such as the painter and celebrated diarist Joseph Farington, and from the portraitist and second President of the Academy, Benjamin West. He spent time copying landscapes by the Old Masters, such as Annibale Carracci, Jacob van Ruisdael and Claude Lorraine, especially examples of the latter's work in the London collection of the connoisseur Sir George Beaumont, whom Constable had first met in the Suffolk village of Dedham around 1795. He also consulted artists' instruction manuals for information on painting materials and techniques, such as Thomas Bardwell's influential *The Practice of Painting and Perspective Made Easy*, first published in 1756 (Cove in Tate 1991, p.494).

In the spring of 1802, Constable exhibited his first picture at the Royal Academy, *A landscape*, which appears to have passed unnoticed by the critics and which today remains unidentified (see Thompson 2005, p.610). However, the occasion offered him the opportunity of evaluating his work alongside that of his contemporaries. It was an experience he found dispiriting, for he regarded their work as distinctly lacking in 'truth'. However, the experience also persuaded Constable that he had himself for too long been 'running after pictures and seeking the truth at second hand', and that he should from now on paint more closely from Nature, 'the fountain's head, the source from whence all originality must spring' (JCC II, p.32).

Although based in London, Constable still continued to regard his parents' house in East Bergholt as home. Indeed until his permanent move to London in 1816 following his marriage to Maria Bicknell, whom he had first met in Suffolk around 1800 (see no.4), Constable would return to East Bergholt each long summer to paint the scenery he had known since childhood. In the summer and early autumn of 1802 he decided to put into effect his new resolve to paint directly from nature. His father had just helped him acquire a small property opposite the family house in the village for use as a studio, and this now provided him with a base from which to go out on sketching expeditions, painting in the open air. He made a sequence of careful studies in oil 'from nature', although some of them were dependent on the landscape formulae he had recently absorbed from studying Old Masters such as Claude Lorraine, or more recent British painters such as Thomas Gainsborough. Indeed, one of them, a view of *Dedham Vale*, is clearly indebted to a small picture by Claude of *Landscape with Hagar and the Angel* that Constable had admired in the collection of Sir George Beaumont (figs.50, 51; Evans 2002).

It would be another six years before Constable returned to open-air sketching in oils in Suffolk. Under pressure from his family to concentrate on portraiture, a more lucrative branch of painting, he accepted a number of commissions to paint the portraits of local Suffolk families. He also undertook commissions to paint local altarpieces, one in 1805 for Brantham parish church and another in 1810 for Nayland, when he also found time to sketch in nearby Stoke-by-Nayland (no.5; see also no.68).

Then in 1805–6, perhaps inspired by a visit to the first exhibition of the newly formed Society of Painters in Watercolour, Constable became interested in experimenting with watercolour for sketching in the open air in Suffolk and on a six-week tour in the Lake District in 1806 (fig.6, p.27). He even painted two finished watercolour compositions at this time, one a marine showing *HMS Victory* at the Battle of Trafalgar, which he exhibited at the Royal Academy in 1806 (Victoria and Albert Museum; R.06.1); and another, a recently discovered view in the Stour Valley (no.3). Together they serve to emphasise that, despite Constable's various forays at this date into portraiture and history painting – religious subjects being regarded as a sub-category of history painting – he nevertheless retained his ambitions to establish himself as a landscape painter in the eyes of his artistic peers. For the next two years, indeed, Constable concentrated on producing a sequence of landscape paintings of Lake District subjects for

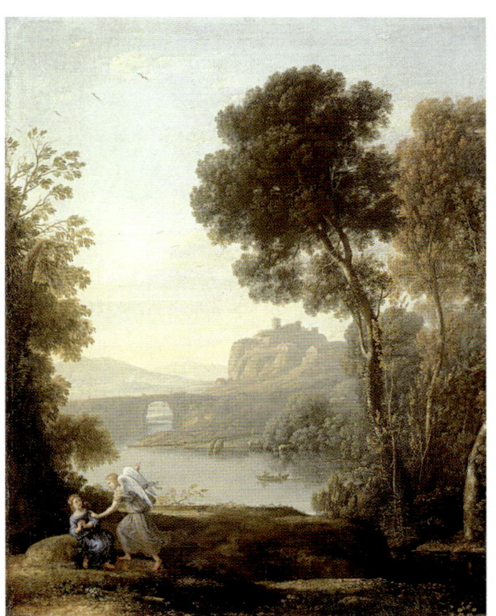

FIGURE 51

Figure 51
Claude Lorraine
**Landscape with Hagar
and the Angel**
1646
Oil on canvas
52.2 × 42.3 (20⅝ × 16⅝)
THE NATIONAL GALLERY,
LONDON

exhibition at the Royal Academy, though none of these are firmly identifiable today. From 1808, however, outdoor painting was to become a regular feature of Constable's work, whether practised in Suffolk until 1817, or in Hampstead, Brighton and Salisbury until about 1829. Although his early Suffolk sketches of c.1808–9 are rather tentative and somewhat flat and uniform in handling, by 1810 they become more expressive, more colourful and more various (nos.5–8). They reveal the intensity of his feelings in front of a landscape that held powerful autobiographical associations. Yet they also functioned as a means of collecting pictorial material, and around the period c.1810–14 Constable often used them in the preparation of pictures he would work up in the studio and then exhibit at the Royal Academy or British Institution (nos.8–14). Letters of encouragement would arrive at regular intervals from his mother in Suffolk. She would urge him to attend to his health but, well aware of her son's tendency to procrastinate, would also encourage him to plan his work in good time for the Academy exhibition in the spring, so that he could bring his pictures to a 'compleat finish [*sic*]', and thus the better 'secure [his] fame' (JCC I, p.77).

As long as Constable restricted himself to an exhibition canvas whose dimensions were no larger than the so-called 'kit-kat' size (36 × 28in/91.5 × 71cm; or 28 × 36in when turned on its side), then this pattern of working, based on intensive sketching and interrelated studio work, appeared to suit him particularly well. His chief exhibit at the Academy in 1810, for example, a canvas of kit-kat size – perhaps identifiable with *The Mill Stream* now in Ipswich (no.9) – was not only well reviewed, but also sold to the Earl of Dysart. Meanwhile, his 1812 Academy exhibit, *Flatford Mill from the Lock* (no.14), a little smaller than a kit-kat size, again

drew favourable reviews from the critics. By May that year, Constable was anxious to embark on another summer sketching campaign, confidently declaring in a letter to Maria:

I am still looking towards Suffolk where I hope to pass the greater part of the summer … You know I have succeeded most with my native scenes … I have now very distinctly marked out a path for myself, and I am desirous of pursing it uninterruptedly (JCC II, p.70).

For the next two Academy exhibitions of 1813 and 1814, Constable now decided to paint canvases on a larger, 'half-length' size (50 × 40in/1.27 × 1.02m). His 1813 Academy exhibit, *Boys Fishing* (National Trust, Anglesey Abbey, Cambridgeshire; R.13.1A) was a canvas on this scale – again turned on its side to form a landscape rather than a portrait format – and was reasonably well received by the critics. Indeed, it even sold the following year. However, when working on this more ambitious scale, Constable was now finding himself up against the problem of how to achieve the right balance of detail and breadth. By 1814, indeed, the year he exhibited *The Ferry* (no.15) at the Royal Academy, he was beginning to receive negative comments from fellow artists and the critics that his pictures were lacking in 'finish'.

To solve this particular problem, Constable realised that he would have to alter his methods and, as far as size was concerned, this would mean a return to painting smaller pictures. Never had the remark that Constable is said to have made to William Purton in later life seemed so true: that, whilst a small canvas would show you what you could do, a large one would show you what you could not (Leslie 1951, p.251, n.1). Constable, it seems, would have to go backwards before he could go forwards again. AL

Self-Portrait

As a young man, Constable was employed for about a year in his father's mills, with a view to taking over the family business. His first biographer, C.R. Leslie, recorded that he performed his duties well, and that,

being remarkable among the young men of the village for muscular strength, and being tall and well formed, with good features, a fresh complexion, and fine dark eyes, his white hat and coat were not unbecoming to him, and he was called in the neighbourhood the 'handsome miller' (Leslie 1951, p.4).

This pencil self-portrait was made some years later in London, in 1806, when Constable had already been training and practising as an artist for seven years. It is executed in the rich tonal style of drawing he had developed by this date chiefly for recording landscape, a style partly influenced by his knowledge of the drawings by the eighteenth-century Suffolk landscapist Thomas Gainsborough. Constable was to become a remarkably fine draughtsman with the pencil, using the medium with astonishing dexterity throughout his life.

Constable was also an accomplished and prolific letter writer, and it is from the wealth of his surviving correspondence, compiled in seven volumes in the 1960s and mid-1970s (see JCC I–VI and FDC 1975), that we gain remarkable insights into his character. He was emotional, self-confessing, affectionate and deeply loyal to family and friends. Yet he could also be over-sensitive, tactless and prone to outbursts of caustic sarcasm, especially in his relations with artistic colleagues or in matters relating to art. He suffered bouts of anxiety and depression, whether brought on by periods of overwork in the studio (exacerbated by a tendency to procrastinate), or when facing personal difficulties, such as the obstacles to his courtship of, and anticipated marriage to, Maria Bicknell. What saw him through these setbacks was an unwavering belief in the direction he wished his art – and life – to go, and a determination to succeed. AL

1

Self-Portrait
1806
Pencil on wove paper
23.7 × 14.5 (9¼ × 5¾)
Inscribed in pencil in lower left-hand corner
'March 1806' (preceded by 'April', subsequently
covered by pencil shading)
R.06.02

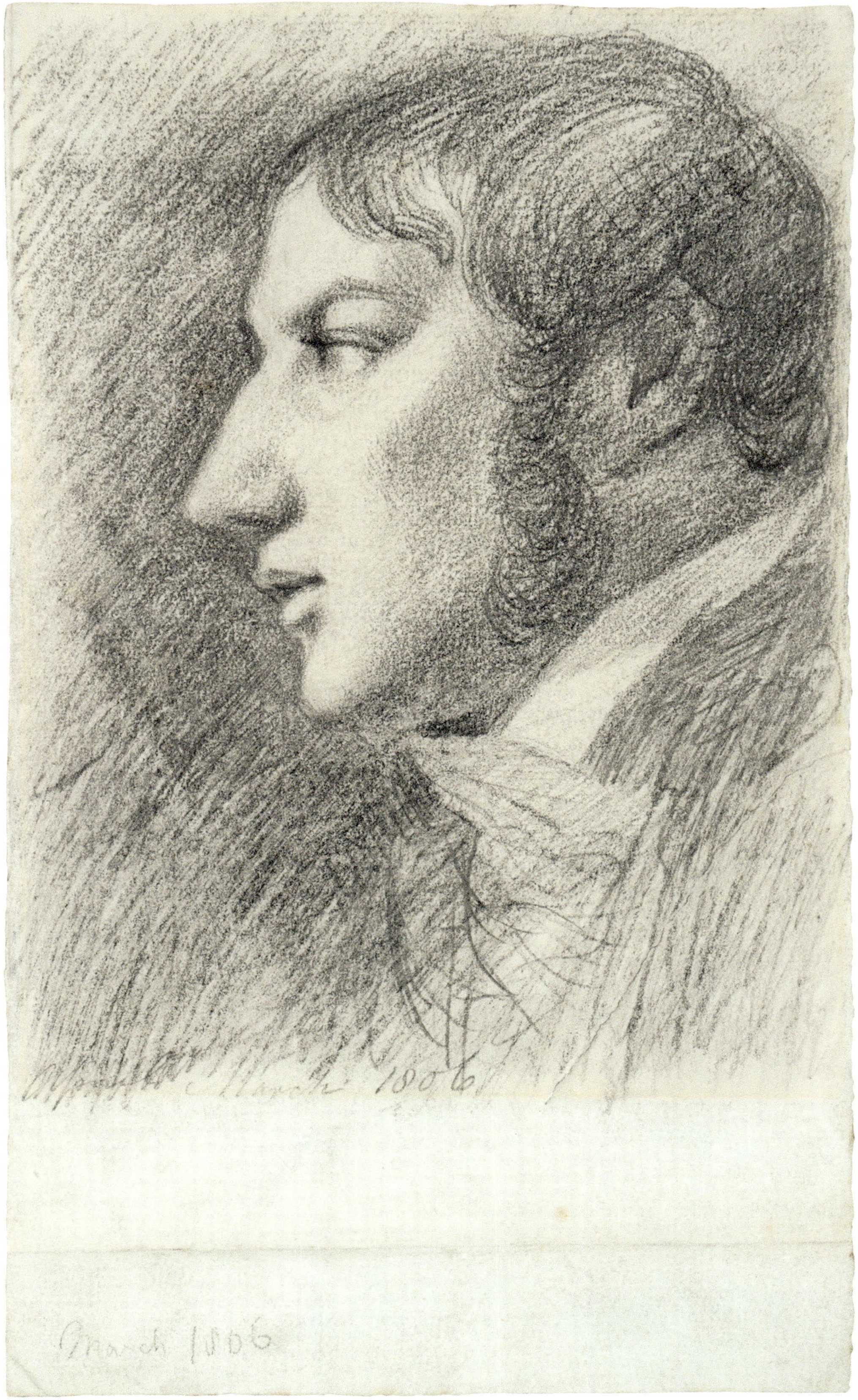

It was to take Constable many years to win full professional recognition. He was already forty-three when he was elected an Associate of the Royal Academy in 1819, and had to wait a further ten years before he achieved full membership. In the months immediately following his long-awaited election as Academician in February 1829, he conceived a project to publish a pictorial overview of his work, engaging the mezzotint engraver, David Lucas, to produce a series of prints from his sketches and paintings. Twenty-two plates were published, in parts, between 1830 and 1832, collectively entitled *Various subjects of Landscape, characteristic of English Scenery, from Pictures Painted by John Constable RA*. Today the series is more generally known as *English Landscape*.

Constable drafted a number of texts to accompany *English Landscape*, and these make it clear that one of its chief aims was to justify his personal conception of landscape painting as demonstrated through his work of the last thirty years. There were two kinds of artist, he wrote. One was an imitator who cleverly recycles the ideas and practices of those who have gone before, and thus gains ready acceptance. The other kind was an innovator, who thinks afresh and charts new territory, adding to art 'qualities of Nature unknown to it before'. However, because 'so few appreciate any deviation from a beaten track', he wrote, the rise of this original artist 'must almost certainly be delayed' – as, indeed, he clearly felt his own had been (JCD, p.10).

It is entirely in keeping with the didactic and highly personal aims of *English Landscape* that Constable should have selected for its frontispiece a print showing the house where he was born. East Bergholt House, a three-storey brick mansion constructed by Golding Constable in 1774, is seen from the garden side on a summer's evening, with an artist conspicuously sketching in the right-hand foreground. The lines of Latin that Constable appended to the title were translated by his friend John Fisher thus:

This spot saw the day spring of my life,
Hours of Joy, and years of Happiness
This place first tinged my boyish fancy with
a love of the art,
This place was the origin of my Fame.

In the introduction to the second edition of *English Landscape* (1833), Constable stated that the subjects were taken from 'Pictures exhibited by the Author at the Royal Academy during the past few years' (JCD, p.10). This was not, however, strictly true. Many of the plates were based on sketches, in some cases going back as far as twenty years (Gage in Paris 2002, p.248). For example, a plate based on a sketch of *Stoke-by-Nayland* of c.1810–11 (no.5) appeared in Part Two in December 1830. Indeed, of those plates that did reproduce pictures Constable had shown at the Academy (as far back, in fact, as at least 1813), only two – *View on the Stour near Dedham* 1822 (no.38) and *Hadleigh Castle* 1829 (no.57) – were examples of the great six-foot landscapes of the 1820s and early 1830s that had helped secure his artistic reputation. Admittedly plates of two further six-footers, *The White Horse* 1819 (no.29) and *The Opening of Waterloo Bridge* 1832 (no.67) had been started for the series, but remained unpublished during his lifetime.

One of the reasons why so few of Constable's great Academy pictures were included in *English Landscape* was perhaps the sheer practical obstacles involved in reducing such large images to a much smaller scale, not to mention the potentially unpromising results. Certainly, later in the 1830s, quite a few of Constable's other six-foot canvases were engraved by Lucas on a substantially larger scale than that for *English Landscape* and published as individual plates (see for example no.62). It is also true that one of the core aims of the project was to capture and promote the 'chiaro'scuro' of landscape (that is, the rich contrasts of light and shade), and this could usually be done equally well, if not actually better, by using sketches rather than pictures. Whatever the exact reasons for the fact that so few of the six-footers were engraved for the project, had they never been painted in the first place, one can assume that Constable would have been unlikely ever to have achieved the very artistic fame he was now so proud to broadcast. AL

2

David Lucas (1802–1881) after John Constable
Frontispiece: East Bergholt, Suffolk
1831
Mezzotint engraving from *English Landscape*,
13.9 × 18.7 (5½ × 7⅜) on India paper laid on
wove paper 26.6 × 36.3 (10½ × 14⅜); plate-mark
23.3 × 23.8 (9⅛ × 9⅜)
Engraved inscriptions: above image:
'FRONTISPIECE./ To Mr. Constable's English
Landscape.'; below image at left and right
respectively: 'Painted by John Constable. R.A.' and
'Engraved by David Lucas'; below image at centre:
'EAST BERGHOLT, SUFFOLK./ Fond recollections
round thy memory twine/ "Hic locus aetatis nostrae
primordia novit/ Annos felices laetitiaeque dies:/
Hic locus ingenuis pueriles imbuit annos/ Artibus,
et nostrae laudis origo fuit."/ London, Published by
Mr. Constable 35, Charlotte St. Fitzroy Square, 1831.'
Shirley no.27 (second state)
TATE. PURCHASED 1985

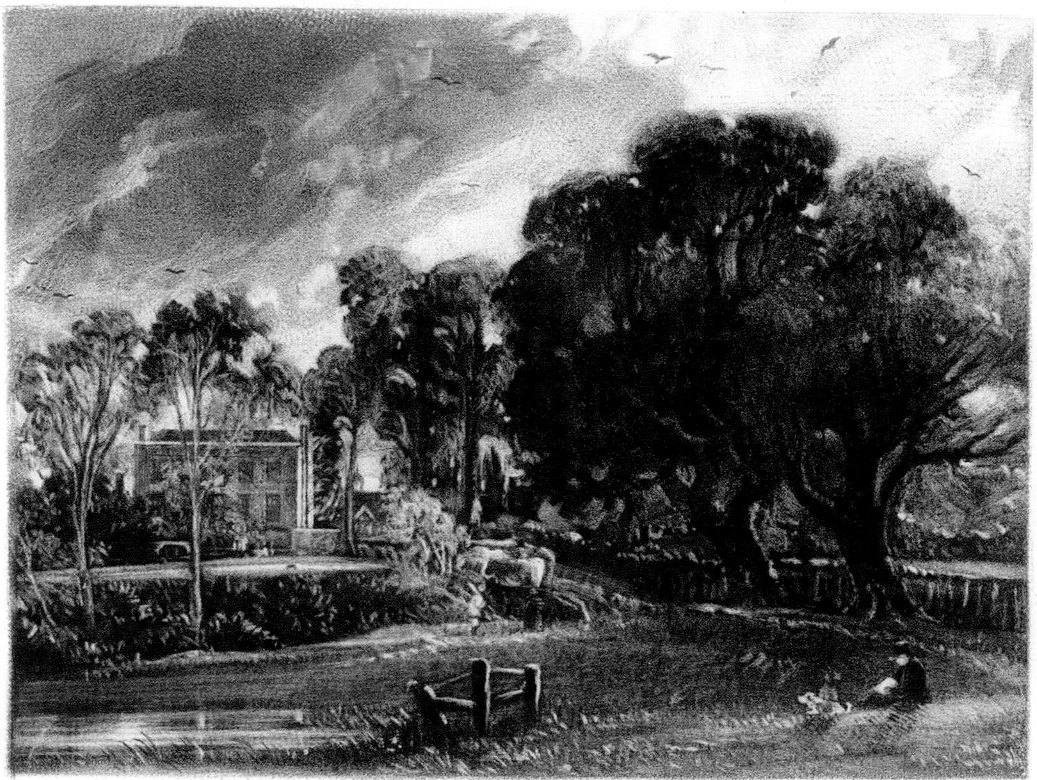

View in the Stour Valley

This signed and dated finished watercolour of 1805 was previously unrecorded in the Constable literature, and adds an exciting new dimension to a phase in the artist's early development that still remains poorly documented. It serves to emphasise the remarkable seriousness of Constable's ambitions as a landscape painter even at this relatively early stage of his career.

Before 1805, Constable had used watercolour only occasionally, and generally only for detailed finished watercolours that follow the conventions of the late eighteenth-century 'tinted' drawing. Around 1805, however, he started using it more frequently and more freely, especially for making *plein-air* sketches in the Stour Valley, as well as on his six-week tour in the Lake District the following year (see fig.6, p.27). Until the appearance of *View in the Stour Valley* (no.3), however, it was assumed that the only finished watercolour painting Constable produced around this time was an ambitious marine subject, *His Majesty's Ship Victory, Capt. E. Harvey, in the Memorable battle of Trafalgar, between two French Ships of the Line*, submitted to the Royal Academy in 1806 (Victoria and Albert Museum; R.06.1).

View in the Stour Valley, a finished watercolour of a pure landscape subject, is a carefully composed painting whose classicising, framing trees recall the work of Claude Lorraine. The inclusion of a hay-cart at centre, meanwhile, is reminiscent of fellow Suffolk landscapist Thomas Gainsborough, and anticipates the core motif of the most famous of Constable's later, mature Suffolk landscapes, *The Hay Wain* 1821 (no.37). The general presentation and mood of the subject, however, is entirely in keeping with Constable's own emerging naturalistic vision; indeed the subject is closely based on a rich tonal pencil drawing of this very same view made by him earlier that same year (*A View near Langham*, Private Collection [not in Reynolds]; repr. Fleming-Williams 1990, p.55).

As this painting is signed and dated and, for a watercolour, on a substantial scale, one might have expected Constable to have exhibited it at the Royal Academy, as he did his watercolour of the *Victory*. J.M.W. Turner had been showing large watercolours of landscape subjects at the Academy since the late 1790s.

This work also bears close comparison with the sort of exhibition watercolour being produced around this time by members of the Old Watercolour Society, whose first exhibition in the spring of 1805 Constable may well have attended, perhaps directly inspiring him to make ambitious watercolours of his own. However, there is no evidence that Constable ever submitted *View in the Stour Valley* for exhibition. It may therefore be that it was a local commission. Alternatively, showing as it does a distant view of Langham church, it is conceivable that Constable painted it as a gift for his early supporter and mentor, Bishop Fisher (1748–1825), through whom he was later to meet the younger John Fisher (1788–1832), the Bishop's nephew, who was to become a lifelong friend and correspondent. Constable first met Bishop Fisher at Dedham in the summer of 1798 when, as Dr John Fisher, he was titular rector of Langham. Indeed, Constable and the elder Fisher are likely to have shared an enthusiasm for the beauties of Dedham Vale in this particular vicinity (Beckett in JCC VI, pp.1–5). AL

3

**View in the Stour Valley looking
towards Langham Church from Dedham**

1805
Watercolour on paper mounted
on a second sheet of paper
48 × 66.4 (18⅞ × 26¼)
Inscribed lower right 'John Constable 1805'
[not in Reynolds]

TATE. PARTIAL PURCHASE AND PARTIAL
LOAN FROM THE AMERICAN FUND FOR THE
TATE GALLERY, COURTESY OF JULIE AND
LAWRENCE SALANDER IN MEMORY OF
JOHN CONSTABLE (1776–1837), DAPHNE
REYNOLDS (1918–2002), EVELYN JOLL
(1925–2001) AND LESLIE PARRIS (1941–2000),
WITH ASSISTANCE FROM THE TATE
PATRONS 2005.

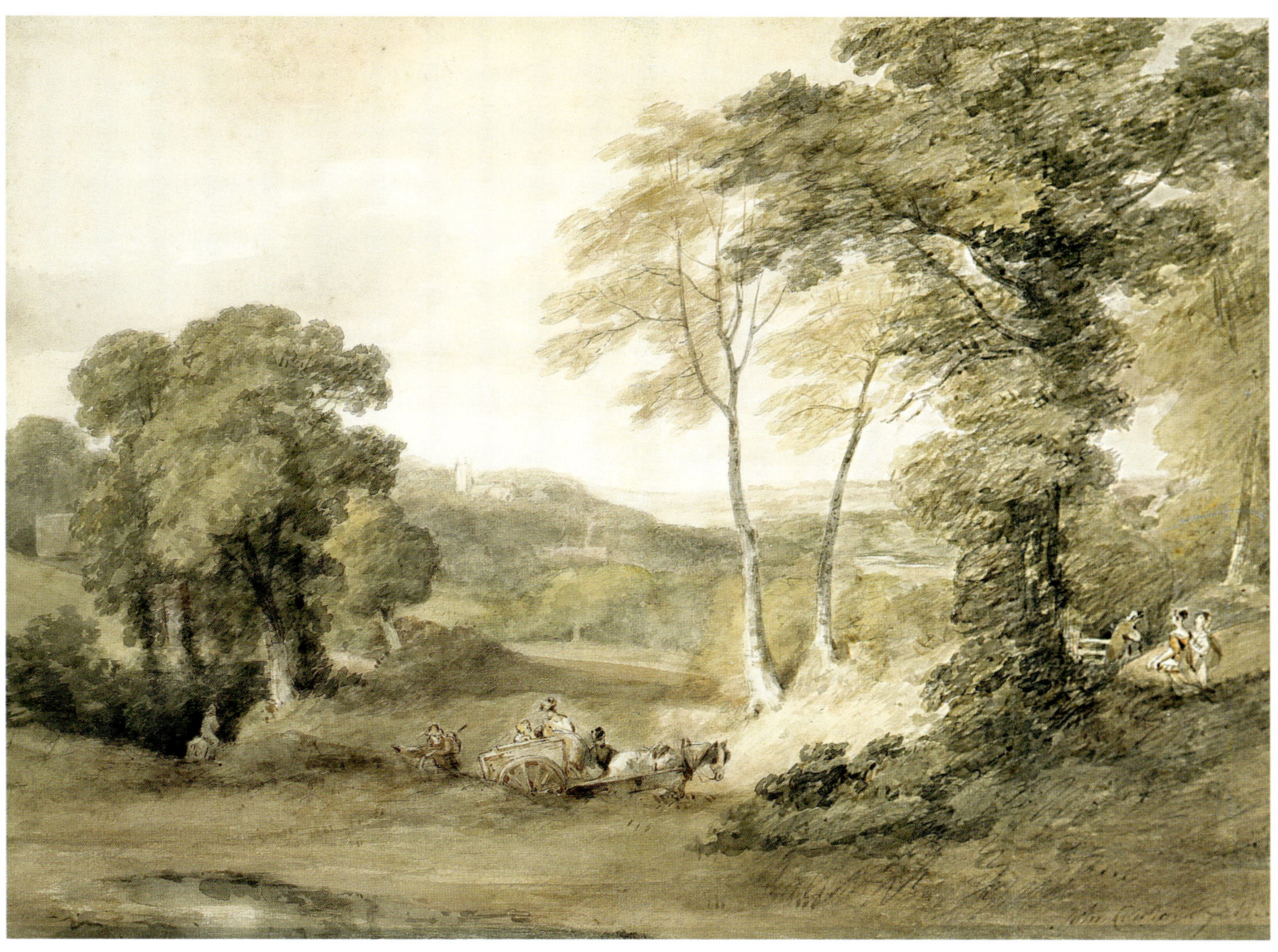

The Church Porch, East Bergholt

St Mary's Church is situated in the heart of East Bergholt village on the High Street, close to the site of East Bergholt House. Constable's father Golding was a church warden for thirteen years and the family had its own pew on the middle aisle. The rector was the formidable Revd Durand Rhudde, whose granddaughter, Maria Bicknell, Constable was to marry in 1816, despite the rector's objections to the match. Constable first met Maria around 1800 on one of her annual visits to East Bergholt to stay with her grandparents at the rectory. At that time she was still a young girl of twelve, whilst Constable was already twenty-four. It was not until 1809, around the time this picture was painted, that he first declared his love (JCC II, p.179).

As a young boy, Constable had been sent to boarding school in Lavenham, and then attended Dedham Grammar School with a view to entering the church, though the idea was abandoned when it was found that he was 'disinclined to the necessary studies' (Leslie 1951, pp.3–4). His mother instilled in him, as she did in all her children, a strong spirit of Christian piety, and a duty to bestow charity without condescension (Beckett in JCC I, p.17). In adulthood Constable was familiar with the writings of the theologian William Paley, to which he was introduced by Archdeacon Fisher, and admired the works of the great Christian poet, John Milton. He was also a staunch supporter of the Anglican Church, and greatly troubled in later life when he saw it threatened by the Catholic Emancipation Act of 1829 and then the Parliamentary Reform Bill, which, when passed in 1832, greatly restricted the role of the established church in public life (Rosenthal 1983, p. 230; Gage in Paris 2002, p.232).

This is the first oil painting by Constable that can certainly be identified as an exhibited picture. Its dimensions correspond closely with those given for the framed size of the picture he sent to the British Institution in 1811, *A Church Porch*, as does C.R. Leslie's evocative description of the 1811 exhibit:

The 'Porch' is that of Bergholt Church, and the stillness of a summer afternoon is broken only by the voice of an old man, to whom a woman and a girl sitting on one of the tombs are listening … such is its extreme simplicity of effect, that it has nothing to arrest the attention, but … once noticed, few pictures would longer detain a mind of any sensibility (Leslie 1845, p.23).

Since we know that Constable would often send to the British Institution pictures he had failed to sell at the previous year's exhibition at the Royal Academy, this painting can also safely be assumed to be his 1810 Academy exhibit, *A church-yard*.

Churchyard imagery was especially popular at this date, thanks to its association with the celebrated poem written by Thomas Gray in 1751, *Elegy Written in a Country Churchyard*. Indeed, Constable had cited some lines from Gray's *Elegy* in an illustration he produced a few years earlier for *A Select Collection of Epitaphs and Monumental Inscriptions* (Ipswich 1806). Although *The Church Porch, East Bergholt* makes no direct reference to Gray's poem, viewers would surely have called it to mind. Constable includes pensive figures gathered around gravestones, as well as the important detail of the afternoon light catching the porch sundial that marks the passing of time. In subsequent years Constable, like many of his contemporaries, would on occasion cite lines of verse to accompany the pictures he exhibited, favouring in particular passages from the epic landscape poem *The Seasons* (first pub. 1727) written by the popular eighteenth-century poet James Thomson (see no.57). AL

4

The Church Porch, East Bergholt
1810
Oil on canvas 44.5 × 35.9 (17 ½ × 14 ⅛)
Exh: RA 1810 (no.116, *A church-yard*);
BI 1811 (no.185, *A Church Porch*,
frame 25 × 22in)
R.10.2
TATE. PRESENTED BY
MISS ISABEL CONSTABLE 1888

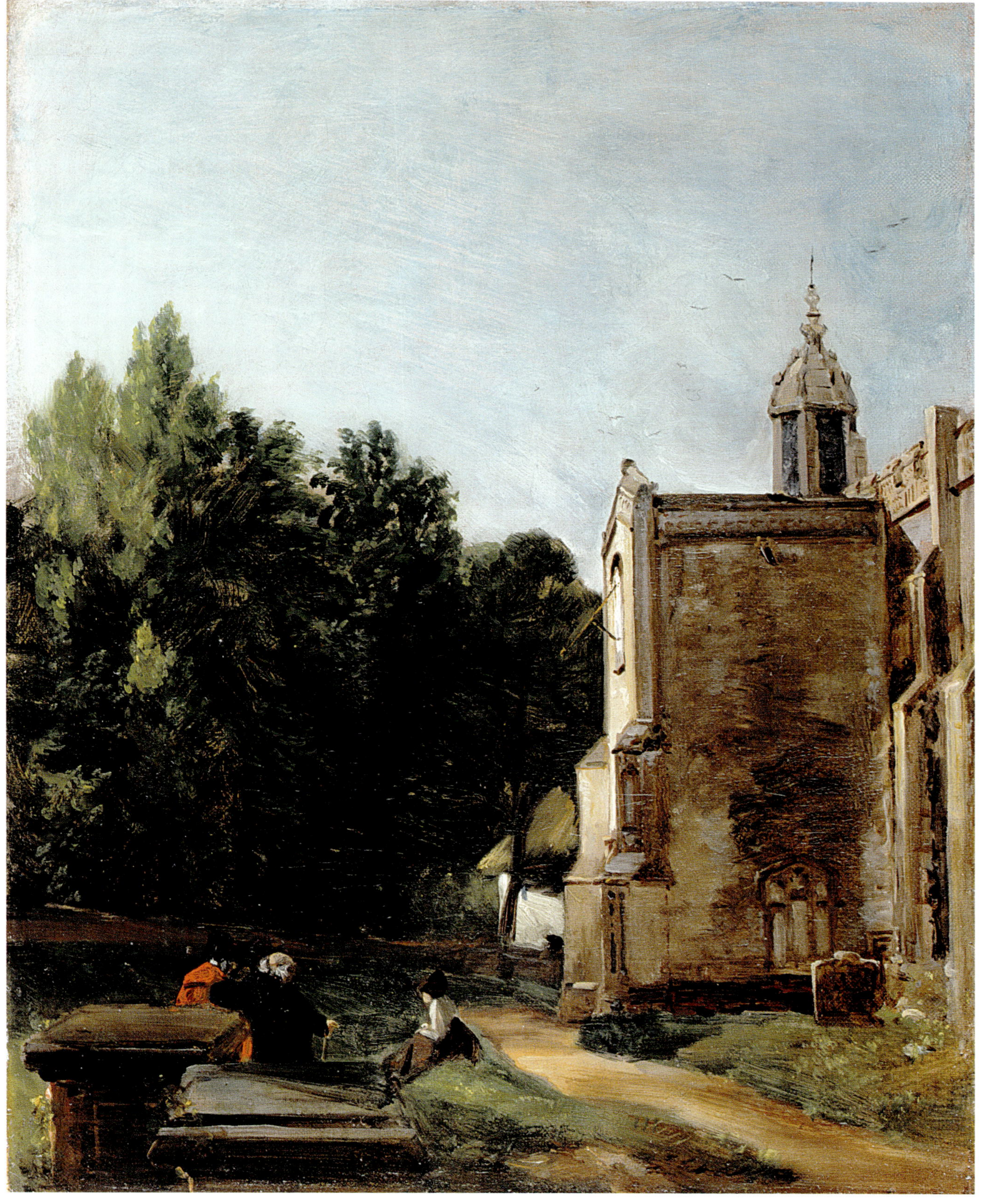

Sketching from Nature

Constable first experimented with oil sketching in the open air in Suffolk in 1802 (see p.77). There then followed a six-year interlude before he took up the procedure again with any regularity. His adoption of the practice was by no means unique for the period. In England in the first two decades of the nineteenth century, there was something of a vogue for painting outdoors, whilst in France *plein-air* sketching in oils had been part of academic practice since the second half of the eighteenth century, and was also widely adopted by the international community of artists then based in Rome (see p.24). However, Constable was to remain more deeply committed to the practice than any of his predecessors or contemporaries, and it was to become a cornerstone of his work until about 1829. During these years, he was to bring to the oil sketch unparalleled new levels of sophistication, inventiveness and sheer brilliance of technique.

In the period 1810 to 1814, in particular, Constable was experimenting with a range of supports – canvas, millboard and paper – and a variety of grounds, as well as different styles of handling (see also nos.7, 8). In *Stoke-by-Nayland* (no.5), for example, the brushstrokes follow an insistent diagonal rhythm, curiously leaning 'backwards' as if applied by a left-handed artist, although Constable was right-handed. *A Lane near Flatford* (no.6), meanwhile, shows a more varied touch, in which a sequence of animated, irregular brushstrokes suggests fast-moving clouds and bristling trees, thus successfully evoking the impression of a breezy summer's day.

In one sense these sketches are equivalents for nature's various moods and effects, and for Constable's responses to them, captured at great speed. However, oil sketching had chiefly evolved in France with the joint functional

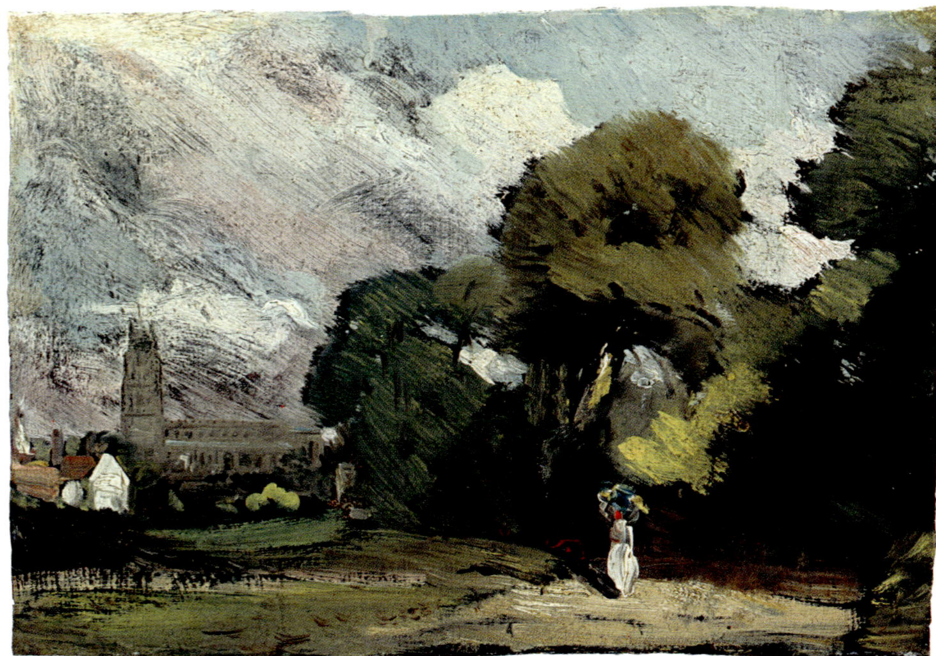

aims of training an artist's eye and supplying a repertoire of pictorial material for later use in the studio. It is, indeed, clear that Constable used *plein-air* oil sketching, and also the humble pencil drawing made in a sketchbook, for just such a purpose, for he regularly composed with a pictorial eye. *Stoke-by-Nayland*, for example, was to be adapted by him many years later for the last of his proposed great landscapes, no.68; and *A Lane near Flatford* (no.6), a lane subject with a young boy bending down to slake his thirst, was adapted for one of his most famous exhibition subjects of the mid-1820s, *The Cornfield* (fig.59, p.116; R.26.1).

Most of Constable's oil sketches include one or two figures, a reminder that, in the words of his biographer, C.R. Leslie, Constable flourished best when dealing with landscapes that 'abound[ed] in human associations' (Leslie 1951, p.18). Leslie also reported the advice that Constable is said to have received in early life from the draughtsman and antiquary, J.T. Smith:

Do not … set about inventing figures for a landscape taken from nature; for you cannot remain an hour in any spot, however solitary, without the appearance of some living thing that will in all probability accord better with the scene and time of day than will any invention of your own (*ibid.* p.6).

In most cases, the inclusion of figures in Constable's sketches does indeed seem consistent with Smith's advice, and thus with the idea that they, and therefore the sketches themselves, were painted on the spot. However, the inclusion in *Stoke-by-Nayland* of a female figure carrying faggots

5

Stoke-by-Nayland
c.1810–11
Oil on canvas remounted
on synthetic board
18.1 × 26.4 (7 ⅛ × 10 ⅜)
R.11.44
TATE. BEQUEATHED BY
HENRY VAUGHAN, 1900

on her head is very close to a similar figure found in a related chalk sketch, as well as two painted variants of the oil sketch itself, made around the same date (R.10.3, p.4; R.11.45 and R.29.61). This raises the question as to whether *Stoke-by-Nayland* (no.5) was indeed painted on the spot, or whether it was worked up in the studio from an existing monochrome sketch. It is an important question to ask, as it prompts us to consider quite to what extent Constable was indeed the 'natural painter' in his early career that so much of the literature written about him would have us believe. AL

6

A Lane near Flatford
c.1811
Oil on paper laid on canvas
20.3 × 30.3 (8 × 11⁷⁄₈)
R.11.30
Tate. Bequeathed by Henry Vaughan, 1900

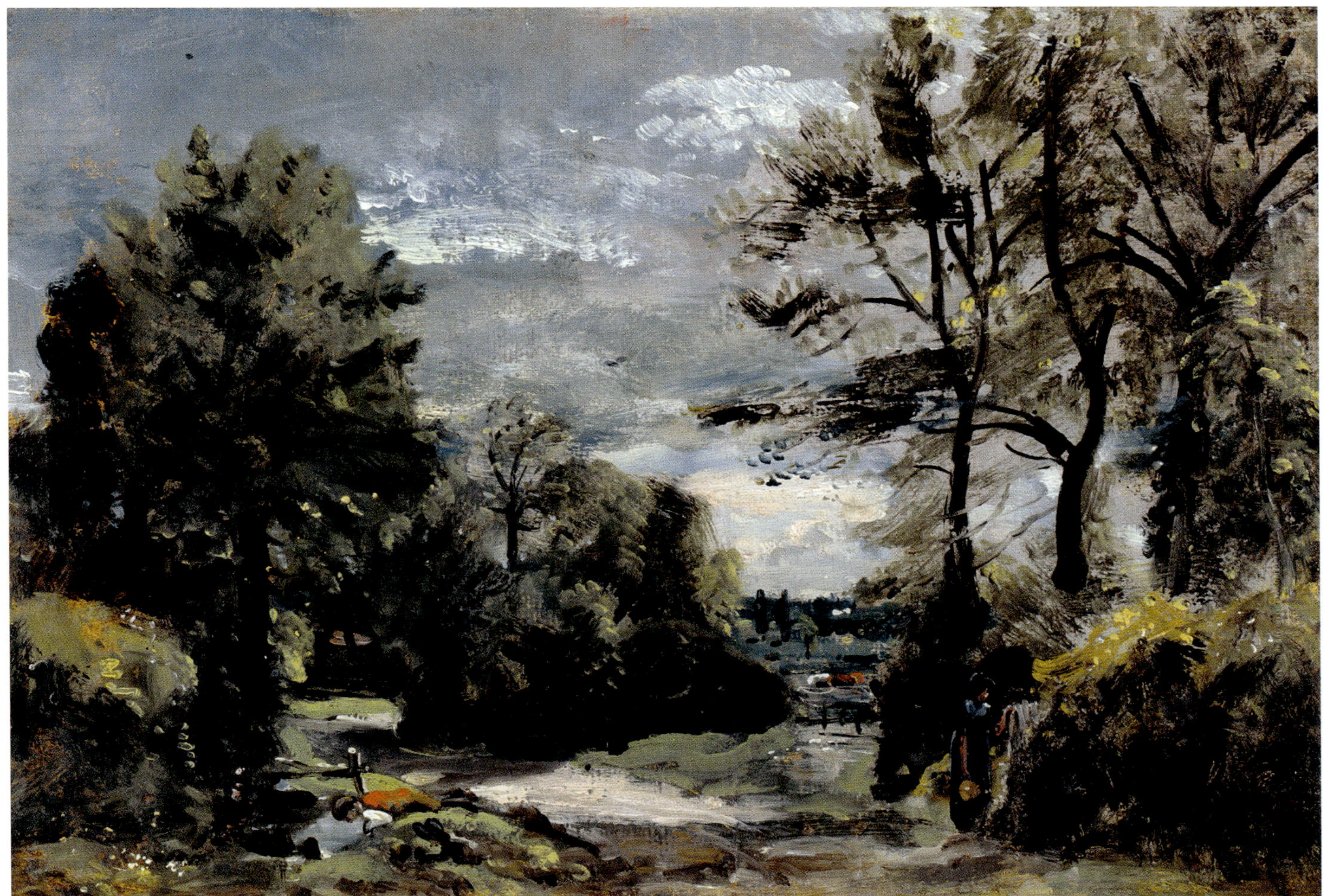

When sketching outdoors in Suffolk, and perhaps also when thinking about suitable subjects for working up into pictures for exhibition, Constable would tend to find himself irresistibly drawn to two distinct types of subject matter. The first embraced the extensive panoramas that could be obtained across Dedham Vale, whether looking westwards from East Bergholt (fig.11, p.34) or, a particular favourite, eastwards from more elevated ground near Langham, as in *Dedham from Langham* (no.7). The second encompassed the more enclosed views along the canalised section of the River Stour close to Flatford Mill, whether looking directly towards the mill itself (nos.10–14) or from a point directly behind it towards Willy Lott's Cottage (nos.8, 9).

These two types of landscape elicited from Constable quite different approaches to composition. His views of Dedham Vale have a much stronger horizontal emphasis, where the landscape extends into depth only gradually, the tower of Dedham church providing a valuable vertical axis in the far distance, as in *Dedham from Langham*. Indeed, in a draft for some text to accompany one of the prints for *English Landscape* based on this very view, *Summer Morning*, Constable wrote thus:

This view of the beautiful valley of the Stour is taken from Langham an elevated spot to the N.W. of Dedham, where the elegance of the tower of Dedham church is seen to much advantage … This tower from all points forms a characteristic feature of the Vale (JCD, p.17).

Indeed, Dedham church tower provides a distant landmark not only in many of Constable's earlier Suffolk landscapes (nos.16, 20, 22–5), but also in many of the six-foot River Stour pictures (nos.38–47).

By contrast, the compositional method Constable adopted for his early views painted near Flatford Mill reveal him projecting the landscape into depth quite suddenly by employing steeply receding lines of perspective that carry the eye towards the motif of two trees, or clumps of trees, which close the vista by meeting (or nearly meeting) in the distance (nos.8–9, 12–14). It is not known when Constable painted this sketch of *The Mill Stream* (no.8) at Flatford, which he subsequently referred to when working on a finished painting of the subject (no.9). However, since the sketch is made on board, a support that Constable tended to use in the period between about 1808 and 1810 (see Cove in Tate 1991, p.500), it might date from as early as 1809. AL

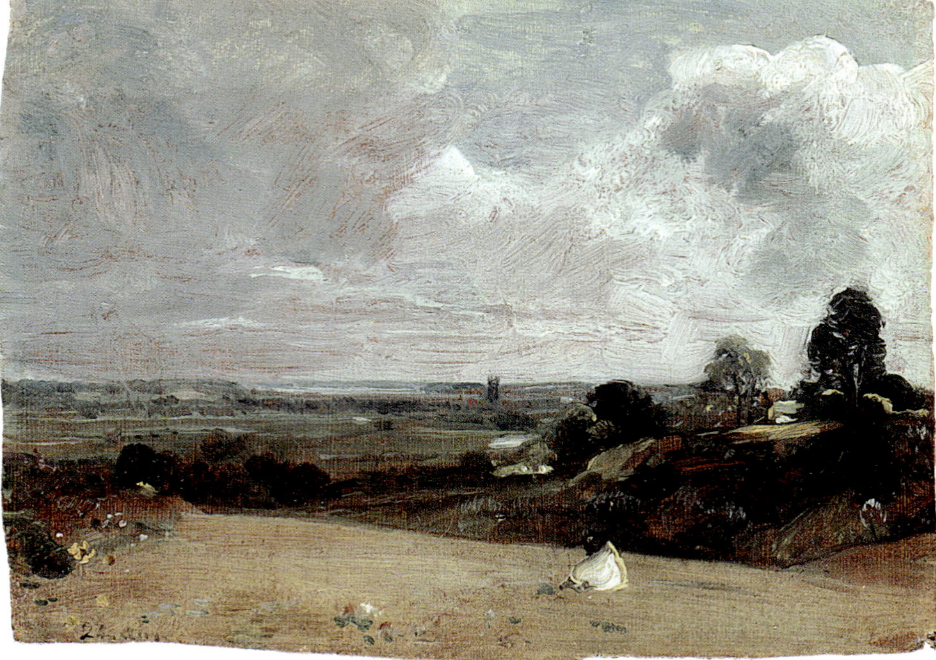

7

Dedham from Langham
c.1813
Oil on canvas remounted
on synthetic panel
13.7 × 19 (5³⁄₈ × 7¹⁄₂)
R.13.15
TATE. BEQUEATHED BY
GEORGE SALTING 1910

8

The Mill Stream
c.1809–14
Oil on board 20.8 × 29.2 (8¹⁄₈ × 11¹⁄₂)
R.14.47
TATE. BEQUEATHED
BY HENRY VAUGHAN, 1900

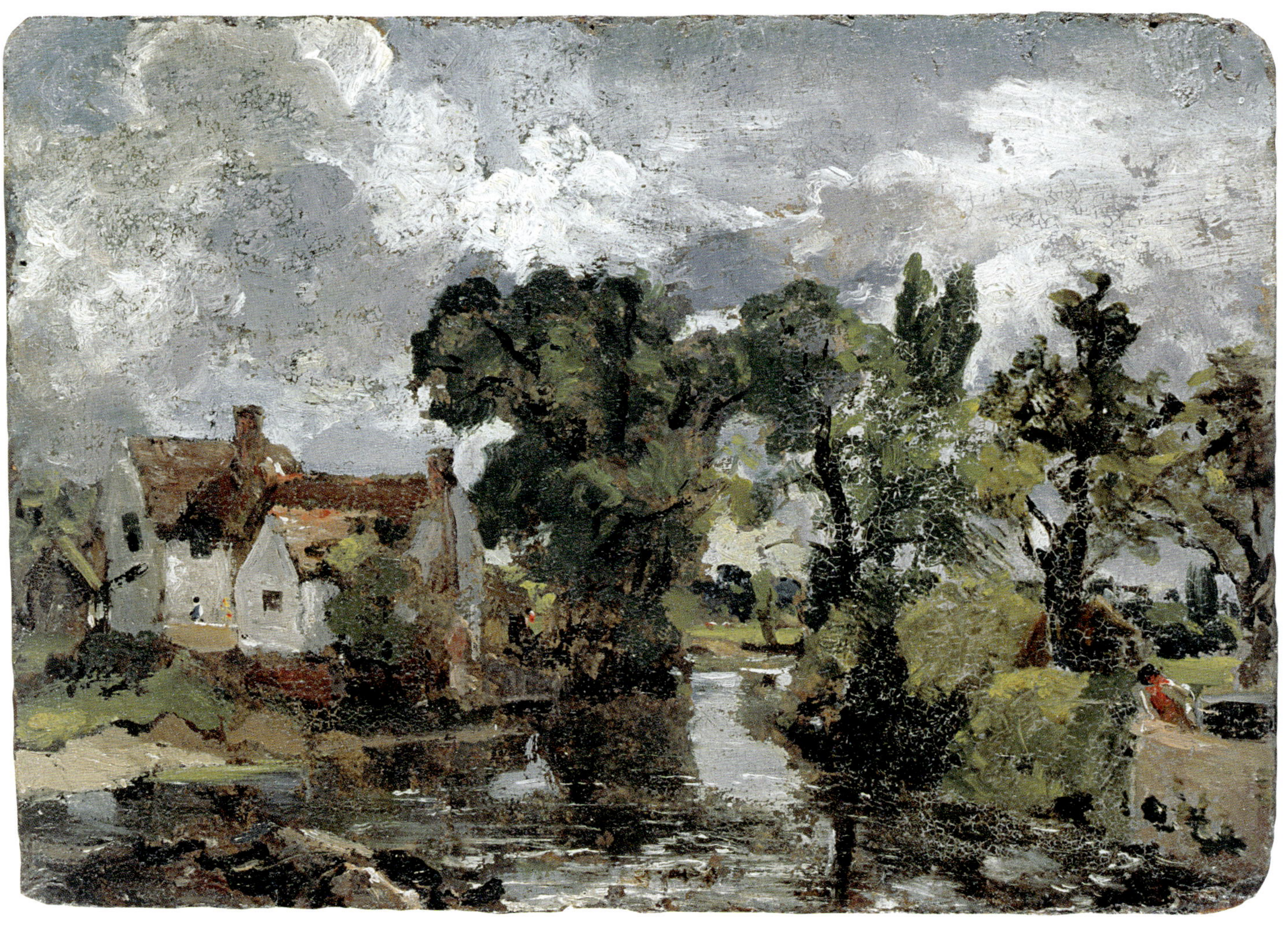

The Mill Stream

The Mill Stream is among the best known of Constable's earlier pictures, thanks to the fact that it was engraved by David Lucas, in 1831, for *English Landscape*.

The mill stream in question is that adjacent to the mill owned by Constable's father at Flatford. Constable's view is taken from the parapet behind Flatford Mill and shows the channel of water that connects the mill stream to the main course of the River Stour (see map, p.72). The house on the left was occupied in Constable's day by a local tenant farmer known as Willy Lott, and has been known ever since as Willy Lott's House (or Willy Lott's Cottage). This same spot was to feature in *The Hay Wain*, the third of the great River Stour pictures that Constable exhibited at the Royal Academy in the 1820s (no.37). Indeed, thanks to the fame that *The Hay Wain* has since acquired, the site itself is today the most familiar among all those that Constable painted, and holds an 'iconic' status in the English landscape.

Constable based the composition of *The Mill Stream* on an earlier oil sketch (no.8). However, he took some of the additional details, such as the ferryman poling a boat at the left, from existing sketchbook drawings (see Tate 1991, pp.137–8). The ferry plied between the bank of the mill stream close to Willy Lott's house and the far bank of the River Stour, using a short cut past the edge of a tree-lined island called 'The Spong' that appears in the composition at the right (see map, p.72). The cutting lay just beyond the parapet in the right foreground, from which a young boy can be seen fishing.

Owing to Constable's inclusion of a ferryboat on the left, *The Mill Stream* was for many years mistakenly identified as the picture that he exhibited at the Royal Academy in 1814 as *Landscape: the ferry*. It is now accepted, however, that a larger, upright version of this subject was the 1814 Academy exhibit (no.15). This raises the question as to why *The Mill Stream* itself, an important and ambitious picture in its own right, has not so far been firmly identified as one of Constable's early exhibits. Whilst it is conceivable that it was painted as a commission whose details are not recorded, the other possibility is that it is still identifiable, albeit under a more generalised title, among Constable's early Academy exhibits.

Two scholars, for example, have recently raised the possibility that *The Mill Stream* may be identifiable with the picture entitled *A Landscape*, which Constable exhibited at the Academy in 1810 (Ivy 1991, pp.26–9, 64–5; Reynolds 1996, p.143). Certainly we know that this 1810 exhibit, like *The Mill Stream*, was a picture of 'kit-kat' size. In addition, two reviews describing the 1810 exhibit are at least consistent with a possible identification of the picture as the *Mill Stream*. One, for example, from the *Repository of Arts*, referred to it as 'a fresh and spirited view of an inclosed [*sic*] fishpond', an idea that might easily have arisen from the presence of the boy fishing at the right; and another, from *The Examiner*, called it 'a pleasing view of water flowing between two trees in the middle of the canvas' (Ivy 10.1, 10.2).

It also seems likely that the *Landscape* that Constable showed at the 1810 Academy exhibition was a Suffolk subject, since the picture was purchased by Wilbraham Tollemache, the 6th Earl of Dysart, whose family seat at Helmingham was located not far from East Bergholt to the north of Ipswich. Indeed Constable had gone sketching in the grounds of Helmingham Hall in 1800, although it was not until 1807 that he was first introduced to Lord Dysart, with a view to making copies of family portraits in London, by a mutual Suffolk acquaintance.

We can also be fairly certain that *The Mill Stream* was a picture that Constable actually sold during his lifetime (see Tate 1991, p.138). If it were to be identifiable with the picture purchased by Lord Dysart at the 1810 exhibition, one would need to be able to establish that Constable was in a position to borrow the painting back in 1831 when David Lucas engraved it for *English Landscape*. In fact, following the 6th Earl's death in 1821, Constable was in regular contact with the Earl's successor, his sister Lady Louisa Manners. Constable painted some portraits for her, and gave advice on her picture collection, whilst she would supply him with venison or invite him to Ham House, the Tollemache family residence on the Thames near Richmond (JCC IV, pp.66–81 *passim*). In such circumstances, Constable would surely have had no problem borrowing the painting back; indeed there is a tantalising reference to some 'Pictures' being exchanged between them in a note that might well date to the period c.1830 to 1831 (FDC 1975, p.137).

The circumstantial evidence suggesting a link between *The Mill Stream* and the Dysart family is, then, certainly promising. If such a link could be established beyond doubt, it would throw fascinating new light on Constable's skills and ambitions as a landscape painter at the relatively early date of 1810. AL

9

The Mill Stream

c.1810–14
Oil on canvas 71.1 × 91.5 (28 × 36)
Exh: ?RA 1810 (no.74, *A Landscape*,
bt Lord Dysart)
R.14.46 (and ?R.10.1)
Ivy: ?10.1–2
IPSWICH BOROUGH COUNCIL
MUSEUMS AND GALLERIES

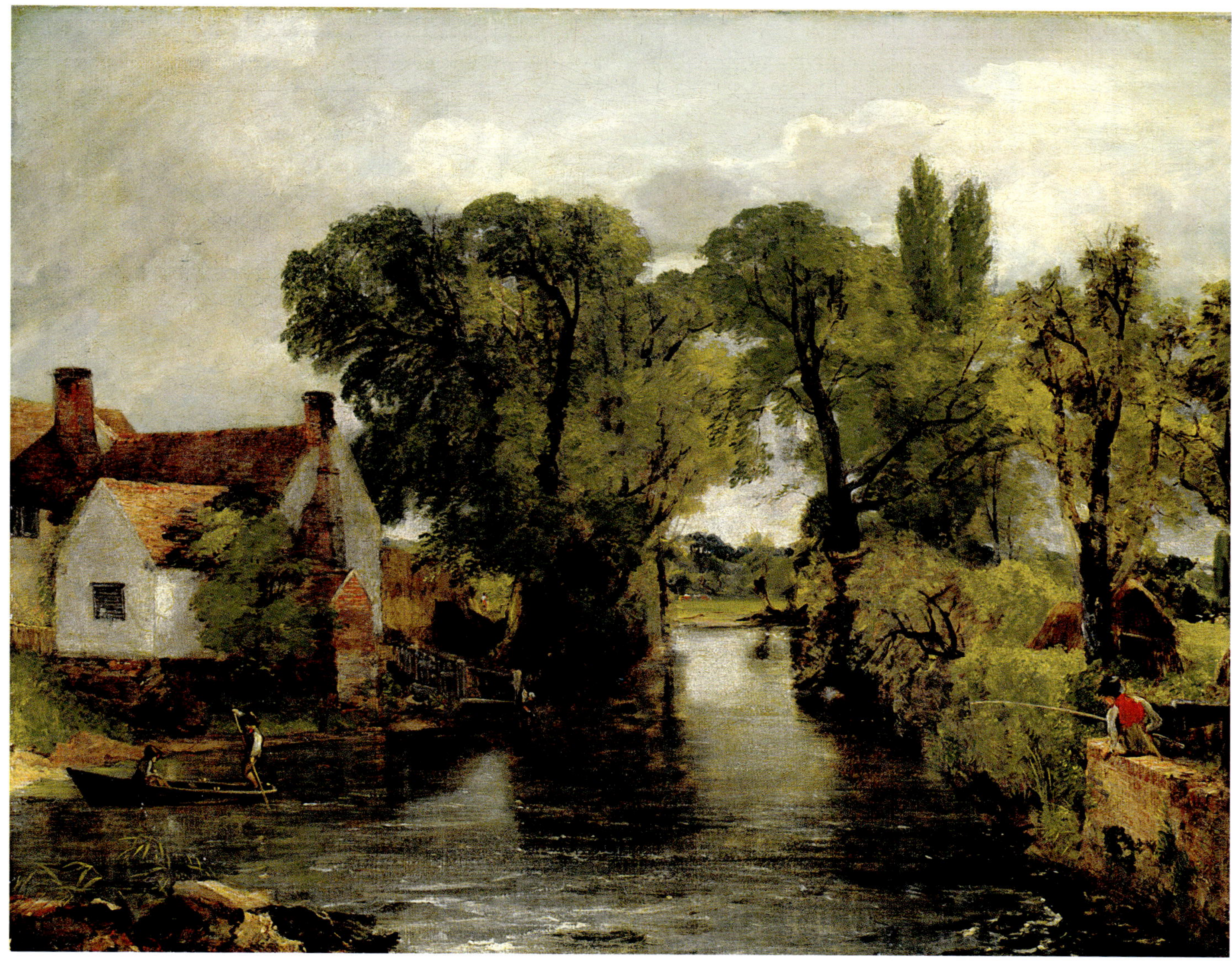

Flatford Mill from the Lock

Flatford Mill from the Lock (no.14) was Constable's main exhibit at the Royal Academy in 1812 and is a key work in his early development. Exhibited under the general title *A water-mill*, it was hailed by the *London Chronicle* as a 'very excellent and promising study' (Ivy 1991, p.66). Furthermore, Constable told Maria that Benjamin West, the Academy's President, even stopped him in the street to tell him how much he admired it (JCC II, p.65).

Whilst *The Mill Stream* (no.9) showed an enclosed corner immediately behind Flatford Mill, this picture, which may pre- or post-date *The Mill Stream*, depicts a more extensive vista looking towards the mill buildings from a point close to the head of the lock from the other side (see map, p.72). It is clear from the many surviving related oil sketches that Constable planned its composition with a great deal of care and deliberation.

No.10 seems to be the first study in the sequence, and shows a lock-keeper or boatman in the process of opening the lock-gate on the left, the mill buildings appearing immediately beyond him (only part of the mill itself is visible on the far left, though the adjacent mill house is seen in full). Like so many of Constable's oil sketches, this may initially have been made by him as a 'one-off', perhaps in the summer of 1810.

By 1811, however, it seems that Constable had already thought of working up a picture of the subject, for that year he decided to explore it in greater detail and from a variety of different angles. For example, no.11 shows him exploring the viewpoint from the other side of the lock. This results in him introducing into the composition not only some trees lining the towpath on the right, which conveniently help frame the view, but also a glimpse of the fields beyond. Two further studies painted that year (no.12; fig.52, p.94) show him then panning further to the right, with the result that even more of the fields come into view, although the mill buildings on the left are now cropped, albeit to a greater or lesser degree.

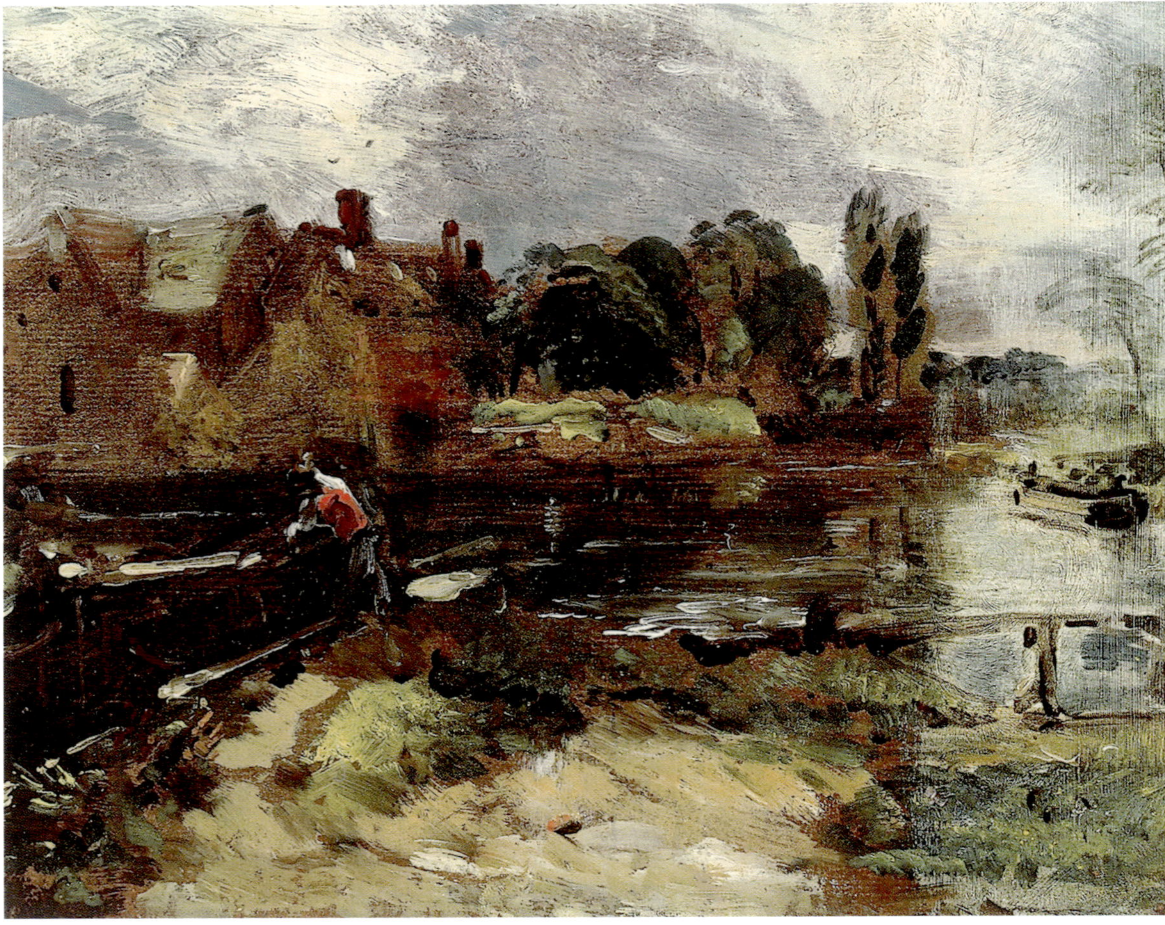

10

Flatford Mill from the Lock
c.1810
Oil on paper 18.4 × 23.5 (7¼ × 9¼)
R.12.5
ESTATE OF SIR EDWIN
A.G. MANTON

Finally, Constable produced an oil sketch, almost certainly in the studio, in which he combined different elements from each of these preceding outdoor studies (no.13; Cove in Tate 1991, p.526). This sketch retains the deep linear perspective he achieved in no.12 and fig.52, but also includes both the framing elements of buildings on the left and of trees and fields on the right, making it a 'composition' in the true sense. This is Constable the 'picture-maker' at work, for he is now distorting actual topography to achieve the most satisfying image. In fact, this compositional type, with sharply receding perspective lines bordered on each side by framing screens of buildings or landscape, is one inspired by his admiration for the seventeenth-century landscape painter Claude Lorraine, above all the latter's 'seaport' subjects (Kitson 1957, p.351).

The final picture (no.14) was then worked up by Constable over a period of about seven months during the winter of 1811–12 (Cove in Tate 1991, p.527). Initially he included the foreground figure opening the lock-gate, but later painted him out (though traces of his red jacket are still visible), replacing him with a youthful angler, perhaps because the latter created a more serene and contemplative mood. He also chose a light for the picture less committed to a particular time of day (Fleming-Williams 1980, p.219).

When compared with the sketches, then, the finished picture is more timeless and universal in character, as one might expect for a picture Constable was preparing for exhibition. Indeed, this method of working – elaborating a more complex composition in the studio from a range of *plein-air* studies and composition sketches – directly anticipates his practice when working on his big six-foot canvases in later years. At this stage, however, Constable had not yet conceived the idea of painting a full-scale studio sketch on the same scale as the anticipated finished picture. AL

11

Flatford Mill from the Lock
1811
Oil on canvas laid on board
15.2 × 21.2 (6 × 8³⁄₈)
R.12.8

DAVID THOMSON

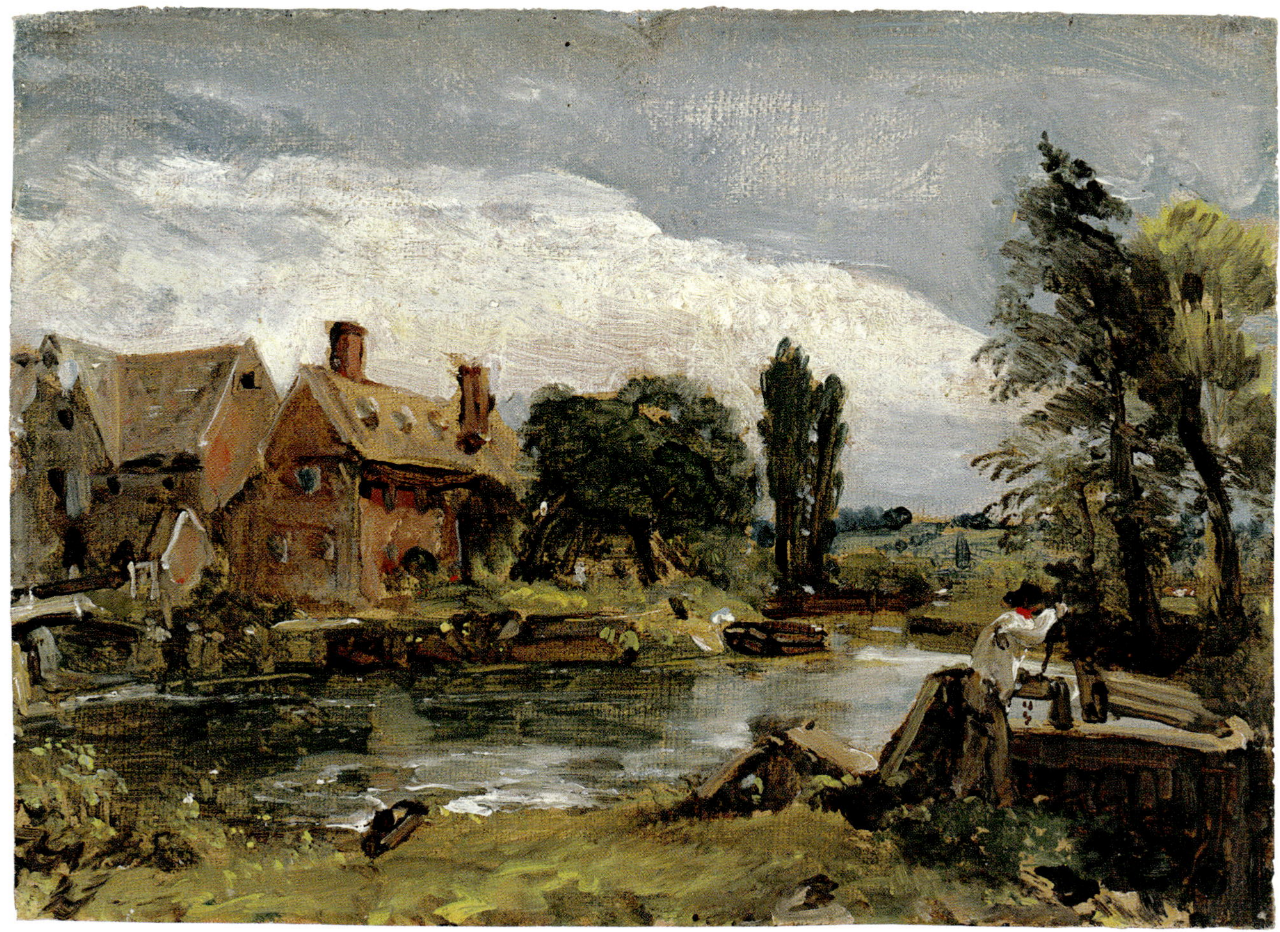

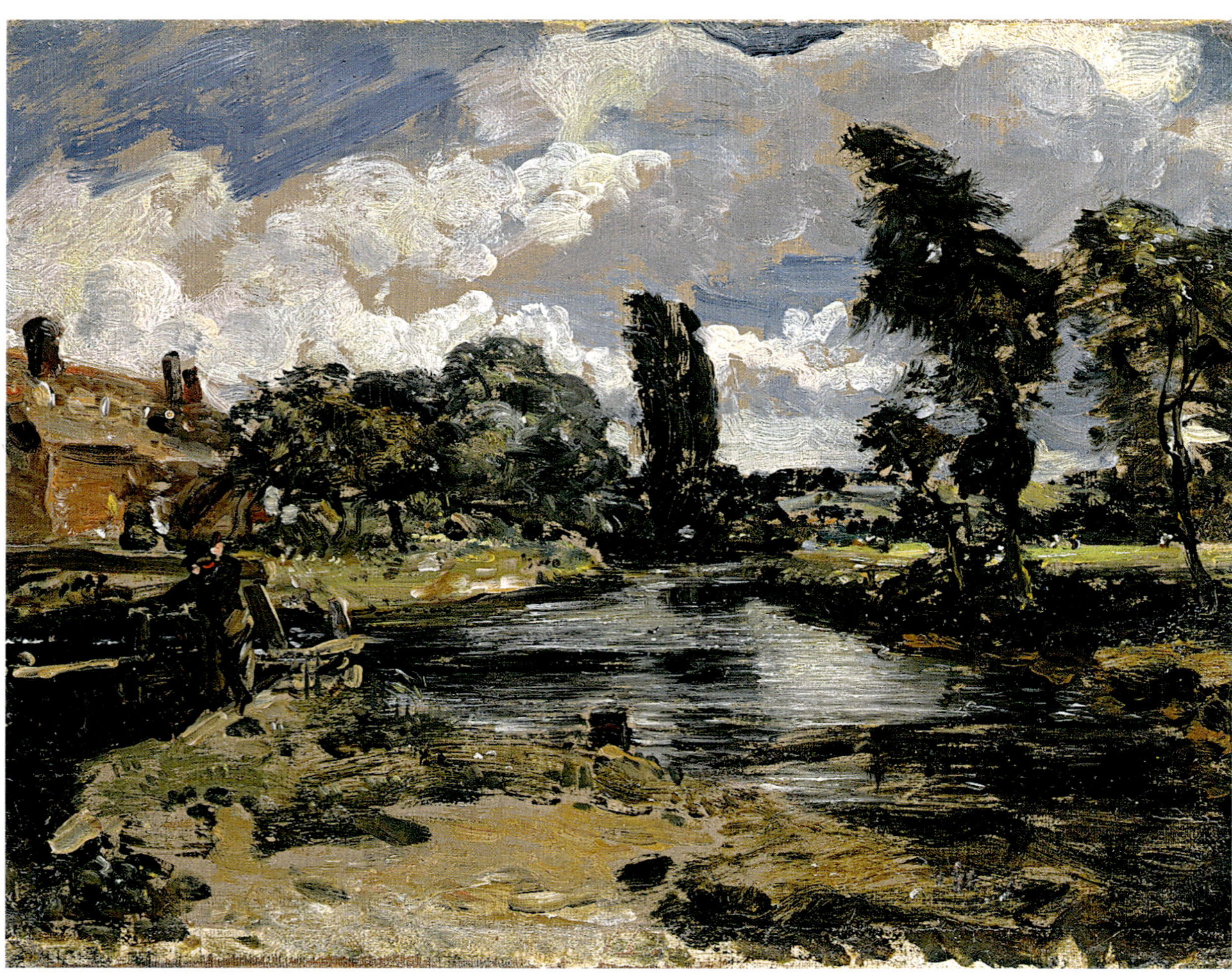

FIGURE 52

Figure 52
Flatford Mill from the Lock
c.1811
Oil on paper laid on canvas
26×35.5 (10¼×14)
ROYAL ACADEMY OF ARTS,
LONDON

12

Flatford Mill from the Lock
c.1811
Oil on canvas 25.4 × 30.5 (10 × 12)
R.12.7
THE HUNTINGTON LIBRARY, ART
COLLECTIONS, AND BOTANICAL
GARDENS

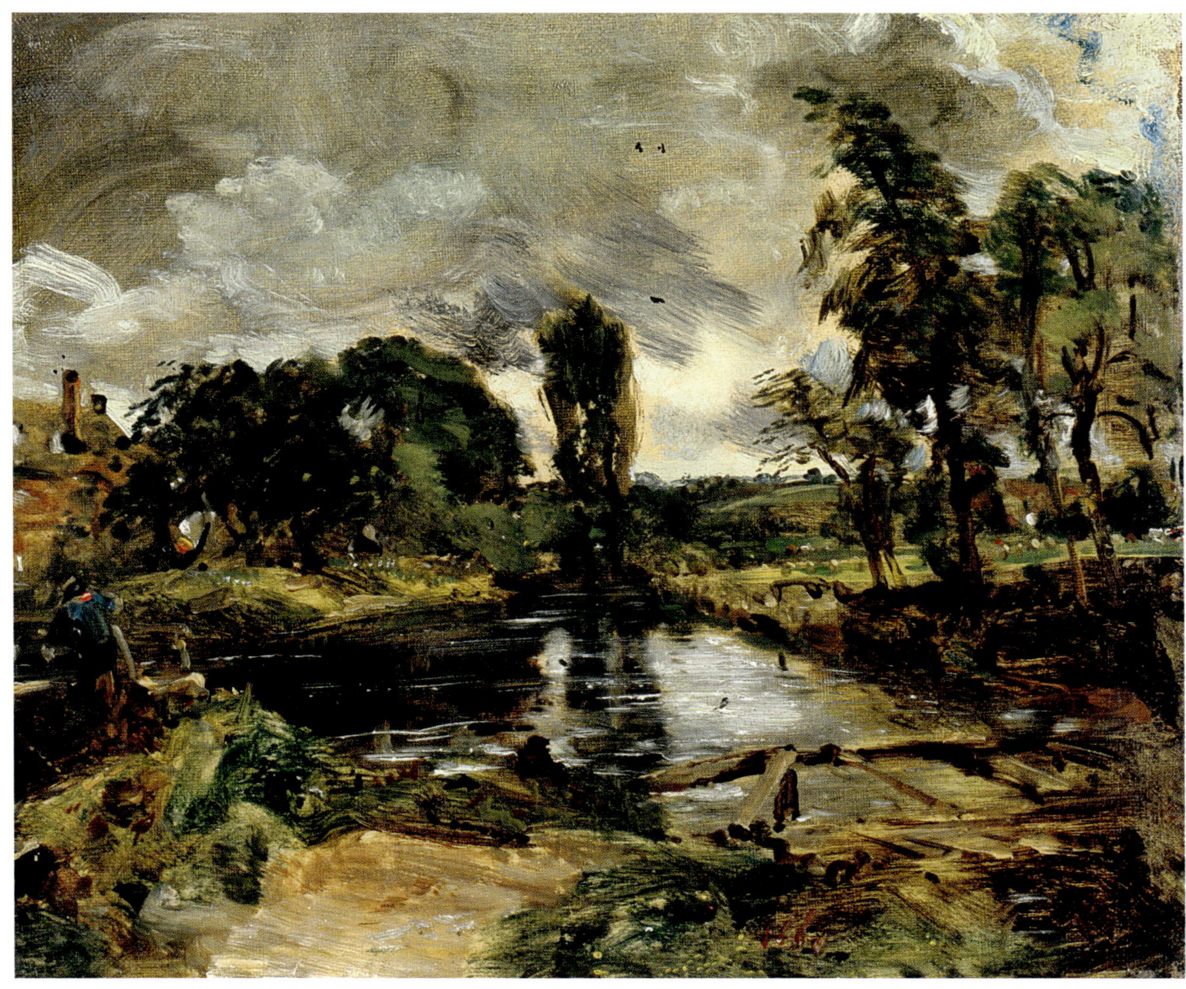

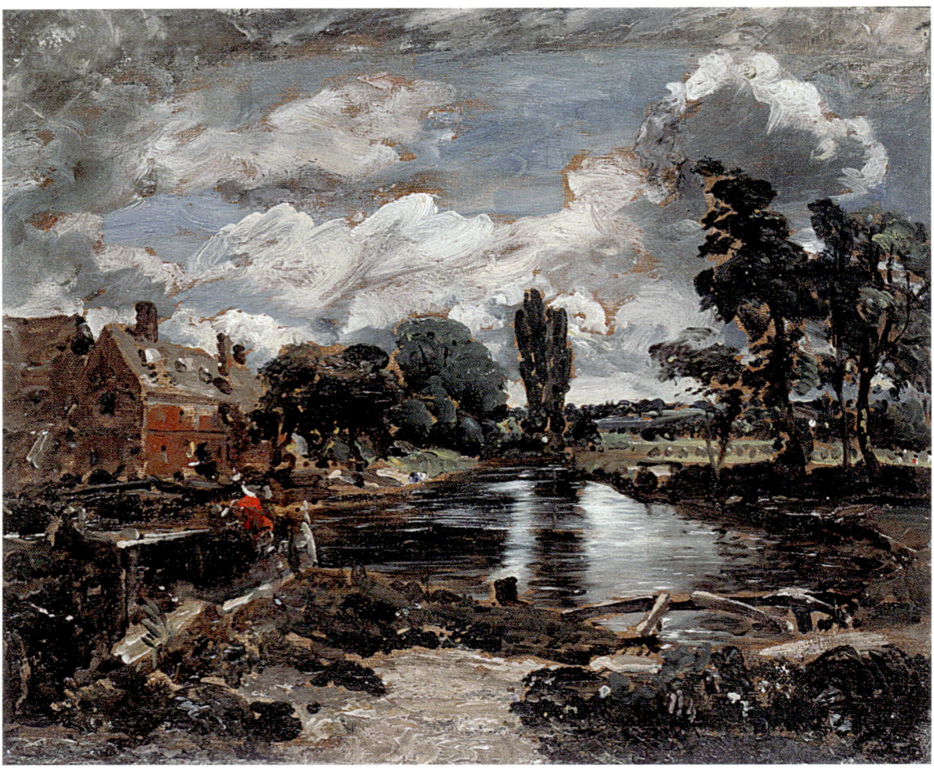

13

**Study for 'Flatford Mill
from the Lock'**
c.1811
Oil on canvas 24.5 × 29.5 ($9^{5}/_{8} × 11^{5}/_{8}$)
R.12. 9
VICTORIA AND ALBERT MUSEUM,
LONDON. GIVEN BY ISABEL CONSTABLE,
DAUGHTER OF THE ARTIST

Flatford Mill from the Lock

1812
Oil on canvas 63.5 × 90.2 (25 × 35½)
Exh: RA 1812 (no.9, *A water-mill*)
R.12.1
Ivy: 12.2–3

DAVID THOMSON

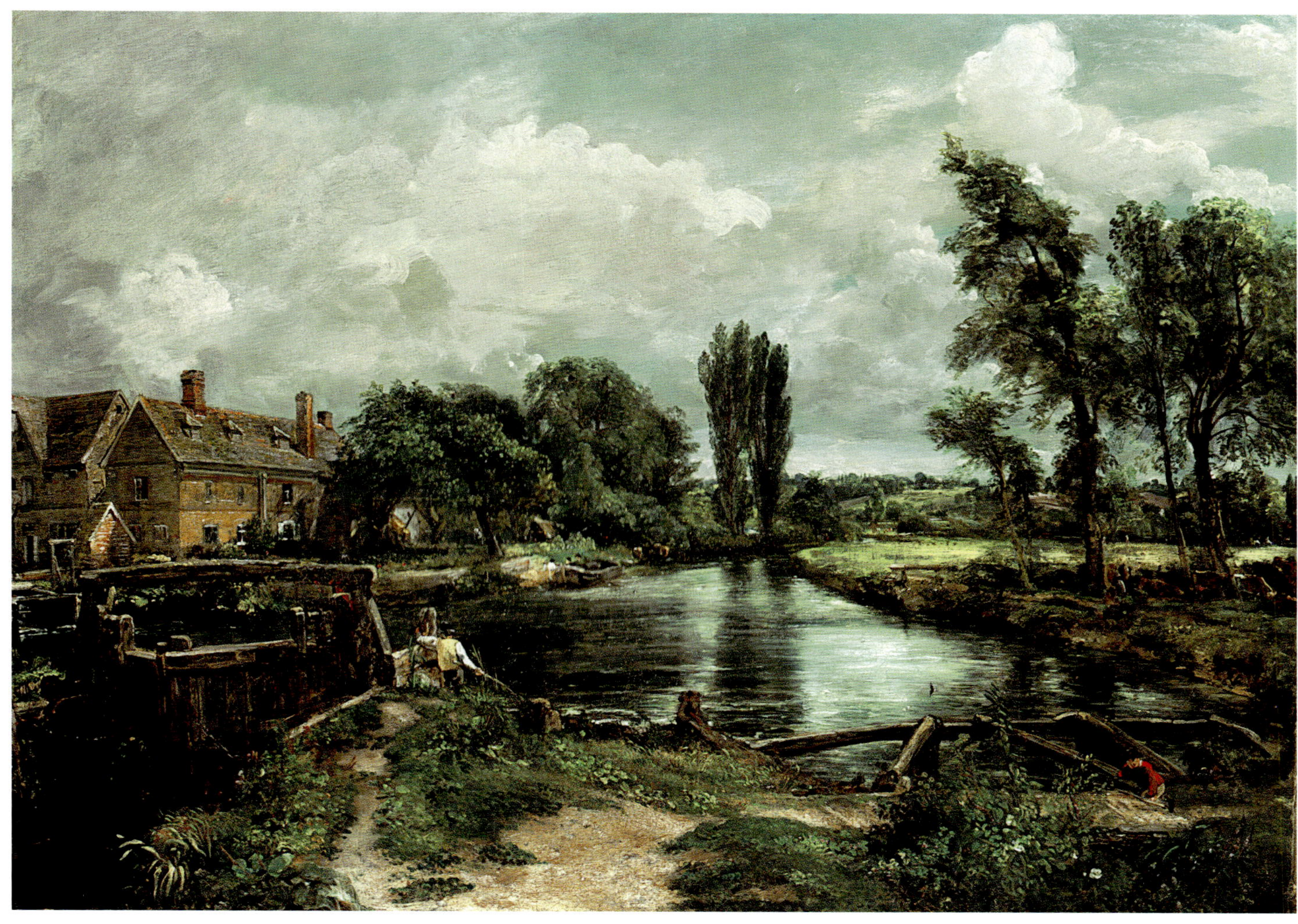

The Ferry

When Constable was translating small oil studies into a medium-sized canvas of, say, roughly a kit-kat size, such as *The Mill Stream* (no.9) or *Flatford Mill from the Lock* (no.14), he was able to do so without having to add too much detail. However, when he attempted to transpose such studies on to a larger canvas like this one, *The Ferry*, he found himself not only having to add more detail but also having to balance this with the requisite amount of 'breadth'. Writing to John Dunthorne in February 1814, Constable confessed:

I am anxious about the large picture, Willy Lott's House, which … promises uncommonly well in masses etc, and tones – but I am determined to detail but not retail it out (JCC I, p.101).

In the event, *The Ferry* was criticised on its exhibition at the Royal Academy in 1814 by *The Examiner* as being 'deficient in finishing' (Ivy 1991, p.69). Constable's uncle, David Pike Watts, also criticised the picture for 'slight of finish', though he had already been reprimanding his nephew on this account for a number of years (JCC IV, pp.9–47 *passim*). Constable did not always take the remarks of critics, or the advice of well-intentioned family, to heart. However, this time it appears that their observations did strike a chord, for soon afterwards he reverted to painting smaller pictures again to improve his skills in finishing. In this respect, it is clear that *The Ferry* is a highly significant transitional work in his development. AL

15

The Ferry
1814
Oil on canvas 125.7 × 100.3 (49½ × 39½)
Exh: RA 1814 (no.261, *Landscape: the ferry*)
R.14.2
Ivy: 14.4

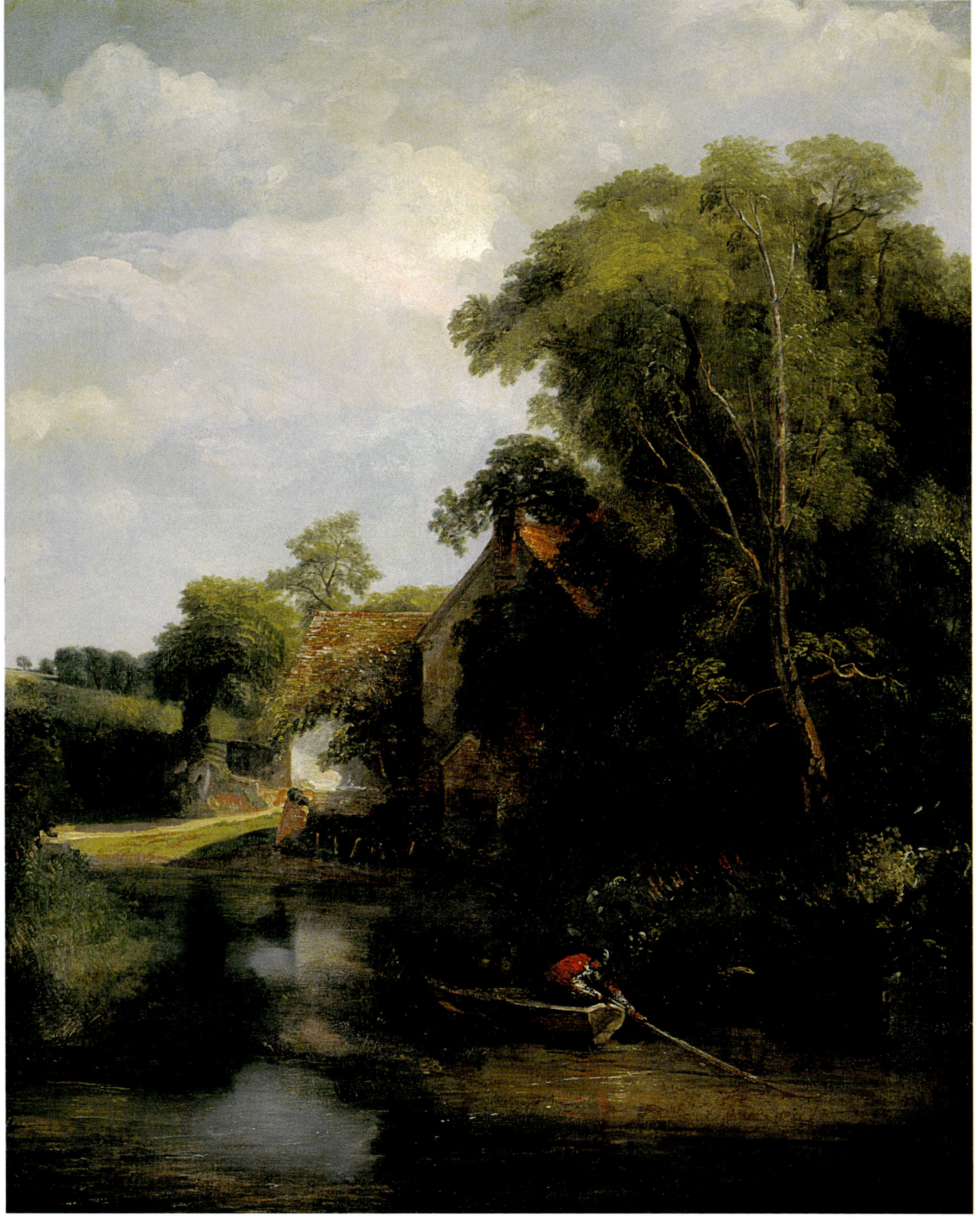

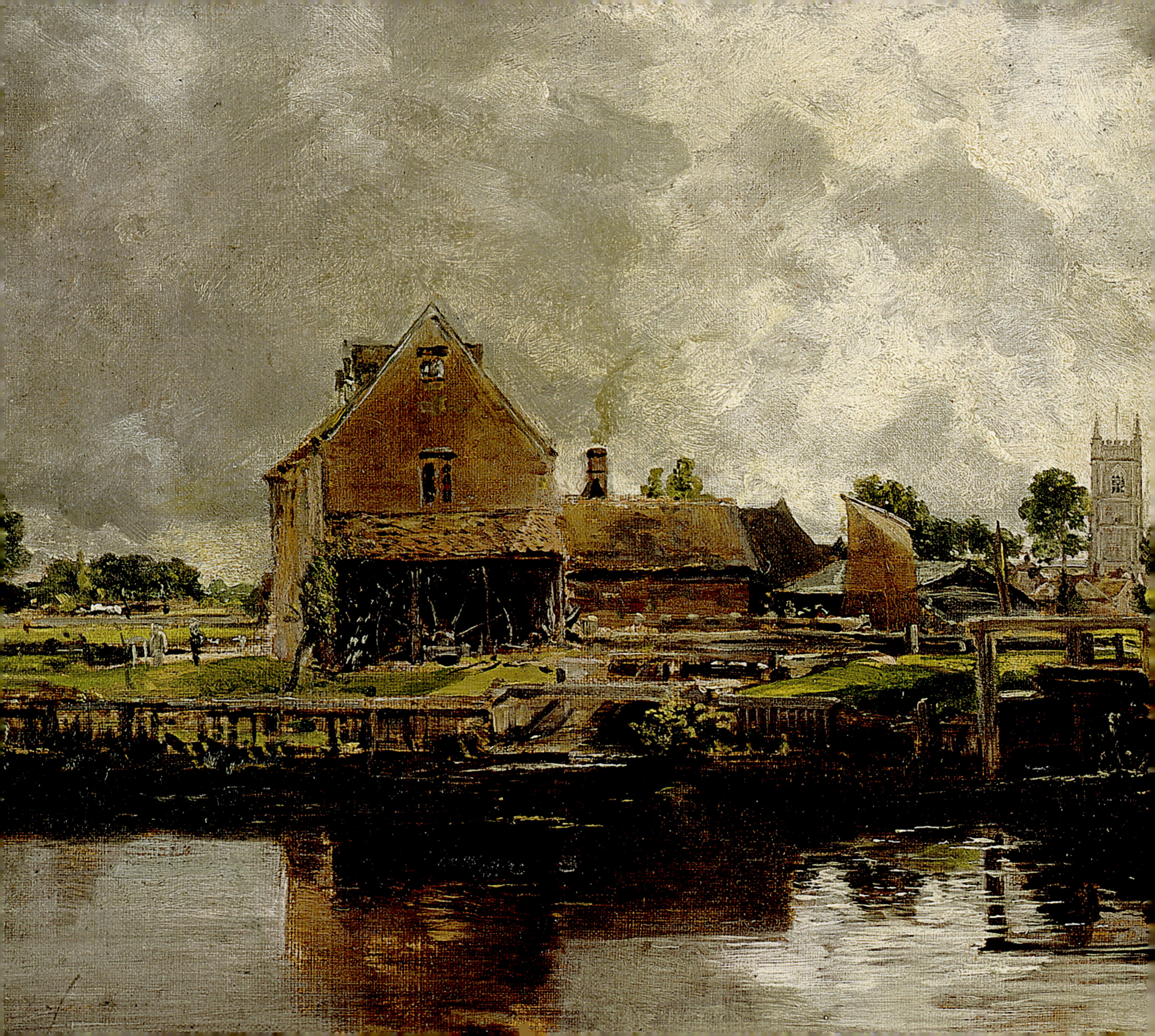

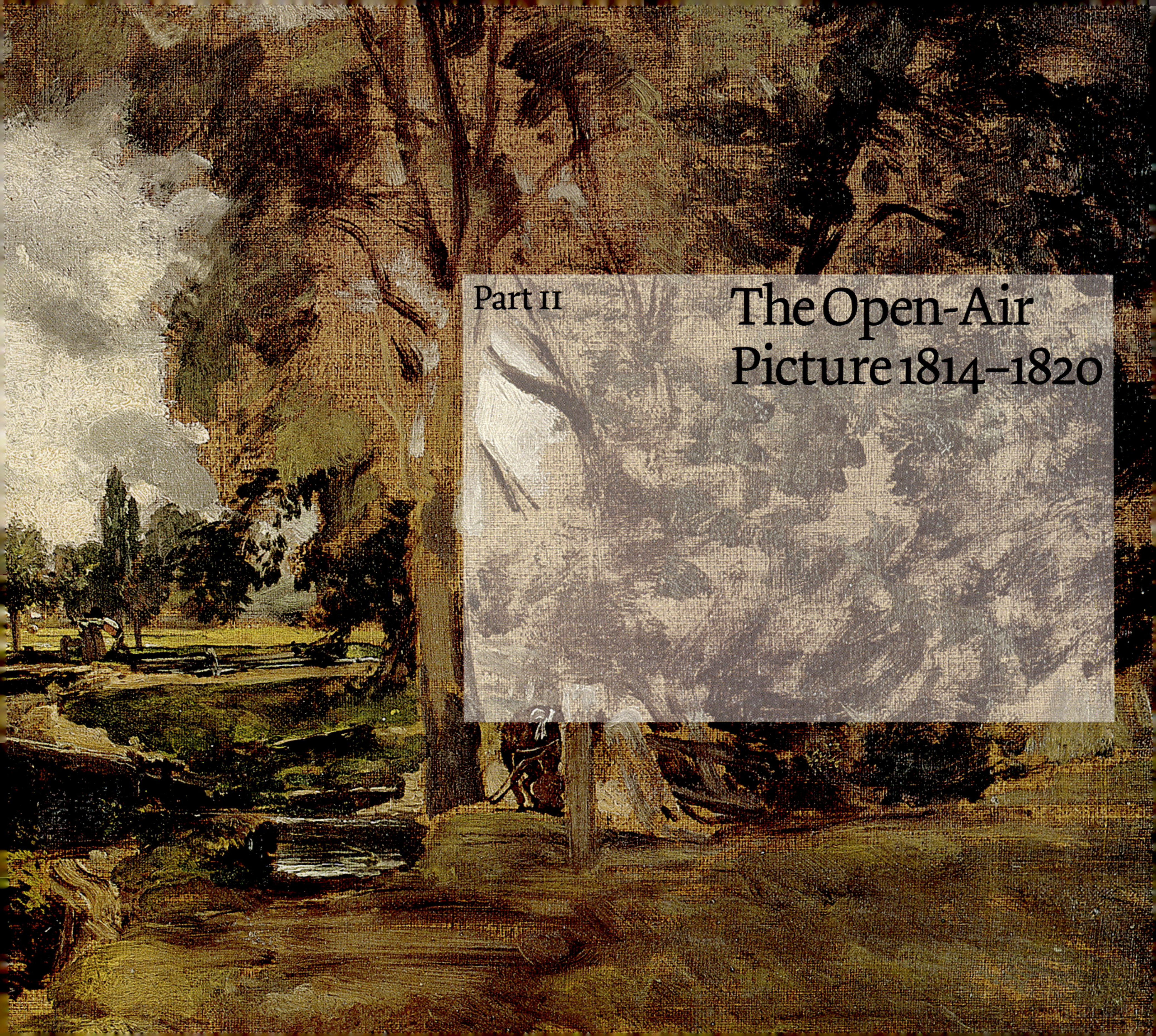

Part II
The Open-Air
Picture 1814–1820

The Open-Air Picture

1814–1820

The year 1814 proved to be something of a watershed for Constable. Not only was he now struggling to resolve the level of 'finish' in his pictures, a problem only exacerbated when he attempted to work on a larger scale, but he was also becoming concerned that his exhibition pictures were tending to look too 'bleak' (JCC I, p.101; see also p.52 for a fuller discussion of 'finish'). This latter problem may have arisen chiefly because Constable was painting them from sketches in the studio over the winter time under a cold, unforgiving light.

In February Constable wrote about these difficulties in a letter to his Suffolk artist friend, John Dunthorne. Addressing in particular the problem of finish in his exhibition pictures, he told Dunthorne that he had arrived at a new resolution: I am determined to finish a small picture on the spot for every one I intend to make in future … this I have always talked about but never yet done … my mind is more settled and determined than ever on this point (JCC I, *ibid.*). The poor reviews Constable received when he exhibited *The Ferry* (no.15) at the Academy in the spring can only have strengthened him in this resolve. So as to improve his powers of finishing he would from now on, he seems to be telling Dunthorne, paint fully worked-up small-scale pictures entirely in the open air. These would then serve as the basis for larger paintings, such as he was evidently still ambitious to paint, albeit still elaborated in the studio.

In the event, only part of this programme of work seems to have materialised. From the summer of 1814 Constable did indeed start painting small pictures in the open air in Suffolk, returning in effect to a practice he had first adopted during his sketching campaign of 1802 (see p.77; also p.34), though this time he was to maintain the practice for a much longer period. Contrary to what Constable had declared in his letter to Dunthorne in February 1814, however, the small *plein-air* pictures he now painted were to serve not as the starting points for larger paintings, but sometimes as the exhibition works themselves. For example, *Boat-Building* (fig.55, p.105), painted during the especially fine summer of 1814, and measuring a modest 20 × 24 inches (51 × 61cm) – a small portrait-size canvas known as a 'head' turned on its side (Carlyle 2001, p.447) – was included among the eight works that Constable sent to the Royal Academy exhibition in the spring of the following year. It shows a barge under construction in Golding Constable's dry dock on a hot summer's afternoon. Indeed, along with another of Constable's Academy exhibits in 1815, *Boat-Building* was singled out by one reviewer for its 'sparkling sun-light' (Ivy 1991, p.70), indicating that, regarding his concern to overcome the 'bleakness' of some of his earlier canvases, his new commitment to painting pictures in the open air was beginning to pay off.

Constable's *plein-air* painting campaign in the summer and autumn of 1814 had undoubtedly proved a very productive one, for in October that year he informed Maria that it was 'many years since I have pursued my studies so uninterruptedly and so calmly – or worked with so much steadiness and confidence' (JCC II, p.133). It is suggested here that the newly discovered picture of *Flatford Lock from the Mill House* (no.16), which shares the same dimensions as *Boat-Building*, albeit turned on its side, and also has a similar level of finish, was probably painted that same season, and might even have been submitted by Constable to the Academy exhibition the following year as well. In the summer of 1815, Constable continued to paint small – and now small- to medium-scale – pictures in the open air, helped once again by the fine weather, for on 27 August we find him writing to Maria that 'I live wholly in the feilds [*sic*] and see nobody but the harvest men' (JCC II, p.149). Indeed, *The Wheatfield* (fig.53), one of the pictures he painted that season, on the small- to medium-scale, non-standard format of 21 × 30 inches (53 × 76cm), actually shows harvest men at work in the distance, together with a group of women gleaning a few remaining wheat sheaves in the foreground. It received reasonably favourable reviews when exhibited at the Royal Academy in 1816, and again at the British Institution in 1817, the critics by now being more or less agreed that Constable had improved in his powers of finishing. Ironically one critic even thought Constable had now moved from a former 'carelessness' of handling to 'the other extreme … the most laboured finish' (Ivy 1991, p.71).

If there was, it appeared, no pleasing the critics, Constable at least no longer needed to concern himself about a perceived lack of finish. What did surely now concern him, however, was how to retain this level of detail when working on a larger scale, the very problem that had defeated him two years earlier with *The Ferry* (no.15). Towards the end of 1815, his confidence apparently now restored, Constable seems to have started work on a much larger Suffolk landscape, as he twice referred to such a work in letters written to Maria from East Bergholt in October and November that year. In one of them he tells her that he has 'put rather a larger landscape on hand than ever I did before' (JCC II, pp.156, 159). Constable's largest landscapes to date were a Lake District subject painted in 1809, whose whereabouts is today unknown, measuring some five feet (1.52m) wide (see p.20); and two, slightly smaller 'half-length' landscapes exhibited in 1813 and 1814 – the latter being

The Ferry – measuring fifty inches (1.27m) in their greater dimension. If the new canvas to which Constable referred in 1815 really was his largest landscape so far, then it might well have been the view of *Dedham from Gun Hill* that he started on a canvas measuring six feet wide, and which today lies under the sketch for *The White Horse* (fig.21, p.45). If so, this would mean that Constable's first attempt at a six-footer dates from as early as 1815.

Having abandoned, or temporarily put aside, this larger landscape, in the summer of 1816 Constable now attempted another one, *Flatford Mill* (no.19), on a more familiar but still substantial scale, the 40 × 50-inch 'half-length' format he had previously used for *The Ferry*, albeit with the canvas now turned on its side. Aware that he could again paint a substantial part of this picture on the spot in Suffolk that summer, but perhaps concerned that the perspective might go awry now that he was working on a significantly larger scale in the open air, Constable appears to have tried something new. He prepared, or turned to an existing, pencil tracing showing Flatford Mill from the towpath, then squared the tracing in preparation for transferring the composition on to a larger 'half-length' canvas (see nos.18, 19). Constable would surely have done the transfer, and other preparatory work on the painting, in the studio, perhaps even in his East Bergholt studio that very summer. However we can be confident that much of the rest of the picture, especially its detail, was painted on the spot in East Bergholt, as we know that Constable, having waited some seven long years to marry Maria, now lingered there on the eve of his wedding. For he was keen to ensure that *Flatford Mill*, which he wanted to send to the Academy the following spring, was, in Maria's words, 'sufficiently forward' (JCC II, p.205).

One of the chief difficulties Constable had encountered during his long courtship of Maria Bicknell was the objection of her grandfather, the rector of East Bergholt, Durand Rhudde. The rector may have felt that a struggling landscape artist would be unlikely to provide adequately for his granddaughter.

He may also have thought that Constable came from an unsuitable family, that is to say a family that worked in trade rather than the professions. In February 1816 he was prompted to a particularly furious outburst of temper on discovering that Constable was still visiting Maria in London and, as ever at these difficult moments, there was an implied threat that he might disinherit her should the couple continue their relationship. This time, however, John and Maria resolved to marry regardless of opposition. Golding Constable's health was failing, and it was looking likely that Constable himself might come into

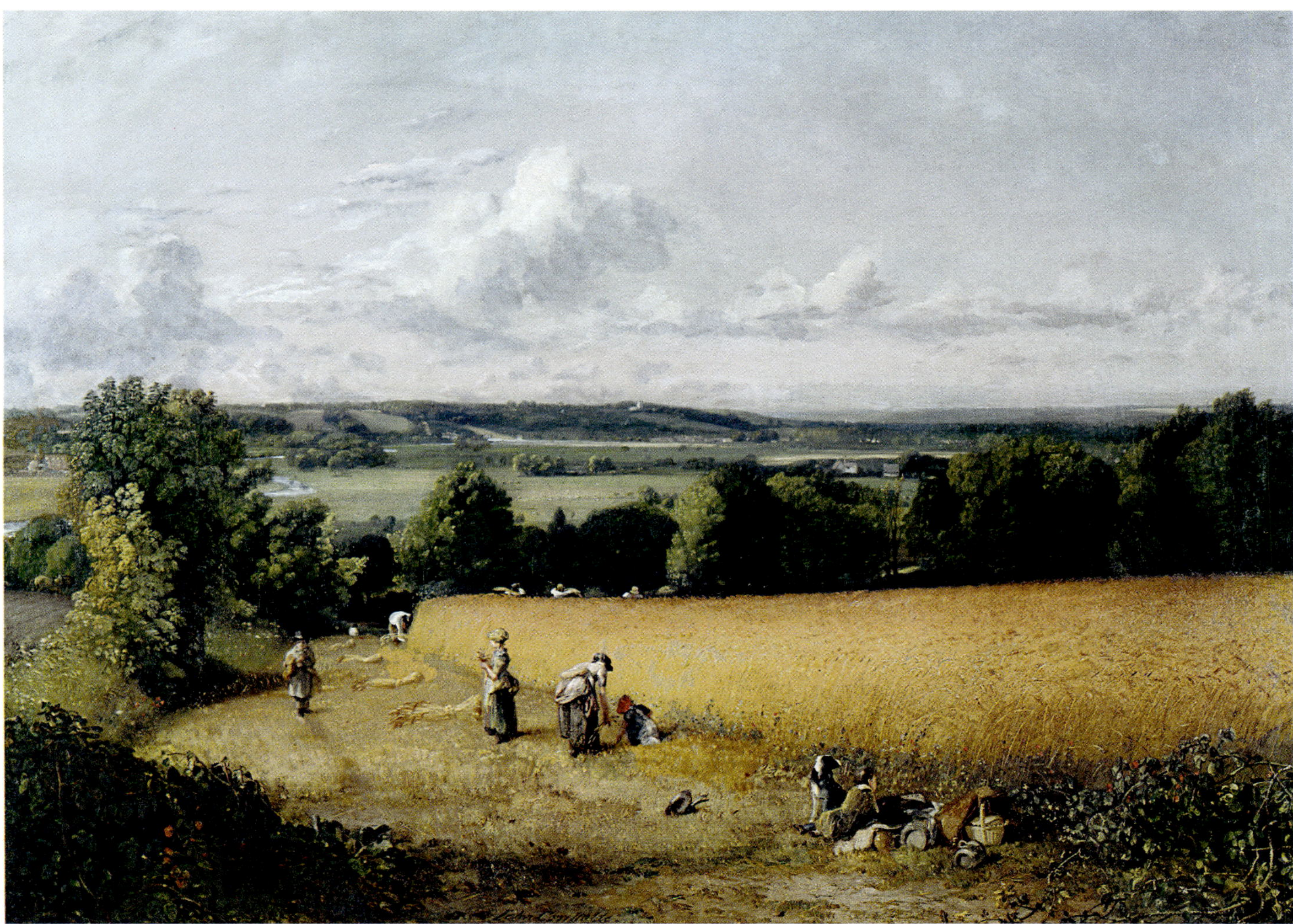

FIGURE 53

Figure 53
The Wheatfield
1815–16
Oil on canvas
53.7 × 72.2 (21⅛ × 28⅜)
ESTATE OF SIR EDWIN
A.G. MANTON

an inheritance in the near future.

When Golding Constable died around the middle of May, however, Constable seemed more anxious to make the best of the summer painting from nature than finally to tie the knot with Maria. For, as well as working on *Flatford Mill*, he also found time over the summer to fulfil a commission to paint two pictures for Major-General and Mrs Rebow of Wivenhoe Park in Essex, one of which was to be a view showing the house across the lake (no.17). Constable was in regular correspondence with Maria during the period he was busy on this commission, and in one of his letters tells her how well his painting of the park is progressing, adding that he thinks he

will in due course 'make a larger picture from what I am now about' (JCC II, p.199). Although no such larger version of the painting ever in fact materialised, assuming this is what Constable actually meant by his stated intention to Maria (see under no.17), it would appear that even in 1816 he had still not abandoned the idea of working up larger studio pictures from smaller *plein-air* ones.

The Rebows had known that the couple were anxious to marry and, as Constable put it in a letter to Maria, were keen to be of 'some service' to them (JCC II, p.196). Another friend anxious to help them out was Constable's friend the Revd John Fisher, now Prebendary of Sarum (Salisbury) who, having himself only very

recently married, now offered to perform the marriage ceremony for Constable and Maria. Following the nuptials at the church of St Martin-in-the-Fields in London in early October, the couple spent an extended honeymoon with John Fisher and his new wife Mary at their home on the coastline near Weymouth in Dorset, where Constable continued to paint, though not always necessarily to finish, pictures in the open air.

A favourite canvas size Constable was using at this time for painting pictures on the spot was the small- to medium-scale format of approximately 21 × 30 inches (53 × 76cm) that he had already employed the previous summer for *The Wheatfield* (fig.53, p.103). Whilst on honeymoon in Dorset that autumn, he used this format not only for a picture of the coast near Osmington, *Osmington and Weymouth Bays* (Museum of Fine Arts, Boston; R.16.81), but also for a view of *Weymouth Bay* (National Gallery, London; R.19.10), although the latter was to remain unfinished. Constable again employed this canvas size for a picture of *Dedham Lock and Mill*, which he probably started to paint during a three-month holiday in Suffolk with Maria in the summer of 1817 (no.23). However, like the *Weymouth* painting, the *Dedham Lock* picture was to remain unfinished, as indeed were two further open-air pictures of Suffolk subjects on different scales that Constable also embarked on that summer, *Fen Lane, East Bergholt* and *A Cornfield* (nos.20, 21).

The existence of these three unfinished pictures painted in Suffolk in 1817 tends to suggest that Constable was deliberately attempting to gather as much material as he could that summer, perhaps aware that this might be his last chance to paint extensively from his much-loved native scenes. He was now putting down firmer roots in London. Indeed, he and Maria had recently taken a new

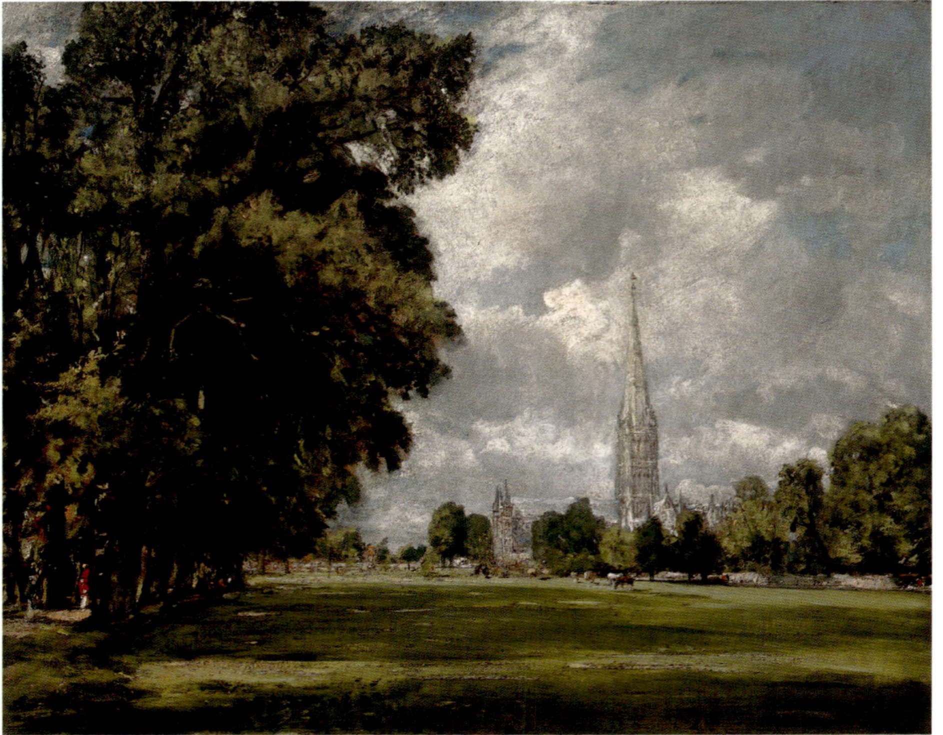

FIGURE 54

Figure 54
Salisbury Cathedral
from the South-West
1820
Oil on canvas
73 × 91 (28³/₄ × 35⁷/₈)
NATIONAL GALLERY OF
ART, WASHINGTON, ANDREW
W. MELLON COLLECTION

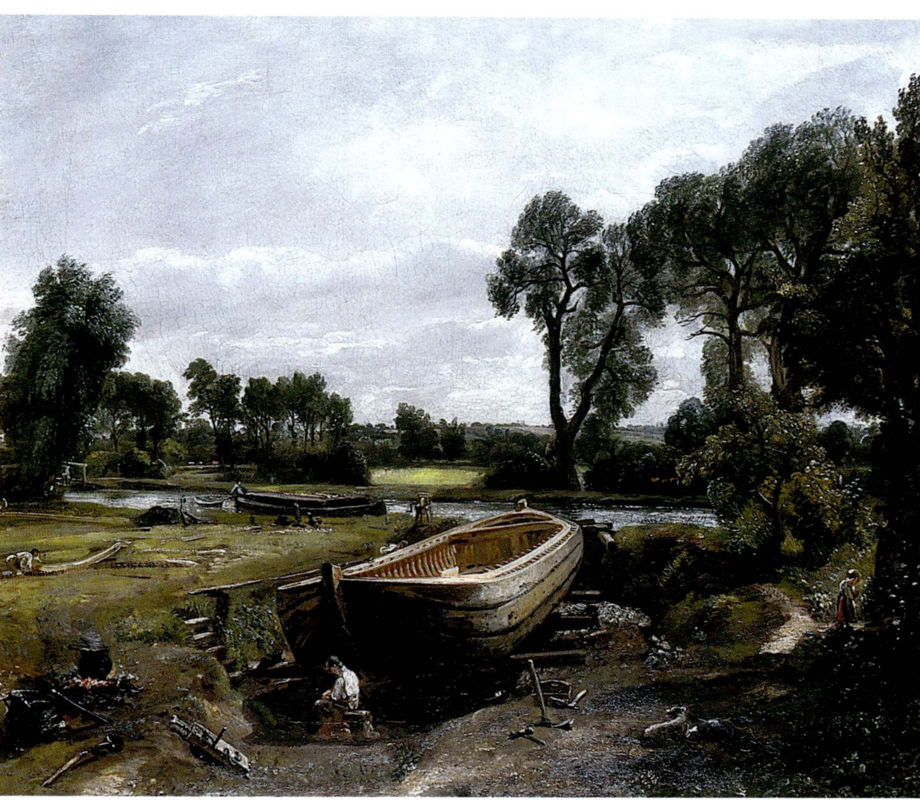

house in Keppel Street in Bloomsbury, and Maria was already expecting their first child. There was also the looming prospect that the family house in East Bergholt would soon have to be sold. All Constable needed to do, it would seem, was to take open-air pictures just far enough for him to be confident that he could then complete them later in his London studio (Parris 1991, p.37).

Unfinished, however, these late Suffolk pictures remained. By the autumn of 1817, newly settled in his house in Keppel Street, and probably using one of the upper rooms as a studio (see p.52), Constable began to radically rethink his methods. As far as his Suffolk landscapes were concerned, he could no longer create images that stemmed from direct observation. Instead, he began to bring his Suffolk material together in a more 'synthetic' way, especially as he was becoming ever more ambitious to project his ideas on a larger and grander scale.

In this context it would appear that one of Constable's unfinished Suffolk pictures from the summer of 1817 may well have played a pivotal role in suggesting to him a new

procedure. In the autumn of 1817 he selected the subject of Dedham Lock to work up for the Academy exhibition the following spring. However, rather than attempt to complete the version he had started on the spot earlier in the summer (no.23), he appears to have made an entirely fresh version on the slightly larger scale of a kit-kat canvas turned on its side, that is, approximately 28 × 36 inches (91.5 × 71cm; see nos.23, 24). He may even have directly transferred the core parts of the composition from the unfinished picture on to the new canvas. In all events he appears to have used an extant *plein-air* painting (no.23) as if it were a near same-scale composition sketch. This might well have suggested to him the idea of purposefully making a composition sketch the following year, in 1818, on the same scale as the next exhibition picture he intended to paint, *The White Horse* (nos.28, 29), even though that picture was now as large as six feet in width.

Constable did not cease painting outdoors after his permanent move to London. Until as late as about 1829 he continued to make oil sketches from nature in Salisbury, Hampstead and Brighton. He even worked on a few more open-air pictures in the early 1820s, in Salisbury (fig.54) and Hampstead (no.27), before finally abandoning the practice around 1822–3. However, from about 1820 his working methods saw a fundamental shift. His studies from nature now began to serve 'as a form of release and refreshment rather than as inspiration', and no longer so directly moulded and informed his studio paintings. If anything, indeed, the influence began to move in the opposite direction, and the more expressive stylistic methods that Constable evolved in the studio from the early 1820s gradually began to find echoes in later sketches and drawings made from the motif (Kitson 1976, p.747). AL

Figure 55
Boat-Building
1814–15
Oil on canvas
50.8 × 61.9 (20 × 24³⁄₈)
VICTORIA AND ALBERT
MUSEUM, LONDON

Flatford Lock

It was in February 1814 that Constable declared to Dunthorne that, in order to improve his 'finishing', he would thenceforward attempt to complete small pictures entirely on the spot. In the earlier years of this campaign, that is to say between about 1814 and 1816, these *plein-air* pictures appear to have measured no more than about 21 × 30 inches (53 × 76cm), and were often as small as 20 × 24 inches (51 × 61cm), the modest portrait-size canvas known as a 'head' that he used for *Boat-Building* (fig.55, p.105).

Flatford Mill from the Mill House, a newly discovered oil by Constable showing the lock at Flatford, shares the same dimensions as *Boat-Building*, and is likely to have been painted in the same year, 1814. The two pictures share a similar level of finish. They also both show the same little girl dressed in red, white and blue that Constable was later to include, in an almost identical pose to the one she strikes in *Flatford Lock*, leaning over a timber parapet close to the water's edge, in his large canvas of *Stratford Mill* (no.31). Furthermore, the foliage of the trees in both works has a similar delicate, feathery appearance that is reminiscent of the work of Claude Lorraine, indicating that Constable had indeed been heeding Farington's recent advice to look long and hard at pictures by Claude and to 'attend to the admirable manner in which all parts of His pictures are completed' (Farington XIII, p.4564). The trees on the far right of no.16 are the same cluster as those that appear in the distance of *Boat-Building* (fig.55), as well as in the foreground of *Flatford Mill* (nos.18, 19). It is only recently that they have been correctly identified by Richard Mabey as black poplars (*Populus nigra*, or water poplars; see Mabey 1996, pp.133–5).

The exact viewpoint in *Flatford Lock*, looking towards the head of the lock at Flatford from a point immediately adjacent to the Mill House, can more readily be appreciated by comparison with the view of the mill and lock seen from the opposite direction that Constable exhibited at the Royal Academy two years before (no.14). Both pictures include the curious construction, clearly visible in the left foreground of no.16, though just a tiny detail in the left-hand distance of no.14, resembling a square well-head with a bell on a chain suspended above. It has been suggested by Anthony Battersby, a mill owner in Somerset in the West of England, that this construction may be connected with a system of self-levelling for locks mentioned on plans dating from 1795 for the proposed Somerset and Dorset Canal (which was never built). These plans describe a device for self-levelling that worked on a ball cock set in a chamber beside the lock. The construction to the left of no.16 may, therefore, be the chamber for such a device, in which case the device itself could well have been attached to a bell to let the miller know when the mechanism was active.

Given the level of finish in no.16, and that Constable's *Boat-Building*, a work on the same scale, was exhibited at the Royal Academy in 1815, one might speculate as to whether no.16 was submitted by him for exhibition that year as well. This is entirely possible, as three oils shown by him at the Academy exhibition in 1815 remain unidentified (see 'List of Constable's Exhibited Works' in Tate 1991, p.39). However, we know from Farington that in November 1814, Constable's uncle David Pike Watts, until this time highly critical of his nephew's work for its 'slight of *Finish*' (JCC IV, p.38), was now sufficiently impressed by Constable's recent 'painted studies … being *more finished*' that he 'bespoke one of them' for himself (Farington XIII, p.4606). Watts might well have been tempted to acquire no.16, having shown interest in another of Constable's oils of Flatford Lock the previous year (JCC IV, p.37).

If no.16 was the work that Watts 'bespoke', then one must assume that it passed back into Constable's possession after his uncle's death in 1816, as the artist would surely have had it close to hand in 1820 when transcribing the detail of the little girl leaning over the timber parapet in *Stratford Mill*. If no.16 was still in Constable's possession in the mid-1820s, one might also imagine that it might have inspired him to adopt an upright format for the much grander, more famous version of this subject, *The Lock* (no.41), which formed part of his remarkable series of large canal scenes painted between 1819 and 1825. AL

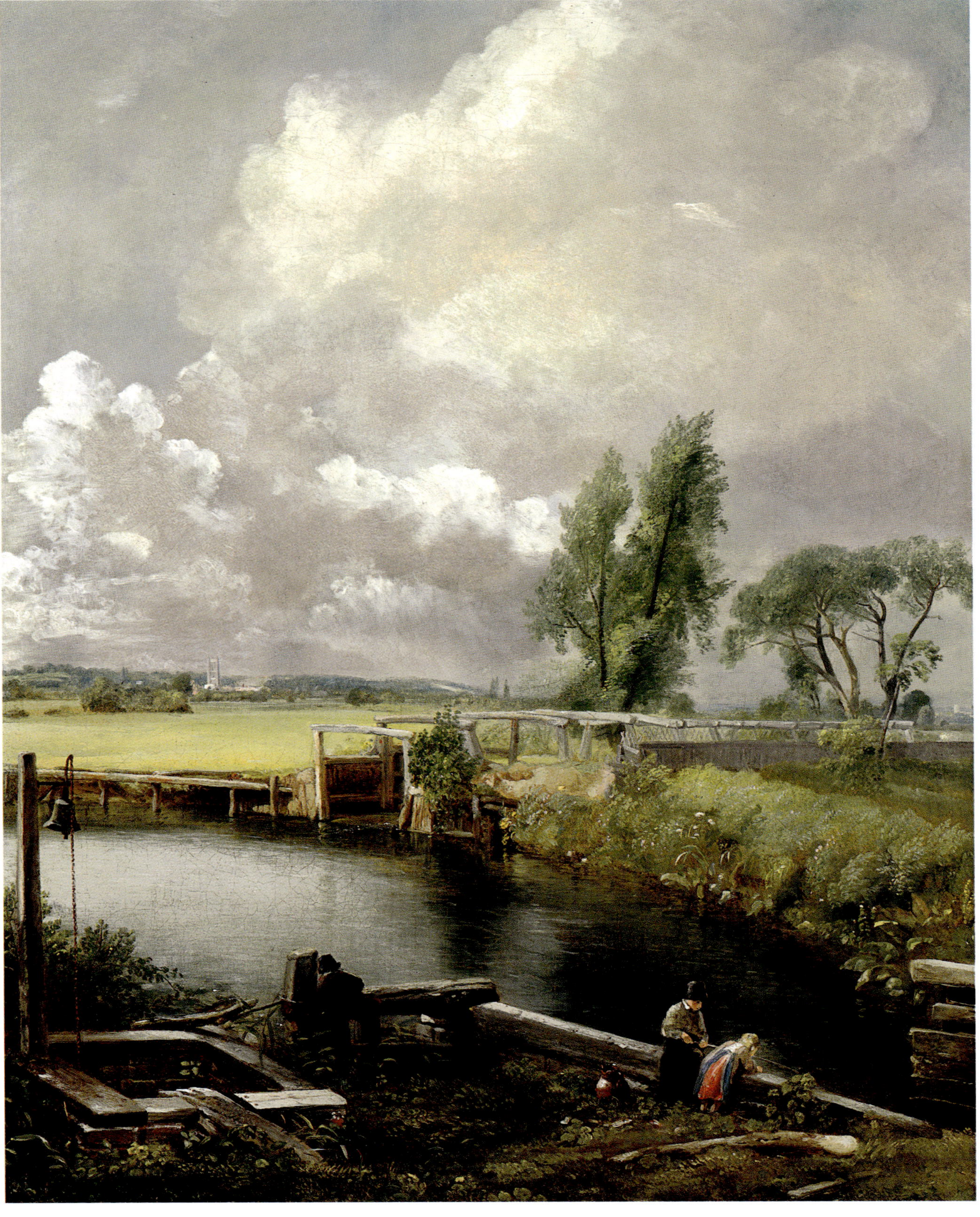

16

**Flatford Lock
from the Mill House**
c.1814
Oil on canvas 61 × 50.8 (24 × 20)
[not in Reynolds]
PRIVATE COLLECTION

Wivenhoe Park

Painted during late August and early September 1816, *Wivenhoe Park* masterfully demonstrates how accomplished Constable had become in painting pictures out of doors within a period of only two years. He received a commission from Major-General Francis Rebow, the owner of the house depicted here and a long-time family friend, for two landscapes, 'one in the park of the house & a beautifull wood and peice [*sic*] of water [i.e. no.17], and another scene in a wood with a beautifull little fishing house' (Constable to Maria Bicknell, 21 Aug. 1816, JCC II, p.196; the second picture, *The Quarters, Alresford Hall*, now in the National Gallery of Victoria, Melbourne, is R.16.30). Various letters from Constable to his fiancée, Maria Bicknell, provide documentation of his work fulfilling the commission. 'They wish me to take my own time about them,' he wrote on 21 August, 'but he will pay me for them when I please, as he tells me he understands from old Driffeild that we may soon want a little ready money' (*ibid.*). On 30 August, a little more than a week into the work, Constable reported on his progress: 'I am going on very well with my pictures … the park is the most forward' (JCC II, p.199). He did, however, make note of an adjustment that would be required to complete the picture to the patron's satisfaction:

The great difficulty has been to get so much in as they wanted to make them acquainted with the scene. On my left is a grotto with some elms, at the head a peice [*sic*] of water – in the centre is the house over a beautifull wood and very far to the right is a deer house, which it was necessary to add, so that my view comprehended too many [distances]. But to day I have got over the difficulty, and begin to like it *myself*. I think however that I shall make a larger picture from what I am now about (*ibid.*).

As discussed in the introduction to this section, Constable's reference to a 'larger picture' may indicate he was contemplating working up a more sizeable studio version of the scene later. If so, he never seems to have done that; indeed, it would have perhaps been a bit odd for him to have chosen a commissioned view as a subject to repeat. Thus, it is worth considering that his words might simply refer to his actual solution to the problem of how to include all the necessary details, which was to increase the size of *Wivenhoe Park* by adding strips of canvas to both its left (4in/10.5cm) and right (3½in/9cm) sides. The addition at the left allowed for a more complete representation of the 'grotto with some elms', along with the charming inclusion of a detail showing the Rebows' daughter driving her donkey cart (another cow, along with an extension of the rail fence, fill in the space at the bottom of the composition). On the right, the added canvas necessitated continuing the surface of the lake, and Constable deftly bridged the transition between the two surfaces by including a fishing boat with two men hauling a net, in this way masterfully continuing the compositional rhythms that he had already established in his initial scheme for the picture (Cooke 1968, p.102).

Judging from both the visual evidence of the painting – which is, in all respects, one of the artist's most marvellously fresh, both in terms of conception and execution – and the information provided by Constable's letters, *Wivenhoe Park* was executed largely, if not entirely out of doors. As has been aptly observed by Michael Kitson: 'It is evident that painting in this manner came a good deal more easily to Constable than working in the studio from previously executed sketches' (Kitson 1991, p.560). At nearly 40 inches (1 m) in width, *Wivenhoe Park* seems to be the largest canvas Constable had yet attempted to execute *en plein air*, albeit, when started, it would have been close to one of the more standard canvas sizes he used for painting from nature, 21 × 30 inches (53.3 × 76.2cm). In a postscript to his letter of 30 August to Maria, he said, 'I live in the park, and Mrs. Rebow says I am very unsociable', which may be taken as evidence of just how much of the time at Wivenhoe he spent working on the picture.

Just how extensively Constable engaged in painting pictures out of doors during his early career, however, has long been debated. C.R. Leslie recorded of *Boat-Building* (fig.55, p.105) that it was a picture he had 'heard him [Constable] say he painted entirely in the open air' (Leslie 1951, p.49). However, recent technical examination has shown that there are a number of adjustments and refinements in the exhibited painting that were probably made in the studio (Cove in Tate 1991, pp.501, 512; also Paris 2002, pp.104, 120–1). In the case of *Wivenhoe Park*, the chronology established by Constable's letters does not conclusively establish whether or not studio work was involved in its creation. He returned from Wivenhoe to East Bergholt on 7 September and remained there until 17 September, and then returned to Wivenhoe for a further two days to finish the painting. It is thus conceivable he might have taken the picture with him to East Bergholt and had time to work on it. He might have worked on the picture at East Bergholt, but there are no easily discernible passages that seem significantly different in terms of finish and execution. Indeed, the consistency of Constable's brushwork agrees with what can be inferred from the accompanying documentation, namely that the canvas was entirely the product of the artist working on site. FK

17

Wivenhoe Park, Essex

1816

Oil on canvas 56.1 × 101.2 (22⅛ × 39⅞)
The canvas has been extended by a strip of
approximately 10.5cm (4⅛in) on the left and
a strip of approximately 9cm (3½in) on the
right. The original canvas would therefore
have measured about 22⅛ × 32¼ inches,
which is close to the small- to medium-sized
format of 21 × 30 inches that Constable
favoured for *plein-air* pictures, especially
when one allows for the fact that the strips
would probably have been joined to the
out- turned tacking edges at left and right.
Exh: RA 1817 (no.85, *Wivenhoe Park, Essex,
the Seat of Major-General Rebow*)
R.17.4
Ivy: 17.6–7
NATIONAL GALLERY OF ART, WASHINGTON,
WIDENER COLLECTION

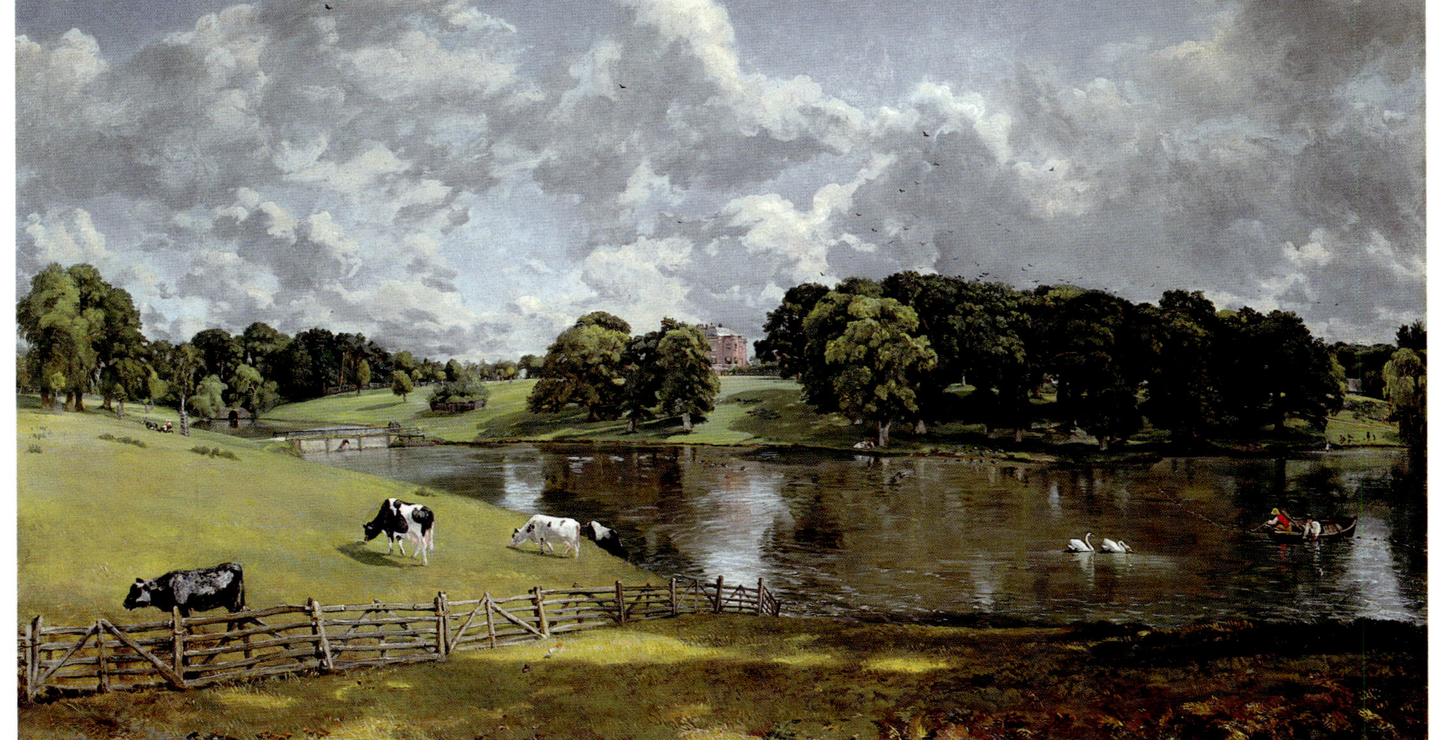

Flatford Mill

The Constable family business based at Flatford flourished under the direction of Golding Constable, the artist's father. Golding had inherited the tenancy of the Flatford corn mill from an uncle in the 1760s, and by 1785 was being described locally as a 'man of fortune … [who] lives in the style of a country squire' (cited Rosenthal 1983, p.8). The business continued to grow in the early years of the nineteenth century. Indeed, between 1806 and 1815, Napoleon's continental blockade forced Britain to depend almost entirely on its own food supplies, and trade in agricultural produce prospered as never before.

Corn ground at Flatford Mill was transported by barges along the canalised Stour to the port of Mistley for onward shipment to London, whilst returning barges brought coal and other cargoes upstream. In no.19, Constable shows a pair, or 'gang', of barges travelling upstream against the current. Having just made their way though Flatford Lock, they are now being disconnected from the tow-horse so that they can be poled under Flatford footbridge (the bridge itself is just out of the composition to the left, though one of its timbers appears in the foreground). Constable's previous representations of the mill had concentrated on more picturesque, close-up corners of the site, with relatively inactive figures in the foreground, usually engaged in fishing (see nos.11, 16). No.19, by contrast, is the first of Constable's paintings to concentrate on the working life of the river. In this respect, as well as in its substantial scale, it is the direct forerunner of the series of six-foot canvases of River Stour subjects that he began exhibiting in 1819 (see nos.28–47).

No.19 has been described as the largest, although not the last, of the pictures that Constable worked on outdoors in Suffolk, albeit it does seem to be his last completed one

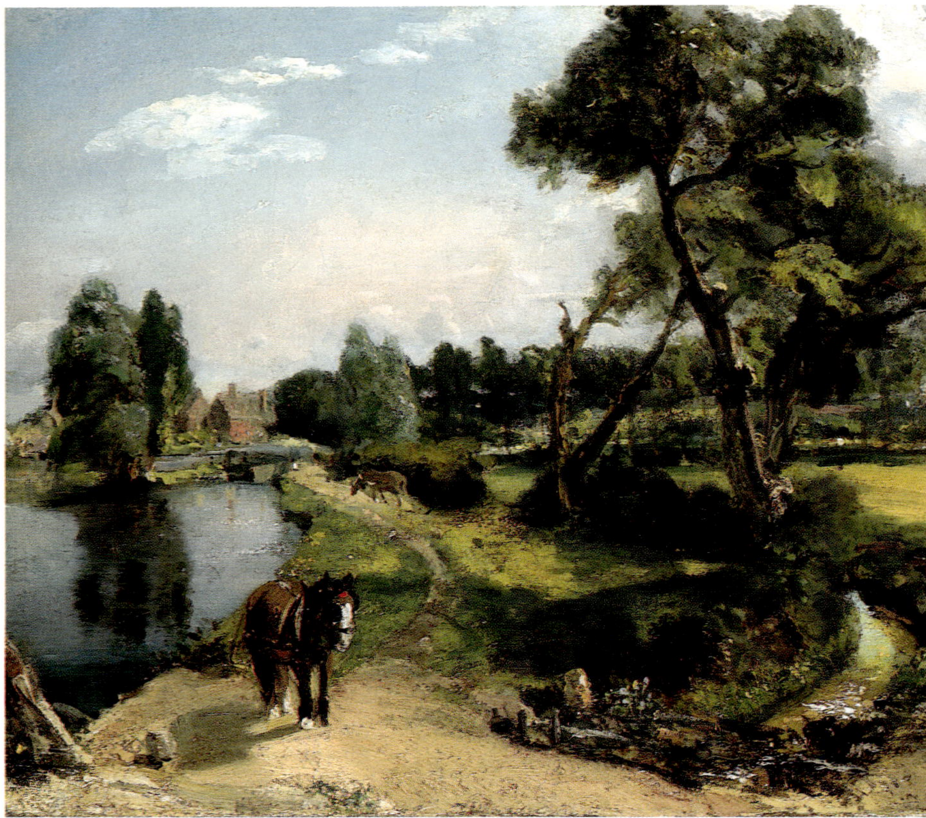

FIGURE 56

(compare nos.20, 21, 23). He made a number of drawings and oil sketches in the vicinity of the mill during the period from 1813 to 1815, before settling on his final viewpoint (Tate 1991, p.179). However, there are only two studies that relate directly to the final composition, and these are likely to date to c.1816. One is a recently authenticated oil study (fig.56; R.16.111), showing the tow-horse in a similar position in the foreground to that it occupies in the finished picture, as well as a second horse further down the towpath in the distance,

which we know from X-rays that Constable originally included in no.19 but then subsequently painted out (see Parris 1981, p.74). The other is a pencil tracing of the scene (no.18), which includes the two barges in the same position as they appear in the finished oil. This is also likely to have been made in the summer of 1816 in direct connection with the picture, and must certainly have been made some time after 14 August 1814 when Constable made another drawing of the same black poplar trees in the foreground, for the

Figure 56
Flatford Mill
c.1816
Oil on canvas
34.3 × 41.3 (13$\frac{1}{2}$ × 16$\frac{1}{4}$)
DAVID THOMSON

Figure 57
Flatford Mill from the Tow-path
1814
Pencil
10.8×8 (4¼×3⅛)
VICTORIA AND ALBERT MUSEUM,
LONDON

foremost tree in the latter (fig.57) bears a large branch that is missing in the tracing.

No.18, and a number of similar tracings by Constable, only came to light a few years ago. The intriguing method that Constable used to make them, said to derive from one described by Leonardo da Vinci in his *Treatise on Painting* (published posthumously in 1580), is described in a little-known contemporary manual on perspective:

The late Mr Constable … when … studying … in his native place … that he might not introduce too much foreground, and that he might sketch the view correctly … attached to the upper part of his easel a frame with a pane of glass in it; … to the four corners he attached four strings, which he brought to his mouth in such a manner as to bring the centre of the glass perpendicular *to his eye*. On this glass … he traced … the outline of his painting and of course his drawing must have been true

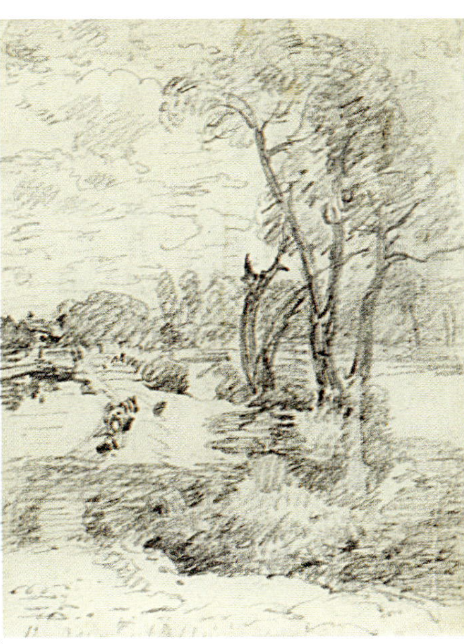

FIGURE 57

(Arthur Parsey, *The Science of Vision*, 1840; cited Fleming-Williams 1990, p.119).

Having traced the outlines of the scene directly on to the glass, probably with brush and printer's ink, Constable would then lay a sheet of paper on to the glass, and retrace the outline with pencil on the paper, probably holding both glass and paper up to the light. An off-print of the original ink tracing, in reverse, would be left on the back of the paper, probably because the ink was still wet (see Fleming-Williams 1990, pp.118–20).

Once Constable had decided he wanted to use this accurate record of the scene in the elaboration of his composition, he needed to transfer the design on to another surface, probably that of the final canvas itself. So he drew a squared grid over the tracing, and with this as a guide he would gradually have been able to work up the composition on a larger scale, section by section, in this way keeping the perspective accurate and also retaining the correct relationship between different elements in the landscape. Constable was often to use transfer grids or threads when elaborating the compositions for his later six-foot landscapes, either when enlarging them from smaller studies as here, or when transferring them from same-scale preparatory sketches (see pp.58–9).

This preparatory work for no.19, and no doubt some of the composition's 'lay-in' as well, would almost certainly have been done by Constable in the studio. However, a great deal of the rest of the picture must have been painted by him on the spot. We know this as, on 12 September 1816, Constable wrote to Maria informing her that he was anxious that the picture was not further advanced, for he was planning to exhibit it at the Academy the following year. Since Constable was now apparently prioritising his painting before

their long-delayed marriage plans, Maria replied to ask him, with more than a hint of sarcasm, whether there was a chance of the picture being 'sufficiently forward, to do without *your copy*', and by '*copy*' she clearly meant the scene itself (JCC II, p.205; Tate 1991, p.180). Of course it is true that painting outdoors on this sort of scale would not have been easy. However, it should be remembered that, in this respect, Constable enjoyed certain practical advantages over other, contemporary landscape painters. Since he was painting scenes associated with his father's milling and farming activities, usually on land owned and operated by his family, he could store his paints, brushes, canvases and easels nearby, either in the studio in East Bergholt that Golding had acquired for him in 1802, or else, no doubt, at his father's mills at Flatford or Dedham (see Cove in Tate 1991, p.510).

It was probably in his London studio over the winter of 1816 to 1817, however, that Constable added, for example, some of the figures in no.19 and the timberwork in the foreground, as well, perhaps, as painting out the distant horse on the towpath and substituting it with the figures of two boys. Before re-exhibiting the picture at the British Institution in January 1818, Constable worked on parts of the picture again, repainting the upper foliage of the black poplars as well as the entire sky (Southall 1982, pp.37–8; Tate 1991, p.181). Constable's practice of reworking details, or entire sections, of pictures after they had been sent to exhibition and were thus notionally 'finished', was something that recurred with increasing regularity in connection with his later large-scale canvases as well. AL

18

Study for 'Flatford Mill'
c.1814–16
Pencil tracing 25.5 × 31.2 (10 × 12¼)
R.16.105
TATE. PURCHASED 1988

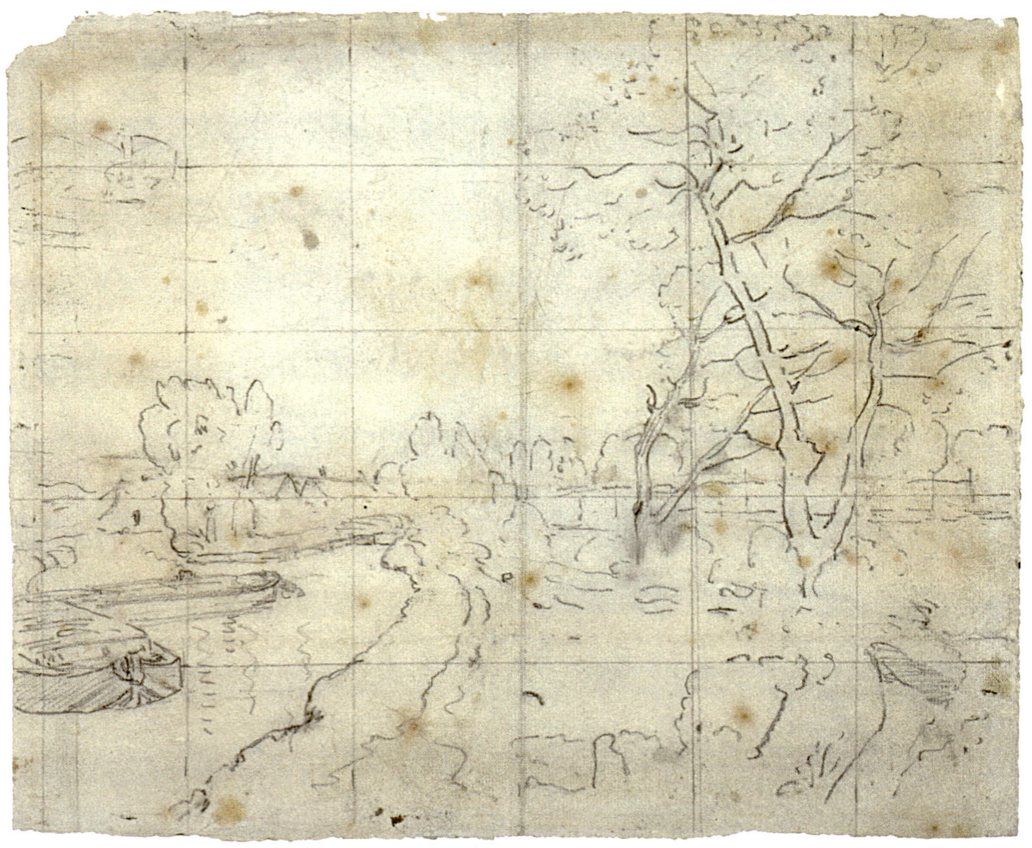

19

Flatford Mill ('Scene on a navigable river')
1817
Oil on canvas 101.7 × 127 (40 × 50)
Inscribed 'Jon Constable.f : 1817'
Exh: RA 1817 (no.255, *Scene on a navigable river*);
BI 1818 (no.91, *Scene on the Banks of a River*,
frame 58 × 68in)
R.17.1
Ivy: 17.6–7; 18.4–5

TATE. BEQUEATHED BY MISS ISABEL
CONSTABLE AS THE GIFT OF MARIA LOUISA,
ISABEL AND LIONEL BICKNELL CONSTABLE
1888

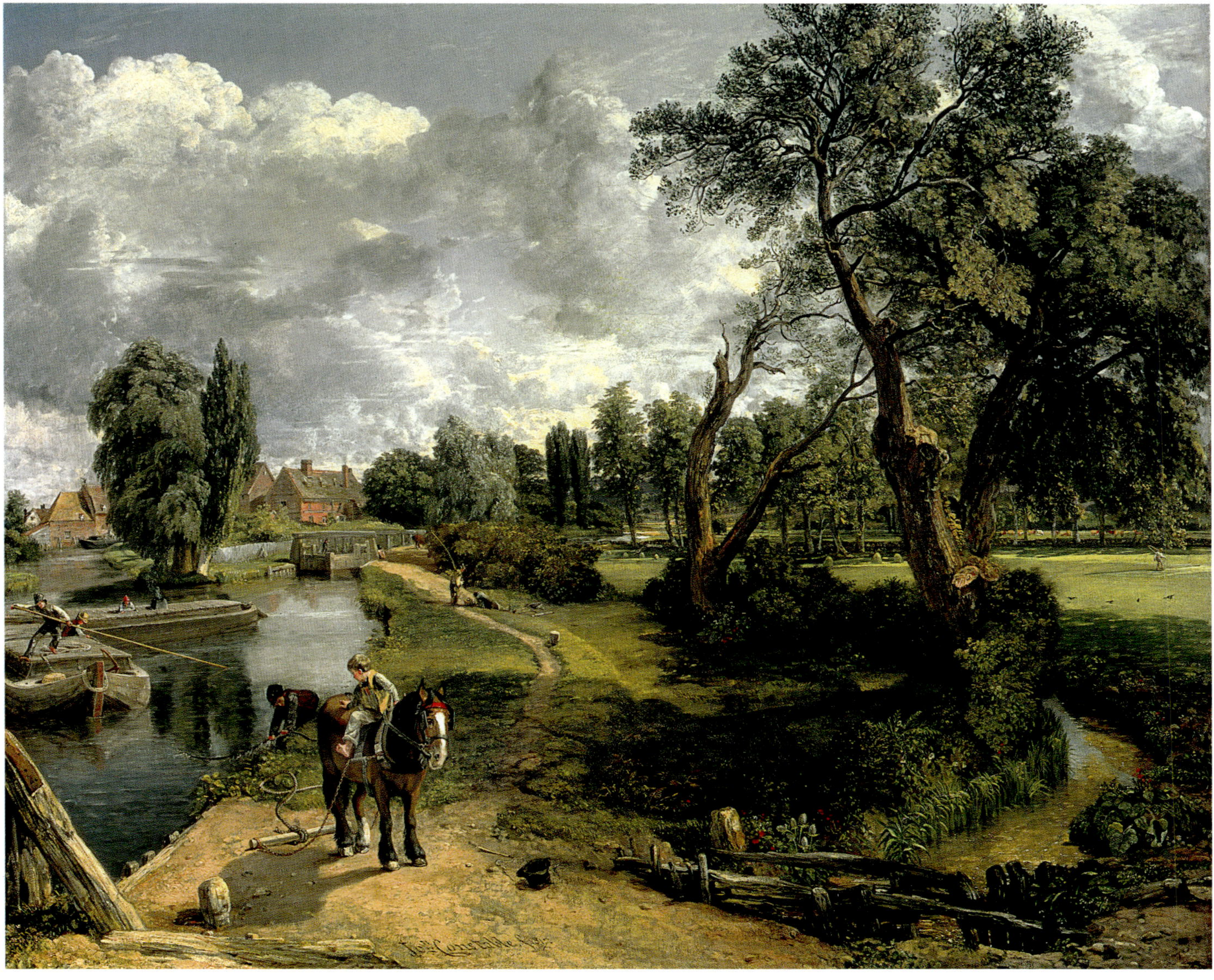

Fen Lane, East Bergholt

Following his marriage to Maria Bicknell in October 1816, Constable's life began increasingly to revolve around London. Nevertheless, in the summer of 1817, when Maria was already expecting their first child, the couple were able to spend a period of some three months together in East Bergholt. Constable profited from this long stay – the last, as it transpired, of his extended summers in Suffolk – by sketching extensively in the open air. On 11 November, Farington noted that 'Constable … had passed 10 weeks at Bergholt … and had painted many studies' (Farington XIV, p.5103).

A number of unfinished outdoor pictures have been associated with this visit to Suffolk, among them *Fen Lane, East Bergholt* (no.20), and also *A Cornfield* (no.21) and *Dedham Lock and Mill* (no.23). All three of these works, and in particular nos.20 and 21, combine areas of highly worked detail, especially in the middle and far distance, with much broader and sketchier passages. It has been plausibly suggested that, if Constable suspected that his 1817 holiday would be his last opportunity to gather a rich supply of Suffolk pictorial material, then leaving the works unfinished in this way, knowing he could complete them later in the studio, would have saved him valuable time (Tate 1991, pp.182, 185). It is also possible, however, that because in the end these works never were finished, they happen to supply us with an interesting record of the approximate point at which Constable might perhaps, as a more general habit, have suspended painting his 'open-air' pictures (with the possible exception of some of the earlier smaller pictures, such as *Wivenhoe Park*, no.17). Constable himself in later life is said to have told an acquaintance that he 'believed most artists sketched their subjects out-of-doors and finished them in; and that he could distinguish the parts of a picture which had been painted *al fresco* from those which had been elaborated in the studio' (Whitley 1930, p.329; cited Gage in Paris 2002, p.104).

As a boy, Constable used to take the route along Fen Lane when walking across the valley from East Bergholt to school in Dedham. *Fen Lane, East Bergholt*, therefore, with its lovingly painted five-bar gate marking the entrance to the lane, holds powerful biographical resonances. As pointed out recently by Ian St John (2002, p.27), and as is confirmed by a pencil study of the site made by Constable the same summer (fig.58), the tower of Dedham church would in reality be just out of sight at this point, hidden by the main cluster of trees just beyond the open gate. Constable perhaps included the tower in *Fen Lane* when working on the painting later in the studio, for pictorial and associative reasons. He was to take even greater liberties with the topography of Dedham church in one of his later six-foot landscapes (see no.47). AL

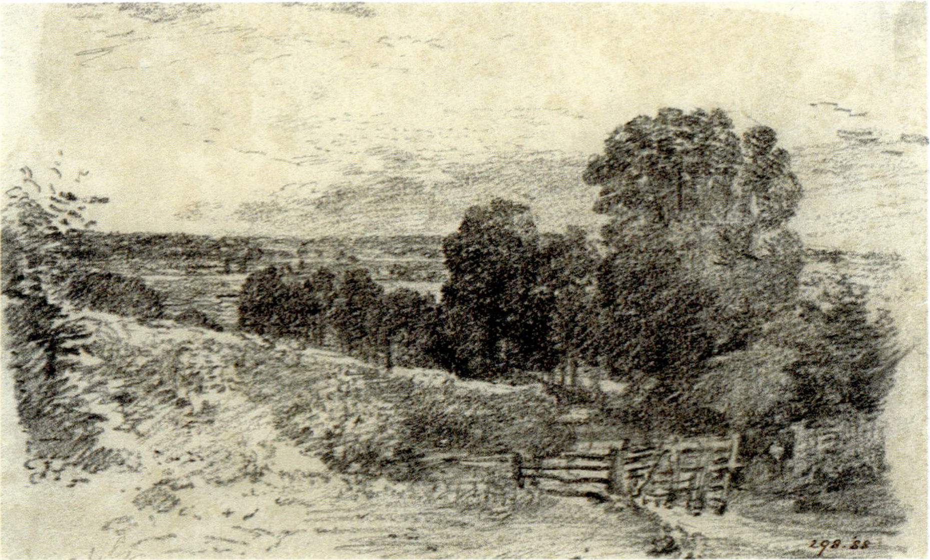

FIGURE 58

Figure 58
Fen Lane
1817
Pencil
11.4 × 18.7 (4½ × 7⅜)
VICTORIA AND ALBERT
MUSEUM, LONDON

20

Fen Lane, East Bergholt

c.1817

Oil on canvas 69.2 × 92.5 (27¼ × 36⅜)

R.16.107

TATE. PURCHASED WITH ASSISTANCE
FROM THE NATIONAL LOTTERY THROUGH
THE HERITAGE LOTTERY FUND AND
THE NATIONAL ART COLLECTIONS FUND
(WITH A CONTRIBUTION FROM THE
WOLFSON FOUNDATION), WITH ADDITIONAL
ASSISTANCE FROM SIR EDWIN AND LADY
MANTON AND TATE MEMBERS IN MEMORY
OF LESLIE PARRIS, DEPUTY KEEPER BRITISH
COLLECTION AND SENIOR RESEARCH
FELLOW COLLECTIONS DIVISION 1974–2000,
AND FROM THE BEQUEST OF ALICE COOPER
CREED, 2002

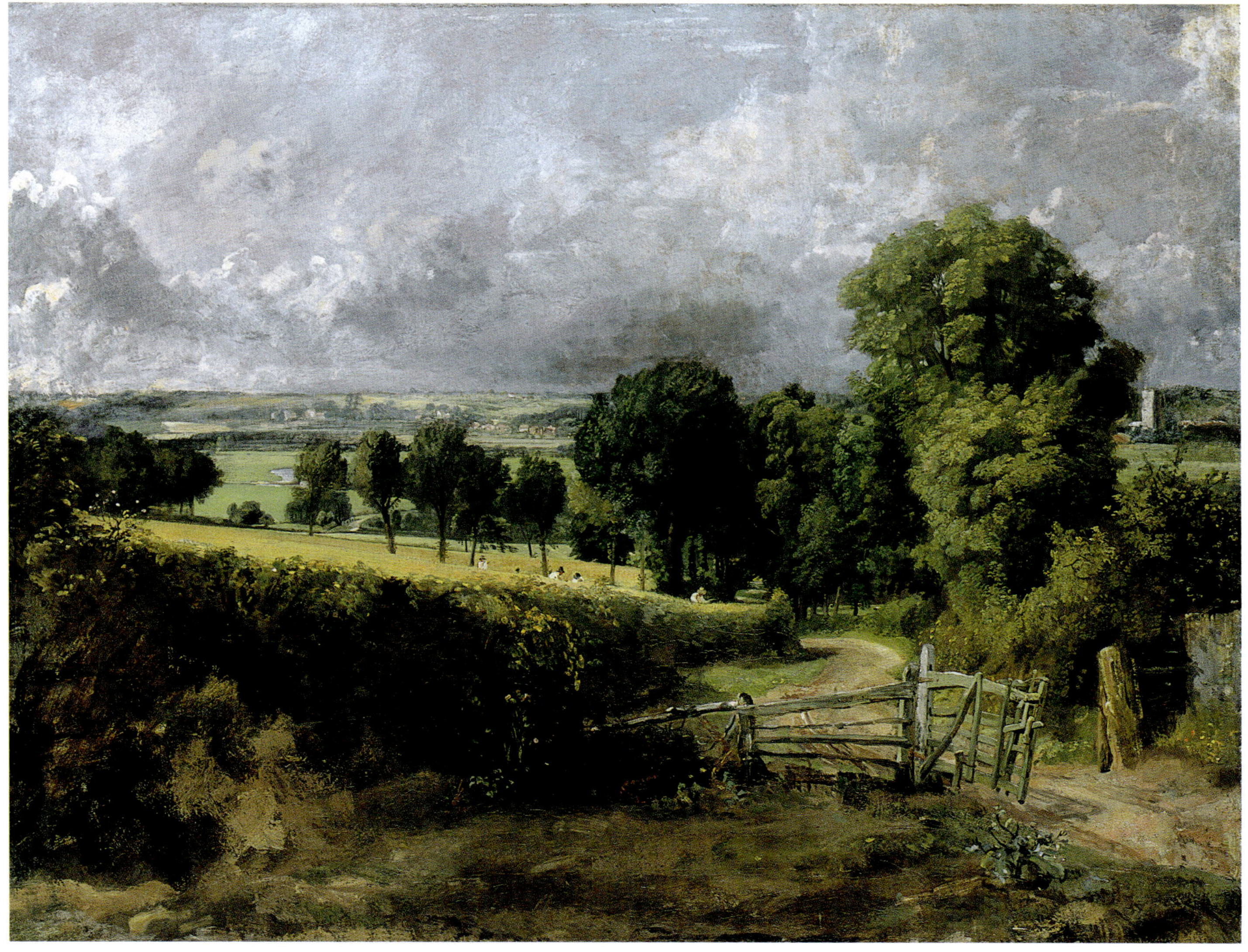

Cornfield

It is perhaps a measure of Constable's ability to select his outdoor material with such effective pictorial potential, that some of his unfinished outdoor Suffolk pictures from the period c.1816–17 have been incorrectly interpreted as later studio compositions.

It was only in 1991, for example, that *A Cornfield* (no.21) was first identified as a work belonging to Constable's Suffolk period, and probably datable to the summer of 1817, on the basis of comparison with other works such as *Fen Lane, East Bergholt* (no.20) and *Dedham Lock and Mill* (no.23), which share the same combination of detail and breadth (see Tate 1991, p.299). Although this interpretation has not been universally accepted (see, for example, Egerton 1998, p.53), the evidence in its favour now seems overwhelming, especially when one bears in mind that the canvas size for *A Cornfield*, approximately 24 × 20 inches (51 × 61cm), was one that Constable especially favoured for outdoor pictures at this time (see *Boat-Building*, fig.55, p.105, and *Flatford Lock from the Mill House*, no.16).

The confusion arises partly, it seems, because Constable certainly did use *A Cornfield* when working on one of the most famous of all his mature Suffolk landscapes, *The Cornfield* (fig.59, R.26.1), a picture he exhibited at the Royal Academy in 1826. *The Cornfield*, however, was produced under particularly pressing circumstances. As late as October 1825, Constable was still hoping to exhibit at the Academy the following spring a large canvas showing *The Opening of Waterloo Bridge* (see nos.63–7). After his progress on the latter was hampered by work on other commissions, by mid-January he found himself in need of a new subject. So he turned to existing studies in stock, and in *A Cornfield* found what has been described as 'a composition almost ready-made, a vista framed by a Claudean balance of unequal masses' (Tate 1991, p.301). Its inherent pictorial possibilities meant that, being so short of time, Constable could manage without having to paint a specific, same-size composition sketch, which by this date

he was generally accustomed to do (see nos.28–47).

Meanwhile, to achieve a finer balance with the larger tree mass at the left, it was probably at this later date that Constable overpainted the tops of the trees to the right of *A Cornfield*, a revision that corresponds closely with the finished picture. In other words, Constable used this work, an abandoned *plein-air* picture of c.1817, as if it were in effect a composition sketch. All he then needed was something to add to the composition by way of narrative detail, and in another earlier *plein-air* sketch, *A Lane near Flatford* (no.6), he found the idea of a young boy bending down to slake his thirst. As incorporated into the finished picture, this figure is often read as one with powerful biographical overtones, an interpretation that is not entirely fanciful when one remembers that both *A Cornfield* and *A Lane near Flatford* almost certainly show Fen Lane, the path Constable used to walk as a young boy to school in Dedham (see also *Fen Lane, East Bergholt*, no.20). AL

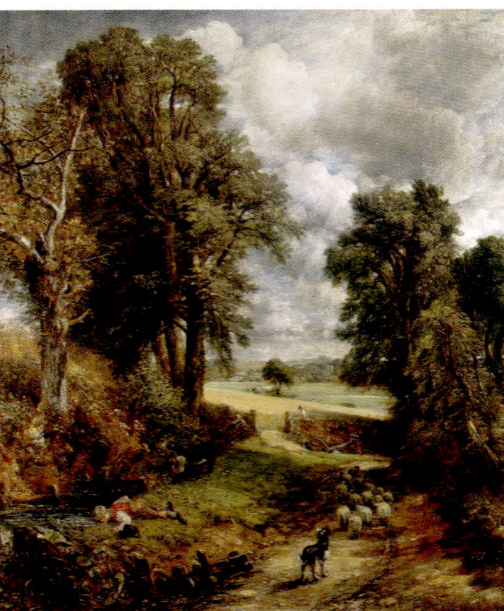

FIGURE 59

Figure 59
The Cornfield
1826
Oil on canvas
143 × 122 (56¼ × 48)
THE NATIONAL GALLERY,
LONDON

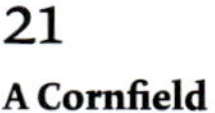

21

A Cornfield

c.1817
Oil on canvas 61.3 × 51 (24⅛ × 20⅛)
R.26.2

TATE. ACCEPTED BY HM GOVERNMENT
IN LIEU OF INHERITANCE TAX AND
ALLOCATED TO TATE 2004

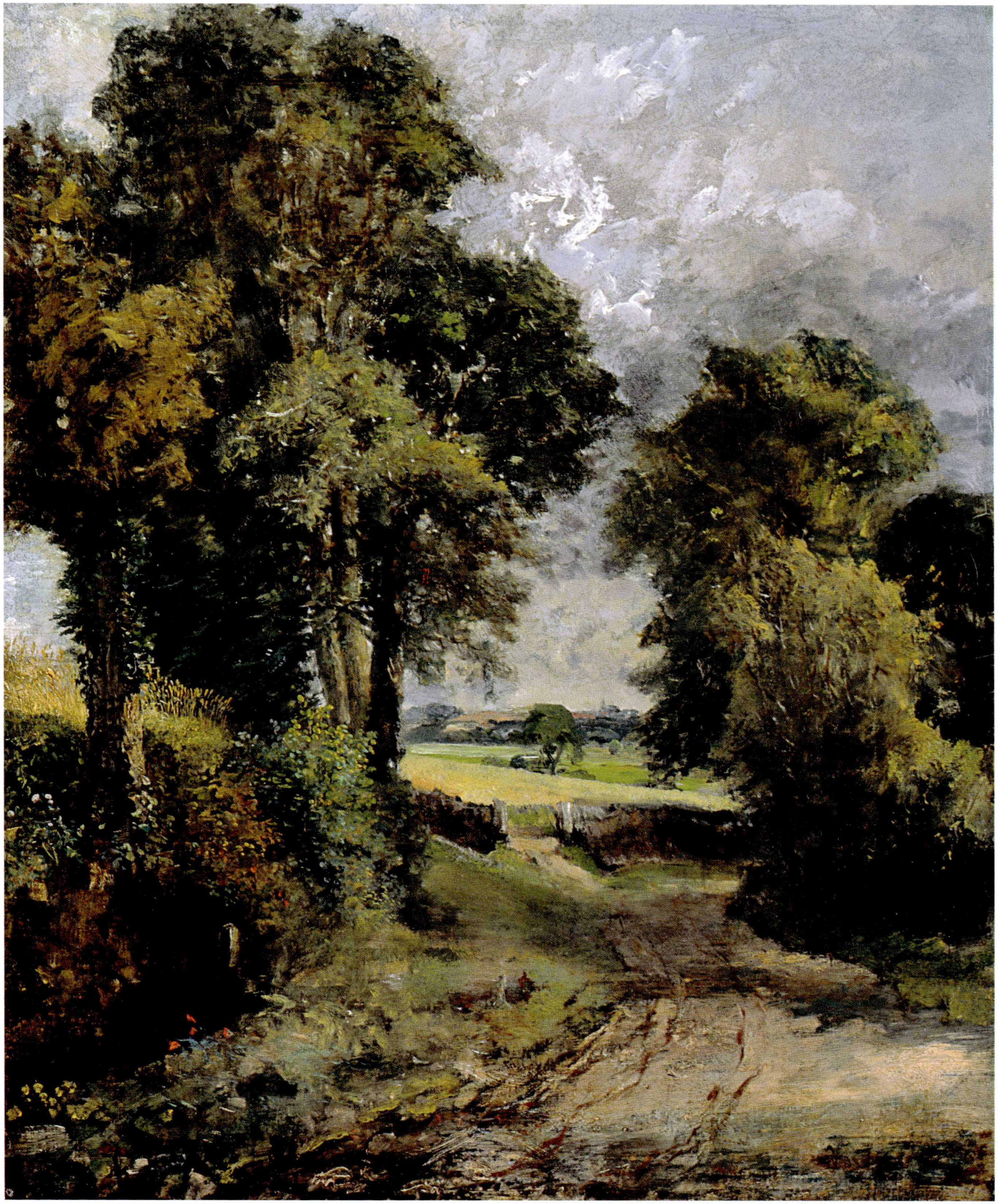

Dedham Lock and Mill

Dedham Mill, like that at Flatford, was owned and operated by Constable's father. However it was situated further upstream from Flatford on the River Stour, and Constable only began to take much notice of it in the summer of 1816 when he made some sketches of the mill in pencil and oil (Private Collection, R.16.4; Victoria and Albert Museum, London, R.16.108). It may have been the death of his father the previous May that had prompted him to turn to a subject that, like the view of the mill at Flatford he painted in 1816 (no.19), was one he closely identified with Golding Constable's memory. However, Constable was hampered by the poor weather from making any serious progress on a Dedham Mill subject that summer; 'you must lament this rain very much', Maria wrote to him on 20 July; 'there can be no going on with Dedham' (JCC II, p.188). Constable returned to the site the following summer and, in no.22, a page from a sketchbook datable to 1817, he explored a viewpoint similar to those he had tried out the previous year.

No.23, meanwhile, is a study in oils of the same subject, which closely resembles *Fen Lane, East Bergholt* (no.20) and *A Cornfield* (no.21) in its handling – combining breadth with detailed finish – and seems similarly to be an unfinished *plein-air* picture. Indeed, like them, it may well have been made in the summer of 1817, for it follows almost exactly the viewpoint that Constable first explored in the preliminary

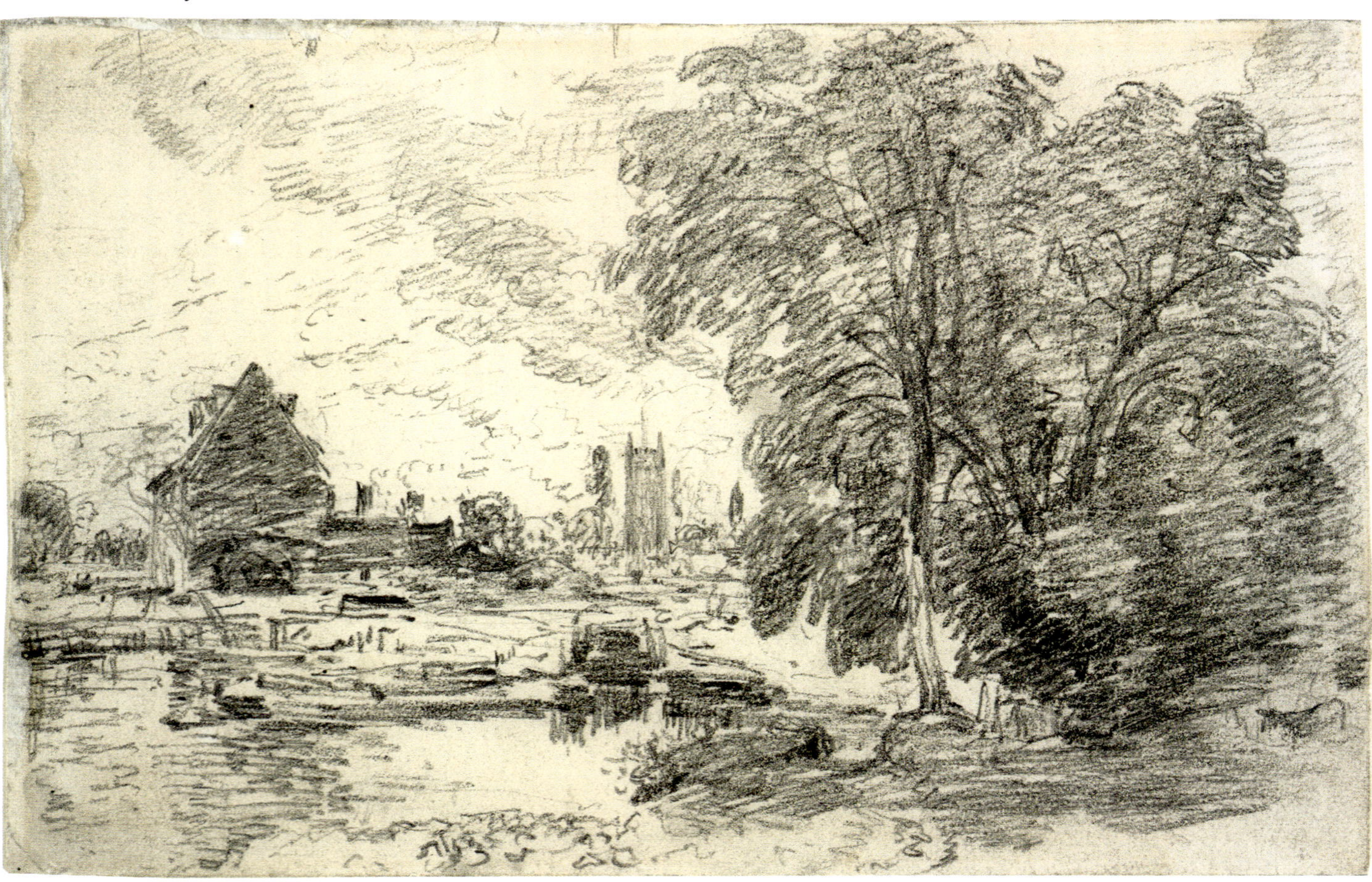

22

Dedham Lock and Mill
1817
Pencil on paper
11.6 × 18.6 (4½ × 7¼)
R.17.25
THE HUNTINGTON
LIBRARY, ART
COLLECTIONS, AND
BOTANICAL GARDENS

pencil study (no.22), as if he had returned to the site with paint and canvas shortly after evaluating its picturesque potential in his sketchbook, just as he had done that summer with *Fen Lane* (no.20). The other possibility is that no.23 was actually made the previous year, and never finished owing to the poor weather. Certainly Constable's method of working in no.23, in which large areas of the foreground are left unpainted so that only the canvas priming is visible, is very close to the unfinished open-air *Weymouth Bay* painted on his honeymoon in Dorset in 1816 (National Gallery, London, R.19.10). Indeed both no. 23 and *Weymouth Bay* are painted on the small- to medium-sized canvas, measuring approximately 21 × 30 inches (53 × 76cm), that Constable especially favoured for outdoor work (see also *The Wheatfield*, fig.53, p.103).

Although no.23 was never finished, Constable was later to rely on it when working up no less than three different versions of the subject in his London studio over the next three or four years. No.24 is the prime version of the picture, measuring approximately 28 × 36 inches (71 × 91.5cm), a kit-kat canvas turned on its side, and almost certainly the painting Constable exhibited at the Royal Academy in 1818 as *Landscape: Breaking up of a shower* (see Fleming-Williams 1990, p.133; Ivy 1991, p.79). No.25 is a second, signed version, this time on an identical scale to no.23, in which Constable has introduced a boat into the left-hand foreground. Then there is a third, the latest of the versions, signed and dated 1820 and very close to no.25, as well as being on the same scale. This was subsequently acquired by the nineteenth-century collector John Sheepshanks, and is now in the Victoria and Albert Museum in London (R.20.10; for a fuller discussion of all three versions, see Tate 1991, pp.185–91).

It is clear, then, that no.23, apparently an abandoned *plein-air* picture, was subsequently used by Constable as if it were, in effect, a same-size (or, for no.24, a near same-size) composition sketch for the three variant versions of the subject. He may have transferred the design, without enlargement, to each of the three individual new canvases in turn, perhaps then adding extra elements of sky, earth, water or foliage to the outer edges of no.24 to allow for the slightly larger scale. Indeed given that no.24, the exhibition version, was elaborated by Constable in the studio during the winter of 1817 to 1818, it seems likely that the experience of working from an existing design on more or less the same scale as the intended finished picture may well have influenced his decision to adopt this procedure purposefully in future years for most subsequent – and larger – exhibition canvases, the first of these being *The White Horse* (nos.28, 29). AL

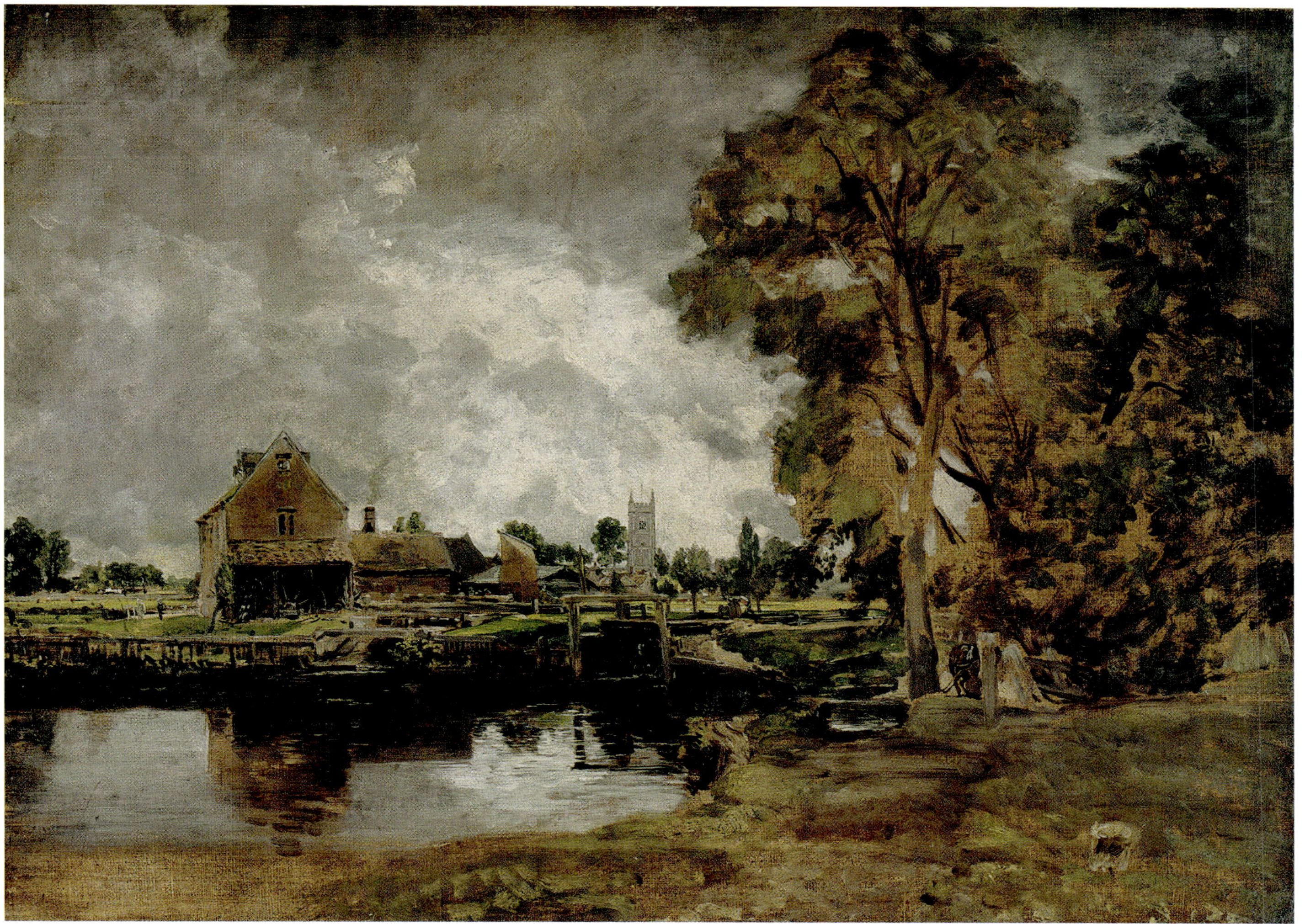

23

Dedham Lock and Mill
c.1816–17
Oil on canvas
54.6 × 76.5 (21½ × 30⅛)
R.20.13
TATE. BEQUEATHED
BY GEORGE SALTING 1910

24

Dedham Lock and Mill
c.1817–18
Oil on canvas
70 × 90.5 (27 ¹/₂ × 35 ⁵/₈)
Exh: ?RA 1818 (no.11, *Landscape:
Breaking up of a shower*);
BI 1819 (no.78, *A Mill*, frame 39 × 47in)
R.20.12
Ivy: ?18.10–12; 19.4–5, 19.7
DAVID THOMSON

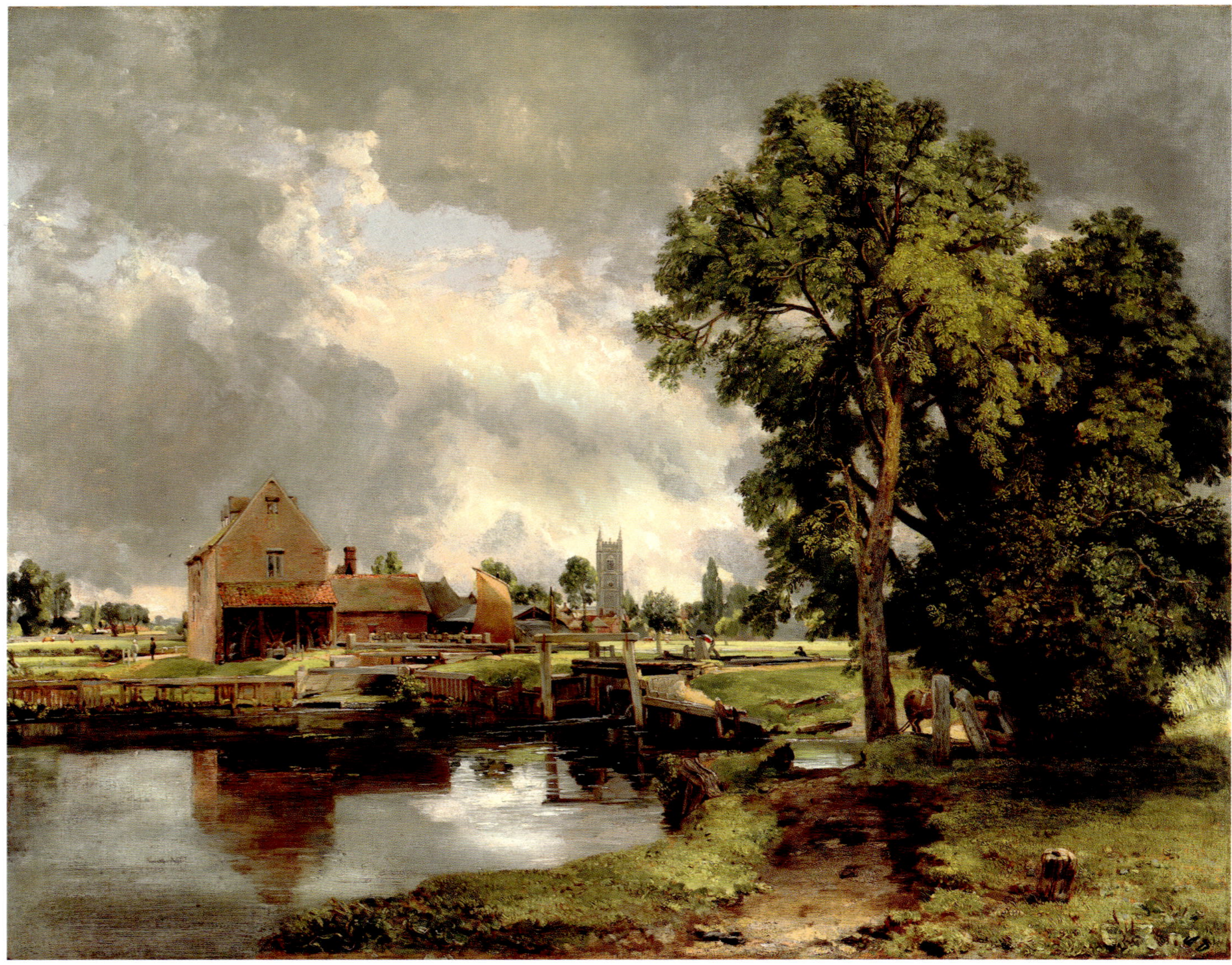

25

Dedham Lock and Mill

c.1818–20
Oil on canvas 54.6 × 77.5 (21½ × 30½)
R.20.11
Inscribed 'John Constable / London'
CURRIER GALLERY OF ART,
MANCHESTER, NEW HAMPSHIRE.
PURCHASE: CURRIER FUND

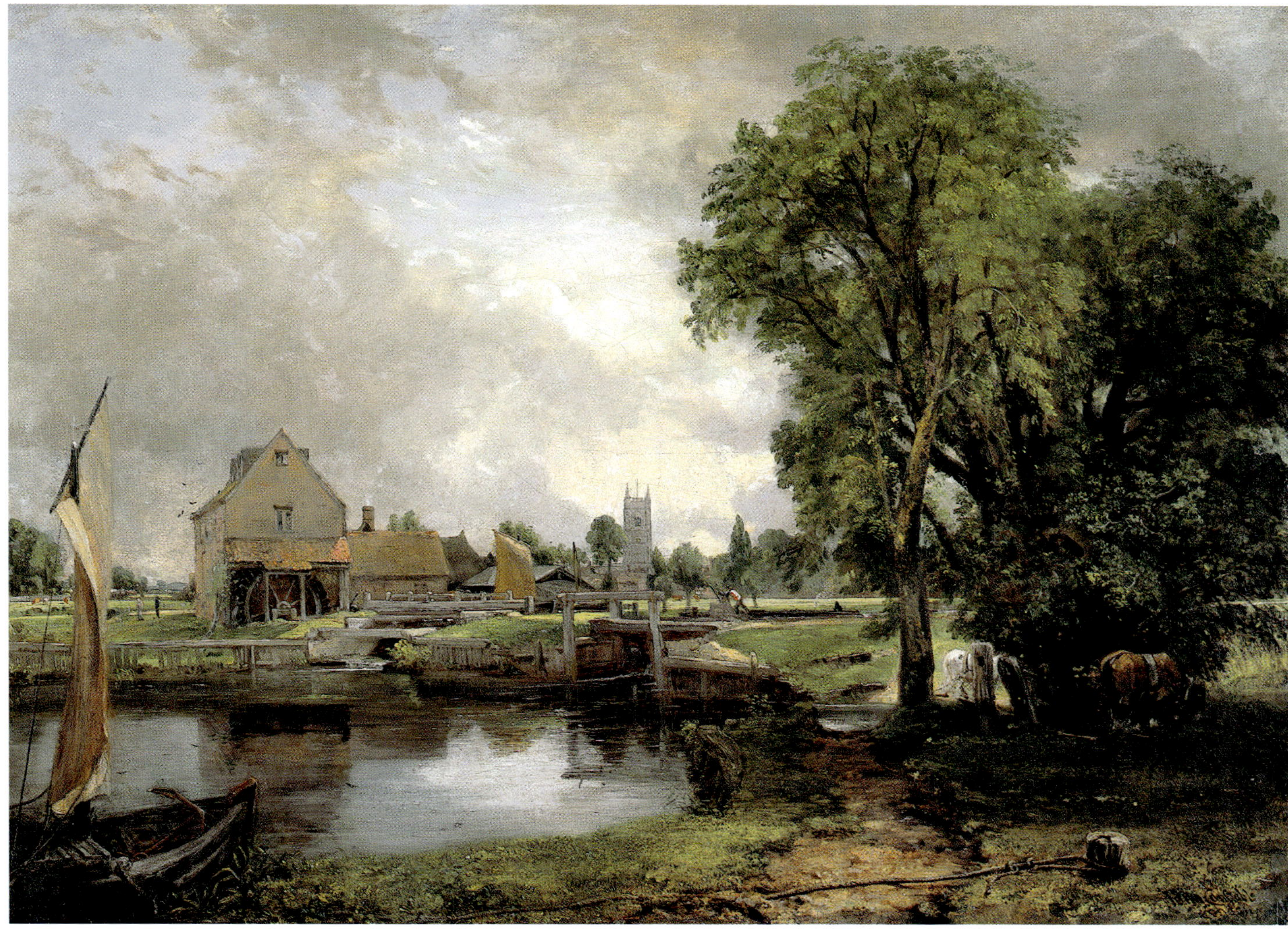

Maria Constable with Two of her Children

Until his marriage to Maria Bicknell in 1816, Constable lived in various lodgings in London, spending long periods of each summer in Suffolk sketching and painting from nature. Following his marriage, however, he rented a house for the first time. He and Maria were to spend the first five years of their married lives in a house in Keppel Street in Bloomsbury, a popular location for artists at that time, and it was there that the first three of their seven children were born. In addition to having a house in the 'West End' of London, from 1819 Constable also took a house most summers to the north of the city in Hampstead, then a small village in rural surroundings, so that Maria and the children could benefit from the cleaner air. The location soon began to play an important role in the development of his art (see no.27).

In this rapidly painted sketch, Maria is shown with two of their children, probably their eldest John Charles (born December 1817) and Maria Louisa ('Minna', born July 1819). It could have been made in their London house in Keppel Street or perhaps in one of the houses they took in Hampstead. Constable painted the sketch on the back of a panel that he had previously used for making a copy of a picture attributed to the seventeenth-century Dutch artist, David Teniers the Younger, which belonged to Sir George Beaumont (see Reynolds 1984, p.63). This suggests that he simply selected the nearest support he could find when wishing to record this tender moment.

On Maria's death in 1828, Constable was to write to his brother Golding that 'nothing [could] supply the loss of such a devoted – sensible – industrious – religious mother – who was all affection' (19 Dec. 1828; FDC 1975, p.81). Constable for his part proved an instinctive, loving father. Leslie recorded that his first child, John Charles, 'might be seen almost as often in his arms as in those of his nurse, or even his mother. His fondness for children exceeded, indeed, that of any man I ever knew' (Leslie 1951, p.71). One of the factors that would no doubt have influenced Constable in his decision to paint larger pictures from 1818 would have been the greater remuneration he hoped to receive in order to support his growing family. AL

26

**Maria Constable with
Two of her Children**
c.1820
Oil on mahogany panel
16.6 × 22.1 (6½ × 8¾)
R.20.86
TATE. PURCHASED 1984

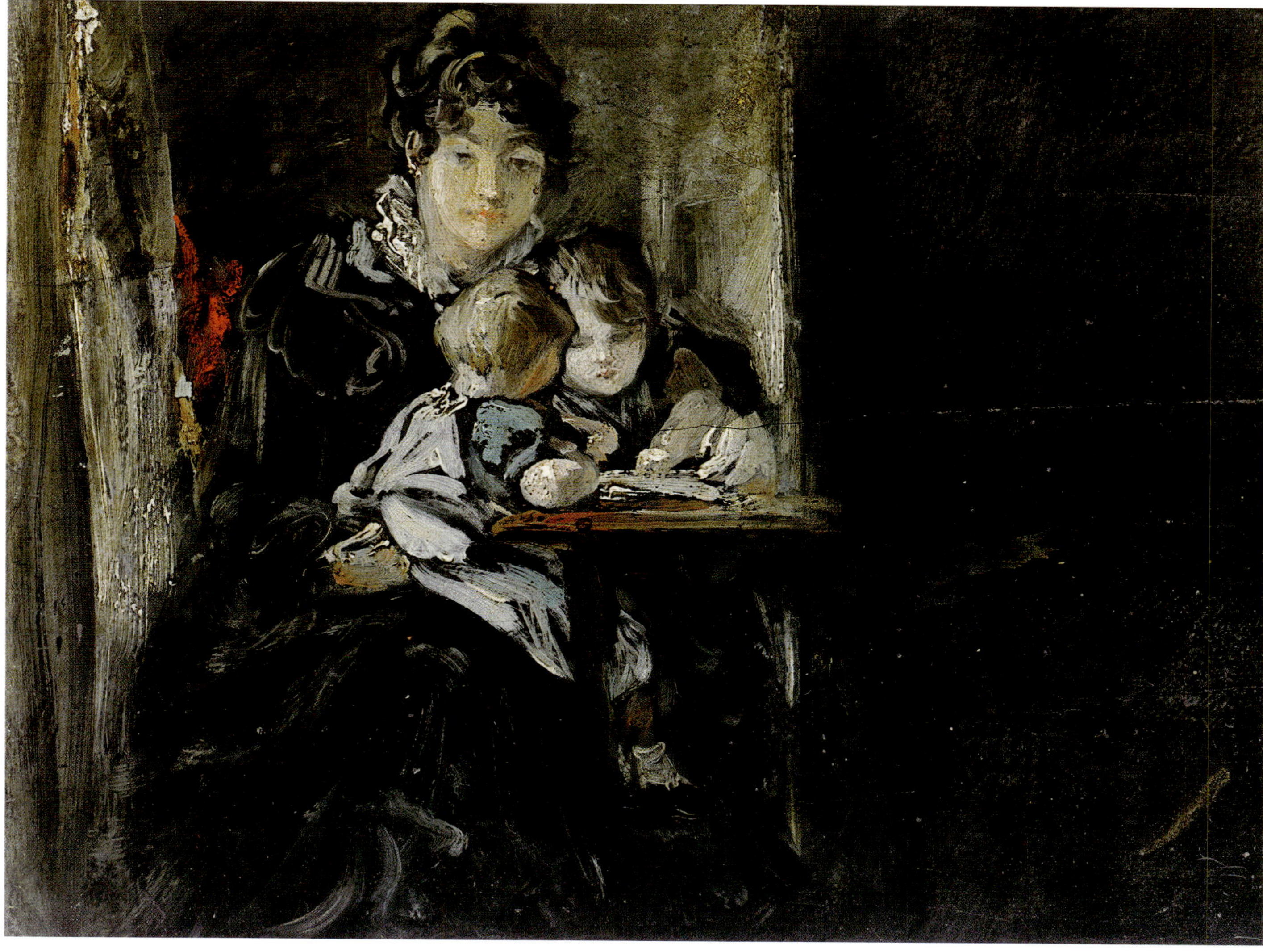

Hampstead Heath

With the exception of 1824, Constable took a house in Hampstead for his family every summer between 1819 and 1826. In 1827 he moved them there permanently, taking a lease on a house in Well Walk. Artists and writers had been settling in Hampstead for over a century. However, Constable decided to retain a studio in London, at first in or near Keppel Street and then, from 1822, at the house and gallery he moved to in Charlotte Street. As he told Fisher in 1826, it was an arrangement that enabled him to 'get always away from idle callers' in London, and 'above all [to] see nature – & unite a town & country life' (JCC VI, p.228).

Constable was greatly stimulated by the new scenery at Hampstead, particularly in the years around 1819 to 1822. He was especially attracted to Hampstead Heath, at this date still a working landscape used by sand-diggers and grazed by cattle, sheep and donkeys, though also partly inhabited by people taking their leisure. From the vantage point of the Heath, Constable could also enjoy the extensive views in all directions, especially those looking northwards or westwards across open countryside towards Harrow on the Hill, which is the viewpoint he has painted in *Hampstead Heath with the House called 'The Salt Box'* (no.27).

Indeed, the location of Hampstead seems to have been of particular importance for Constable in the period 1819 to 1822, in some ways perhaps serving as a substitute sketching ground for Suffolk and thus helping him to adapt to the idea of a permanent life in the metropolis. Certainly it has been convincingly argued that at Hampstead during these years, Constable continued to paint small and small-to medium-sized pictures partly in the open air (see Tate 1991, pp.215–17). *Hampstead Heath* has been proposed as such a work, as have two other, slightly larger pictures of the Heath (Fitzwilliam Museum, Cambridge, R.21.8; Victoria and Albert Museum, London, R.21.10), both of which are indeed painted in one of Constable's favourite *plein-air* formats (measuring approximately 21 × 30in/ 53.5 × 76.2cm). One of the latter (R.21.8) includes the same red-jacketed labourer emptying a wheelbarrow who appears on the far right of no.27. However, this is the sort of detail that Constable would have added later in the studio. At some stage, Constable unfolded the left and right tacking edges of no.27 to extend the surface available for painting, something he was often to do in his later career, especially when working on the full-scale sketches for the six-footers.

Constable also loved to record the dynamic, blustery skies over the Heath, and indeed between the years 1821 and 1822 he painted about a hundred individual oil sketches of clouds and skies at Hampstead, which are rightly celebrated for their remarkable range, quality and aesthetic or meteorological interest (see Liverpool and Edinburgh 2000 and New York 2004). Although Hampstead never featured as the subject of one of his six-foot canvases, Constable's experience of observing and recording the skies there in the early 1820s was crucial in helping him resolve the problems he was facing at that date when attempting to integrate the skies into the compositions of his large River Stour subjects painted for exhibition at the Royal Academy (New York 2004, p.35). AL

27

Hampstead Heath with the House called 'The Salt Box'
c.1820
Oil on canvas
38.4 × 66.8 (15 ⅛ × 26 ⅜)
R.21.7

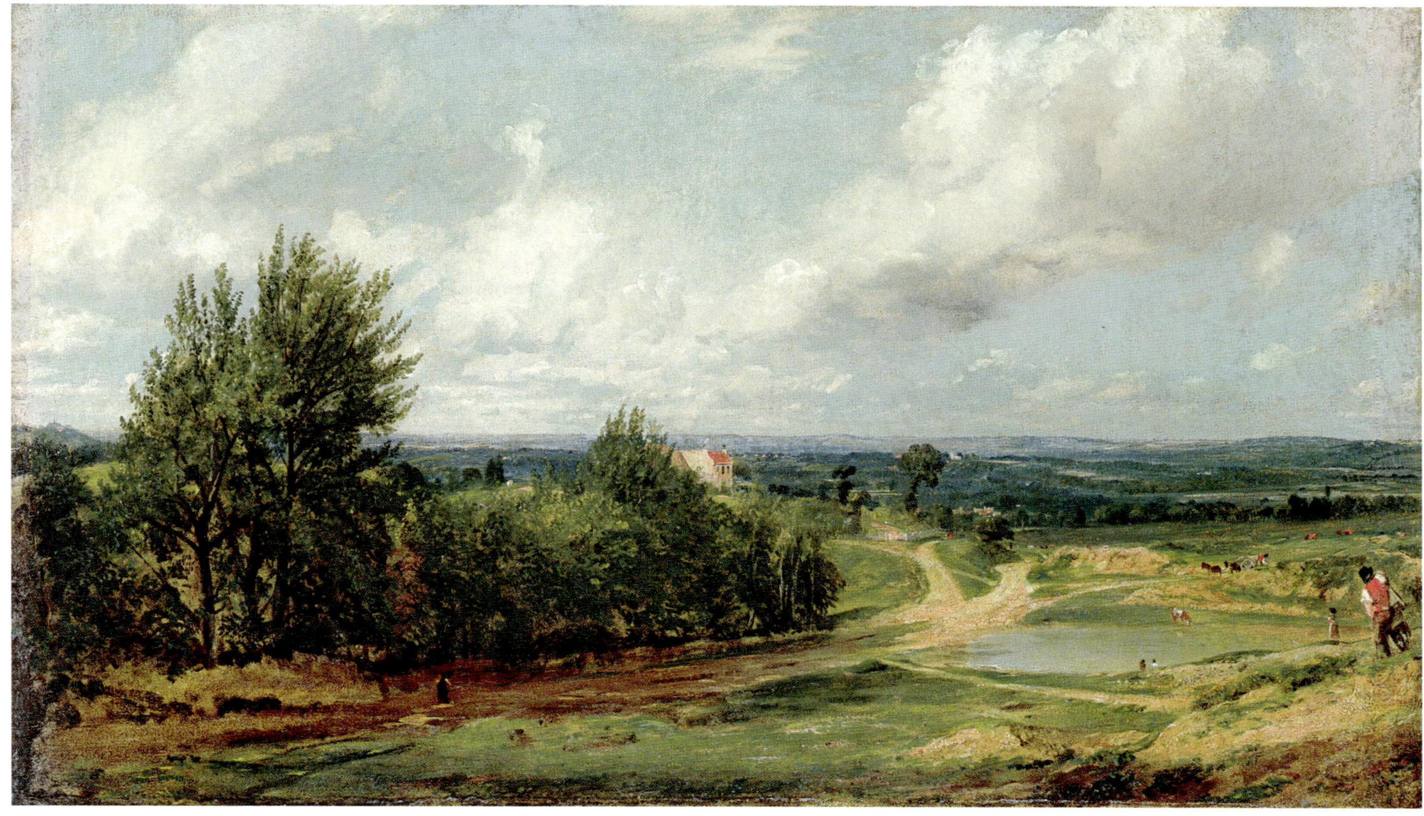

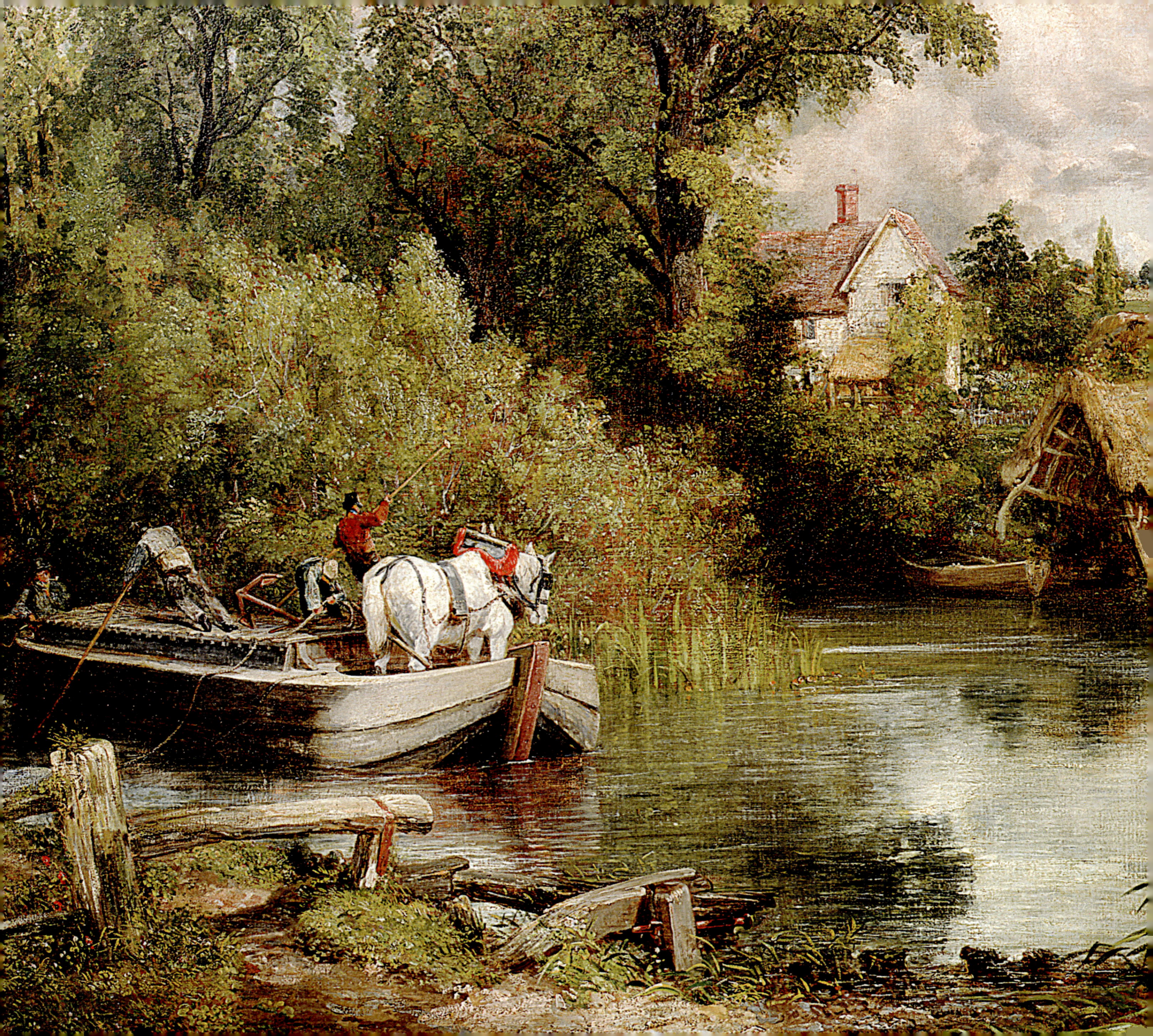

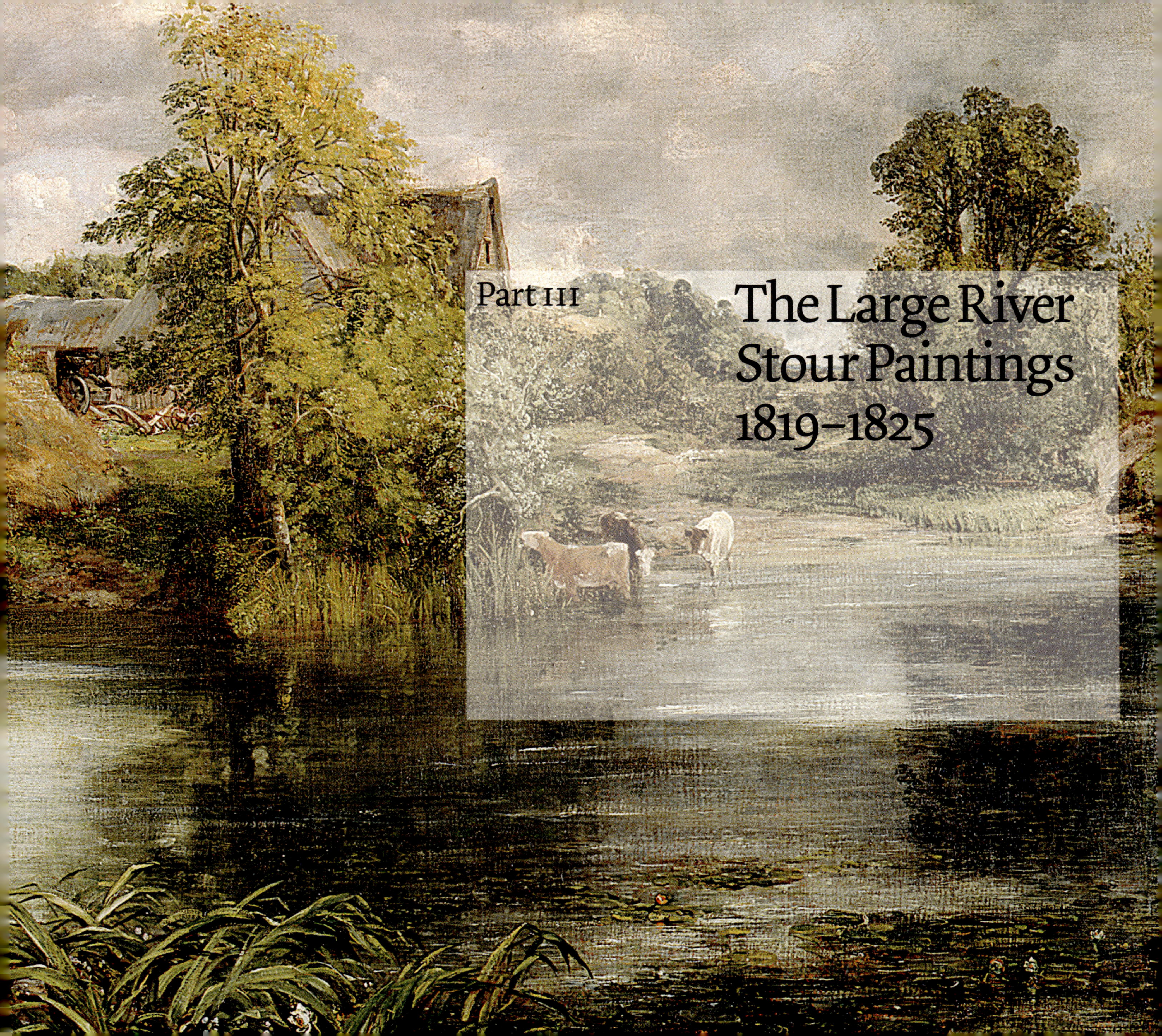

Part III

The Large River Stour Paintings 1819–1825

'I do not consider myself at work without I am before a six-foot canvas' (Constable to John Fisher, 23 October 1821, JCC VI, p.76)

Painting 'finished' pictures – as opposed to sketches or studies – in the open air was ultimately to prove unsustainable for Constable. This was less to do with the practical difficulties he faced in handling his materials outdoors, it seems, than for his need to be in front of, or close to, the landscape itself. Once he had married in the autumn of 1816, and was to settle more permanently in London, this was of course no longer possible, though a three-month holiday in Suffolk in the summer of 1817 provided him with a temporary stay of execution.

Working partly in the open air, with direct access to the scene before him, by 1817 Constable had managed to paint an Academy picture, *Flatford Mill* (no.19), as large as 40 × 50 inches (1.01 × 1.27m), a 'half-length' turned on its side. He exhibited the picture at the Royal Academy in 1817, and then again, having repainted the sky, at the British Institution the following year. It is perhaps significant, however, that Constable appears to have sent nothing larger than a kit-kit sized canvas, *Dedham Lock and Mill* (no.24), to the Academy exhibition in 1818. Certainly as late as 31 January that year, Farington mentioned in his diary that Constable 'had not any principal work in hand' (Farington XV, pp.5147–8). Recently married, and with his first child born in December 1817, Constable clearly had many distractions that year. However, he also appears to have been struggling with the challenge of how best to paint large landscapes now that he was removed from those very scenes he wished to record.

In all events, the autumn and winter of 1818 to 1819 clearly marked an important turning point for Constable, perhaps partly prompted by the disappointing news in November of his only receiving one vote in the election of new associate members of the Royal Academy. For it was around this time that he started painting the first of the famous six-foot canvases that he was to send to the Academy exhibitions at regular intervals until the early 1830s, *The White Horse* (no.29), and, in planning this new picture, he also started painting the first of his full-scale sketches (no.28). For now that he was distanced from his native scenes, he needed to recreate his Suffolk material synthetically in the studio from sketches and studies made in earlier years, and the large sketch clearly represented for him a means of 'knitting' together these disparate elements. Constable's use of large preliminary designs, purposefully painted with the sole intention of them functioning as full-scale compositional sketches prior to his undertaking an additional, finished painting of the same subject, appears to be unique in Western art (Rhyne 1990b, pp.118–19). Indeed, it has been said that it is Constable's use of the full-scale studio sketch, rather than his smaller outdoor nature studies, that establishes him as an avant-garde painter, determined to rethink the demands of his art and to address them in an entirely original way (Gage in Paris 2002, p.137).

With *The White Horse*, Constable continued to concentrate on the working life of the River Stour that had provided him with the subject matter not only of his most ambitious recent Academy exhibit, *Flatford Mill* 1817 (no.19), but of so many of his earlier pictures as well (nos.9, 14, 15). The subject of this painting, and of those of the other large River Stour scenes that followed, were of course familiar ones: 'I should paint my own places best', he told Fisher in 1821 (JCC VI, p.78). Indeed, although now settled permanently in London, Constable probably still continued to regard himself primarily as a Suffolk artist, albeit his love of his boyhood haunts was now a recollected love, 'an emotion at once sweetened and saddened by nostalgia', as Michael Kitson so aptly put it (Kitson 1976, p.746). However, it was also the case that this section of the canalised Stour with its busy river traffic also offered Constable a wealth of incident from which he could select a narrative episode for his landscapes: a horse being ferried in a barge towards the tow-path on the opposite side of the river in *The White Horse*, for example; barges manoeuvring past each other in *View on the Stour near Dedham* 1822 (no.39); or a barge-horse leaping over a barrier on the tow-path in *The Leaping Horse* 1825 (no.47). Indeed, one of the reasons he may have abandoned the first of his six-foot landscapes, *Dedham from Gun Hill*, which lies underneath the full-size sketch for *The White Horse* (fig.21, p.45), is that its subject was an open panoramic landscape offering little in the way of obvious potential for narrative incident. When he reworked the Dedham Vale subject on an upright format in the late 1820s, he was to add a gypsy mother and child in the foreground, seated next to a fire and makeshift shelter (fig.74, p.164). Nevertheless, her presence in the landscape feels more marginal than that of the figures who occupy Constable's River Stour landscapes.

The White Horse was warmly received by the critics when exhibited at the Academy in 1819, and played a large part in securing Constable's election as an Associate Academician towards the end of the year. On 2 November, Constable wrote to his brother Abram proudly declaring that 'I was last night by a large majority elected an *Associate* of the *Royal Academy* – therefore I am now *J. Constable A.R.A.*' (FDC 1975, pp.73–4). As later noted by his biographer, C.R. Leslie – who himself received five votes in the final ballot for the election of Associates in 1819 to Constable's eight – *The White Horse* was 'too large to remain unnoticed' on the Academy walls (Leslie 1951, p.73). Indeed, Constable's success with the picture encouraged him to try to submit a similarly large landscape to the Academy exhibition in most subsequent years. For he had now proved to himself that he was capable of painting a Suffolk landscape on a more monumental scale, whilst still managing to retain the sense of fidelity to nature that had characterised his previous work, as well as the requisite level of detail and 'finish'.

Until 1825, all the large landscapes that Constable sent to the spring Academy exhibitions – *The White Horse* 1819 (no.29), *Stratford Mill* 1820 (no.31), *The Hay Wain* 1821 (no.37), *View on the Stour near Dedham* 1822 (no.39), *The Lock* 1824 (no.41) and *The Leaping Horse* 1825 (no.47) – featured scenes on the River Stour taken from within a small geographical radius of about three miles (see map, p.72). On the one hand, these pictures deserve to be appreciated on their own individual merits, for each shows a different episode from the working life of the river, and each has its own very distinctive representation of the weather and thus its own particular mood. Yet, as Graham Reynolds has pointed out, together they reveal a 'successive and progressive exploration of a particular *idée fixe*', and for this reason they also need to be examined and understood as a group (Reynolds 1965, p.61). Indeed, when examined as a series, it is clear that not only is there significant progression in terms of their narrative and dramatic content, but also in the coherence and force of their presentation.

For example, in *The White Horse*, the first of the pictures in the series, the chief incident, the ferrying of the tow-horse in a boat from one side of the river to the other, is relegated to the far left-hand side of the painting. Furthermore, the composition could be said to break too easily into three separate parts (Kitson 1976, p.749). In the next painting in the series, *Stratford Mill*, meanwhile, the composition is certainly more unified. However, the viewer's attention tends to wander between the scattered figures of the rider on the left, the anglers in the foreground and the men in the barge on the right, insufficiently engaged by a single narrative episode (Tate 1991, p.197). With the third picture in the series, *The Hay Wain*, however, Constable succeeded in creating a strong visual focus at the heart of the composition in the form of a hay-cart crossing a ford, and this also supplies a more significant, if as yet still understated, narrative element in the picture. For if we look closely we see that one of the cart's wheels is beginning to turn to the right, indicating that it will shortly swing round to continue its journey across the ford to collect another load of hay from the distant fields, before returning to complete the cycle once again. In *The Hay Wain*, we also sense that we are looking at a particular scene at a particular time of day. Dense clusters of cumulus clouds have formed, indicating that the time is around noon – the title, indeed, under which Constable exhibited the picture – though the billowing clouds suggest from their depth of convection that showers will follow later in the afternoon (Thornes 1999, p.46).

In the first three of the large River Stour pictures, then, the figurative element is rather underplayed by Constable, and the viewer has to look quite hard to unravel the narrative threads. With the next three paintings in the series, however, he strove to give the figures a more emphatic role, and also to create landscapes with more strenuous and dynamic action. The fourth picture in the group, *View on the Stour near Dedham*, was clearly a pivotal work in this development, and here the full-scale sketch for the picture (no.38) also played a critical role. In previous full-scale sketches, Constable had tended first to transfer most of the figures from sketch to finished picture. If he subsequently decided some of them were surplus to requirements, perhaps because they detracted from the central incident, he would simply paint them out on the finished canvas itself, as he did for example with the main boy fishing in *Stratford Mill* or a second horse in *The Hay Wain*, as the x-radiographs of these two pictures reveal (fig.64, p.137; fig.65, p.140). With *View on the Stour*, however, even though Constable still made changes between the sketch and the picture, it would appear that most of his important alterations to the figures in the scene were made on the sketch itself.

The recent x-radiograph taken of the full-scale sketch for *View on the Stour near Dedham* shows that Constable originally envisaged a much busier foreground, not dissimilar to that of *Stratford Mill*, with two boys fishing and a young girl close to the river's edge on their right (fig.69, p.149). His reason for subsequently painting them out would almost certainly have been connected with his desire to create a more powerful visual and narrative focus at the heart of the composition, for in a letter of April 1822 he told Fisher that he had made many changes to the picture over the last two or three months, with a view to giving it a 'rich centre' (JCC VI, p.89). Although Constable did not mention painting out the figures – he may perhaps have done this at quite an early stage – he did tell Fisher he had 'taken away the sail' and then added a second barge 'in the middle of the picture, with a principal figure' (*ibid.*). Now that both the sketch and the exhibition version of *View on the Stour* have been X-rayed, it can safely be assumed that the sail that Constable told Fisher he had painted out belonged to the barge in the sketch – where it is clearly visible in the X-ray – rather than to either of the barges in the finished picture. This is a particularly revealing discovery, as it tells us that Constable must have worked on, and continued to make changes to, both sketch and picture in tandem during the evolution of *View on the Stour*, and thus perhaps during the genesis of other large canvases as well.

Constable also told Fisher that he had 'endeavoured to paint with more delicacy' when working on the exhibition version of *View on the Stour* (Leslie 1951, p.90). Making so many of his changes on the full-scale sketch rather than on the exhibition version would have helped him ensure that the surface of the latter was fresher because less heavily worked, and indeed it has been suggested by John Gage that this may have been one of the chief reasons for Constable's adoption of the full-scale sketch in the first instance (Gage in Paris 2002, p.137). However, despite his attempt to produce a more delicate painted surface for *View on the Stour*, Constable complained to Fisher that 'hardly anybody has seen it' (Leslie 1951, p.90). This was not strictly true, since the critic for the *Morning Chronicle* actually commented on the 'finished merit' of the picture, whilst even drawing attention to 'too much minuteness in the pencilling [i.e. brushwork] of the trees in the middle distance' (Ivy 1991, p.95). Nevertheless, when Constable came to paint the next of his large River Stour canvases, *The Lock*, two years later, he seems to have been less concerned to create a pristine surface on the finished canvas. For not only does *The Lock* have some remarkable passages of free and vigorous brushwork but, as Sarah Cove has noted, it is the first of Constable's large exhibited pictures (as opposed to full-scale sketches) in which his use of the palette knife can be detected (see p.64). From this date onwards, indeed, the distinction between sketch and picture appears to be narrowing in Constable's work, and the exhibition canvas now begins to take on some of the characteristics of the sketch.

In *The Lock*, Constable also produced one of his most dynamic and successful compositions, the athletic figure of the lock-keeper straining forward to open the lock gates, against a backdrop of briskly moving clouds and shimmering trees. As Andrew Hemingway observed of the figure moving a barge in *View on the Stour*, so here in *The Lock* rural labour is given a dramatic quality, if not actually presented in heroic guise (Hemingway 1992, p.253). Something similar could be said of *The Leaping Horse*, the last of Constable's large River Stour scenes, where a rider urges a barge horse to jump over a barrier on the tow-path in a manner that recalls some of the great equestrian portraits of the past. Again, the turbulent sky seems to echo the energetic movement of horse and rider. However nature is here seen not at a specific moment – not, for example, under a noon-day sky as in *The Hay Wain* – but rather in terms of the essences of the elements, in particular wind and light. This more abstracted, generalised conception of nature reflects a distinct shift in Constable's practice, from one concerned with transcribing appearances to one that aims for the recreation of sensations (Rosenthal 1983, p.166). Constable is no longer aiming for an idea of overall truth. The black poplars along the tow-path of *Flatford Mill* (no.19) have given way to large clumps of weightier and more generalised species in *View on the Stour* and *The Lock*. In *The Leaping Horse*, meanwhile, Constable even introduces the spire of Dedham

church in a position far from the one it occupies in reality, an anachronism unthinkable in his work only a few years before. It is effective and ambitious picture-making, not naturalism, that is now Constable's primary concern.

Although it is undoubtedly right to consider the six large River Stour landscapes as a group, it is unlikely that Constable himself ever planned them as such from the outset, even if he may gradually have begun to see them in this way. There were, for example, many occasions in the early 1820s when he thought of interrupting the series by submitting to the Academy a London subject featuring the opening of Waterloo Bridge, a scene he had witnessed and sketched in 1817. In September 1820, for example, he was seriously contemplating working up a composition on this theme for the Academy exhibition the following spring. However, he was eventually persuaded by Farington in November to paint another Suffolk subject instead, one 'more corresponding with his successful picture exhibited last May', by which he meant *Stratford Mill* (Farington XVI, p.5582). Heeding Farington's advice, it was then at some speed that Constable proceeded to paint the third of his River Stour pictures, *The Hay Wain*, for exhibition at the Academy in 1821.

In the meantime, however, Constable continued to nurture aspirations to produce a large Waterloo Bridge subject. Not only did he start and attempt to finish such a work, almost certainly identifiable today as no.65, but in 1821 and 1822 he even got as far as releasing advertisements announcing that the picture would be shown at the Academy exhibition in those years (Ivy 1991, pp.87, 93). Given the pressure of time, it was always unlikely that Constable would manage to finish and send two large exhibition pictures to the Academy

in any given year. One must therefore assume that in 1821, and then again in 1822, Constable was still hoping, until quite a late stage, to prioritise a Waterloo Bridge subject for exhibition over a River Stour view. In the event, his main 1822 exhibit was again a River Stour subject, *View on the Stour near Dedham* (no.39), and it was not until a decade later that he finally managed to finish and exhibit a large picture – now a different version – of a Waterloo Bridge subject (no.67).

Another factor indicating that Constable is unlikely to have planned the six River Stour pictures as a series from the outset is that it appears that he was not always confident he could actually afford to paint a large exhibition canvas every year, least of all in the early 1820s. These substantial pictures, complete with full-scale sketches, were costly and time-consuming to paint, and had to be juggled with regular commissions he received for smaller landscapes or even portraits. In addition, alongside his larger landscapes for the Academy exhibitions, most years Constable would send some smaller, cabinet-sized pictures (measuring approximately 13×20in/33×51cm), which he could hope to sell more readily as they could be accommodated more easily in the average domestic home and were also more modestly priced. It is true that Fisher had purchased the first two of Constable's large River Stour subjects, *The White Horse* for himself, and *Stratford Mill* for his lawyer J.P. Tinney. However *The Hay Wain* and *View on the Stour* were left in Constable's hands until April 1824, when they were purchased together in a special financial package by the Anglo-French dealer John Arrowsmith, who exhibited them to great excitement at the Paris Salon later in the year (see nos.32–9).

Indeed by April 1822, Constable was

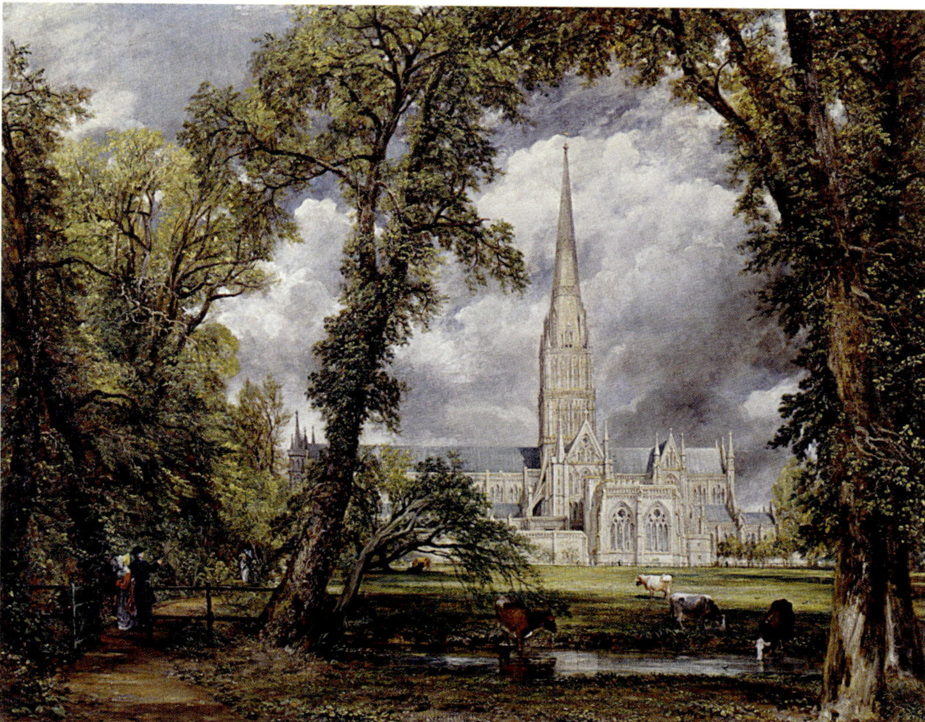

struggling so badly with his financial affairs that he told Fisher that although 'a large picture … was necessary this year – the next may take its chance' (13 April 1822, JCC VI, p.88). Thanks, perhaps, to Fisher meanwhile bending Tinney's ear, Constable soon afterwards told Fisher of an arrangement he had come to with Tinney that, he said, would 'enable me to do another large work as a certainty – thus to keep up & add to my reputation' (JCC VI, p.92). In fact, Constable was both too busy and too unwell that autumn and winter to produce any large landscape for the Academy exhibition in 1823, and the River Stour series was thus interrupted for the first time. His main exhibit

Figure 60
Salisbury Cathedral from the Bishop's Grounds
1823
Oil on canvas
87.6 × 111.8 (34½ × 44)
VICTORIA AND ALBERT
MUSEUM, LONDON

that May was a mid-size picture, *Salisbury Cathedral from the Bishop's Grounds* (fig.60) that he had recently painted on commission for his old friend Bishop Fisher, John Fisher's uncle. Constable's inability to send a 'large picture' to the Academy that year evidently troubled him. 'I am hurt this year for the want of one,' he told Fisher in July, 'the Church should have been an offset only' (JCC VI, p.124). Straightaway he began making plans for his next large picture, *The Lock*, and when it was finally ready for despatch to the Academy exhibition in the spring of 1824, his luck turned, for it sold on the first day. Perhaps spurred on by this success, Constable then painted another large

River Stour subject for the Academy exhibition the following year, *The Leaping Horse*. As it turned out, however, this was to be the only picture in the River Stour series that was never to find a buyer in Constable's lifetime. It was also to be the last of his large paintings on a River Stour theme.

Constable's motives in painting his larger pictures were clearly mixed. He seems to have been equally, if not more, committed to painting the six-footers with a view to furthering his reputation at the Academy as he was with an eye to remuneration, though no doubt he would have hoped to achieve both at the same time. However, with *The Leaping Horse* it was looking as though he had now exhausted the narrative potential of his River Stour scenes (Hemingway 1992, p.257). Indeed, the picture may even have come to haunt him. For, having made substantial changes to the canvas after its return from the Academy exhibition in order to make it more 'saleable' (JCC II, p.397; see also nos.42–7), it was the only painting in the River Stour series that Constable failed to send on at some stage for further exhibition at the British Institution. His tampering with the picture, something that was to become an almost obsessive habit in later years, may have rendered it unexhibitable.

The six large paintings that together form the River Stour series undoubtedly form one of the great high points of Constable's career. Painted during some of the happiest and most settled years of his life, they reveal careful planning, remarkable creative resourcefulness and the application of determined willpower. Indeed, in their entirety it has been said that they amount to 'Constable's appropriation and exaltation of his own countryside' (Reynolds 1965, p.75). By the mid-1820s, however, the time had come for him to move on to different subjects. AL

The White Horse

Constable's interest in painting ever larger pictures, presumably because he knew they would attract more attention at the annual exhibitions of the Royal Academy and could be priced higher, was already evident by the mid-1810s. Up until 1817, the largest work he is known to have shown was *Flatford Mill* (no.19), which cost him considerable time and effort. Painted just before his marriage and subsequent move to London, it has been deemed a paean to his 'careless boyhood' spent in the valley of the River Stour (Tate 1991, p.181). That it may have been, but it also forcefully demonstrated for the artist that the difficulties and time required in executing such works out of doors were indeed substantial, and that he would need to reconsider the very fundamentals of his painting methods if he wished to undertake even larger canvases.

With the exhibition of *The White Horse* (under the title *A scene on the river Stour*) at the Royal Academy in 1819, Constable began a new phase in his career, one in which his primary efforts each year would be expended in creating a large landscape for public display. His contemporary J.M.W. Turner had been painting and showing landscapes of such scale (and even larger) for some years by this time, as had other artists such as John Martin. It is likely that Constable, now in his early forties and with more than a decade of work as a professional landscape painter behind him, felt some urgency to push his own art to a comparable level if he were to hope for greater recognition and greater economic benefits. Newly married and facing the increased costs of maintaining a household in London, he would have been well motivated in these ambitions. Whatever the case, his efforts paid off: following the successful exhibition of *The White Horse* he was elected an Associate of the Royal Academy, and the painting itself was

purchased by his friend Archbishop John Fisher for £100. It was Fisher who coined the name by which the picture became known for posterity. In July, before the exhibition at the Academy had closed, he wrote to Constable: Will you have the goodness to tell me what price you put upon your great picture now in the exhibition. We will call it if you please '*Life* and the pale Horse', in contradistinction to Mr. West's painting [i.e. *Death on a Pale Horse*] (JCC VI, p.44). Fisher was obviously contrasting the naturalistic vitality of Constable's landscape to the apocalyptic gloom of Benjamin West's gigantic canvas, which had received widespread attention during its exhibition in London in 1818; his name for the picture was soon adapted to simply *The White Horse*.

Only in recent years, and thanks especially to the efforts of Charles Rhyne, has it become clear just how complex Constable's process was in conceiving and executing the exhibited version of *The White Horse*, and the precise role of preliminary studies in its creation. No. 28, having long occupied an uncertain place in evaluations of Constable's oeuvre, is now accepted as a full-size sketch. The earliest known record of its existence dates only from 1872 – thirty-five years after Constable's death – when it was shown at a Royal Academy exhibition and where, significantly, it was not identified as a sketch (Reynolds 1984, p.29; see also pp.25–6 above). Ten years later it was shown once again, in a commercial London gallery; the following year (1883) it was reproduced as an engraving in the *Magazine of Art* (see fig.16, p.43). Judging from that print, the painting by then resembled a fully finished work, and was generally consonant in appearance with the exhibited version, which was then in a private English collection. There were, however, certain differences, including

the location of the thatched boathouse, the addition of a dovecote near the central (i.e. Willy Lott's) house, and the absence of a plough in front of the barn. These variations might, on their own, be reasonably reconciled with Constable's usual practice of refining and adjusting elements between sketch and finished composition. However, one point of divergence was more difficult to understand: the contours of the roof of Willy Lott's house are clearly different from the corresponding details in the finished painting, where the gable is shown at the proper angle to the river. Constable knew perfectly well the form and orientation of the house from a variety of viewpoints; by this time he had painted and sketched it many times (see, for example, nos.8–9). It is difficult to imagine why he would have seen fit to alter its shape.

In 1893 no.28 was purchased by P.A.B. Widener of Elkins Park, near Philadelphia, Pennsylvania. In a 1915 catalogue of the Widener Collection it was described as 'a variant of the famous picture exhibited at the Royal Academy' (W. Roberts, *Pictures in the Collection of P.A.B. Widener at Lynnewood Hall, Elkins Park, Pennsylvania* 1915 [n.p.]). The differences between the two pictures were noted, but no attempt was made to account for the existence of a finished 'variant' of one of Constable's famous six-footers, even though no other comparable cases of such replication were known (a second version of *The Lock*, see no.41, presumably being overlooked). Nor, at this point, was the possibility that the painting might be a sketch, even one considerably compromised by later interventions, introduced.

After the painting entered the collection of the National Gallery of Art, Washington, John Walker, the gallery's second director, observed in 1944: 'It seems to me a full size sketch made as a preliminary study for the Frick painting' (letter to Herbert L. Satterlea, curatorial files, National Gallery of Art; cited in Swicklik 1998). That assessment, in the absence of other proposals, more or less remained until the 1970s. In 1976, the organisers of the major exhibition of Constable's works at the Tate Gallery, wrote:

With the publication of Robert Hoozee's catalogue raisonné in 1979, the painting was rejected from Constable's oeuvre, and declared 'probably a later copy' (Hoozee 1979, p.149). Then, in 1983, Leslie Parris proposed that the discontinuities between the picture and the finished version might be explicable because it was a sketch that had, at some point, been repainted in order to make it appear a finished, and thus more readily saleable, work (see Swicklik, p.376). The question remained as to when the picture was reworked and, more importantly, whether the repainting might have been done by Constable himself. In 1984 Charles Rhyne requested the picture be examined with infrared and x-radiography, hoping these questions might at last be answered. That examination led to significant revelations about Constable's creative process at the very moment he was embarking on this important new phase in his art.

The most intriguing of these findings was that Constable initially contemplated a completely different scene, one closely similar to some of his earlier views of the Stour Valley from the Coombs, with Stratford bridge in the middle distance, Dedham church at the upper right, and the river's estuary in the far distance. In light of this new information, it could no

longer be assumed that no. 28 was unquestionably begun purely as part of Constable's preparations for painting the exhibition version of *The White Horse*. He had been interested in the view of the valley from the area of the Coombs and Gun Hill from as early as 1802 (see, for example, his *Dedham Vale* of that year, see fig.50, p.76). It is thus possible he might have begun a large picture of the subject many years before starting work on *The White Horse*, only to abandon it and put the canvas aside for reuse later. Although there is no certain evidence that Constable ever attempted anything on the scale of a six-footer before *The White Horse*, the matter is complicated by the fact that he wrote from East Bergholt to Maria in October and November 1815 that he was working on 'a larger landscape … than ever I did before' (JCC II, p.156). The identity of this work remains unknown, leaving the possibility it might have been the painting the artist first attempted on the canvas of no.28 (Tate 1991, p.69). The question is not easily resolved, but Rhyne has argued, convincingly in my view, that this is unlikely. In his opinion the character of the view of Dedham, as it can be judged from the X-rays, suggests a studio production more in keeping

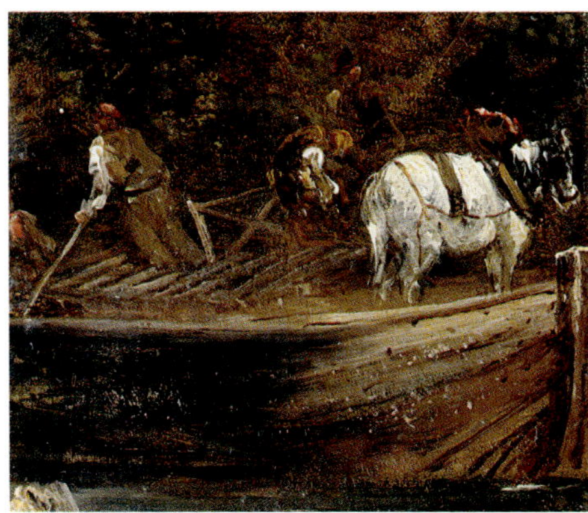

Figure 61
Study of men and tow-horse on a barge
c.1812–16
Oil on millboard
13.4 × 14.5 (5¼ × 5¾)
PRIVATE COLLECTION

with Constable's work of around 1817 to 1818 (correspondence with FK, 10 Oct. 2005). Moreover, he feels it would have been out of character for Constable to have made such a radical jump in the size and concept of his exhibition pieces as early as 1815, when he was still working largely *en plein air* and had yet to attempt anything approaching this size.

Just when Constable began no.28 is of relevance, because it could help explain why he decided to do something he had never done before, namely execute a full-size sketch for a planned exhibition piece. If we assume, following Rhyne, that the Dedham Vale image was begun soon after the artist's move to London and that it was his first attempt to paint a work that large – and to do so based only on his sketches and studies (that is, without the ability to refresh his vision by looking at the actual scene itself) – it is not difficult to imagine that he may have encountered difficulties in completing it. After all, up to this point he had trained himself largely to work from nature and on a comparatively smaller scale, and he was now doing something very different. His decision to abandon his first attempt may, then, have been determined by the recognition that he would now need to work out the overall composition of a painting in advance, exploring various possibilities in a large sketch before turning to the creation of the finished picture. Whatever the case, and no matter when Constable may have started the Dedham image, there is technical evidence that is important in determining the nature of what came next on the canvas. There is no intermediate ground layer between the Dedham view and the sketch for *The White Horse* over it; in fact, certain elements of the former, such as the vine encircling the tree stump at the lower left, are incorporated in the latter. It seems highly unlikely that Constable

would have started a picture he intended for exhibition in this way, for the textures and colours of the first level of paint would inevitably have affected the appearance of overlying layers of pigment without an intervening ground layer.

Rhyne had not yet published his findings in 1984, when Graham Reynolds published the volume of his Constable catalogue raisonné devoted to the second half of the artist's career, but Reynolds did refer to Rhyne's research in a note. Even before having benefit of this new information, Reynolds' judgment was that no.28 was a fully authentic work by the artist, although one much compromised in appearance by damage, later repaintings, and the presence of a thick, heavily discoloured varnish (Reynolds 1984, p.30). In 1992 the curators and conservators at the National Gallery of Art decided to undertake a complete conservation treatment of the picture, with the goal of removing all layers of the painting that were demonstrably not by Constable himself (see Swicklik 1998). From the technical examination it now seemed increasingly clear that much of the paint seen on the surface of the canvas was put there before the publication of the engraving by someone who attempted to 'finish' the work, but who had little understanding of Constable's own handling of paint and certain details of the composition of the exhibited *White Horse*. On the other hand, it was equally clear that the complex relationships between the paint layers of the sketch for *The White Horse* and those of the abandoned view of Dedham Vale, would have to be carefully analysed and understood once the later repainting was removed. The fortuitous result of the treatment was that a very well-preserved and stunningly lively oil sketch was revealed. Although differences between the sketch and finished painting were still evident, some of the ones that had long been most troubling to observers were now resolved. In particular, the sketch turned out (as X-rays had suggested) to have Willy Lott's house in its proper orientation, and the improperly located boathouse was now gone altogether, having been completely the work of a later artist. The 'rediscovery' of this remarkable painting was one of the prime catalysts in encouraging the undertaking of the present exhibition.

The scene depicted in both sketch and finished painting is a view from the right (south) bank of the Stour, looking back across the river just below Flatford. The barge (or lighter) at the left has just taken on board the horse from the towpath on the right bank, and is setting up to go downstream to a spot where the path resumes on the opposite bank. Just beyond the barge is a small island called 'The Spong', which lies between the river and the mill stream running out from Flatford Mill (see map, p.72). Willy Lott's house is visible just to the left of centre in the middle distance and, to the right, partially obscured by trees, is the farmhouse now known as Gibbonsgate Farm.

The origins of Constable's interest in the scene are found in a drawing of the left-hand portion of it, from approximately the area of the boathouse to the left edge, in an 1814 sketchbook (Victoria and Albert Museum, R.14.32, p.66) and in two oil sketches from about the same vantage point (c.1817, Private Collection, R.19.3, R.19.4); there also exist a pencil drawing of the boathouse seen in the final painting (c.1817, Private Collection; R.19.5) and a chalk drawing of the boat moored nearby (see no.34). A small oil sketch of the barge with several figures and the horse has recently been discovered (fig.61, p.133). FK

28

The White Horse (full-size sketch)
c.1818
Oil on canvas
127.5 × 183 (50¼ × 72)
R.19.2
NATIONAL GALLERY OF ART,
WASHINGTON, WIDENER COLLECTION

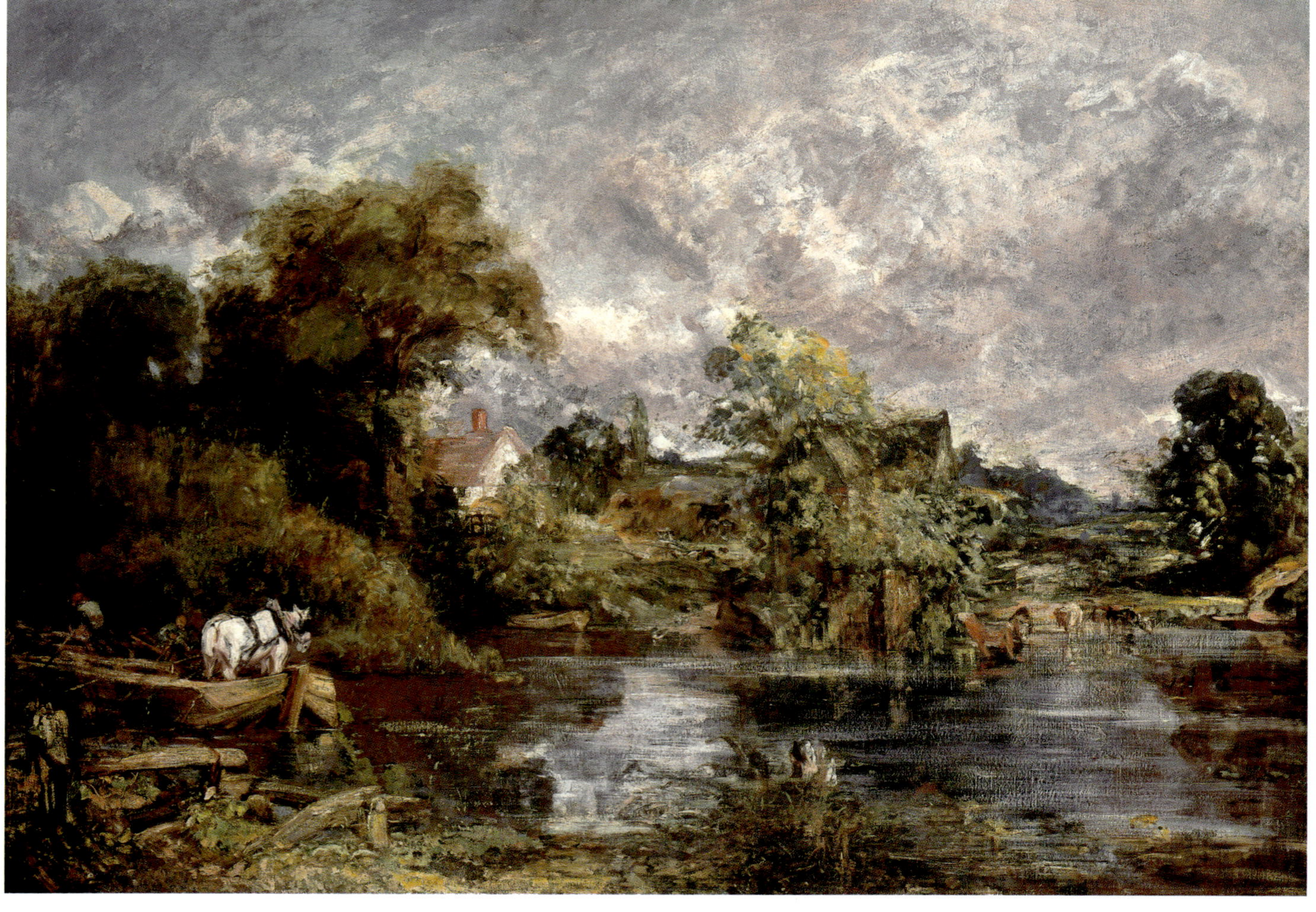

29

The White Horse
1819
Oil on canvas
131.5 × 187.8 (51¾ × 74), including extension
at right where the tacking edge has been
incorporated into the picture plane
Signed and dated along the bottom edge
(left of centre) in sloping script 'I C John Constable
London. F.1819' (the 'I C' may represent
a first and less complete signature)
Exh: RA 1819 (no.251, *A scene on the river Stour*);
Living Artists of the English School, BI 1825 (no.118,
River Scene); Salon, Lille 1825 (no.98, one of two
works entitled *Deux vues des Canaux d'Angleterre*)
R.19.1
Ivy 19.10–12; 19.14; 19.16–17
THE FRICK COLLECTION, NEW YORK. PURCHASE

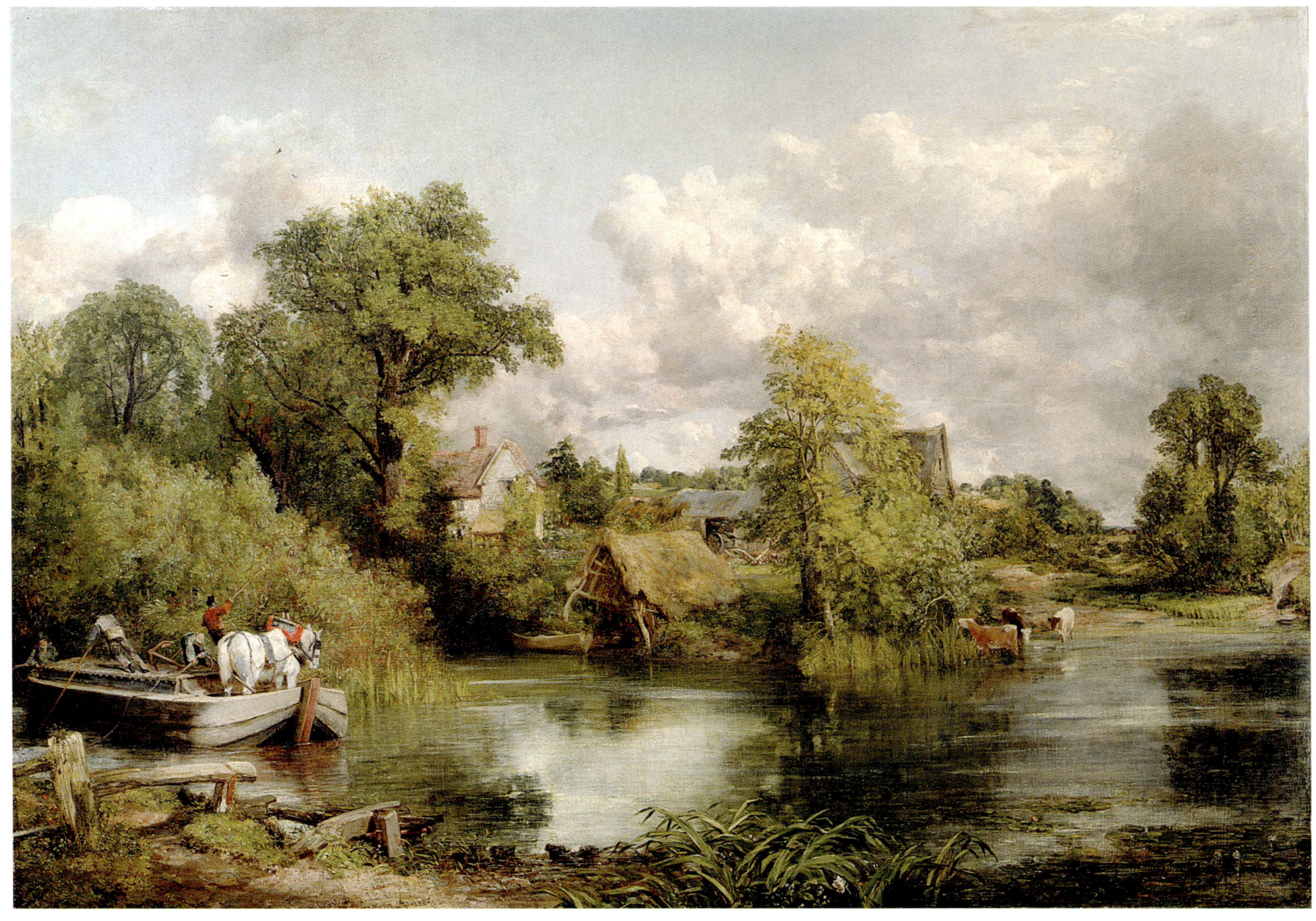

Stratford Mill

Constable followed the success of *The White Horse* by submitting a second six-foot canvas of River Stour scenery, *Stratford Mill* (exhibited originally as simply *Landscape*) to the Royal Academy in 1820. Perhaps some measure of his increasing self-confidence is revealed by the fact that he told Farington he felt no need to consult others, as he had often done in the past, for their opinions of the new picture before placing it on exhibition (1 April 1820, Farington XVI, pp.5487–8). For *Stratford Mill* he chose a different site from the locale of Flatford, which otherwise provided the inspiration for his large-scale river pictures. Stratford St Mary, about two miles west, was the site of a picturesque old timber-framed watermill (part of it is visible at the left of nos.30 and 31). The slightly elevated point of view was provided by a footbridge that crossed the river there; its modern replacement still affords visitors a

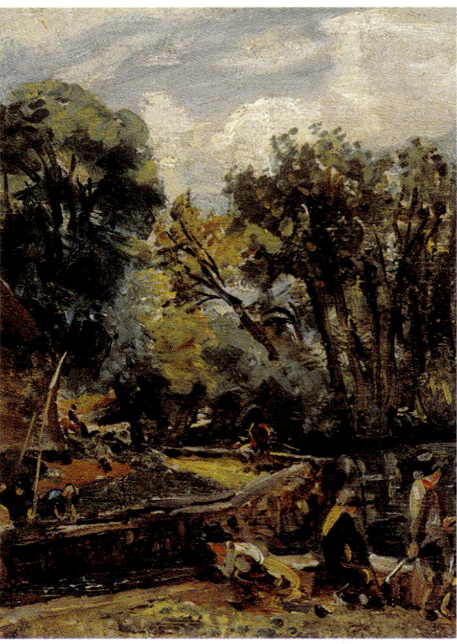

Figure 62
Anglers at Stratford Mill
1811
Oil on panel
18.7 × 14.6 (7³⁄₈ × 5³⁄₄)
PRIVATE COLLECTION

similar view, although without the mill, which was replaced by a brick structure in 1825 that operated into the 1890s (it was demolished in 1948 and the site remains vacant; a concrete and steel bulkhead has long since replaced the wooden banking visible at the left of Constable's painting; see St John 2005, p.21). It was (and is) a particularly lovely spot, where the river ran broad and calm and was flanked by graceful trees and verdant watermeadows. Constable would develop the compositional type he first essayed here, with a left half largely filled with trees and architecture and a right opened to an expansive view of land and sky, to even greater effect in *The Hay Wain* the following year (no.37).

Constable apparently first explored the subject in a vertically orientated oil sketch, which only came to modern attention in 1982, made *en plein air* on 17 August 1811 (fig.62); a more fully developed horizontal study (at 12 × 16¹⁄₂in/30.5 × 42cm slightly smaller than one-quarter scale of the finished picture) likely made in the studio dates from 1819 (fig.63). However, only within the last twenty-five years or so has it been accepted that the finished picture was, as in the case of *The White Horse*, preceded by a full-scale oil sketch (i.e. no.30). As Reynolds wrote in 1984 (p.45), the sketch for *Stratford Mill* 'has long been viewed with suspicion, and the probable falsity of the "signature" has cast doubt on the authenticity of the whole work'. The inscription, which reads, 'John Constable RA London', has been questioned on the grounds that its character is inconsistent with accepted signatures by the artist, which are generally rare on his finished works, let alone his sketches; there is also the fact that the 'RA' suggests a date of 1829 or later (following Constable's election to full membership), which is obviously inconsistent on a work painted before 1820 (Rhyne 1990a,

p.73, has suggested the picture may have been reworked by the artist himself at a later date, at which point the signature may have been added; others, however, think that the signature was added after Constable's death). However, certain differences between the oil sketches mentioned above and the full-size sketch have been convincingly analysed to support the authenticity of the latter. In particular, seven children are seen (three with fishing rods) in the vertical sketch of 1811, two of whom are on the bank near the mill at the left edge of the image; one holds a fishing pole and the other leans forward and gazes into the water. In the horizontal studio study the two figures at the left are absent. In the large sketch both were reintroduced, but the boy fishing at the extreme left was subsequently painted out (the pole he held is still visible). Neither of these figures is present in the finished canvas, so it is highly unlikely a copyist would have included them and then painted over one of them in the sketch (Reynolds 1984, p.45).

The main differences – other than, of course, the level of finish and the nature of the paint handling – between the full-size sketch for *Stratford Mill* and the exhibited version are found in the group of young fishermen at the lower centre. In the sketch a standing boy wielding his pole dominates, his form rising up against the river and establishing a pronounced vertical accent in that part of the composition, which is accentuated by the trees on the far bank and, less obviously, by the sweep of the clouds to the right in the distant sky. He is gone in the final version – though X-rays (fig.64) reveal that Constable originally included him, and then painted him out – and without him the visual rhythms and energies of the painting seem less staccato and more relaxed and consonant with a peacefully bucolic mood. The calmer feeling in the finished picture is also accented by its more restrained

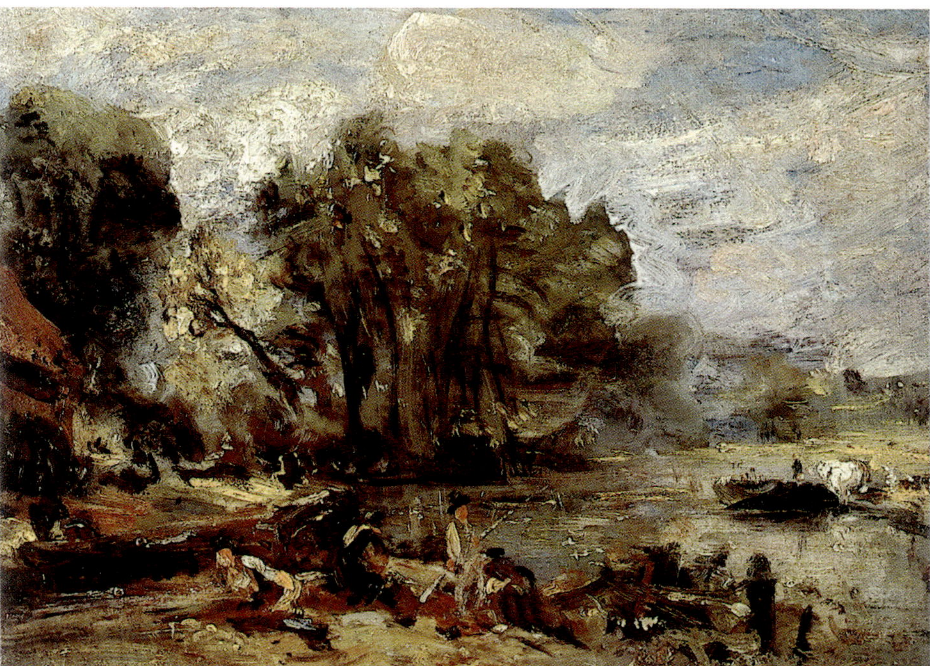

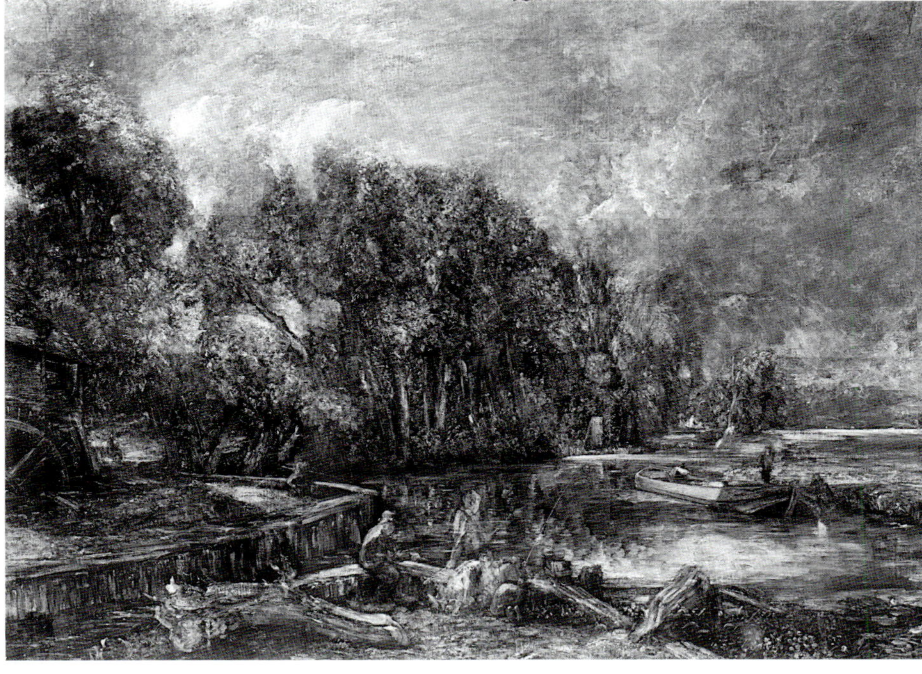

paint handling. Throughout the sketch forms are described with remarkably free and vibrant brushwork, giving its overall surface a nervous energy that is visually exhilarating in its own right. The disparities between the boldness of a preliminary sketch and the more subdued handling of an exhibition picture diminish somewhat over the following years, as Constable increasingly worked out how to integrate the informal qualities of the sketch with the more considered demands of a finished picture.

Stratford Mill has little in the way of subject or incident beyond the foreground youths fishing; a second angler is situated on the bank beyond the mill at the left, and a horse and rider are visible in a patch of light beyond. The barge on the far bank of the river is anchored, having neither a tow-horse to move it upstream nor any sign of its occupants working to guide it downriver. A white tow-horse does appear by the barge in the quarter-scale sketch; in the full-scale sketch a brown horse is shown grazing in the field nearby at the right. The true subject is the expansive beauty of the scenery of the Stour Valley. The visual combination of the limpid river, its richly forested banks on the one side and its meadows on the other, with a grandly realised sky filled with billowing clouds, results in an undeniably stirring and affecting image of the English countryside.

The picture was well received by the press when shown in 1820, although there were some complaints about its lack of finish; the critic for *The Examiner*, for example, felt it had a 'more exact look of nature than any picture we have seen by an Englishman, and has been unequalled by very few of the boasted foreigners of former days, except in finishing' (cited in Reynolds 1984, p.44). Constable himself held the picture in extremely high regard and once observed that it was grander than *The Hay Wain*. The painting did not, however, sell at the exhibition and, once Constable had it back in his studio, he apparently worked on it once more. In January 1821 his friend John Fisher arranged to buy it as a present for John Pern Tinney, a lawyer who had recently won a lawsuit for him. In subsequent years Constable clashed with Tinney over his desire to borrow the picture back for his own purposes. He succeeded in doing so late in 1823 and proceeded to work 'a good deal in toning & improving' it the following June (JCC II, p.324). In 1825 he was allowed to borrow it for exhibition with *The White Horse* at the British Institution, but Tinney denied his request to send it to the opening exhibition of the Scottish Royal Academy, and had it back in his possession by November of the same year.

The sky in *Stratford Mill* was harshly judged by someone described by Fisher as 'a grand critical party' who saw the picture in Tinney's home in Salisbury in 1821. Constable responded to this criticism with a defence of his methods that has since become well known:

Figure 63
Sketch for 'Stratford Mill'
c.1819
Oil on canvas
30.5 × 41.9 (12 × 16½)
PRIVATE COLLECTION

Figure 64
Composite x-radiograph of
Stratford Mill 1820 (no.31)
THE NATIONAL GALLERY,
LONDON

Stratford Mill

That Landscape painter who does not make his skies a very material part of his composition – neglects to avail himself of one of his greatest aids. Sir Joshua Reynolds speaking of the 'Landscape' of Titian & Salvator & Claude – says *'Even their skies seem to sympathise with the Subject'*. I have often been advised to consider my *Sky* – as a *'White Sheet drawn behind the Objects'*. Certainly if the Sky is *obtrusive* – (as mine are) it is bad, but if they are *evaded* (as mine are not) it is worse, they must and always shall with me make an effectual part of the composition. It will be difficult to name a class of Landscape, in which the sky is not the *'key note'*, the *standard of 'Scale'*, and the chief *'Organ of sentiment … The sky is the 'source of light'* in nature – and governs everything. Even our common observations on the weather of every day, are suggested by them but it does not occur to us. Their difficulty in painting both as to composition and execution is very great, because with all their brilliancy and consequence, they ought not to come forward or be hardly thought about in a picture (JCC VI, pp.76–7). **FK**

30

Stratford Mill (full-size sketch)
c.1819
Oil on canvas 131 × 184 (51½ × 72½)
Inscribed bottom right (probably not by the artist) 'John Constable RA/ London'
R.20.2
YALE CENTER FOR BRITISH ART,
PAUL MELLON FUND

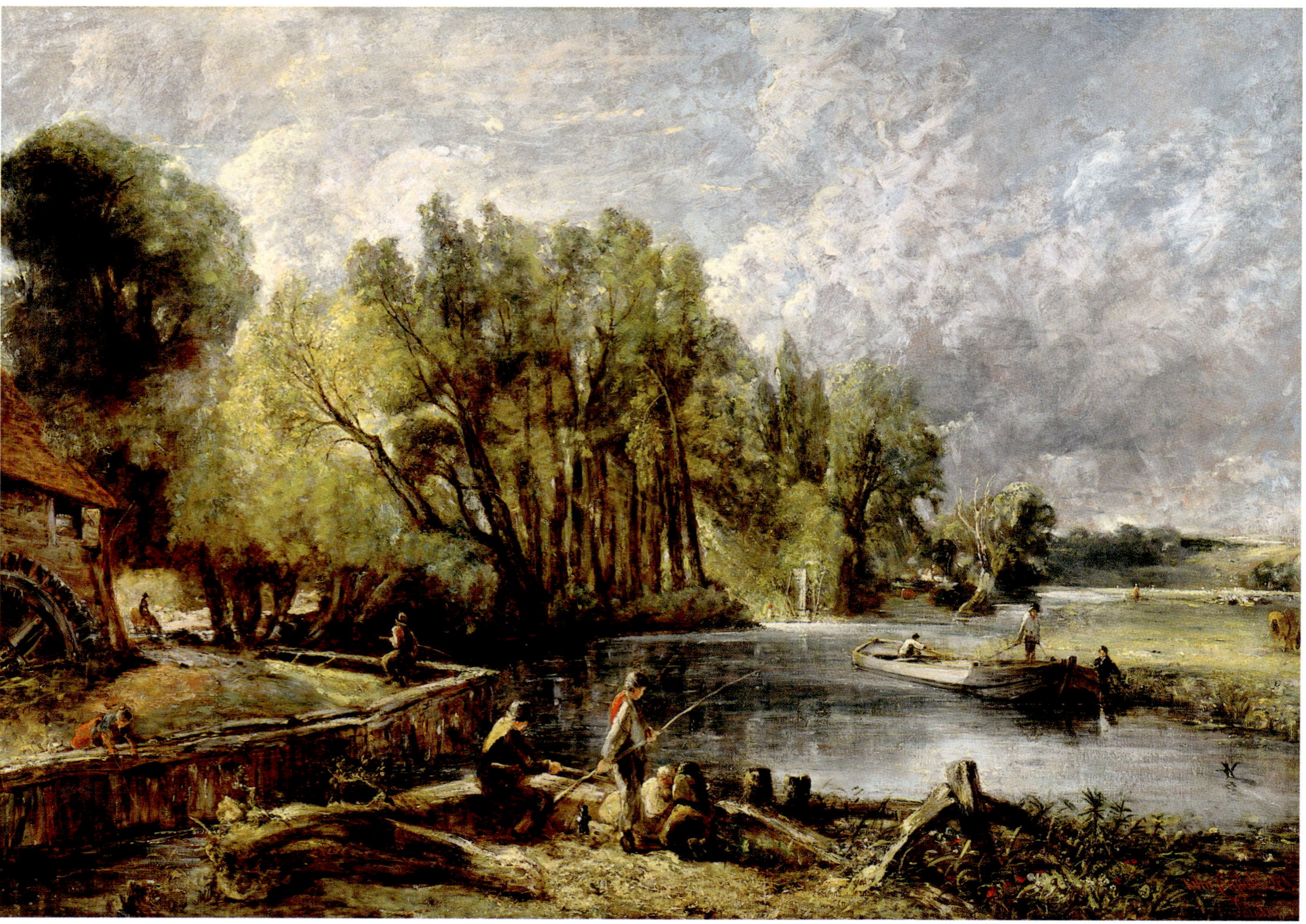

31

Stratford Mill

1820
Oil on canvas 129 × 184.8 (50¾ × 72¾)
Exh: RA 1820 (no.17, *Landscape*);
Living Artists of the English School,
BI 1825 (no.114, *Landscape: a Water-mill,
with Children angling*)
R.20.1
Ivy 20.3; 20.8–9; 20.11–15; 25.10
THE NATIONAL GALLERY, LONDON

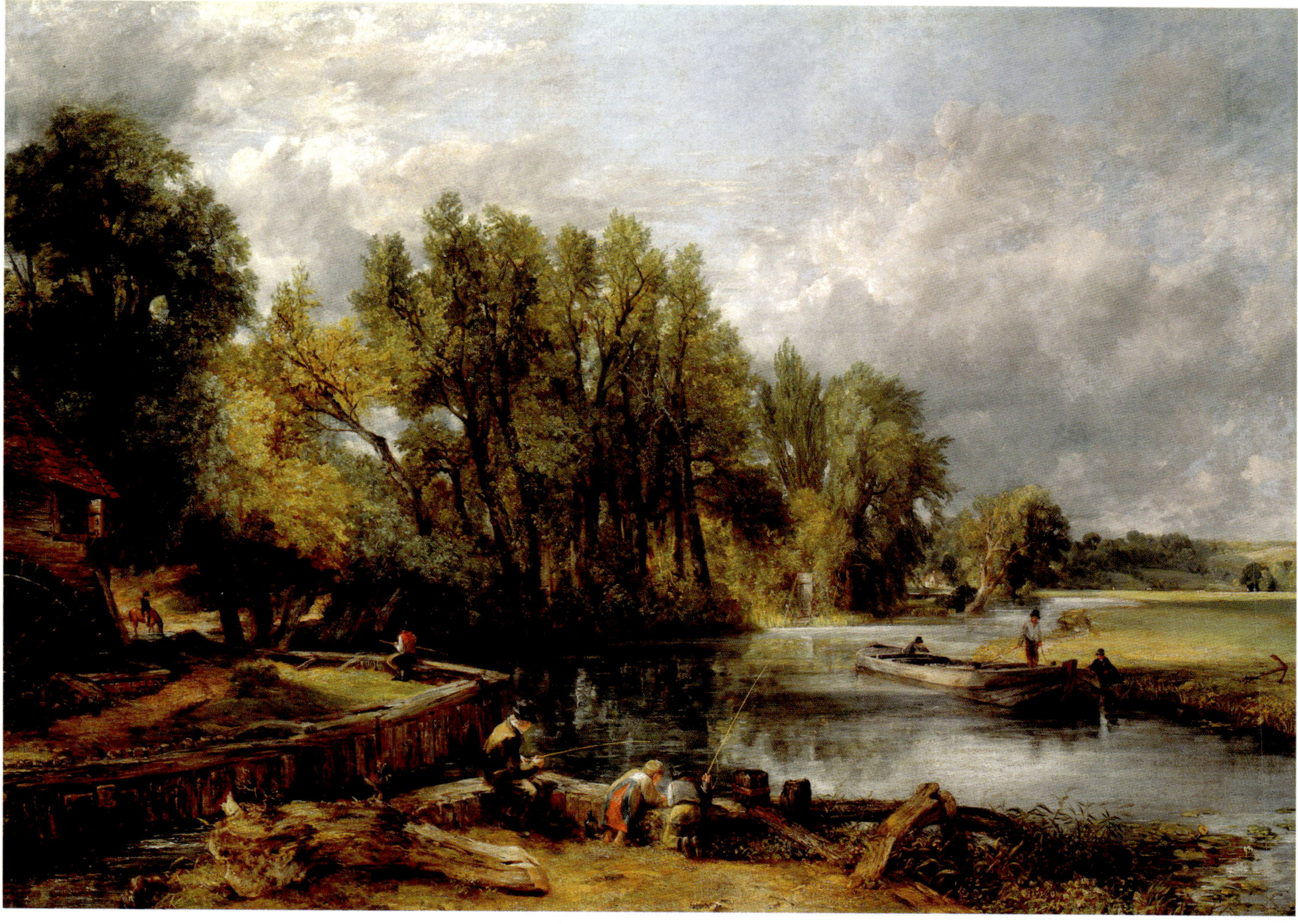

The Hay Wain

Since its donation to London's National Gallery in 1886, *The Hay Wain* has become not only Constable's best-known work, but also one of the most admired paintings in all Britain. Given the iconic status *The Hay Wain* has assumed in Constable's oeuvre, it is perhaps surprising to realise he was somewhat uncertain in choosing it as the subject to follow *Stratford Mill* of 1820 (no.31). He initially considered, as he told Farington in a letter of 21 November 1820, painting a scene in London, rather than one in Suffolk, a view 'on the Thames on the day of the opening of Waterloo Bridge' (Farington XVI, p.5582). Farington, however, advised him 'to proceed on & complete for the Exhibition a subject more corresponding with his successful picture exhibited last may [i.e. *Stratford Mill*]'. Once Constable had decided to undertake a new River Stour scene, he had less than five months to have the picture ready to go on public display in April 1821.

The view in *The Hay Wain* is taken from below Flatford Mill, with Willy Lott's house anchoring the left side of the composition. Slightly to the right of centre, a horse-drawn hay wagon with a man and a boy aboard is traversing the stream of water discharged from the mill, and turning to negotiate a passage across the main channel of the river across the shallow ford that gave Flatford its name. Just to the right of Lott's house a woman bends down to gather water; a dog walks along the foreground bank and, just beyond the moored rowing boat near the right edge of the picture, an angler makes his way through the reeds. In the meadow in the right middle distance are workers cutting hay and another loaded wagon.

In depicting this particular scene, Constable returned to a place with which he was thoroughly familiar. Flatford Mill was his father's first home, and his oldest sister and

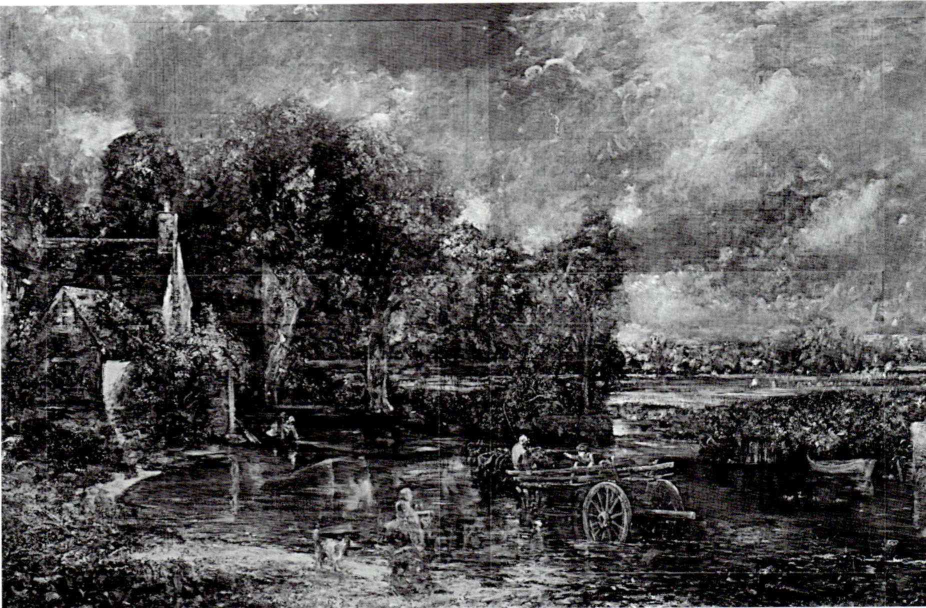

brother were born there; he had sketched and drawn the place many times before 1820. Perhaps it was the short time available to him to execute the new picture that led him to choose such a familiar subject. It was certainly one he had considered before, albeit from a somewhat different viewpoint (see nos.8, 9). In composing the new picture, he consulted sketches depicting Lott's cottage from a point of view a little further downstream from the mill. The vertically orientated *Willy Lott's House* (no.32) relates closely to the left side of the finished painting, although it shows less of the house itself; it also introduces the motif of the dog on the bank. On the verso of this sketch is a similar one, but with a horse rather than a dog. In a horizontal format sketch dated 1816 (no.33), Constable expanded the scene to the left to include most of the house. It was most likely in

his London studio that Constable used these two sketches in working up a small, vigorously executed study (no.35) where virtually all of the principal elements of the final painting, including the cart fording the stream, are introduced for the first time. The study also includes a barge with a raised sail on the river in the right-hand distance, a motif that calls to mind similar vessels that Constable included in his earlier *Dedham Lock and Mill* subjects, especially no.25. Although no barge with raised sail is included in the full-scale sketch for *The Hay Wain*, nor, apparently, in the finished picture, the x-radiograph of the latter (fig.55) indicates that Constable in fact originally included such a vessel on the left, but subsequently painted it out.

Constable expanded the main elements of the small sketch in no.36, a six-foot canvas that

Figure 65
Composite x-radiograph of *The Hay Wain* 1821 (no.37), showing details originally introduced in to the picture – a boy and horse in the foreground, and a barge with raised sail in the distance – and subsequently painted out
THE NATIONAL GALLERY, LONDON

has been aptly characterised as 'the most generalised and least detailed of his extant full-size sketches' (Reynolds 1984, p.69). Most of the elements from no.35 are present, along now with a figure on horseback near the dog on the bank; the central chimney of Willy Lott's house has, however, been omitted. In the large sketch, Constable seems to have been most concerned with working out the overall elements of the composition on a greatly enlarged scale, and with organising the overall patterns of light and shade (Reynolds 1965, p.66). It is truly remarkable in its freedom of handling and boldness of surface effects, and for the way Constable allowed the brown ground layer on the canvas to be plainly visible in numerous passages. It certainly gives every indication of having been executed quickly and with exceptional creative energy (see also pp.60–1).

Constable largely followed the template established by the full-size sketch in the finished picture. At the lower centre he initially included the mounted rider, then replaced him with a barrel, and finally painted that out as well; pentimenti of these forms are clearly visible today with the naked eye and are yet more visible in the X-ray (fig.65). He returned the central chimney to Willy Lott's house and substantially reworked the form of the hay wagon. For the latter he consulted a drawing (now unlocated) he had requested from the son of his friend John Dunthorne, no doubt because he lacked sketches of his own and questioned his visual memory regarding specific details of the shape and construction of such wagons. These were typically used for hauling timber and other heavy goods, and were converted for carrying hay in harvest season by running extra boards along both sides to increase capacity (St John 2000, p.7). The wagon depicted in the full-scale sketch lacked these boards and the long beam running

underneath the frame of the wagon; these details were presumably in Dunthorne's drawing, and Constable carefully added them in the final picture. Otherwise, most of the artist's efforts seem to have been devoted to sharpening the image's overall clarity of form, and to transforming the somewhat summarily depicted atmospherics found in the sketch into a masterfully realised sweep of clouds and sky.

Given the constraints of time allowed for its completion, Constable must have worked on *The Hay Wain* with unusual speed and assuredness. In late February 1821 Constable's brother Abram, having apparently seen the picture not long before, worried: 'I hope you will have your picture ready but from what I saw I have faint hopes of it, there appear'd everything to do' (JCC I, p.193). Even as late as 1 April, little more than a week before it was due at the Royal Academy, he said he still had 'much to do on it' (JCC VI, p.65). Nevertheless, the painting was generally well received by critics, one of whom considered that it 'approaches nearer to the actual look of rural nature than any modern landscape whatever' (*The Examiner*, see Ivy 1991, p.88, no.21.11). Constable himself seems to have been at least a little surprised at what he had managed to pull off, observing to Fisher that it was 'not so grand as Tinney's [i.e. *Stratford Mill*, no.31] owing perhaps to the masses not being so impressive – the power of Chiaro Oscuro is lessened – but it has rather a more novel look than I expected' (1 April 1821, JCC VI, p.65).

As was the case with his two previously exhibited six-footers, Constable chose a simple descriptive title for the new painting: *Landscape: Noon*. The first known use of the title by which it has become universally known is in a letter to the artist from Fisher of 14 February 1821: 'And how thrives the "hay wain … ?"' (JCC VI, p.62). Fisher had earlier coined the name for

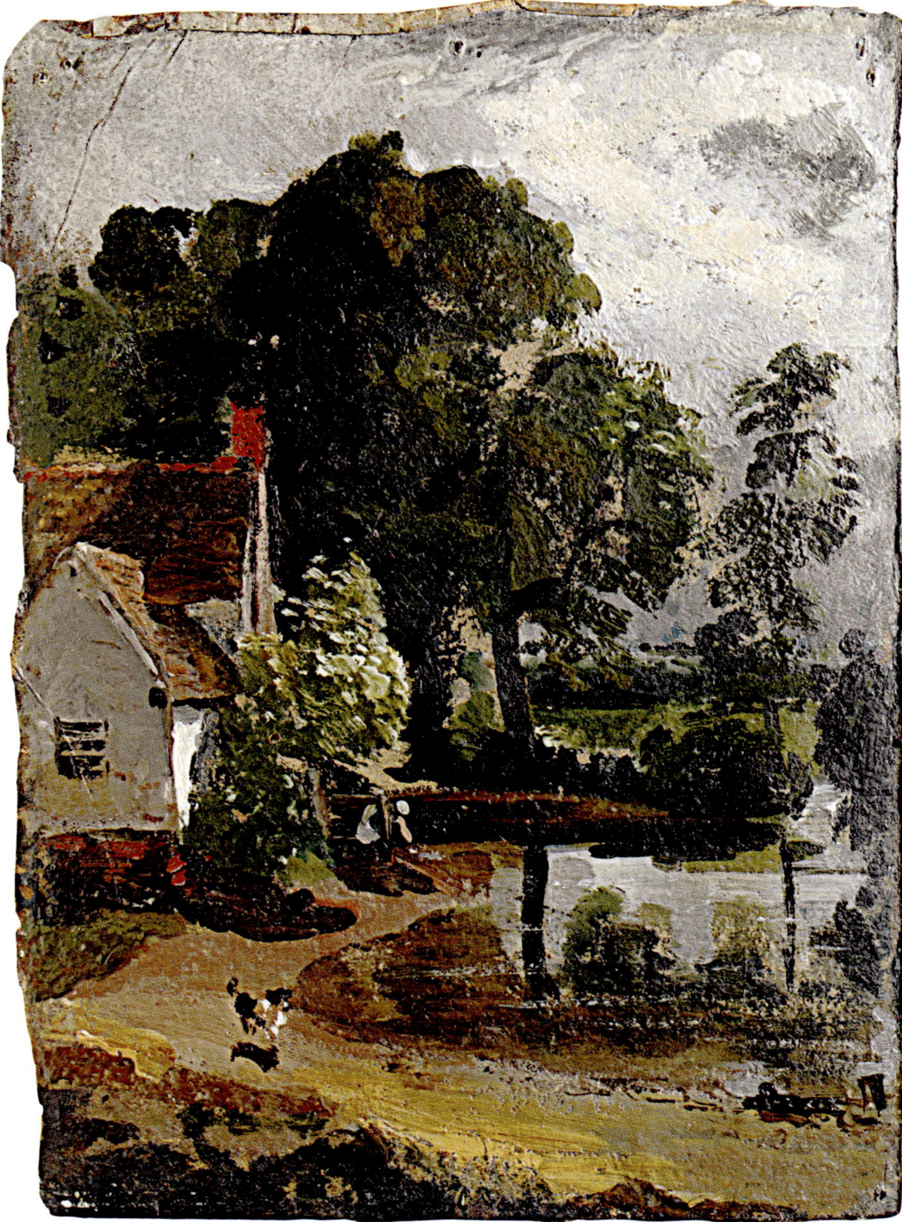

32

Willy Lott's House
c.1811
Oil on paper
24.1 × 18.1 (9$\frac{1}{2}$ × 7$\frac{1}{8}$)
R.11.37

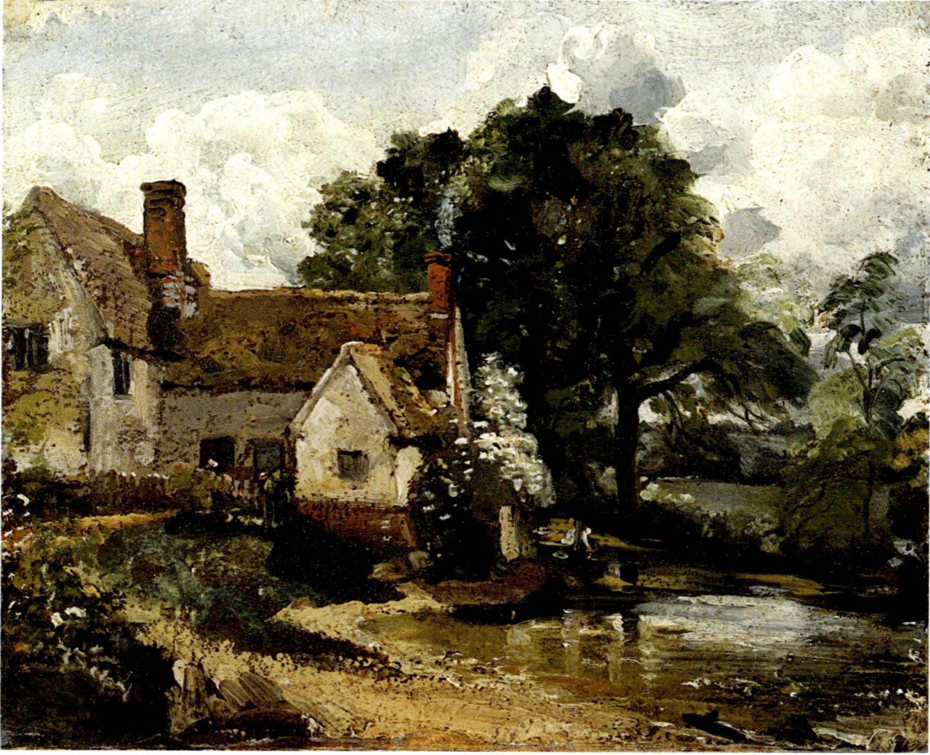

John Arrowsmith offered to purchase it for £70, which Constable did not accept. They subsequently agreed on a transaction in which Arrowsmith received three pictures, *The Hay Wain*, *View on the Stour Near Dedham* (no.39) and one of Constable's views of *Yarmouth Jetty* (it is unclear which one) for £250. In 1824 the three paintings were shown at the Paris Salon and greatly admired, earning Constable a gold medal from Charles X. As has been much discussed in the literature both on Constable and on French painting of the nineteenth century, *The Hay Wain* proved influential for a number of French artists, including Eugène Delacroix, who applied lessons he learned from it in repainting parts of his *Massacre at Chios* (Louvre), which was also shown at the 1824 Salon (see especially Florisoone 1957 and Noon 2003, p.192). Constable's art was also far reaching in its influence on French landscape painters; Constant Troyon, in particular, became deeply enamoured of his work, as is evident in paintings such as *The Approaching Storm* 1849 (fig.15, p.42). Fisher summed the situation up well when he told Constable:

The purchase of your two great landscapes for Paris is surely a stride up three or four of the steps of the ladder of popularity. English boobies, who dare not trust their own eyes, will discover your merits when they find you admired at Paris (JCC VI, p.158). **FK**

The White Horse and had also called *Stratford Mill* 'The Touchwood Tree', although the latter did not stick.

The Hay Wain remained unsold at the Academy and Constable had it back in his studio by late summer, when he told Fisher 'I shall do more to it' (JCC VI, p.71). In October he seems to have finished working on the picture, observing to Fisher that it was now 'much *together*' (JCC VI, p.78). Precisely what Constable did in reworking the painting is unclear, but it has reasonably been speculated that he may have taken advantage of the knowledge he had gained in painting studies of clouds at Hampstead during the preceding months in improving the sky (Reynolds 1984, pp.68–9). However, it has also been noted that the sky in *The Hay Wain* had already been admired when it was first exhibited the previous spring, with one critic praising its 'noble volume of cloud and clear light' (Ivy 1991, p.88).

Among those who were impressed by *The Hay Wain* in 1821 were two Frenchmen, the author Charles Nodier, who declared 'The palm of the exhibition belongs to a very large landscape by Constable', and the painter Théodore Géricault, who was said to have been 'quite stunned' by it (Reynolds 1984, p.69). The following year, when the painting was shown at the British Institution, the Parisian dealer

33

Willy Lott's House
1816
Oil on paper laid on canvas
19.4 × 23.8 (7⅝ × 9⅜)
Inscribed on the back
'J. Constable – 29 July 1816'
R.16.23
IPSWICH BOROUGH COUNCIL
MUSEUMS AND GALLERIES

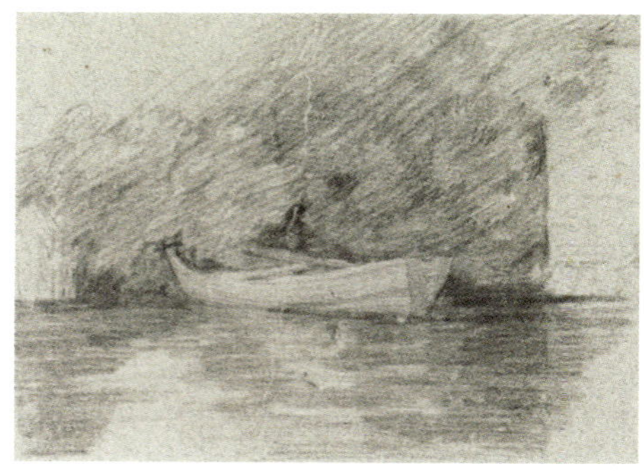

34

A rowing boat moored by a river bank
c.1809–11
Black chalk on blue-grey paper
9 × 12.6 (3½ × 5)
R.09.77
COURTAULD INSTITUTE
OF ART GALLERY, LONDON

35

Sketch for 'The Hay Wain'

c.1820

Oil on paper on panel

12.5 × 18 (4⅞ × 7)

R.21.3

YALE CENTER FOR BRITISH ART,
PAUL MELLON COLLECTION

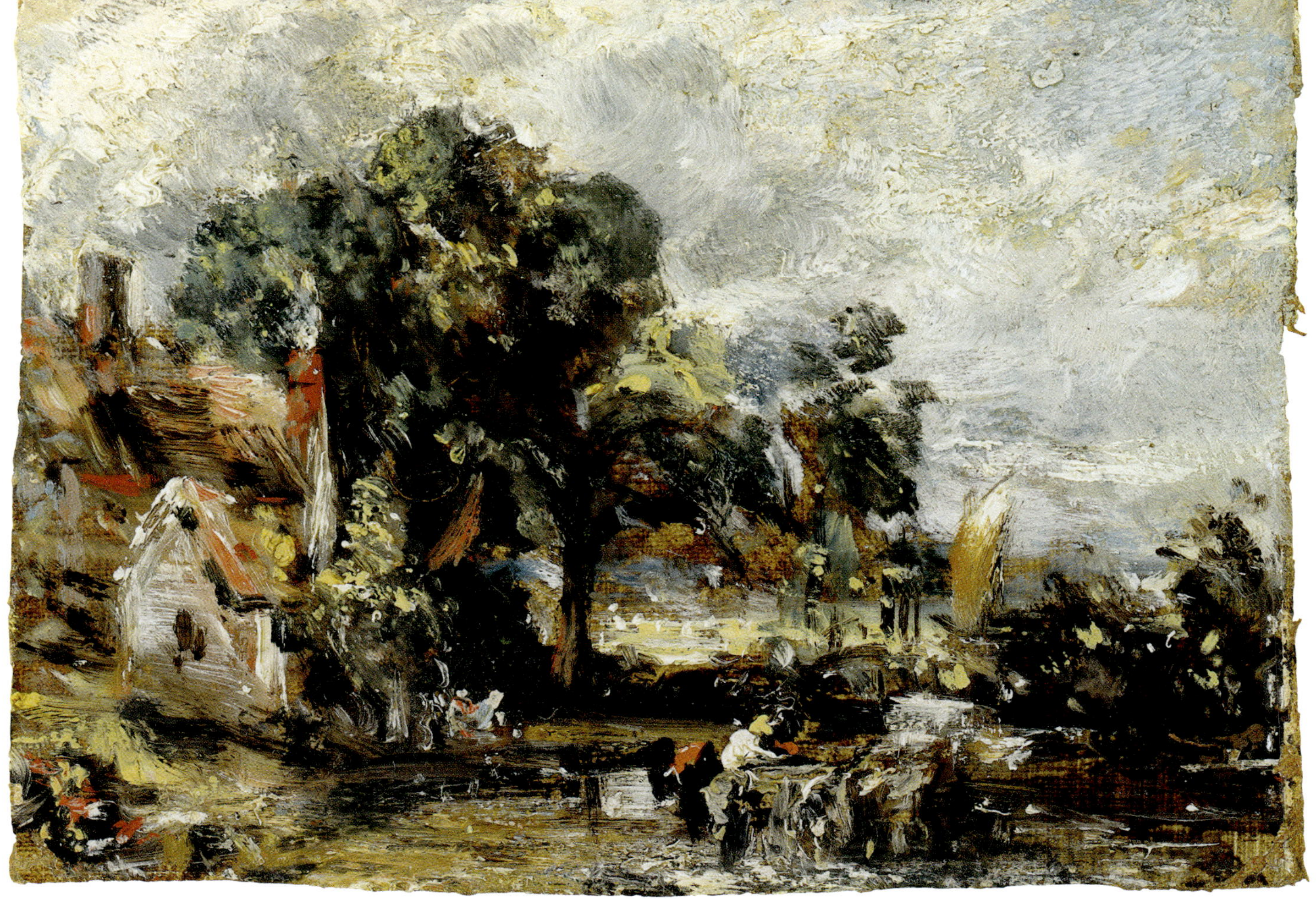

36

The Hay Wain (full-size sketch)
c.1820
Oil on canvas 128 × 184 (50⅜ × 72½)
R.21.2

VICTORIA AND ALBERT MUSEUM,
LONDON. BEQUEATHED
BY MR HENRY VAUGHAN

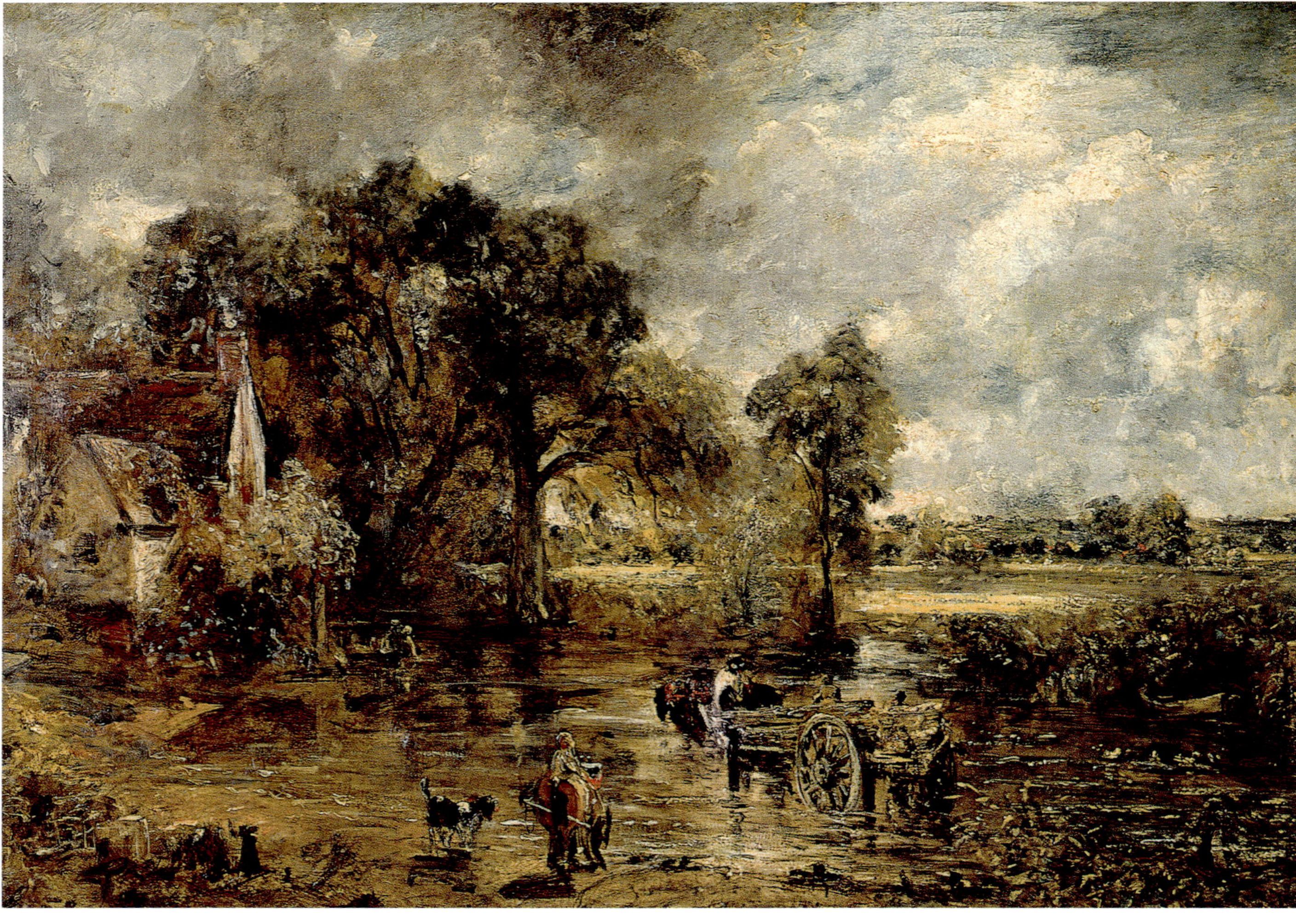

37

The Hay Wain

1821

Oil on canvas 130.5 × 185.5 (51¼ × 73)
Inscribed along bottom edge 'John
Constable pinx^t. London 1821'
Exh: RA 1821 (no.339, *Landscape: Noon*);
BI 1822 (no.197, *Landscape; Noon*; frame
68 × 91 in); Salon, Paris, Aug. 1824–Jan.
1825 (no.358, *Une charrette à foin
traversant un gué au pied d'une ferme;
paysage*)
R.21.1
Ivy 21.3–6; 21.8–9; 21.11–14; 21.16–17; 21.19;
24.21–4
THE NATIONAL GALLERY, LONDON

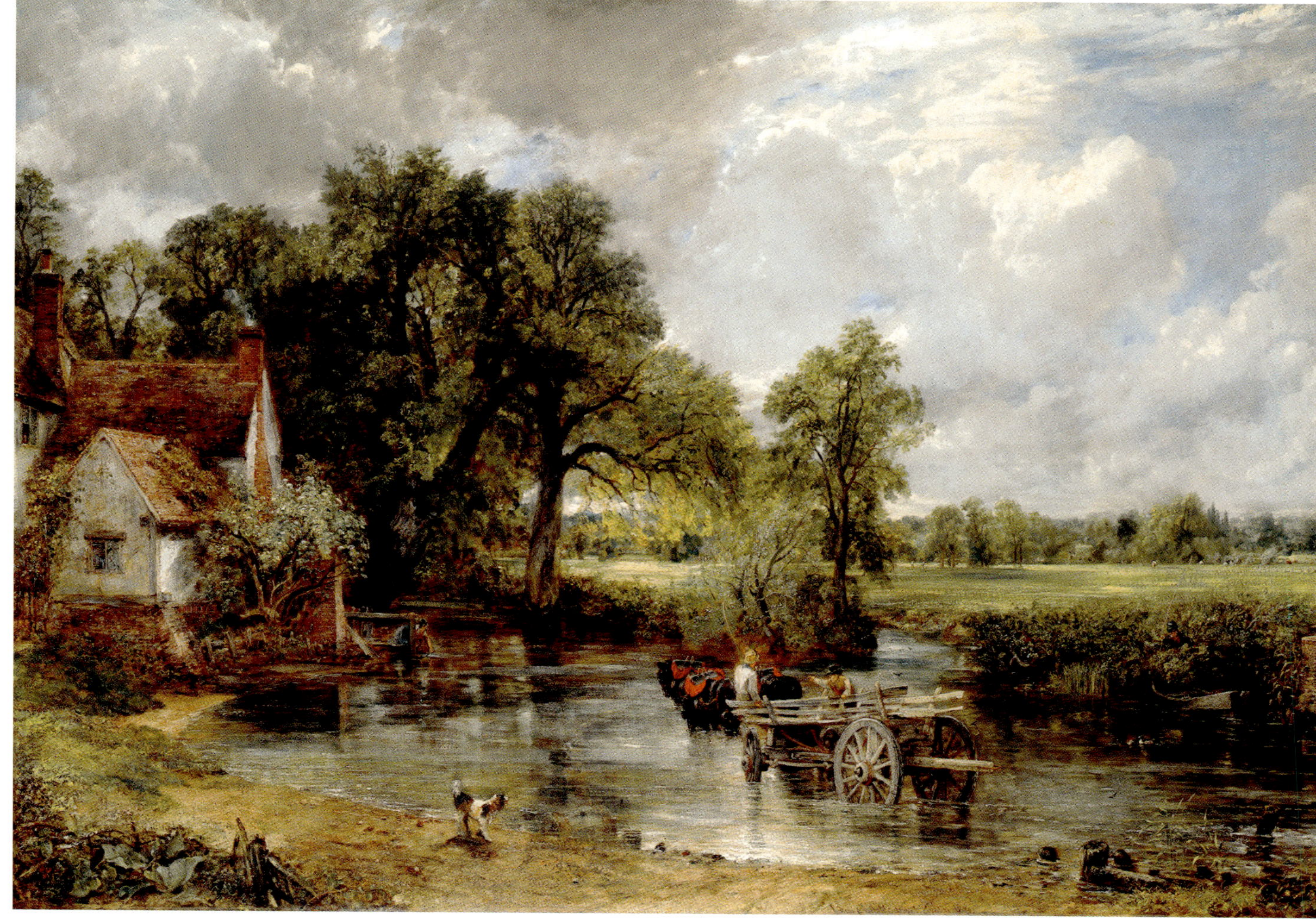

View on the Stour near Dedham

For the first three of his six-foot canvases featuring scenes on the canalised Stour, *The White Horse*, *Stratford Mill* and *The Hay Wain* (nos.29, 31, 37), Constable had allocated a marginal role to its commercial river craft. Indeed in *The Hay Wain*, a scene set in a quiet backwater of the river, barges do not feature at all. In the next three six-footers, by contrast, this one, no.39 – the fourth in the series – and also *The Lock* and *The Leaping Horse* (nos. 41, 47), Constable made the river's traffic the primary focus of attention.

In *View on the Stour near Dedham* (no.39), for example, a barge is being poled into the middle of the stream away from a second barge behind it, so as to continue its journey downstream through Flatford Lock, which is just out of the composition to the left. A third, moored barge on the left is waiting to make its way upstream. Constable's viewpoint is looking towards Flatford footbridge, with Bridge Cottage on the right and Dedham church tower in the distance. In the right-hand foreground we can just see the wooden beam marking the edge of the boatbuilding yard that had been the subject of one of his earlier *plein-air* pictures (see fig.55, p.105).

Constable appears to have started work on the picture in the early autumn of 1821, in a room he had taken for use as a studio in a glazier's shop in London (JCC VI, p.71). He was now spending more time with Maria and their three children in Hampstead, at their residence at No.2 Lower Terrace and, although he had cleared a small shed in the garden there for use as a workshop, it would have been too small to accommodate a six-foot canvas, least of all a full-size sketch as well. Family obligations, however, made it difficult for him to leave Hampstead and thus make any headway on the painting. 'I am … much behind with the Bridge,' he told Fisher on 20 September, referring to the picture by the affectionate name he had himself coined for it, and announcing his resolution to 'leave my family & work in London' (*ibid.* p.74). By 23 October he was again writing to Fisher from Hampstead that he was anxious to get to his London painting room, declaring 'I do not consider myself at work without I am before a six-foot canvas' (*ibid.* p.76). It would seem, therefore, that Constable was unable to make serious progress on *View on the Stour* until he had finally settled his family back into their Keppel Street house towards the end of the month, and was much closer to his rented London studio.

As was the case for his previous six-foot River Stour scenes, when planning no.39 Constable made a preliminary full-scale compositional sketch in oils (no.38). Whilst his earlier full-size sketches had been based on a variety of *plein-air* oil studies and other compositional material, no.38 by contrast seems to have been based on little more than three tiny pencil studies that Constable had made along this stretch of the river in a sketchbook in 1814 (R.14.32). One of these studies, on p.59 of the sketchbook (fig.66), also sketched on p.29, was used by him for the left-hand side of the composition. Fig.67, meanwhile, made on p.52 of the book and showing a view just slightly further upstream so that Bridge Cottage has now come into

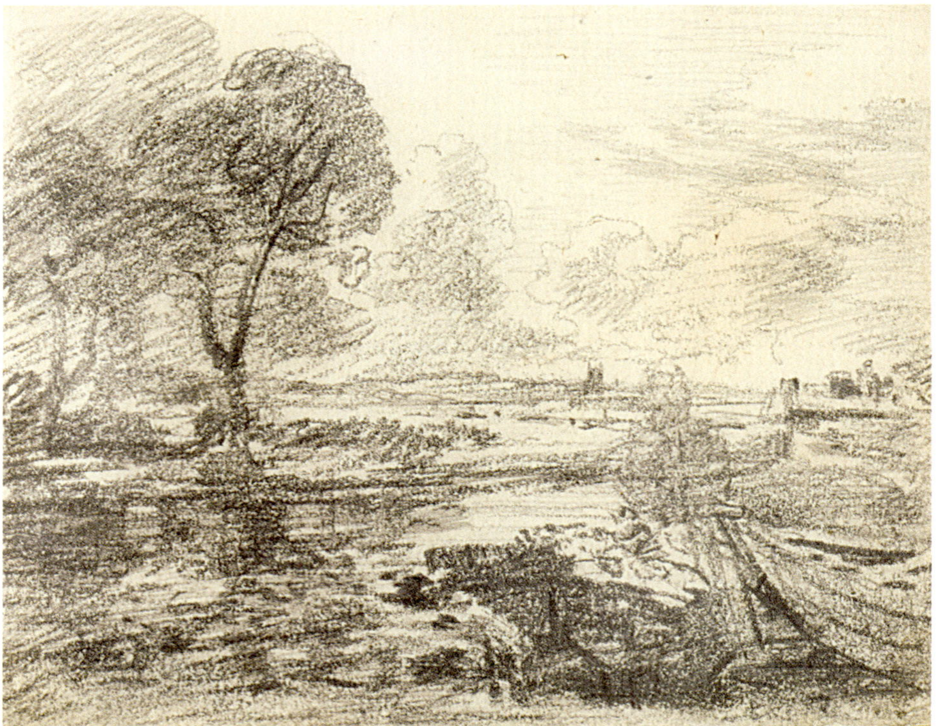

FIGURE 66

Figure 66
Flatford Old Bridge and Dedham Church from the barge-building dock
Page 59 from intact sketchbook used in Suffolk and Essex 1814
8×10.8 ($3^{1}/_{8} \times 4^{1}/_{4}$)
VICTORIA AND ALBERT MUSEUM, LONDON

view, served for the right-hand side.
Constable's decision to integrate here two
different viewpoints into one is indicative of a
growing willingness on his part to favour the
interests of picture-making over any concern
with topographical accuracy.

During the course of the picture's
evolution, indeed, Constable was to make more
changes to the full-scale sketch, as well as
between sketch and finished picture, than
for any of his previous large River Stour
landscapes. Perhaps his procedures were more
complex in this case owing to the slightness
of the preliminary material from which he was
working. However, it would also seem that,
at this particular juncture in the River Stour
series, he was striving to secure a more
ambitious and focused design.

Some of the changes Constable made to
the sketch for *View on the Stour* (no.38) involved
painting out individual details. A number of
these changes (pentimenti) have been known
about for some time, as traces of them can
still be seen with the naked eye. For example,
by careful examination of the painted surface
one can deduce that Constable originally
painted three cows and a figure on the bridge,
as well as a sail on the left of the barge
(its outline can still be seen underneath the
forms of the trees, see fig.40, p.61) and a figure
at its stern.

It was not until 2005, however, that an
x-radiograph of the sketch was taken for the
first time (fig.69, p.149), and it is therefore only
now that the full implications of these changes
can be appreciated. For what the x-radiograph
also revealed is that Constable had originally
included many more figures in the foreground
of the composition. Not only, for example, did
he originally show two young boys fishing in
the sketch – one of which, wearing a hat, looks
as though he was directly adapted from the

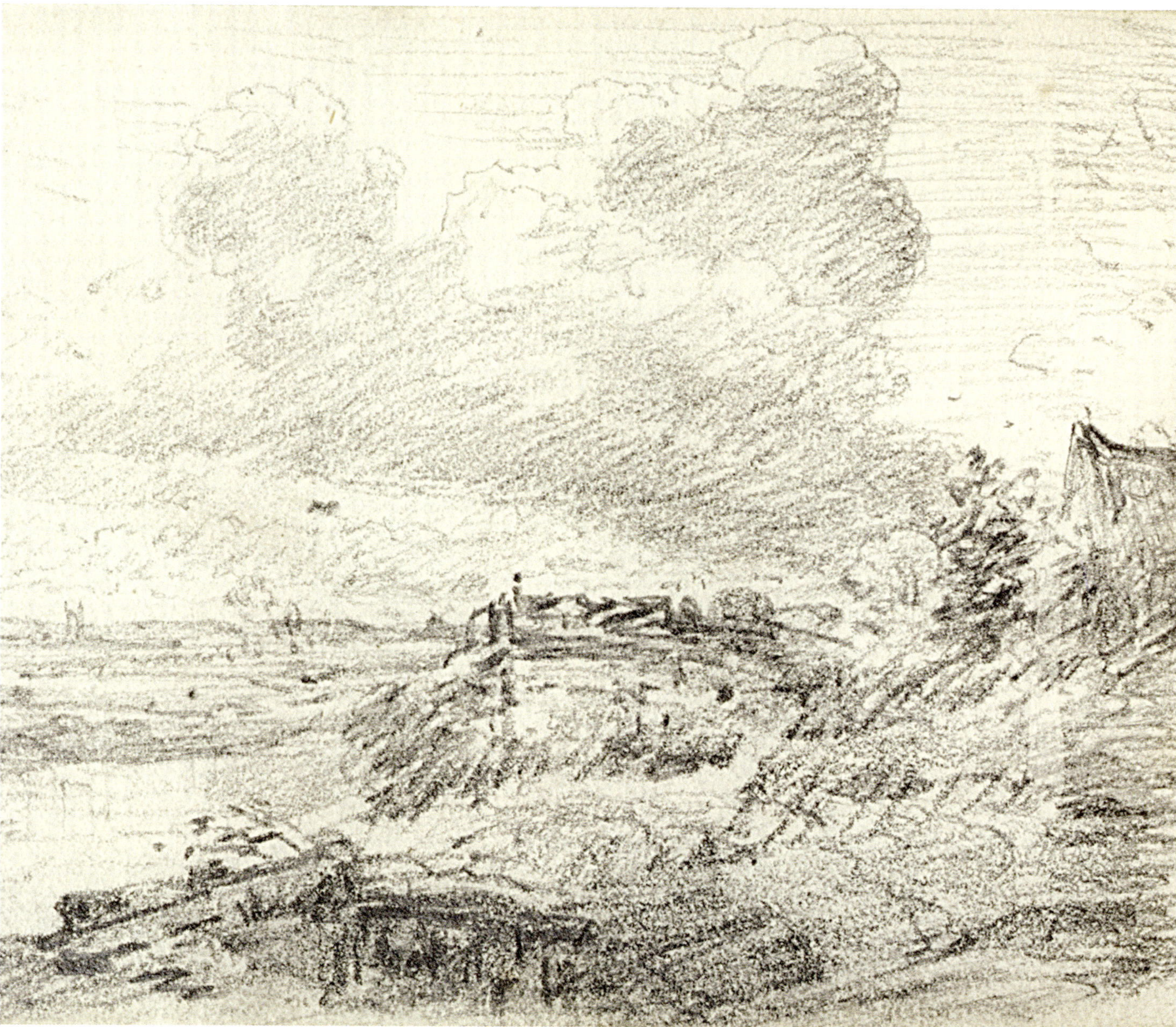

FIGURE 67

Figure 67
Flatford Old Bridge
and Bridge Cottage
Page 52 from intact
sketchbook used in
Suffolk and Essex 1814
8 × 10.8 ($3^1/_8$ × $4^1/_4$)
VICTORIA AND ALBERT
MUSEUM, LONDON

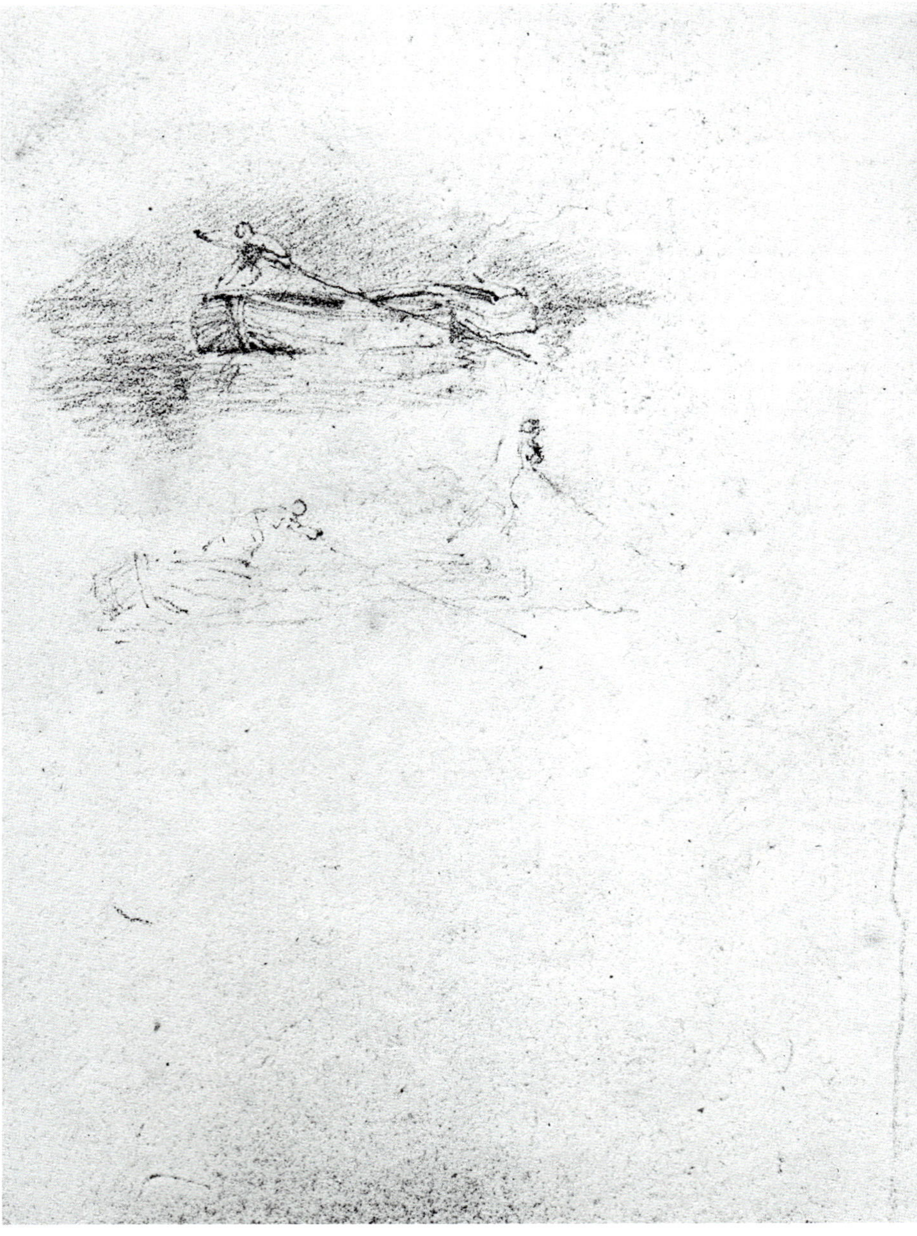

FIGURE 68

Figure 68
**Two sketches of
men or boys
propelling barges**
Page 11 from intact
sketchbook used in
Suffolk and Essex 1813
12 × 8.9 (4¾ × 3½)
VICTORIA AND ALBERT
MUSEUM, LONDON

single figure who appears on the left-hand
side of *Stratford Mill* 1820 (no.31). In addition,
beyond them to the right, he also originally
included the same little girl who had appeared
on the far right-hand side of *Boat-Building*
(fig.55, p.105) as well as, in a leaning position,
in both *Flatford Lock from the Mill House* c.1814
(no.16) and *Stratford Mill*. His subsequent
elimination of figurative detail, then, was
more draconian than previously thought.
Interestingly, the x-radiograph of the sketch
also reveals that Constable originally painted
a boat immediately under the bridge, in a
position not far away from where he was later
to reintroduce it in the finished picture,
indicating that sometimes his changes of
mind might come full circle.

Not all of the changes in the sketch would
necessarily have been made at the same time,
and indeed some of them, including perhaps
the painting out of the sail on the left, may
even have been made at quite a late stage.
Constable then made further changes to the
composition between sketch and finished
picture, and these are evident simply by
comparing the two as they now appear. The
most significant alteration was the addition of
a second barge in the centre of no.39, together
with a lighterman strenuously poling it
towards mid-stream, taken from a tiny study
Constable had made in a sketchbook in 1813
(R.13.17, fig.68). In the finished painting, the
lighterman wears a conspicuous white shirt
and red cap, and his pole sets up a diagonal
movement across the picture plane, which is
then echoed by a long-handled eel spear
strategically placed by Constable close to the
river's edge in the foreground (Asleson and
Bennett 2001, p.62).

As Constable explained in a letter to Fisher
on 1 April 1822, these latter changes, and also
the painting out of the sail in the sketch, were

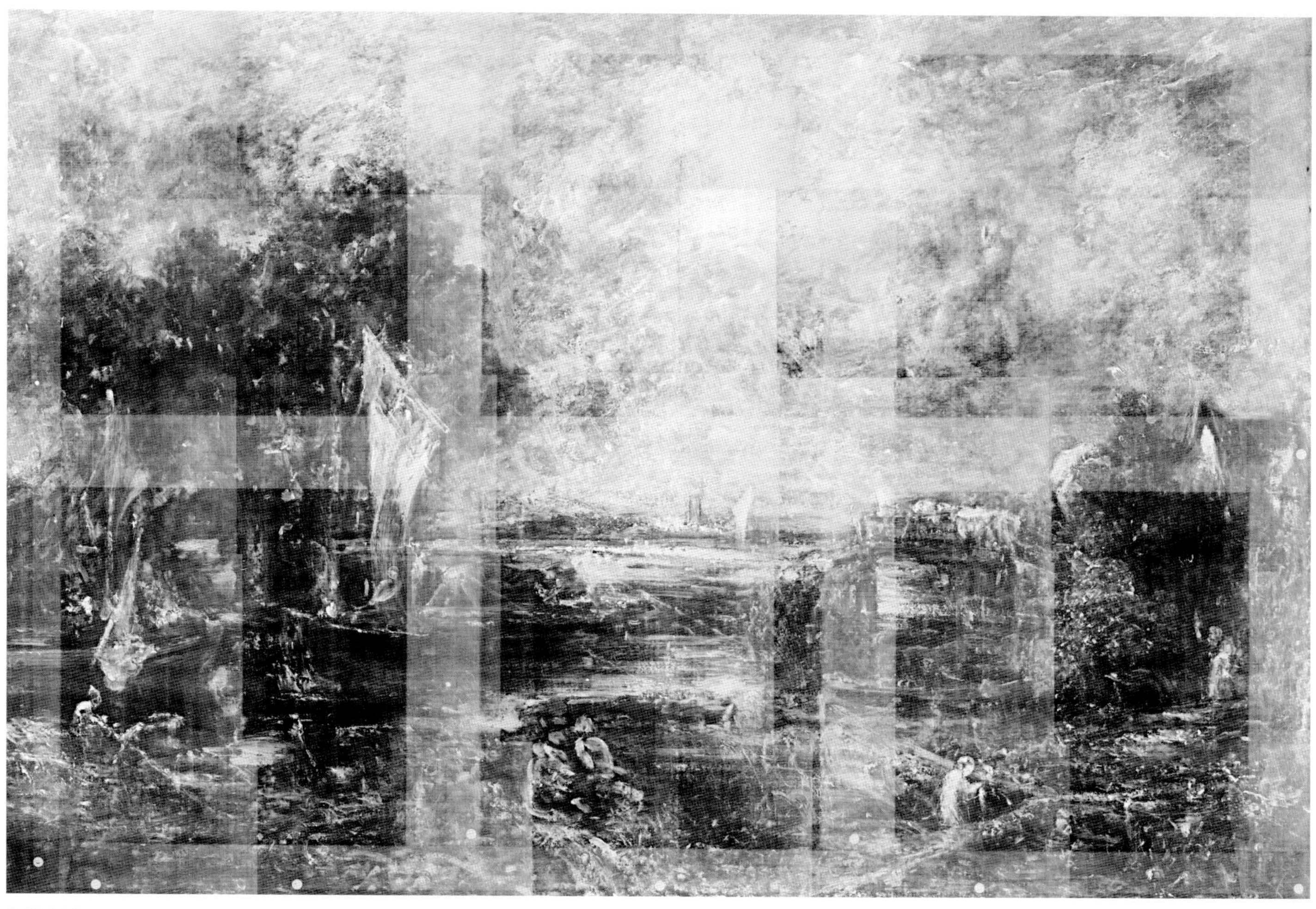

tower of Dedham church. Further small changes can be seen in an X-ray of the finished picture (Asleson and Bennett 2001, p.53; fig.22).

Despite all these changes, and the fact that he had encountered severe delays in getting started on the picture the previous year, Constable seems to have been satisfied he had brought *View on the Stour* to a satisfactory level of finish before submitting it to the Academy in April. 'My conscience acquits me as to any neglect of [my] last picture', he told Fisher in a letter dated 13 April (JCC VI, p.89). Although it failed to find a buyer at either the Academy in 1822 or on its exhibition at the British Institution in 1823, the following year it was purchased, together with *The Hay Wain*, by John Arrowsmith, and on their exhibition at the Paris Salon in 1824 the paintings famously earned Constable a gold medal (see under nos.32–7). The original medal is now in the collection of the National Gallery, London (see Noon 2003, cat.6, p.56). However, inset into the frame of *View on the Stour* is an electrotype of both sides of the medal. On the obverse is a portrait of Charles X of France, and on the reverse is engraved: 'Exposition au Salon de 1824. M. CONSTABLE PEINTRE DE PAYSAGE.'

View on the Stour (no.39) was still in France when, in the early 1830s, Constable selected the subject for inclusion in *English Landscape*. David Lucas therefore made the print (Shirley 1930, no.19) from the full-scale sketch instead. AL

primarily designed to give the picture a 'rich centre'; he wanted to ensure that the right-hand side of the composition did not draw the eye away from the heart of the design (JCC VI, p.89). To hold his 'rich centre', however, as Robert Wark has pointed out (1971, p.116), Constable also needed to eliminate any

distracting features from the periphery of the composition. So he omitted from no.39 the man rowing in a skiff on the left as well as the two boys fishing on the lower right, although he then inserted into the reedbeds just beyond them a less conspicuous moored boat. Meanwhile, the cow on Flatford footbridge was

replaced with a woman in a bonnet, and the bridge itself was made 'entire'; that is, Constable ensured the whole of its structure was visible by removing some of the foliage at the right. Finally, he reduced the size of the sail belonging to the boat in the distance, probably because it otherwise threatened to dwarf the adjacent

Figure 69
Composite
x-radiograph of full-size
sketch for *View on the
Stour near Dedham* c.1821
(no.38)
PRIVATE COLLECTION

38

**View on the Stour near Dedham
(full-size sketch)**

c.1821

Oil on canvas

129.4 × 184 (51 × 72½), including extensions at
top, bottom and left where the original tacking
edges were incorporated into the picture
surface. Original dimensions of the canvas
before these extensions were approximately
127 × 182.8 (50 × 72). There are sufficient tack
holes visible along the top, left and right edges,
located approximately 5cm (2in) apart, to
suggest that the sketch was squared up with
threads at these intervals when Constable
transferred the design to the finished canvas.

R.22.2

PRIVATE COLLECTION

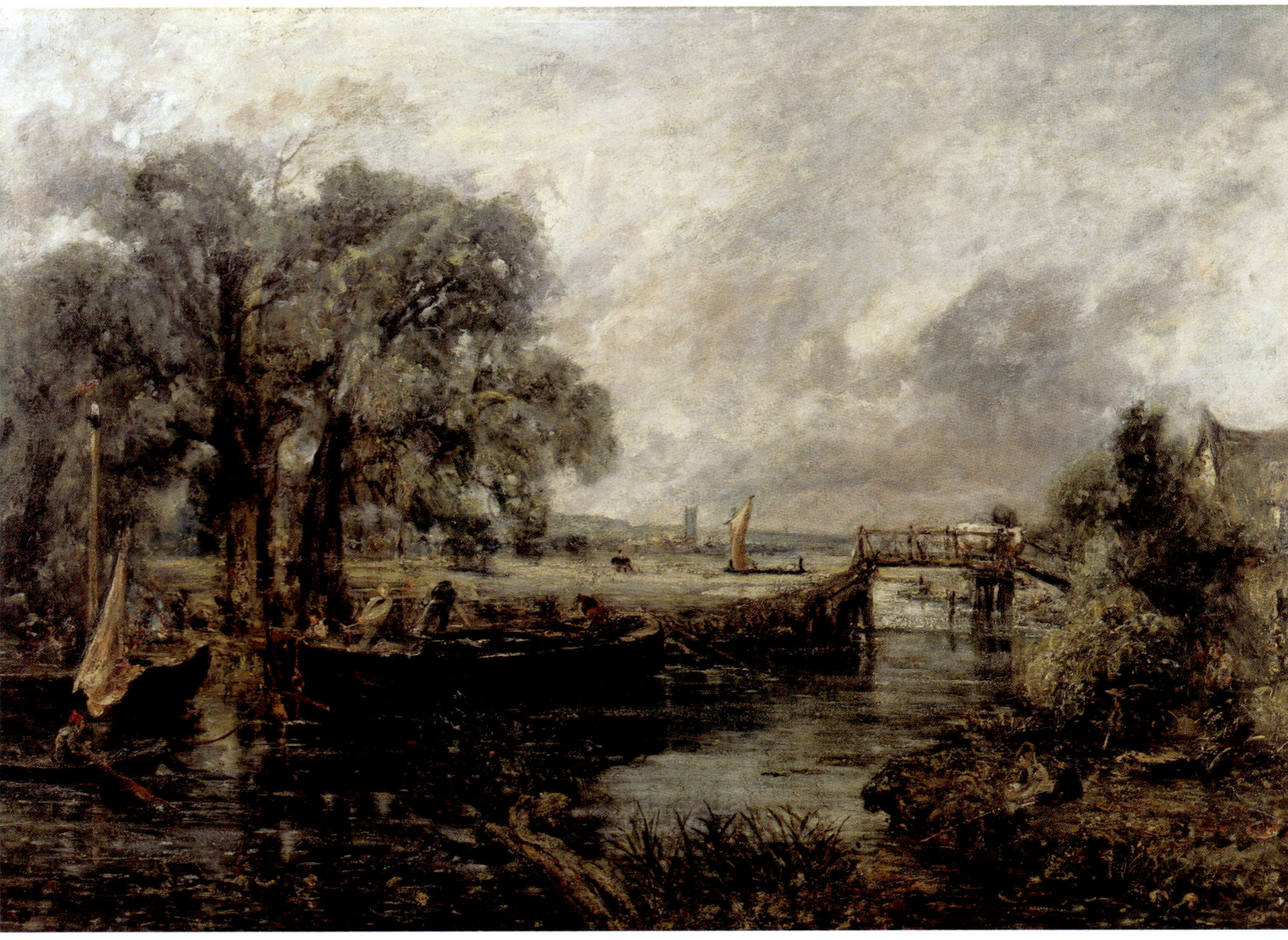

39

View on the Stour near Dedham

1822

Oil on canvas

130 × 188 (51 × 74), including extensions at top, bottom, left and right where the original tacking edges were incorporated into the picture plane (probably by the artist, though possibly done during lining)

Signed and dated in the bottom right-hand corner in sloping letters 'John Constable pinx. London 1822'

Exh: RA 1822 (no.183, *View on the Stour, near Dedham*); BI 1823 (no.35, *Landscape*); Salon, Paris, Aug. 1824–Jan. 1825 (no.359, *un canal en Angleterre; paysage*)

R.22.1

Ivy 22.7; 22.14; 22.17–20; 22.22–3; 23.1–5; 25.19

THE HUNTINGTON LIBRARY, ART COLLECTIONS, AND BOTANICAL GARDENS

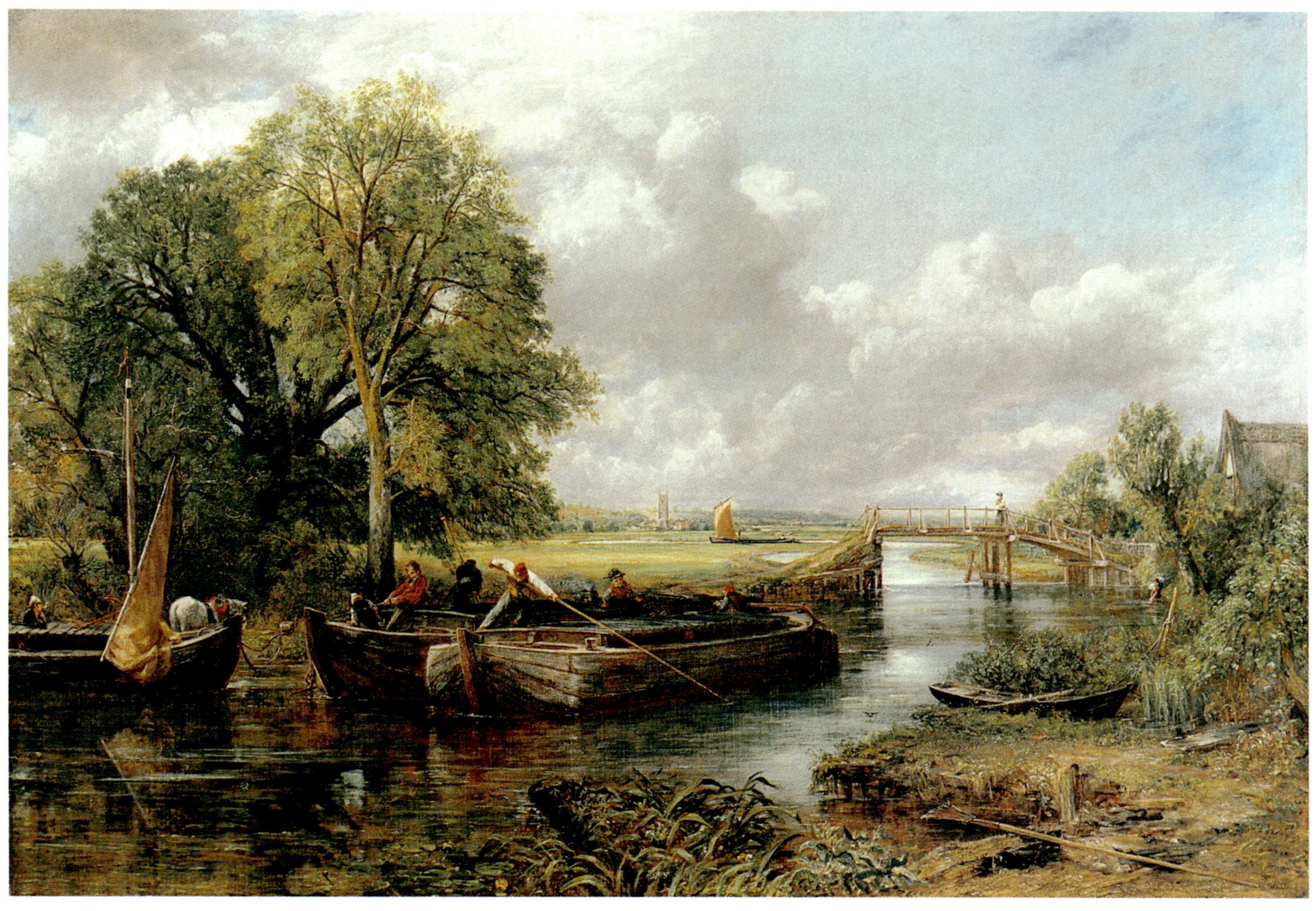

The Lock

The subject in these paintings is the lower (i.e. downstream) gate of Flatford Lock seen from a close vantage point looking westward, with the tower of Dedham church visible in the distance. The upstream gate, and much of the structure of the lock itself, may be easily discerned in the background of *Flatford Mill* (no.19). In *The Lock*, a barge waits in the flooded chamber of the lock, steadied by a man who pulls firmly on a line passed around a bollard on the bank. At the centre of the composition, a man in a red waistcoat heaves on a crowbar to work the mechanism that allows water to rush from the lock into the river. On the opposite side of the lock are a brown tow-horse, a dog, and a boy who prepares to assist with the opening of the gates. Constable was deeply enamoured of scenes such as this. As he wrote in 1821:

the sound of water escaping from Mill dams … Willows, Old rotten Banks, slimy posts, & brickwork. I love such things … As long as I do paint I shall never cease to paint such Places (JCC VI, p.77).

Except for *The Lock*, all of Constable's major exhibition pictures of Stour scenery (nos.29, 31, 37, 39, 47) were horizontal canvases, and it is not clear when he made the decision to change formats. On 21 February 1823 he told Fisher: 'I have put a large upright Landscape in hand, and I hope to get it ready for the Academy' (JCC VI, p.112), which might refer to a lock subject. However, in the first known reference where Constable specifically identifies the subject, it is only as 'my Lock' (6 Dec. 1823; JCC VI, p.146), with nothing to indicate whether it was horizontally or vertically orientated. Not until a letter to Fisher of 17 January 1824 do we find conclusive evidence of the canvas's format: 'I am about my upright Lock' (JCC VI, p.150). What is known with certainty, however, is that the shape of the canvas used for the large sketch of the subject (no.40) was altered at some point. A strip of canvas was added at the top to increase the height by about 11 1/4 inches (28.5cm), and the right side was cut down (by exactly how much is unknown, although it is not believed to have been more than about 6 inches (15cm; Tate 1991, p.284, citing Cove thesis). Thus, the canvas was originally horizontally configured, which suggests Constable's initial thoughts may have been of a composition similar to that seen in two subsequent variants on the theme (fig.8, p.28; fig.70, R.26.15). It has been suggested (Tate 1991, p.290) that a pen and ink studio sketch (fig.71, R.26.17) may indicate what Constable first envisaged in depicting the scene, and may have been used as inspiration for the initial composition of no.41 in its horizontal format.

Without question, the bold handling of the large sketch, where the forms are laid in largely with the use of a palette knife, indicate that it was always intended as a study and never thought of by Constable as something that could be finished for exhibition. On the reverse is a sketch of the head of a girl (R.24.3), which suggests it was an abandoned canvas now reused. X-radiographs (fig.72) show that Constable originally painted horizontal beams spanning the lock; these beams, which helped support the wooden walls of the lock, were actually present and may be seen in *Flatford Mill*. In the pen and ink drawing (fig.71), Constable did include one of the beams at the end of the lock, but angled it up towards the

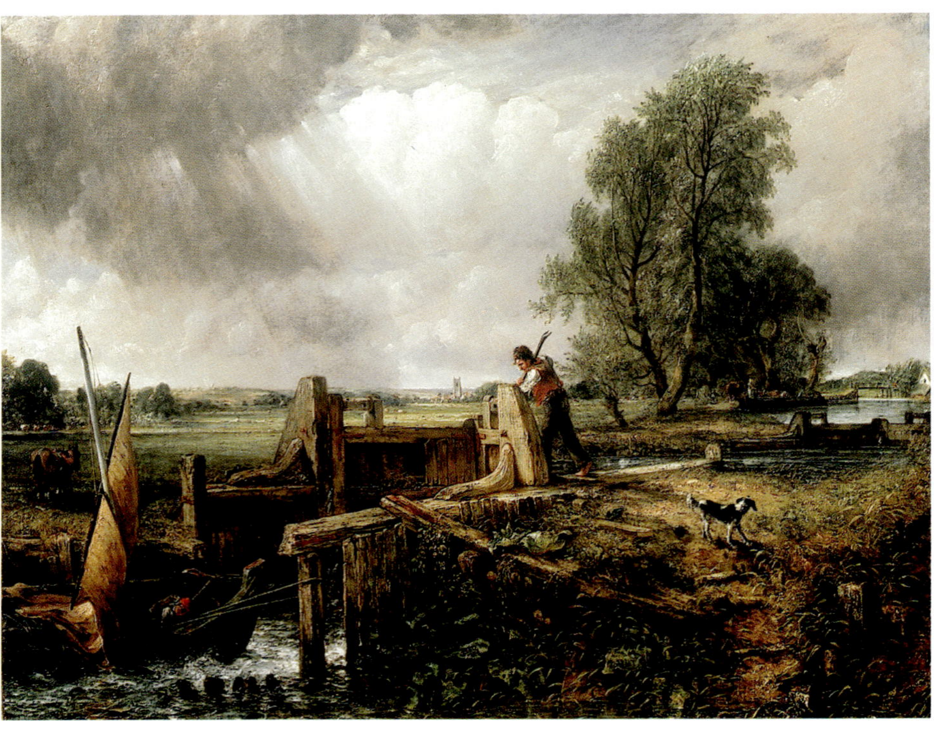

Figure 70
A Boat Passing a Lock
1826 (exh.1829)
Oil on canvas
101.6 × 127 (40 × 50)
ROYAL ACADEMY OF ARTS,
LONDON

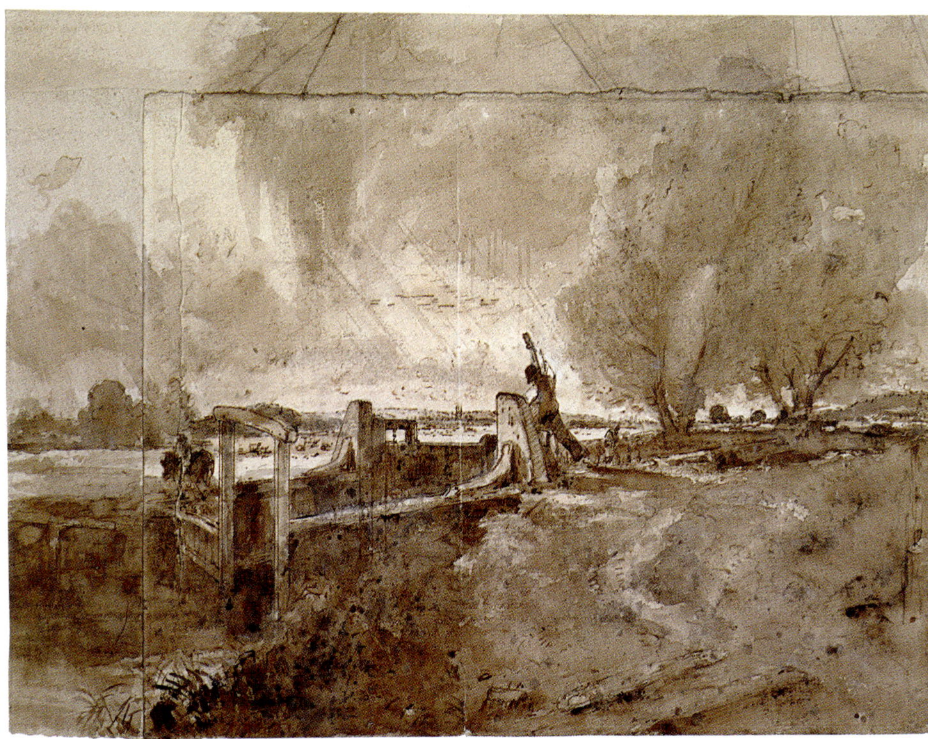

left so that it did not intersect with the horizon line. His decision to paint over the beams in the sketch and eliminate them altogether in the subsequent pictures must have been due to his realisation that they created a distracting visual rhythm that conflicted with the view across the meadows to Dedham.

Constable's choice to shift to a vertical format was likely made so that the motif of the man working the lock could become the painting's centre of interest, both literally in placement, and also aesthetically in establishing a focus for the picture's compositional energies. Furthermore, thanks to the recent discovery of *Flatford Mill from the*

Figure 71
Flatford Lock
c.1824
Pen and ink
28.7 × 36.4 (11¹/₄ × 14³/₈)
FITZWILLIAM MUSEUM,
CAMBRIDGE

Mill House c.1814 (no.16), we now know that he had already treated the subject of Flatford Lock on an upright format, albeit on a much smaller scale. In his earlier *Dedham Lock and Mill* paintings (see nos.23–5), a similarly posed man working the lock is included in the middle distance, but he is only a tiny detail in the overall composition; now he becomes the protagonist. In the sketch the man's hands are placed at the exact centre of the canvas, and his arms are aligned precisely on the diagonal between the top left and bottom right corners. They thus establish a dramatic vertical vector of sight within the composition. A countering lateral movement is established by the

diagonal of the canal running from right to left, while the exertions of the man on the barge create a contrasting torque to the energies of the man at the lock.

The exhibited version follows the sketch rather closely, although with certain refinements and adjustments. Constable's handling of paint, similar to that he used in preceding exhibition pictures, is more restrained and less openly expressionistic than in the sketch, and the details throughout are brought to a higher level of finish (although, as Cove points out above, p.64, this is the first of Constable's 'finished' six-footers to show any conspicuous use of the palette knife). The structure of the lock itself is revealed with greater specificity, and the fishing pole lying on its foremost horizontal beam has been replaced by another large timber running perpendicular to it. The deletion of the rod removed a certain sense of genre-like incident (the suggestion being that the man has just stopped fishing in order to attend to his duties), and thus helped suppress the particular in favour of the timeless (Dorment 1986, p.50).

The Lock, which was first shown with the title *A boat passing a lock*, was completed by 15 April 1824, when Constable wrote to Fisher:

I was never more fully bent on any picture than on that which you left me engaged upon – It is gone to its audit with all its deficiencies in hand – my *friends* all tell me it is my best. be that as it may I have done my best. It is a good subject and an admirable instance of the picturesque (JCC VI, p.155).

The picture was well received and generally praised by critics. As the reviewer for the *Literary Gazette* wrote:

We have always had occasion to remark the skill with which this artist, in a style peculiar to himself, effects the most perfect representation of the objects of his study,

whether of foreground or of distance. The character of his details, like those of Wilson, appear as if struck out with a single touch; but this we are well aware, comes only by great practice and much previous thought and calculation. In none of his former works have these essential qualities been more distinctly visible than in this picture. It is a fine example of the picturesque, with which its striking and powerful execution well accords (Ivy 1991, p.107).

Constable was clearly pleased, writing in May 1824 to Fisher:

My picture is liked at the Academy. Indeed it forms a decided feature and its light cannot be put out, because it is the light of nature – the Mother of all that is valuable in poetry, painting, or anything else – where an appeal to the soul is required. The language of the heart is the only one that is universal – and Sterne says that he disregards all rules – but makes his way to the heart as he can. My execution annoys most of them and all the scholastic ones – perhaps the sacrifices I make

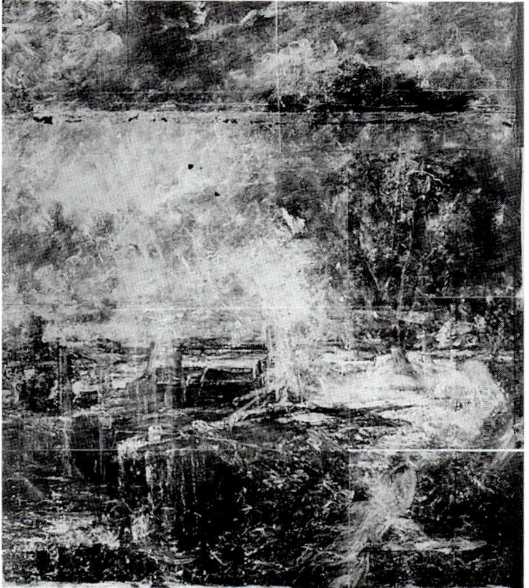

Figure 72
Composite x-radiograph of the full-size sketch of *The Lock* c.1823 (no.40)
PHILADELPHIA MUSEUM OF ART.
THE JOHN HOWARD MCFADDEN
COLLECTION

for *lightness* and *brightness* is too much, but these things are the essence of landscape. Any extreem is better than white lead and oil and *dado* painting (JCC VI, p.157).

The Lock sold on the opening day of the Academy exhibition – a first for Constable – to James Morrison, a successful entrepreneur who had become wealthy through importing a variety of goods and investing in railroads. Fisher congratulated his friend: 'I am not surprised that "The Navigator" sold on a first inspection, for it was one of your best pictures' (JCC VI, p.158). As was the case with *Stratford*

Mill, Fisher's nickname for the picture did not stick, as had the ones he coined for *The White Horse* and *The Hay Wain*. It would be some time before Morrison actually received the picture, for Constable had it back in his studio in November 1824, working to prepare it for the engraver S.W. Reynolds, who had proposed making a print of it at his own expense. 'My Lock is now on my easil,' he wrote to Fisher in April 1825. 'It looks most beautifully silvery, windy & delicious – it is all health – & the absence of everything stagnant, and is wonderfully got together after only this one

year' (JCC VI, p.200). Constable was represented by the picture in the exhibition of *Living Artists of the English School* at the British Institution in May 1825, after which it was finally released to Morrison, with whose descendants it remained until 1990. Reynolds never completed the print. However, a large engraving was made by Reynolds's pupil, David Lucas, from a second version of the picture that Constable made with the help of his studio assistant, John Dunthorne (R.25.33; for the print by Lucas, see Shirley 1930, no.35). FK

40

The Lock (full-size sketch)
c.1823
Oil on canvas
141.7 × 122 (55³⁄₄ × 48). The canvas has been extended by the artist at the top by approximately 28.5cm (11 1/4in) and cut down at the right by no more than approximately 15cm (6in)
R.24.2
PHILADELPHIA MUSEUM OF ART: THE JOHN HOWARD MCFADDEN COLLECTION

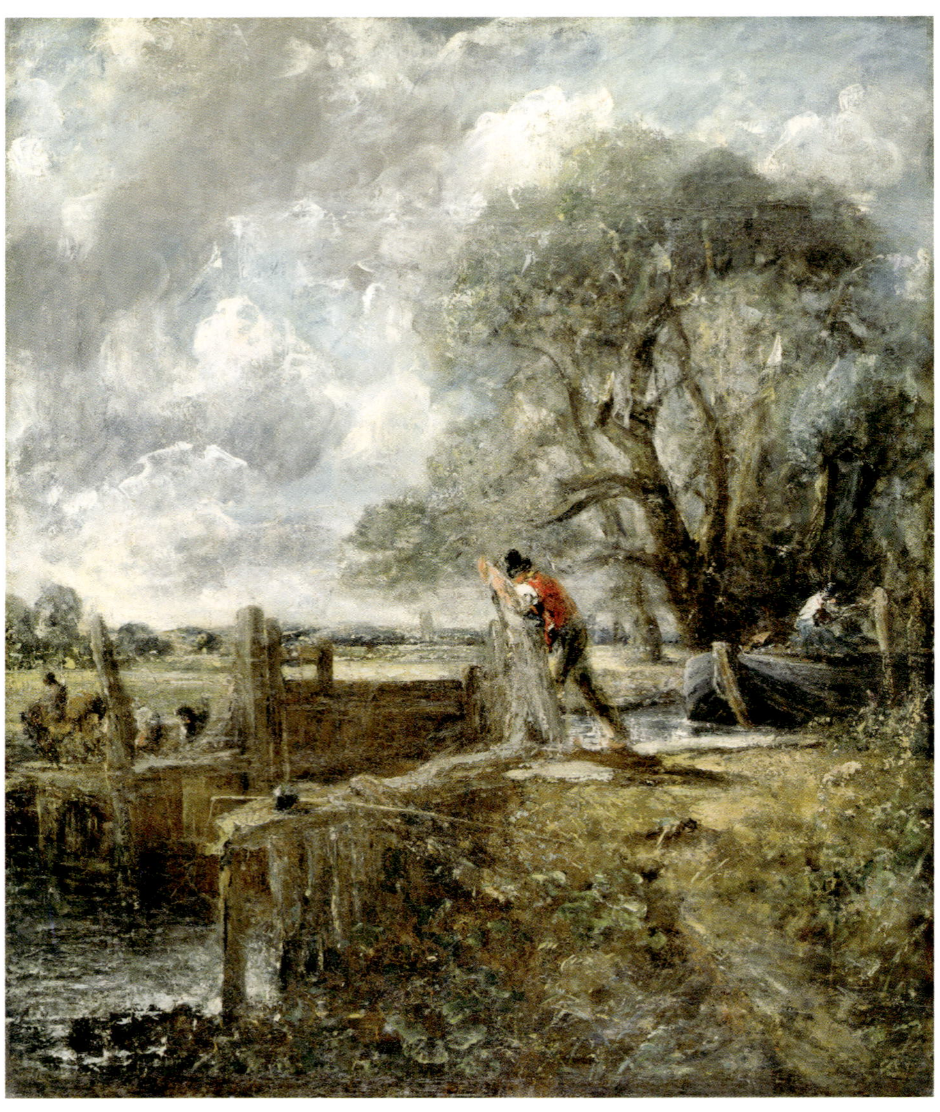

41

The Lock
1824
Oil on canvas 142.2 × 120.7 (56 × 47½)
Exh: RA 1824 (no.180, *A boat passing a lock*);
Living Artists of the English School,
BI 1825 (no.129, *The Lock*)
R.24.1
Ivy 24.10–12; 24.14–16; 24.18–20
COLLECTION OF CARMEN THYSSEN-
BORNEMISZA, ON LOAN TO THE THYSSEN-
BORNEMISZA MUSEUM, MADRID

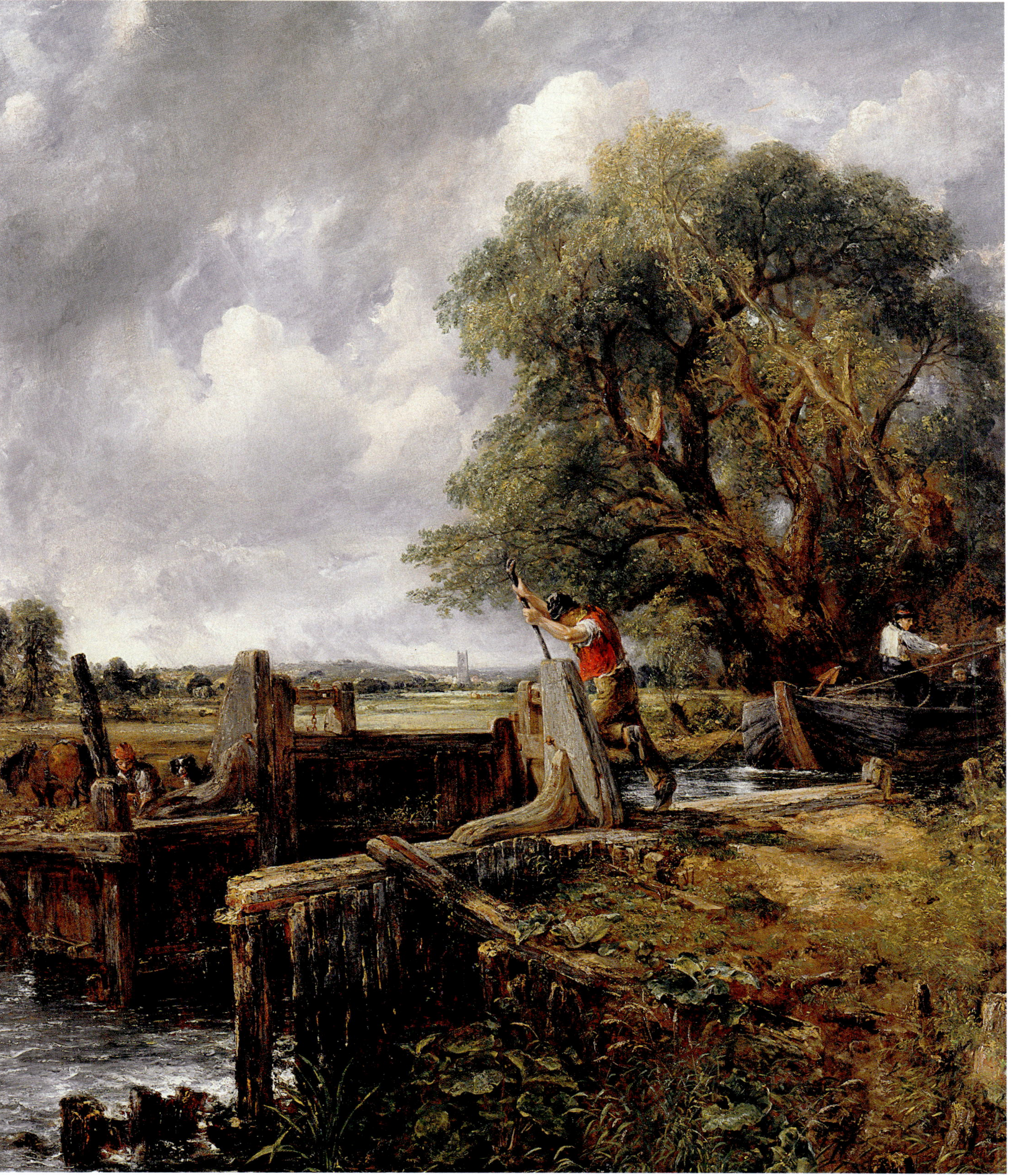

The Leaping Horse

The Leaping Horse is the sixth and last of the large River Stour scenes that Constable exhibited at the Royal Academy between 1819 and 1825. Arguably the most powerful of all his Suffolk river views, it also forms what has been described as the 'pictorial and emotional climax' of the entire series (Reynolds 1965, p.77).

Dealing once again with the traffic on the River Stour, this time Constable chose a site further upstream from Flatford towards Dedham. The site, sometimes known as the Float Bridge or the Float Jump, features a sluice on the south bank of the Stour at a point where the course of the old river temporarily left the navigable section (see map, p.72). Here, over a small wooden bridge (Float Bridge) on the towpath immediately above the sluice, a three-foot high (91cm) wooden barrier had been constructed to prevent cattle straying. Local Suffolk barge-horses were specially trained to leap over such barriers, hence both the title of Constable's painting and the alternative name of the site, the Float Jump.

In a letter of 17 November 1824, Constable told Fisher he was planning another 'large picture' in his series of River Stour scenes, and by 17 December he confirmed he was actually 'putting a 6-foot canvas in hand' (JCC VI, pp.181, 187). He first explored his ideas for the composition in two studio sketches in pen and ink. The earlier of the two studies (no.42) shows two barges manoeuvring past the Float Jump, one of which is still waiting for its stationary horse to be ridden over the barrier. In the second drawing, however (no.43), which now shows a single boat, the horse has become a prancing steed, but as yet it carries no rider. Only in the full-scale sketch (no.46) does Constable develop the key dramatic idea of introducing a rider to urge the leaping horse forwards over the jump. It has often been remarked, indeed, that seen from a low viewpoint on the timber framework of the bridge, Constable's horse and rider take on a resemblance to an equestrian monument on a high architectural base, recalling Renaissance prototypes by artists such as Leonardo da Vinci (Clark 1960, p.120). The rearing horse and rider have also been compared with other great equestrian portraits of the past such as Diego Velázquez's *Count Duke Olivares on Horseback* (Prado, Madrid; see Tate 1991, p.295).

Constable continued to inform Fisher about his progress on the picture in January the following year. At first he spoke of his 'usual anxieties' in getting himself properly 'launched' on the picture, though towards the end of the month he was making better progress, telling him that the subject was now 'most promising' (JCC VI, pp.190–1). As had been the case for his preceding large River Stour pictures, Constable made various changes to the composition during the course of its evolution, both on the full-scale sketch and between sketch and exhibition picture. For example, the x-radiograph of the sketch reveals that Constable originally included a young boy striding out towards the main barge at the left, perhaps assisting it to clear the bank (Young and Parkinson 1992, p.311, fig.37), as well as, apparently, ropes being thrown towards it from the prow of the second barge just entering the scene from the left. Neither of these features was to be carried over into the finished picture. However, x-

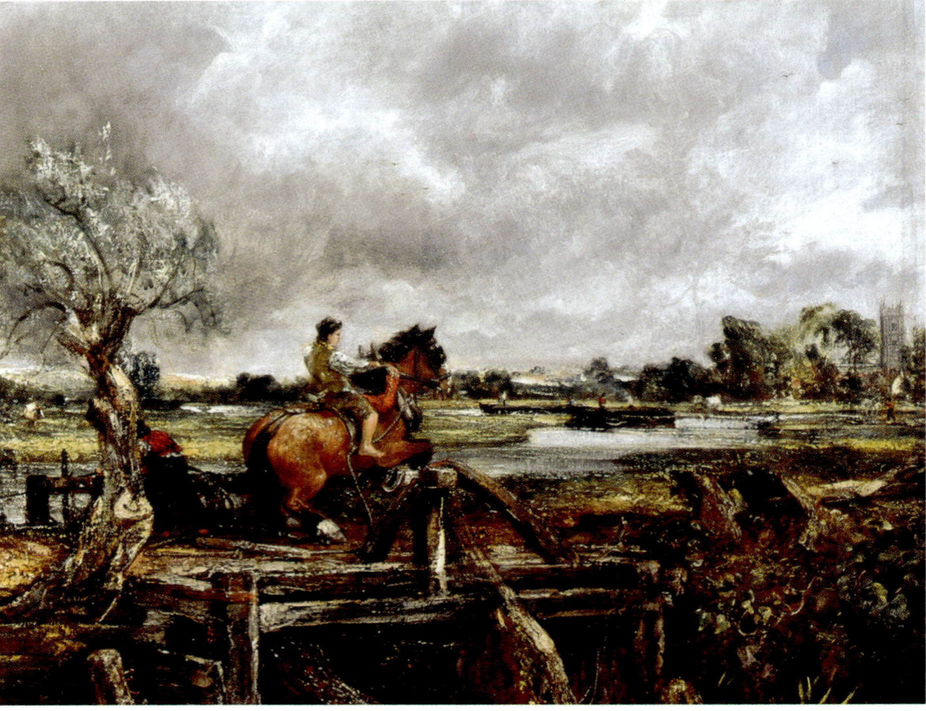

FIGURE 73

Figure 73
Detail from 'The Leaping Horse' 1825 (no.47), showing traces of the painted-out willow to the right of the horse under the sky
ROYAL ACADEMY OF ARTS, LONDON

radiographs of the latter reveal that other details from the sketch, such as the boat entering from the left, one of the figures in the main barge manoeuvring the boat with a pole, and a cow on the far river bank just to its right, were initially carried over into the exhibited picture by Constable and then later painted out.

By early April, Constable informed Fisher that he had recently submitted the painting to the Academy, but was nevertheless unhappy about its state of completion. 'It is a lovely subject, of the canal kind,' he told him, 'lively – & soothing – calm and exhilarating, fresh – & blowing, but it should have been on my easil a few weeks longer' (JCC VI, pp.197–8). One of the key differences between the sketch and the finished picture as it appears today is in the respective positions of the willow stump. In the sketch the willow is placed to the right of the horse, but in the exhibited painting it is to the horse's left, thus opening up the vista, and thus the momentum of the picture, on the right. We know however that Constable originally painted the willow stump in no.47 to the right of the horse, in roughly the same position as it appears in the sketch. Indeed it would surely have been in this latter form that Constable would have submitted the picture to the Academy exhibition at the end of March 1825. For in September of that year – that is, after the picture had returned from the Academy exhibition unsold – Constable noted in his journal that he 'took out the old willow stump by my horse' (JCC II, p.385). Having overpainted the willow on the right, he then reintroduced it to the left of the horse instead (fig.73). Sarah Cove has established that other alterations to the picture, such as adding a strip to the upper edge of the canvas and the extension of the tall tree on the far bank of the river at the left, would have been made by

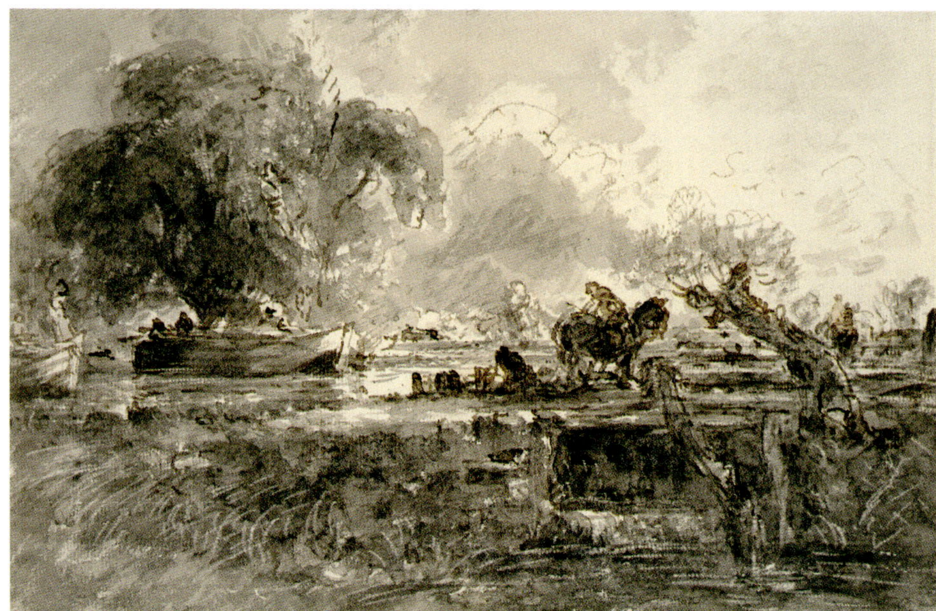

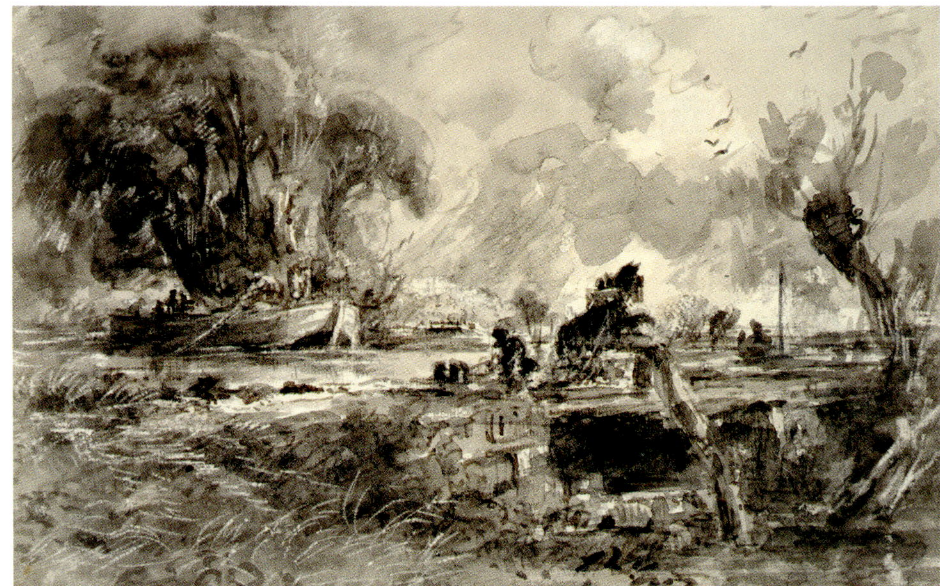

Constable around the same time (see p.64).

Only a month before he embarked on these alterations, Constable had received a letter of enquiry from a potential purchaser, Francis Darby of Coalbrookdale, Shropshire, in the English Midlands, son of the famous Abram Darby who built the world's first cast-iron bridge. Darby expressed an interest in acquiring one or more of Constable's exhibits shown in the recent Academy exhibition, which included not only *The Leaping Horse* itself but also two companion pictures of Hampstead Heath (*Branch Hill Pond, Hampstead* and *Child's Hill*, R.25.5–6; see also Tate 1991, pp.235–7). In due course, Darby decided to buy the two views of Hampstead Heath. However the description Constable sent Darby of *The Leaping Horse* at this time is of particular interest in highlighting some important features relevant to its narrative content that might otherwise, one suspects, be in danger of passing unnoticed. He wrote:

Scene in Suffolk – banks of a Navigable River – barge Horse leaping on an old Bridge. under which is a flood Gate and an Eli bray. river plants and weeds – a more-Hen frightened from her nest – near by in the meadows is the fine Gothic tower of Dedham (JCC IV, p.97).

'Eli bray' or elibray is probably local vernacular for an eel-trap, and indeed a net can be seen in no.47 trailing in the sluice under the bridge, almost certainly set to trap eels (Tate 1991, p.296). The moorhen frightened from her nest by the thunder of hoofs on the wooden bridge, meanwhile, adapted by Constable from no.45, is just visible at the lower right-hand edge of the picture, whilst the 'fine Gothic tower of Dedham ' can just be made out on the very far right-hand side. Neither of these two details is included in the full-scale sketch, and indeed Dedham church actually stands behind the

42

**First Study for
'The Leaping Horse'**
1824
 Pen, brown ink, grey and brown wash on laid paper
20.2 × 30 (8 × 11¾)
R.25.3
THE BRITISH MUSEUM,
LONDON

43

**Second Study for
'The Leaping Horse'**
1824
Pencil, pen and grey wash on laid paper
20.2 × 30.1 (8 × 12⅞)
R.25.4
THE BRITISH MUSEUM,
LONDON

viewer at this point of the river (see map, p.71), as Constable himself was well aware, having regularly walked this route to school in Dedham as a young boy.

The idea of including Dedham church here to close the composition at the right may have been suggested to Constable by an earlier pencil study he had made of the church next to a willow stump, albeit taken from the opposite bank (no.44). However, its function in the finished picture is likely to be primarily of symbolic rather than pictorial value, expressing something of Constable's religious feeling for the harmony of nature, as well, perhaps, as the significance of the established church as a focus of order in the traditional rural world (Honour 1979, p.90; Hemingway 1992, p.247). There may also have been further significance for Constable in the fact that the barge-horse is leaping over a barrier situated directly over the course of the old river that marks the county boundary, and thus that it is in the process of crossing from Essex into the artist's native Suffolk (see Smart and Brooks 1976, p.105). AL

44

A Willow Stump
c.1821
Pencil on paper
9.3 × 11.9 (3⁵⁄₈ × 4³⁄₄)
R.21.14
COURTAULD INSTITUTE
OF ART GALLERY, LONDON

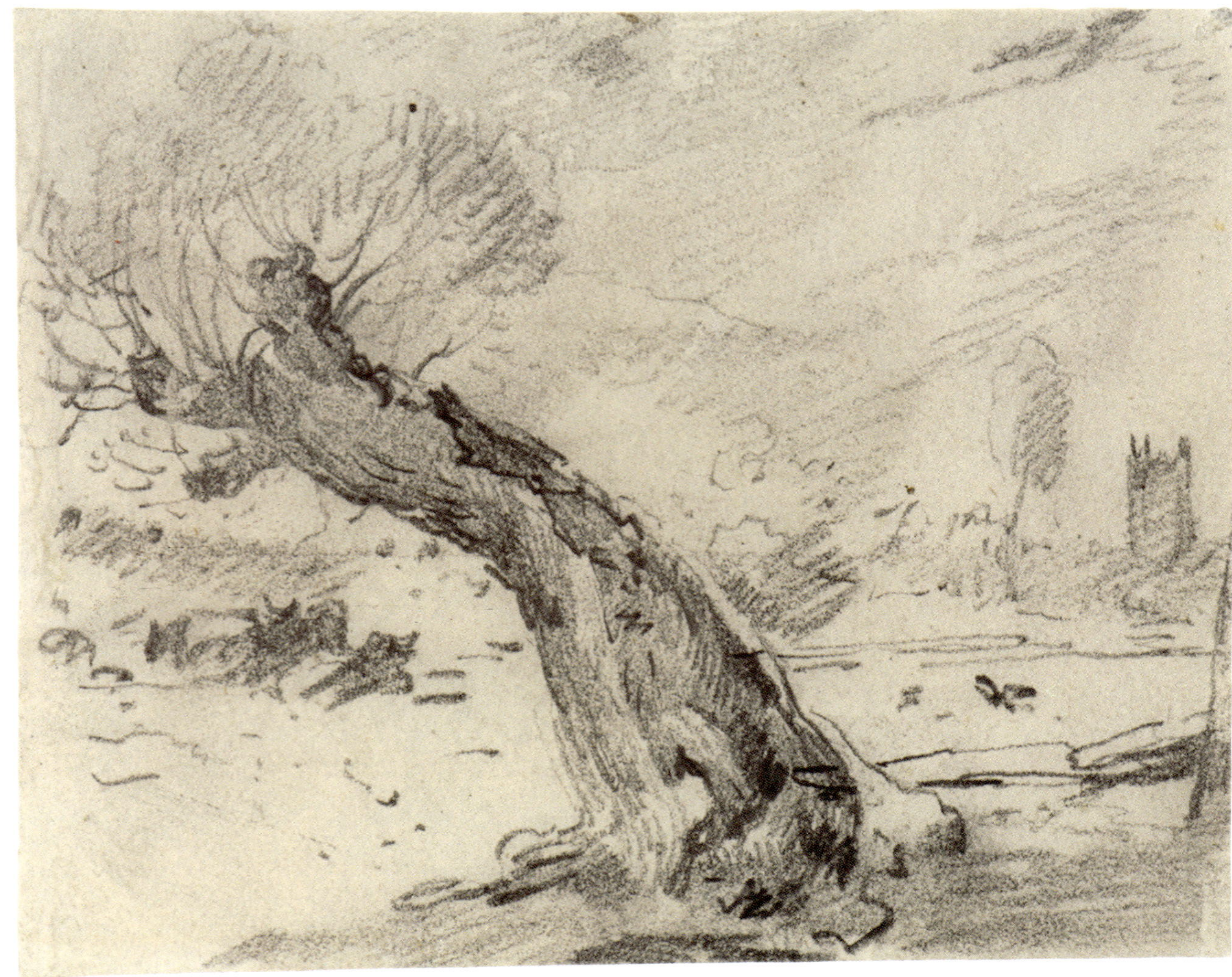

45

**A Moorhen startled
from its nest**

c.1824
Oil on board
14.6 × 15.2 (5¾ × 6)
R.24.84
PRIVATE COLLECTION

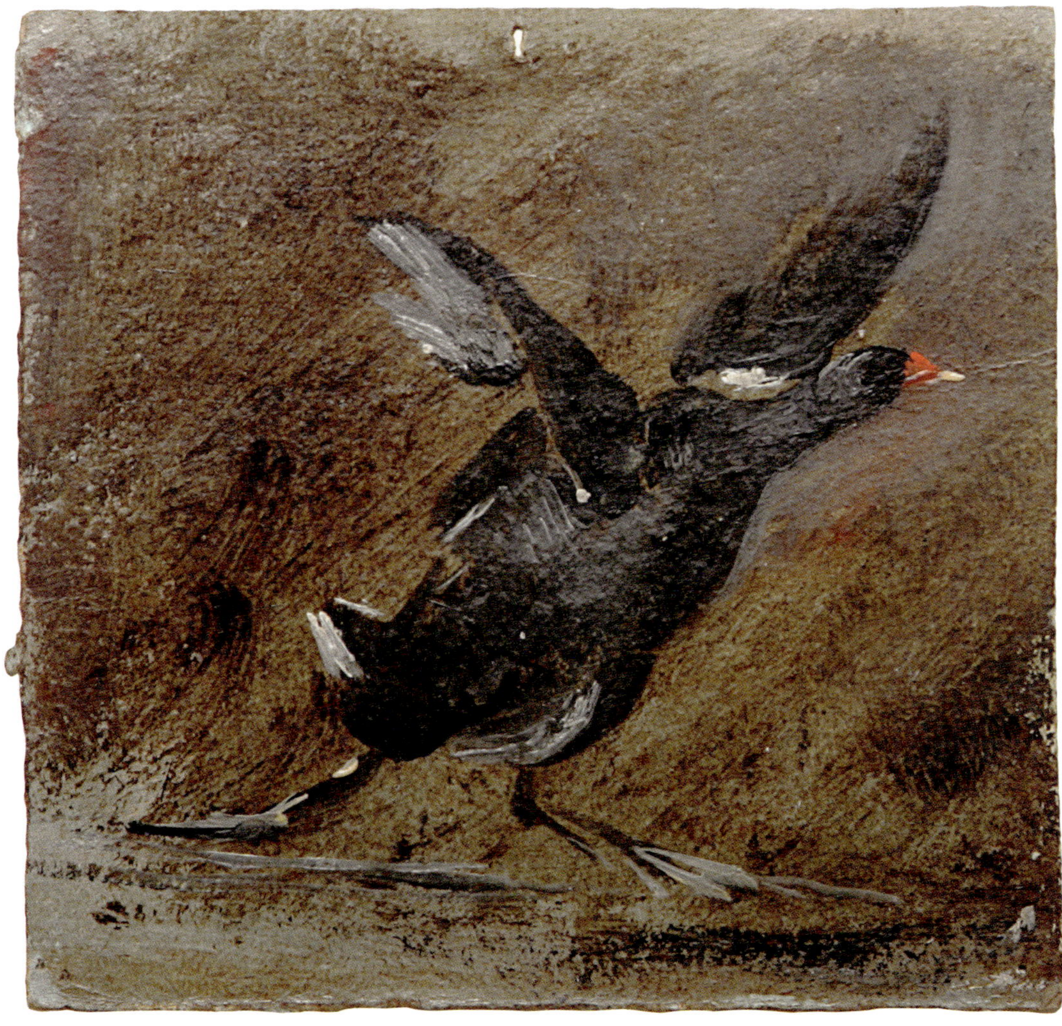

46

The Leaping Horse (full-size sketch)
c.1824
Oil on canvas
129.4 × 188 (48 × 72), including extensions at top
and right, where the original tacking edges were
incorporated into the picture surface, and further
butt-joined extensions at top and lower edges,
probably added after Constable's death
R.25.2

VICTORIA AND ALBERT MUSEUM, LONDON.
BEQUEATHED BY MR HENRY VAUGHAN

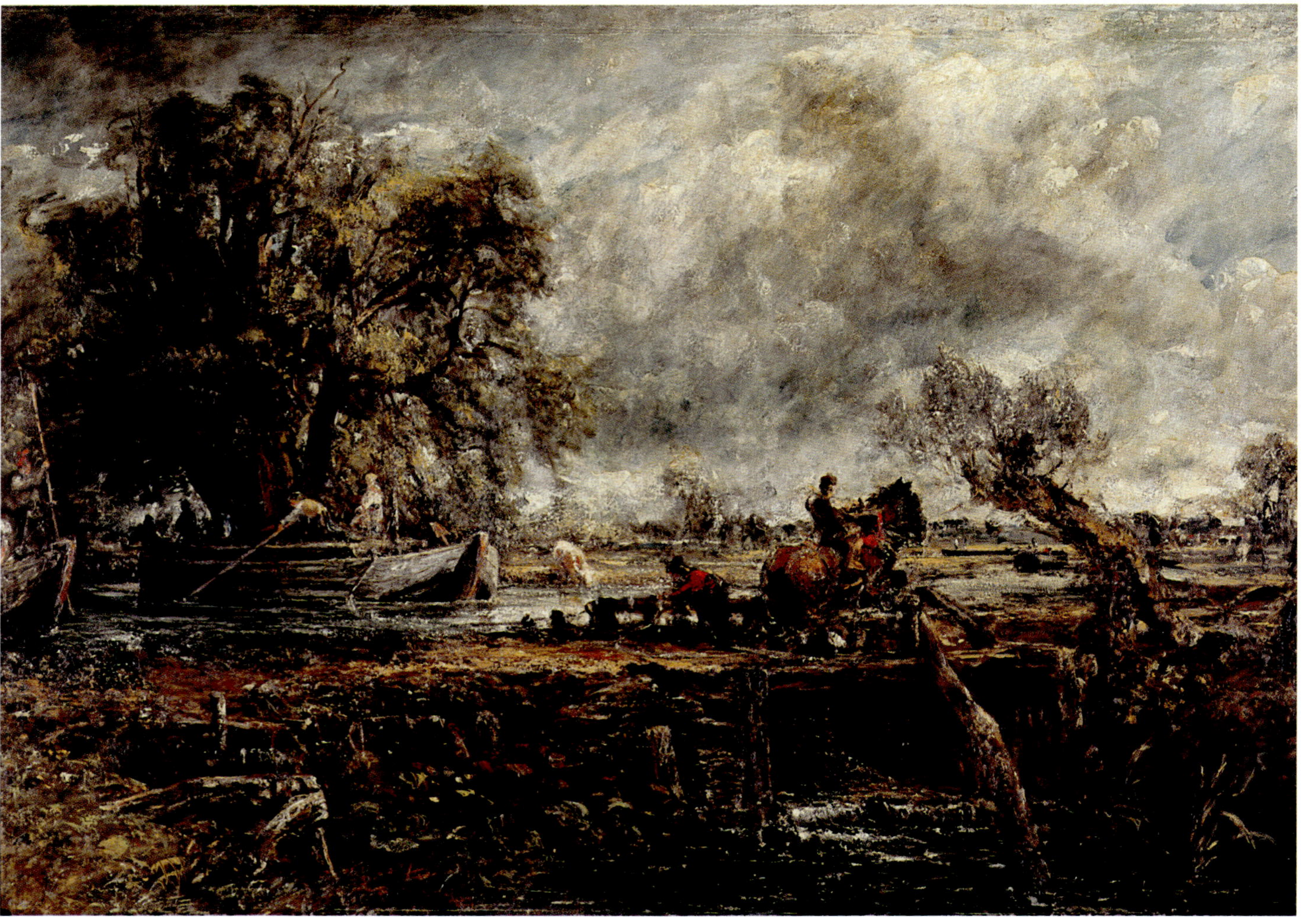

47

The Leaping Horse

1825

Oil on canvas

139.7 × 185.4 (55 × 73), including extensions
made by incorporating the original tacking
edges in the picture surface and by the later
addition of a separate 6.3cm (2 ¹⁄₂-in) strip at
the top. Original dimensions of the canvas
before these extensions and additions would
have been approximately 127 × 177.8cm
(50 × 70 in). The right-hand side of the canvas
also has a modern butt-joined extension added
when the picture was lined in 1965.

Exh: RA 1825 (no.224, *Landscape*)

R.25.1

Ivy 25.4; 25.9; 25.14–15

ROYAL ACADEMY OF ARTS, LONDON

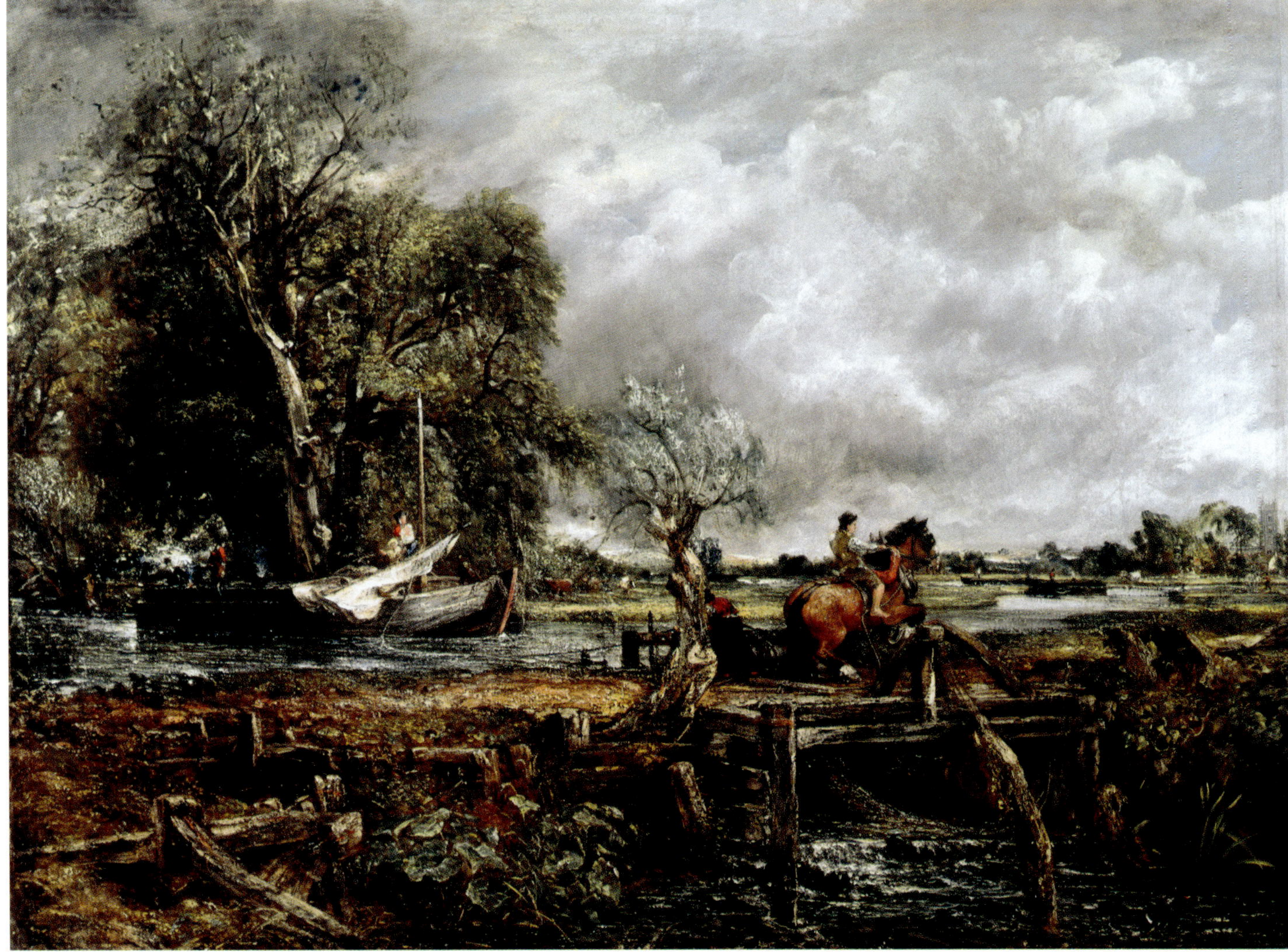

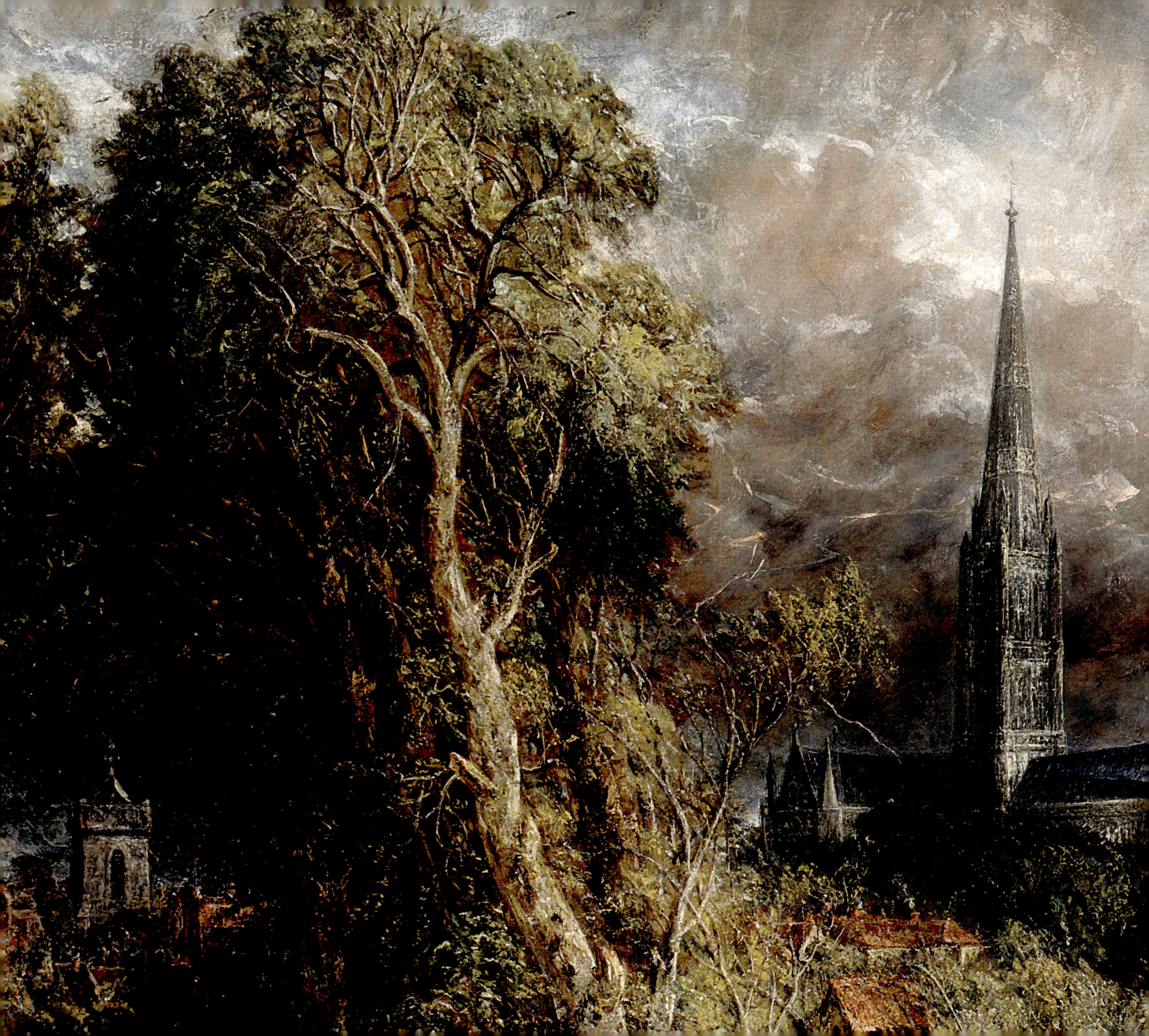

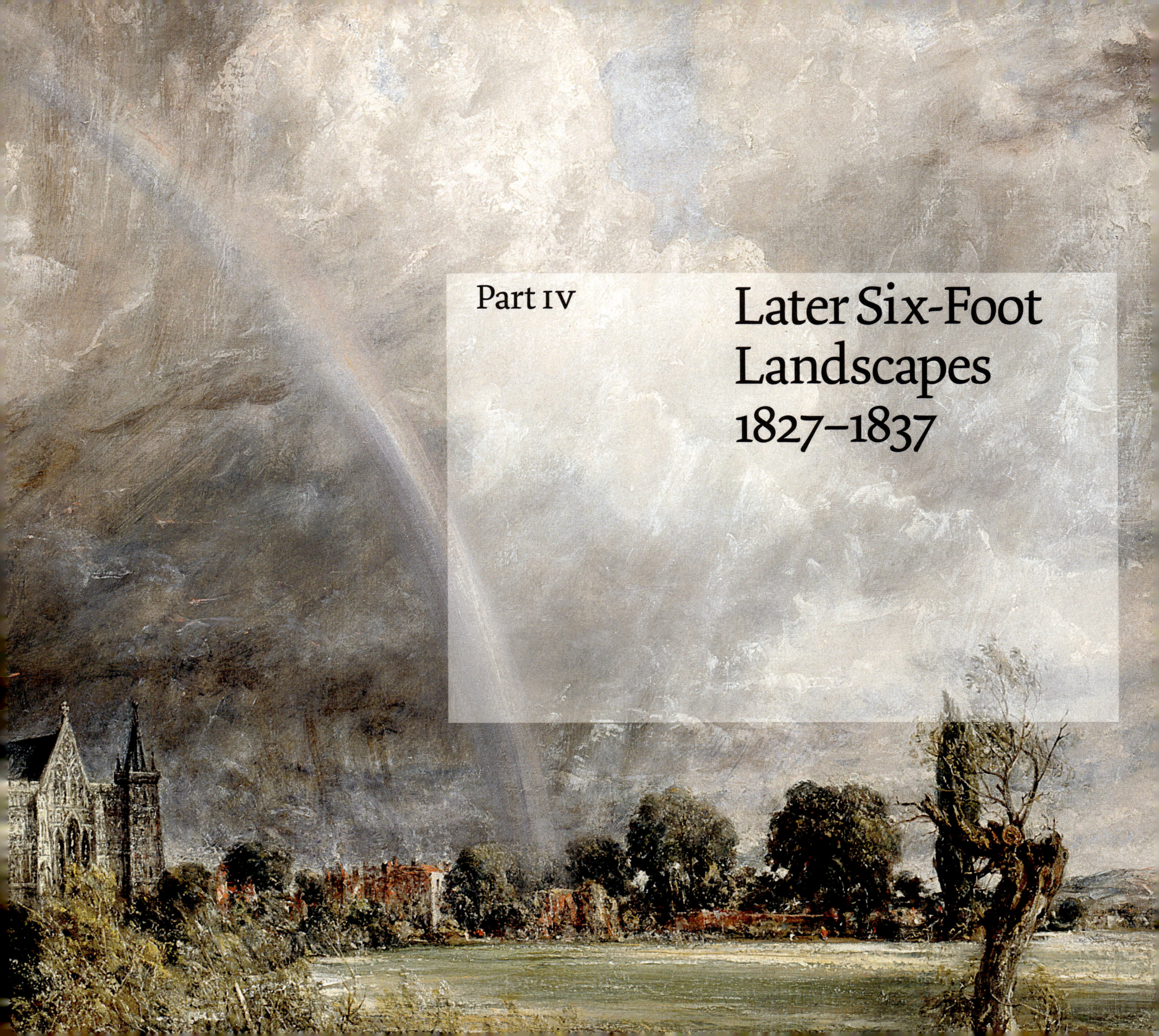
Part IV
Later Six-Foot
Landscapes
1827–1837

Later Six-Foot Landscapes 1827–1837

In November 1824 Constable wrote to John Fisher telling him he was planning another large picture for next year's Academy exhibition, the sixth and, as it was to transpire, the last of his great River Stour scenes, *The Leaping Horse* (no.47). In his letter of reply, Fisher expressed his hope that:

Although urging Constable to diversify in terms of the 'time of day' he represented in his landscapes, which was almost invariably around noon, Fisher might well have thought that Constable should think of varying his subject matter as well. Certainly when Constable was to paint a large marine subject two years later, the *Chain Pier, Brighton* (no.51), Fisher told him he believed it to be 'a usefull

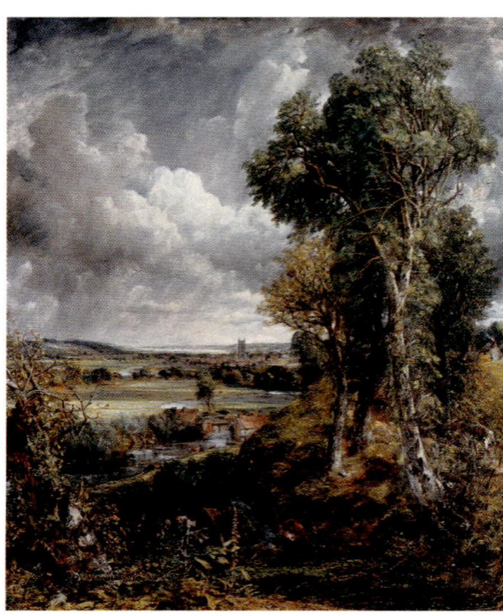

Figure 74
Dedham Vale
1828
Oil on canvas
145 × 122 (57⅛ × 48)
NATIONAL GALLERY OF
SCOTLAND, EDINBURGH

change of subject' (JCC IV, p.155).

Of course, as far as Constable was concerned, his true subject was not the specific location of a given landscape but rather Nature herself in all her various moods. In his riposte to Fisher's suggestion that he might in future diversify 'as to time of day', he stated that it was actually 'subject and change of weather and effect', by which he meant the subject of the weather and its various changes and effects, that 'afford variety in Landscape'; and thus, whilst he acknowledged Fisher's advice, he was not prepared to 'enter into that notion of varying ones plan to keep the Publick in good humour' (JCC VI, p.181). Nevertheless, having painted River Stour landscapes for all the large pictures he had exhibited at the Academy between 1819 and 1825, the time had now come for Constable to consider selecting new subjects for his exhibition landscapes.

From 1826, for example, although still sometimes adopting Suffolk locations for his large exhibition pictures, Constable now almost exclusively selected them from what he called 'Inland scenery', that is to say from locations situated away, or 'inland', from the River Stour itself. His Academy exhibit in 1826, for example, *The Cornfield* (see fig.59, p.116), is a pastoral landscape showing the lane in East Bergholt he used to walk along to school in Dedham as a young boy. He was to paint further 'inland' Suffolk subjects for exhibition over the coming years, including another *Dedham Vale* subject for the Academy in 1828 (fig.74, p.164), a landscape of *Helmingham Dell* in 1830 (Nelson-Atkins Museum of Art, Kansas City, R.30.1), and a full-size sketch for a painting of *Stoke-by-Nayland* in the mid-1830s (no.68), from which he probably intended to work up another Academy picture. Meanwhile, with his *Salisbury Cathedral from the Meadows* (no.61), Constable returned to a theme he had

first treated for exhibition in 1823 when, chiefly due to illness, his main exhibit had been the somewhat smaller version of a *Salisbury Cathedral* subject commissioned from Bishop Fisher following an extended stay in Salisbury in 1820 (fig.60, p.131). However, quite a few of the subjects Constable painted for his later six-foot exhibition landscapes reveal him moving in entirely new directions. In 1827, for example, he exhibited a large marine subject, the *Chain Pier, Brighton* (no.51); in 1829 a 'picturesque' ruin, *Hadleigh Castle* (no.57); and in 1832, after many years of planning and false starts, a thoroughly urban, 'modern' subject, *The Opening of Waterloo Bridge* (no.67). Indeed, it was only in 1835 with *The Valley Farm* (Tate; R.35.1) that Constable was ever again to return to a River Stour subject for an exhibition canvas, and this was in any case a variant of a subject he had treated many years earlier in *The Ferry* of 1814 (no.15).

Following favourable reviews of *The Leaping Horse* at the Academy in 1825 – indeed, one critic argued that the artist was now 'gradually rising to the head of his department' (Ivy 1991, p.115) – in the autumn and winter of 1825 to 1826 Constable revived a long-standing ambition to send to the Academy a large canvas showing *The Opening of Waterloo Bridge*. In October he started 'getting … the large picture of the Waterloo – on the Real canvas' (JCC II, p.407). However, by the following January he was telling Fisher that the picture was 'at a stand – owing in some measure to the ruined state of my finances' (JCC VI, pp.212–13). At short notice, he therefore decided to work up an alternative subject for the 1826 exhibition, *The Cornfield* (fig.59, p.116). Owing to pressure of time, instead of preparing a full-scale sketch for *The Cornfield*, as had now become his usual working method, he found himself able to manage chiefly by depending on an existing unfinished *plein-air* picture dating from his Suffolk period, which he now used as if it were, in effect, a preparatory sketch (no.21).

Now that Constable had proved to himself, by force of circumstance, that he could manage to paint an ambitious Academy exhibit without a full-scale preparatory sketch, he seems to have developed the confidence sometimes to make do in future with a purposefully painted half-scale sketch instead of one painted on the same scale as the intended picture. In the autumn and winter of 1826 to 1827, for example, he deliberately painted only a half-scale preparatory sketch for his coastal subject of the *Chain Pier, Brighton* (fig.77, p.171; no.51), and in future years he was to do the same for the *Dedham Vale* of 1828 (fig.74) and also for the second version of *The Opening of Waterloo Bridge* (nos.66, 67). At this particular moment, however, from around 1826 to 1827, making composition sketches on a somewhat smaller scale could only have been an advantage for Constable, as his life was becoming increasingly complicated on a practical level and ever more unsettled.

From 1819 Constable had started taking lodgings in Hampstead so that Maria could escape the pollution of the West End. By 1824, however, her health was showing signs of further deterioration, no doubt exacerbated by the strain of frequent childbearing; their fourth child, Isabel, had been born in 1822, and six years later their 'quiver', to use Constable's term, was to rise to seven. So from 1824 until 1828, on numerous occasions Constable settled his growing family into accommodation in Brighton in Sussex on the southern coast of England, so they could benefit from the sea air. For Constable this meant constant travelling between London, Hampstead and Brighton during these years, which must have made it very difficult for him to settle into any one,

single working space, never mind the prospect of having to juggle two large works alongside each other when not in his London studio. The *Chain Pier* was painted at a house he rented in Hampstead in Downshire Hill. Temporary accommodation, however, is unlikely to have supplied him with a space as suitable as that provided by a purpose-designed studio and gallery like the one he had taken over from Farington in Charlotte Street. Indeed, bearing in mind that the *Chain Pier* originally measured a substantial seven feet (2.13m) wide, rather than the six feet (1.83m) it measures today, a full-scale sketch for it would have been even more cumbersome to accommodate than earlier six-foot ones.

At the time Constable was staying in Brighton, between 1824 and 1828, the old fishing town was fast developing into a fashionable seaside resort, thanks chiefly to its association with the Prince Regent, now George IV, who had remodelled the Royal Pavilion in an extravagant orientalist style. His first impressions of the town were distinctly unfavourable. In August 1824 he told Fisher that the magnificence of the sea was drowned by the noise of stage coaches filled with visitors, although the 'breakers – & sky – [were] lovely indeed'. It may therefore seem surprising that Constable should have decided to paint a large canvas of Brighton at all, the more so, indeed, as in the same letter to Fisher as he decried the town itself, he also dismissed as 'hackneyed' the coastal subjects currently being shown at the Academy by artists like Augustus Wall Callcott and William Collins, writing:

These subjects are so little capable of that beautifull sentiment that landscape is capable of or which rather belongs to landscape, that they have done a great harm to the art – they form a class of art much easier than landscape

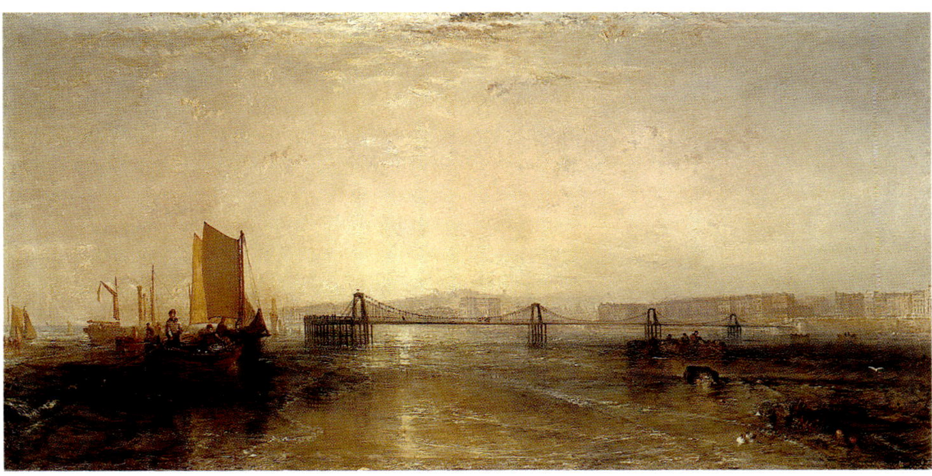

& have in consequence almost supplanted it, and have drawn off many who would have encouraged the growth of a pastoral feel in their own minds (JCC VI, pp.171–2).

In fact, in the early 1820s, Constable had already tried his own hand at marine subjects, albeit on a much smaller, 'cabinet-size' scale, producing views of *Harwich Lighthouse* in Essex and *Yarmouth Jetty* in Norfolk which proved so popular with collectors that he was to repeat them in several versions (R.20.7–9, R.22.36–8). He surely hoped to sell the *Chain Pier*, and he may also have thought that to paint a coastal subject on a six-foot (or, in its original form, on a seven-foot) scale would serve to demonstrate his versatility and range as a landscape painter and thus increase his chances for election as a full Academician. The picture did not in fact find a buyer, even when exhibited at the British Insitution the following year, 1828. Furthermore the critics were divided about its merits, *The Times* arguing that it was 'one of his best works', whilst, for example, the *New Monthly Magazine* felt it only proved how much

better suited his style of painting was to rustic landscape, declaring: 'Mr Constable's style is rural, adapted to rural objects amost exclusively' (Ivy 1991, pp.122, 124). Evidently Constable's fellow Academicians inclined to the latter view as well, at least judging by the outcome of the voting for new candidates the following year, when Constable received only five votes to the eighteen garnered by the subject painter, William Etty. Neverthetheless, the *Chain Pier* does seem to have played a part in provoking J.M.W. Turner to consider at one stage treating his own version of *Brighton from the Sea* (fig.75) for Lord Egremont from the same direction (see nos.48–52). Furthermore, Andrew Hemingway has pointed out that, by comparison with the more traditional marines painted by contemporaries such as Callcott and Collins, Constable's *Chain Pier* is refreshingly original, presenting explicit evidence of the way that the new town at this date had encroached on the old, and thus directly engaging with the 'modern' Brighton (Hemingway 1992, pp.190–3).

Figure 75
J.M.W. Turner
Brighton from the Sea
c.1829
Oil on canvas
63.5 × 132 (25 × 52)
PETWORTH HOUSE, SUSSEX.
RECEIVED IN LIEU OF DEATH
DUTIES BY THE TATE GALLERY
1984

By the summer of 1828, it was clear that the sea air was failing to make any impression on Maria's advancing tuberculosis. Constable therefore took her back to Hampstead where, the previous year, they had acquired a permanent residence in Well Walk (although Constable continued to retain his Charlotte Street studio). Her health continued to decline, however, and towards the end of November she died. Constable was inconsolable, telling a friend that 'a void is made in my heart that can never be filled again in this world' (JCC IV, p.282). Among the many letters of support he received was one from John Fisher who, aware that 'words will not ward off irreparable loss', advised Constable that 'you should apply yourself rigidly to your profession. Some of the finest works of art have been the result of periods of distress' (JCC VI, pp.239–40). By the following January, indeed, Constable was telling C.R. Leslie that 'could I get afloat on a canvas of six feet, I might have a chance of being carried away from myself' (JCC III, p.18). He should have been buoyed by the news just three weeks later – news he had so keenly sought in the past – that he had now finally been elected an Academician. However, as he told Leslie, the good news came tinged with sadness, having been 'delayed until I am solitary and cannot impart it'. Salt was then rubbed into the wound when the President of the Royal Academy, Sir Thomas Lawrence, told Constable he was lucky to have been elected at a time when there were so many talented history painters on the shortlist of candidates (Leslie 1951, pp.171–3; see also nos.53–7).

All this – the loss of his wife and now his election as an Academician, carrying with it a sense of higher expectations – made Constable especially anxious about the reception of his next main exhibit at the Academy the following spring. The 'canvas of six feet' he had chosen to 'get afloat on' to distract himself from his grief following Maria's death was a landscape showing the ruined medieval fortifications of Hadleigh in Essex. Perhaps feeling under pressure to justify his new academic status, in *Hadleigh Castle* (no.57) Constable produced an image ostensibly more conventional than any he had previously submitted for exhibition at the Academy, for ruined castles and crumbling abbeys had for many years been part of a vogue for 'picturesque' and antiquarian landscape, though their height of popularity dated back from a decade or two earlier when adopted by artists such as J.M.W. Turner. Turner had also made a speciality of historical and 'sublime' landscapes, and by appending to the title of the picture in the Academy catalogue a quotation from Thomson's *Seasons*, and thus lending it a literary emotion, Constable may have hoped that *Hadleigh Castle* would be appreciated in a similar vein (Cormack 1986a, p.190). However it is hard to avoid the impression that the subject of the ruin at Hadleigh, with its overtones of isolation and decay, also served for Constable as a metaphor for his own profoundly bleak mood in the months after Maria's death. This seems particularly so in the case of the large composition sketch for the picture, with its cool tonality, ferocious strokes of the palette knife and savagely worked paint (no.56).

With *Hadleigh Castle*, Constable had again reverted to the practice of using a full-scale sketch, or in this particular case a little less than a full-scale sketch, for at approximately 48 × 66 inches (1.22 × 1.68m) the sketch is a little smaller than the finished picture. He was again to use a full-size sketch for his Academy exhibit of *Helmingham Dell* the following year, though the latter is not strictly one of Constable's 'great' landscapes, being much closer to a 'half-length' size (40 × 50in/1.02 × 1.27m). To the next exhibition in 1831, however, Constable was once again to send a true six-footer, *Salisbury Cathedral from the Meadows* (no.61), and for this he again produced a full-scale sketch, the last indeed of his full-scale sketches for which there also survives an equivalent finished painting. Although the exhibition picture of *Salisbury Cathedral from the Meadows* is unlikely to have been painted until the autumn and winter of 1830 to 1831, the subject had actually been in Constable's mind since 1829, when he twice stayed with Fisher at Leadenhall in Salisbury Close. Indeed, before his second visit in November, Fisher told Constable he had set up for him at Leadenhall a 'great easil' so that he could start as soon as he arrived, and thus enjoy proximity to his 'material drawn from nature herself' (JCC VI, pp.250–1).

This raises the intriguing question as to whether, on this occasion, and thus uniquely for any of his full-scale sketches, Constable may have started the large compositional sketch for *Salisbury Cathedral from the Meadows* with close, if not direct, access to the very scene he was painting. On balance, however, this seems unlikely. As John Gage has pointed out, not only in the full-scale sketch is the perspective of the cathedral decidedly awkward (and the spire particularly so, which no doubt explains why at one stage it was subsequently overpainted by another hand, see fig.17, p.44). Furthermore, in all his preliminary studies and sketches for the final picture, including the full-scale sketch, Constable substantially misrepresented the structure of the west front, where the flanking pinnacles are in fact each separated from the gable of the nave by a broad crenellated parapet. When Constable came to correct his mistake in the final picture, he may perhaps have consulted the antiquarian John Britton, a copy of whose *Beauties of England and Wales: Wiltshire* (1814) at some stage entered his library, and to whom in July 1830 he presented a part work of his series of prints, *English Landscape*. Given that Constable had known Salisbury for so long, and painted the cathedral so many times before (though admittedly not from this side), this seems a surprising mistake. Not only does it suggest that Constable is unlikely to have started the full-scale sketch at Salisbury in 1829 despite Fisher's best intentions, but it may also be an indication of an increasingly abstracted state of mind (Gage in Paris 2002, pp.232–3).

The 1830s were in fact to prove a very difficult period for Constable. He was just beginning to come to terms with the death of Maria when, in August 1832, came the further blow of the death of his greatest friend and confidante, John Fisher, and then Fisher's death was followed in November by that of Constable's former studio assistant, the younger John Dunthorne. Meanwhile, Constable was beginning to suffer serious bouts of ill health himself. He found it increasingly difficult to apply himself to the painting of a large exhibition canvas every year, and around this time therefore began to send a greater number of watercolours and drawings to the Academy alongside, or sometimes instead of, his large exhibition canvases. On a more positive note, during these years he was also involved in other professional activities that took up increasing amounts of his time, inevitably affecting his productivity as a painter. In 1829 until his death, he devoted much of his time, energy and money to the production and publishing of the twenty-two mezzotints for *English Landscape*. For although it was David Lucas who actually engraved the subjects, it was Constable who first selected them, corrected the many proof impressions and who also drafted an accompanying letterpress (see no.2). From 1833, Constable was also committed to giving a series of lectures on the history and importance of landscape painting to the Hampstead Literary and Scientific Society, to the Worcestershire Institution for Promoting Literature, Science and the Fine Arts, and to the Royal Institution in London. Not only did these lectures involve much preparation in the way of reading, but Constable also made diagrams of compositions by the Old Masters to use as illustrations. In the 1830s he also twice served as Visitor at the Royal Academy Schools, developing a new teaching course in the Life School.

Given these other pressures and commitments, in the 1830s Constable only completed four exhibition canvases on a substantial scale, *Salisbury Cathedral from the Meadows* 1831 (no.61), *The Opening of Waterloo Bridge* 1832 (no.67), *The Valley Farm* 1835 (Tate) and *The Cenotaph* 1836 (fig.13, p.138), the first two of these being the largest and most ambitious. Indeed *The Opening of Waterloo Bridge*, at approximately seven feet wide, is actually the largest of all Constable's landscapes, although the *Chain Pier* would originally have been similar in size when originally shown at the Royal Academy in 1827 and then again at the British Institution in 1828. The *Waterloo Bridge* subject had first been mooted by Constable, of course, as early as 1819 and, following many years of procrastination and changes of heart, he finally brought it to completion for the Academy exhibition of 1832. In 1826 he had achieved an apparent breakthrough when he managed to get access to a new viewpoint for the subject from the terrace of Pembroke House, a viewpoint he was subsequently to use in the finished painting. However, the indifferent reaction he received on exhibiting his marine of the *Chain Pier* in 1827 may have discouraged him from proceeding to exhibit an uncharacteristic urban subject as well. When he finally did submit the *Waterloo Bridge* picture to exhibition in 1832, he was very nervous about its reception, not only, he told Leslie, because it was so unfinished, but also as 'it has not my redeeming voice (the rural)' (JCC III, p.68).

As it happened, *The Opening of Waterloo Bridge* was to be the last of the great landscapes that Constable was ever to send to the Academy. Nevertheless, he frequently refers to his intention of painting another 'large canvas' in the period 1834 to 1835, and he would no doubt have done so had he found the time, as well, perhaps, as the strength. There was also the difficulty Constable faced of finding a suitable subject, especially bearing in mind that any chosen theme would have to hold its own when projected on a large scale. In 1834, he wrote to his friend and namesake George Constable of Arundel of the difficulty of finding 'a subject fit for the largest of my sizes', adding that he was considering 'a canal or a rural affair, or a wood, or a harvest scene' (JCC V, p.17). It would seem that in the end Constable settled for 'a rural affair'. For Charles Rhyne has convincingly argued that the late canvas of *Stoke-by-Nayland* in Chicago (no.68) is not in fact an unfinished painting but rather a full-scale sketch for a picture that Constable never got round to starting (Rhyne 1987; see also p.47 of present catalogue).

After his large landscapes had returned from exhibition at the Royal Academy, Constable would often retouch them, even substantially repaint them, especially if he was intending to re-exhibit them elsewhere, whether perhaps at the British Institution in London, or elsewhere in the country such as in Birmingham or Worcester. Early in 1833 he retouched the large *Salisbury Cathedral from the Meadows* (no.61) before sending it to the British Institution, confidently telling Leslie:

I have got the Great Salisbury into the state I always wished to see it – 'it is a rich and most impressive canvas' if I see it free from self-love (JCC III, p.89).

In July 1834 Constable worked on the picture again before sending it to the Birmingham Society of Arts, telling a Hampstead friend, William Purton, that he had now 'much increased its power and effect … I have no doubt of this picture being my best now' (JCC V, p.42). On 29 March 1837, meanwhile, only two days before he died, Constable was still correcting proof impressions of the large mezzotint that David Lucas was making from the Salisbury picture (no.62). To some extent this was a routine activity for Constable, but in retrospect it is also a very poignant one. For C.R. Leslie was later to write that Constable himself thought it was his *Salisbury Cathedral from the Meadows* that would in future be considered his greatest picture, believing that it conveyed 'the fullest impression of the compass of his art' (Leslie 1951, p.237). AL

Chain Pier, Brighton

The *Chain Pier, Brighton* (no.51) is the only picture that Constable produced of Brighton – in fact of any marine subject – on a monumental scale. Indeed given his initial, unfavourable reaction to the resort, it is perhaps surprising that he should have decided to paint a substantial exhibition picture of Brighton at all. In August 1824, just three months after first settling Maria and their four children in lodgings at the resort, Constable described it to his friend John Fisher in the following unflattering terms:

Brighton is the receptacle of the fashion and offscouring of London. The magnificence of the sea, and its ... everlasting voice, is drowned in the din & lost in the tumult of stage coaches – gigs – 'flys' &c.– and the beach is only piccadilly ... by the sea-side. Ladies dressed & *undressed* – Gentlemen in morning gowns & slippers on, or without them altogether about *knee deep* in the breakers – footmen – children – nursery maids, dogs, boys, fishermen – *preventive service men* [i.e. customs officials] (with hangers & pistols) rotten fish & those hideous amphibious animals the old bathing women, whose language both in oaths & voice resembles men – all are mixed together in endless & indecent confusion. The genteeler part, the marine parade, is still more unnatural – with its trimmed and neat appearance & the dandy jetty or chain pier, with its long & elegant strides into the sea a full 1/4 mile. In short there is nothing here for a painter but the breakers – & sky – which have been lovely indeed ... The fishing boats are picturesque (JCC VI, p.171).

Maria and the children were to stay in Brighton at regular intervals until her death in 1828 so as to benefit from the sea air, and Constable would visit them as often as he could, taking advantage of the frequent coach service from London. Not only were the sea and sky to prove irresistible subjects when he came to take up his paintbrush or pencil, but so were the 'picturesque' fishing boats, for he clearly enjoyed the pictorial contrast between the verticals of their masts and sails with the horizontals of the sea and beach (fig.76, no.48). In fact it was not long before he was even tempted to sketch the 'dandy jetty' or chain suspension pier itself, which had been constructed chiefly to supply a landing place for steam packets arriving from Dieppe and had only opened in 1823, the year before Constable first arrived in Brighton. One can safely assume that he must have made the detailed pencil study of *Marine Parade and Chain Pier, Brighton* (no.49) on one of his earliest visits to Brighton in 1824, as it includes the buoys linked by chains to the pier-head. These were set up to protect the pier from boats being swept against it, but were destroyed in a storm in November 1824 and then never replaced (Tate 1991, p.281).

It would appear that Constable's initial hostile reaction to Brighton softened over time. For around 1826 he was beginning to explore possibilities for making a larger landscape on a Brighton theme, painting a small, very broadly handled compositional sketch (no.50) modelled on the panoramic drawing of the Marine Parade he had made two years earlier (no.49). In the compositional sketch, however, Constable's view is taken from further back (that is, further west). As a result the wooden pump house, which in the drawing is seen highlighted in ink and partly framing the composition at the extreme left, has now receded further back into the composition, appearing immediately to the right of a substantial building, the Albion Hotel, which opened in August 1826. He has also disposed various figures across the beach, including in the central middle distance a man in profile standing close to the water's edge wearing white trousers and a yellow cap, directly adapted from the figure seen on the left in *Beaching a Boat, Brighton* (no.48). Meanwhile, infrared reflectography of the compositional sketch has also revealed that, at some stage, Constable shortened the pier, perhaps to make room for the boat on the right (Tate 1991, p.277). The length of the pier was to give him further problems in the final picture as well, when he decided to extend it, and the changes he made near the pier-head are still visible today with the naked eye.

The *Sketch for 'Chain Pier, Brighton'* (no.50) represents Constable's first idea for the composition of his Brighton subject in the same way, for example, as the smaller composition sketches for *Stratford Mill* (fig.63, p.137) and for *The Hay Wain* (no.35) show the early genesis of those compositions. As was the case for the latter two, one would have expected Constable then to use this smaller study as the basis for a full-scale sketch painted on the same scale as the final canvas. Instead, however, this time he produced a second compositional sketch only about half the size of the intended picture (fig.77, p.171). More thinly painted than his previous full-scale sketches, this half-scale study was nevertheless designed, like them, to function as the last stage in the preparatory process before he started on the exhibition picture itself.

The half-scale sketch (fig.77) shows Constable developing his ideas for the final composition in a number of important ways. The buildings lining Marine Parade in the distance, for example, are now more carefully delineated. The Albion Hotel is seen from an oblique angle instead of towards its side. The boat on the left with raised sail is now more fully developed, apparently painted with

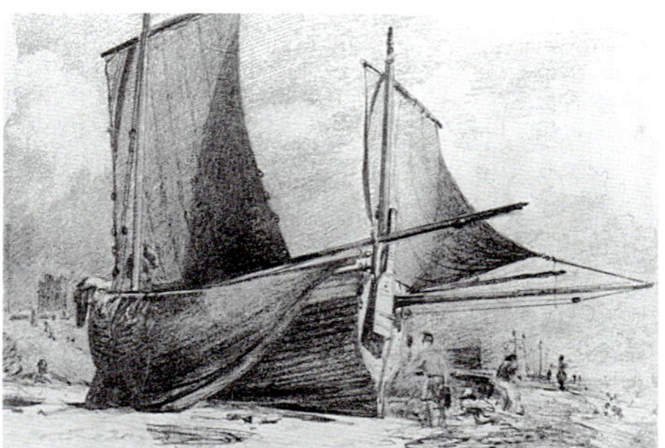

Figure 76
A Brighton Lugger
1824
Pencil
17.8 × 26.1 (7 × 10¼)
PRIVATE COLLECTION

FIGURE 76

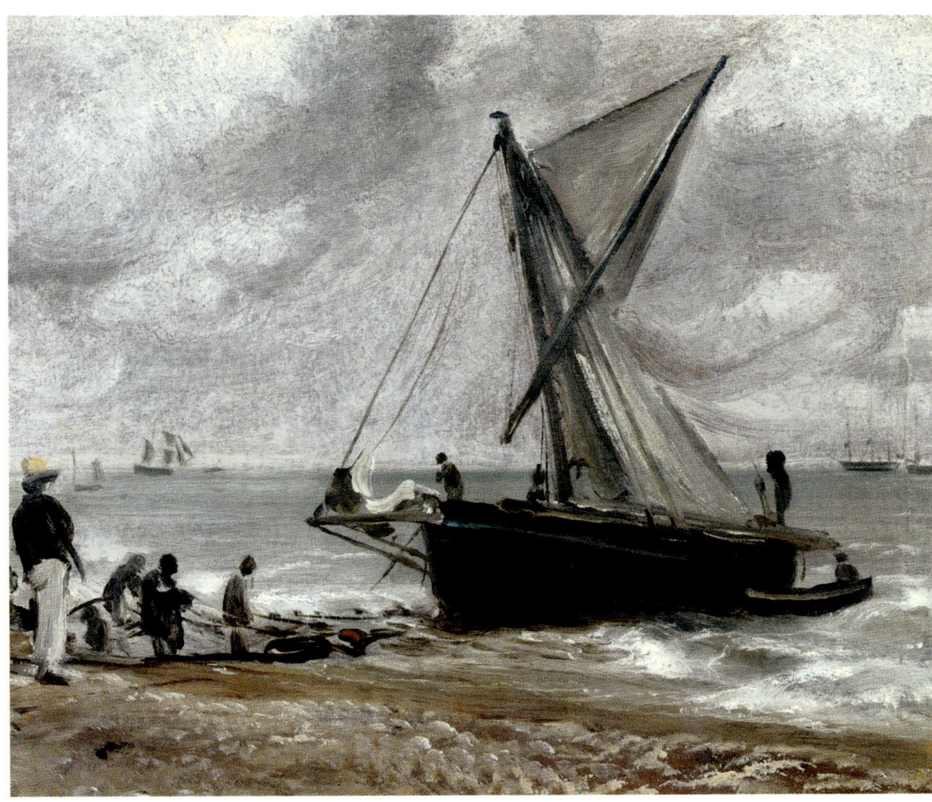

reference to the pencil drawing of a Brighton lugger that Constable had made on the beach in 1824 (fig.76). Meanwhile, the man on the foreshore in the yellow hat has been brought closer to the viewer to watch the boat beaching episode, this time both man and boat directly taken from no.48. In fact, the main purpose of this half-scale sketch seems to be to establish the relative groupings of the boats, figures and buildings, for Constable has done very little, for example, to develop the sky. Indeed in the final painting, the powerful impression of the wind blowing inland off the sea, with the sun casting shadows to the left, is adapted more

closely from the smaller sketch, no.50, than from the half-scale study.

Constable appears to have painted the final picture (no.51) in Hampstead, in a house he had taken on Downshire Hill, between the end of 1826 and the beginning of 1827. For in April 1827 he mentioned to the printseller and publisher Dominic Colnalghi, who was later to publish an engraving of the *Chain Pier* (no.52), that he would shortly be bringing the picture from Hampstead to London for the opening of the Academy exhibition (JCC IV, p.155). The final painting is a brilliant synthesis of ideas that Constable gathered together from the

preliminary sketches and existing studies. He even seems to have selectively squared for transfer to the final canvas the careful drawing he had made of the *Marine Parade and Chain Pier* in 1824 (no.49), as is suggested by the evidence of pin holes both on the back of the drawing itself, and also on the upper and lower tacking margins of the finished picture that occur only in the area corresponding to the equivalent passage in the drawing (see p.60). Meanwhile, Constable decided to abandon the boat beaching episode shown in both of the preliminary sketches, perhaps because it threatened to close off this side of the composition. Certainly in the finished picture there is a stronger suggestion of an open expanse of sea stretching out and away from the crowded beach and shoreline on the left (Dorment 1986, p.59). Finally, he added one or two further details, such as the mooring post, anchor, ropes and other fishing tackle in the left-hand foreground, from earlier *plein-air* drawings (for example R.24.36, R.27.1A).

These additional features in the left-hand foreground – among them are also an upturned boat, drying nets and an overturned basket of skate – together evoke a vivid impression of Brighton's traditional fishing industry and the life of the shore. Beyond them a boy carries in the rope of an approaching boat, and a fisherman pulls in a net. Mingled among the fishermen, however, Constable shows one or two fashionable visitors braving the blustery conditions. As well as the man in the yellow hat from the earlier sketches, now returned to his original position in the middle distance, there are two women closer to the viewer carrying parasols and being buffeted by the wind. Together with the recently opened Albion Hotel on the left, the houses on Marine Parade picked out in sunlight beyond it, and the chain pier itself in the far distance forming an elegant

sihouette on the horizon, these figures are a reminder of the 'modern' Brighton, which has encroached on the life of the old fishing town. Indeed the pictorial structure of the painting, with its distinct contrasts of colour and of light and shade, serves to dramatise this relationship between old and new (Hemingway 1992, p.190). In the *Chain Pier*, then, Constable creates a memorable portrait of a coastal town at a key moment of historical transition.

Constable's friend John Fisher was staying with him in Hampstead just before the artist sent the *Chain Pier* to the Academy for exhibition, and Fisher reported to his wife that the picture was 'most beautifully executed & in a greater state of finish and forwardness, than you can ever before recollect'. He also added that 'Turner, Calcott and Collins will not like it', by which he meant that these artists would surely regard it as an intrusion into their own territory of marine subjects (JCC VI, p.230). The picture received mixed reviews on its exhibition at the Academy in 1827, and though in August Constable told Fisher he had had an enquiry about its price from 'a man of rank', it failed to find a buyer (*ibid.* p.231). As for Fisher's comment that some of Constable's artistic colleagues would not welcome his showing a marine painting, in Turner's case this appears to have been the case. When 'provoked' in this manner, Turner's usual response was to produce a similar subject of his own by way of riposte and, indeed, soon afterwards he painted a canvas of *Brighton from the Sea* for the carved room at Petworth House (fig.75, p.165). Although this shows the Chain Pier from the opposite side to Constable's version, Ian Warrell has shown that Turner's first exploration of this subject was actually a large colour study showing the view looking east,

49

**Marine Parade and
Chain Pier, Brighton**
1824
Pencil, with pen additions
11.1 × 42.5 (4³⁄₈ × 16³⁄₄), including
extension of an extra strip of paper 5.4cm
(2¹⁄₈in) on left
Inscribed by the artist in pencil over the
roofs of the houses with colour notes
Brown Red and others that are illegible
R.27.2
VICTORIA AND ALBERT MUSEUM,
LONDON. GIVEN BY ISABEL CONSTABLE,
DAUGHTER OF THE ARTIST

50

Sketch for 'Chain Pier, Brighton'
c.1826
Oil on paper laid on canvas
33 × 61 (13 × 24)
R.27.3
PHILADELPHIA MUSEUM OF ART:
THE JOHN G. JOHNSON COLLECTION

that is in the same direction as Constable's *Chain Pier*, and thus almost certainly directly inspired by it (Warrell 1995, pp.36–7, fig.8).

Prospective purchasers of Constable's *Chain Pier* may have been deterred by the picture's stormy mood and vigorous handling. After it again failed to sell when shown at the British Insititution in 1828, Fisher urged Constable to 'put it on an easil by your side, Claude fashion, & so mellow its ferocious beauties' (JCC VI, p.241). Technical analysis by Sarah Cove and Natasha Duff indicates that Constable did indeed work on the picture again around this time. Not only, for example, did he repaint part of the sky on the upper right using the palette knife (though this can hardly have been supposed to temper the picture's 'ferocious beauties'); he also – and indeed it is now very clear that it was Constable himself who was responsible for this – reduced the width of the canvas by removing approximately nine inches (22.8cm) on the left, and a further inch (2.5cm) on the right. The engraving of the *Chain Pier* published by Dominic Colnaghi in 1829 (no.52) gives an indication of what the picture would have looked like before it was cut down. More of the boat on the left was visible, for example, with its main mast and sail again taken from the earlier drawing of the Brighton lugger (fig.76, p.168); and the dog who now stares vacantly out of the painting was once watching a fisherman smoking a pipe on the extreme left.

When reducing the width of the canvas, Constable may have wanted to make it closer to a standard six-footer. However, he may also have hoped to build a stronger *repoussoir* effect, that is, to strengthen the sense of recession in the picture (Tate 1991, pp.279–81).

As Andrew Hemingway has noted, the engraving of the *Chain Pier* (no.52) includes on the right-hand horizon the unmistakable if miniscule profile of the Brighton–Dieppe steam ferry, a detail never included in Constable's picture. This probably reflects the fact that the print was published jointly by Colnaghi and 'Mr Folker' of Brighton, and thus aimed at visitors to the resort receptive to its recent development (Hemingway 1992, p.191). AL

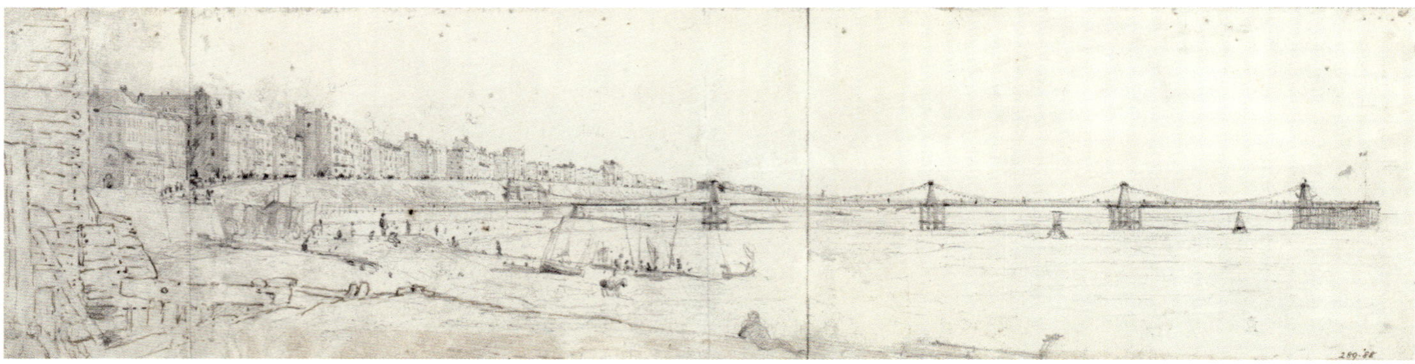

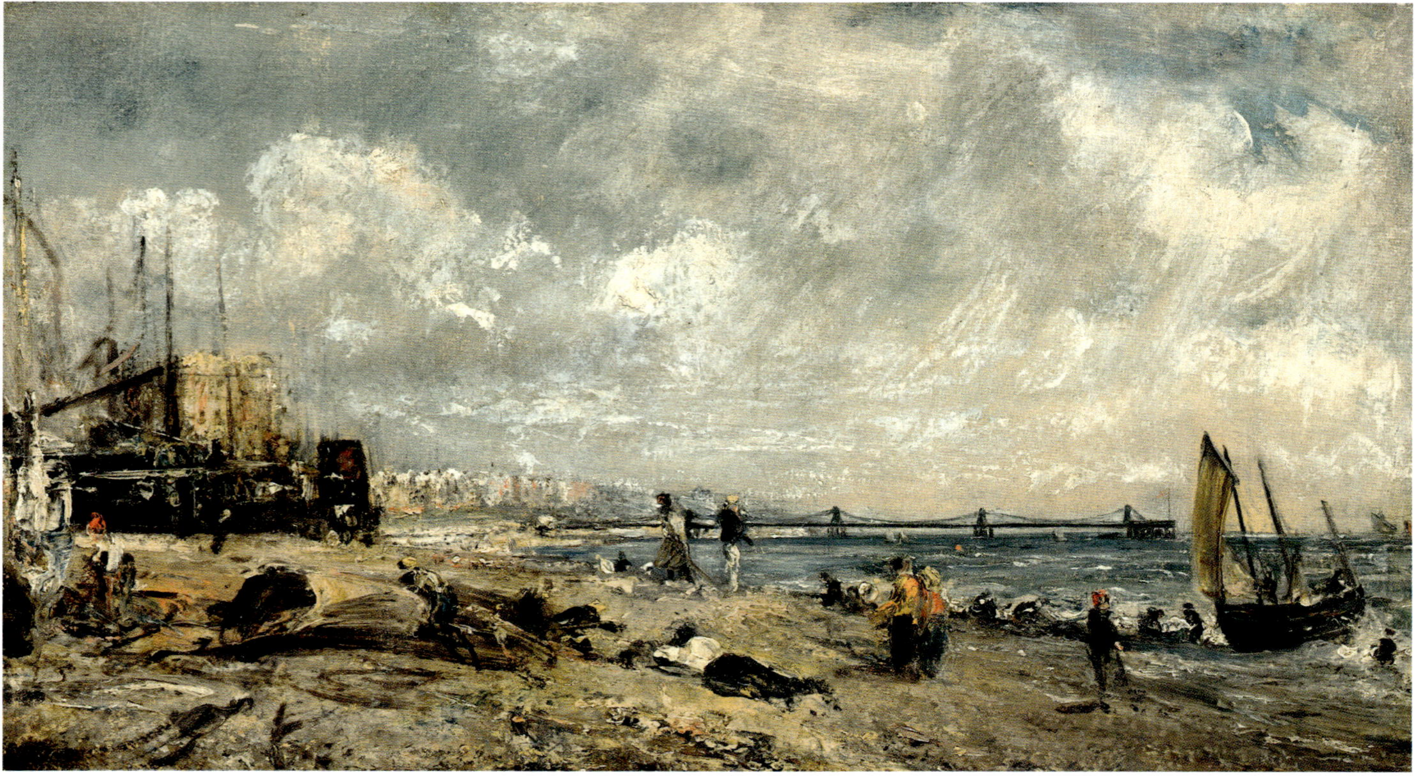

Figure 77
Sketch for 'Chain Pier, Brighton'
c.1826–7
Oil on canvas 60.6 × 98.8 (23³⁄₄ × 38⁷⁄₈)
R.27.4
PHILADELPHIA MUSEUM OF ART:
THE WILLIAM P. WILSTACH COLLECTION

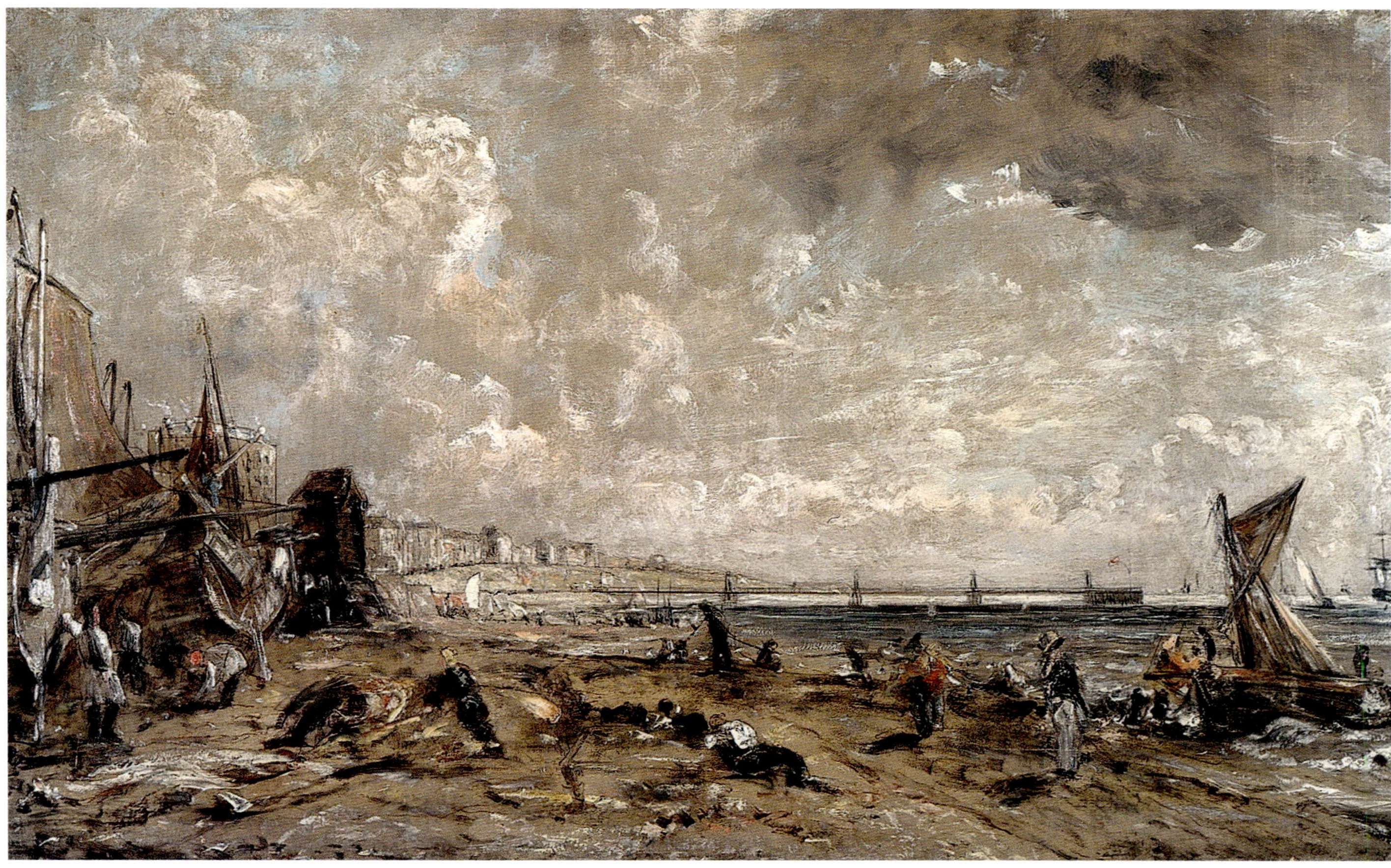

FIGURE 77

51

Chain Pier, Brighton

1827

Oil on canvas

127 × 183 (50 × 72), including flattened tacking
edges at right-hand side and bottom. The picture
has been cut down on the left by approximately
23 cm (9 in), and a narrow strip of canvas added to
the right tacking edge, indicating that the canvas
once measured about 81 in, almost 7 ft wide
(205 cm). There are also sets of small square holes
on the upper and lower tacking margins,
probably associated with the use of threads
to create a 'squaring-up' grid.

Exh: RA 1827 (no.186, *Chain Pier, Brighton*); BI 1828
(no.64, *The Beach at Brighton, The Chain Pier in the
distance*, frame 68 × 99 in)

R.27.1

Ivy 27.12–18; 27.22; 28.2–5; 28.7

TATE. PURCHASED 1950

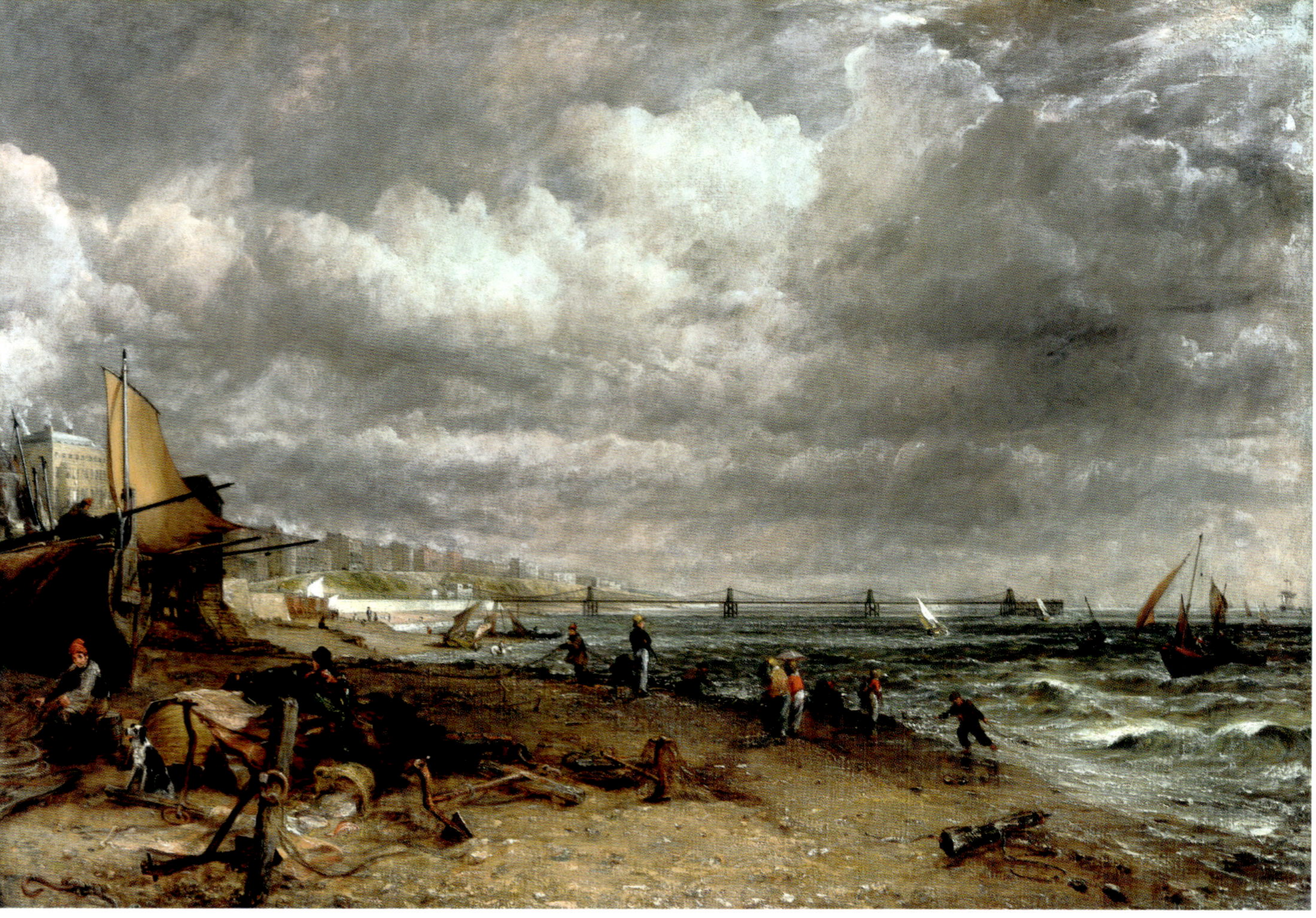

52

Frederick William Smith (1797–1835)
after John Constable
View of Brighton with the Chain Pier
1829
Line-engraving 19 × 31.1 (7¹⁄₂ × 12¹⁄₄) on
India paper laid on wove paper 40.2 × 55
(15⁷⁄₈ × 21⁵⁄₈)
Engraved inscriptions below image:
'Painted by John Constable' (left);
'Engraved by Frederick Smith' (right).
Also with publication line: 'London
Published August 12th 1829 by Colnaghi
Son & Co Printsellers to the King Pall Mall
East & by Mʳ. Folker Brighton'.

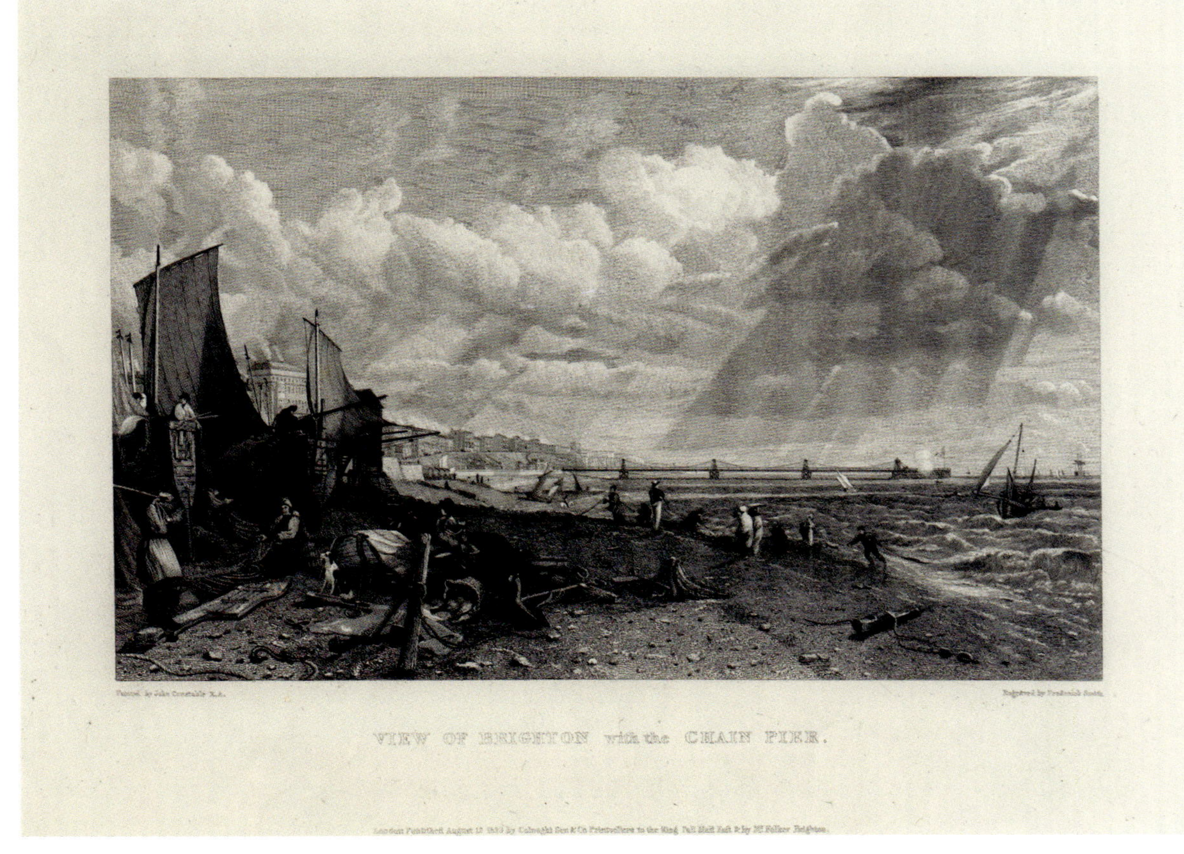

Hadleigh Castle

Constable first visited Hadleigh Castle in the summer of 1814, on a tour with his family's old friend and his early supporter, the Revd Walter Wren Driffield (Hawes 1983, p.458). Situated near the mouth of the River Thames, Hadleigh was more notable for the views it offered than for its remnants of medieval castle architecture, as relatively little of the fortifications remained standing. As Constable wrote to Maria:

there is a ruin of a castle which from its situation is really a fine place – it commands a view of the Kent hills, the Nore and the North Foreland & looking many miles to sea (JCC II, p.127).

On the 1814 visit he made a small pencil sketch (no.53), showing the remains of two of the castle's circular towers against a summarily rendered landscape. There is no evidence Constable ever returned to Hadleigh. In this modest drawing, then, were the seeds of inspiration he would later use in creating one of his most memorable landscapes, exhibited at the Royal Academy in 1829 as *Hadleigh Castle. The mouth of the Thames – morning, after a stormy night* (no.57).

Constable left us no evidence why he chose the subject. In the previous year he had submitted the upright *Dedham Vale* (fig.74, p.164) to the Academy, which turned out to be his last major exhibition piece inspired by the scenery of the Stour Valley. It was also the last of his great works fully informed by an affirming sense of nature's ameliorative beauty and vitality. As has been observed, with *Hadleigh Castle*:

We feel ourselves in a different world. Instead of an invigorating celebration of benign, sustaining nature, fully in harmony with man, the painting enshrines the desolate, melancholy remnants of a once-proud royal stronghold, forlornly

silhouetted against a turbulent sky (Hawes 1983, pp.455–6).

It has often been suggested that the death of Constable's beloved Maria in November 1828 may have led him to think once again of this lonely place. In the letter quoted above, which was written to her during an especially difficult time in their courtship, he had spoken of walking by the sea and musing about its 'melancholy grandeur'; perhaps her death did, in fact, bring the ruins of Hadleigh once again to mind. In December 1828, when he may have already begun painting *Hadleigh Castle*, he admitted: 'Hourly do I feel the loss of my departed Angel … I shall never feel again as I have felt the face of the world is totally changed to me' (Hawes 1983, p.456, citing FDC 1975, p.81).

Although we do not know precisely when, at some point Constable translated his 1814 drawing into an oil sketch (no.54), now adding the figure of a shepherd with his flock at the lower left. In both the 1814 drawing and the oil sketch there is a substantial gap between the two towers (they are, however, shown closer together than they are in reality). In a pen and ink drawing (no. 55), a dog appears next to the shepherd, a tree is introduced beside the left-hand tower, and the view is greatly expanded to the right. The large oil sketch (no.56) closely follows the pen and ink sketch. It has been called 'one of the most astonishing pieces of pure painting ever to emerge from Constable's hand' (Lyles in Paris 2002, p.169). Painted with bold strokes of the palette knife, its surface is vividly and richly textured. Remarkably, in the early 1930s, and for a brief period after it was acquired by the National Gallery in 1935, this sketch was believed to be the final version, so great was the notion that Constable's late works had become ever more freely and loosely painted.

In 1936, Charles Holmes observed:

No work by Constable on a considerable scale, not even the magnificent *Leaping Horse* in the Diploma Gallery at Burlington House, conveys so directly the impression of masterful energy as does this *Hadleigh Castle*. Rubens himself could not have slashed in that dazzling sky of blue and white with more vehemence; to carry the same audacious vigour into the middle distance and foreground was a technical feat no less astonishing (Holmes 1936a, p.107; see also Fleming-Williams and Parris 1984, p.125).

The primary area of development in this sketch was in the sky, which has been aptly described as 'powerfully luminous and alive with agitated cloud forms … energizing the mood of the whole scene' (Hawes 1983, p.459). Of course, it is impossible to imagine that Constable could have painted this extraordinarily expressive sky without benefit of the studies of clouds he made at Hampstead in 1821 and 1822 (see also no.27). Indeed, there is an energy and vitality here that simply has no real precedent in Constable's art other than in his cloud studies. In the finished painting the sky is painted with less agitated brushwork, but it remains nonetheless a tour de force, almost, as Reynolds has observed, 'an enormous sky study' in its own right (Reynolds 1984, p.200).

Constable was nervous about placing *Hadleigh* on exhibition in the spring of 1829. That February he had at last been elected to full membership of the Royal Academy, but under less than ideal circumstances. The election was close, and Thomas Lawrence, the Academy's President, told him that he 'considered him peculiarly fortunate in being chosen an academician at a time when there were historical painters of great merit on the list of candidates' (Leslie 1951, p.173). As he

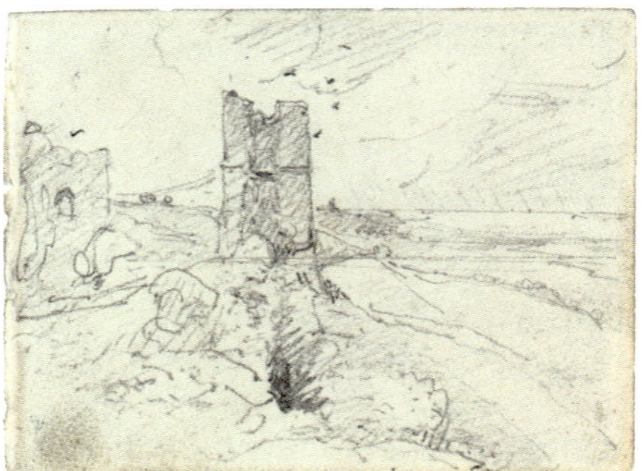

53

Hadleigh Castle
1814
Pencil on paper
8.1 × 11.1 (3¼ × 4⅜)
R.14.13
VICTORIA AND ALBERT
MUSEUM, LONDON.
GIVEN BY ISABEL
CONSTABLE, DAUGHTER
OF THE ARTIST

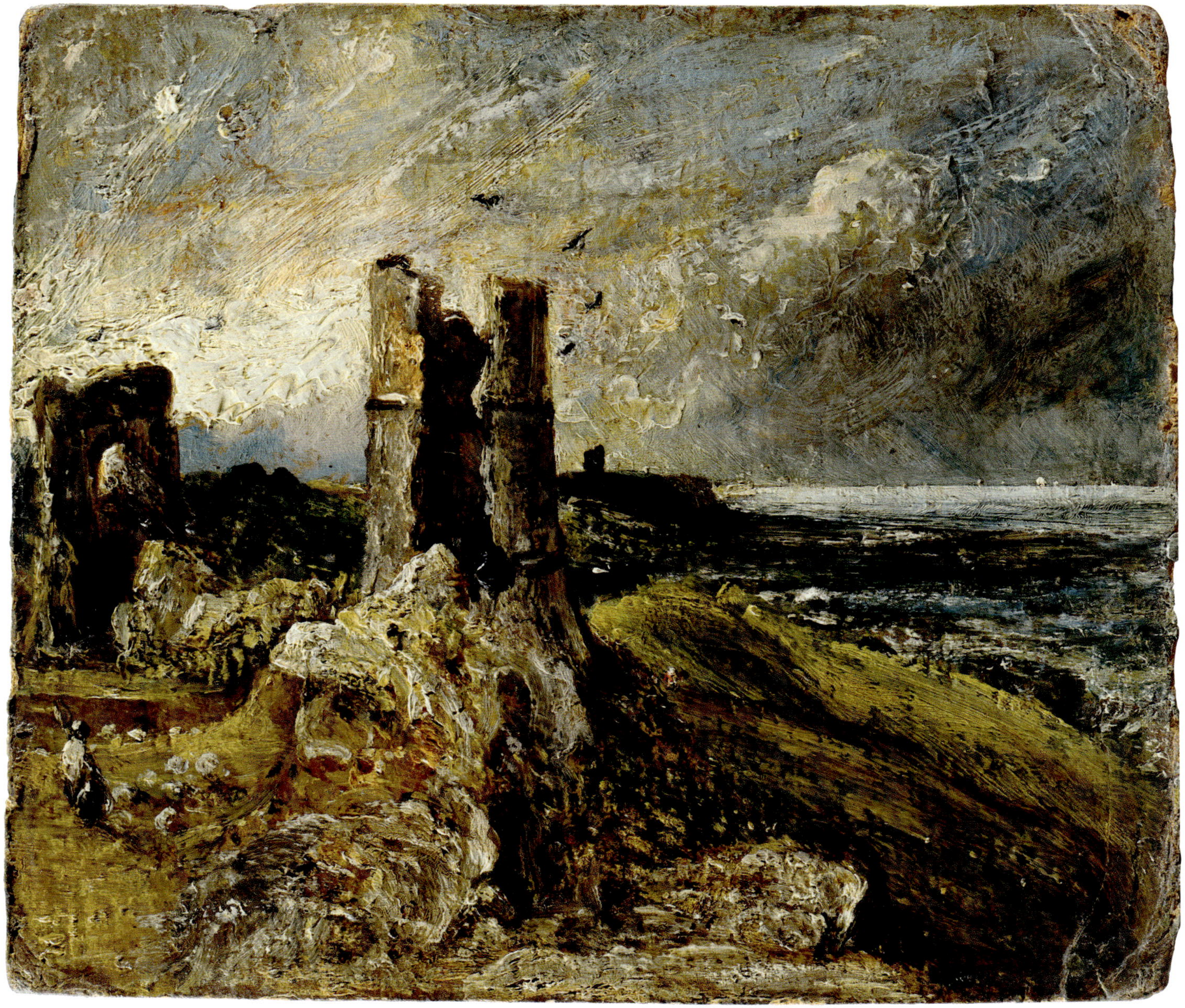

prepared to send the picture to the Academy, Constable wrote to Leslie: 'I am grievously nervous about it – as I am still smarting under my election' (JCC III, p.20). Nevertheless, the picture was generally well received, although there were some adverse comments about his wide use of flickering white highlights across the surface of the canvas. Turner was said to have observed sarcastically that these highlights reminded him of splashes of whitewash that might have dripped from a newly painted ceiling.

Constable arranged to have lines from James Thomson's poem *The Seasons* quoted in the exhibition catalogue, perhaps in an effort to ensure the painting would be seen as a kindred celebration of nature's power:

The desert joys
Wildly, through all his melancholy bounds
Rude ruins glitter; and the briny deep,
Seen from some pointed promontory's top
Far to the blue horizon's utmost verge,
Restless, reflects a floating gleam.
('Summer', from *The Seasons* (1727), 1744 edn,
lines 165–70; cited in Kroeber 1975, p.51)

As Michael Rosenthal has noted, these lines are not only descriptively similar to the painting, but also suggest that what the painting is ultimately about is light and its power to animate and vitalise the landscape (1983, pp.215–17). Indeed, the sombre towers, which speak of decay and the failed ventures of the past, strike a dramatic contrast to the vibrant expanse of light and air against which they are juxtaposed. As the title indicates, the storm has passed and a new day is beginning. Whatever the state his own emotions may have been when he painted *Hadleigh Castle*, Constable seemed intent on his audience finding in it a decidedly optimistic meaning. FK

54
**Sketch for
'Hadleigh Castle'**
c.1828
Oil on board
20 × 24 (7⁷⁄₈ × 9¹⁄₂)
R.29.3
Yale Center for British Art, Paul Mellon Collection

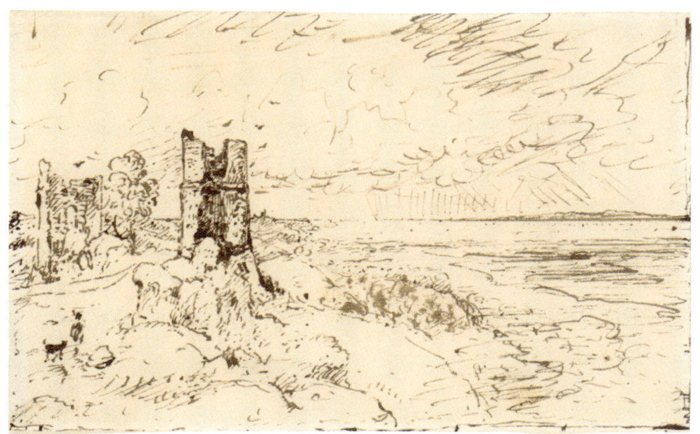

55
**Sketch for
'Hadleigh Castle'**
c.1828
Pen and iron-gall ink
on wove paper
10.1 × 16.6 (4 × 6¹⁄₂)
R.29.4
David Thomson

56

Hadleigh Castle (full-size sketch)
c.1828–9
Oil on canvas 122.5 × 167.4 (48¼ × 65⅞)
The canvas was extended after Constable's
death, by strips of approximately 10cm (4in)
at the left and along the bottom edge. The
additions seem to have been chiefly intended
to repair earlier damage to these areas.
R.29.2

TATE. PURCHASED 1935

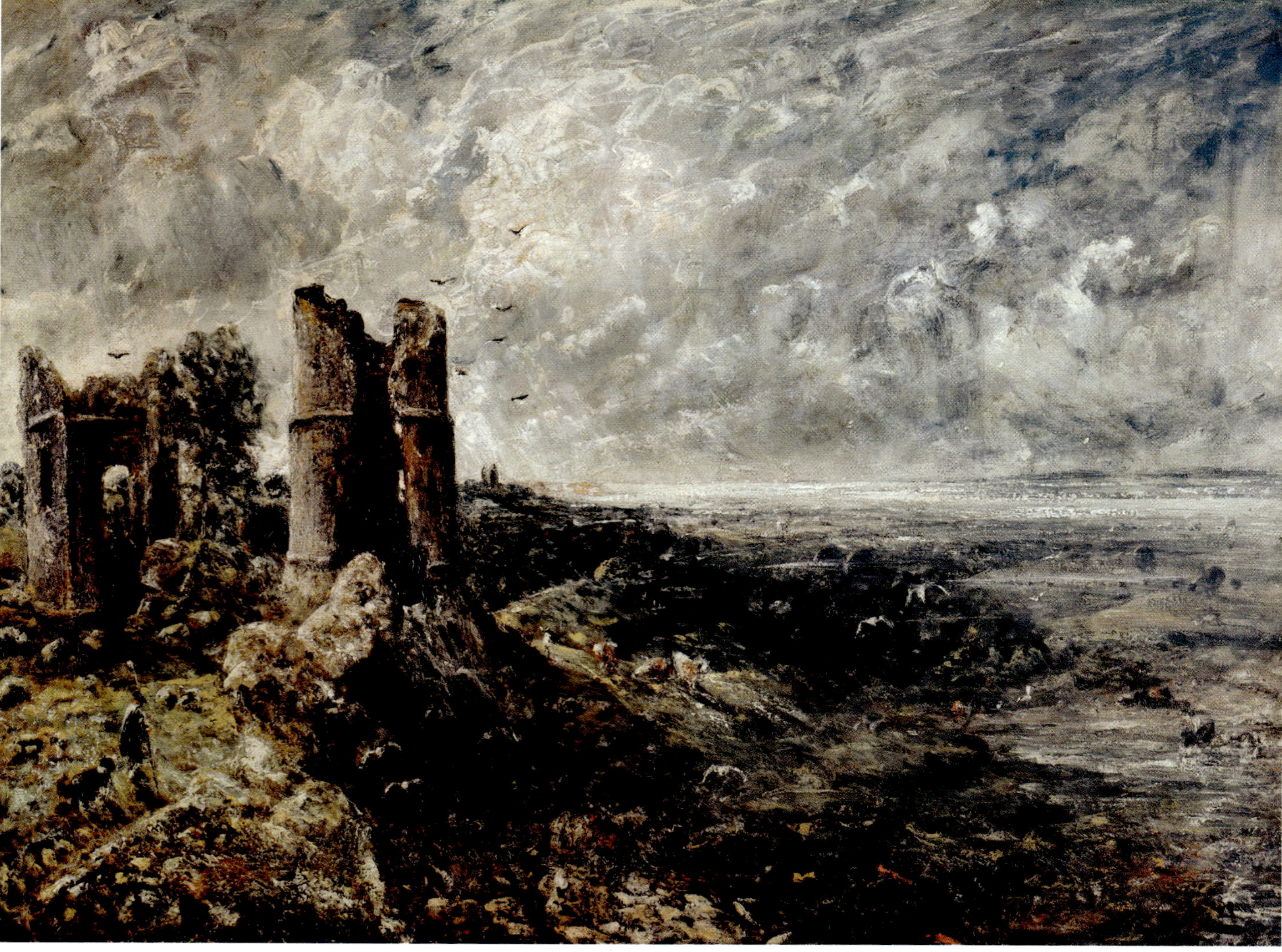

57

Hadleigh Castle

1829

Oil on canvas 122 × 164.5 (48 × 64¾)

Exh: RA 1829 (no.322, *Hadleigh Castle.
The mouth of the Thames – morning, after a stormy
night*; exhibited with quotation from James
Thomson's *The Seasons* [cited on p.175])

R.29.1

Ivy 29.10–11; 29.14; 29.18–20; 29.22–6

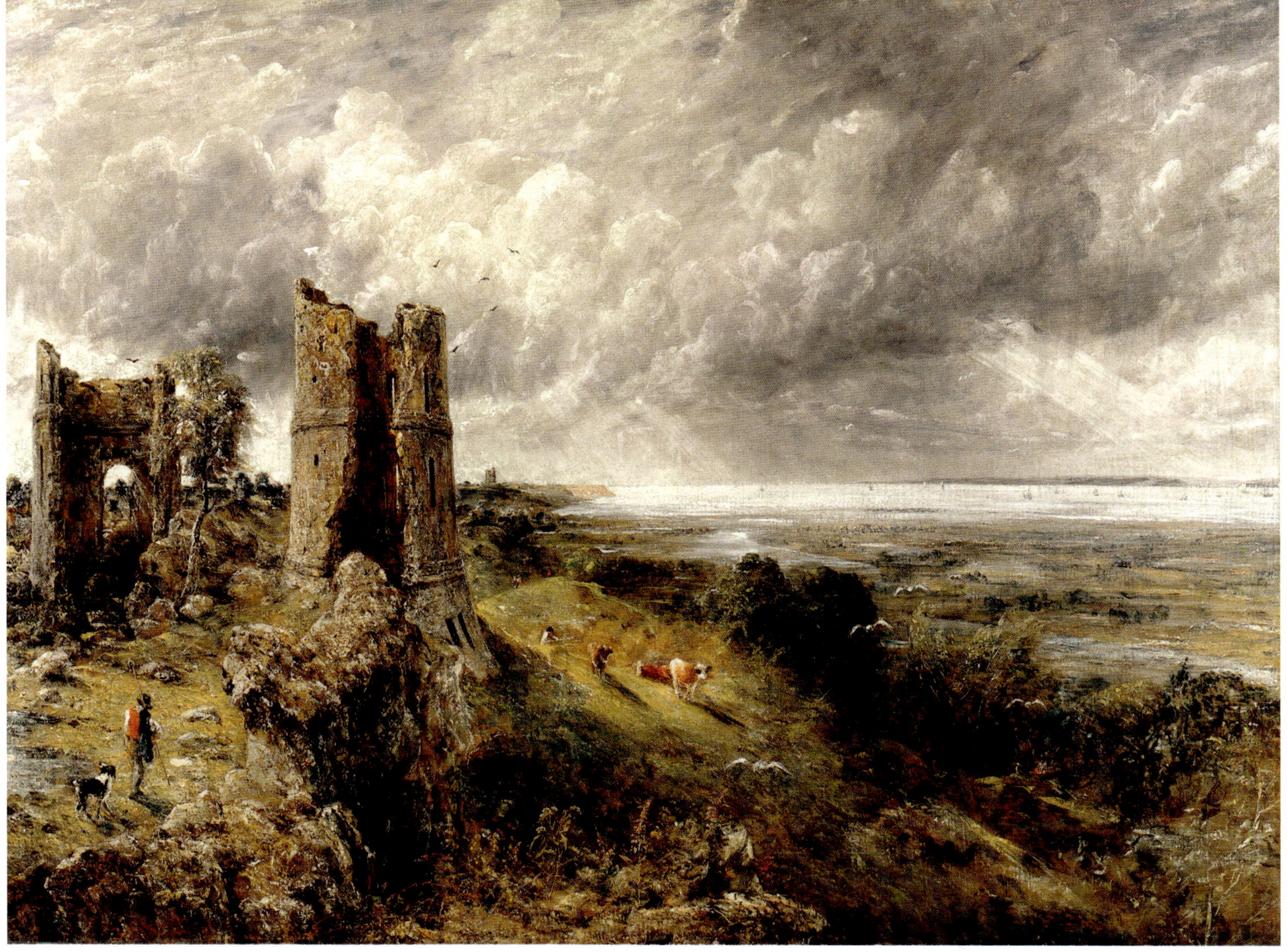

In 1811 Constable made his first trip to Salisbury, where he visited Dr John Fisher, the Bishop, whom he had first met some years earlier on one of his visits to Dedham (see no.3). While there his friendship with the Bishop's nephew, also named John, strengthened and, in Constable's words, 'first took so deep a root' (JCC VI, p.207). The younger Fisher became one of the painter's most important friends, and their correspondence over the years has provided scholars with an invaluable and lively source of information (as the number of references to it in this catalogue plainly attests). Constable would visit him at Leadenhall, his home in Salisbury Close, a number of times, and the view of the cathedral became a favourite subject and one with particularly positive personal meanings for him.

The genesis of Constable's greatest painting of the scene, *Salisbury Cathedral from the Meadows* (no.61), lay in his last visits there, made in July and November 1829. During July he made drawings of the cathedral from across the River Avon looking over the intervening meadows (Tate 1991, pp.360–7). At that time he seems to have discussed the idea of a large picture from this vantage point with Fisher, because the latter wrote to him on 9 August that:

The great easil has arrived & waits … Pray do not let it be long before you come & begin your work. I am quite sure the 'Church under a cloud' is the best subject you can take. It will be an amazing advantage to go every day & look afresh at your materials drawn from nature herself (JCC VI, pp. 250–1).

Implicit in Fisher's words is the recognition that Constable's practice in painting large pictures in his London studio based on studies had, inevitably, deprived him of the vital inspiration that experiencing an actual scene could provide. It also seems that Fisher expected Constable to paint this next large exhibition piece at his, Fisher's, home, but in the end that did not happen. His stay in November seems to have been relatively brief and it is hard to imagine that he could have accomplished much then on the 'great' easel (Reynolds 1984, p.226). Nevertheless, it has been suggested that he may well have started work on the full-scale sketch (no.60) while at Leadenhall (Tate 1991, p.364), and certainly the extraordinary vitality and vigorous nature of its surface makes it at least conceivable it was executed over a very short span of time.

What we do know, however, is that less than two years later, in 1831, Constable had no.61 sufficiently complete to send it to the Academy for exhibition. On 23 March 1831 Constable wrote to David Lucas, who was later to make an engraving of the picture (no.62):

I have made a great impression to my large canvas. Beechey was here yesterday, and said, 'Why *damn* it Constable, what a *damned* fine picture you are making, but you look *damned* ill – and you have got a *damned* bad cold.' So that you have evidence on *oath* of my being about a fine picture & that I am ill (JCC IV, p.346).

In creating the composition Constable made use of three drawings of the view he had made while at Salisbury and three small oil sketches derived from them (nos.58, 59; see also Tate 1991, pp.360–3). In no.58, which was probably made on the November visit, many

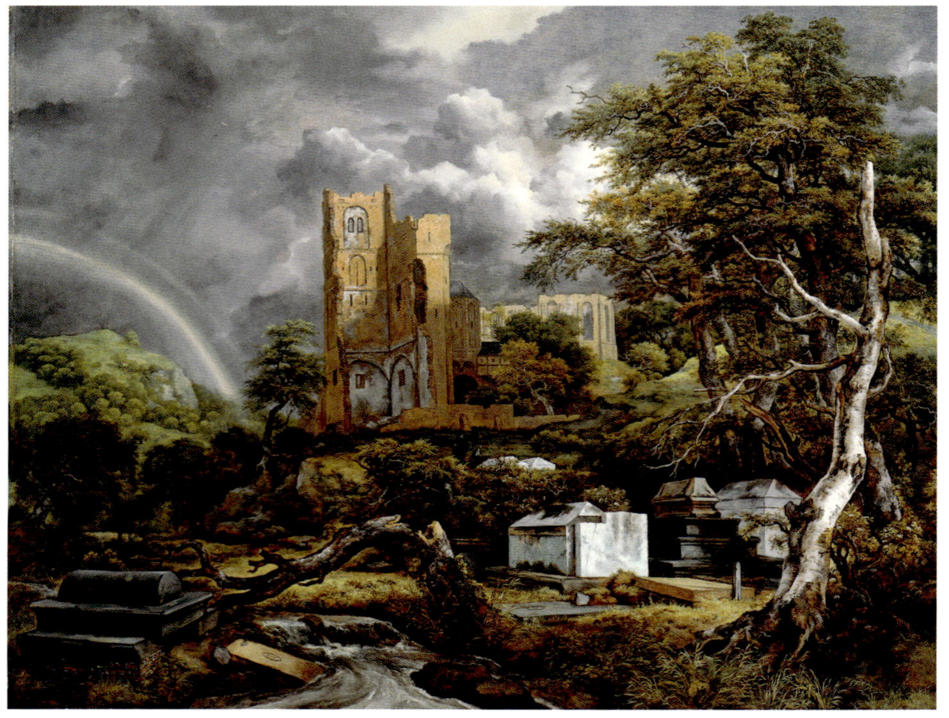

Figure 78
Jacob van Ruisdael
The Jewish Cemetery
c.1654–5
Oil on canvas
142 × 189 (55⅞ × 74⅜)
DETROIT INSTITUTE OF ARTS.
GIFT OF JULIUS H. HAASS IN
MEMORY OF HIS BROTHER DR
ERNEST W. HAASS

of the main elements are in place, most notably the motif of the wagon fording the river. A man and a dog make their appearance at the lower right, setting out to cross a footbridge. Constable developed the composition further in a vigorous oil sketch (no.59), before turning to make the full-scale sketch itself (no.60). As Sarah Cove has shown (see p.59), there are traces of transfer grids – using horizontal, vertical and diagonal pencil lines – on each and all of these, as Constable transferred the composition from one to the other in sequence.

Painted with a boldness and vigour that recall the sketch for *Hadleigh Castle* (no.56), the full-scale sketch has often been viewed with suspicion since it entered the collection of the Guildhall Art Gallery in 1902. Writing in 1904, C.J. Holmes noted: 'There seems to be a general feeling that the large picture attributed to Constable which was recently given to the Guildhall gallery is of very doubtful authenticity' (Holmes 1904, p.53). By that time someone had painted over the cathedral and substituted an ill-proportioned castle (see fig.17, p.44); this was removed during the process of conservation of the canvas in 1951 ('Constable's "Fording the River" Transformed: Cleaning Reveals Salisbury Cathedral in Place of the Castle', *Illustrated London News*, 19 July 1952, p.107). Even in its newly cleaned and now original state the painting continued to be doubted; Hoozee, for instance, considered it a dubious attribution in his 1979 catalogue raisonné (Hoozee 1979, p.151). However, in recent years, as Constable's methods and intentions in painting these large sketches have become more fully understood, it has won general acceptance. It logically continues his working out of the composition in no.59, with the dog moved to the left side, the man left out altogether, and the group of trees anchoring the left side increased in mass. The wagon itself

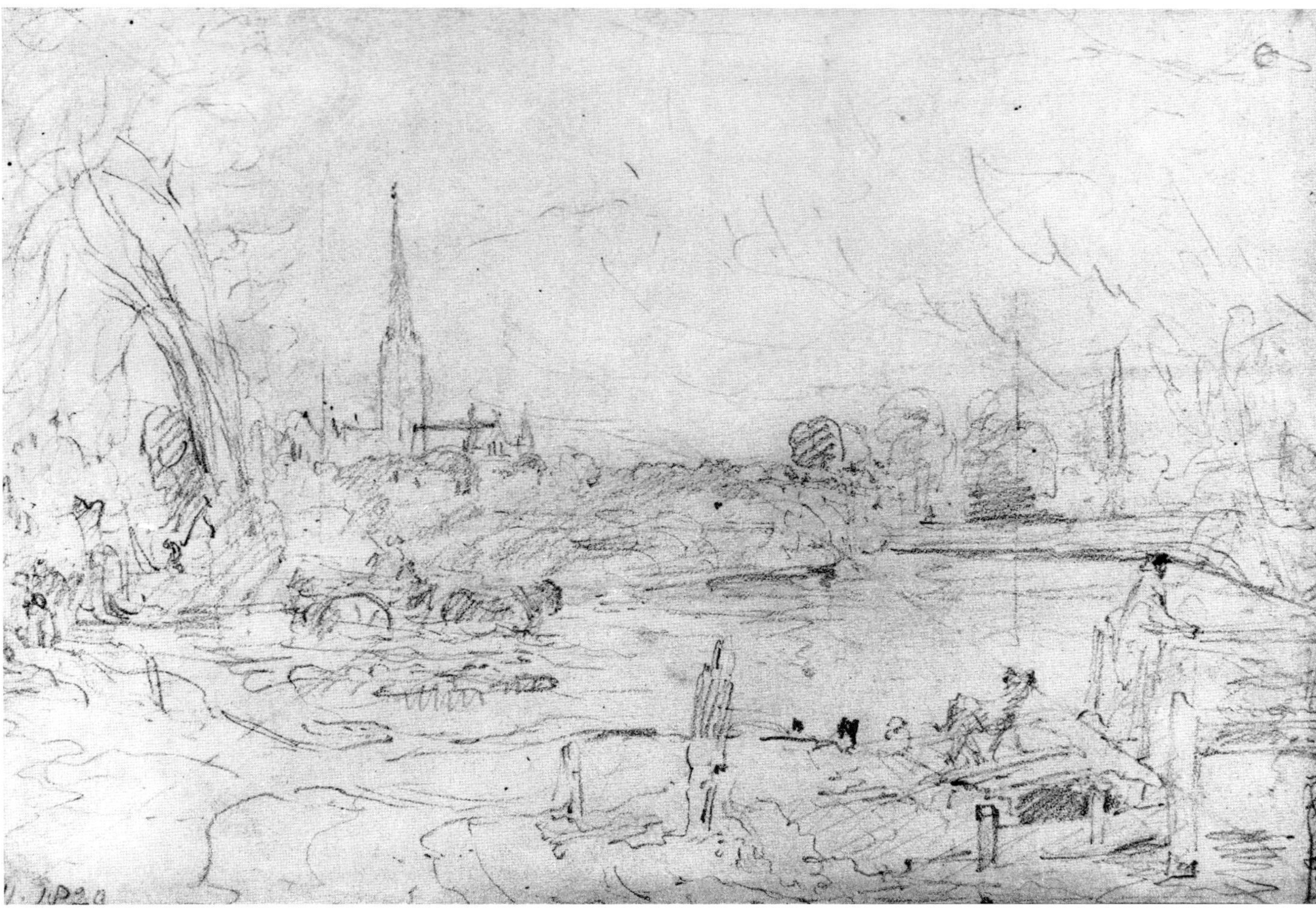

is now a more dominant motif and is more clearly described. It is different in form from the wagon in *The Hay Wain* (no.37) and others he had earlier drawn and painted in Suffolk and Hampstead; this was a 'bow-wagon', which were only used in England's southern and south-western counties, and thus appropriate to the locale (Tate 1991, p.364). The cathedral is oddly situated so that it rises dramatically in elevation from the east to the west, seeming on the one hand to be ploughing into the pictorial space like some great surging ship and on the other about to slide backwards out of view altogether (see fig.41, p.62).

Once on view at the Academy the final picture was met with mixed critical reception. In particular, the colouring of the sky and Constable's by now well-established use of white highlights were faulted. As a critic for *The Times* observed:

A very vigorous and masterly landscape, which somebody has spoiled since it was painted, by putting in such clouds as no human being ever saw, and by spotting the

58

Salisbury Cathedral from Long Bridge
1829
Pencil on paper 23 × 32.5 (9 × 12¾)
Inscribed in pencil in lower left-hand
corner '[?]11.1829'
R.29.13
LADY LEVER ART GALLERY, NATIONAL
MUSEUMS LIVERPOOL

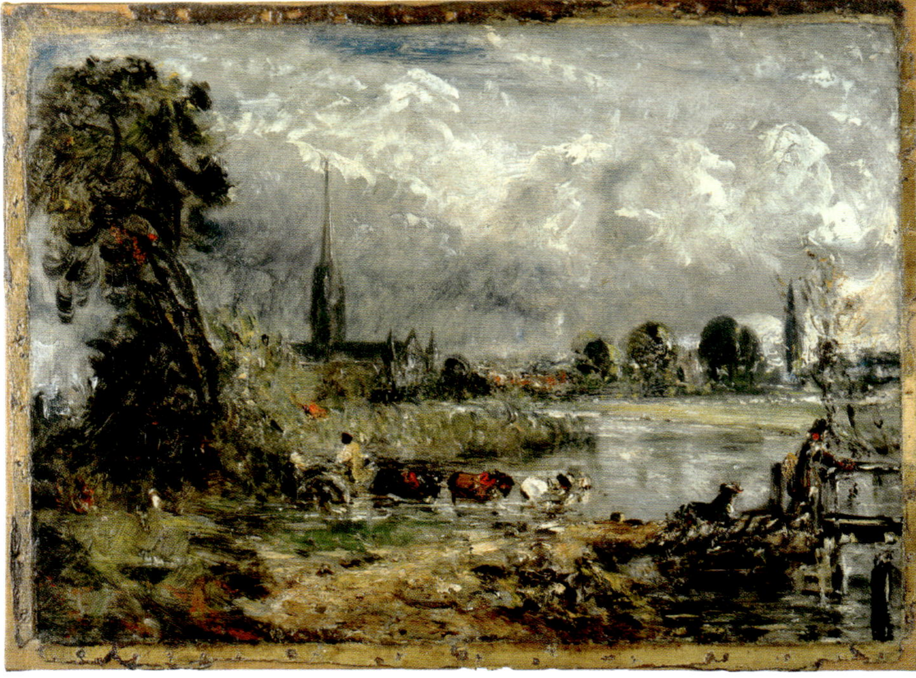

aesthetic sense of instability and disquieting energy in no.61, have led some observers to suggest the painting had for Constable an underlying meaning that related to his and Fisher's unease about what they perceived as threats to the stability of the Anglican Church due to proposed Parliamentary Reform measures (for a summary, see Rosenthal 1983, p.230). This seems plausible, although others have also argued that Constable's art rarely, if ever, obviously engaged issues of contemporary politics, and was all but inevitably personal in its associative meanings (see Tate 1991, p.367, following Harwood 1985). The latter view is supported, perhaps, by the fact that when Constable exhibited the picture at the Royal Academy in 1831, he chose to include lines from James Thomson's *The Seasons* (from which he had also quoted for *Hadleigh Castle*) that seem to be more informed by a sense of life's turmoils and despairs being assuaged by faith and a hope for renewed and refreshed beginnings than any political considerations:

As from the face of heaven the scatter'd clouds
Tumultuous rove, th'interminable sky
Sublimer swells, and o'er the world expands
A purer azure. Through the lightened air
A higher lustre and a clearer calm
Diffusive tremble; while, as if in sign
Of danger past, a glittering robe of joy,
Set off abundant by the yellow ray,
Invests the fields, and nature smiles reviv'd.
('Summer', from *The Seasons* [1727], 1744 edn, lines 1223–31, with many variations)

Both interpretations – and, indeed others – may be relevant, but it is worth remembering that Constable himself observed of Jacob van Ruisdael's *The Jewish Cemetery* (fig.78, p.178), which he knew at first hand and was surely on his mind when composing

foreground all over with whitewash. It is quite impossible that this offence can have been committed with the consent of the artist (Ivy 1991, p.150).

Constable made a number of significant adjustments in translating the full-scale sketch into an exhibition picture. The canvas he selected is 6 inches (15cm) taller than that used for the sketch, and the additional area it provided was primarily used to add to the amount of river bank visible at the bottom. As had been the case with his practice previously, Constable employed a comparatively subdued handling of paint to describe the forms in greater detail, so that elements such as the wagon and its horses and the cathedral now resolve more legibly into focus. Nevertheless, the brushwork overall is broken and staccato in feeling, establishing a nervous visual energy across the canvas that gives the whole a certain sense of agitated animation (see p.64). The sky – to which Constable has now added a great rainbow (on which see the fine study by Schweizer 1982) arching from left to right and terminating exactly at Fisher's home, Leadenhall – is one of the artist's most powerfully unsettled and grandly expressive. Lest we miss the attention – and honour – the artist paid to his friend, the line of sight from the dog at the lower centre leads the eye across the red highlight on the harness of the lead horse and directly to the house itself.

Fisher's description of the subject (cited above) as the 'Church under a cloud', and the

59

Sketch for 'Salisbury Cathedral from the Meadows'
c.1829
Oil on canvas 36.5 × 51.1 (14³/₈ × 20¹/₈)
Regularly spaced tack holes are visible along the edges, indicating that the sketch was squared-up with threads, so that Constable could transfer the composition to the full-scale sketch (no.60)
R.31.5

Salisbury Cathedral from the Meadows, that its implied allegory of life was easily overlooked. As he wrote:

he attempted to tell that which is outside the reach of art … there are ruins to indicate old age, a stream to signify the course of life, and rocks and precipices to shadow forth its dangers. But how are we to discover all this? (JCD, p.64).

Still, we may well wonder how Constable had been able to discern the very meanings in Ruisdael's painting that he felt were 'outside the reach of art'. Works such as *Salisbury Cathedral from the Meadows* leave us with the sense that Constable knew that the province of landscape painting was, on the most obvious and general level, the realm of nature, but that he also knew that it was inevitable, and indeed to be expected and encouraged, that it would also embrace the realms of imaginative interpretation. FK

60

Salisbury Cathedral from the Meadows (full-size sketch)
c.1829–31
Oil on canvas 133.5 × 186 (52⅝ × 73¼)
The canvas has been extended at left and right, where both tacking edges have been turned out
R.31.2
GUILDHALL ART GALLERY, CITY OF LONDON

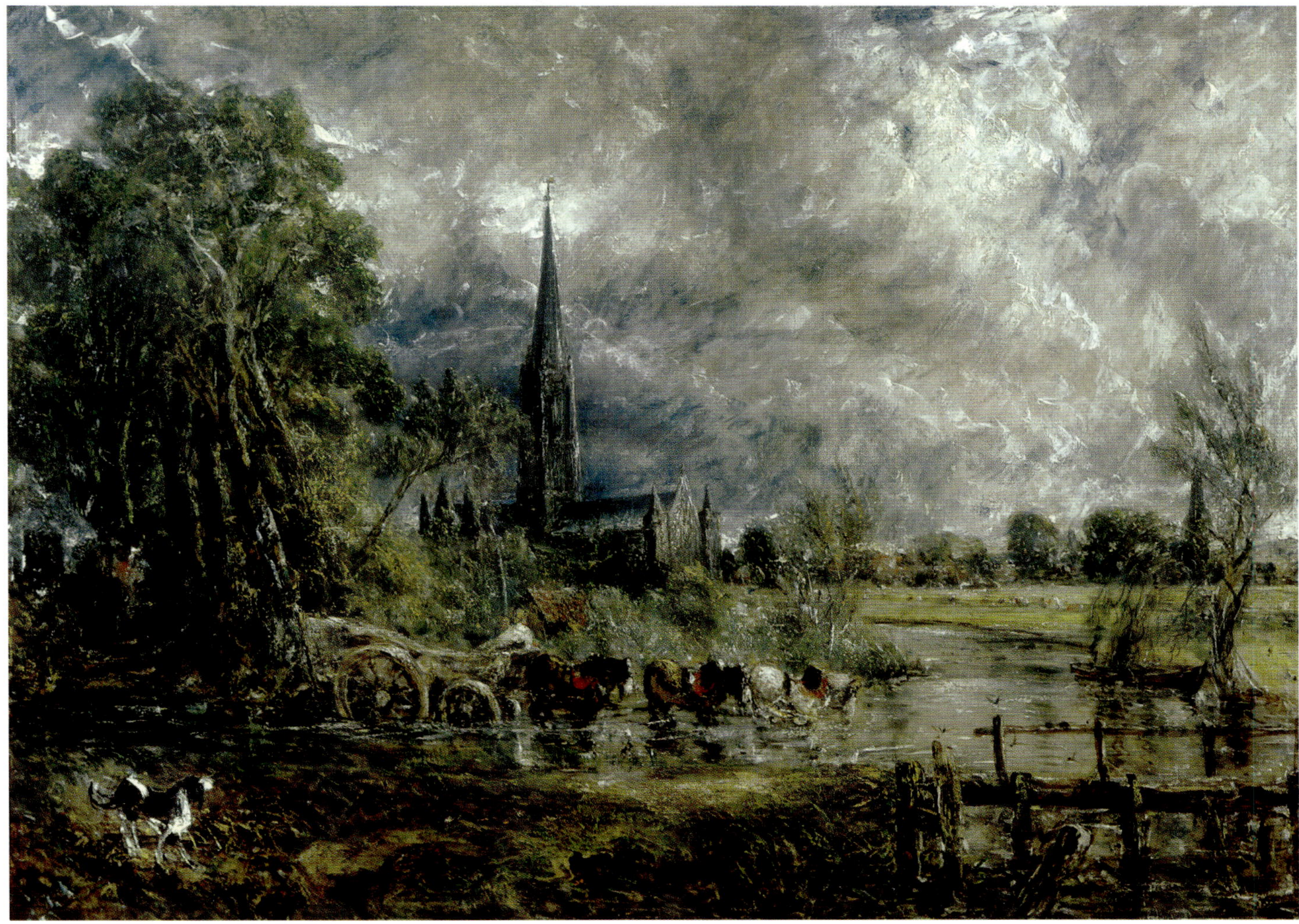

61

Salisbury Cathedral from the Meadows
1831
Oil on canvas 151.8 × 189.9 (59¾ × 74¾)
Exh: RA 1831 (no.169, *Salisbury Cathedral,
from the meadows*); BI 1833 (no.155, *Salisbury
from the meadows*, frame 72 × 82in);
Birmingham Society of Arts 1834 (no.317,
*Salisbury Cathedral, from the Meadows,
Summer Afternoon, A retiring Storm*);
Worcester Institution 1836 (no.2, *Salisbury
Cathedral from the Meadows – Summer
Afternoon – A retiring Tempest*)
R.31.1
Ivy 31.8–12; 31.14–17; 31.20–4; 31.26–9; 31.31–2;
33.1; 33.3–4; 33.6–8; 33.12; 34.39; 36.28
PRIVATE COLLECTION

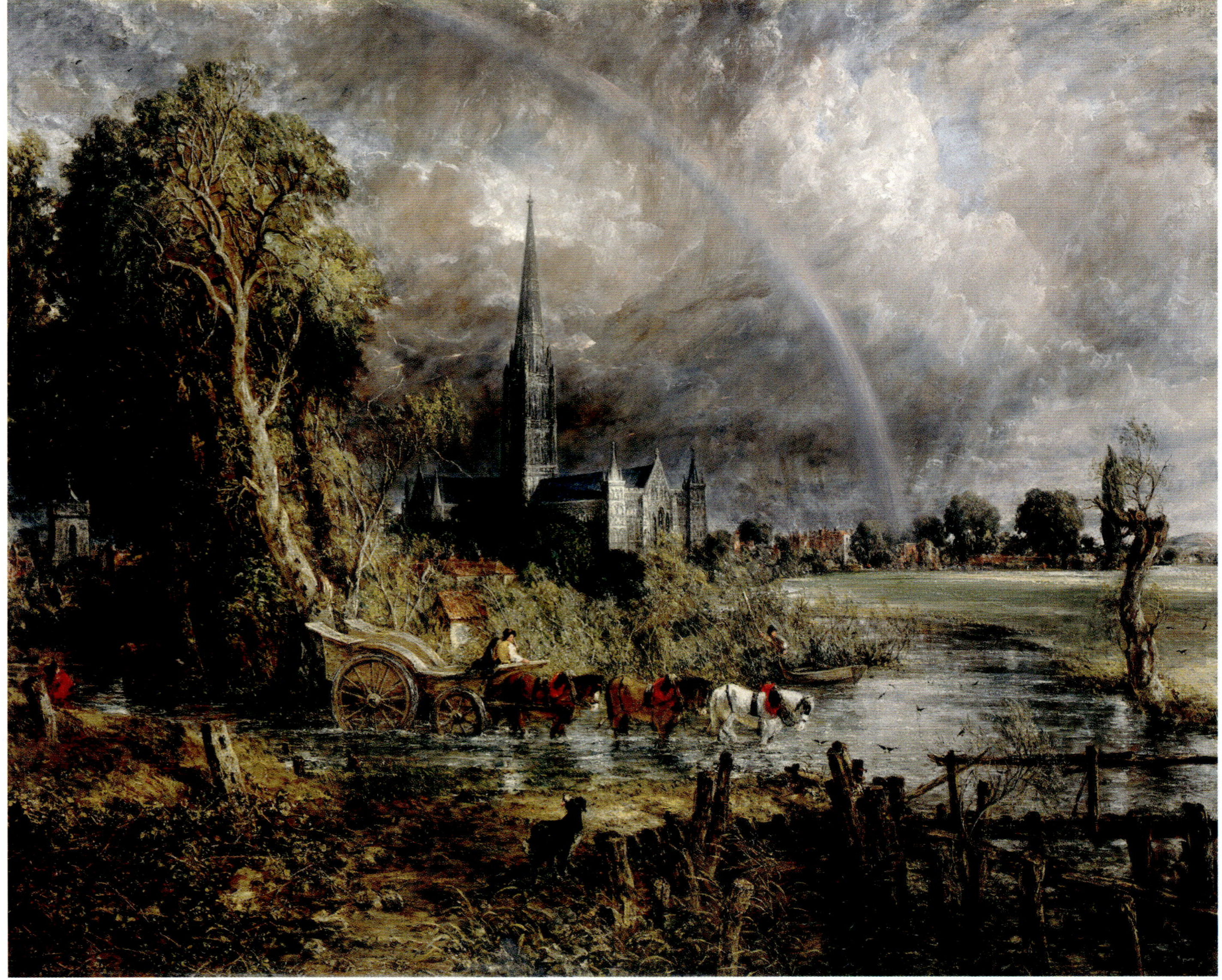

62

David Lucas after John Constable
**Salisbury Cathedral from the Meadows:
The Rainbow**
c.1835
Mezzotint engraving (image size) 55.1 × 69.2
(21³⁄₄ × 27¹⁄₄), touched with pencil, chalk and
grey wash; white paper collage on post at lower
left Shirley no.39, ?progress proof e
Private Collection

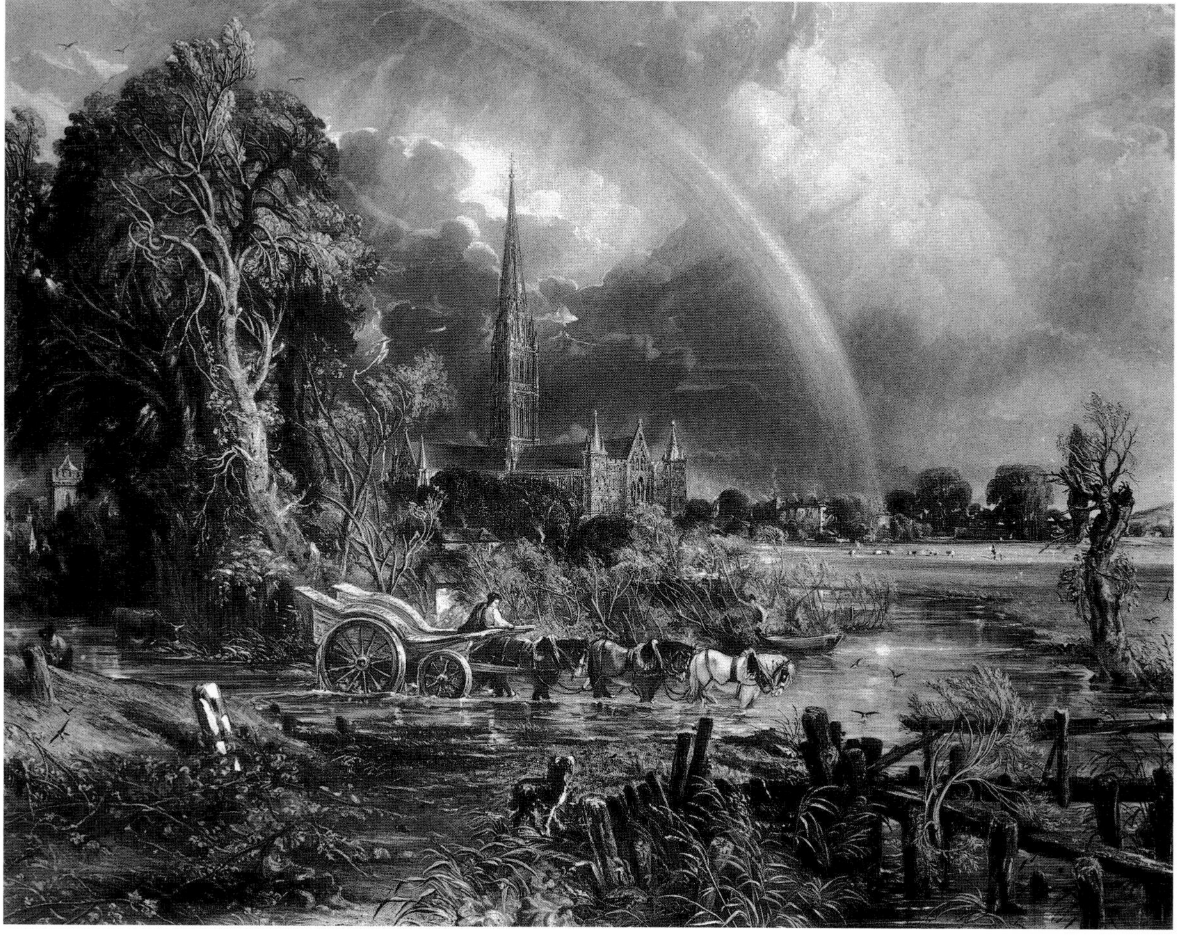

The Opening of Waterloo Bridge

Three years after his marriage to Maria Bicknell in 1816 and his permanent move to London, Constable decided to paint a large picture of a London subject, the ceremonial opening by the Prince Regent of Waterloo Bridge on the second anniversary of the battle, 18 June 1817. As a patriot and royalist, he would have been attracted by this historic event, and in choosing to paint a picture of it he may have been angling for royal patronage, bearing in mind that his father-in-law, Charles Bicknell, was solicitor to the Prince Regent. Alternatively, he may simply have wished to tackle a great 'historical' landscape that would recall the seaport subjects of the seventeenth-century French painter Claude Lorraine, with their scenes of embarkation (Tate 1991, p.206) or the more recent Thames subjects by the Venetian artist Canaletto (see fig.79). Yet the unfamiliar subject matter caused Constable no end of difficulty. His first ideas for the composition date from around 1819 (see fig.80, nos.63–4). However it was to be another thirteen years before he managed to bring the picture to completion, finally exhibiting it at the Royal Academy in 1832 (no.67). Of all Constable's great landscapes, it was this one that had the longest gestation and by far the most complex evolution.

The new bridge was designed by John Rennie, and its opening in 1817 proved a popular and highly colourful public event. The Prince Regent was accompanied by escorts of Foot Guards, Horse Guards and representatives of the Navy, as well as the Lord Mayor, whose festive, bedecked barge, the *Maria Wood*, appears in Constable's finished picture on the right (no.67). The Prince embarked on one of the royal barges from Whitehall Stairs, shown on the left of the composition, and then made the short river journey to the southern end of the bridge (on the far right). Salutes were fired

from the bridge as they progressed and, upon landing, the Prince marched in procession with the Dukes of York and Wellington across the bridge, lined for the occasion with Waterloo veterans (Parris 1994–5 [n.p.]). Crowds of spectators lined both sides of the river. Places could be hired on the upper floors or roofs of buildings on the north side , including presumably those shown in Constable's picture close to Whitehall Stairs, and the festive atmosphere was heightened by the consumption of beer and gin (Sutton 1955, p.249).

Although it is not known for certain whether Constable actually witnessed the day's events, circumstantial evidence suggests that he did. He was certainly in London at that time, being a regular attender at the Royal Academy's spring exhibition at Somerset House, situated just to the east of the new bridge; its extensive river façade is clearly visible in Constable's final picture on the left (no.67). Furthermore three pencil drawings by Constable of the bridge, or made in its immediate vicinity, are thought to come from a sketchbook he used in the early summer of 1817 (R.17.5–7).

One of Constable's initial problems when planning this subject was to decide from what height and from which angle it should be shown. His first idea seems to have been to present it from a very high viewpoint, as is indicated by a drawing he made about 1819 (fig.80), which was probably taken from an upper floor of the bow-fronted house (No.5 Whitehall Yard); this was to come just into view in the first version of the painting (no.65), and then fully into view in the exhibition version (no.67). Earlier topographical artists, including Canaletto himself (fig.79), had often adopted an elevated viewpoint of this sort as a way of ensuring a high horizon line and thus plenty of space to depict the exact details of, say, country houses and their estates or – in the case of river

scenes – pageants on the water. However it was probably this elevated viewpoint, or at least a 'painted sketch' of it, that Farington criticised in the summer of 1819 as being too much of a '"Bird's eye view" and thereby lessening [the] magnificence of the bridge and buildings' (Farington XV, p.5396).

In response to Farington's criticism, around 1819 Constable then made a composition sketch in oils showing the scene from a lower viewpoint, and from a position further to the right (no.63). Compared with his previous pencil study, which was purely a portrait of the site itself, here Constable has started planning his ideas for how to present the launch of the river procession. The royal barge can be seen drawn up at Whitehall Stairs on the left, and the Regent and his entourage are shown lining the quay. Immediately behind them is the garden wall of Fife House, at that time the home of the Prime Minister Lord Liverpool, and on the far left soldiers line the wall of Grantham House. Meanwhile, a puff of smoke on the bridge indicates the firing of a salute, and just beyond this appears the spire of St Paul's Cathedral. All these details were to be carried over by Constable into the finished picture (no.67). There is also a drawing by Constable from around this time, or perhaps slightly later, which shows him experimenting with a position from slightly further back (no.64). It appears to have been made by him originally in pencil on tracing paper, and then effectively redrawn more freely in pen and ink in a style recalling Canaletto. The Venetian artist might have been in Constable's mind not only because he was known for his pictures of river processions, but also because he had often painted this stretch of the Thames looking eastwards towards St Paul's.

Having established that the lower of these two viewpoints was the most suitable,

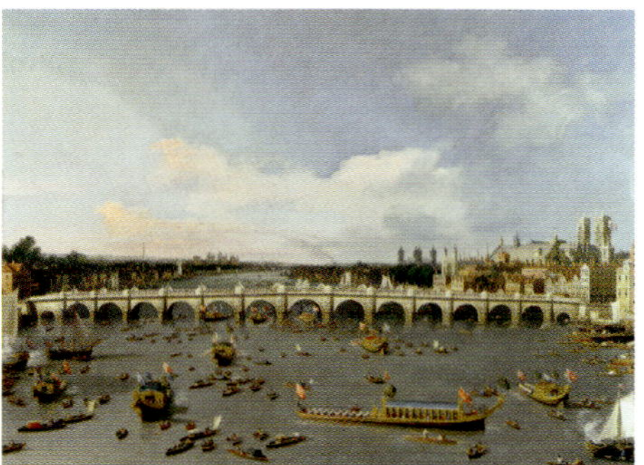

Figure 79
Giovanni Antonio Canal
(Canaletto)
**London: Westminster Bridge
from the North on Lord
Mayor's Day**
c.1746–7
Oil on canvas
95.8 × 127.5 (37³⁄₄ × 50¹⁄₄)
YALE CENTER FOR BRITISH ART,
NEW HAVEN; PAUL MELLON
COLLECTION

FIGURE 79

Constable then began working towards a finished picture. 'I am putting my river Thames on a large canvas,' he told Fisher on 1 September 1820, 'I think it promises well' (JCC VI, p.56). This 'large canvas' is likely to be the 'new begun picture; "A view on the Thames on the day of opening Waterloo Bridge"' that Constable took to show Farington in November (though being so large he would presumably have had to roll it up first). However, Farington advised him to set it aside and paint another large Suffolk subject for the following year's exhibition instead (Farington XVI, p.5582). Even though Constable followed Farington's advice and painted *The Hay Wain* (no.37) as an alternative exhibit, an advertisement appeared in the press that year announcing that a picture of 'the opening of Waterloo Bridge' by Constable would be exhibited at the Academy that spring, as did a similar advertisement the following year (Ivy 1991, pp.87, 93). However by May 1822, when Bishop Fisher saw the picture at Constable's house in Keppel Street, it was clearly still unfinished, though the Bishop admired it enough to declare it 'equal to Canaletti [*sic*]' (JCC II, p.276).

For many years, the identity of this earlier version of *The Opening of Waterloo Bridge* has puzzled scholars. The only other large-scale painting of the subject known to exist, apart from the exhibited version, is the one at Anglesey Abbey (no. 65), and this had generally been assumed to be the full-scale sketch for the Tate picture (despite its being uncharacteristically larger than the exhibition version) and thus dateable to c.1828–32. In 1991, however, Leslie Parris and Ian Fleming-Williams pointed out that the Anglesey Abbey version does not include the tall, white cylindrical shot tower, built in 1826 for the manufacture of lead shot, which appears in the far right-hand distance of Constable's later version of the subject and its

related sketches (nos.66, 67), and thus that it was almost certainly dateable to before 1826 (see Tate 1991, p.369). They also pointed out that the viewpoint in no.65 was lower than that adopted for the later sketch and painting (nos.66, 67). Meanwhile, in 2002 it was noted that no.65 actually looked for stylistic reasons to be a work painted in the early 1820s (Paris 2002, p.173). Now, for the first time, it can be stated with some degree of confidence that the Anglesey Abbey version of *The Opening of Waterloo Bridge* is indeed the one that Constable started around 1820, as Sarah Cove has shown that it is painted on a canvas prepared with a reddish-brown priming, which is only characteristic of works dating up to around 1820 (see p.57).

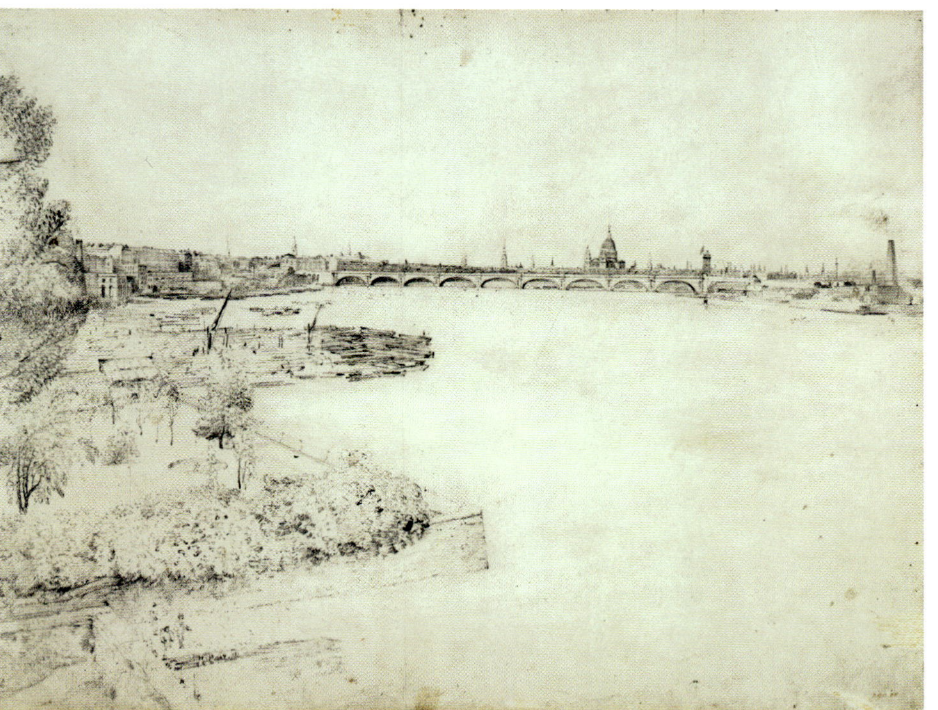

FIGURE 80

If, however, the Anglesey Abbey version (no.65) of *The Opening of Waterloo Bridge* is indeed the version started by Constable around 1820, when he had already been making full-scale sketches for large pictures for a period of two years, one then needs to ask whether no.65 is the full-scale sketch for a picture that was never started (or no longer survives); or whether it is actually the intended exhibition picture itself that was never finished (in which case perhaps a full-scale sketch was never made, or else no longer survives). At this stage, the evidence is inconclusive. On the one hand there are arguments in favour of interpreting no.65 as a full-scale sketch. The handling, for example, is fairly uniform in its breadth whereas we know that, at least for exhibition

pictures painted partly in the open air, Constable would tend to work up areas to different levels of finish at different stages in their evolution (see nos.20, 21, 23). Furthermore, most of the tacking edges of no.65 have been turned out to extend the surface available for painting, which is something Constable tended to do more readily with his sketches than for pictures destined for exhibition – although in this case it is possible that he turned out the edges many years later when using no.65 as an aid in the preparation of the second version of the subject (no.67). On the other hand, despite its 'sketchy' appearance, no.65 may actually have been started by Constable with the intention of becoming a 'finished' version (and thus he would have hoped in this instance to have managed without a full-scale sketch). If this were the case, Sarah Cove has suggested that Constable might have taken the picture too far ever to have been able to 'bring it back' again to the finesse required for a finished picture. This would explain not only why he then abandoned the painting, but also why in the subsequent versions of the composition he paid so much attention to painstaking and laborious underdrawing.

Whether the Anglesey Abbey version of *The Opening of Waterloo Bridge* (no.65) is a full-size sketch or an unfinished picture, by May 1824 there are indications that Constable had in any case decided to start on another version. For he told Fisher that month that he had now ordered some new canvas for the painting. However, by July he was already bemoaning to Fisher that he had 'no inclination to pursue my Waterloo, I am impressed with an idea that it will ruin me' (JCC VI, pp.161, 168). Then in the autumn of 1825 the artist Thomas Stothard suggested a 'capital alteration' to the picture, which Constable enthusiastically embraced in the hope that it

Figure 80
Waterloo Bridge from above Whitehall Stairs
c.1819
Pencil on trimmed wove paper
30.6 × 41 (12 × 16⅛)
VICTORIA AND ALBERT MUSUEM, LONDON

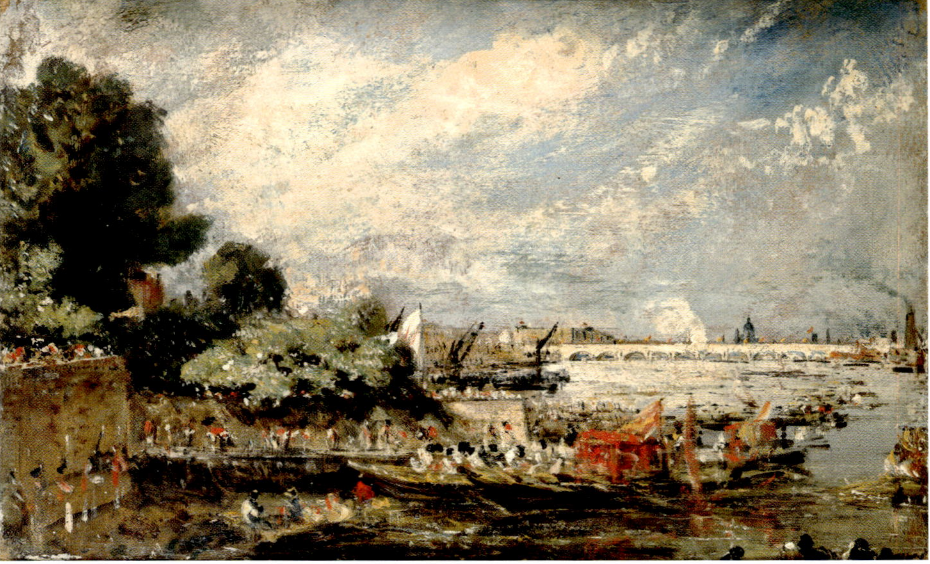

63

**Sketch for 'The Opening
of Waterloo Bridge'**

c.1819
Oil on board
29.2 × 48.3 (11½ × 19)
R.19.23
VICTORIA AND ALBERT
MUSEUM, LONDON. GIVEN
BY ISABEL CONSTABLE,
DAUGHTER OF THE ARTIST

64

**Sketch for 'The Opening
of Waterloo Bridge'**

c.1819–20
Pen and brown ink over
pencil on tracing paper laid
on card
16.5 × 27.3 (6½ × 10¾)
R.19.25
VICTORIA AND ALBERT
MUSEUM, LONDON. GIVEN
BY ISABEL CONSTABLE,
DAUGHTER OF THE ARTIST

would 'increase its consequence and do everything for it' (JCC IV, p.243). With the help of his studio assistant, the younger John Dunthorne, in September or October 1825 he set about 'getting the outline on the Waterloo', presumably on the new canvas that was destined to become the new exhibition version (JCC II, p.397). By 12 November he was insisting to Fisher that 'my *Waterloo … shall be done* for the next exhibition – saving only the fatalities of life' (JCC VI, p.206). Only a week later, however, he confessed to Fisher that 'My Waterloo like a blister begins to stick closer & closer & to my disturb my nights' (JCC VI, p.207). As it transpired, Constable did not manage to finish the picture in time for the following year's exhibition in 1826, sending *The Cornfield* (fig.59, p.116) to the Academy instead.

In the summer of 1826, however, a new opportunity presented itself, which meant that Constable may well have put the old version aside and started a new one. That summer, he was able to sketch the entire scene again from the terrace of Pembroke House, which explains the higher viewpoint that appears in the final picture and its related preliminary sketch (nos. 66, 67). He wrote excitedly to Fisher in July 1826:

I have made several visits to the terrace at Lord Pembroke's; it was the spot of all others to which I wanted to have access. I have added two feet to my canvas (JCC VI, p.223).

Constable would certainly have made fresh drawings at this point, though none survive today, and no doubt they would have included in the distance the silhouette of the newly constructed shot tower that appears in the subsequent version of, and sketches for, the picture (nos.66, 67). As his new position was a little further away as well as higher than his previous one, not only did it now serve to bring into full view the bow-fronted house on the left, but also part of the façade of another house adjacent, either Pembroke House itself or perhaps the house of Michel Angelo Taylor,

which lay between Pembroke House and the bow-fronted building (Tate 1991, p.371).

One might have imagined that Constable's visit to Pembroke House in 1826 would have given him the new impetus he so badly needed to bring the picture at long last to completion. However, his work on *The Opening of Waterloo Bridge* now appears to have come to a standstill again until 1829. Whether between 1826 and 1829 he may have proceeded any further with the old 'outline' he had started with John Dunthorne is not known for sure. Sarah Cove has suggested (personal communication, March 2006) that the earlier pencil 'outline' was now worked on again, in a second campaign, being reinforced in ink. However, it is also possible that Constable started an entirely new canvas at this point. Nor is the significance of the extra 'two feet' (60.9cm) he told Fisher he had added to his canvas fully understood. There are no signs of any additions on the left, or even in part on the right, of the final exhibition picture (no.67). Indeed, it is entirely possible that Constable's statement about the extra two feet expressed only another intention, this time to extend the canvas, rather than a fait accompli (Tate 1991, p.371). As it happens, the final version of the picture in the Tate is some ten inches narrower than the first version in the collection of Anglesey Abbey. Had Constable ever finished a version from no.65 it would have been, at approximately eight feet wide (2.43m), by far the largest of all Constable's great landscapes.

What we do know is that in 1829 Constable turned his attention to the Waterloo Bridge painting once again. This time his revived interest in the subject seems to have been connected with his plans to include it, as a substitute for *Hadleigh Castle*, in *English Landscape*, the series of mezzotint engravings after his paintings that he was working on at

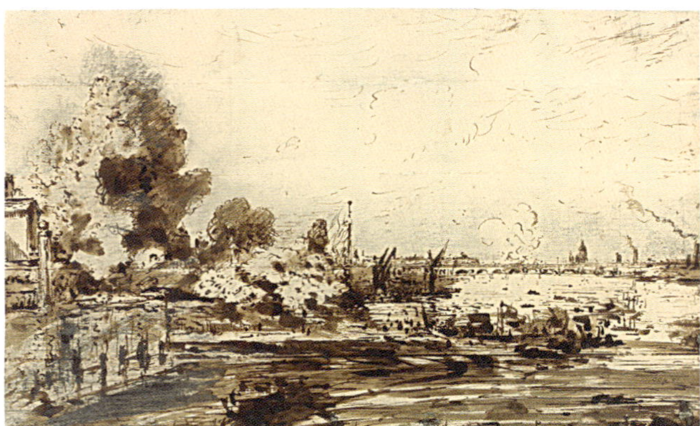

this time with David Lucas (see no.2). The print is based, or at least early 'proof' impressions of it are closely based, on no.66, a compositional sketch for a Waterloo Bridge subject that Constable made around 1829 (Parris 1994, p.69). However, since no.66 is approximately half the size of the finished Tate picture, and relates directly to it, once can probably assume that it was originally conceived and executed as a half-scale sketch for a new picture of a Waterloo Bridge subject, in the same way, for example, that the half-scale sketch for the *Chain Pier* (fig.77, p.171) was purposefully painted in preparation for a finished version of that subject. The situation is, however, complicated by the existence of a second, almost identical, version of no.66 in a private collection on a very similar scale, though less colourful and more thinly painted (R.29.64; see also Parris 1994, no.23, p.67, colour repr.). The explanation for the existence of this second version seems to lie in the fact that Constable was working on a new, large painting of *The Opening of Waterloo Bridge* at the same time as Lucas was preparing a print of the subject, and each needed a version of the composition to hand. The more monochrome version in a private collection may, then, have been painted as a substitute for Lucas, so that Constable could retrieve no.66 when working up the final picture.

The half-scale sketch for *The Opening of Waterloo Bridge* (no.66) was not, however, the only study Constable appears to have referred to when working up the final version of the picture (no.67). He still had in the studio his earlier, abandoned version of the composition, no.65. Indeed, it may have been around this time, in the late 1820s, that he now restretched it, incorporating the tacking edges into the picture plane. Sarah Cove has observed that no.65 was extensively reworked by Constable

using some of his later, brighter pigments belonging to the period c.1828–37, for example 'scarlet vermilion' and the bright orange (perhaps Field's 'orange vermilion') seen on the barges (see p.194; also Cove in Tate 1991, pp.506–7). If no.65 is no longer identifiable as the full-scale sketch for the Tate picture, there is nevertheless every indication that Constable referred to it, as well as reworking it, when elaborating his 1832 exhibit, even though he would have had other sketches to hand,

such as no.66, as well.

The finished picture differs from the earlier version, no.65, not only in its viewpoint, but also in its addition of one or two extra details. The inclusion of the Lord Mayor's barge on the right in the exhibition version has already been noted, as has the shot tower beyond it on the horizon. When one remembers that Constable is here representing an event that took place in 1817, the appearance of the shot tower is actually an anachronism. It is therefore curious

that Constable decided to retain it, unless, perhaps, he was intending to hint at British martial qualities, the picture in effect celebrating a famous British military battle at one remove (Rosenthal 2001, p.152). Another difference between the two works, and even between the finished picture and its related half-scale sketch, no.66, is that in the exhibition version Constable included in the foreground a parapet surmounted by urns. The parapet was probably designed to serve

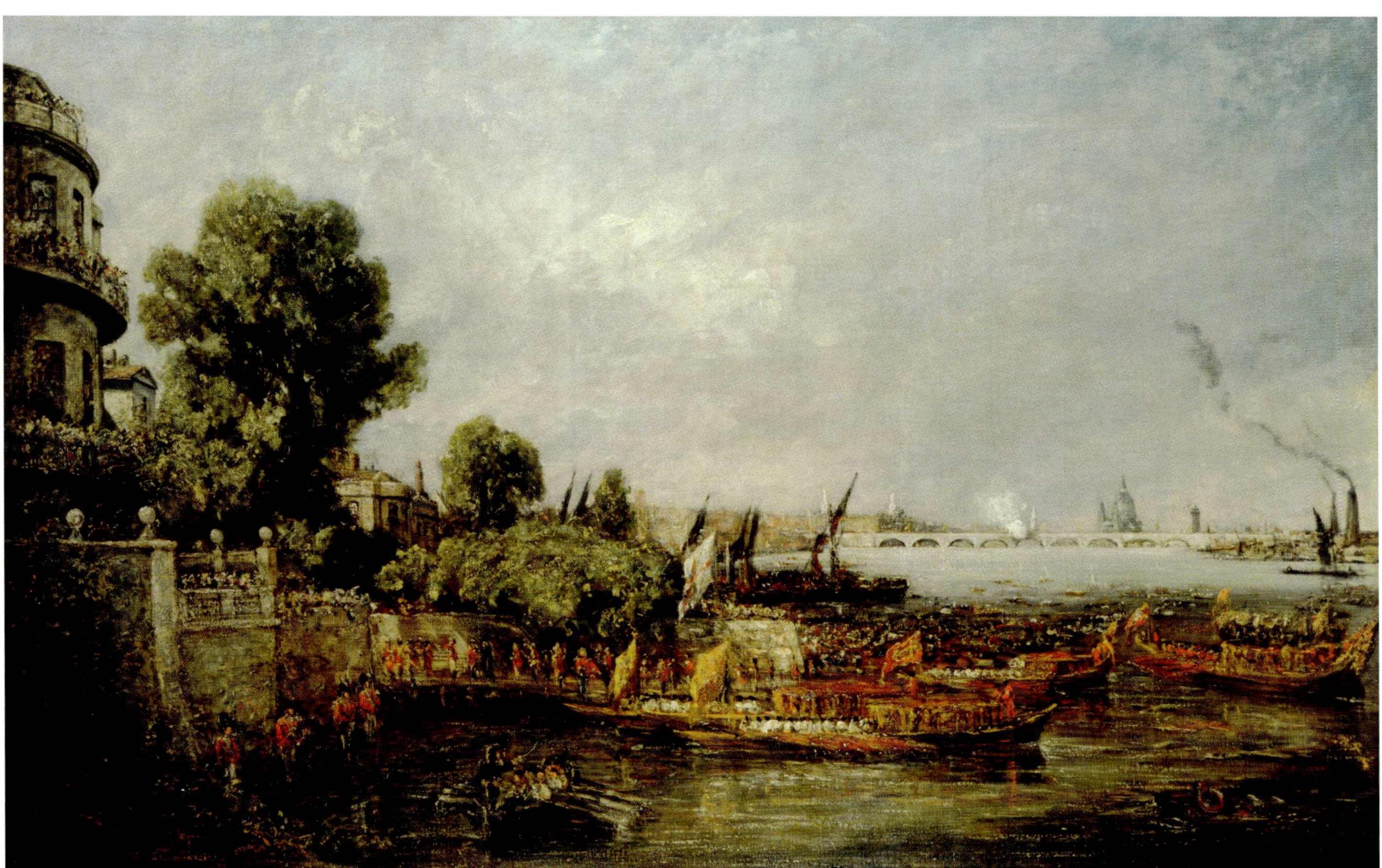

65

The Opening of Waterloo Bridge (first version)

c.1820–5

Oil on canvas

153.7 × 245.4 (60$\frac{1}{2}$ × 9 $\frac{5}{8}$), including flattened tacking edges at left, right and bottom sides, and probably also upper side as well. These appear to have been incorporated into the picture plane after the canvas was restretched, conceivably as late as c.1828–30

R.32.2

ANGLESEY ABBEY, THE FAIRHAVEN COLLECTION
(THE NATIONAL TRUST)

as a *repoussoir*, that is to add depth to the picture, and it certainly helps project the eye of the viewer beyond the scene of the royal embarkation and further into the distance, towards the sky and river as well indeed to the line at which they meet, the bridge itself. Here, immediately above the bridge, Constable portrays a rare atmospheric phenomenon, which he explained to C.R. Leslie: 'when the spectator stands with his back to the sun, the rays may be sometimes seen *converging* in perspective towards the opposite horizon' (Leslie 1845, p.310). John Thornes has explained that this observed effect is actually due to the sun's rays passing through a gap in the clouds at a shallow angle, but that due to perspective the slightly diverging rays actually appear to converge as anticrepuscular rays (Thornes 1999, p.142).

By March 1832, a month or two before the picture was due to be sent to the Academy, Constable appears to have been in good spirits, telling Lucas that he was 'dashing away at the great London' (JCC IV, p.368). However, by late April he was thrown by Thomas Stothard's remark that the picture was 'very unfinished Sir – much – to do', and became nervous about its reception at the forthcoming exhibition (JCC III, pp.67–8). It cannot have helped that, on one of the 'varnishing' days set aside for Academicians to retouch their pictures before the exhibition opened to the public, J.M.W. Turner, put out by the high-colour key of *The Opening of Waterloo Bridge*, added an intense red buoy to his own cool, grey marine, *Helvoetsluys* (fig.14, p.39), which hung adjacent. This is said to have prompted Constable to remark that 'He [Turner] has been here and fired a gun' (Leslie 1860, I, pp.202–3).

When the Academy exhibition finally opened, reviews of *The Opening of Waterloo Bridge* were mixed. Even though Constable had given it the title *Whitehall Stairs, June 18th, 1817*, many of the critics confused the event it represented with the subject of paintings sent in by other artists showing the opening of London Bridge in 1831 by William IV. Either because of the mixed reviews, or because the picture required too much extra work to it, Constable did not submit it to the British Institution exhibition in 1833. Although in 1834 he told a friend, George Constable of Arundel (no relation), that he was 'brushing up my Waterloo Bridge, and shall make it look like something before I have done with it' (JCC V, p.17), the picture does not seem to have been exhibited again in Constable's lifetime. AL

66

Sketch for 'The Opening of Waterloo Bridge'

c.1829
Oil on canvas 62 × 99 (24³⁄₈ × 39)
R.29.63
YALE CENTER FOR BRITISH ART,
PAUL MELLON COLLECTION

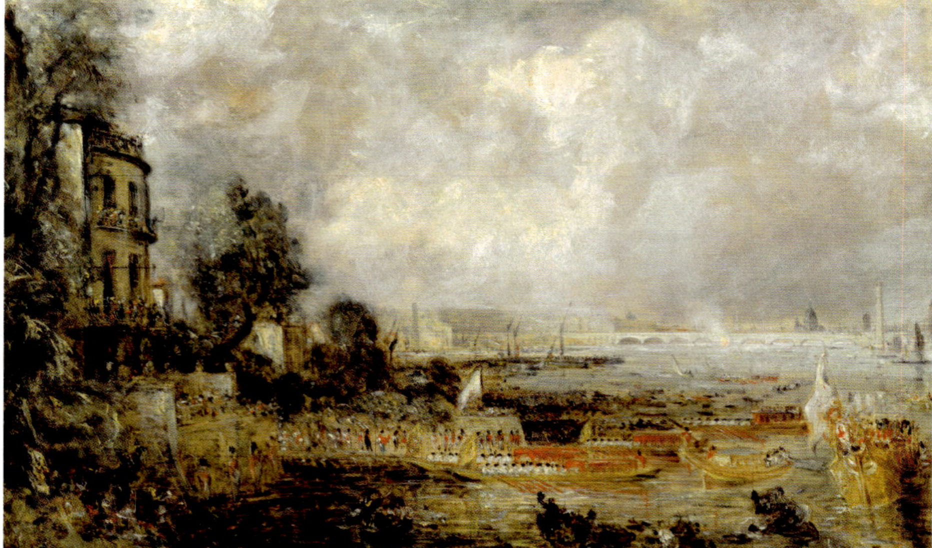

67

**The Opening of Waterloo Bridge
('Whitehall Stairs, June 18th, 1817')**
1832
Oil on canvas 130.8 × 218 (51$\frac{1}{2}$ × 85$\frac{7}{8}$)
Exh: RA 1832 (no.279, *Whitehall Stairs,
June 18th, 1817*)
R.32.1
Ivy 32.8–12; 32.14; 32.16; 32.19–24; 32.27;
32.29–31

TATE. PURCHASED WITH
ASSISTANCE FROM THE NATIONAL
HERITAGE MEMORIAL FUND,
THE CLORE FOUNDATION,
THE NATIONAL ART COLLECTIONS
FUND, THE FRIENDS OF THE TATE
GALLERY AND OTHERS 1987

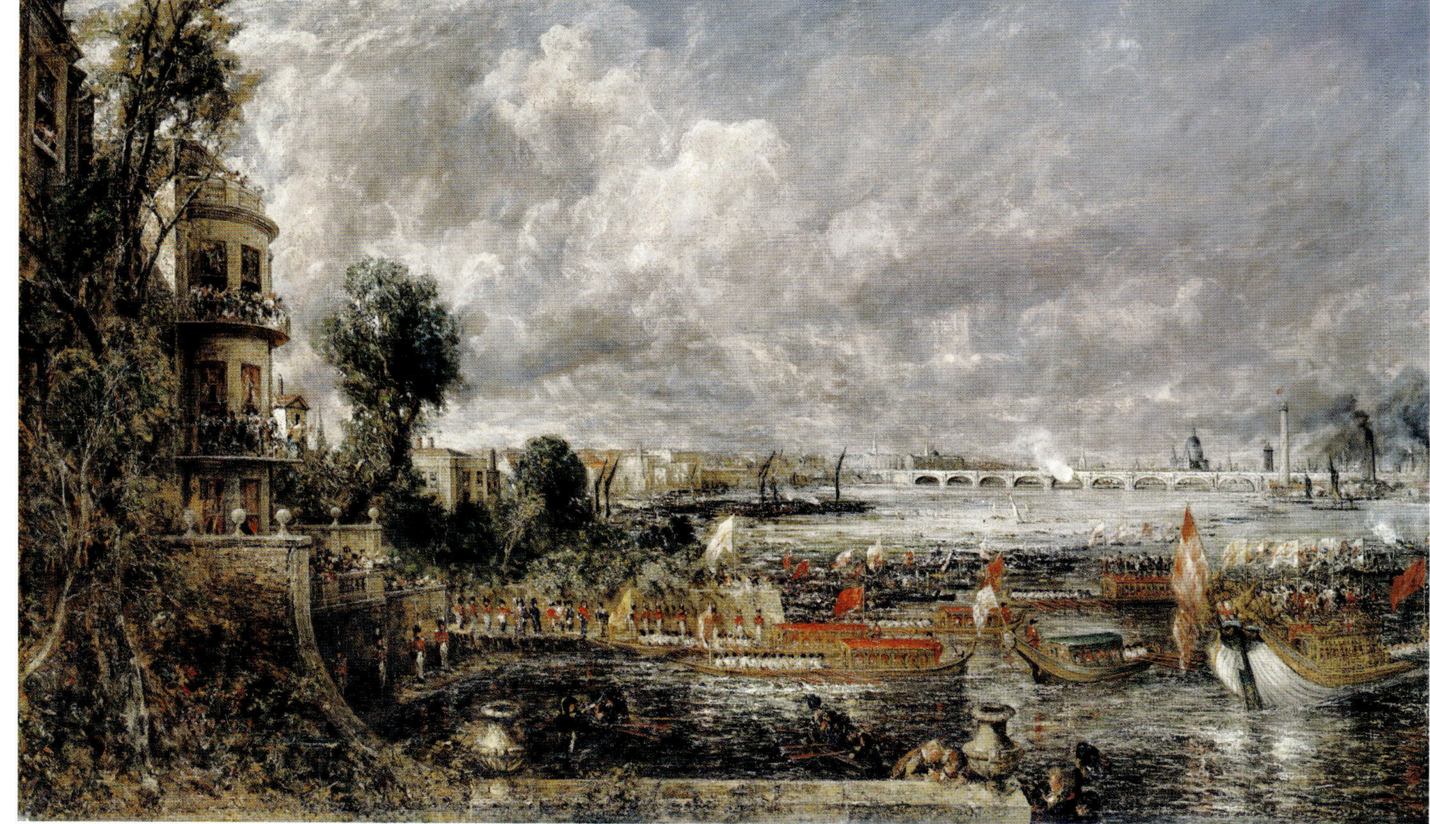

Stoke-by-Nayland

This extraordinary canvas long posed some of the most vexing questions about the very nature of Constable's late style and his aesthetic intentions in painting his large exhibition pieces. In 1834 Constable stated in a letter to his friend William Purton that he was 'foolishly bent on a large canvas' (JCC V, p.43), which may have been a reference to the present picture. The following year he wrote to Purton: I am glad you encourage me with 'Stoke'. What say you to a summer morning? July or August, at eight or nine o'clock, after a slight shower during the night, to enhance the dews in the shadowed part of the picture, under 'Hedge row elms and hillocks green', then the plough, cart, horse, gate, cows, donkey, &c are all good paintable material for the foreground, and the size of the canvas sufficient to try one's strength, and keep one at full collar (JCC V, p.44).

C.R. Leslie, in his *Memoirs of the Life of John Constable*, stated that no large picture of this subject was ever painted (Leslie 1951, p.251). Presumably he would have known of no.67, given his role in advising Constable's family about the sale of the works remaining in the artist's studio, so perhaps his statement should be understood as meaning that Constable never completed a *finished* picture of Stoke-by-Nayland. Thanks to the researches of Charles Rhyne (see, most especially, Rhyne 1987), it is now clear that no.68 was, in fact, a large-scale sketch that Constable was likely to have used as the basis for painting a finished picture had he lived.

The origins of the composition were probably laid in 1810, when Constable was commissioned to paint an altarpiece for Nayland church and is known to have gone sketching at Stoke-by-Nayland nearby. The village of Stoke-by-Nayland is a few miles west of East Bergholt and Dedham, located on a high ridge overlooking the Stour Valley. The church of St Mary, with its 36-metre (120ft) tall west tower, dominates the site, and is visible from miles around; Constable would have seen it from afar throughout his life. Oil sketches he made in around 1810 to 1811 (for example, no.5 and *Stoke-by-Nayland* c. 1811, Victoria and Albert Museum, R.29.61) establish the basic format he would develop more fully a quarter of a century later in no.68. The church and several nearby houses, adjusted from their positions in reality, are situated at the far left with an expanse of cloud-filled sky opening above them; large trees fill the right side. Constable included a similar view of the scene in *English Landscape* (see fig.81), although here with a rainbow arching over the church and the figure of a man at a gate added in the foreground. In a text accompanying the print the artist wrote:

The solemn stillness of Nature in a Summer's Noon, when attended by thunder-clouds, is the sentiment attempted in this print; at the same time, an endeavour has been made to give an additional interest to this Landscape by the introduction of the Rainbow (cited in Parris 1981, pp.62–3; see also JCD, p.21). After a discussion of the rainbow's significance, he turned to the church itself, noting the grand visual impact of its tower. Constable felt that a landscape view that included a motif of this kind 'imparts a peculiar sentiment, and gives a solemn air to even the country itself, and they cannot fail to impress the mind … with … mingled emotions of melancholy and admiration' (Parris 1981, pp.62–3; JCD, p.22).

It has often and reasonably been suggested that Constable's revisiting of the subject of Stoke-by-Nayland in conceiving the mezzotint for *English Landscape* must have been a factor in leading him to contemplate a large picture

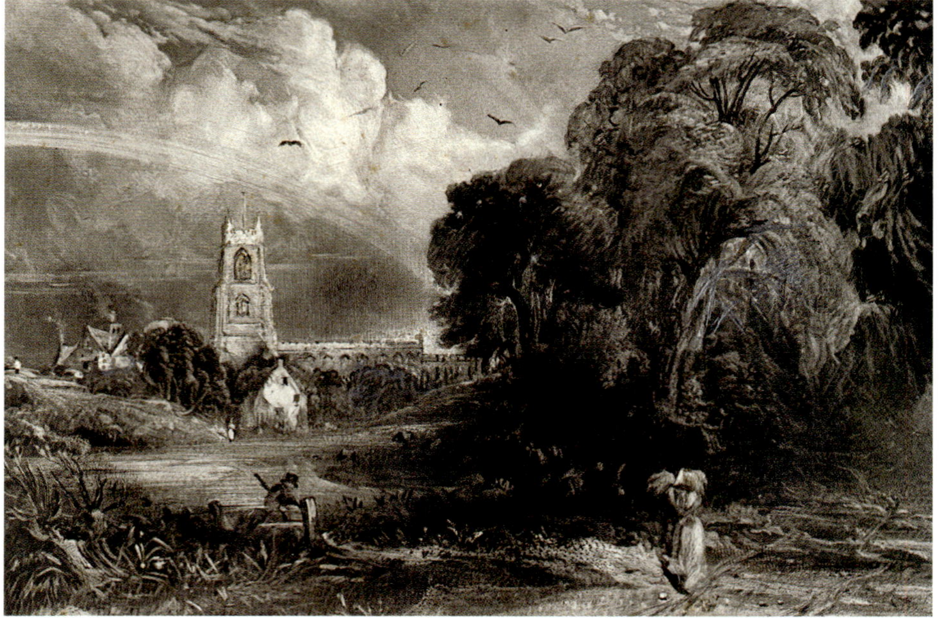

FIGURE 81

Figure 81
Stoke by Nayland, Suffolk
1830
Mezzotint engraving (progress proof 'e');
image size 14.4×21.9 (5¾×8⅝)
FITZWILLIAM MUSEUM, CAMBRIDGE

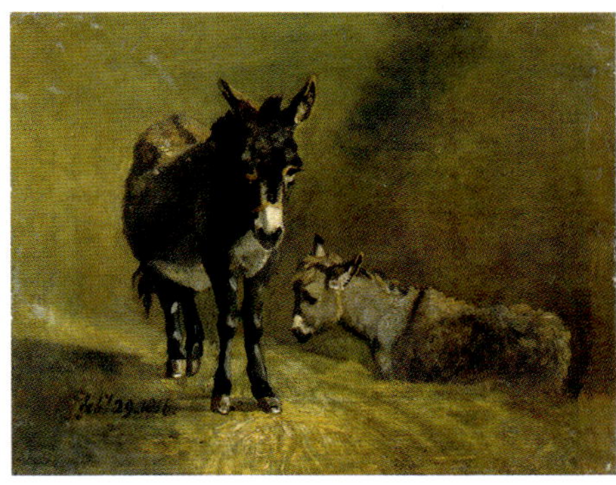

FIGURE 82

based on a view of the church. As the correspondence cited above indicates, he was likely at work on the full-size sketch by the period 1834 to 1835 and consulting his earlier studies; a 'blot' drawing (fig.83) may have been made in connection with the mezzotint, or possibly later in connection with work on no.68 (Tate 1991, p.472). The plough at the lower centre was based on an 1814 oil sketch (R.14.14), and the two donkeys just above the reclining man at the centre derive from a sketch in Philadelphia only recently identified as a work by Constable (fig.82; see also Thompson 2005, p.611). The anatomically impossible position of the reclining man suggests that Constable was considering at least two different poses for him; only in a sketch never intended to be exhibited would he have experimented in this way.

No.68 manifests some of Constable's most inspired use of the palette knife. As Rhyne (1987, p.10) has written:

Nowhere in Constable's art does he use the palette knife with more skill to suggest the character of an object with such specificity.

Similarly rich and impressive handling is visible in two other medium-sized sketches that must date from roughly the same time as no.68, *A Farmhouse near the Water's Edge* c.1834 (Phillips Collection, Washington, DC; R.34.76) and *Cottage at East Bergholt* (fig.84, p.192). For a sense of what the surface of a finished *Stoke-by-Nayland* might have looked like, a suggestion may be offered by Constable's *Hampstead Heath with a Rainbow* 1836 (fig.85, p.192). There the flickering play of his brushwork in describing the landscape combines with the more sweeping strokes of paint in the sky to create a shimmering, energised portrayal of nature's beauty. Constable was pleased with the result, writing of it, 'I have lately turned out one of my best bits of Heath, so fresh – so bright – dewy & sunshiny' (16 Sept. 1836, JCC V, p.35). It is also worth noting that a rainbow appears in *Hampstead Heath*, as was the case with the 1830 mezzotint of *Stoke-by-Nayland* and the 1831 *Salisbury Cathedral from the Meadows* (no.61). Even though the *Stoke* sketch does not include one (nor does, for that matter, the Guildhall sketch for *Salisbury*, no.60), Constable might well have intended to include a rainbow in the finished picture.

For Reynolds, the fact that the atmospheric mood of the Chicago *Stoke* was less troubled and oppressive than the imagery found in the 1830 mezzotint suggested that the artist's own 'gloom was lifting', and this represented a 'more optimistic account of the scene' (Reynolds 1984, p.292). Rhyne, while not discounting this reading, has argued that the sentiments expressed in Constable's text accompanying the mezzotint might equally have informed his thoughts about the painting. His awareness of the associations

of the past and history evoked by the ancient building may have combined with his deeply personal beliefs about the landscape in which it was sited, to establish complex and multi-layered meanings. Thus, it is Constable's own words that perhaps offer us the best guide to understanding the image:

The venerable grandeur of these religious edifices, with the charm that the mellowing hand of time hath cast over them, gives them, an aspect of extreme solemnity and pathos; and they stand lasting and impressive monuments of the power and munificence of our Ecclesiastical Government. The Church of Stoke, though by no means one of the largest, must be classed with these: it was probably erected about the fifteenth century … The nave of Stoke church, with its long continued line of embattled parapet, the finely proportioned chancel, with the bold projection of the buttresses throughout the building, would be the admiration of the student, while its grandest feature the Tower, from its commanding height, seems to impress on the surrounding country its own sacred dignity of character (letterpress to *English Land*scape, JCD, pp.22–3). **FK**

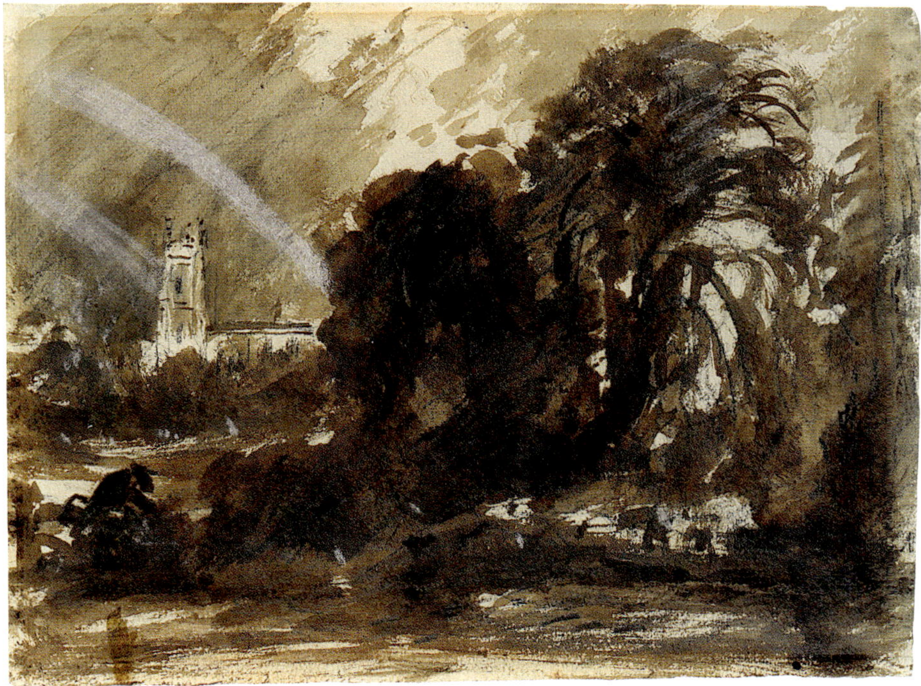

FIGURE 83

Figure 82
Two Donkeys
1816
Oil on canvas mounted on panel
19 × 25 (7½ × 9⅞)
PHILADELPHIA MUSEUM OF ART.
JOHN G. JOHNSON COLLECTION,
1917

Figure 83
Stoke by Nayland
c.1829–35
Pencil and ink wash with white
heightening
12.2 × 16.5 (4⅞ × 6½)
DAVID THOMSON

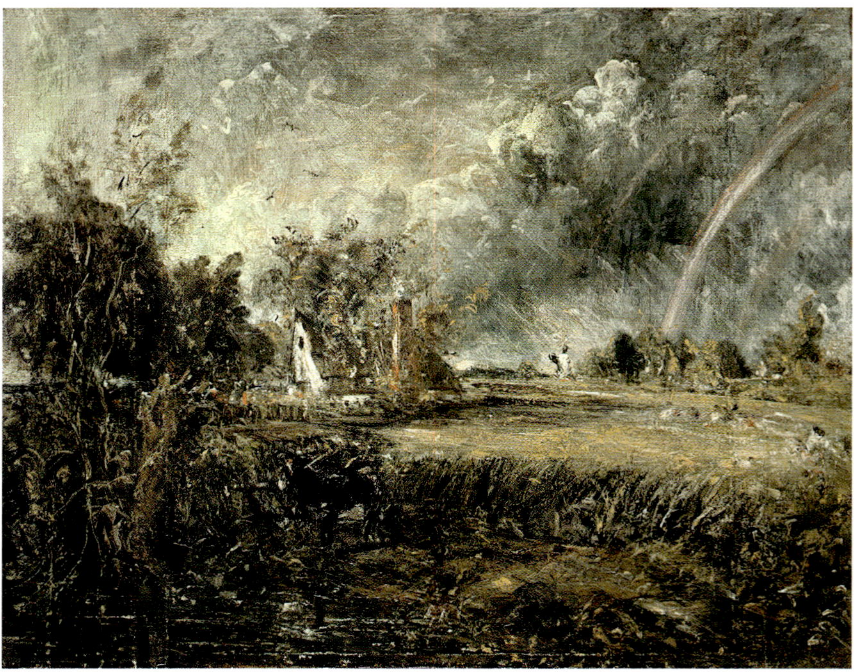

FIGURE 84

Figure 84
Cottage at East Bergholt
1830s
Oil on canvas
84.5 x 112 (33¼ × 44⅛)
LADY LEVER ART GALLERY,
NATIONAL MUSEUMS
LIVERPOOL

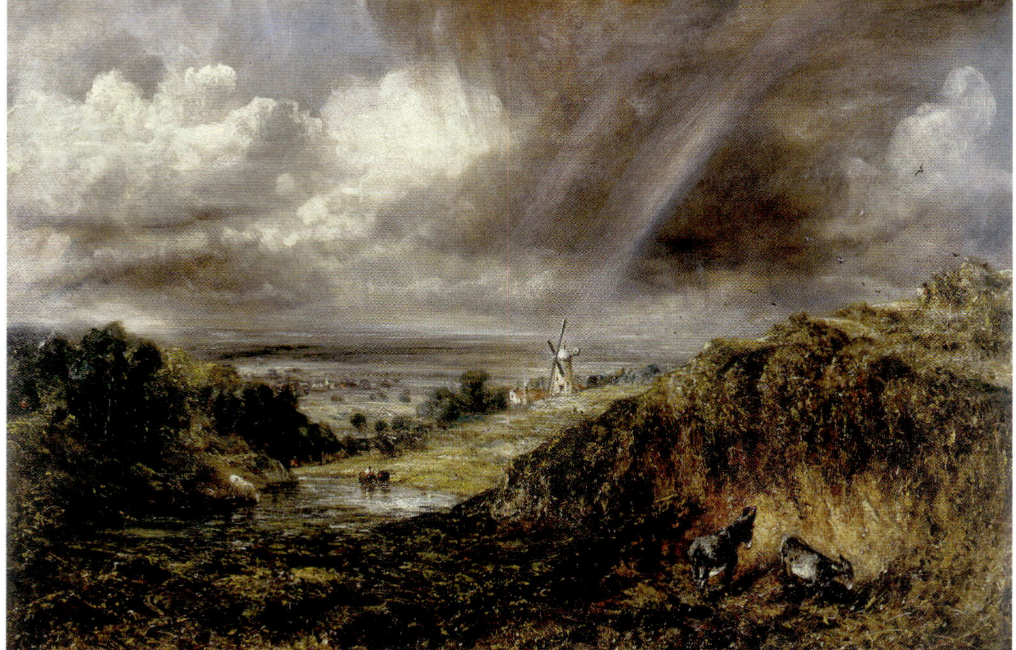

FIGURE 85

Figure 85
Hampstead Heath
with a Rainbow
1836
Oil on canvas
50.8 × 76.2 (20 × 30)
TATE. BEQUEATHED BY MISS
ISABEL CONSTABLE AS THE GIFT
OF MARIA LOUISA, ISABEL AND
LIONEL BICKNELL CONSTABLE
1888

68

Stoke-by-Nayland (full-size sketch)
c.1835–7
Oil on canvas 125.8 × 168.5 (49$^{1}/_{2}$ × 66$^{3}/_{8}$)
R.36.19
ART INSTITUTE OF CHICAGO,
MR AND MRS W.W. KIMBALL COLLECTION

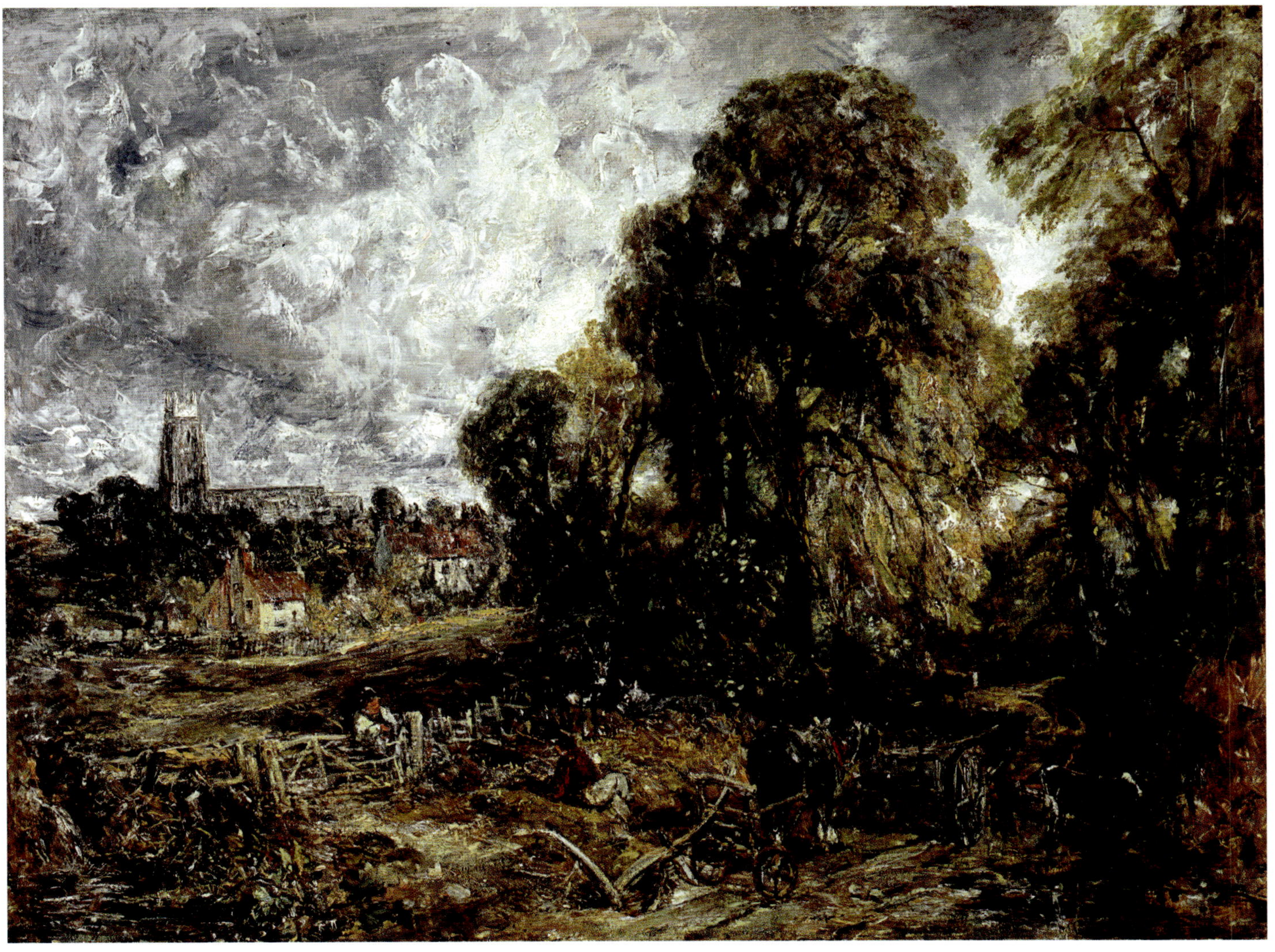

Constable's Studio Materials

Constable died unexpectedly during the night of 31 March 1837, having been hard at work in his studio on *Arundel Mill and Castle*, his forthcoming Academy exhibit (Tate 1991, no.202, pp.384–5). His sudden death meant that his studio was just as he had left it the previous evening. When an artist is as revered as Constable, one imagines that his studio equipment and materials will be retained in the condition in which he last used them. However, where there is a family of painters, as in every subsequent generation of Constable's family, or where objects pass out of the family collection, as with nos.69, 70, it is possible that later materials may have crept in with those belonging to the famous deceased. This is aptly illustrated by a recollection from the memoirs of the late Hugh Golding Constable, Constable's grandson: 'In 1891 I sold a clean palette … Colchester has the palette and somebody has put silly little dabs of paint on it' (H.G. Constable, 'Memoirs', c.1937–49, personal communication, R. Constable 1997).

John Constable's sons Alfred and Lionel both possessed genuine artistic talent and might have been tempted to use their father's materials and palettes, though the bladders of pigment were probably unusable by the time they were grown up. However, this does not appear to have happened, as no inconsistent materials have been found among Constable's paints or on his palette.

The contents of Constable's studio were divided among his children and close friends, including the artist C.R. Leslie and his engraver, David Lucas. There were at least four palettes, including no.69; a wooden sketching box with brushes, a chalk-holder, a palette knife and some pigments in glass phials (Constable family collection; Cove in Tate 1991, p.507, col. illus. p.501, fig.166); a metal paint box containing eleven paint bladders (no.70);

various prepared canvases, rolls of canvas, easels and frames (sold 1838; personal communication, Leslie Parris 1997); and 'a large wooden box full of bottles of colours and battered old brushes in another box, stolen by Sinn Fein in 1921' (H.G. Constable c.1937–49). Sadly, much of the material that remained in the family collection was destroyed by fire or stolen from the family home in Ireland in the early twentieth century.

One of Constable's surviving palettes (no.69) is covered with original impasted blobs of smeared paint and a darkened brown substance that is probably a spilled medium or varnish. Analysis of the materials was first carried out at the Tate for the *Paint and Painting* exhibition (Tate 1982b); the catalogue lists vermilion, Emerald green, chrome yellow and madder as having been identified (*ibid.* p.65). Further pigment analysis by Sarah Cove (1990, 1998) assisted by Rachel Grout (2003) has also identified Patent yellow (lead oxychloride), cobalt blue, lead white, a bright scarlet (probably a commercially prepared mixture of vermilion and the organic red 'lake' pigment madder), Mars yellow (synthetic iron oxide), black (possibly bone black) and various red, brown and orange earths. These were ground in a variety of mediums, including linseed oil mixed with pine resin, and either walnut oil or a mixture of poppy and linseed oils with a lot of pine resin mixed in. The spilled medium is a resin varnish, probably dammar or mastic, with a small addition of a 'drying' oil. Sarah Cove has identified these pigments and mediums in the 'finishing' layers of Constable's late works, c.1828–37, and they closely correspond to those identified in the metal paint box (no.70). The pigments include both translucent colours that were used for final glazing in a lush, glossy, slow-drying linseed oil/pine resin medium, and opaque yellows and whites, bound in poppy oil, probably with the addition of egg, to create the crisp highlights used to add the distinctive 'sparkle' to Constable's exhibited paintings. Cobalt blue is particularly significant as it is rarely found in Constable's oils, though it has been identified in some works from the 1820s and the large *Stoke-by-Nayland* sketch (no.68; Cove in Tate 1991, pp.502, 507). It may also have been used in the uncharacteristically bright blue sky of *Arundel Mill and Castle*, in the place of natural ultramarine, suggesting that this may be the palette that Constable was using to 'finish' the picture, in preparation for exhibition, on the last day of his life.

Constable's paint box of c.1837 (no.70) is a rectangular metal box with a hinged lid, originally divided into eighteen compartments, in two rows. There are now seventeen compartments, as one of the 'dividers' has been removed to make a double-sized space. It is probably a 'Japanned Tin Oil Colour Box', such as were commonly available from artists' colourmen in the nineteenth century (Cove 1998, p.211). It is similar to an early nineteenth-century paint box containing dried bladders acquired by the Victoria and Albert Museum and believed to have belonged to a 'William Turner' (P.65-1920; Darrah 1995, illus. p.72). The present author's analysis of the contents of the box belonging to Constable was carried out and published (Cove 1998), and can be summarised as follows. The glass phial with cork stopper contains the powdered blue-glass pigment smalt, some of which has spilled out. Smalt was routinely used by Constable in conjunction with the very expensive blue pigment natural ultramarine, probably as an 'extender', to make the colour go further. Similar phials containing two shades of ultramarine are in Constable's other surviving paint box (Cove in Tate 1991, p.507, fig.166).

69

Constable's palette

c.1837

24.5×40.5 (9¾×16)

Reddish hardwood, traditionally cherry wood
or walnut, though not identified by analysis

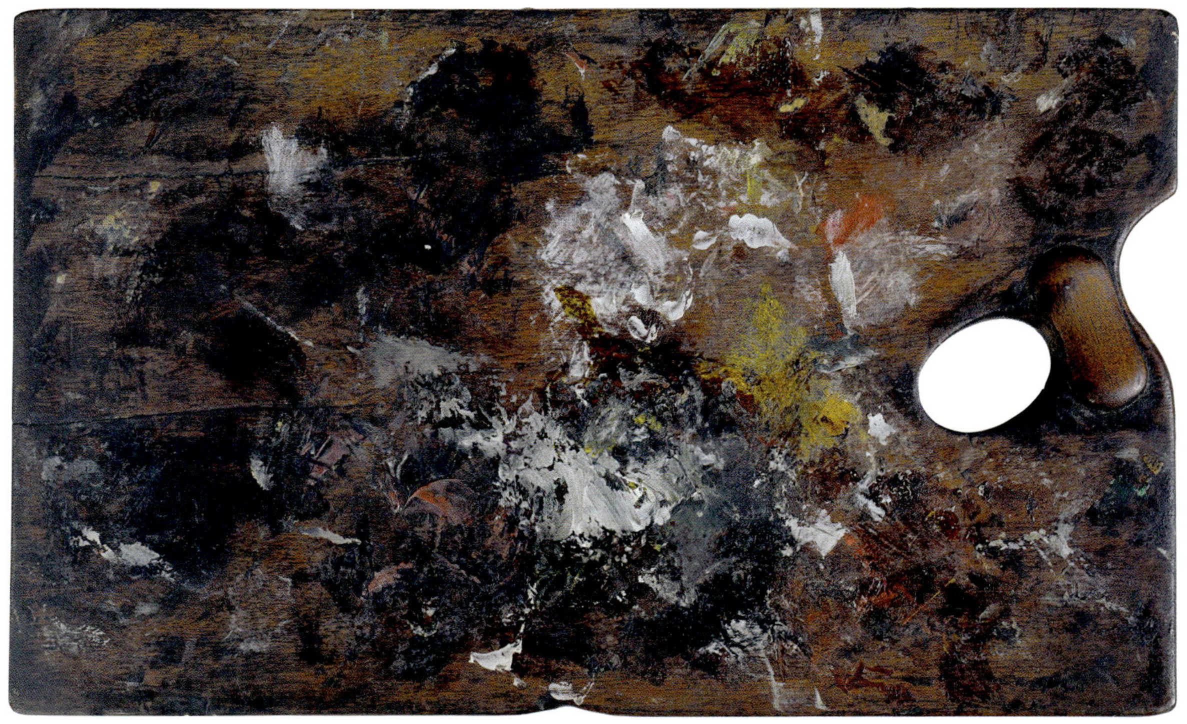

The white stone is a piece of gypsum (mainly calcium sulphate, containing a small proportion of natural chalk), which may be a lump of wall plaster that served a variety of purposes: roughening the surface of paper or canvas or rubbing down grounds; drawing, like 'chalk'; or powdered up and used as an extender to make colours more translucent whilst thickening the paint. There are eleven bladders of paint in the box, some with illegible paper labels. Bladders were used by artists for storing paint until the mid-nineteenth century, when the collapsible metal paint tubes we use today were invented. Paint was ground up with oil to a stiff consistency and a small blob was put into a piece of pig-skin, like that used for making sausages, and tied up with twine. To get the paint out, the bladder was pierced with a small tack, usually wood or bone (ivory for the wealthy), a small amount of paint was squeezed out and the hole plugged with the tack to stop the paint drying out. The paint in these bladders is hard and dry now due to age and the oil medium has darkened the skins, though some colour is still visible in places (fig.86). The bladders contain the following: verdigris; a mixed yellow-brown glaze containing a yellow lake with small additions of black, vermilion, Patent yellow and orange earths; chrome yellow (lead chromate); a blue-green containing verdigris and Prussian blue;

a transparent orange iron oxide (Mars orange); an orangey-brown mixed from two translucent earths; a reddish-brown mixture of earths and black; umber; a dark red-brown mixture of umber and vermilion; Emerald green (copper aceto-arsinate). These are both pure pigments and mixtures that may have been purchased under proprietary names describing the colour rather than the constituent pigments. The paint in the bladders is primarily bound with slow-drying poppy oil, which extends the 'shelf-life', sometimes with additions of thickened linseed oil and possibly pine resin. Heat-treated linseed oil is used for slow-drying pigments such as umber. The bladders are covered in bright specks of dried paint that were also analysed to discover Constable's 'working' mixtures. These include the pigments listed above, together with lead white, bone brown/black, synthetic red and yellow iron oxides (Mars colours) and two different red 'lakes'. The pigment splashes contained a mixture of the mediums found in the bladders together with the additives: zinc sulphate 'driers' in poppy oil, lead-based 'driers' in linseed oil, mastic varnish, egg yolk, beeswax and pine resin. Many of the pigments and mediums found here are also present on the palette (no.69) and have been identified in Constable's 'late' works from c.1828 to 1837 (see pp.61–2; Cove in Tate 1991, p.507).

The analysis of the paint box sheds considerable light on Constable's materials and working practice at the end of his life, and demonstrates both his practical skill and his willingness to manipulate traditional painting materials to create a personal range of 'effects'. We find that in his 'late' studio works he used proprietary paints and mediums such as 'drying oils', which could be bought off-the-shelf, mixed with a range of commercial and home-made additives to create 'working'

mediums. These were precisely formulated to obtain the required consistency of paint for each area of a picture. The primary 'late' medium, poppy oil, dries more slowly than other oils, and was ideal for an artist who reworked his surfaces constantly, over a period of months, making a feature of dragged, partially dry brushwork to create a lattice of flickering colour. Egg and beeswax were added to create stiff highlights, and pine resin and heat-treated linseed oil gave a lush, glossy medium for glazing. Mastic varnish was used for glazing as well, and could also be used to make a 'gelled' medium that creates an impasto with 'soft flow'. The paints identified here are clearly featured in two of Constable's last great Academy works, shown in this exhibition: *Salisbury Cathedral from the Meadows* 1831 (no.61) and *The Opening of Waterloo Bridge* 1832 (no.67). SC

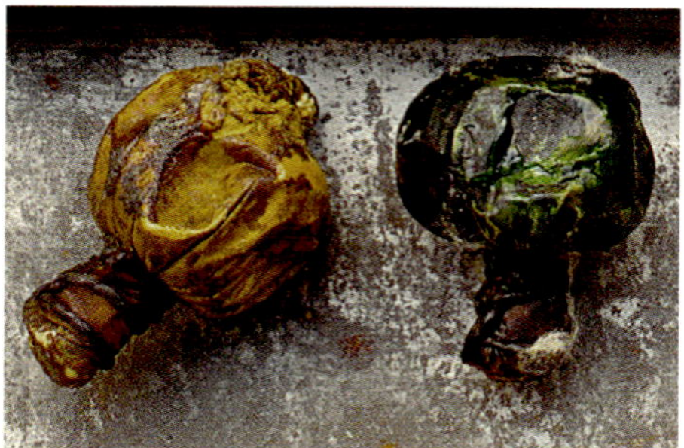

FIGURE 86

Figure 86
Two bladders from the
paint box (no.70) containing
chrome yellow and
Emerald green
SARAH COVE, WITH THE
PERMISSION OF SIR EDWIN
A.G. MANTON

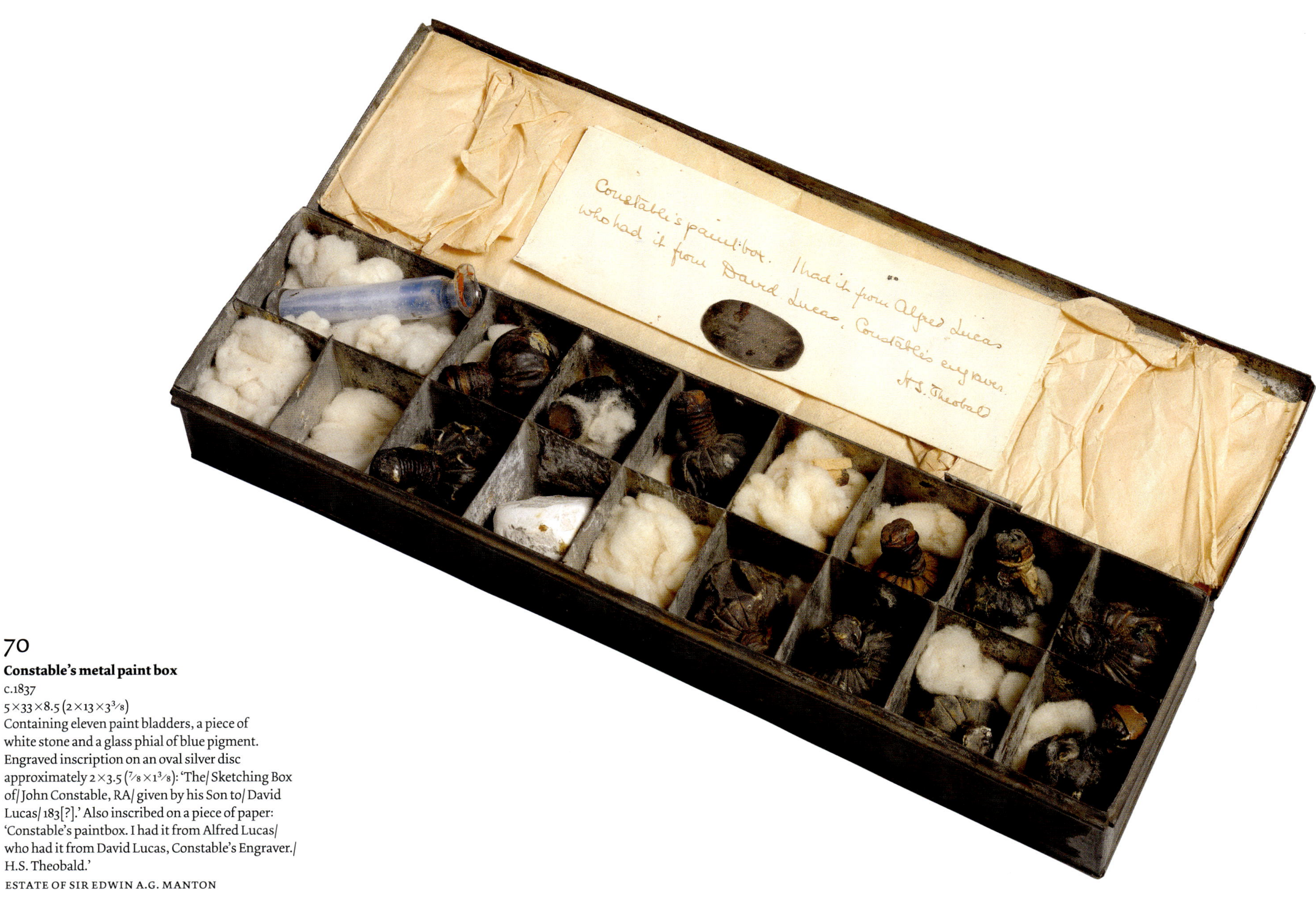

70

Constable's metal paint box

c.1837

5×33×8.5 (2×13×3⅜)
Containing eleven paint bladders, a piece of
white stone and a glass phial of blue pigment.
Engraved inscription on an oval silver disc
approximately 2×3.5 (⅞×1⅜): 'The/ Sketching Box
of/ John Constable, RA/ given by his Son to/ David
Lucas/ 183[?].' Also inscribed on a piece of paper:
'Constable's paintbox. I had it from Alfred Lucas/
who had it from David Lucas, Constable's Engraver./
H.S. Theobald.'

ESTATE OF SIR EDWIN A.G. MANTON

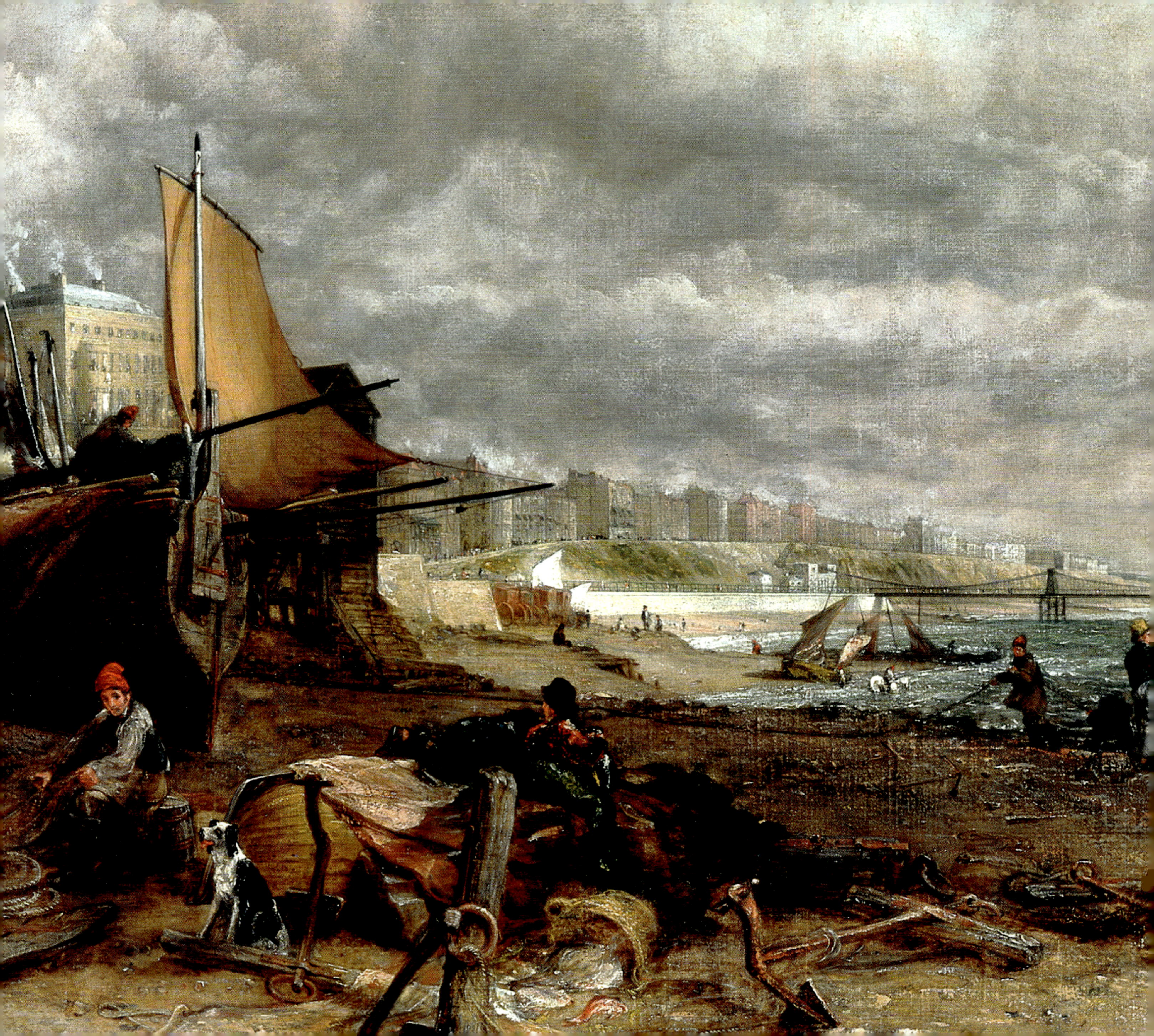

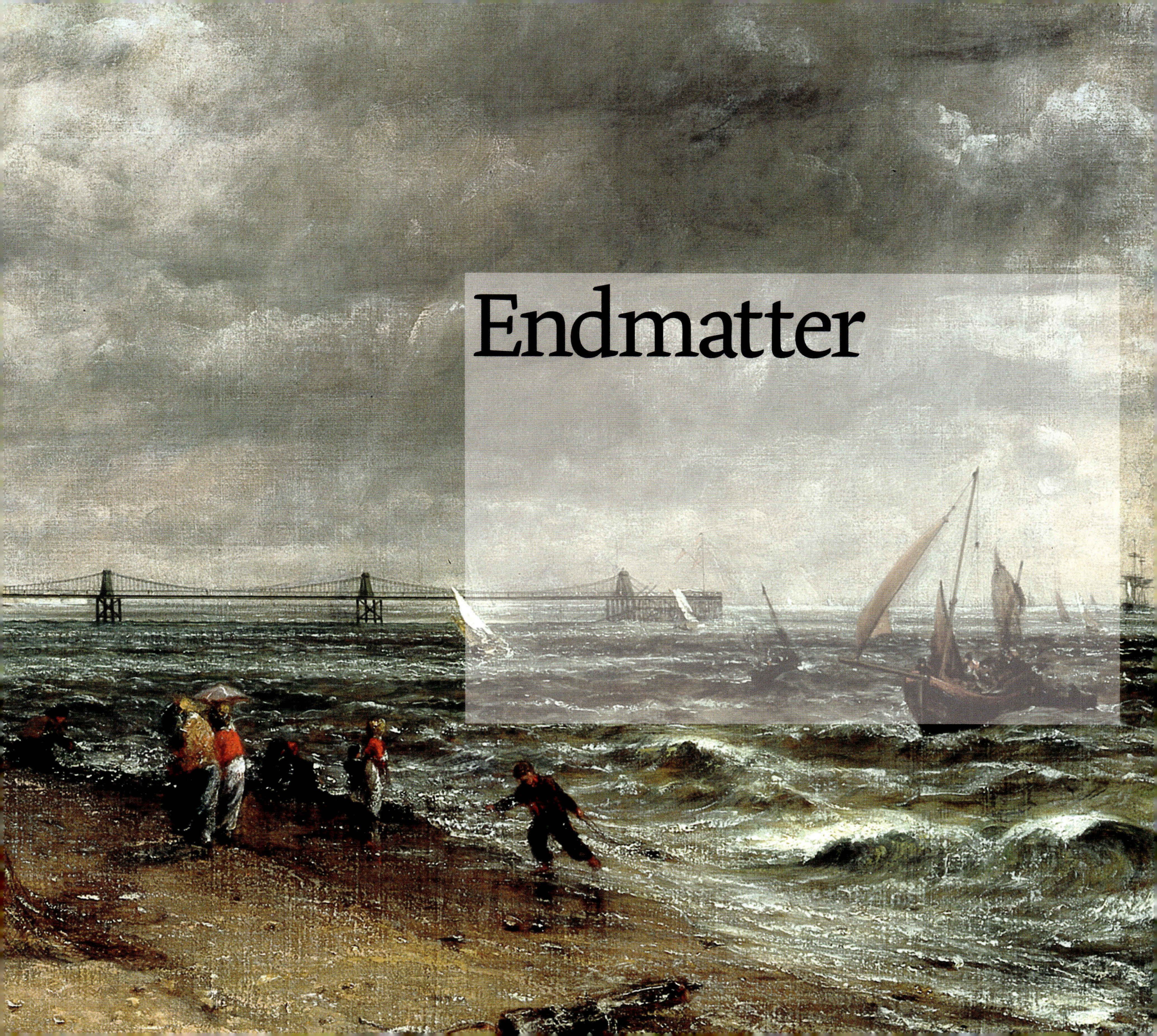
Endmatter

Constable:
The Big Picture
John Gage

Short forms of publications are
given in full in the bibliography

1 Fry 1934, pp.136, 140–1, cited in
Fleming-Williams and Parris 1984,
p.124. This is the best-documented
discussion of Constable's
posthumous reputation.
2 Clark 1961, p.88.
3 JCC VI, p.76: JC to JF, 23 Oct. 1821.
4 JCC V, p.11: JC to GC, 14 Dec. 1832.
5 Farington IX, pp.3431–2, 3 April 1809.
Farington noted that the scene was
in Borrowdale, and Constable had
exhibited a *Borrowdale* at the RA in
1808 (no.103), and possibly the same
one at the British Institution in 1809
(no.248), but this was an upright
composition half the size of the
one described by Farington. In 1807
and 1808 he had shown (the same?)
Westmorland scene, which was
four feet (1.2m) wide, including
the frame. None of them have so
far been traced.
6 *Dedham Vale* was first discussed by
Charles Rhyne 1990b, pp.109–29.
Constable's academic aspirations are
noted by Farington XIII, p.4564, 23
July 1814.
7 Quoted by Whitley 1928, II, pp.162–3.
8 Farington IV, p.1288, 19 Oct. 1799.
The painting Farington sketched at
Dance's on 28 Jan. 1794 (fig.1, p.20),
which he described as 'very clear',
and with the shade areas as detailed
as the lights, was almost certainly
the one described to him by J.S.
Copley on 11 April as 'of the Camera
Obscura kind, a direct imitation'. A
critic described it as showing 'an

extensive track of country, admirably
varied by trees, shrubs, hills, vales
and water, with a flock of sheep equal
to Berchem' (Whitley 1928), but
another observer commented that
the greens were not true (Farington I,
p.185, 30 April 1794; cf. *ibid.* p.175,
2 April 1794).
9 Farington VIII, p.2988, 13 March;
p.3001, 2 April 1807. For the painting,
David Blayney Brown, *Augustus Wall
Callcott*, exh. cat., Tate Gallery,
London, 1981, no.5.
10 Farington VI, p.2239, 10 Feb.1804.
11 Farington VI, p.2039, 27 May 1803.
12 Cove in Tate 1991, pp.497–8. Cove also
notes the Rubensian origin of the
dark translucent priming in
Constable's late painting, p.498.
The sketches are R.12.25 and 51.
13 See now C. Brown, *Making and
Meaning: Rubens's Landscapes*,
1996, p.69.
14 JCD, p.61.
15 For the whole affair, Blayney Brown
in Tate 1981, note 9, no.13.
16 JCC VI, p.92: JC to JF, April 1822;
cf. JC to JF, 7 Oct. 1822, p.98.
17 JCC VI, p.124: JC to JF, ?10 July 1823;
cf. also JF to JC, 18 Jan. 1824, p.151.
18 Egerton 1998, p.46. This is the most
important discussion of Constable
and Rubens to date.
19 Redgrave 1947, pp.365–6.
20 Leslie 1951, p.280. This sounds
remarkably like an observation by
the seventeenth-century Bolognese
painter Francesco Albani (Albano):

'in nature brushstrokes are not seen'
(*nella natura, non si vedono le
pennellate*), C.C. Malvasia, *Felsina
Pittrice* (1678), 1841 edn, Bologna, II,
p.166, cited P. Sohm, *Pittoresco:
Marco Boschini, his Critics, and their
Critiques of Painterly Brushwork in
Seventeenth- and Eighteenth-Century
Italy*, 1991, p.85. Constable included a
discussion of Albano in his lectures
on the history of landscape, but his
notes are now lost (Leslie 1951, p.307;
FDC 1975, p.9).
21 JCC VI, p.185: JC to JF, 17 Dec. 1824.
22 JCC VI, p.78: Leslie 1951, p.86.
23 JCC VI, p.142: JC to JF, 2 Nov. 1823.
24 Redgrave 1947, note 19, p.371.
25 See L. Whiteley, 'Constable et le
Salon de 1824', and O. Meslay,
'Collectionner Constable: une longue
habitude française', in Paris 2002,
pp.47–56.
26 The classic study is still P. Conisbee,
'Pre-Romantic *Plein-air* painting', *Art
History*, vol.2, no.4, 1979, pp.413–28.
27 JCC II, p.32: JC to JD, 29 May 1802.
28 E. Robertson (ed.), *Letters and Papers
of Andrew Robertson, A.M.*, 2nd edn.
1898, pp.84, 114. On Robertson and
Constable, FDC 1975, pp.276–8.
29 Clark 1961, note 2, p.89.
30 JCC VI, p.88: JC to JF, 13 April 1822.
31 Redgrave 1947, note 19, pp.370–1.
32 JCC VI, pp.44–5: JC to JF, 2 July 1819;
JC to JF, 17 June 1819.
33 S. Smetham and W. Davies (eds.),
*Letters of James Smetham, with an
Introductory Memoir*, 1902, pp.290–1.

Ruskin's attacks on Constable are
discussed in Fleming-Williams
and Parris 1984, note 1, pp.49–51.
34 JCC VI, p.89: JC to JF, ?1 April 1822.
35 JCC VI, p.87: JC to JF, 13 April 1822.
36 JCC VI, p.157: JC to JF, 8 May 1824.
37 Allen Staley in *Romantic Art in
Britain: Paintings and Drawings,
1760–1860*, exh. cat., Detroit Institute
of Arts, 1968, p.205. The best
discussion of this series is in
Tate 1991, nos.157–60.
38 JCC VI, p.191: JC to JF, 23 Jan. 1825.
39 JCC VI, p.198: JC to JF, April 1825.
40 Clark 1944, p.8.
41 C. Rhyne 1990b, note 6, p.120.
42 Leslie 1860, vol.1, p.115. Leslie had
witnessed the making of two
Constable death-masks, one of
which was discussed at a meeting
of the Phrenological Society in 1843,
when the painter's small 'organ
of Form' was contrasted with the
remarkably large organs of Self-
Esteem and Love of Approbation.
Whitley 1930, 1973 edn, p.331.
43 JCC VI, p.258: JC to JF, 24 May 1830.
44 cf. JCD, p.68 (Royal Institution);
FDC 1975, p.20 (Hampstead).
45 JCC V, p.17: JC to GC, 2 July 1834.
46 JCC V, p.42: JC to WP, 29 July 1834;
Leslie 1951, p.267 (in the event,
however, *The Cornfield* [R.26.1;
fig.59, p.116] was chosen instead).
47 Leslie 1951, p.251, note 1.
48 JCC V, pp.43–4: JC to WP, 17 Dec.
1834, ?Feb.1835.
49 Leslie 1951, pp.285–8.

Soliciting Attention: Constable, the Royal Academy and the Critics
Anne Lyles

1   Leslie 1951, p.3.
2   JCC II, pp.22–3: 4 Feb. 1799.
3   M.A. Stevens, 'The Royal Academy in the Age of Queen Victoria', in H. Valentine and MaryAnne Stevens (eds.), *Art in the Age of Queen Victoria*, exh. cat., Royal Academy of Arts, London, 1999–2000, p.26; and D.B. Brown, *The Art of J.M.W. Turner* (1990), London 2002, p.15. In the 1780s the exhibitions lasted five weeks, then gradually increased to twice that length by the 1830s (D. Solkin, 'Introduction: This Great Mart of Genius', in London 2001, p.5).
4   J. Murdoch, 'Architecture and Experience: the Visitor and the Spaces of Somerset House 1780–1796', in London 2001, pp.15–17; and J. Sunderland and D. Solkin, 'Staging the Spectacle', *ibid.* pp.23–4. For a general discussion of the architecture of the Royal Academy rooms, see J. Newman, *Somerset House: Splendour and Order*, London 1990.
5   Sunderland and Solkin, in London 2001, note 4, p.37.
6   G. Smith, 'Watercolourists and Watercolours at the Royal Academy, 1780–1836', in London 2001, pp.194–5. As Smith points out, complaints about reflections from side-lit windows were actually made in connection with watercolours hung in the Council Room. However, since the Library and Antique Academy were also side-lit, the same problem would have arisen in these rooms as well.
7   Farington V, p.1764, 6 April 1802.
8   For a full listing of Constable's pictures, see 'Constable's Exhibited Works 1802–1837', Tate 1991, pp.39–42; details of where individual pictures were hung are given in the original Royal Academy catalogues. The painting exhibited in 1802 with the title, *A landscape*, known to have been painted on a canvas of 'kit-kat' size (36×28in/91.5×71cm) was identified until recently with a picture in the Art Gallery of Ontario, *Edge of a Wood* (R.02.1: see Tate 1991, no.1; and Paris 2002, no.1). However, the recent attribution to Constable of a study of *Two Donkeys* dated 1816 in the Philadelphia Museum of Art by Jennifer Thompson – a study used for the donkeys in the Ontario picture – now makes such an identification highly unlikely (see Thompson 2005, pp.610–11). Furthermore, Sarah Cove has also noted that the ground, priming, pigments and medium in *Edge of a Wood* are more characteristic of Constable's work of about 1814 to 1816; see Cove in New York 2004, p.139.
9   Ivy 1991, p.63.
10 Ivy 1991, pp.64–5 (10.1–10.4).
11 Tate 1991, p.70; and Farington X, p.3666, 8 June 1810.
12 Farington XI, p.3916.
13 *Ibid.*
14 Ivy points out (1991, p.65) that, although Andrew Shirley claimed that *Dedham Vale: Morning* was among the first of Constable's exhibited paintings 'to achieve favourable notice or indeed any notice at all from the contemporary critics' (Shirley 1946, p.6), no reviews have been found.
15 J. Knowles, *The Life and Writings of Henry Fuseli*, vol.2, London 1831, p.217.
16. For Constable's admiration of Reynolds, see Rosenthal 1983, pp.27–9; Gage in Paris 2002, pp.38, 257, 271–3; and Lambert 2005, pp.29–37. For Reynolds's *Discourses*, delivered at the Royal Academy between 1769 and 1790, *Sir Joshua Reynolds: Discourses on Art*, ed. R.R. Wark, New Haven and London 1975.
17 For Constable's appreciation of the Old Masters, see especially his 'Lectures on Landscape', JCD, pp.28–74.
18 JCC II, pp.31–2, 29 May 1802.
19 Draft for third lecture, on *The Dutch and Flemish Schools*, delivered at the Royal Institution, 1836; JCD, p.65.
20 Leslie 1951, p.18.
21 JCC III, p.59: JC to C.R. Leslie, 14 Jan. 1832.
22 The present whereabouts of this picture is not known; see Reynolds 1996, 12.4, p.166.
23 Hemingway 1992, p.246.
24 JCC VI, p.18, early Nov. 1812.
25 Draft for third lecture, on *The Dutch and Flemish Schools*, delivered at the Royal Institution, 1836; JCD, p.61.
26 Farington XII, p.4328, 8 April 1813; for West's comment, see JCC II, p.104, letter from JC to Maria Bicknell, 3 May 1813.
27 Constable sold *Landscape: Boys Fishing* to the Bond Street bookseller James Carpenter, who paid 20 guineas and 'Books to a certain amount beyond that sum'; Farington XIII, pp.4487–8.
28 Farington XIII, p.4564, 23 July 1814.
29 Ivy 1991, p.73 (no.17.4), p.75 (no.18.4).
30 Ivy 1991, p.79.
31 Ivy 1991, pp.82–3 (nos.19.14 and 19.16 respectively).
32 Ivy 1991, pp.95–6 (nos.22.20 and 22.17 respectively).
33 Ivy 1991, p.86 (no.20.15, written by William Carey).
34 Note by Lucas in his copy of Leslie's *Life*, quoted in FDC 1975, p.57, and discussed in greater length in Cormack 1986b, see pp.79–80.
35 For black poplars in *Flatford Mill* and *The Hay Wain*, identifiable by their large forked trunks, see Mabey 1996, pp.133–5; and under entry for *Flatford Mill* (no.19) in present catalogue. Peter Kennedy Scott (in conversation with the author) has suggested that the slanting sunlit tree with amber foliage in *Stratford Mill* may be identifiable with a hybrid black poplar, an example of which he once observed growing in a hedgerow above the Stour valley towards the end of May 2001. The main group of trees along the river bank in *Stratford Mill*, meanwhile, are probably small-leaved elms, as suggested to Peter Kennedy Scott by Richard Mabey.
36 The uncertainty over the placement of *Dedham Vale* (R.28.1) arises from the fact that it was exhibited under the title *Landscape*, the same title used for another work Constable exhibited that year (*Hampstead Heath: Branch Hill Pond*, R.28.2). It is impossible to deduce from the content of the reviews which picture was hung in the Great Room and which in the School of Painting (see Ivy 1991, pp.127–8).
37 JCC VI, p.158: Fisher to JC, 10 May 1824.
38 Ivy 1991, p.106 (no.24.16; *London Magazine*, IX, June 1824).
39 As Sarah Cove has pointed out (pp.54, 65–6), Constable often submitted his paintings to the Academy before he was ready to do so, and thus before he had time to refine his 'finishing' touches. When his pictures returned from exhibition, he would therefore invariably start work on them again, especially toning them down. The passage of time also served to mellow some of the most glaring effects of his technique, as some of his more sympathetic critics were prepared to admit (see Ivy 1991, pp.49–50).
40 For the surface of *Hadleigh Castle* 'communicating … the appearance of having been scattered over … with a huge quantity of chopped hay', see Ivy 1991, p.133 (no.29.12; *Gentleman's Magazine*, May 1829).
41 Ivy 1991, pp.42–3.
42 See, for example, Ivy 1991, p.89 (no.21.14); p.114 (no.25.14); p.135 (no.29.24); p.160 (no.32.19); pp.162–3 (32.27).
43 JCC VI, p.185: JC to John Fisher, 17 Dec. 1824.
44 Ivy 1991, p.49.
45 M. Rosenthal, 'Turner Fires a Gun', in London 2001, p.149.
46 Ivy 1991, p.163 (no.32.27; *Morning Post*, 9 June 1832).
47 Ivy 1991, p.201 (no.35.14, *The Athenaeum*, 23 May 1835).
48 Michelangelo's marble tondo, *The Virgin and Child with St John*, was gifted to the Royal Academy in Beaumont's will, 'unless otherwise disposed of by his successors', and in 1830, three years after his death, his wishes were honoured. Constable made a sketch of the tondo that year in pen and ink (R.30.09), and wrote a description of the tondo, and an account of its gift to the Academy, in *The Athenaeum* in July 1830; JCD, pp.79–80.
49 JCC V, p.32, 12 May 1836.
50 Ivy 1991, p.233 (no.37.19; *John Bull*, 30 April 1837).

The Remarkable Story of the 'Six-Foot Sketches'
Charles Rhyne

1 Fry 1934, p.141.
2 Clark 1961, p.77 (1949 edn); and Amsterdam 1936, p.19.
3 Leslie 1855, p.276.
4 *The White Horse* (6 ft, R.19.2; no.28), *Stratford Mill* (6 ft, R.20.2; no.30), *The Hay Wain* (6 ft 2 in, R.21.2; no.36), *View on the River Stour near Dedham* (6 ft 1 in, R.22.2; no.38), *The Leaping Horse* (6 ft 2 in, R.25.2; no.46), and *Salisbury Cathedral from the Meadows* (6 ft 2 in, R.31.2; no.60).
5 *The Opening of Waterloo Bridge* (8 ft, R.32.2; no.65).
6 *Hadleigh Castle* (5 ft 5⅞ in, R.29.2; no.56) and *Stoke-by-Nayland* (5 ft 6⅜ in, R.36.19; no.68).
7 *The Lock* (4 ft 7⅞ in, R.24.2; no.40), *A Boat Passing a Lock* (4 ft 2½ in, R.26.16; fig.70, p.152) and *Helmingham Dell* (4 ft 2¾ in, R.30.3; Louvre, Paris).
8 *Salisbury Cathedral from the Meadows* (R.31.2; no.60) and *Stoke-by-Nayland* (R.36.19; no.68). The full-size sketch for *The Opening of Waterloo Bridge* was presumably begun much earlier (R.32.2; no.65).
9 As described in the text, *View on the Stour near Dedham* (R.22.2; no.38) must be referred to in a letter and note to Fisher (JCC VI, pp.74, 89). Because Constable never painted the finished painting of *Stoke-by-Nayland*, the sketch (R 36.19; no.68) must be that described in the letter from Constable to William Purton (Leslie 1843, p.104; JCC V, p.44). *The White Horse* sketch (R.19.2; no.28) seems likely to have been referred to, because Constable's statement that he had a six-foot canvas in hand comes just one month after his statement that he was planning a large picture (JCC VI, pp.181, 187). *Salisbury Cathedral from the Meadows* (R.31.2; no.60) may be the 'sketch of Salisbury' referred to by Constable in a letter to David Lucas, Constable's mezzotint engraver, written towards the end of October 1830 (JCC IV, p.336).
10 For Constable's meeting with Delacroix, see JCC IV, pp.199–201. Malcolm Cormack proposed that 'As well as seeing Constable's studio, with its unsold works, he would also have seen Constable's major exhibit at the Royal Academy of 1825, *The Leaping Horse*, and further Hampstead Heath scenes' (Cormack 1986a p.161).
11 Tate 1976, p.119.
12 Recorded in Leslie 1843, p.30. Beckett quotes Constable's note and reviews the evidence (JCC VI, p.89).
13 Foster and Sons, 1838.
14 Leslie 1843, p.51. Leslie seems to have been uncertain about the two often quoted sentences, because he eliminated them from the middle of a paragraph in his 1845 edition, p.155.
15 Quoted in Reynolds 1973a, pp.132–3.
16 Redgrave 1866, vol. 2, pp.394–6. In my view it is a misreading of this passage to claim that in them 'we see the beginnings of that preference for the large sketch over the finished picture' (Fleming-Williams and Parris 1984, pp.53–4).
17 The history of the gifts of Henry Vaughan, Isabel Constable and others to the Victoria and Albert Museum and the Tate Gallery are recounted authoritatively by Reynolds 1973a, pp.1–5, and by Parris 1981, pp.11–16.
18 *Old Masters*, exh. cat., Royal Academy of Arts, London, 1872, no.14.
19 Reproduced in Rhyne 1990b, p.111, fig.4.
20 Described by Michael Swicklik in Swicklik 1998.
21 First published by C.J. Holmes, who argued for its authenticity. His article included a full-page illustration (reversed) of the sketch as it appeared at the time. Holmes wrote that 'Constable was evidently dissatisfied with the design and painted out the church, rainbow, and cathedral, leaving only a small piece of the west front which he turned into a castellated house'; Holmes 1904, pp.45, 53.
22 Holmes 1902, appendix D, pp.238–52.
23 *Ibid.* p.121.
24 Fry 1934, pp.140–1.
25 Amsterdam 1936, p.19.
26 Venturi 1947b, pp.144–7, figs.31, 32. Venturi 1947a, pp.47–53, figs.28–37. These pages are a must-read for anyone interested in the reception of Constable's full-size sketches by European scholars.
27 Leslie 1951, 'Preface' by Mayne, p.xiii.
28 Smart and Brooks 1976, p.89.
29 Taylor 1973, p.38.
30 Rhyne 1990b.
31 Reproduced with details in *ibid.* The 1984 examination was conducted in the Paintings Conservation Department of the National Gallery of Art, by Sarah Fisher, Charlotte Hale and Eugena Ordonez. The results of this and other technical examinations are described in the article, notes 11–18. An x-radiograph is the image created when X-rays are transmitted through an artwork on to a specially coated polyester film.
32 Michael Swicklik presented alternative interpretations in his article, Swicklik 1998, pp.362–72.
33 Sunderland 1981, p.36.
34 Leslie 1855, p.276.
35 H.W. Janson, *History of Art*, New York 1962, p.469, fig. 705. This quote and illustration remained unchanged through the 1986 revised edition, p.594, fig.821.
36 Frederick Hartt, *Art, A History of Painting, Sculpture, and Architecture*, 2 vols., Englewood Cliffs, New Jersey, 4th edn, 1993, vol.2, p.897, fig.31-21. The text and colour image are unchanged from the first edition, 1976, vol.2, p.328, pl.53.
37 Rhyne 1987.
38 Leslie 1843, p.104. It is unclear whether or not Beckett had a full-size sketch in mind when he wrote that Leslie 'may mean only that it was never finished according to academic standards, for a large study is known' (JCC V, p.45).
39 Reynolds 1984, R.31.1, 32.1, 33.1, 35.1, 36.1; and 36.7, 37.1.
40 Rhyne 1990a, p.77, note 34; Rhyne 1990b, p.128, note 45.
41 Tate 1991, pp.380–1.
42 At the Art Institute of Chicago, my thanks especially to David Kolch, who carried out the cleaning, tragically his last, and to Inge Fiedler, who conducted the technical examination.
43 Bermingham 1986, p.128.
44 Especially important for study of the full-size sketches have been comprehensive technical studies at individual museums in whose collections the works reside. Sarah Cove has carried out and published in-depth technical research on Constable's work. Although her publications to date do not deal with any of the full-size sketches, her recent examination of some of these in preparation for this exhibition has produced important discoveries, described in her essay in this catalogue (pp.51–67).
45 *Seventeenth, Eighteenth and Nineteenth Century British Paintings*, 6 July 1983, Sotheby, Parke Bernet & Co., London, 1983, lot 267, pp.96–101.
46 Reynolds 1984. The changing view of this sketch by various scholars over the years is highly informative, but too detailed to recount here.
47 Reynolds 1973a.
48 Tate 1976.
49 Taylor 1973, figs.120–3.
50 In Venturi 1947a, *The Hay Wain* sketch and painting are on one page (figs.28–9), with *The Leaping Horse* sketch and painting on the facing page (figs.30–1).
51 Hoozee 1979, nos.460, 474, 618, 662.
52 Hoozee's catalogue was partly based on his M.A. (Hoozee 1971) and Ph.D (Hoozee 1975) theses, each two volumes, unreferenced in the Constable literature. In both theses, Hoozee focuses on Constable's creative process, arguing that the full-size sketches take on an increasingly conflicted relationship both to his open-air sketches and finished paintings.
53 Parris 1981.
54 *Ibid.* no.33, pp.128–33.
55 Carefully reasoned arguments for and against the attribution to Constable of these strips and the painting on them are presented in *ibid.* pp.128–30, with two X-ray photographs, under no.33; and in Reynolds 1984, p.201 under GR 29.2.
56 Reynolds 1984; Reynolds 1996.
57 Reynolds 1984, plates 68–9, 129–30, 213–14, 334–5, 475–6, 572–3, 626–7, 704–5, 792–3, 819–20.
58 Tate 1991.
59 *Ibid.* p.201.
60 *Ibid.* p.364.
61 *Ibid.* p.380.

The Painting Techniques of Constable's 'Six-Footers'
Sarah Cove

I would like to thank the following curators, colleagues and friends for their kind assistance in the preparation of this essay: Paul Ackroyd, Zoe Allen, Shelley Bennett, Rachel Billinge, Lucia Borgea, Peter Bower, Nicola Costaras, Natasha Duff, Mark Evans, Theresa Fairbanks-Harris, Rachael Fenton, Inge Fiedler, Sarah Fisher, Susan Foister, John Harrison, Isabel Horovitz, Rica Jones, Frank Kelly, Vivien Knight, Kate Kooistra, Alastair Laing, Allison Langley, Vicky Leanse, Edwina Mulvany, John Murdoch, Judith Nesbitt, Mandy Paulley, Cathy Putz, Tony Reeve, Charles Rhyne, Jacqueline Ridge, Ashok Roy, Nick Savage, Becky Shanks, Conal Shields, Tina Sitwell, Lesley Stevenson, Michael Swicklik, Rachel Tant, Jennifer Thompson, John Thornes, Mark Tucker, Phillip Warner, Martin Wyld and Frank Zuccari. I would especially like to thank David Thomson for his foresight and generosity in helping to establish the Constable Research Project in 1986, and for twenty years of enthusiasm and friendship. Thanks to Anne Lyles for many fruitful discussions, and to both her and Nicola Bion for their encouragement and tolerance of numerous drafts and missed deadlines! I am very grateful to my close friend and colleague Leslie Carlyle for editing the final draft and for additional 'nuggets' of information that help bring the text to life. Profound thanks to my husband, Alan Cummings, for deconstructing my arguments and incisive editing of this text. Finally, my deepest gratitude to Alan, Ollie and Eliza for living with my Constable mania.

1 The Constable Research Project was established by the author in 1986, in collaboration with the Victoria and Albert Museum, London, and private collector David Thomson, to study John Constable's oil painting materials and techniques. The research was registered for Ph.D. (1987–96) in the Department of Conservation and Technology, the Courtauld Institute of Art, University of London, under the supervision of the late Caroline Villers and the late Leslie Parris. To date, 124 oils from 1799 to 1837, plus two paint boxes and Constable's palette, have been examined, with full technical examination and scientific analysis having been carried out on about three-quarters of them. For full references, Cove in Tate 1991, p.529; Cove in New York 2004.

2 See Appendix.

3 *John Constable's Correspondence*, 7 vols.; for full references, see JCC I–VI and FDC in bibliography. Constable's personality is laid bare in his letters to his wife Maria (vol.II) and his correspondence with Archdeacon John Fisher (vol.VI). He wrote to Maria with great emotion, telling her of his daily activities, but never with the philosophical depth of his letters to Fisher. These are the most open and far reaching, revealing deep friendship, mutual respect and support, and diverse interests, including all aspects of art, and Constable's progression in particular. After Fisher's death in 1832, this mantle was taken up by C.R. Leslie, but with less intensity.

4 For a more detailed discussion of nineteenth-century 'finish', see Cove in Tate 1991, pp.509–10.

5 *Literary Gazette*, 3 July 1819, p.428 in Ivy 1991, p.83.

6 JCC III, pp.67–8: 24 April 1832.

7 See p.29.

8 See p.42; Leslie 1951, pp.89–90. See also Appendix, no.16.

9 JCC V, pp.43–4; also cited p.190 of present catalogue; see also p.42.

10 A similar point is made by Mayne in Leslie 1951, p.xiii.

11 Farington XIV, pp.5030–1, 6 June 1817; also JCC II, pp.223–4.

12 JCC VI, p.99: 7 Oct. 1822.

13 JCC II, p.229: 14 July 1817.

14 JCC VI, p.65: 1 April 1821. There are numerous references in the correspondence to 'cases' and 'boxes' for paintings. These were wooden crates, made to order, in which paintings were transported, probably wrapped in paper or fabric and padded with straw or felt wadding. In an unpublished letter of 1 June 1829 (David Thomson), Constable wrote to a client, Thomas Simcox-Lea, regarding the delivery of the portrait of *Mrs Elizabeth Lea with her three children* (64 × 51 cm/26¹⁄₂ × 21¹⁄₄ in; R.30.19). He intended to 'take care that the Group [portrait] shall be safely packed and sent to You 36.Newgate Street. in good time – The frame with the Case I suppose will be about £3.10.0ᵈ. which I will send You a receipt for.' Constable does not elaborate on the packing procedure; however Gainsborough mentions a 'packing case cost me 7 shillings' and that he protected a picture from dust in transit by 'paper[ing] up' the surface before it was packed in its case. J. Hayes, *The Letters of Thomas Gainsborough*, New Haven and London 2001, nos.7, 28. Dust in cases was perennially problematic: Wright of Derby instructed a client to 'wipe it off with a clean dry cloth (fine and not linty)' after unpacking a picture; 4 June 1780 to D. Daulby, Derby Public Library, Local History, 2962, letter 4. I am grateful to Conal Shields and Rica Jones respectively for these references.

15 JCC VI, p.71: 4 Aug. 1821.

16 JCC VI, p.74: 20 Sept. 1821; also JCC VI, p.99: 7 Oct. 1822.

17 JCC VI, p.204: 10 Sept. 1825.

18 In Aug. 1827 the Constable family moved to 'a comfortable little house' at Well Walk in Hampstead, though he kept the ground floor and studio at Charlotte Street while renting out the rest of the house. JCC VI, p.230–1: 26 Aug. 1827.

19 Whereabouts unknown, Tate 1991, p.43.

20 JCC VI, p.100: 31 Oct. 1822.

21 *Ibid.*

22 JCC II, p.402: 22 Oct. 1825.

23 JCC II, p.411: 23 Nov. 1825.

24 Annotations to the drawing of Constable's house (figs.27, 28) at No.76 (formerly 35) Charlotte Street, by Claude Rogers, occupier from 1939 to 1940, Tate 1991, p.43.

25 JCC II, p.402: 22 Oct. 1825.

26 1 Jan. 1821: sunrise 8.07am, sunset 4.02pm; realistically this means only six hours of good daylight in mid-winter. This improves to between nine and ten hours in October and March. I am grateful to Dr John E. Thornes (University of Birmingham) for sunrise and sunset times for 1821. See also Cove in Tate 1991, p.510.

27 JCC II, p.421: 12 Dec. 1825.

28 JCC VI, p.252: 3 Sept. 1829.

29 Cove in Tate 1991, p.510.

30 JCC VI, p.84: 16 Feb. 1822.

31 JCC VI, p.123: 5 July 1823.

32 JCC VI, p.209: 19 Nov. 1825.

33 JCC II, p.297: 9 Nov. 1823.

34 Cove in Tate 1991, pp.494–6, 498–504,

fig.50; Cove 1992, pp.123–8; Cove in New York 2004, pp.124–5. See also P. Bower, 'Catching the Sky: The Papers and Boards Used by John Constable for his Studies of Sky and Cloud', in New York 2004, pp.153–79.

35 Canvas 'weight' is often referred to as fine, medium, coarse or heavy, and is usually measured in this context by counting the number of threads per centimetre, horizontally and vertically, on exposed canvas or on an x-radiograph.

36 CRP 1986–2005 and Appendix: most canvases have fifteen to nineteen threads per centimetre (⅖in) horizontally and vertically. For Constable's earlier canvases, see Cove in Tate 1991, pp.494–6.

37 Appendix, no.9.

38 Rhyne 1990b, pp.109–29; also Swicklik 1998, pp.362–72.

39 Nineteen to twenty-two threads per centimetre (⅖in) horizontally, and fifteen to nineteen threads per centimetre vertically.

40 Twill fabric is woven with the weft (horizontal) thread going over two and under one warp (vertical) thread such that a diagonal pattern is created in the weave. Cove in Tate 1991, p.494, fig.151.

41 Natasha Duff, Paintings Conservator at Tate, agrees with the authors of Tate 1991 that the additions are not by Constable, Appendix, no.24; see also Duff 2006; Tate 1991, p.312–14. Reynolds does not agree and thinks the strips are autograph Constable, Reynolds 1984, R.29.2, p.201.

42 JCC III, p.18: 21 Jan 1829.

43 Cove in Tate 1991, pp.494–5.

44 Catalogue dimensions are frequently misleading, as they do not indicate whether they refer to the size of the original canvas, the painted image or the present stretcher size, which

in most cases is not original and has often been enlarged. Reliable dimensions from the reports listed in the Appendix are the basis for this essay.

45 Anon., *A Compendium of Colours*, 1808, and Hayter 1815; Appendix 22: Standard Canvas Dimensions, in Carlyle 2001, p.447.

46 *Ibid.* p.185.

47 A 'kit-kat' is the nickname for a portrait canvas measuring 36 × 28 inches (91.4 × 71.1cm). This comes from its use in a series of portraits of members of the 'Kit-Kat Club', who met at the house of Christopher Kat, painted by Sir Godfrey Kneller in the early eighteenth century. See Gullick and Timbs (1859), cited in Carlyle 2001, p.216–17.

48 See p.21.

49 Constable is quite blasé about transporting paintings. He once suggested sending two large versions of *Salisbury Cathedral* to Fisher in Salisbury (83 miles from London, three to four days' journey by horse-drawn wagon) so that Fisher could choose one, JCC VI, p.207: 12 Nov. 1825. By this date established carriers ran services to and from major towns. Wright of Derby sent a partially worked painting of Vesuvius to a client 'on approval' using the carrier Shawcross, and Gainsborough regularly used Walter Wiltshire's 'flying waggon' (*sic*), which took four days from Bath to London; see Wright to D. Daulby, 11 Jan. 1780, Derby Public Library, Local History, mss.8962, letter 3; and J. Hayes, *The Letters of Thomas Gainsborough*, New Haven and London 2001, nos.19, 62. Paintings appear to have fared reasonably well in transit despite the comparatively crude conditions,

though semi-dry paint was susceptible to damage from careless handling and packing. Gainsborough and Wright of Derby both mention large paintings being rolled 'upon a cylinder' and packed in 'cases' for transport, with concerns over the paint being dry enough not to be damaged by the rolling; Wright to Boydell, 12 March 1789, Bemrose 1885, p.97; and Hayes 2001, no.98. I am grateful to Rica Jones for these references.

50 Carlyle 2001, p.186.

51 Until 1869 Winsor & Newton sold canvas in nine or ten different roll widths, from 27 inches wide to 7ft 2in wide. A width of 4ft 6in (54in) is listed in the 1851 catalogue. The general trend suggests that the ten choices of width listed in 1851 are likely to be the same as those in earlier catalogues. Dr Leslie Carlyle, personal communication, Oct. 2005.

52 *The Valley Farm*, 1835, oil on canvas, 58 × 49¼ in (1.47 × 1.25m; R.35.1), Tate, Reynolds 1984, p.273, pl. 987. This and *The Cornfield* (fig.59, p.116) and *Dedham Vale* (fig.74, p.164) have not been measured by the author. Dimensions are taken from Reynolds 1984.

53 The painting was extensively reworked in the late 1820s to 1830s, as much of it is painted using Constable's 'late' pigments (c.1828–37), which are very distinctive (see nos.69, 70; note 138). These were identified using a hand-held viewer at 25 × magnification and comparisons made with pigments identified by analysis, Appendix nos.33, 34. Also Cove in Tate 1991, pp.504–7, figs.169–70; Cove 1998, pp.211–16.

54 Constable sometimes ordered canvases to his own specifications

and occasionally for friends, such as Bishop Fisher who asked him to 'order two canvasses [*sic*] to be got ready and primed' for his daughter in March 1819, Bishop Fisher to JC, JCC VI p.41.

55 Appendix nos.19, 21. A black-and-white photograph in the *Chain Pier* Conservation File, Tate, shows a Duty Code, '01 28 15', the number '2' probably the canvas size, and 'T. Brown/linen' stencilled in black on the back of the canvas, Natasha Duff, personal communication, Oct. 2005. Thomas Brown's canvas stamps are much more common than those of any other colourman from c.1805 to 1830. See C. Proudlove, 'London Artists' Colourmen: Part I: A–D', *The Picture Restorer, Journal of the British Association of Paintings Conservator-Restorers*, no.10, autumn 1996, pp.10–12.

56 JCC VI, p.161: late May 1824.

57 For example, Callcott's *Market Day* (fig.2, p.21). Also John Martin's *The Delivery of Israel out of Egypt*, 1824–5, 1.49 × 2.4m (58¾ × 94½in), Harris Museum and Art Gallery, Preston, reproduced in L. Parris, *Landscape in Britain 1750–1850*, exh. cat., Tate Gallery, London, 1973, no.284, p.117.

58 These were revealed by x-radiography, as they have been filled and painted over by a later hand.

59 After use they could have been stretched, pinned out, kept flat face to a wall, or rolled up. The x-radiograph of the full-size sketch of *Hadleigh Castle* 1829 (no.56) shows that, along the bottom and left side of the original canvas, the paint had flaked off before the edges were extended. It could have been stored rolled, with the right edge inside, standing upright on the bottom edge. If it was wrapped in a narrow

band of canvas or paper around the centre, and tied to stop it unrolling, this would have protected the central part of the outside (left) edge, where paint has not been lost. Ultimately over time a painting stored in this way would have flaked along the bottom and outside edges from poor handling and storage. If it was unrolled relatively soon after Constable's death (minimum eight years) and given a harsh nineteenth-century glue lining, the characteristic cracks that often develop during rolling would not necessarily be evident today. Alternatively, it may not have been extended until the 1930s. See Duff 2006.

60 Oil paintings on linen canvas do not usually need lining for eighty to a hundred years, by which time the original canvas is degraded and no longer fully supports the work. If a painting is lined relatively early, especially if the paint is still somewhat soft, considerable damage can be done to the paint structure. Nineteenth-century liners used hot, heavy irons to laminate the original canvas to a new backing, often face downwards, and this could cause raised paint to be smeared, flattened and 'moated' – pushed back into the canvas forming a dip, or 'moat' around an impasto.

61 JCC II, p.397: 1 Oct. 1825.

62 JCC III, p.62: 29 Feb. 1832 (n.b. it was a leap year).

63 JCC III, p.69: 27 April 1832.

64 Natasha Duff, Tate, personal communication, May 2005.

65 Sold by the Artist's Administrators, Foster, 16 May 1838, lot 68, bt. Tiffin, see p.170.

66 Cove in Tate 1991, Cove 1998, Cove in New York 2004.

67 Swicklik 1998, p.370.

68 *Study of a Girl's Head* (R.24.3), Reynolds 1984, p.135, pl. 477.

69 Appendix, no.18.

70 See p.157.

71 *A Wooded Bank with an Open Book and Distant View of Water*, c.1829–36, is made from five pieces of canvas joined in this manner. Conservation Report, The Metropolitan Museum of Art, New York, Cove in Tate 1991, p.495. See also New York 1988, no.2, p.21, col. plate 2.

72 The Roberson Archive (nineteenth-century London colourman) shows that artists had their pictures enlarged by this company, Dr L. Carlyle, personal communication, Nov. 2005. For details of the Archive see Carlyle 2001, pp.279–80.

73 Carlyle 2001, p.186.

74 Cove in Tate 1991, pp.496–8.

75 *The White Horse* sketch c.1818 (no.28) and *Stratford Mill* sketch c.1819 (no.30) have white/off-white grounds, and *The White Horse* 1819 (no.29) has a pink ground. All three have an opaque reddish-brown priming. Appendix, nos.8, 9, 11.

76 JCC VI, p.56: 1 Sept. 1820.

77 Cove in New York 2004, pp.142–6.

78 The off-white grounds consist of a single thick layer of chalk and lead white; pale pink grounds consist of chalk and lead white pigmented with finely ground red, brown and orange iron oxides (synthetic earth pigments), sometimes with a small amount of charcoal black. Appendix, nos.14–16, 20; CRP 1986–2005: *A Boat Passing a Lock*, 1826, exh.1829 (R.26.15; fig.70, p.152): full technical examination, pigment analysis, Libby Sheldon, University College, London, 1996.

79 Claessens of Belgium, established in the early twentieth century, still hand-prime canvases in the traditional manner, using a wooden roller covered in a plush fabric that creates a 'stippled' texture in their grounds. Dr L. Carlyle, personal communication, Nov. 2005. Rollers are not currently thought to have been used for decorating purposes as early as the 1820s, Helen M. Hughes, Historic Interiors, English Heritage, personal communication, Nov. 2005.

80 A 'stippler' is a wide, flat, soft brush that is held flat in the palm of the hand by a leather strap, used by today's 'high-class' decorators for smoothing out brushmarks. It reduces streaks and gives a lightly 'stippled' texture, Helen M. Hughes, Historic Interiors, English Heritage, personal communication, Nov. 2005.

81 The ground of the *Chain Pier, Brighton* is mainly chalk, a pipe-clay 'extender' and lead white pigmented with ochres, Appendix, no.21. Staining tests, carried out in 1990 by the author and Anna Southall, former Paintings Conservator, Tate, on the 'stippled' priming of *Hampstead Heath with the house called 'The Salt Box'*, c.1820–1 (no.27) indicate a proteinaceous medium, probably egg, Cove in Tate 1991, pp.496–8, fig.153. Egg-bound grounds were recommended in artists' manuals of the period and were also used by Turner, Cove in Tate 1991, p.496; Carlyle 2001, pp.170–1.

82 Carlyle 2001, pp.178–9.

83 Dunthorne worked occasionally for Constable as early as 1812–14: JCC II, p.79: 22 June 1812; JCC I, p.101: 22 Feb. 1814. I am grateful to Anne Lyles for the latter reference. Abram Constable's suggestion of bringing him to London in 1819 indicates that he was not permanently employed before then, JCC I, p.183: 6 Sept. 1819. Paintings from the early 1820s suggest Dunthorne's work in the studio from that time, Cove in Tate 1991, p.508.

84 Artists' manuals often recommended home-prepared grounds over commercially prepared ones due to problems with cracking and lifting of the latter. A recipe published by Merimée in 1830 describes an absorbent distemper ground, which includes 'a little oil', recommended on the basis of its speed and ease of preparation, Carlyle 2001, pp.165–7.

85 Constable's 'late' absorbent white ground consists of one or two layers of chalk with additions of lead white, gypsum and pipe-clay as extenders. The smooth pink priming under skies consists of lead white and chalk coloured with small amounts of red and brown iron oxides, vermilion, earths, charcoal black and an unidentified brown (possibly Vandyke brown). Appendix, nos.29, 30, 32. Also CRP 1986–2005, *The Glebe Farm* c.1832–5 (R.27.9A),* *The Valley Farm* 1835 (R.35.1) and *Hampstead Heath with a Rainbow* 1836 (R.36.7).* *Analysis by optical microscopy and EDX carried out for the author by Rachel Grout, 2002–3.

86 Appendix, no.30. Also Cove in Tate 1991, p.496, fig.155.

87 Carlyle 2001, p.166.

88 Fielding (1839) in *ibid.* p.168.

89 *Ibid.* p.166.

90 Miss Cleaver was the daughter of William Cleaver, Bishop of Bangor. She had been researching the Venetian 'method' for twenty years according to Constable, who is somewhat scathing on the subject, JCC II, pp.347–8: 30 June 1824.

91 Carlyle 2001, pp.166–7.

92 This consists of umber, bone/ivory and charcoal blacks, often warmed with a little vermilion, red lake and red/brown iron oxides. Appendix, nos.29, 30, 32. Also CRP 1986–2005: *A Boat Passing a Lock* (R.26.15; fig.70, p.152), *The Glebe Farm* (R.27.9A),* *The Valley Farm* (R.35.1) and *Hampstead Heath with a Rainbow* (R.36.7).* *Analysis by optical microscopy and EDX carried out for the author by Rachel Grout, 2002–3.

93 Leslie 1951, p.207.

94 Farington noted Benjamin West saying Rubens's ground 'might be made by glazing over a *white ground* with a thin coat of Burnt Umber softened by a little blue', see pp.21–2. For Rubens's influence on Constable's technique, Cove in Tate 1991, p.498.

95 *The Mill Stream* (R.14.50).

96 A virtually identical method is described by Kingston (1835) in Carlyle 2001, pp.45–6.

97 Cove in Tate 1991, p.509.

98 JCC IV, p.429: 11 Nov. 1836.

99 JCC IV, p.363: 26 Dec. 1831. See also nos.201–2, Tate 1991, pp.353–4.

100 Appendix, no.21. Noted by Natasha Duff, Tate.

101 Chalk drawing cannot be detected using infrared reflectography that is usually used to identify and enhance carbon-based underdrawing (charcoal, graphite and some inks).

102 Artists' painting manuals of the early nineteenth century 'were remarkably consistent in calling for "white chalk" or "pipe-clay" for the first drawing on the canvas' (Carlyle 2001). 'White chalk' did not necessarily mean a simple lump of calcium carbonate, as Roberson sold a 'white chalk' consisting of whiting, pipe-clay, lead white and

Plaster of Paris (gypsum) bound with gum. 'Italian chalk' was the best, 'Spanish chalk' was crumbly and inferior and 'French chalk' was coarse and only suitable for larger works. *Ibid.* pp.207–8. Chalk was also recommended for rectifying the image during painting, and we know that Constable used it for this purpose from John James Chalon, who wrote regarding a painting of his own that he intended showing to Constable: 'I shall require one of your Scrutinizing looks, and will take care to have White Chalk ready,' FDC, p.190: 14 Nov. 1832.

103 Carlyle 2001, pp.207–8.

104 Appendix, no.31.

105 JCC VI, pp.180–3: 17 Nov. 1824.

106 Cove in Tate 1991, p.508.

107 Appendix, no.15.

108 Constable appears to have used a method recommended in eighteenth- and early nineteenth-century sources, in which pencil drawing was reinforced with watercolour 'fixed or strengthened with very dilute oil colour', consistently recommending 'warm tones including burnt sienna, burnt and raw umber, Vandyke brown and on one occasion umber and a choice of various reds', Carlyle 2001, p.208.

109 Appendix, no.21. Infra-red reflectography and image processing carried out by Natasha Duff, Tate.

110 *Marine Parade and Chain Pier, Brighton* (no.49).

111 The underdrawing in the landscape and foreground may have become more visible with the increased transparency of the *imprimatura* with age, but it would certainly have always been somewhat visible in the more thinly painted areas.

112 Constable wrote frequently to Maria

in Brighton mentioning the 'outline': JCC II: pp.396–7, 1 Oct. 1825; p.407, 31 Oct. 1825; p.415, 28 Nov. 1825; pp.416–17, 6 Dec. 1825; pp.421–2, 12 Dec. 1825. He also mentioned progress on the work to Fisher, though not specifically regarding the 'outline': JCC VI, p.206: JC to JF, 12 Nov. 1825; p.207, 19 Nov. 1825. It was admired by Thomas Lawrence in mid-Jan. 1826, JCC II, p.424.

113 Appendix, no.29, noted by Roy Perry, former Head of Paintings Conservation, Tate.

114 Farington XVI, pp.5582–3, in Egerton 1998, p.42.

115 Consisting of lead white, a translucent white, Prussian blue and vermilion (optical identification only), Appendix, no.14.

116 Note 60.

117 A mixed green (Prussian blue and an opaque yellow, possibly Naples), vermilion, a red lake, red and brown iron oxides, charcoal black, lead white and a translucent white (visual identification only). Appendix, no.14.

118 13 April 1822, Leslie 1951, pp. 89–90; p.42 of present catalogue.

119 Appendix, no.11.

120 S. Cove, *Rolf on Art, The Big Event: The Hay Wain*, BBC1, 26 Sept. 2004.

121 Scumbling is the opposite of glazing. It describes the uneven working of a thin layer of opaque or semi-opaque paint over a layer of a different colour, usually with a hog's hair brush, so that the underlayer shows through. *The Penguin Dictionary of Art & Artists*, Penguin Books, 1979 edn, p.412. For its nineteenth-century context and technique, Carlyle 2001, pp.220–1.

122 For earlier uses and a discussion of the pigment, see Cove in Tate 1991,

p.506. George Field, colourmaker, noted that Patent yellow was 'soon injured by both the sun's rays and impure air', *Chromatography*, 1835, pp.77–8, in Carlyle 2001, pp.519–20.

123 This contains large coarse particles of charcoal, the 'bluest' of the blacks, mixed with small amounts of vermilion, lead white, natural earth and synthetic iron oxides, Appendix, no.32.

124 The 'turbid medium effect' is an optical effect created by applying a thin semi-opaque light colour over a dark underlayer, which creates a 'bluer' appearance in the upper paint layer, Cove in New York 2004, p.142.

125 Appendix, no.32. Verdigris has also been identified in the Manton paint-box bladders, Appendix, no.33, and Cove 1998, table 1, p.211. It is also identified on *Edge of a Heath by Moonlight*, oil on panel, 17.8 × 27.3cm (7 × 10¾ in), David Thomson (R.10.41), redated to the 1830s following technical examination in 2003 (CRP 1986–2005).

126 In 1821 Constable considered the sky to be the ' "*key note*", the *standard of "Scale"*, and the chief Organ of Sentiment' in a picture. He expressed the importance of this to Fisher, JCC VI, pp.76–8: 23 Oct. 1821.

127 *Hove Beach* (R.24.72).

128 The exceptional blue pigment natural ultramarine is made from the expensive semi-precious stone lapis lazuli, ground into powder form. Constable used it with smalt (possibly an adulterant) in skies, horizons and distant landscape on 'finished' paintings throughout his career. 'French' (synthetic) ultramarine, was developed in 1826–8, Carlyle 2001, pp.472–3,

478–9. It is not certain whether Constable ever used it, as he considered it inferior, Cove in Tate 1991, pp.507, 512.

129 Areas of glazing in *Stratford Mill* (no.31), notably the blue 'glaze' over the trees on the left, appear slightly milky. This may indicate the use of a resin/resin-oil medium, which is more brittle than straight oil, that has slightly crystallised and become desaturated with age. This is the opposite of Constable's intention in 'toning' the landscape. Appendix, no.10.

130 Constable did some of the 'toning' with his mentor Sir George Beaumont, an amateur painter notorious for the 'mellow' appearance of his oils, JCC II, p.324: 3 June 1824.

131 Farington XVI, p.5487.

132 *Annals of the Fine Arts*, V, 1820, pp.388–90 in Ivy 1991, pp.85–6.

133 'Oiling-out' layers are present in cross-sections from numerous paintings. There are also several specific references to 'oiling-out', and to washing the surfaces of paintings before repainting, in the JC Correspondence; CRP 1986–2005; Cove in Tate 1991, p.512; see also Appendix.

134 Egerton 1988, p.30.

135 Appendix, no.13, and Egerton 1988, p.42.

136 Cove in Tate 1991, p.527.

137 JCC II, pp.385: 7 Sept. 1825.

138 Appendix, no.19.

139 John Cawse, a pupil of John Opie and contemporary of Constable, commented on the particular suitability of poppy oil for 'finishing' paintings, as 'it is of such a nature as to admit of painting on for days before it completely dries', J. Cawse, *Introduction to the Art of Painting in Oil Colours*, London 1827, p.171. For a detailed discussion of Constable's 'late' painting mediums, Cove 1998, pp.211–16.

140 Constable's palette expanded from c.1828. New additions to his previous range of pigments include two 'true' greens, Emerald green and verdigris, cobalt blue in skies, a commercially prepared brilliant scarlet that is an intimate mixture of vermilion and a red lake, red and pink madder lakes and Field's 'orange-vermilion'. Appendix, nos.29, 30, 32–4; CRP 1986–2005, *The Glebe Farm* (R.27.9A),* *The Valley Farm* (R.35.1) and *Hampstead Heath with a Rainbow* (R.36.7).* *Analysis by optical microscopy and EDX carried out for the author by Rachel Grout, 2002–3.

141 For a summary of Constable's 'late' oil paint mediums see Cove 1998, table 4, p.215.

142 Without studio examination of the paint surface, it is possible to confuse palette-knife work with brushwork that has been accidentally squashed while wet or smeared by lining. This creates a 'hard edge' similar to the appearance of palette-knife work, and is especially deceptive on x-radiographs. There are numerous incorrect references to palette-knife work in the Constable literature, including the author's own, regarding *The Hay Wain* (no.37), Cove in Tate 1991, p.513.

143 Ivy 1991, p.145,

144 Leslie Carlyle and Joyce Townsend, 'An investigation of lead sulphide darkening of nineteenth century paintings', in papers for the conference 'Dirt and Pictures Separated', United Kingdom Institute for Conservation (UKIC), London 1990, pp.40–3. See also Leslie Carlyle, 'The artists' anticipation of change as discussed in British nineteenth century instruction books on oil painting' and 'Appearance, Opinion, Change: Evaluating the Look of Paintings', UKIC, London 1990, pp.62–7. See also Carlyle 2001, pp.259–60.

145 Constable described the 'mellowing hand of time' to Solomon Hart, in Alexander Brodie (ed.), *Reminiscences of Solomon Hart, R.A.*, 1882, p.58, in JCC IV, p.129. The combination of lead-based pigments and a very lean oil-egg medium meant that these paints were particularly susceptible to lead-sulphide darkening, Cove 1998, pp.214, table 4, p.215, see also note 144 above.

146 JCC VI, pp.197–8: 13 April 1825; and 'My last years work has got much *together*', JCC VI, pp.76–8: 23 Oct. 1821.

147 JCC VI, p.100: 31 Oct. 1822.

148 For example, regarding *The White Horse* (no.29), JCC VI, p.45: 17 July 1819; in respect of *The Hay Wain* (no.37), JCC VI, p.71: 4 Aug. 1821.

149 JCC VI, p.70: JF to JC, 19 July 1821.

150 FDC, p.85: JF to JC, 1 Sept. 1833.

151 Carlyle 2001, p.239.

152 *Ibid.* pp.233–6. A disfiguring and relatively insoluble 'grey' layer, which may be a denatured egg-based 'temporary' varnish combined with dirt, has been identified during cleaning by the author on two Constable 'finished' oils, including *Dedham Lock and Mill 1817–18* (no.24). These varnishes were not lasting and were meant to be removed by washing with water – a practice Constable is known to have carried out – before a spirit varnish was applied. This may have occasionally been overlooked and, as a result, the darkened 'layer' remained present beneath later varnish applications.

153 For a more detailed discussion of Constable's varnishing practices, Cove in Tate 1991, pp.515–16.

154 *The White Horse* (no.29), JCC VI, pp.221–2: 1 July 1826.

Amsterdam 1936 *Twee Eeuwen Engelsche Kunst*, exh. cat. with foreword by Kenneth Clark, Stedelijk Museum, Amsterdam, 1936

Asleson and Bennett 2001 R. Asleson and S.M. Bennett, *British Paintings at the Huntington*, 2001

Bermingham 1986 A. Bermingham, *Landscape and Ideology: the English Rustic Tradition 1740-1860*, Berkeley and Los Angeles 1986

Boulton 1984 S. Boulton, 'Church under a cloud: Constable and Salisbury', *Turner Studies*, 1984, vol.3, no.2, pp.29-44

Carlyle 2001 Dr L. Carlyle, *The Artist's Assistant: Oil Painting Instruction Manuals and Handbooks in Britain 1800-1900 with Reference to Selected Eighteenth Century Sources*, London 2001

Chicago 1946 K. Clark, 'Hogarth, Constable and Turner', in *Masterpieces of English Painting: William Hogarth, John Constable, J.M.W. Turner*, exh. cat., Art Institute of Chicago, 1946, pp.9-16

Clark 1944 K. Clark, *John Constable: The Hay Wain in the National Gallery, London*, London 1944

Clark 1960 K. Clark, *Looking at Pictures*, New York 1960

Clark 1961 K. Clark, *Landscape into Art* (1949), London 1961

Cooke 1968 H.L. Cooke, *Painting Lessons from the Great Masters*, London 1968

Cormack 1986a M. Cormack, *Constable*, Cambridge 1986

Cormack 1986b M. Cormack, 'Constable's Stratford Mill', in John Wilmerding (ed.), *Essays in Honor of Paul Mellon*, Washington 1986, pp.71-83

Cove 1988 S. Cove, 'An Experimental Painting by John Constable R.A', *The Conservator*, no.12, 1988, pp.52-6

Cove 1992 S. Cove, 'Constable's Oil Sketches on Paper and Millboard', Manchester Conference Papers, Institute of Paper Conservation (IPC-UK), 1992, pp.123-8

Cove 1998 S. Cove, 'Mixing and Mingling: John Constable's Oil Paint Mediums, c. 1802-37, including analysis of the "Manton" Paint Box', in 'Painting Techniques: History, Materials and Studio Practice', Contributions to the Dublin Congress, International Institute for Conservation of Historic & Artistic Works (IIC), 1998, pp.211-16

CRP 1986-2005 S. Cove, 'The Constable Research Project', unpublished Technical Examination Reports, 1986-2005

Darrah 1995 Josephine A. Darrah, 'Connections and Coincidences: Three Pigments', in *Preprints of a Symposium, Historical Painting Techniques, Materials and Studio Practice, University of Leiden, The Netherlands*, ed. A. Wallert, E. Hermens and M. Peek, California 1995, pp.70-7

Dorment 1986 R. Dorment, *British Painting in the Philadelphia Museum of Art*, 1986

Duff 2006 Natasha Duff, 'Constable's Sketch for *Hadleigh Castle*: A Technical Examination', Tate Papers, London 2006, www.tate.org.uk/ research/ tateresearch/ tatepapers

Egerton 1998 J. Egerton, *National Gallery Catalogues, the British School*, London 1998

Evans 2002 M. Evans, ' "A More Lasting Remembrance": Constable's paintings of *Dedham Vale* from the Coombs and Claude's *Landscape with Hagar and the Angel*', in *British Art Journal*, vol.3, no.3, autumn 2002, pp.43-7

Farington J. Farington, *Diary 1793-1821*, 16 vols., vols.1-6 ed. Kenneth Garlick and Angus Macintyre; vols.7-16 ed. Katherine Cave, New Haven and London 1978-84; index Evelyn Newby 1998

FDC 1975 L. Parris, C. Shields and I. Fleming-Williams (eds.), *John Constable, Further Documents and Correspondence*, Ipswich, Suffolk, 1975

Fleming-Williams 1980 I. Fleming-Williams, 'John Constable at Flatford', *Connoisseur*, vol.204, July 1980, pp.216-19

Fleming-Williams 1990 I. Fleming-Williams, *Constable and his Drawings*, London 1990

Fleming-Williams and Parris 1984 I. Fleming-Williams and L. Parris. *The Discovery of Constable*, London 1984

Florisoone 1957 M. Florisoone, 'Constable and the *Massacre of Scios* by Delacroix', *Journal of the Warburg and Courtauld Institutes*, no.20, 1957, pp. 180-5

Foster 1838 Foster and Sons, London, *A Catalogue of the Valuable Finished Works, Studies and Sketches, of John Constable, Esq. R.A., Deceased ... Which Will be Sold by Auction by Messrs. Foster and Sons ... on Tuesday the 15th of May 1838, and following Day*, London 1838

Fry 1934 R. Fry, *Reflections on British Paintings*, London 1934, pp.134-48, figs.34, 59, 62-6

Harwood 1985 E.S. Harwood, 'Constable's "Church under a Cloud": some further observations', *Turner Studies*, 1985, vol.5, no.1, summer 1985, pp.27-9

Hawes 1983 L. Hawes, 'Constable's *Hadleigh Castle* and British Romantic Ruin Painting', *Art Bulletin*, vol. 65, Sept. 1983, p.455-70

Hayes 1992 J. Hayes, *British Paintings of the Sixteenth through Nineteenth Centuries: the Collections of the National Gallery of Art Systemic Catalogue*, National Gallery of Art, Washington, and Cambridge, UK, 1992

Hemingway 1992 A. Hemingway, *Landscape Imagery and Urban Culture in Early Nineteenth-Century Britain*, Cambridge, UK, 1992

Hind 1909 C. Lewis Hind, *Constable*, London 1909

Holmes 1902 C.J. Holmes, *Constable and His Influence on Landscape Painting*, London 1902

Holmes 1904 C.J. Holmes, 'The Gassiot Constable', *Burlington Magazine*, IV, no.10, Jan. 1904, p.53

Holmes 1931 C. Holmes, 'Introduction', *The Letters of John Constable, R.A. 1826-1837, to C.R. Leslie, R.A., 1826-1837*, ed. Peter Lewis, London 1931, pp.xv-xxxv

Holmes 1936a C.J. Holmes, 'Constable's *Hadleigh Castle*', *Burlington Magazine*, LXVIII, March 1936, pp.107-8, 113, 294-5

Holmes 1936b C.J. Holmes, *Self & Partners (Mostly Self), Being the Reminiscences of C.J. Holmes*, London 1936

Honour 1979 H. Honour, *Romanticism*, London 1979

Hoozee 1971 R. Hoozee, 'John Constable 1776-1837: Het Realizatie-proces', 2 vols., MA thesis, University of Ghent, 1971

Hoozee 1975 R. Hoozee, 'John Constable 1776-1837: Kritische Stijlstudie van Zijn Werken en analyse van het Realisatieproces in Zijn Kunst Bijdrage tot de Geschiedenis van de Landschapschilderkunst in de Negentiende Eeuw', 2 vols., Ph.D thesis, University of Ghent, 1975

Hoozee 1979 R. Hoozee, *L'opera completa di Constable*, Milan 1979

Ivy 1991 J. Ivy, *Constable and the Critics 1802-1837*, Ipswich, Suffolk, 1991

JCC I *John Constable's Correspondence I*, ed. R.B. Beckett, Ipswich, Suffolk, 1962

JCC II *John Constable's Correspondence II, Early Friends and Maria Bicknell (Mrs. Constable)*, ed. R.B. Beckett, Ipswich, Suffolk, 1964

JCC III *John Constable's Correspondence III, The Correspondence with C.R. Leslie*, ed.R.B. Beckett, Ipswich, Suffolk, 1965

JCC IV *John Constable's Correspondence IV, Patrons, Dealers and Fellow Artists*, ed. R.B. Beckett, Ipswich, Suffolk, 1966

JCC V *John Constable's Correspondence V, Various Friends, with Charles Boner and the Artist's Children*, ed. R.B. Beckett, Ipswich, Suffolk, 1967

JCC VI *John Constable's Correspondence VI, The Fishers*, ed. R.B. Beckett, Ipswich, Suffolk, 1968

JCD *John Constable's Discourses*, ed. R.B.Beckett, Ipswich, Suffolk, 1970

Key 1948 Sydney J. Key, *Constable: His Life and Work*, London 1948

Kitson 1957 M. Kitson, 'John Constable, 1810-1816: A Chronological Study', *Journal of the Warburg and Courtauld Institutes*, vol.20, 1957, pp.338-57

Kitson 1976 M. Kitson, 'The Inspiration of John Constable', Fred Cook Memorial Lecture, *Journal of the Royal Society of Arts*, Nov. 1976, pp.738-53

Kitson 1991 M. Kitson, 'London: John Constable at the Tate', exhibition review, *Burlington Magazine*, CXXXIII, Aug. 1991, vol.133, no.106, pp.559-62

Kroeber 1975 K. Kroeber, *Romantic Landscape Vision: Constable and Wordsworth*, Wisconsin 1975, pp. 44-60

Lambert 2005 R. Lambert, *John Constable and the Theory of Landscape Painting*, Cambridge, UK, 2005

Leslie 1843 C.R. Leslie, *Memoirs of the Life of John Constable, Esq. R.A., Composed Chiefly of the Letters*, London 1843

Leslie 1845 C.R. Leslie, *Memoirs of the Life of John Constable, Esq. R.A., Composed Chiefly of the Letters*, London 1845

Leslie 1855 C.R. Leslie, *Hand-Book for Young Painters*, London 1855, pp.273-9

Leslie 1860 C.R. Leslie, *Autobiographical Recollections*, 2 vols, London 1860.

Leslie 1896 Robert C. Leslie, 'Introduction', *Life and Letters of John Constable, R.A. by C.R. Leslie, R.A.*, London 1896

Leslie 1951 C.R. Leslie, *Memoirs of the Life of John Constable* (1843 and 1845), ed. Jonathan Mayne, London 1951

Liverpool and Edinburgh 2000 *Constable's Clouds*, ed. E. Morris, with contributions from J. Gage, A. Lyles, M. Suggett, J.E. Thornes and T. Wilcox, exh. cat., Walker Art Gallery, Liverpool, and National Gallery of Scotland, Edinburgh, 2000

London 1872 *Exhibition of the Works of the Old Masters, together with the Works of Deceased Masters of the British School*, exh. cat., Royal Academy of Arts, London, 1872

London 2001 D. Solkin (ed.), *Art on the Line: the Royal Academy Exhibitions at Somerset House 1780-1836*, exh. cat., Courtauld Institute of Arts, London, 2001

Mabey 1996 R. Mabey, *Flora Britannica:*

The Definitive New Guide to Wild Flowers, Plants and Trees, London 1996
Murdoch 1998 J. Murdoch, 'Introduction' to *The Courtauld Gallery at Somerset House*, London 1998, pp.7–24
New York 1988 *John Constable, R.A.*, exh.cat., Salander-O'Reilly Galleries, New York, 1988
New York 2004 *Constable's Skies*, ed. F. Bancroft, with contributions from F. Constable, G. Reynolds, A. Lyles, L. Weiseltier, D. Shapiro, F. Skloot, C. Shields, S. Cove and P. Bower, exh.cat., Salander-O'Reilly Galleries, New York, 2004; including S. Cove, 'Very Great Difficulty in Composition and Execution: the materials and techniques of Constable's sky and cloud studies of the 1820s', pp.123–52
Noon 2003 *Constable to Delacroix: British Art and the French Romantics*, ed. P. Noon, with contributions from Stephen Bann, David Blayney Brown, Rachel Meredith, Christine Riding and Marie Watteau, exh.cat., Tate Britain, London; Minneapolis Institute of Arts; and The Metropolitan Museum of Art, New York, 2003
Paris 2002 *Constable: le Choix de Lucian Freud*, exh.cat. with contributions by W. Feaver, J. Gage, A. Lyles, O. Meslay, L. Whitely and R. Ur, Grand Palais, Paris, 2002
Parris 1981 Leslie Parris, *The Tate Gallery Constable Collection*, London 1981
Parris 1986 Leslie Parris, *The 'English Landscape' Prints of John Constable and David Lucas*, exh. cat., Tate Gallery, London, 1986
Parris 1991 Leslie Parris, *Constable: Pictures from the Exhibition*, Tate, London, 1991
Parris 1994 Leslie Parris, *Constable, A New York Private Collection*, New York 1994
Parris 1994–5 Leslie Parris, *Constable: the Opening of Waterloo Bridge*, exh. leaflet, Tate Gallery, London, 1994
Redgrave 1866 Richard and Samuel Redgrave, *A Century of Painters of the English School, with Critical Notices of Their Works, and an Account of the Progress of Art in England*, London 1866, vol.2, pp.381–99
Redgrave 1947 Richard and Samuel Redgrave, *A Century of British Painters*, London 1947
Reynolds 1965 G. Reynolds, *Constable: the Natural Painter*, London and New York 1965
Reynolds 1973a G. Reynolds, *Catalogue of the Constable Collection: Victoria and Albert Museum* (1960), London 1973

Reynolds 1973b G. Reynolds, *John Constable the Natural Painter*, exh. cat., Auckland City Art Gallery, New Zealand, 1973
Reynolds 1983 G. Reynolds, *Constable's England*, exh. cat., The Metropolitan Museum of Art, New York, 1983
Reynolds 1984 G. Reynolds, *The Later Paintings and Drawings of John Constable*, 2 vols., New Haven and London 1984
Reynolds 1996 G. Reynolds, *The Early Paintings and Drawings of John Constable*, 2 vols., New Haven and London 1996
Rhyne 1987 Charles Rhyne, 'Constable's Last Major Oil Sketch: The Chicago *Stoke-by-Nayland*', ms. on deposit in the Department of European Paintings, Art Institute of Chicago, 1987 (copies also held in library/archive of Tate, London, and National Gallery of Art, Washington)
Rhyne 1988 Charles Rhyne, 'Constable and Dunthorne: Oil Sketches and Paintings by Dunthorne Jr. (1798–1832), Dunthorne's Role in the Paintings of John Constable (1776–1837)', 1988, ms. on deposit in the Paintings Department of Tate, London, and National Gallery of Art, Washington
Rhyne 1990a Charles Rhyne, 'Changes in the Appearance of Paintings by John Constable', in *Appearance, Opinion, Change: Evaluating the Look of Paintings*, London 1990, pp.72–84
Rhyne 1990b Charles Rhyne, 'Constable's First Two Six-Foot Landscapes', *Studies in the History of Art*, vol.24, National Gallery of Art, Washington, 1990, pp.109–29
Rhyne 1990c Charles Rhyne, *John Constable: Toward a Complete Chronology*, Portland, Oregon, 1990 www.reed.edu/~crhyne/papers/ jc_chronology.pdf
Rhyne 1990d Charles Rhyne, *A Proposal for the Creation of Comprehensive Archives of Information on the Working Procedure of Individual Artists and on the Visual Appearance and Physical Character of Their Art: A Trial Study, John Constable*, Portland, Oregon, 1990, www.reed.edu/~crhyne/papers/ jc_procedure.pdf
Rosenthal 1983 M. Rosenthal, *Constable: the Painter and his Landscape*, New Haven and London 1983
St John 2000 I. St John, *Flatford: Constable Country*, East Bergholt, Suffolk, 2000
St John 2002 I. St John, *East Bergholt: Constable Country*, East Bergholt, Suffolk, 2002
St John 2005 I. St John, *Dedham: Constable Country*, East Bergholt, Suffolk, 2005

Schweizer 1982 Paul D. Schweizer, 'John Constable, Rainbow Science, and English Color Theory', *Art Bulletin*, col.64, no.3, Sept. 1982, pp.424–45
Shirley 1930 A. Shirley, *The Published Mezzotints by David Lucas after John Constable, R.A.*, Oxford 1930
Shirley 1937 A. Shirley, *Memoirs of the Life of John Constable, R.A., by C.R. Leslie, R.A.*, ed. and enlarged by A. Shirley, London 1937
Shirley 1946 A. Shirley, *John Constable, R.A.*, 1946
Smart and Brooks 1976 Alastair Smart and Attfield Brooks, *Constable and His Country*, London 1976
Southall 1982 A. Southall, 'John Constable … *Flatford Mill (Scene on a navigable River)*' in S. Hackney (ed.), *Completing the Picture*, London 1982, pp.34–8
Sunderland 1981 J. Sunderland, *Constable*, London (1971), 2nd much enlarged edn 1981
Sutton 1955 D. Sutton, 'Constable's "Whitehall Stairs", or "The Opening of Waterloo Bridge"', *Connoisseur*, CXXXVI, 1955, pp.249–55
Swicklik 1998 M. Swicklik, 'Interpreting Artist's Intent in the Treatment of John Constable's *The White Horse Sketch*', *Journal of the American Institute for Conservation*, vol.37, no.3, Fall–Winter 1998, pp.362–72
Tate 1937 *Centenary Exhibition of Paintings and Water-colours by John Constable R.A.*, exh. cat., Tate Gallery, London, 1937
Tate 1976 L. Parris and I. Fleming-Williams, *Constable: Paintings, Watercolours and Drawings*, with an essay by C. Shields, exh. cat., Tate Gallery, London, 1976
Tate 1982a L. Parris and I. Fleming-Williams, *Lionel Constable*, exh. cat., Tate Gallery, London, 1982
Tate 1982b *Paint and Painting*, exh. cat., Tate Gallery, London, 1982
Tate 1991 L. Parris and I. Fleming-Williams, *Constable*, exh. cat., Tate Gallery, London, 1991; including S. Cove, 'Constable's Oil Painting Materials and Techniques', pp.493–518, and S. Cove, 'Case Study 2: *Flatford Mill from the Lock*, 1811–12: Preparatory Sketch, Study and "Finished" Picture', pp.523–9
Tate 2005 D. Brown, 'The Flatlands: "The Nature of our Looking"', in *A Picture of Britain*, exh.cat., ed. D. Dimbleby, Tate Britain, London, 2005, pp.157–81
Taylor 1973 B. Taylor, *Constable: Paintings, Drawings and Watercolours*, London 1973

Thompson 2005 Jennifer Thompson, 'A rediscovered oil-sketch by John Constable', *Burlington Magazine*, Sept 2005, vol. CLXVII, pp.608-12
Thornes 1999 J. Thornes, *John Constable's Skies: A Fusion of Art and Science*, Birmingham 1999
Vaughan 1996 W. Vaughan, 'Constable's Englishness', *Oxford Art Journal*, 1996, vol.19, no.2, pp.17–27
Vaughan 2002 W. Vaughan, *Constable*, London 2002
Venturi 1947a L. Venturi, *Modern Painters: Goya, Constable, David, Ingres, Delacroix, Corot, Daumier, Courbet*, New York and London 1947
Venturi 1947b L. Venturi, *Painting and Painters: How to Look at a Picture, from Giotto to Chagall*, New York and London 1947, pp.142–7, figs.31–2
Walker 1979 J. Walker, *John Constable* (New York 1978), London 1979
Wark 1971 R.W. Wark, *Ten British Pictures 1740-1840*, San Marino 1971; see 'Constable's *View on the Stour near Dedham*', pp.111–21
Warrell 1995 I. Warrell, ' "Piccadilly by the Seaside"; John Constable at Brighton' and 'J.M.W. Turner in Brighton', essays in D. Beevers (ed.), *Brighton Revealed through Artists' Eyes c.1760-c.1960*, exh. cat., Brighton Museum and Art Gallery, Sussex, 1995, pp.17–31, 32–9
Whitley 1928 W.T. Whitley, *Artists and Their Friends in England*, London 1928
Whitley 1930 W.T. Whitley, *Art in England 1821-1837*, Cambridge, UK, 1930
Young and Parkinson 1992 P. Young and R. Parkinson, 'Another Pentimento in Constable's *Leaping Horse*', *Burlington Magazine*, CXXXIV, May 1992, p.311

Sources of Technical Information and Status of Examination Reports on Paintings, Palette and Paint Box in the Exhibition
Sarah Cove

Catalogue numbers are given in parentheses after the title of each work.

Pictures shown by Constable at the Royal Academy are dated to the year of their exhibition, even though often started the previous year or, conceivably, earlier.

Dimensions listed here were taken by the author, or directly from technical reports supplied by the lenders.

An 'R' number indicates the listing of the work in the catalogue raisonné of Constable's work compiled by Graham Reynolds in 1984 and 1996 (see bibliography).

1 Flatford Mill from the Lock (no.14)
1812, oil on canvas, 63.5 × 90.2 (25 × 35 ½), R.12.1. Full technical examination and analysis, Sarah Cove, 1988.

2 Flatford Mill from the Lock (sketch) (no.10)
c.1810, oil on paper, 18.4 × 23.5 (7¼ × 9¼), R.12.5. Examined off the wall, Sarah Cove, 2004.

3 Flatford Mill from the Lock (sketch) (no.11)
1811, oil on canvas, 15.2 × 21.2 (6 × 8³⁄₈), R.12.8. Full technical examination and analysis, Sarah Cove, 1988.

4 Study for 'Flatford Mill from the Lock' (no.13)
c.1811, 24.5 × 29.5 (9⁵⁄₈ × 11⁵⁄₈), R.12.9. Full technical examination and analysis, Sarah Cove, 1989.

5 Wivenhoe Park, Essex (no.17)
1816, oil on canvas, 56.1 × 101.2 (22¹⁄₈ × 39⁷⁄₈), R.17.4. Examined on the wall, Sarah Cove, 1989.

6 Dedham Lock and Mill (no.24)
c.1817–18, oil on canvas, 72.4 × 92.75 (28 × 36), R.20.12. Full technical examination and analysis, Sarah Cove, 1989.

7 Dedham Lock and Mill (no.25)
c.1818–20, oil on canvas, 54.6 × 77.5 (21½ × 30½), R.20.11. Studio examination with infrared photography, no X-ray or analysis, Sarah Cove, 1989.

8 The White Horse (no.29)
1819, oil on canvas, 131.5 × 187.8 (51³⁄₄ × 73¹⁵⁄₁₆), R.19.1. Examined on the wall, Sarah Cove, Paris, 2002 and Tate, 2003.

9 The White Horse (full-size sketch) (no.28)
c.1818, oil on canvas, 127 × 183 (50 × 72), R.19.2. Full technical examination and analysis, Charlotte Hale 1984 and Michael Swicklik and Barbera Berrie, 1990s.

10 Stratford Mill (no.31)
1820, oil on canvas, 127 × 182.9 (50 × 72), R.20.1. Studio examination and X-ray, no infrared reflectography or analysis, Sarah Cove, 2005.

11 Stratford Mill (full-size sketch) (no.30)
c.1819, oil on canvas, 131 × 184 (51½ × 72½), R.20.2. Technical examination and analysis, Herbert Lank, 1983; Examined on the wall, Sarah Cove, 1989; Supplementary notes on technique and condition, Gay Myers, YCBA, 2004.

12 Hampstead Heath with the House called 'The Salt Box' (no.27)
c.1820, oil on canvas, 38.4 × 66.8 (15¹⁄₈ × 26³⁄₈), R.21.7. Technical examination and analysis carried out by Anna Southall and Joyce Townsend, Tate, 1990. Further examination by Sarah Cove at Tate to help determine status of edges, 1991.

13 The Hay Wain (no.37)
1821, oil on canvas, 130.5 × 185.5 (51³⁄₈ × 73¹⁄₁₆), R.21.1. Medium analysis report, R. White and J. Pilc 1997; studio examination and X-ray, no infrared reflectography or analysis, Sarah Cove, 2005.

14 The Hay Wain (full-size sketch) (no.36)
c.1820, oil on canvas, 137 × 188 (53¹⁵⁄₁₆ × 74), R.21.2. Studio examination, no infrared reflectography, X-ray or analysis, Sarah Cove in collaboration with Nicola Costaras, V&A Paintings Conservator, 2005.

15 View on the Stour near Dedham (no.39)
1822, oil on canvas, 130 × 188 (51³⁄₁₆ × 74), R.22.1. Studio examination with infrared reflectography and X-ray, Shelley Svoboda, freelance conservator, 1994; supplementary notes, Rosamond Westmoreland, freelance conservator, 2002.

16 View on the Stour near Dedham (full-size sketch) (no.38)
c.1821, oil on canvas, 129.4 × 185.3 (50¹⁵⁄₁₆ × 72¹⁵⁄₁₆), R.22.2. Full technical examination and analysis, Sarah Cove in collaboration with Natasha Duff, Tate Paintings Conservator. Analysis Natasha Duff and Joyce Townsend, Tate Conservation Scientist, 2005.

17 The Lock (no.41)
1824, oil on canvas, 142.2 × 120.7 (56 × 47½), R.24.1. Examined on the wall, Sarah Cove, at Sotheby's, London 1990 and off the wall by daylight, Sarah Cove, Paris, 2002.

18 The Lock (full-size sketch) (no.40)
c.1823, oil on canvas, 141.7 × 122 (55¹³⁄₁₆ × 48¹⁄₁₆), R.24.2. Studio examination (no analysis), Jean Rosston in collaboration with Charles Rhyne, 1984; notes by M.H. Butler, 1984; supplementary information supplied at Sarah Cove's request by Mark Tucker, PMA Paintings Conservator, 2005.

19 The Leaping Horse (no.47)
1825, oil on canvas, 142.2 × 187.3 (56 × 73³⁄₄), R.25.1. Examined off the wall and X-ray, Sarah Cove in collaboration with Mandy Paulley, RA Paintings Conservator. X-ray interpretation Sarah Cove with Isabel Horovitz, RA, Nicola Costaras, V&A, Anne Lyles, Tate, 2005.

20 The Leaping Horse (full-size sketch) (no.46)
c.1824, oil on canvas, 129.4 × 188 (50¹⁵⁄₁₆ × 74), R.25.2. Full technical examination, Sarah Cove in collaboration with Nicola Costaras, V&A, and Natasha Duff, Tate. Analysis Natasha Duff and Joyce Townsend, Tate. X-ray interpretation Sarah Cove with Isabel Horovitz, RA, Nicola Costaras, V&A, Anne Lyles, Tate, 2005.

21 Chain Pier, Brighton (no.51)
1827, oil on canvas, 127 × 183 (50 × 72), R.27.1. Full technical examination and analysis, Sarah Cove in collaboration with Natasha Duff. Analysis Natasha Duff and Joyce Townsend, Tate, 2005.

22 Sketch for 'Chain Pier, Brighton' (fig.77, p.171)
c.1826–7, oil on canvas, 60.6 × 98.8 (23³⁄₄ × 38⁷⁄₈), R. 27.4. Structure and condition notes from the Curatorial and Conservation files compiled by K. Kooistra, NGA Washington Conservation Intern, 2004, including a brief report by David Skipsey, PMA Paintings Conservator, 1991; supplementary notes supplied by Jennifer Thompson, Curator, and Mark Tucker, Conservator, 2005.

23 Hadleigh Castle (no.57)
1829, oil on canvas, 122 × 164.5 (48¹⁄₁₆ × 64³⁄₄), R.29.1. Examined on the wall, Sarah Cove, 1989.

24 Hadleigh Castle (full-size sketch) (no.56)
c.1828–9, oil on canvas, 122.5 × 167.4 (48¹⁄₄ × 65⁷⁄₈), R.29.2. Full technical examination and analysis, Natasha Duff, Tate, 2005.

25 Sketch for 'Hadleigh Castle' (no.54)
c.1828, oil on board, 20 × 24 (7⁷⁄₈ × 9½), R.29.3. Studio examination for loan, Lance Mayer, 2004.

26 Salisbury Cathedral from the Meadows (no.61)
1831, oil on canvas, 151.8 × 189.9 (59³⁄₄ × 74³⁄₄), R.31.1. Studio examination and infrared reflectography, no X-ray or analysis, Sarah Cove, 1988.

27 Salisbury Cathedral from the Meadows (full-size sketch) (no.60)
c.1829–31, oil on canvas, 135.8 × 188 (53½ × 74), R.31.2. Studio examination, no X-ray, infrared reflectography or analysis, Sarah Cove, 2005.

28 Salisbury Cathedral from the Meadows (studio study) (no.59)
c.1829, oil on canvas, 34.2 × 48.4 (14¹⁄₄ × 20¹⁄₈), R.31.5. Studio examination and X-ray, no analysis, Sarah Cove, 2005.

29 The Opening of Waterloo Bridge (no.67)
1832, oil on canvas, 130.8 × 218 (51½ × 85⁷⁄₈), R.32.1. Full technical examination and analysis, Sarah Cove, 1988.

30 The Opening of Waterloo Bridge (half-size sketch) (no.66)
c.1829, oil on canvas, 62 × 99 (24³⁄₈ × 39), R.29.63. Full technical examination and analysis, Sarah Cove, 1989.

31 Sketch for 'The Opening of Waterloo Bridge' (no.63)
c.1819, oil on board, 29.2 × 48.3 (11½ × 19), R.19.23. Full technical examination and analysis, Sarah Cove, 1989.

32 Stoke-by-Nayland (no.68)
c.1835–7, oil on canvas, 125.8 × 168.5 (49½ × 66³⁄₈), R.36.19. Full examination and extensive analysis, Allison Langley and Inge Fiedler, 1986 and 2005. Examined on the wall, Sarah Cove, Paris, 2002.

33 Constable's metal paint box (no.70)
c.1837, a tin box divided into seventeen compartments containing eleven paint bladders, chalk and a glass phial of blue pigment, 5 × 33 × 8.5 (2 × 13 × 3³⁄₈). Extensive analysis of pigments and mediums carried out by Sarah Cove, assisted by Catherine Hassall, Libby Sheldon, J. Boon and Brian Singer, 1996–7, published in Cove 1998, pp.211–16.

34 Constable's wooden palette (no.69)
c.1837, 24.5 × 40.5 (9³⁄₄ × 16). Analysed by Anna Southall, Tate, and J. Mills and R. White, National Gallery, c.1981–2, see Tate 1982b, pp.65–6 (illus). Extensive analysis was carried out by Sarah Cove in 1990, see Cove in Tate 1991, pp.501, 507, fig.168, p.501. See also Cove 1998, pp.211–16. Further analysis by optical microscopy and EDX carried out for Sarah Cove by Rachel Grout, 2002–3 (unpublished).

Sarah Cove's specific queries on the ground/priming of *Salisbury Cathedral from the Bishop's Grounds* 1823 (R.23.1; fig.60, p.131), *The Cornfield* 1826 (R.26.1; fig.59, p.116) and *Dedham Vale* 1828 (R.28.1; fig.74, p.164) were answered by Paintings Conservators: Zoe Allen, Victoria and Albert Museum, Paul Ackroyd, The National Gallery, and Lesley Stevenson, National Gallery of Scotland, respectively.

1

Self-Portrait
1806
Pencil on wove paper
23.7 × 14.5 (9¼ × 5¾)
Inscribed in pencil in lower left-hand
corner 'March 1806' (preceded by
'April', subsequently covered by
pencil shading)
R.06.02
TATE. PURCHASED 1984

2

David Lucas (1802–1881) after
John Constable
Frontispiece: East Bergholt, Suffolk
1831
Mezzotint engraving from *English
Landscape*, 13.9 × 18.7 (5½ × 7⅜) on India
paper laid on wove paper 26.6 × 36.3
(10½ × 14⅜); plate-mark 23.3 × 23.8
(9⅛ × 9⅜)
Engraved inscriptions: above image:
'FRONTISPIECE./ To Mr. Constable's
English Landscape.'; below image at
left and right respectively: 'Painted by
John Constable. R.A.' and 'Engraved by
David Lucas'; below image at centre:
'EAST BERGHOLT, SUFFOLK./ Fond
recollections round thy memory twine/
"Hic locus aetatis nostrae primordia
novit/ Annos felices laetitiaeque dies:/
Hic locus ingenuis pueriles imbuit
annos/ Artibus, et nostrae laudis origo
fuit."/ London, Published by Mr.
Constable 35, Charlotte St. Fitzroy
Square, 1831.'
Shirley no.27 (second state)
TATE. PURCHASED 1985

3

**View in the Stour Valley looking
towards Langham Church from
Dedham**
1805
Watercolour on paper mounted
on a second sheet of paper
48 × 66.4 (18⅞ × 26¼)
Inscribed lower right
'John Constable 1805'
[not in Reynolds]
TATE. PARTIAL PURCHASE AND
PARTIAL LOAN FROM THE AMERICAN
FUND FOR THE TATE GALLERY,
COURTESY OF JULIE AND LAWRENCE
SALANDER IN MEMORY OF JOHN
CONSTABLE (1776–1837), DAPHNE
REYNOLDS (1918–2002), EVELYN JOLL
(1925–2001) AND LESLIE PARRIS
(1941–2000), WITH ASSISTANCE FROM
THE TATE PATRONS 2005

4

The Church Porch, East Bergholt
1810
Oil on canvas 44.5 × 35.9 (17½ × 14⅛)
Exh: RA 1810 (no.116, *A church-yard*);
BI 1811 (no.185, *A Church Porch*,
frame 25 × 22in)
R.10.2
TATE. PRESENTED BY
MISS ISABEL CONSTABLE 1888
London only

5

Stoke-by-Nayland
c.1810–11
Oil on canvas remounted on synthetic
board 18.1 × 26.4 (7⅛ × 10⅜)
R.11.44
TATE. BEQUEATHED BY HENRY
VAUGHAN, 1900

6

A Lane near Flatford
c.1811
Oil on paper laid on canvas
20.3 × 30.3 (8 × 11⅞)
R.11.30
TATE. BEQUEATHED BY
HENRY VAUGHAN, 1900

7

Dedham from Langham
c.1813
Oil on canvas remounted on synthetic
panel 13.7 × 19 (5⅜ × 7½)
R.13.15
TATE. BEQUEATHED BY GEORGE
SALTING 1910
London only

8

The Mill Stream
c.1809–14
Oil on board 20.8 × 29.2 (8⅛ × 11½)
R.14.47
TATE. BEQUEATHED BY
HENRY VAUGHAN, 1900

9

The Mill Stream
c.1810–14
Oil on canvas 71.1 × 91.5 (28 × 36)
Exh: ?RA 1810 (no.74, *A Landscape*,
bt Lord Dysart)
R.14.46 (and ?R.10.1)
Ivy: ?10.1–2
IPSWICH BOROUGH COUNCIL
MUSEUMS AND GALLERIES

10

Flatford Mill from the Lock
c.1810
Oil on paper 18.4 × 23.5 (7¼ × 9¼)
R.12.5
ESTATE OF SIR EDWIN A.G. MANTON
London only

11

Flatford Mill from the Lock
1811
Oil on canvas laid on board
15.2 × 21.2 (6 × 8⅜)
R.12.8
DAVID THOMSON
London only

12

Flatford Mill from the Lock
c.1811
Oil on canvas 25.4 × 30.5 (10 × 12)
R.12.7
THE HUNTINGTON LIBRARY, ART
COLLECTIONS, AND BOTANICAL
GARDENS
London only

13

**Study for 'Flatford Mill
from the Lock'**
c.1811
Oil on canvas 24.5 × 29.5 (9⅝ × 11⅝)
R.12. 9
VICTORIA AND ALBERT MUSEUM,
LONDON. GIVEN BY ISABEL
CONSTABLE, DAUGHTER OF
THE ARTIST
London only

14

Flatford Mill from the Lock
1812
Oil on canvas 63.5 × 90.2 (25 × 35½)
Exh: RA 1812 (no.9, *A water-mill*)
R.12.1
Ivy: 12.2–3
DAVID THOMSON
London only

15

The Ferry
1814
Oil on canvas 125.7 × 100.3 (49½ × 39½)
Exh: RA 1814 (no.261, *Landscape: the ferry*)
R.14.2
Ivy: 14.4
TRUSTEES OF THE DUPPLIN TRUST,
ON LONG LOAN TO TATE
London only

16

**Flatford Lock
from the Mill House**
c.1814
Oil on canvas 61 × 50.8 (24 × 20)
[not in Reynolds]
PRIVATE COLLECTION

17

Wivenhoe Park, Essex
1816
Oil on canvas 56.1 × 101.2 (22⅛ × 39⅞)
The canvas has been extended by a strip
of approximately 10.5cm (4⅛in) on the
left and a strip of approximately 9cm
(3½in) on the right. The original canvas
would therefore have measured about
22⅛ × 32¼ inches, which is close to the
small- to medium-sized format of 21 ×
30 inches that Constable favoured for
plein-air pictures, especially when one
allows for the fact that the strips would
probably have been joined to the out-
turned tacking edges at left and right.
Exh: RA 1817 (no.85, *Wivenhoe Park,
Essex, the Seat of Major-General Rebow*)
R.17.4
Ivy: 17.6–7
NATIONAL GALLERY OF ART,
WASHINGTON, WIDENER COLLECTION

18

Study for 'Flatford Mill'
c.1814–16
Pencil tracing 25.5 × 31.2 (10 × 12¼)
R.16.105
TATE. PURCHASED 1988

19

**Flatford Mill
('Scene on a navigable river')**
1817
Oil on canvas 101.7 × 127 (40 × 50)
Inscribed 'Jon Constable.f : 1817'
Exh: RA 1817 (no.255, *Scene on a navigable
river*); BI 1818 (no.91, *Scene on the Banks of
a River*, frame 58 × 68in)
R.17.1
Ivy: 17.6–7; 18.4–5
TATE. BEQUEATHED BY MISS ISABEL
CONSTABLE AS THE GIFT OF MARIA
LOUISA, ISABEL AND LIONEL
BICKNELL CONSTABLE 1888

20

Fen Lane, East Bergholt
c.1817
Oil on canvas 69.2 × 92.5 (27¼ × 36⅜)
R.16.107
TATE. PURCHASED WITH ASSISTANCE
FROM THE NATIONAL LOTTERY
THROUGH THE HERITAGE LOTTERY
FUND AND THE NATIONAL ART
COLLECTIONS FUND (WITH A
CONTRIBUTION FROM THE WOLFSON
FOUNDATION), WITH ADDITIONAL
ASSISTANCE FROM SIR EDWIN AND
LADY MANTON AND TATE MEMBERS
IN MEMORY OF LESLIE PARRIS,
DEPUTY KEEPER BRITISH COLLECTION
AND SENIOR RESEARCH FELLOW
COLLECTIONS DIVISION 1974–2000,
AND FROM THE BEQUEST OF ALICE
COOPER CREED, 2002

21

A Cornfield
c.1817
Oil on canvas 61.3 × 51 (24⅛ × 20⅛)
R.26.2
TATE. ACCEPTED BY HM
GOVERNMENT IN LIEU OF
INHERITANCE TAX AND ALLOCATED
TO TATE 2004
London only

22

Dedham Lock and Mill
1817
Pencil on paper 11.6 × 18.6 (4½ × 7¼)
R.17.25
THE HUNTINGTON LIBRARY, ART
COLLECTIONS, AND BOTANICAL
GARDENS

23

Dedham Lock and Mill
c.1816–17
Oil on canvas
54.6 × 76.5 (21½ × 30⅛)
R.20.13
TATE. BEQUEATHED BY
GEORGE SALTING 1910

24

Dedham Lock and Mill
c.1817–18
Oil on canvas 70 × 90.5 (27½ × 35⅝)
Exh: ?RA 1818 (no.11, *Landscape:
Breaking up of a shower*); BI 1819
(no.78, *A Mill*, frame 39 × 47in)
R.20.12
Ivy: ?18.10–12; 19.4–5, 19.7
DAVID THOMSON
London only

25

Dedham Lock and Mill
c.1818–20
Oil on canvas 54.6 × 77.5 (21½ × 30½)
R.20.11
Inscribed 'John Constable / London'
CURRIER GALLERY OF ART,
MANCHESTER, NEW HAMPSHIRE.
PURCHASE: CURRIER FUND
Washington and San Marino only

26

**Maria Constable with
Two of her Children**
c.1820
Oil on mahogany panel
16.6 × 22.1 (6½ × 8¾)
R.20.86
TATE. PURCHASED 1984
London only

27

**Hampstead Heath with the
House called 'The Salt Box'**
c.1820
Oil on canvas
38.4 × 66.8 (15⅛ × 26⅜)
R.21.7
TATE. PRESENTED BY
MISS ISABEL CONSTABLE 1887

28

The White Horse (full-size sketch)
c.1818
Oil on canvas 127.5 × 183 (50¼ × 72)
R.19.2
NATIONAL GALLERY OF ART,
WASHINGTON, WIDENER
COLLECTION

29

The White Horse
1819
Oil on canvas
131.5 × 187.8 (51¾ × 74), including
extension at right where the tacking
edge has been incorporated into the
picture plane. Signed and dated along
the bottom edge (left of centre) in
sloping script 'I C John Constable
London. F.1819' (the 'I C' may represent a
first and less complete signature)
Exh: RA 1819 (no.251, *A scene on the river
Stour*); *Living Artists of the English School*,
BI 1825 (no.118, *River Scene*); Salon, Lille
1825 (no.98, one of two works entitled
Deux vues des Canaux d'Angleterre)
R.19.1
Ivy 19.10–12; 19.14; 19.16–17
THE FRICK COLLECTION, NEW YORK.
PURCHASE

30

Stratford Mill (full-size sketch)
c.1820
Oil on canvas 131 × 184 (51½ × 72½)
Inscribed bottom right (probably not
by the artist) 'John Constable RA/
London'
R.20.2
YALE CENTER FOR BRITISH ART,
PAUL MELLON FUND

31

Stratford Mill
1820
Oil on canvas 129 × 184.8 (50¾ × 72¾)
Exh: RA 1820 (no.17, *Landscape*);
Living Artists of the English School,
BI 1825 (no.114, *Landscape: a Water-mill,
with Children angling*)
R.20.1
Ivy 20.3; 20.8–9; 20.11–15; 25.10
THE NATIONAL GALLERY, LONDON

32

Willy Lott's House
c.1811
Oil on paper
24.1 × 18.1 (9½ × 7⅛)
R.11.37
VICTORIA AND ALBERT MUSEUM,
LONDON. GIVEN BY ISABEL
CONSTABLE, DAUGHTER OF
THE ARTIST

33

Willy Lott's House
1816
Oil on paper laid on canvas
19.4 × 23.8 (7⅝ × 9⅜)
Inscribed on the back
'J. Constable – 29 July 1816'
R.16.23
IPSWICH BOROUGH COUNCIL
MUSEUMS AND GALLERIES

34

**A rowing boat moored
by a river bank**
c.1809–11
Black chalk on blue-grey paper
9 × 12.6 (3½ × 5)
R.09.77
COURTAULD INSTITUTE
OF ART GALLERY, LONDON

35

Sketch for 'The Hay Wain'
c.1820
Oil on paper on panel
12.5 × 18 (4⅞ × 7)
R.21.3
YALE CENTER FOR BRITISH ART,
PAUL MELLON COLLECTION

36

The Hay Wain (full-size sketch)
c.1820
Oil on canvas 128 × 184 (50⅜ × 72½)
R.21.2
VICTORIA AND ALBERT MUSEUM,
LONDON. BEQUEATHED
BY MR HENRY VAUGHAN

37

The Hay Wain
1821
Oil on canvas 130.5 × 185.5 (51¼ × 73)
Inscribed along bottom edge 'John
Constable pinxᵗ. London 1821'
Exh: RA 1821 (no.339, *Landscape: Noon*);
BI 1822 (no.197, *Landscape; Noon*; frame
68 × 91 in); Salon, Paris, Aug. 1824–Jan.
1825 (no.358, *Une charrette à foin
traversant un gué au pied d'une
ferme; paysage*)
R.21.1
Ivy 21.3–6; 21.8–9; 21.11–14; 21.16–17; 21.19;
24.21–4
THE NATIONAL GALLERY, LONDON

38

**View on the Stour near Dedham
(full-size sketch)**
c.1821
Oil on canvas
129.4 × 184 (51 × 72½), including
extensions at top, bottom and left where
the original tacking edges were
incorporated into the picture surface.
Original dimensions of the canvas
before these extensions were
approximately 127 × 182.8 (50 × 72).
There are sufficient tack holes visible
along the top, left and right edges,
located approximately 5cm (2in) apart,
to suggest that the sketch was squared
up with threads at these intervals when
Constable transferred the design to the
finished canvas.
R.22.2
PRIVATE COLLECTION

39

View on the Stour near Dedham
1822
Oil on canvas 130 × 188 (51 × 74),
including extensions at top, bottom, left
and right where the original tacking
edges were incorporated into the
picture plane (probably by the artist,
though possibly done during lining)
Signed and dated in the bottom
right-hand corner in sloping letters
'John Constable pinx. London 1822'
Exh: RA 1822 (no.183, *View on the Stour,
near Dedham*); BI 1823 (no.35, *Landscape*);
Salon, Paris, Aug. 1824–Jan. 1825 (no.359,
un canal en Angleterre; paysage)
R.22.1
Ivy 22.7; 22.14; 22.17–20; 22.22–3; 23.1–5;
25.19
THE HUNTINGTON LIBRARY,
ART COLLECTIONS,
AND BOTANICAL GARDENS

40

The Lock (full-size sketch)
c.1823
Oil on canvas 141.7 × 122 (55¾ × 48)
The canvas has been extended by the
artist at the top by approximately
28.5cm (11 1/4in) and cut down at the
right by no more than approximately
15cm (6in)
R.24.2
PHILADELPHIA MUSEUM OF ART:
THE JOHN HOWARD MCFADDEN
COLLECTION

41

The Lock
1824
Oil on canvas 142.2 × 120.7 (56 × 47½)
Exh: RA 1824 (no.180, *A boat passing a
lock*); *Living Artists of the English School*,
BI 1825 (no.129, *The Lock*)
R.24.1
Ivy 24.10–12; 24.14–16; 24.18–20
COLLECTION OF CARMEN
THYSSEN-BORNEMISZA,
ON LOAN TO THE THYSSEN-
BORNEMISZA MUSEUM, MADRID

42

**First Study for
'The Leaping Horse'**
1824
Pen, brown ink, grey and brown wash on
laid paper 20.2 × 30 (8 × 11¾)
R.25.3
THE BRITISH MUSEUM, LONDON

43

**Second Study for
'The Leaping Horse'**
1824
Pencil, pen and grey wash on laid paper
20.2 × 30.1 (8 × 12⅞)
R.25.4
THE BRITISH MUSEUM, LONDON

44

A Willow Stump
c.1821
Pencil on paper 9.3 × 11.9 (3⅝ × 4¾)
R.21.14
COURTAULD INSTITUTE
OF ART GALLERY, LONDON

45

A Moorhen startled from its nest
c.1824
Oil on board 14.6 × 15.2 (5¾ × 6)
R.24.84
PRIVATE COLLECTION

46

The Leaping Horse (full-size sketch)
c.1824
Oil on canvas 129.4 × 188 (48 × 72),
including extensions at top and right,
where the original tacking edges were
incorporated into the picture surface,
and further butt-joined extensions at
top and lower edges, probably added
after Constable's death
R.25.2
VICTORIA AND ALBERT MUSEUM,
LONDON. BEQUEATHED BY MR
HENRY VAUGHAN

47

The Leaping Horse
1825
Oil on canvas 139.7 × 185.4 (55 × 73),
including extensions made by
incorporating the original tacking edges
in the picture surface and by the later
addition of a separate 6.3cm (2 ½-in)
strip at the top. Original dimensions of
the canvas before these extensions and
additions would have been
approximately 127 × 177.8cm (50 × 70 in).
The right-hand side of the canvas also
has a modern butt-joined extension
added when the picture was lined in
1965.
Exh: RA 1825 (no.224, *Landscape*)
R.25.1
Ivy 25.4; 25.9; 25.14–15
ROYAL ACADEMY OF ARTS, LONDON

48

Beaching a Boat, Brighton
c.1824
Oil on paper laid on canvas 24.8 × 29.4
(9¾ × 11⅝)
R.24.64
TATE. PRESENTED BY
MRS P.M. RAINSFORD 1986

49

**Marine Parade and
Chain Pier, Brighton**
1824
Pencil, with pen additions 11.1 × 42.5
(4⅜ × 16¾), including extension of an
extra strip of paper 5.4cm (2⅛in) on left.
Inscribed by the artist in pencil over the
roofs of the houses with colour notes
Brown Red and others that are illegible
R.27.2
VICTORIA AND ALBERT MUSEUM,
LONDON. GIVEN BY ISABEL
CONSTABLE, DAUGHTER OF
THE ARTIST

50

Sketch for 'Chain Pier, Brighton'
c.1826
Oil on paper laid on canvas
33 × 61 (13 × 24)
R.27.3
PHILADELPHIA MUSEUM OF ART:
THE JOHN G. JOHNSON COLLECTION

51

Chain Pier, Brighton
1827
Oil on canvas 127 × 183 (50 × 72),
including flattened tacking edges at
right-hand side and bottom. The picture
has been cut down on the left by
approximately 23cm (9in), and a narrow
strip of canvas added to the right
tacking edge, indicating that the canvas
once measured about 81 in, almost 7ft
wide (205cm). There are also sets of
small square holes on the upper and
lower tacking margins, probably
associated with the use of threads to
create a 'squaring-up' grid.
Exh: RA 1827 (no.186, *Chain Pier,
Brighton*); BI 1828 (no.64, *The Beach at
Brighton, The Chain Pier in the distance*,
frame 68 × 99in)
R.27.1
Ivy 27.12–18; 27.22; 28.2–5; 28.7
TATE. PURCHASED 1950

52

Frederick William Smith (1797–1835)
after John Constable
**View of Brighton with
the Chain Pier**
1829
Line-engraving 19 × 31.1 (7½ × 12¼) on
India paper laid on wove paper 40.2 × 55
(15⅞ × 21⅝)
Engraved inscriptions below image:
'Painted by John Constable' (left);
'Engraved by Frederick Smith' (right).
Also with publication line: 'London
Published August 12th 1829 by Colnaghi
Son & Co Printsellers to the King Pall
Mall East & by Mʳ. Folker Brighton'.
THE BRITISH MUSEUM, LONDON

53

Hadleigh Castle
1814
Pencil on paper 8.1 × 11.1 (3¼ × 4⅜)
R.14.13
VICTORIA AND ALBERT MUSEUM,
LONDON. GIVEN BY ISABEL
CONSTABLE, DAUGHTER OF THE
ARTIST

54

Sketch for 'Hadleigh Castle'
c.1828
Oil on board 20 × 24 (7⅞ × 9½)
R.29.3
YALE CENTER FOR BRITISH ART,
PAUL MELLON COLLECTION

55

Sketch for 'Hadleigh Castle'
c.1828
Pen and iron-gall ink on wove paper
10.1 × 16.6 (4 × 6½)
R.29.4
DAVID THOMSON

56

Hadleigh Castle (full-size sketch)
c.1828–9
Oil on canvas 122.5 × 167.4 (48¼ × 65⅞)
The canvas was extended after
Constable's death, by strips of
approximately 10cm (4in) at the left and
along the bottom edge. The additions
seem to have been chiefly intended to
repair earlier damage to these areas.
R.29.2
TATE. PURCHASED 1935

57

Hadleigh Castle

1829
Oil on canvas 122 × 164.5 (48 × 64³/₄)
Exh: RA 1829 (no.322, *Hadleigh Castle.
The mouth of the Thames – morning, after
a stormy night*; exhibited with quotation
from James Thomson's *The Seasons*
[cited on p.175])
R.29.1
Ivy 29.10–11; 29.14; 29.18–20; 29.22–6
YALE CENTER FOR BRITISH ART,
PAUL MELLON COLLECTION

58

**Salisbury Cathedral
from Long Bridge**

1829
Pencil on paper 23 × 32.5 (9 × 12³/₄)
Inscribed in pencil in lower left-hand
corner '[?]11.1829'
R.29.13
LADY LEVER ART GALLERY,
NATIONAL MUSEUMS LIVERPOOL

59

**Sketch for 'Salisbury Cathedral
from the Meadows'**

c.1829
Oil on canvas 36.5 × 51.1 (14³/₈ × 20¹/₈)
Regularly spaced tack holes are visible
along the edges, indicating that the
sketch was squared-up with threads, so
that Constable could transfer the
composition to the full-scale sketch
(no.60)
R.31.5
TATE. BEQUEATHED BY
HENRY VAUGHAN 1900

60

**Salisbury Cathedral from the
Meadows (full-size sketch)**

c.1829–31
Oil on canvas 133.5 × 186 (52⁵/₈ × 73¹/₄)
The canvas has been extended at left and
right, where both tacking edges have
been turned out
R.31.2
GUILDHALL ART GALLERY, CITY OF
LONDON

61

**Salisbury Cathedral from the
Meadows**

1831
Oil on canvas 151.8 × 189.9 (59³/₄ × 74³/₄)
Exh: RA 1831 (no.169, *Salisbury Cathedral,
from the meadows*); BI 1833 (no.155,
Salisbury from the meadows, frame 72 ×
82in); Birmingham Society of Arts 1834
(no.317, *Salisbury Cathedral, from the
Meadows, Summer Afternoon, A retiring
Storm*); Worcester Institution 1836 (no.2,
*Salisbury Cathedral from the Meadows –
Summer Afternoon – A retiring Tempest*)
R.31.1
Ivy 31.8–12; 31.14–17; 31.20–4; 31.26–9;
31.31–2; 33.1; 33.3–4; 33.6–8; 33.12; 34.39;
36.28
PRIVATE COLLECTION
London only

62

David Lucas after John Constable
**Salisbury Cathedral from the
Meadows: The Rainbow**

c.1835
Mezzotint engraving (image size)
55.1 × 69.2 (21³/₄ × 27¹/₄), touched with
pencil, chalk and grey wash; white paper
collage on post at lower left
Shirley no.39, ?progress proof e
PRIVATE COLLECTION
London only

63

**Sketch for 'The Opening
of Waterloo Bridge'**

c.1819
Oil on board 29.2 × 48.3 (11¹/₂ × 19)
R.19.23
VICTORIA AND ALBERT MUSEUM,
LONDON. GIVEN BY ISABEL
CONSTABLE, DAUGHTER OF
THE ARTIST

64

**Sketch for 'The Opening
of Waterloo Bridge'**

c.1819–20
Pen and brown ink over pencil
on tracing paper laid on card
16.5 × 27.3 (6¹/₂ × 10³/₄)
R.19.25
VICTORIA AND ALBERT MUSEUM,
LONDON. GIVEN BY ISABEL
CONSTABLE, DAUGHTER OF THE
ARTIST

65

**The Opening of Waterloo Bridge
(first version)**

c.1820–5
Oil on canvas 153.7 × 245.4 (60¹/₂ × 9 ⁵/₈),
including flattened tacking edges at left,
right and bottom sides, and probably
also upper side as well. These appear to
have been incorporated into the picture
plane after the canvas was restretched,
conceivably as late as c.1828–30
R.32.2
ANGLESEY ABBEY, THE FAIRHAVEN
COLLECTION (THE NATIONAL TRUST)
London only

66

**Sketch for 'The Opening
of Waterloo Bridge'**

c.1829
Oil on canvas 62 × 99 (24³/₈ × 39)
R.29.63
YALE CENTER FOR BRITISH ART, PAUL
MELLON COLLECTION

67

**The Opening of Waterloo Bridge
('Whitehall Stairs, June 18th, 1817')**

1832
Oil on canvas 130.8 × 218 (51¹/₂ × 85⁷/₈)
Exh: RA 1832 (no.279, *Whitehall Stairs,
June 18th, 1817*)
R.32.1
Ivy 32.8–12; 32.14; 32.16; 32.19–24; 32.27;
32.29–31
TATE. PURCHASED WITH ASSISTANCE
FROM THE NATIONAL HERITAGE
MEMORIAL FUND, THE CLORE
FOUNDATION, THE NATIONAL ART
COLLECTIONS FUND, THE FRIENDS OF
THE TATE GALLERY AND OTHERS 1987

68

Stoke-by-Nayland (full-size sketch)

c.1835–7
Oil on canvas 125.8 × 168.5 (49¹/₂ × 66³/₈)
R.36.19
ART INSTITUTE OF CHICAGO, MR
AND MRS W.W. KIMBALL COLLECTION

69

Constable's palette

c.1837
24.5 × 40.5 (9³/₄ × 16)
Reddish hardwood, traditionally cherry
wood or walnut, though not identified
by analysis
TATE LIBRARY AND ARCHIVE.
PRESENTED TO THE NATIONAL
GALLERY IN 1887 BY ISABEL
CONSTABLE AND TRANSFERRED
TO TATE IN 1953
London only

70

Constable's metal paint box

c.1837
5 × 33 × 8.5 (2 × 13 × 3³/₈)
Containing eleven paint bladders, a
piece of white stone and a glass phial of
blue pigment.
Engraved inscription on an oval silver
disc approximately 2 × 3.5 (⁷/₈ × 1³/₈):
'The/ Sketching Box of/ John Constable,
RA/ given by his Son to/ David Lucas/
183[?].' Also inscribed on a piece of
paper: 'Constable's paintbox. I had it
from Alfred Lucas/ who had it from
David Lucas, Constable's Engraver./
H.S. Theobald.'
ESTATE OF SIR EDWIN A.G. MANTON
London only

Public Collections

Anglesey Abbey, The National Trust 65
Chicago, IL, USA, Art Institute of Chicago 68
Ipswich Borough Council Museums & Galleries 9, 33
Liverpool, National Museums Liverpool, Lady Lever Art Gallery 58
London, The British Museum 42, 43, 52
London, Courtauld Institute of Art Gallery 34, 44
London, Guildhall Art Gallery, City of London 60
London, The National Gallery 31, 37
London, The Royal Academy of Arts 47
London, Tate 1, 2, 3, 4, 5, 6, 7, 8, 18, 19, 20, 21, 23, 26, 27, 48, 51, 56, 59, 67, 69
London, Victoria and Albert Museum 13, 32, 36, 46, 49, 53, 63, 64
Manchester, NH, USA, Currier Museum of Art 25

New Haven, CT, USA, Yale Center for British Art 30, 35, 54, 57, 66
New York, NY, USA, The Frick Collection 29
Philadelphia, PA, USA, Philadelphia Museum of Art 40, 50
San Marino, CA, USA, The Huntington Library, Art Collections, and Botanical Gardens 12, 22, 39
Washington, DC, USA, National Gallery of Art 17, 28

Private Collections

The Dupplin Trust, on long loan to Tate 15
Estate of Sir Edwin A.G. Manton 10, 70
Private Collection 16, 38, 45, 61, 62
David Thomson 11, 14, 24, 55
Collection of Carmen Thyssen-Bornemisza, on loan to the Thyssen-Bornemisza Museum, Madrid 41

Catalogue Illustrations

The Art Institute of Chicago 68
© Copyright The Trustees of The British Museum, London 42, 43, 52
Courtauld Institute of Art Gallery, London 34, 44
Currier Museum of Art, Manchester, New Hampshire 25
David Thomson 11, 55
David Thomson/photography by Prudence Cuming Associates Ltd 14
David Thomson/photograph © Sarah Cove 24
Copyright The Frick Collection, New York 28
Guildhall Art Gallery, City of London 60
The Huntington Library, Art Collections and Botanical Gardens, San Marino 12, 22, 39
Ipswich Museums and Galleries 9, 33
Lady Lever Gallery, National Museums Liverpool 58
Museo Thyssen-Bornemisza, Madrid 41
© The National Gallery, London 31, 37, 61
© 2005 Board of Trustees, National Gallery of Art, Washington 17, 28
© NTPL/Christopher Hurst 65
Philadelphia Museum of Art: The John G. Johnson Collection, 1917 50
Philadelphia Museum of Art: John Howard McFadden Collection/Photography by Graydon Wood, 1994 40
Private Collection 16
Private Collection 49
Private Collection/Vincent Photographic Ltd 45
Private Collection/photograph © Sarah Cove 70
Private Collection 38
© 2003 Royal Academy of Arts, London/photography by John Hammond 47
Tate 1, 2, 3, 4, 5, 6, 7, 8, 15, 19, 20, 21, 23, 26, 27, 48, 51, 56, 59, 67
Tate Photography/Rodney Tidnam 69
V & A Images/Victoria and Albert Museum 13, 32, 36, 46, 53, 63, 64
Yale Center for British Art: Paul Mellon Collection/photography by Richard Caspole 30, 35, 54, 57, 66

Figure Illustrations

© The Bridgeman Art Library fig.11
© Copyright The Trustees of The British Museum fig.10
Photograph © 1996 The Detroit Institute of Arts fig.78
Photograph © Copyright Fitzwilliam Museum, University of Cambridge figs.71, 81
Guildhall Art Gallery, City of London/photograph © Sarah Cove figs.35, 41, 42
© Rose M. Merrill fig.29
Photograph © 1991 The Metropolitan Museum of Art, New York fig.46
© Musée Royaux des Beaux Arts de Belgique fig.43
© Board of Trustees, National Gallery of Art, Washington fig.19
© Board of Trustees, National Gallery of Art, Washington/photography by José A. Naranjo fig.54
© Board of Trustees, National Gallery of Art, Washington/photography by Bob Grove fig.15 National Gallery Australia fig.35
© National Gallery of Scotland fig.74
© The National Gallery, London figs.4, 13, 51, 59, 64
The National Gallery, London/photograph © Sarah Cove figs.32, 39, 44, 48
© National Museum of Wales fig.45
Philadelphia Museum of Art: John G. Johnson Collection, 1917/photography by Lynn Rosenthal fig.82
Philadelphia Museum of Art: Purchased with the W.P. Wilstach Fund, 1896/photography by Graydon Wood 1994 fig.77
Private Collection fig.86
Private Collection/X-ray taken by Mark Heathcote. Image mosaic compiled by Helen Spande fig.69
© Royal Academy of Arts, London figs.52, 70
Royal Academy of Arts, London/photograph © Sarah Cove figs.30, 37
The Royal Collection © 2006 Her Majesty Queen Elizabeth II fig.1
Salander-O'Reilly Galleries, New York fig.6
© Tabley House Collection, University of Manchester, UK fig.2

Tate Photography/Rodney Tidnam fig.26
Tate/photograph © Sarah Cove figs.31, 38, 47, 49
© Tokyo Fuji Art Museum fig.14
V & A Images/Victoria and Albert Museum figs.7, 50, 55, 57, 58, 60, 66, 67, 73, 80
Yale Center for British Art: Paul Mellon Collection/photography by Richard Caspole fig.5
Yale Center for British Art/photograph © Sarah Cove fig.36

Tate relies on a large number of supporters – individuals, foundations, companies and public sector sources – to enable it to deliver its programme of activities, both on and off its gallery sites. This support is essential in order to acquire works of art for the Collection, run education, outreach and exhibition programmes, care for the Collection in storage and enable art to be displayed, both digitally and physically, inside and outside Tate. Your donation will make a real difference and enable others to enjoy Tate and its Collection both now and in the future. There are a variety of ways in which you can help support Tate and also benefit as a UK or US taxpayer. Please contact us at:
The Development Office
Tate
Millbank
London SW1P 4RG
Tel: 020 7887 8945
Fax: 020 7887 8098

American Patrons of Tate
1285 6th Avenue (35th fl)
New York, NY 10019
USA
Tel: 001 212 713 8497
Fax: 001 212 713 8655

Donations
Donations, of whatever size, from individuals, companies and trusts are welcome, either to support particular areas of interest, or to contribute to general running costs.

Gifts of Shares
We can accept gifts of quoted shares and securities. These are not subject to capital gains tax. For higher rate taxpayers, a gift of shares saves income tax as well as capital gains tax. For further information please contact the Development Office.

Gift Aid
Through Gift Aid, you can provide significant additional revenue to Tate. Gift Aid applies to gifts of any size, whether regular or one-off, since we can claim back the tax on your charitable donation. Higher rate taxpayers are also able to claim additional personal tax relief. Contact us for further information and a Gift-Aid Declaration.

Legacies
A legacy to Tate may take the form of a residual share of an estate, a specific cash sum or item of property such as a work of art. Legacies to Tate are free of Inheritance Tax, and help to secure a strong future for the Collection and galleries.

Offers in lieu of tax
Inheritance Tax can be satisfied by transferring to the Government a work of art of outstanding importance. In this case the amount of tax is reduced, and it can be made a condition of the offer that the work of art is allocated to Tate. Please contact us for details.

Tate Annual Fund
A donation to the Annual Fund at Tate benefits a variety of projects throughout the organisation, from the development of new conservation techniques to education programmes for people of all ages and abilities.

American Patrons of Tate
American Patrons of Tate is an independent charity based in New York that supports the work of Tate in the United Kingdom. It receives full tax exempt status from the IRS under section 501(c)(3) allowing United States taxpayers to receive tax deductions on gifts towards annual membership programmes, exhibitions, scholarship and capital projects. For more information contact the American Patrons of Tate office.

Membership Programmes
Tate Members enjoy unlimited free admission throughout the year to all exhibitions at Tate Britain, Tate Liverpool, Tate Modern and Tate St Ives, as well as a number of other benefits such as exclusive use of our Members' Rooms and a free annual subscription to *Tate Etc*.

Whilst enjoying the exclusive privileges of membership, you are also helping secure Tate's position at the very heart of British and modern art. Your support actively contributes to new purchases of important art, ensuring that the Tate's Collection continues to be relevant and comprehensive, as well as funding projects in London, Liverpool and St Ives that increase access and understanding for everyone.

Tate Patrons
Tate Patrons are people who share a strong enthusiasm for art and are committed to giving significant financial support to Tate on an annual basis. The Patrons support the acquisition of works from across Tate's broad collecting remit, as well as other areas of Tate activity such as conservation, education and research. The scheme provides a forum for Patrons to share their interest in art and to exchange knowledge and information in an enjoyable environment. United States tax payers who wish to receive full tax exempt status from the IRS under Section 501 (c) (3) may want to pay through our American office. For more information on the scheme please contact the Patrons office.

Corporate Membership
Corporate Membership at Tate Modern, Tate Liverpool and Tate Britain offers companies opportunities for corporate entertaining and the chance for a wide variety of employee benefits. These include special private views, special access to paying exhibitions, out-of-hours visits and tours, invitations to VIP events and talks at members' offices.

Corporate Investment
Tate has developed a range of imaginative partnerships with the corporate sector, ranging from international interpretation and exhibition programmes to local outreach and staff development programmes. We are particularly known for high-profile business to business marketing initiatives and employee benefit packages. Please contact the Corporate Fundraising team for further details.

Charity Details
The Tate Gallery is an exempt charity; the Museums & Galleries Act 1992 added the Tate Gallery to the list of exempt charities defined in the 1960 Charities Act. Tate Members is a registered charity (number 313021). Tate Foundation is a registered charity (number 1085314).

Mr David Cohen CBE
Sarah and Gerard Griffin
The Hite Foundation
ICAP plc
ICI
The Kirby Laing Foundation
Robert and Mary Looker
Mr and Mrs David Mirvish
Anthony and Deirdre Montagu
Paul and Alison Myners
Oliver Prenn
Mr and Mrs James Reed
Simon and Virginia Robertson
The Judith Rothschild Foundation
Keith and Kathy Sachs
Mrs Coral Samuel CBE
Pauline Denyer-Smith and Paul
  Smith
The Starr Foundation
Hugh and Catherine Stevenson
Aroldo Zevi
and those who wish to remain anonymous

**Tate Britain Corporate
Members 2006**

Accenture
American Express
Apax Partners Ltd
Aviva plc
Barclays plc
BNP Paribas
Clifford Chance
Credit Suisse
Deutsche Bank
Drivers Jonas
EMI
Ernst & Young
Fidelity Investments
Freshfields Bruckhaus Deringer
Friends Provident PLC
GAM
GLG Partners
HSBC
Lehman Brothers
Linklaters
Nomura
Pearson
Reckitt Benckiser
Reuters
Shearman & Sterling LLP
Sotheby's
Tishman Speyer
UBS

Tate Britain Corporate Supporters
Founding Sponsors

BP PLC
Campaign for the creation of Tate
  Britain (1998-2000)
BP Displays at Tate Britain
  (1990-2007)
Tate Britain Launch (2000)

BT
Tate Online (2001-2008)

CHANNEL 4
The Turner Prize (1991-2003)

ERNST AND YOUNG
Picasso: Painter/Sculpture (1994)
Cézanne (1996)
Bonnard (1998)
Art of the Garden (2004)
Turner Whistler Monet (2005)

Benefactor Sponsors

EGG PLC
Tate & Egg Live (2003)

GLAXOSMITHKLINE PLC
Turner on the Seine (1999)
William Blake (2000)
*American Sublime: Landscape
  Painting in the United States,
  1820-1880* (2002)

GORDON'S gin
Turner Prize (2004, 2005)

PRUDENTIAL PLC
*The Age of Rossetti, Burne-Jones
  and Watts: Symbolism in
  Britain 1860–1910* (1997)
The Art of Bloomsbury (1999)
Stanley Spencer (2001)

TATE & LYLE PLC
Tate Members (1991-2000)
*Tate Britain Community
  Education* (2001-2007)

Major Sponsors

AIG
Constable: The Great Landscapes
  (2006)

BARCLAYS PLC
Turner and Venice (2003)

THE BRITISH LAND COMPANY PLC
Joseph Wright of Derby (1990)
Ben Nicholson (1993)
Gainsborough (2002)
Degas, Sickert, Toulouse-Lautrec
  (2005)

THE DAILY TELEGRAPH
Media Partner for *American
  Sublime* (2002)
Media Partner for *Pre-Raphaelite
  Vision: Truth to Nature* (2004)
Media Partner: for *In-A-Gadda-
  Da-Vida* (2004)

THE GUARDIAN
Media Partner for *Intelligence*
  (2000)
Media Partner for *Wolfgang
  Tillmans if one thing matters,
  everything matters* (2003)
Media Partner for *Bridget Riley*
  (2003)
Media Partner for Tate & Egg Live
  Series (2003)
Media Partner for *20 years of the
  Turner Prize* (2003)
Media Partner for *the Turner Prize*
  (2004, 2005)

MORGAN STANLEY
*Visual Paths: Teaching Literacy in
  the Gallery* (1999-2002)

TATE MEMBERS
Exposed: The Victorian Nude
  (2001)
Bridget Riley (2003)
*A Century of Artists' Film in
  Britain* (2003-2004)
In-A-Gadda-Da-Vida (2004)
Art Now: Nigel Cooke (2004)
Gwen John and Augustus John
  (2004)
Michael Landy – Semi Detached
  (2004)
Picture of Britain (2005)

VOLKSWAGEN
*Days like these: Tate Triennial of
  Contemporary Art* (2003)

Sponsors

DIESEL
Late at Tate Britain (2004)
Art Now (2004, 2005)

THE TIMES
Media partner for *Art and the 60s:
  This Was Tomorrow* (2004)